NEW YORK, *New York* 1/2

Marimo Ragawa

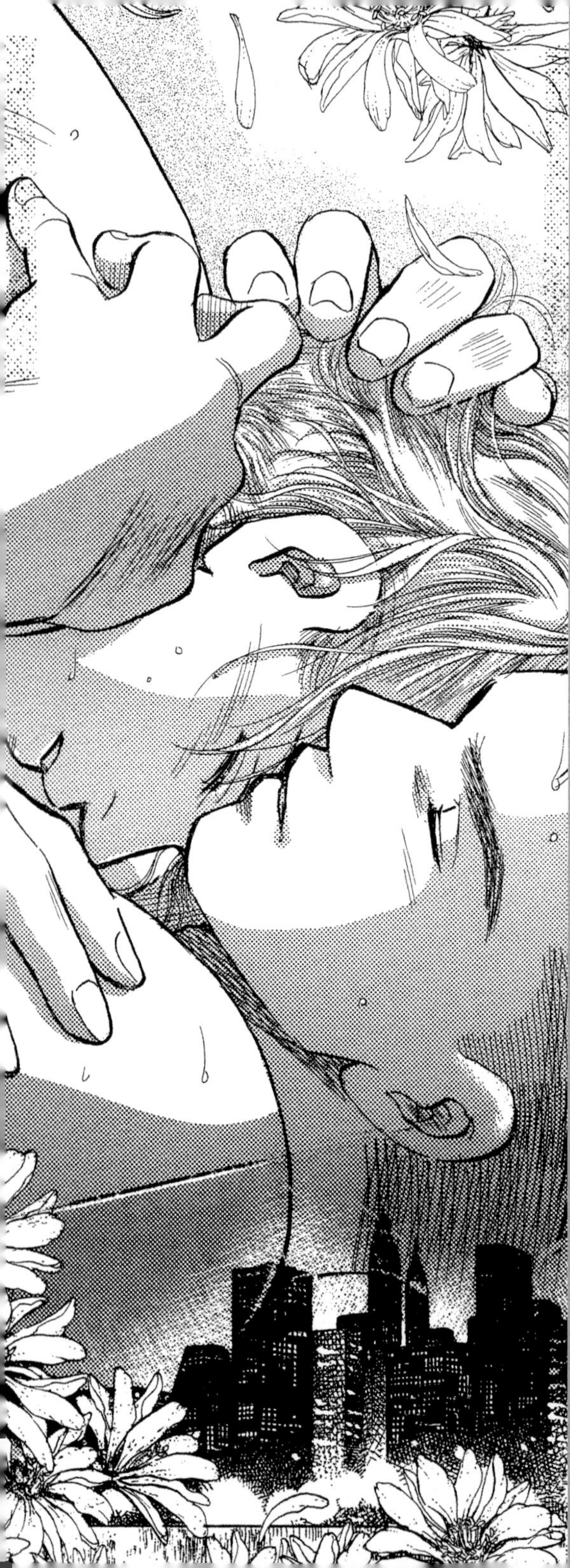

CONTENTS

NEW YORK, New York

Marimo Ragawa

This English-language edition of *New York, New York* contains certain words and phrases that are currently considered outdated in LGBT culture and in Jewish culture. *New York, New York* originally began publication in Japan in 1995 and portrays the culture of 1990s New York City, including language commonly used both inside and outside the gay community at the time.

NEW
YORK,
New York'

EPISODE I

SCENE 1

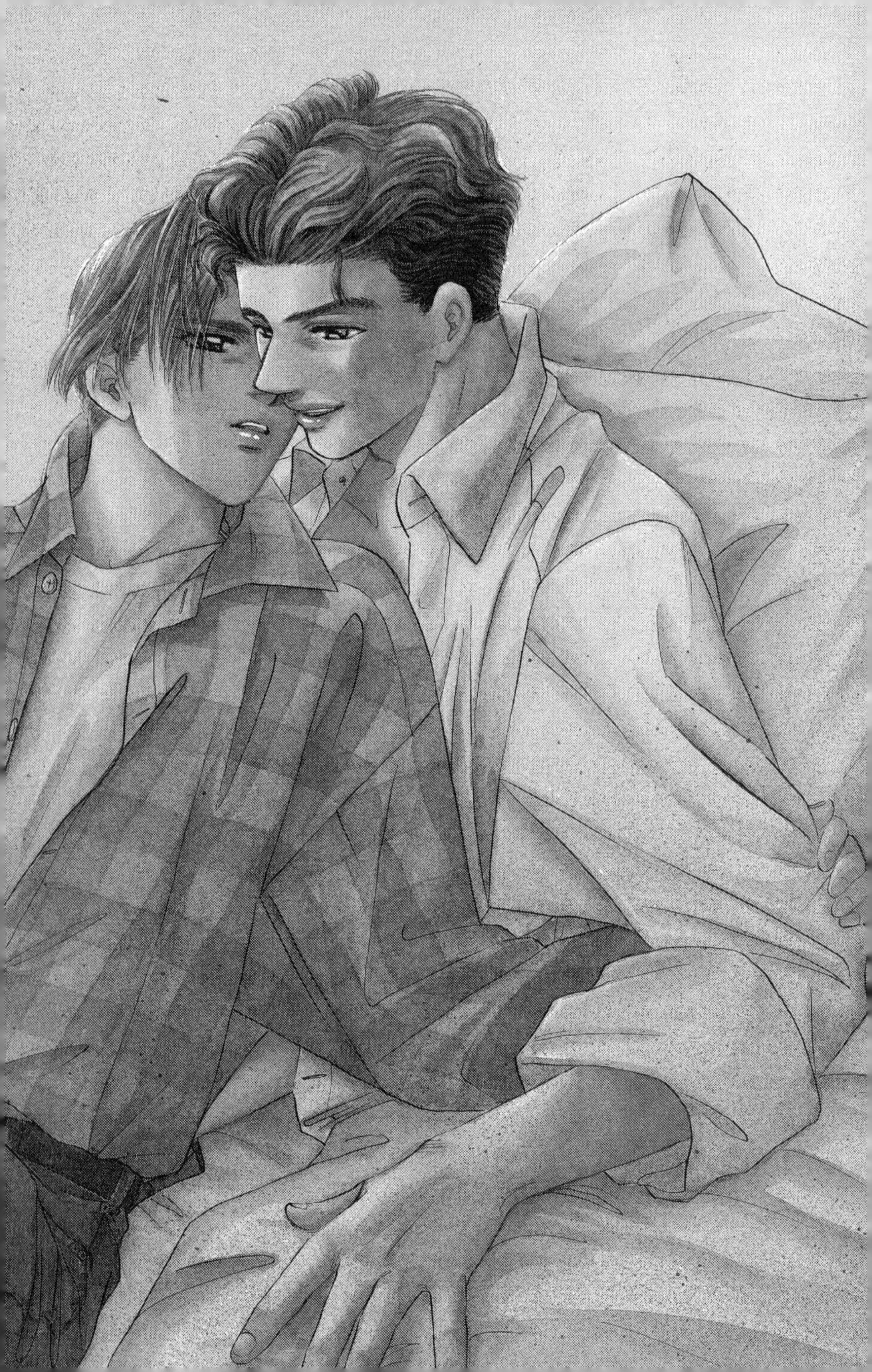

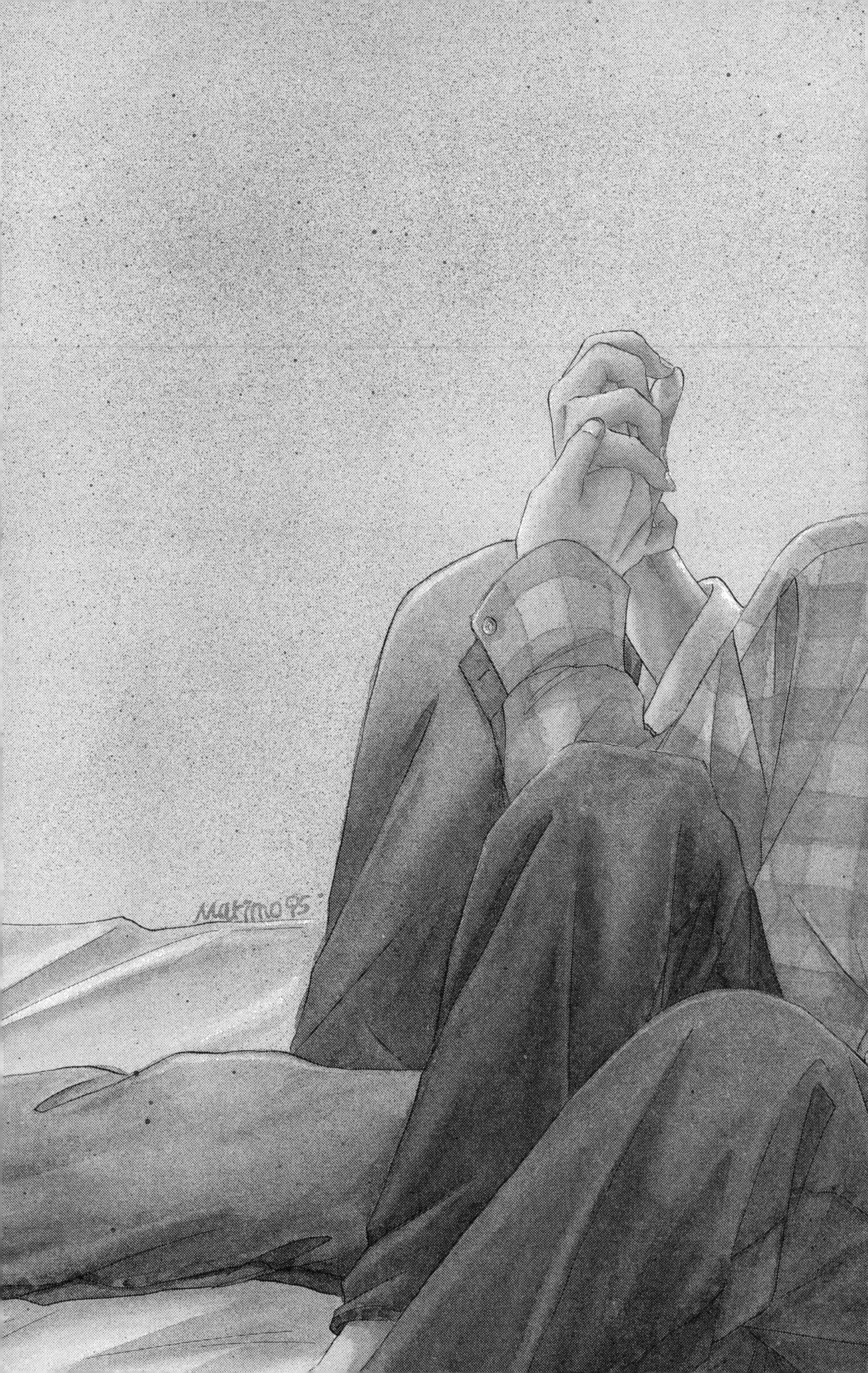
Makino'95

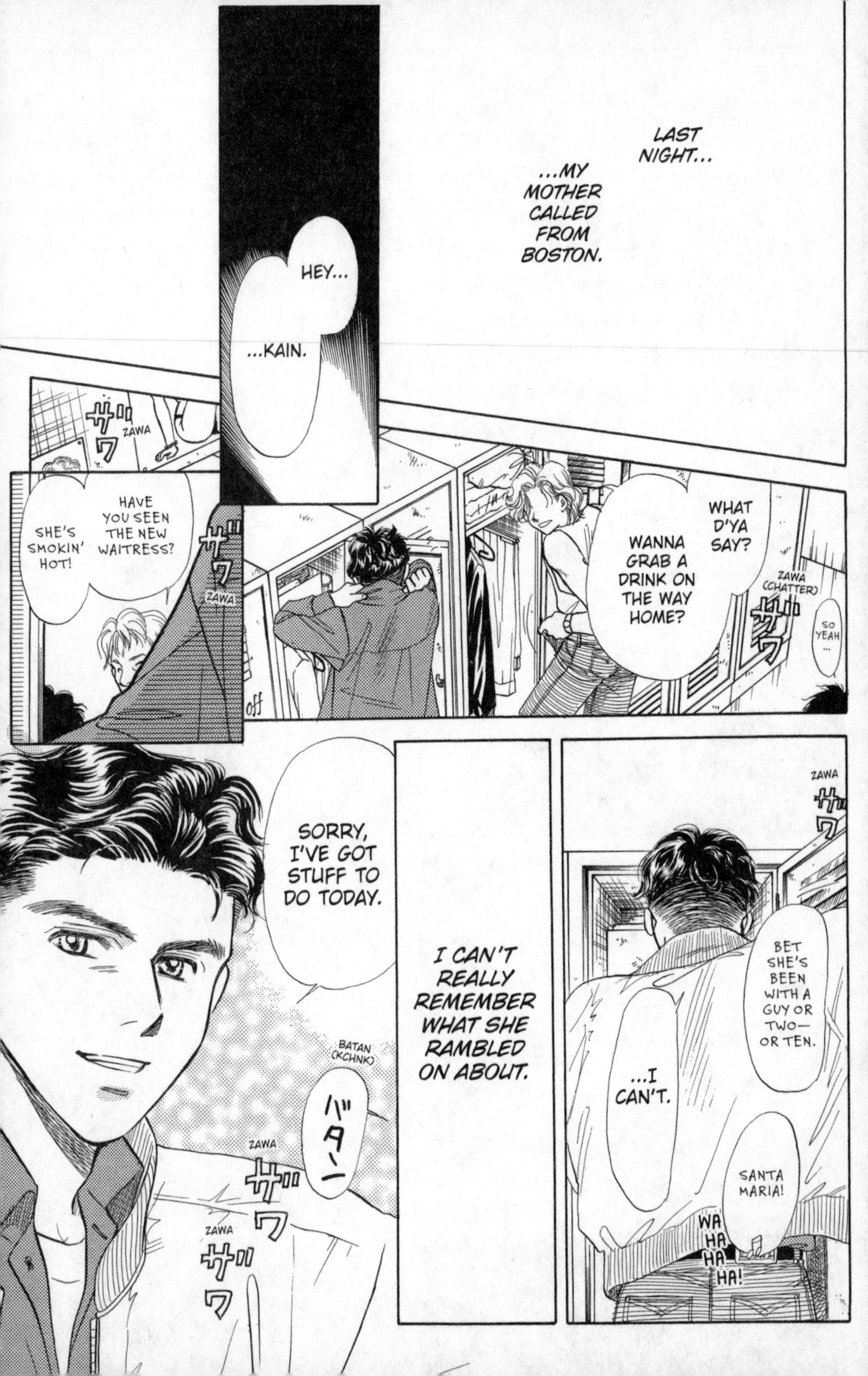
LAST NIGHT...
...MY MOTHER CALLED FROM BOSTON.
HEY...
...KAIN.
WHAT D'YA SAY?
WANNA GRAB A DRINK ON THE WAY HOME?
ザワ
ZAWA (CHATTER)
SO YEAH...
ザワ
ZAWA
HAVE YOU SEEN THE NEW WAITRESS?
SHE'S SMOKIN' HOT!
ザワ
ZAWA
ZAWA
ザワ
BET SHE'S BEEN WITH A GUY OR TWO—OR TEN.
...I CAN'T.
SANTA MARIA!
WA HA HA HA!
I CAN'T REALLY REMEMBER WHAT SHE RAMBLED ON ABOUT.
SORRY, I'VE GOT STUFF TO DO TODAY.
BATAN (KCHNK)
バタン
ZAWA
ザワ
ZAWA
ザワ

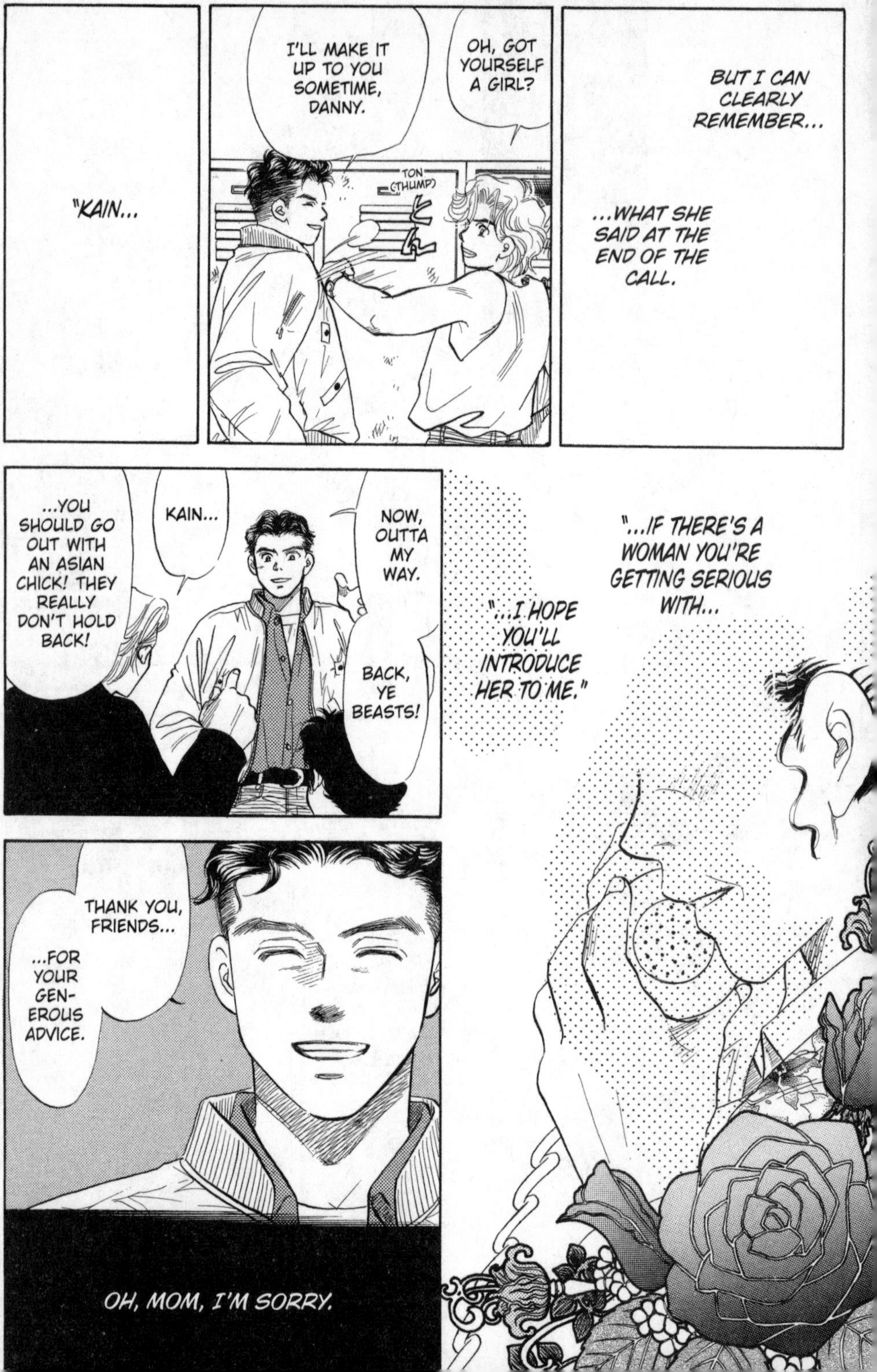
BUT I CAN CLEARLY REMEMBER...
...WHAT SHE SAID AT THE END OF THE CALL.
OH, GOT YOURSELF A GIRL?
I'LL MAKE IT UP TO YOU SOMETIME, DANNY.
TON (THUMP)
とん
"KAIN...
"...IF THERE'S A WOMAN YOU'RE GETTING SERIOUS WITH...
"...I HOPE YOU'LL INTRODUCE HER TO ME."
NOW, OUTTA MY WAY.
BACK, YE BEASTS!
KAIN...
...YOU SHOULD GO OUT WITH AN ASIAN CHICK! THEY REALLY DON'T HOLD BACK!
THANK YOU, FRIENDS...
...FOR YOUR GENEROUS ADVICE.
OH, MOM, I'M SORRY.

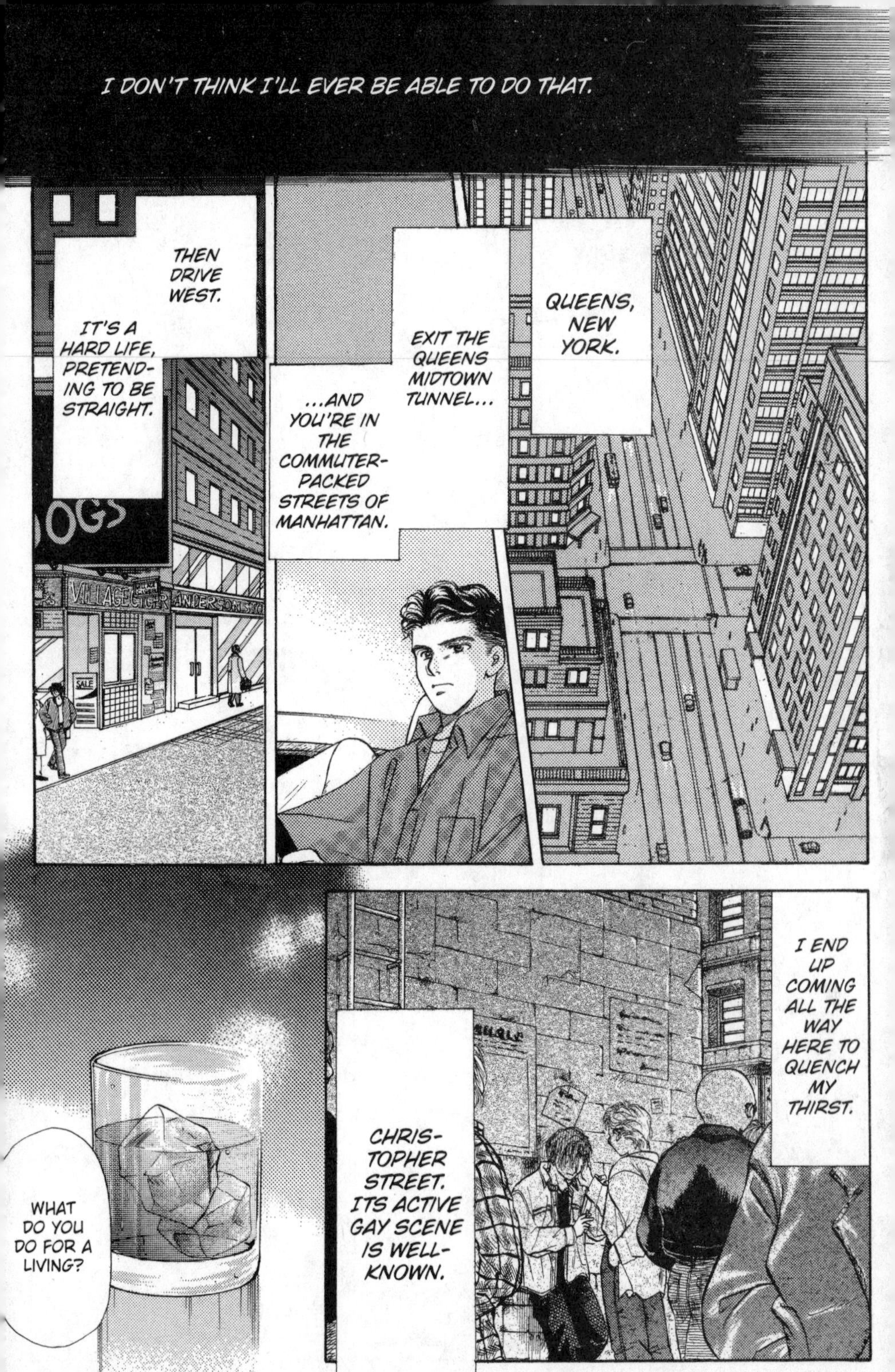
I DON'T THINK I'LL EVER BE ABLE TO DO THAT.
QUEENS, NEW YORK.
EXIT THE QUEENS MIDTOWN TUNNEL...
...AND YOU'RE IN THE COMMUTER-PACKED STREETS OF MANHATTAN.
THEN DRIVE WEST.
IT'S A HARD LIFE, PRETENDING TO BE STRAIGHT.
VILLAGE CIGAR
SALE
I END UP COMING ALL THE WAY HERE TO QUENCH MY THIRST.
CHRISTOPHER STREET. ITS ACTIVE GAY SCENE IS WELL-KNOWN.
WHAT DO YOU DO FOR A LIVING?

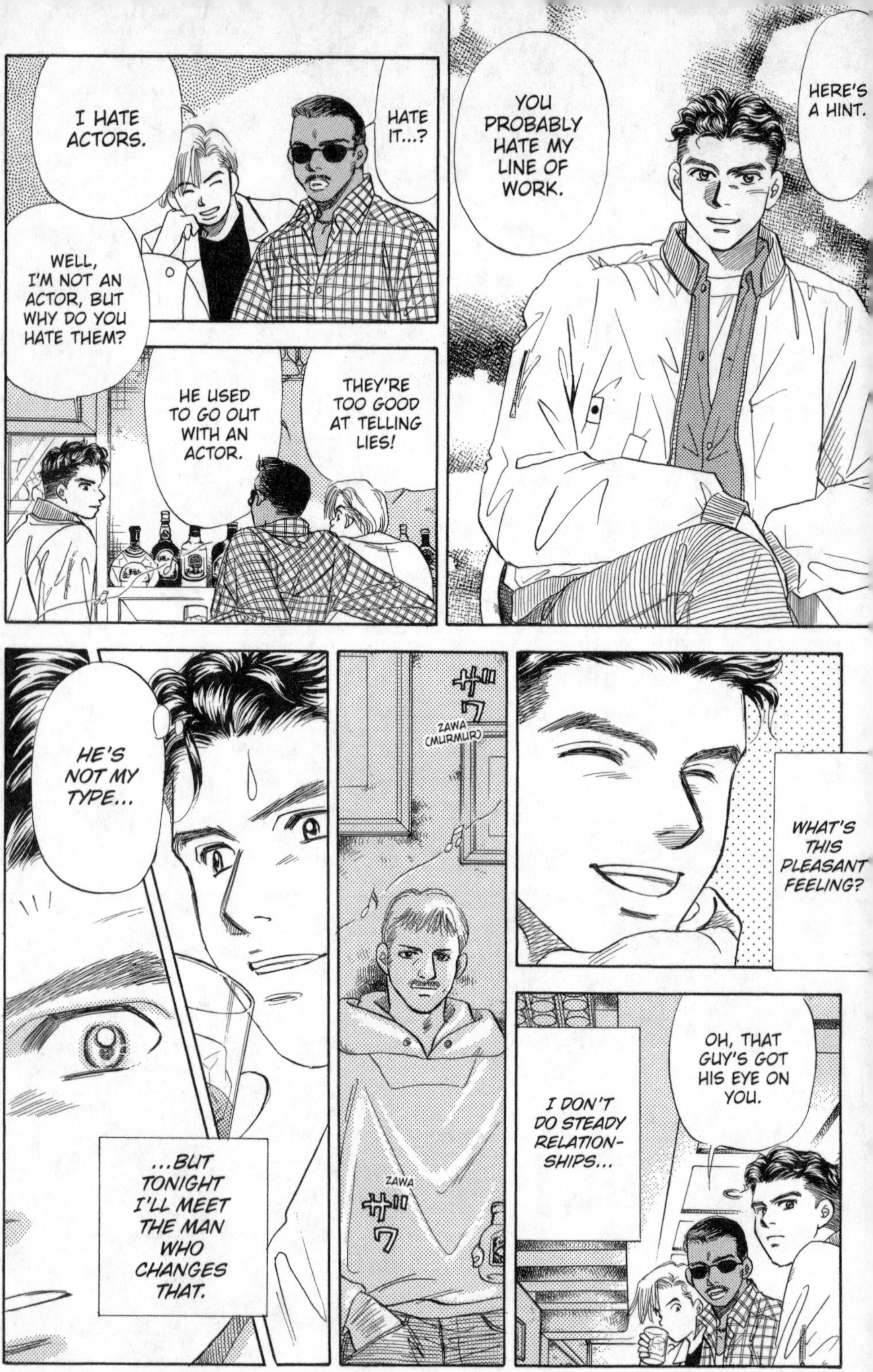
HERE'S A HINT.
YOU PROBABLY HATE MY LINE OF WORK.
HATE IT...?
I HATE ACTORS.
WELL, I'M NOT AN ACTOR, BUT WHY DO YOU HATE THEM?
THEY'RE TOO GOOD AT TELLING LIES!
HE USED TO GO OUT WITH AN ACTOR.
WHAT'S THIS PLEASANT FEELING?
OH, THAT GUY'S GOT HIS EYE ON YOU.
I DON'T DO STEADY RELATION-SHIPS...
ザワ
ZAWA (MURMUR)
ZAWA
ザワ
HE'S NOT MY TYPE...
...BUT TONIGHT I'LL MEET THE MAN WHO CHANGES THAT.

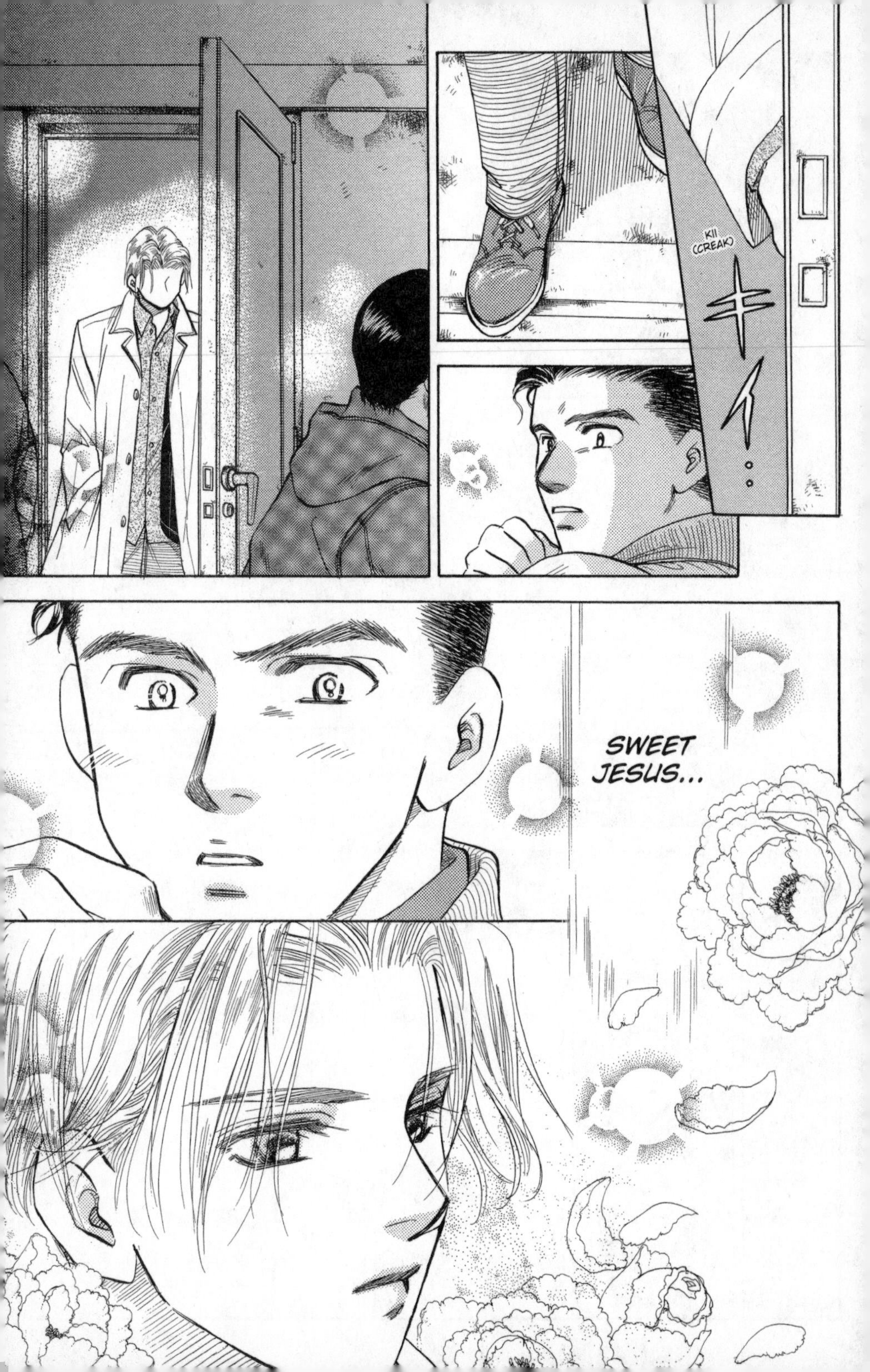
KII
(CREAK)
キィ…
SWEET
JESUS...

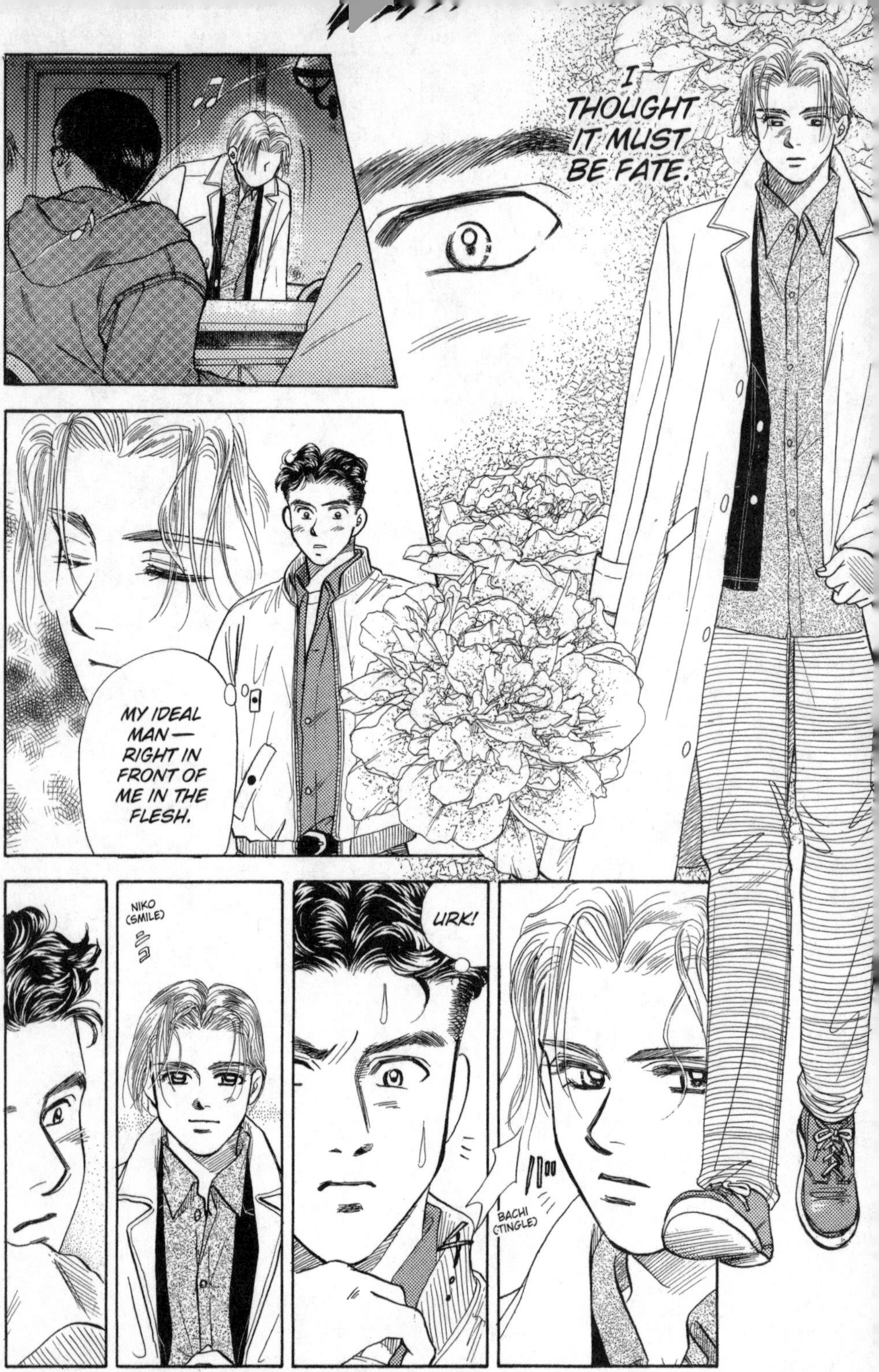
I THOUGHT IT MUST BE FATE.
MY IDEAL MAN—RIGHT IN FRONT OF ME IN THE FLESH.
BACHI (TINGLE)
URK!
NIKO (SMILE)

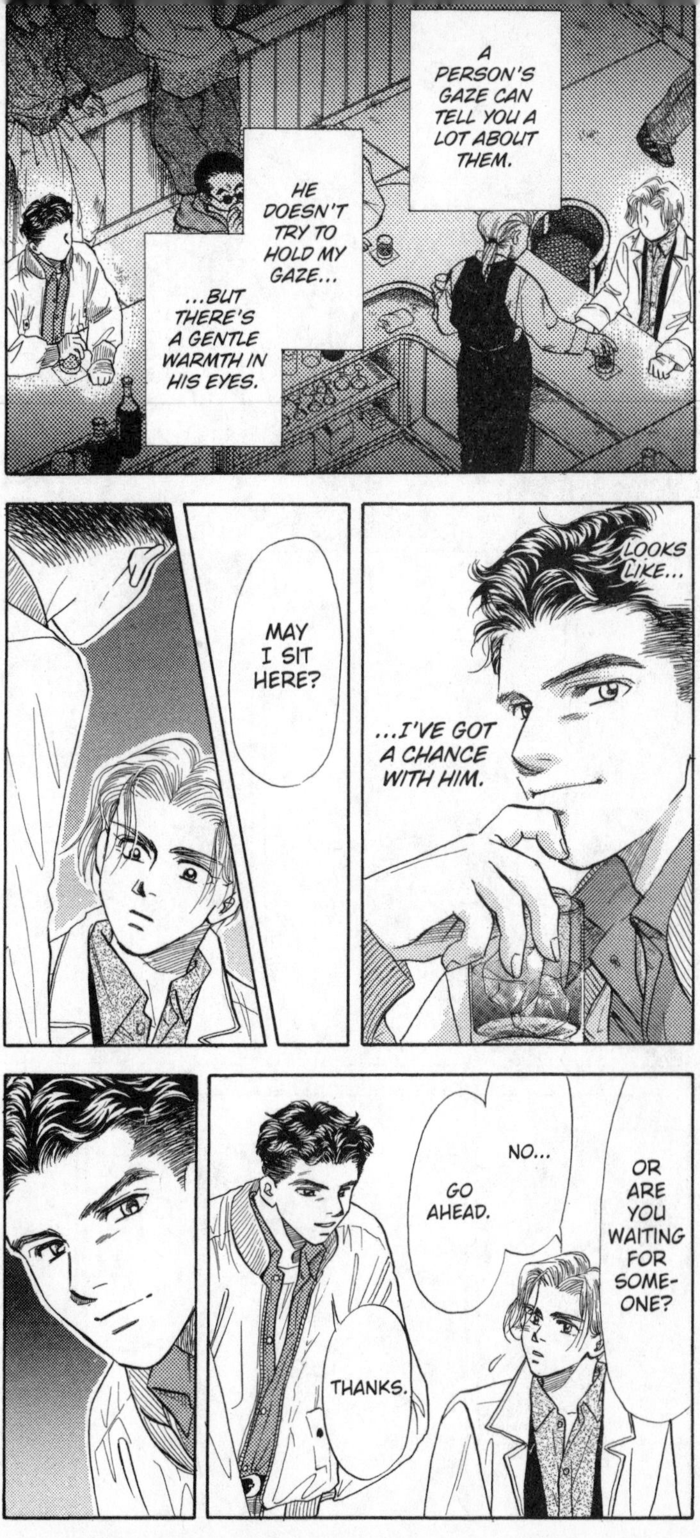
A PERSON'S GAZE CAN TELL YOU A LOT ABOUT THEM.
HE DOESN'T TRY TO HOLD MY GAZE...
...BUT THERE'S A GENTLE WARMTH IN HIS EYES.
LOOKS LIKE...
...I'VE GOT A CHANCE WITH HIM.
MAY I SIT HERE?
OR ARE YOU WAITING FOR SOME-ONE?
NO...
GO AHEAD.
THANKS.

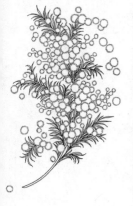

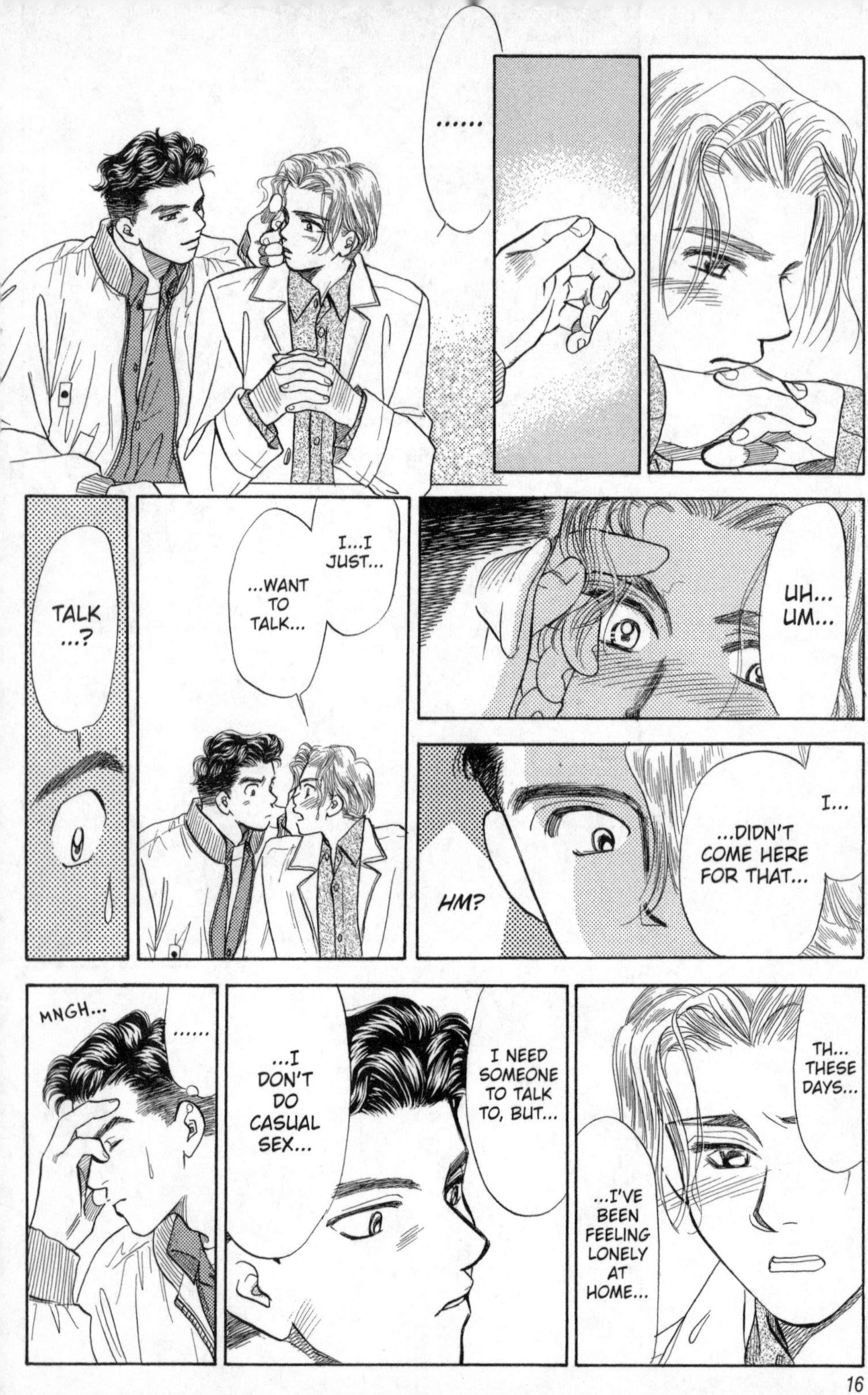
......
UH... UM...
I...
...DIDN'T COME HERE FOR THAT...
HM?
I...I JUST...
...WANT TO TALK...
TALK ...?
TH... THESE DAYS...
...I'VE BEEN FEELING LONELY AT HOME...
I NEED SOMEONE TO TALK TO, BUT...
...I DON'T DO CASUAL SEX...
......
MNGH...

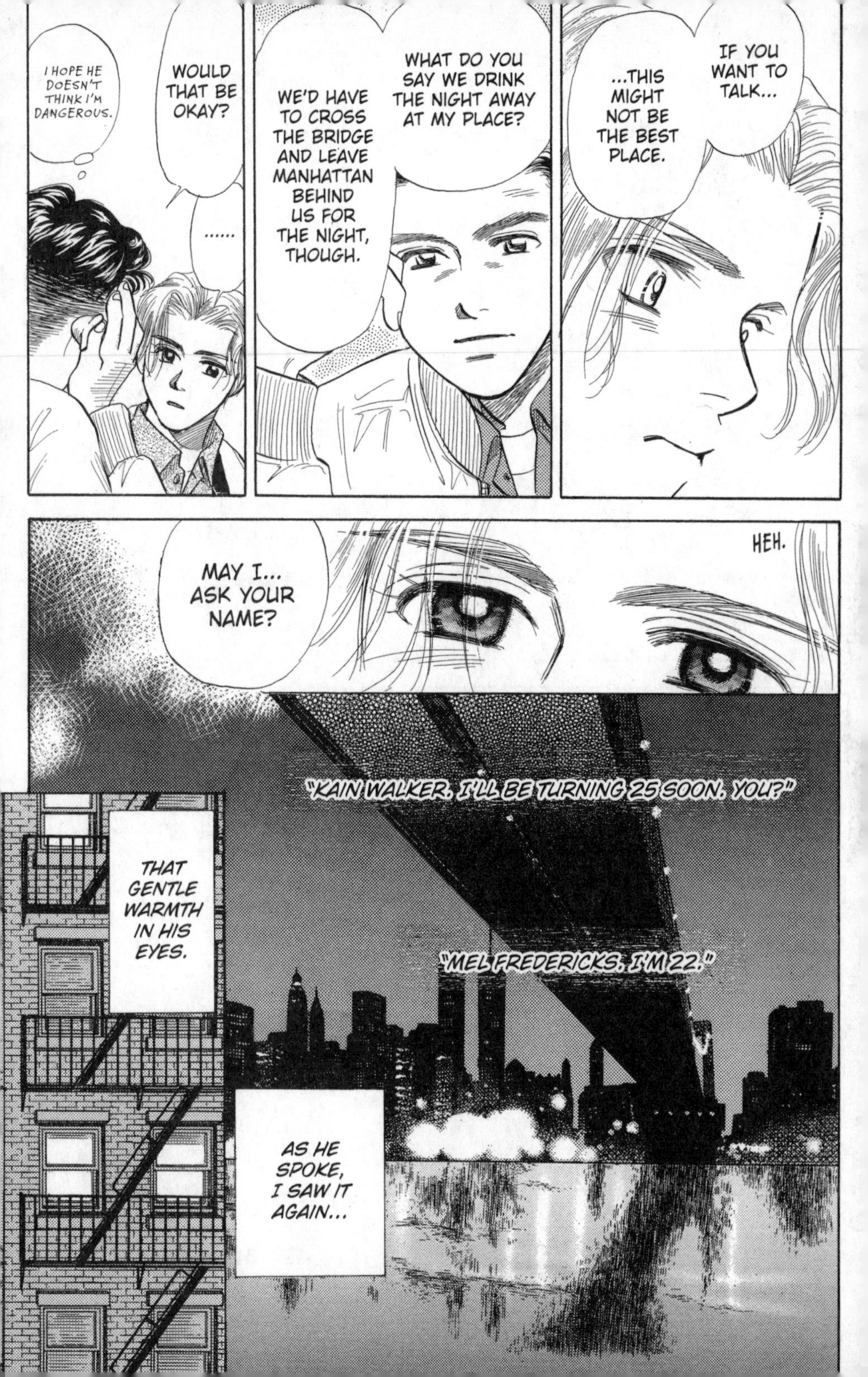
IF YOU WANT TO TALK...
...THIS MIGHT NOT BE THE BEST PLACE.
WHAT DO YOU SAY WE DRINK THE NIGHT AWAY AT MY PLACE?
WE'D HAVE TO CROSS THE BRIDGE AND LEAVE MANHATTAN BEHIND US FOR THE NIGHT, THOUGH.
WOULD THAT BE OKAY?
I HOPE HE DOESN'T THINK I'M DANGEROUS.
......
HEH.
MAY I... ASK YOUR NAME?
"KAIN WALKER. I'LL BE TURNING 25 SOON. YOU?"
"MEL FREDERICKS. I'M 22."
AS HE SPOKE, I SAW IT AGAIN...
THAT GENTLE WARMTH IN HIS EYES.

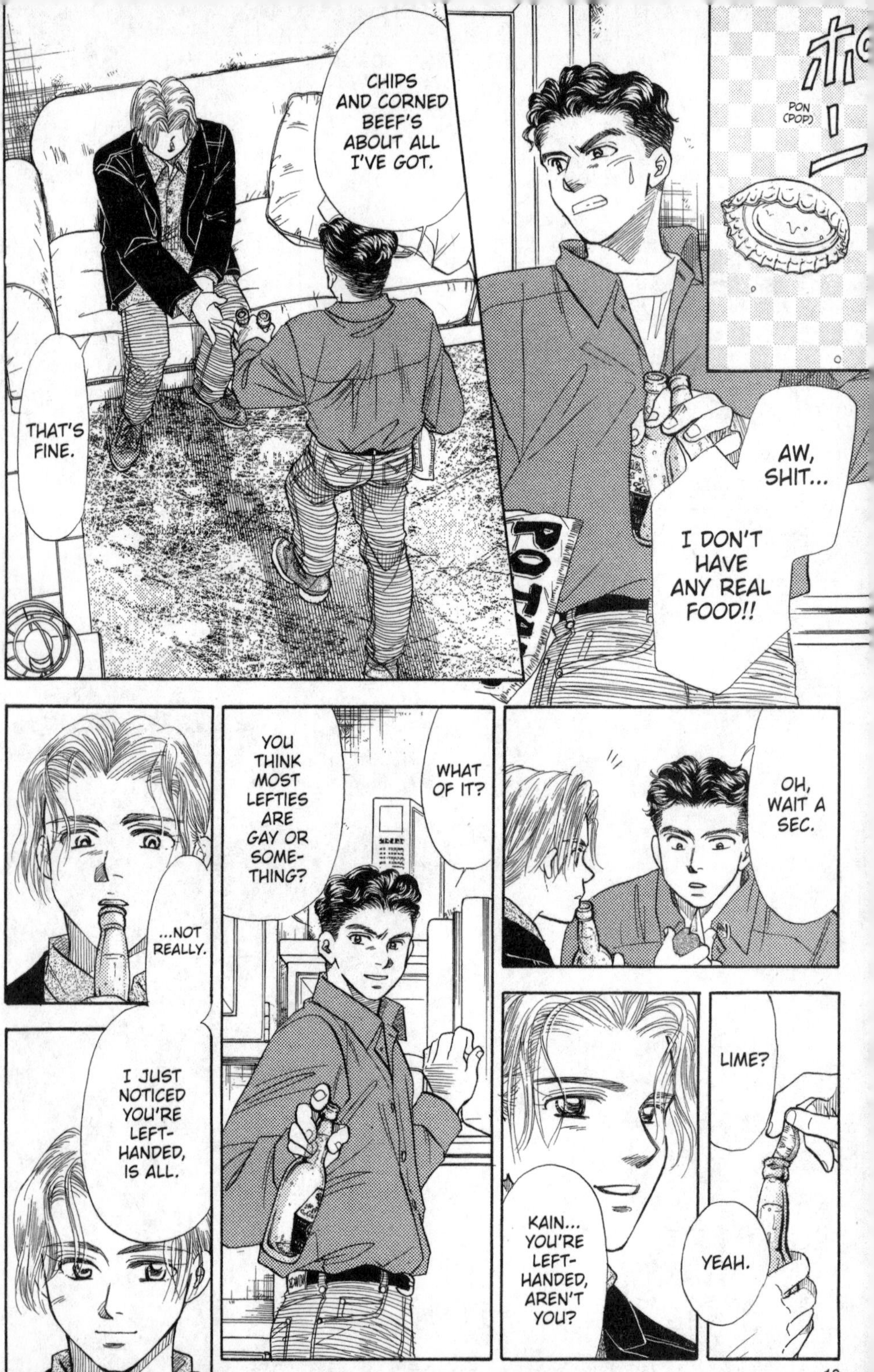
PON (POP)
AW, SHIT...
I DON'T HAVE ANY REAL FOOD!!
CHIPS AND CORNED BEEF'S ABOUT ALL I'VE GOT.
THAT'S FINE.
OH, WAIT A SEC.
LIME?
YEAH.
KAIN... YOU'RE LEFT-HANDED, AREN'T YOU?
WHAT OF IT?
YOU THINK MOST LEFTIES ARE GAY OR SOME-THING?
...NOT REALLY.
I JUST NOTICED YOU'RE LEFT-HANDED, IS ALL.

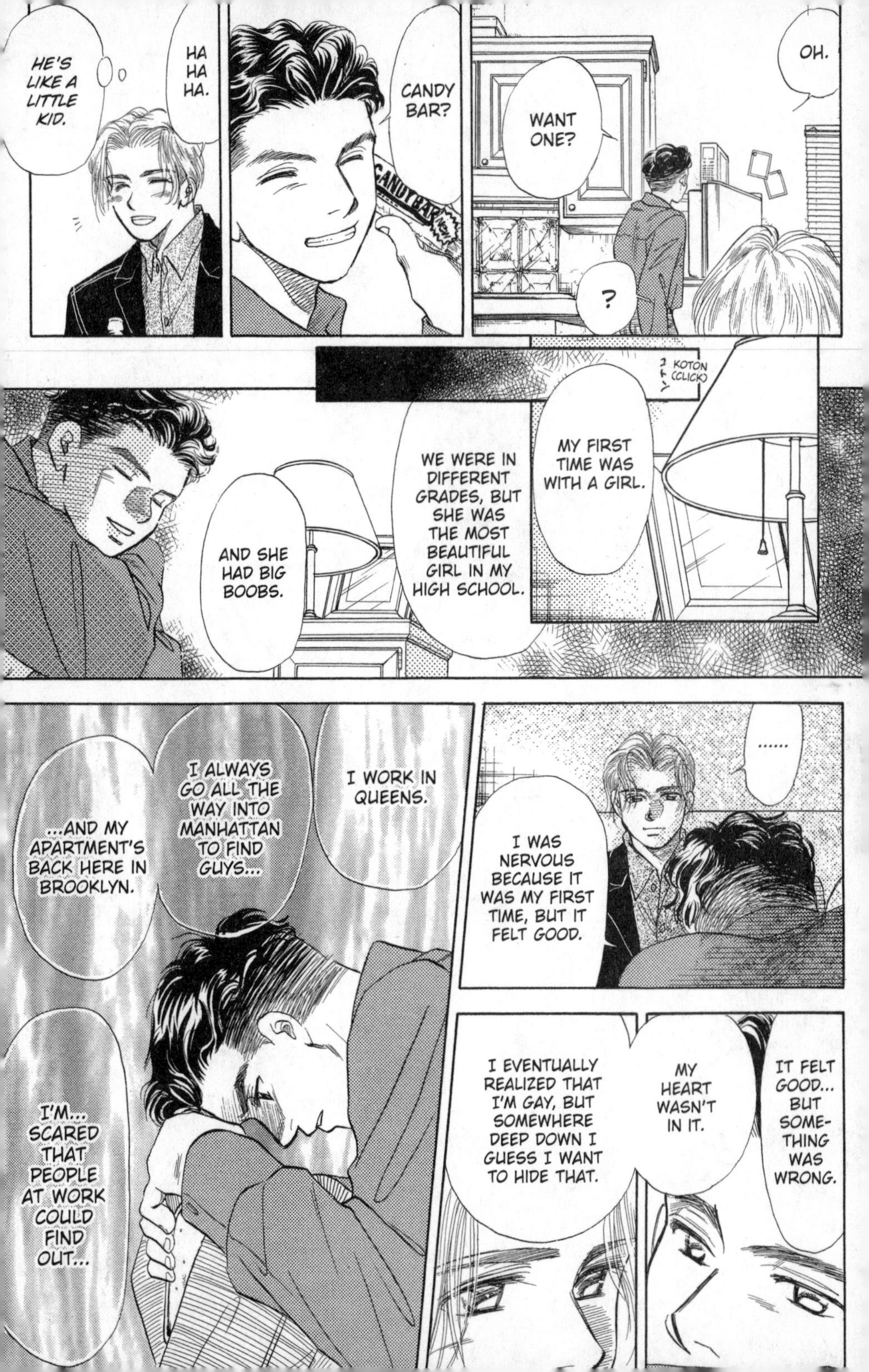
OH.
WANT ONE?
?
CANDY BAR?
CANDY BAR NEW!
HA HA HA.
HE'S LIKE A LITTLE KID.
KOTON (CLICK)
MY FIRST TIME WAS WITH A GIRL.
WE WERE IN DIFFERENT GRADES, BUT SHE WAS THE MOST BEAUTIFUL GIRL IN MY HIGH SCHOOL.
AND SHE HAD BIG BOOBS.
......
I WAS NERVOUS BECAUSE IT WAS MY FIRST TIME, BUT IT FELT GOOD.
IT FELT GOOD... BUT SOMETHING WAS WRONG.
MY HEART WASN'T IN IT.
I EVENTUALLY REALIZED THAT I'M GAY, BUT SOMEWHERE DEEP DOWN I GUESS I WANT TO HIDE THAT.
I WORK IN QUEENS.
I ALWAYS GO ALL THE WAY INTO MANHATTAN TO FIND GUYS...
...AND MY APARTMENT'S BACK HERE IN BROOKLYN.
I'M... SCARED THAT PEOPLE AT WORK COULD FIND OUT...

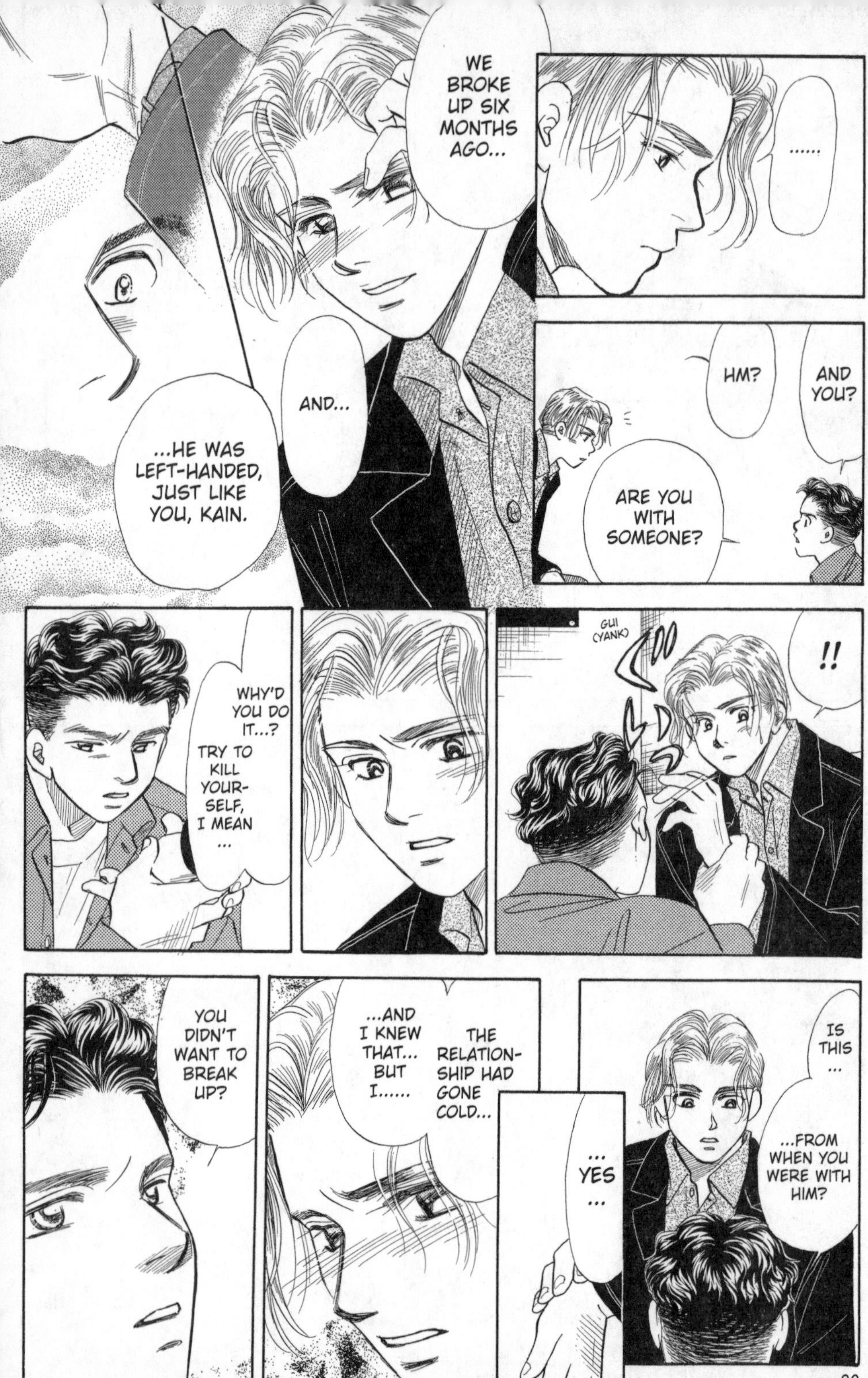
......
AND YOU?
HM?
ARE YOU WITH SOMEONE?
WE BROKE UP SIX MONTHS AGO...
AND...
...HE WAS LEFT-HANDED, JUST LIKE YOU, KAIN.
!!
GUI (YANK)
WHY'D YOU DO IT...? TRY TO KILL YOURSELF, I MEAN ...
IS THIS ...
...FROM WHEN YOU WERE WITH HIM?
... YES ...
THE RELATIONSHIP HAD GONE COLD...
...AND I KNEW THAT... BUT I......
YOU DIDN'T WANT TO BREAK UP?

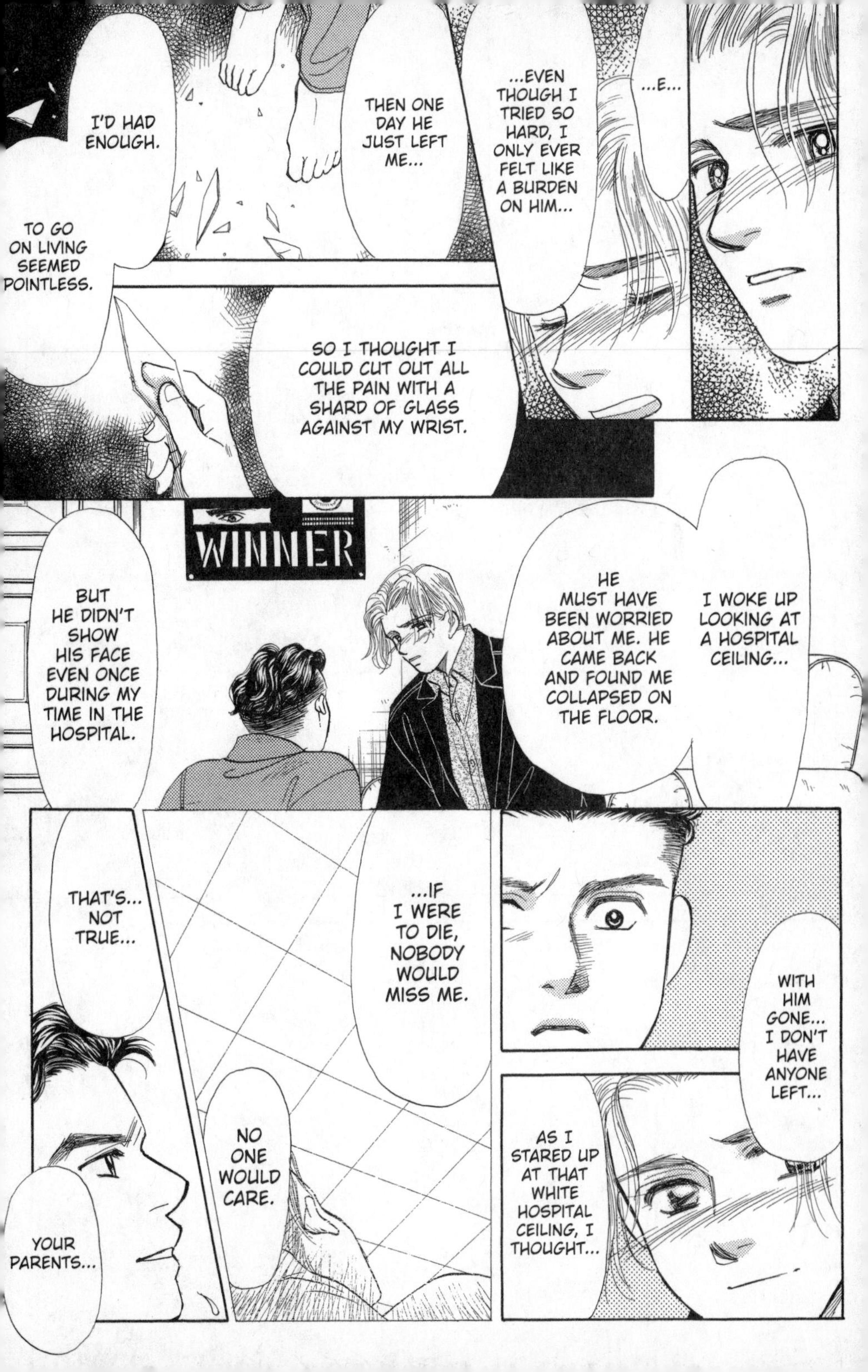
...E...
...EVEN THOUGH I TRIED SO HARD, I ONLY EVER FELT LIKE A BURDEN ON HIM...
THEN ONE DAY HE JUST LEFT ME...
I'D HAD ENOUGH.
TO GO ON LIVING SEEMED POINTLESS.
SO I THOUGHT I COULD CUT OUT ALL THE PAIN WITH A SHARD OF GLASS AGAINST MY WRIST.
I WOKE UP LOOKING AT A HOSPITAL CEILING...
HE MUST HAVE BEEN WORRIED ABOUT ME. HE CAME BACK AND FOUND ME COLLAPSED ON THE FLOOR.
WINNER
BUT HE DIDN'T SHOW HIS FACE EVEN ONCE DURING MY TIME IN THE HOSPITAL.
WITH HIM GONE... I DON'T HAVE ANYONE LEFT...
AS I STARED UP AT THAT WHITE HOSPITAL CEILING, I THOUGHT...
...IF I WERE TO DIE, NOBODY WOULD MISS ME.
NO ONE WOULD CARE.
THAT'S... NOT TRUE...
YOUR PARENTS...

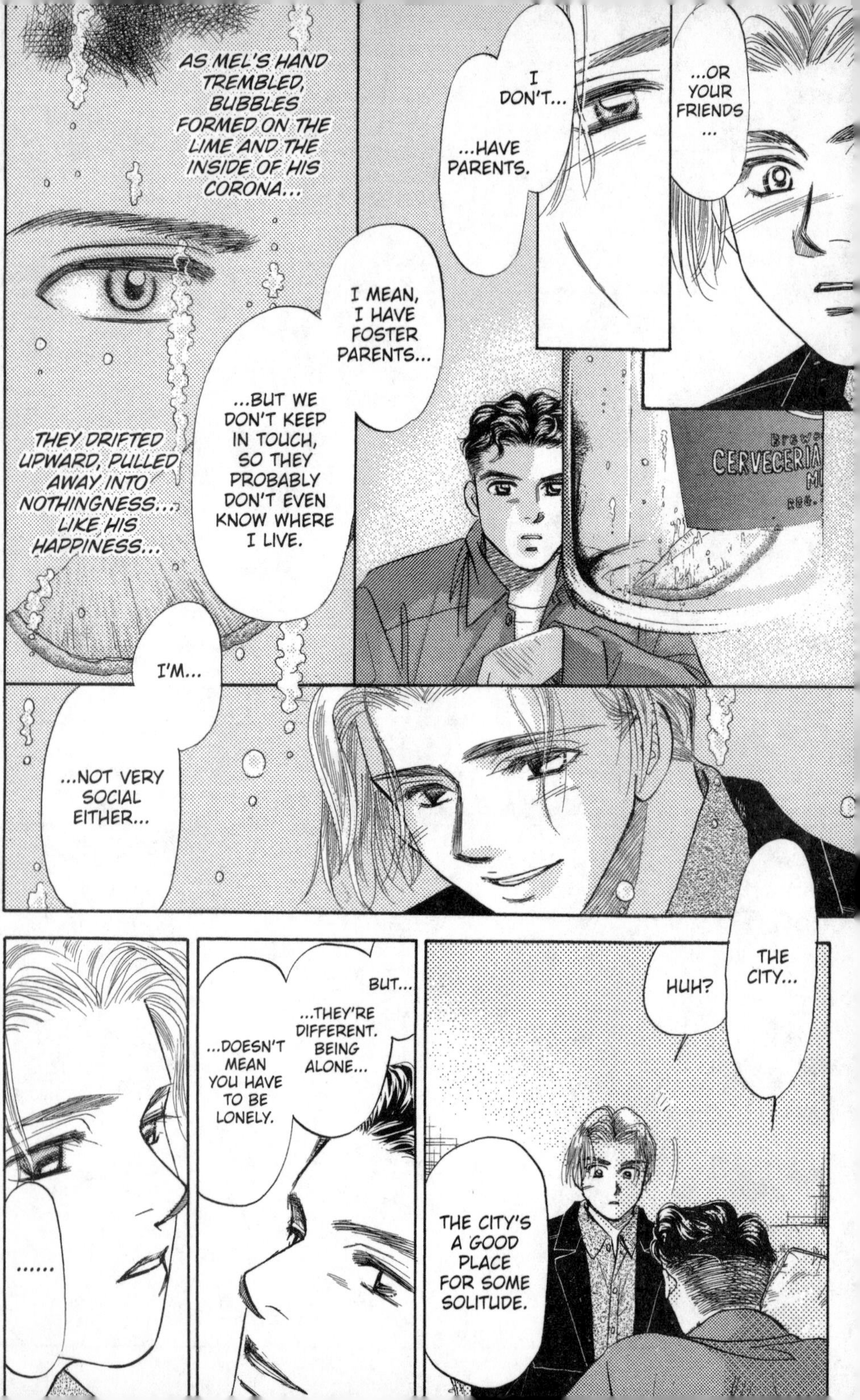
...OR YOUR FRIENDS ...
I DON'T...
...HAVE PARENTS.
I MEAN, I HAVE FOSTER PARENTS...
...BUT WE DON'T KEEP IN TOUCH, SO THEY PROBABLY DON'T EVEN KNOW WHERE I LIVE.
CERVECERIA
AS MEL'S HAND TREMBLED, BUBBLES FORMED ON THE LIME AND THE INSIDE OF HIS CORONA...
THEY DRIFTED UPWARD, PULLED AWAY INTO NOTHINGNESS... LIKE HIS HAPPINESS...
I'M...
...NOT VERY SOCIAL EITHER...
THE CITY...
HUH?
THE CITY'S A GOOD PLACE FOR SOME SOLITUDE.
BUT...
...THEY'RE DIFFERENT. BEING ALONE...
...DOESN'T MEAN YOU HAVE TO BE LONELY.
......

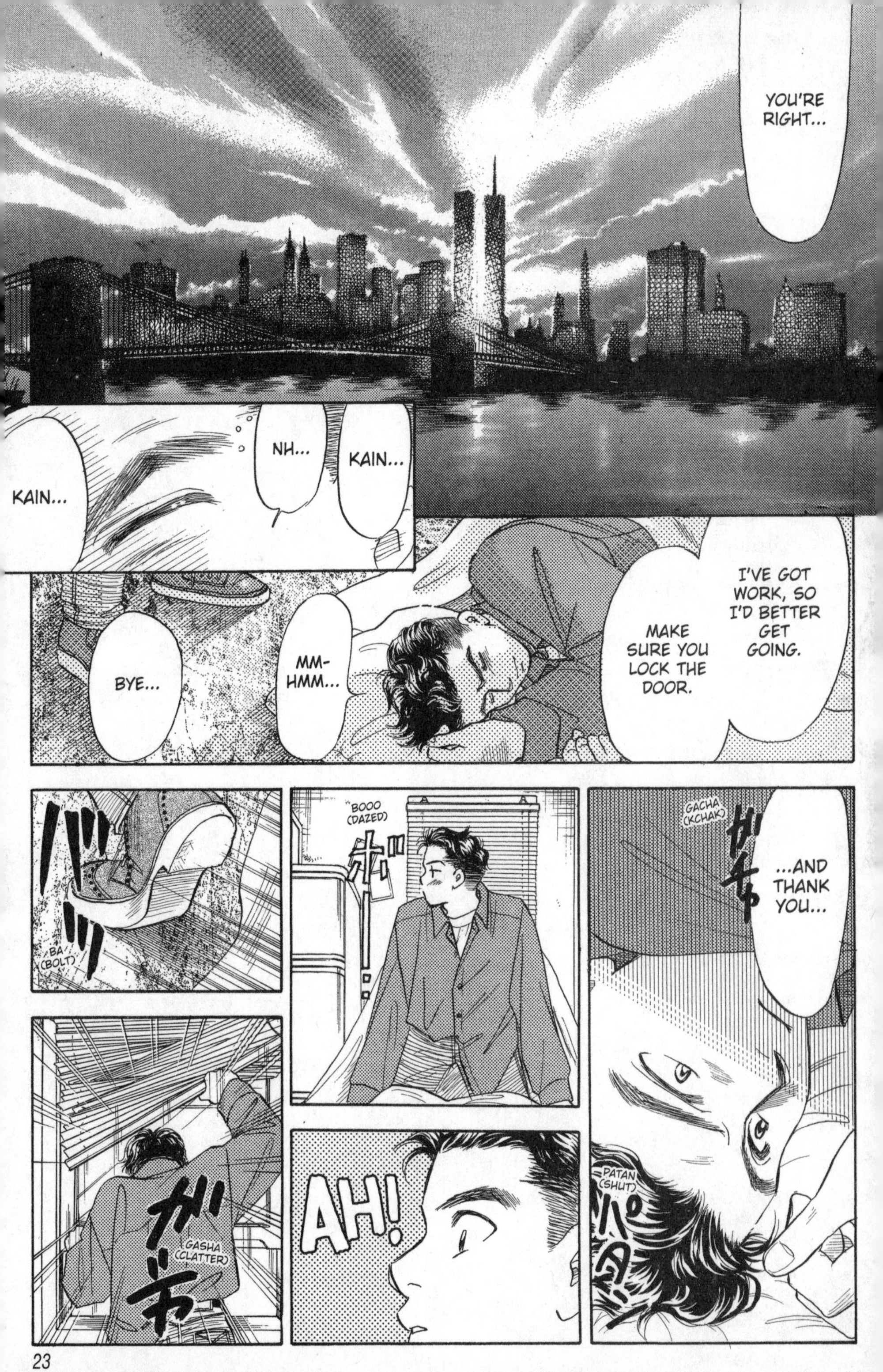
YOU'RE RIGHT...
KAIN...
NH...
KAIN...
I'VE GOT WORK, SO I'D BETTER GET GOING.
MAKE SURE YOU LOCK THE DOOR.
MM-HMM...
BYE...
GACHA (KCHAK)
...AND THANK YOU...
PATAN (SHUT)
BOOO (DAZED)
BA (BOLT)
AH!
GASHA (CLATTER)

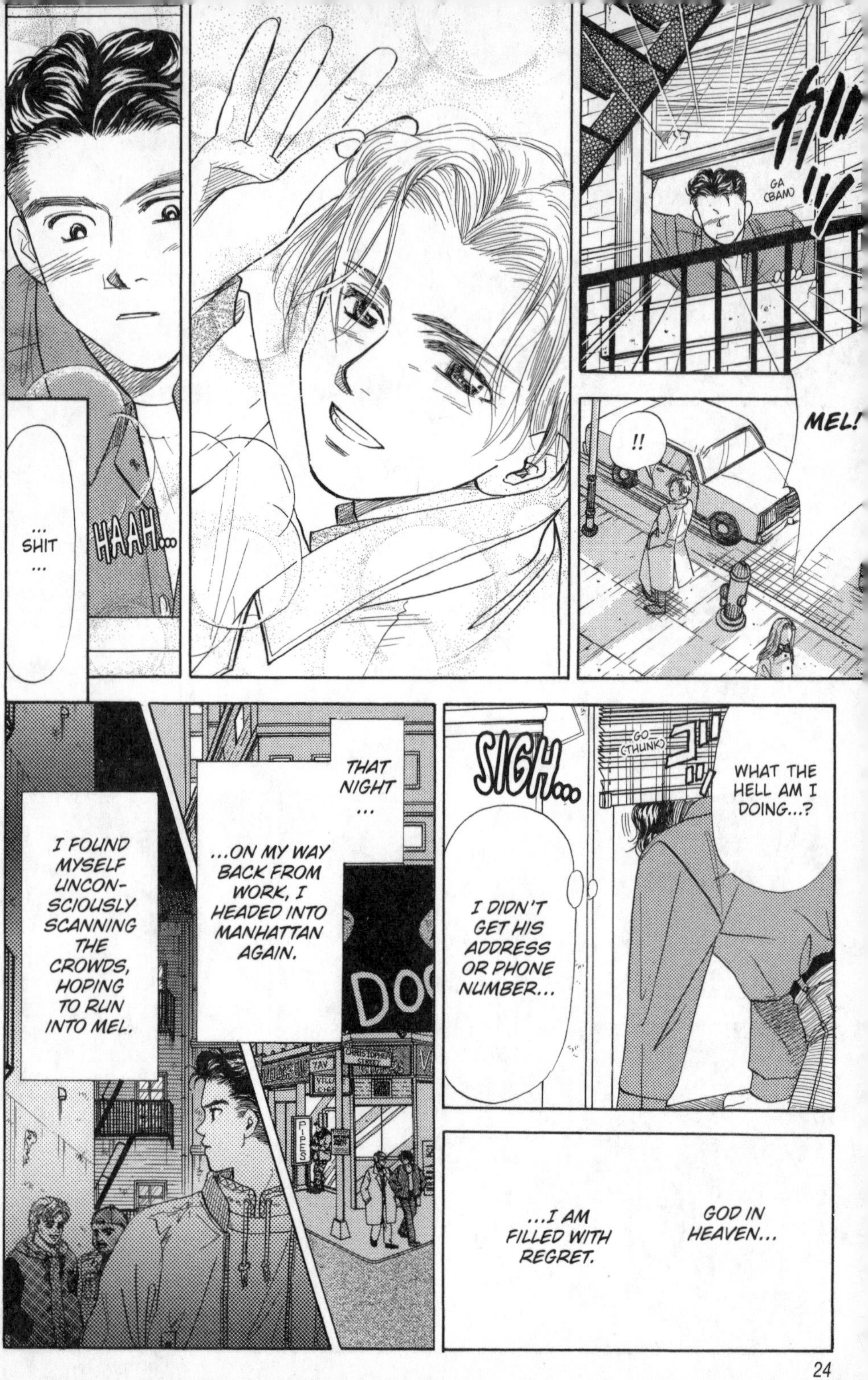
GA (BAM)
MEL!
!!
HAAH...
... SHIT ...
SIGH...
GO (THUNK)
WHAT THE HELL AM I DOING...?
I DIDN'T GET HIS ADDRESS OR PHONE NUMBER...
GOD IN HEAVEN...
...I AM FILLED WITH REGRET.
THAT NIGHT ...
...ON MY WAY BACK FROM WORK, I HEADED INTO MANHATTAN AGAIN.
I FOUND MYSELF UNCONSCIOUSLY SCANNING THE CROWDS, HOPING TO RUN INTO MEL.
PIPES

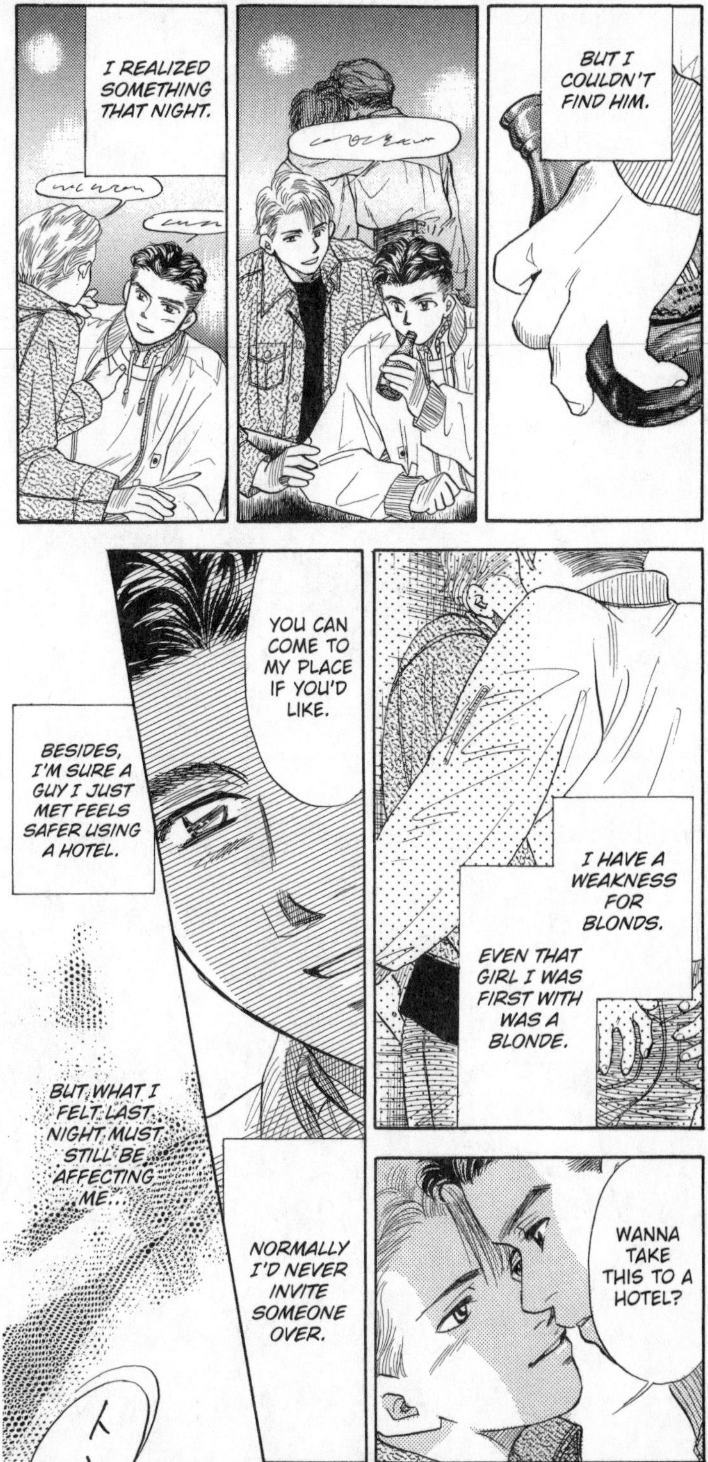
BUT I COULDN'T FIND HIM.
I REALIZED SOMETHING THAT NIGHT.
I HAVE A WEAKNESS FOR BLONDS.
EVEN THAT GIRL I WAS FIRST WITH WAS A BLONDE.
WANNA TAKE THIS TO A HOTEL?
NORMALLY I'D NEVER INVITE SOMEONE OVER.
YOU CAN COME TO MY PLACE IF YOU'D LIKE.
BESIDES, I'M SURE A GUY I JUST MET FEELS SAFER USING A HOTEL.
BUT WHAT I FELT LAST NIGHT MUST STILL BE AFFECTING ME...
TON (TMP)

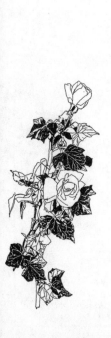

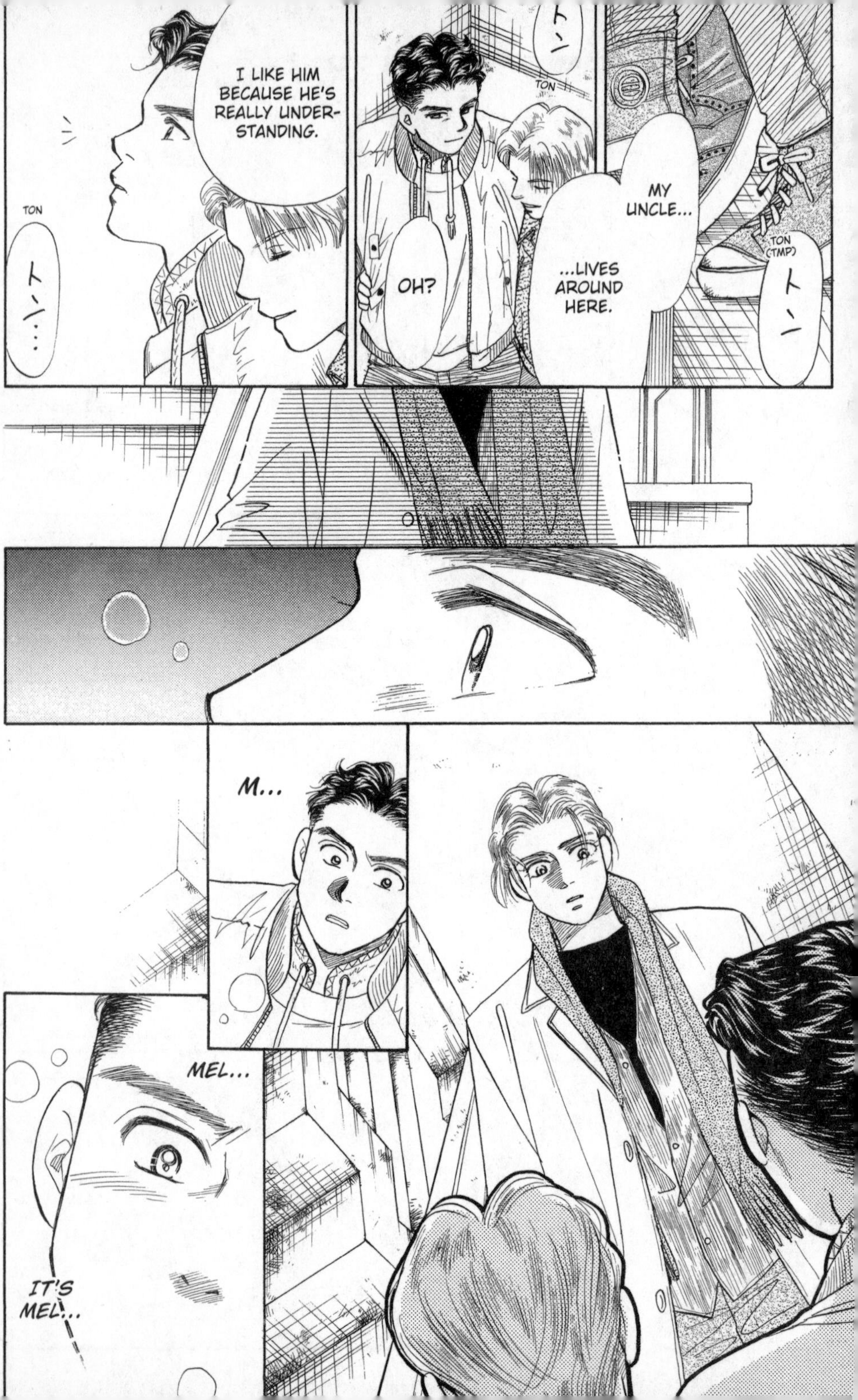
MY UNCLE...
TON (TMP)
トン
...LIVES AROUND HERE.
トン
TON
OH?
I LIKE HIM BECAUSE HE'S REALLY UNDER-STANDING.
TON
トン…
M...
MEL...
IT'S MEL...

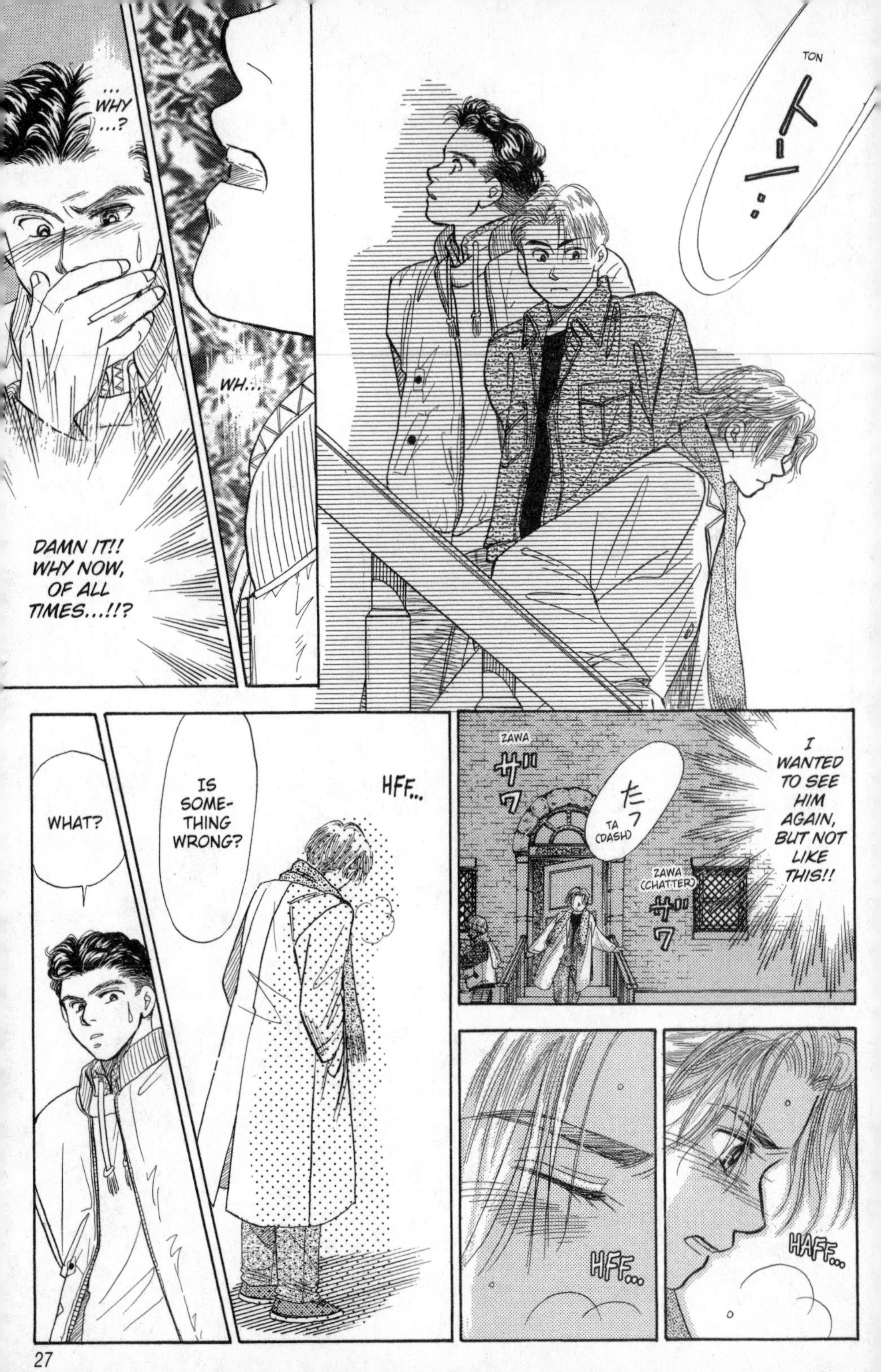
TON
トン…
...WHY...?
WH...
DAMN IT!! WHY NOW, OF ALL TIMES...!!?
I WANTED TO SEE HIM AGAIN, BUT NOT LIKE THIS!!
ZAWA
ザワ
たっ
TA (DASH)
ZAWA (CHATTER)
ザワ
HAFF...
HFF...
HFF...
IS SOME-THING WRONG?
WHAT?

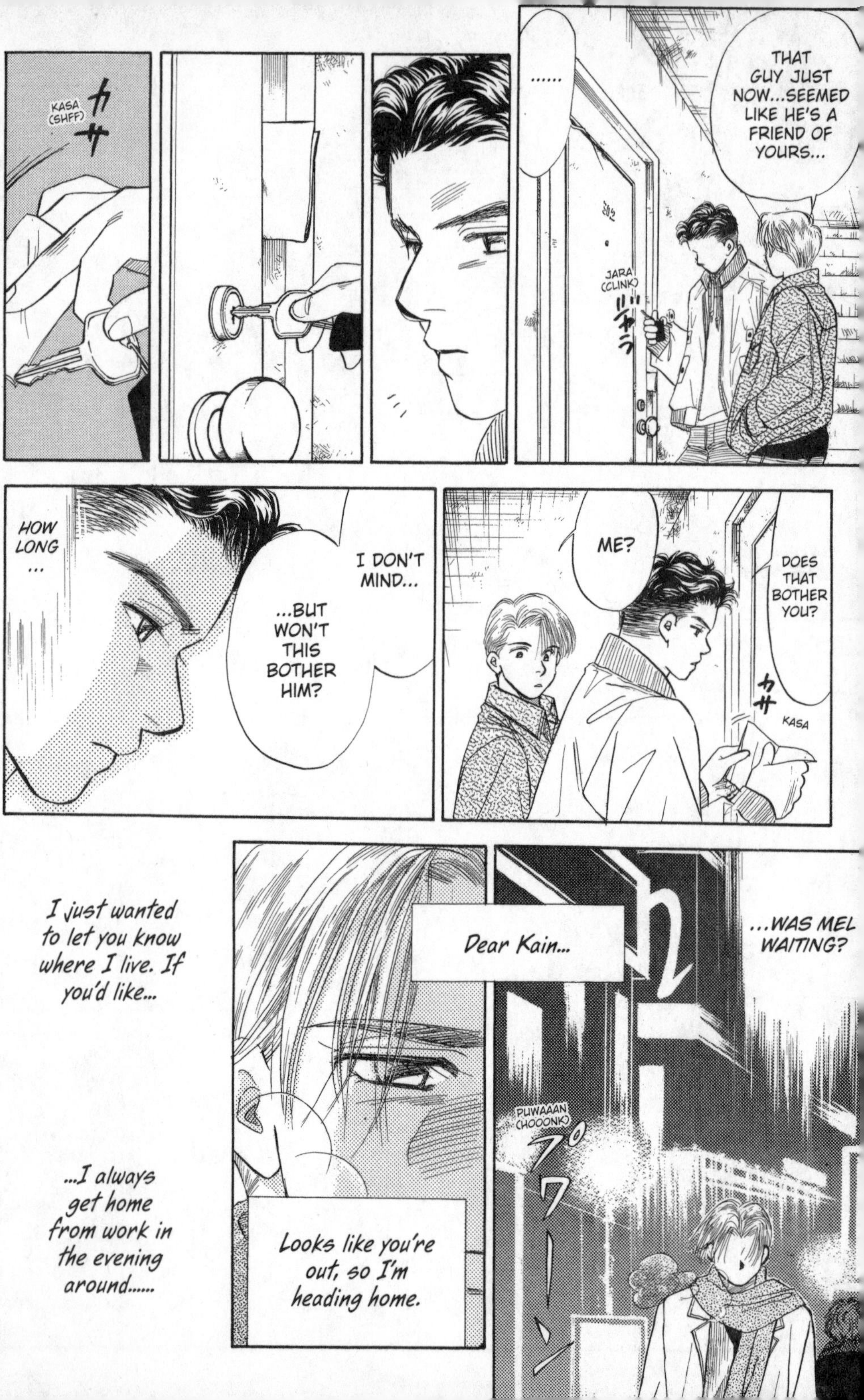
THAT GUY JUST NOW...SEEMED LIKE HE'S A FRIEND OF YOURS...
......
JARA (CLINK)
ジャラ
KASA (SHFF)
カサ
DOES THAT BOTHER YOU?
ME?
カサ
KASA
I DON'T MIND...
...BUT WON'T THIS BOTHER HIM?
HOW LONG ...
...WAS MEL WAITING?
Dear Kain...
PUWAAAN (HOONK)
プワーン
Looks like you're out, so I'm heading home.
I just wanted to let you know where I live. If you'd like...
...I always get home from work in the evening around......

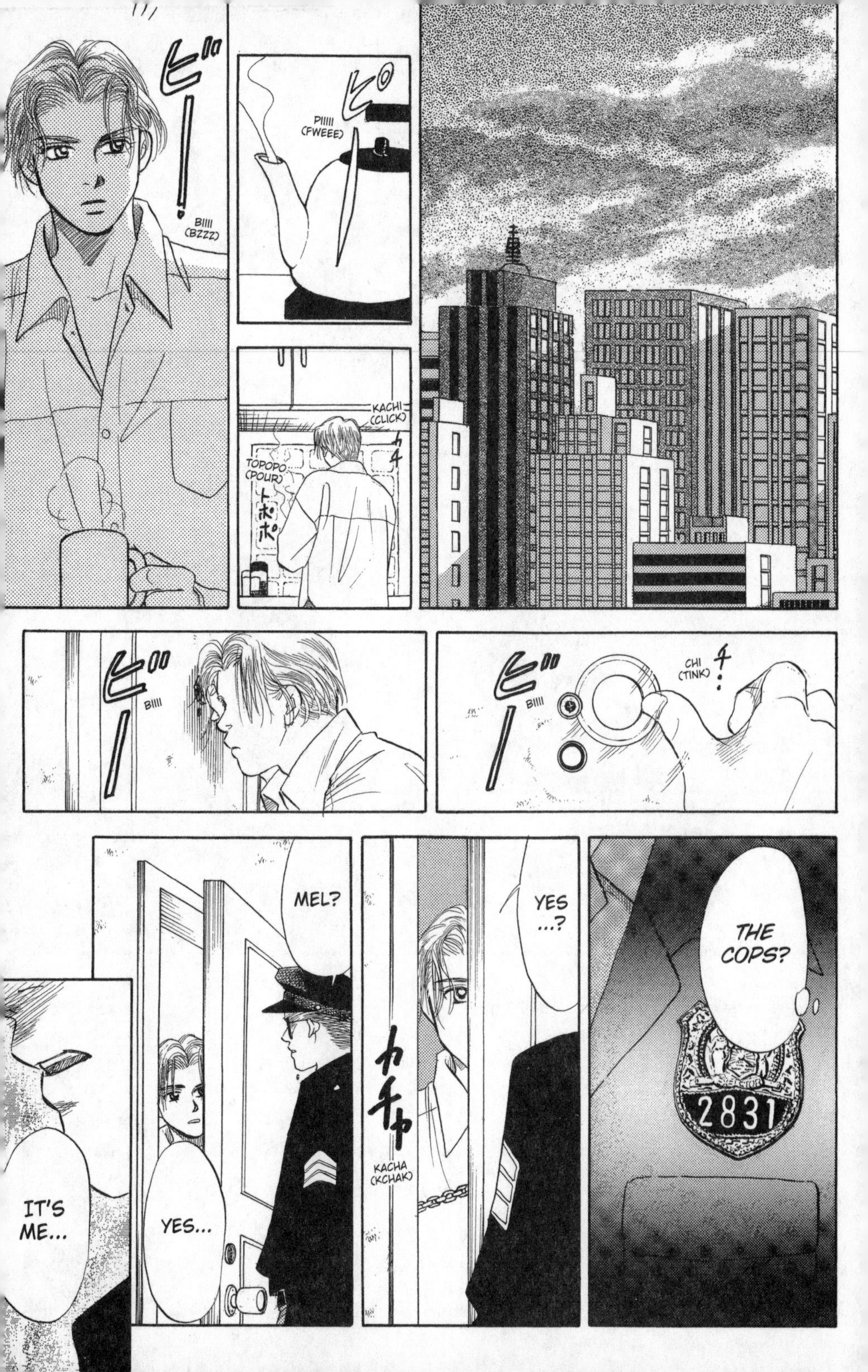
PIIII
(FWEEE)
KACHI
(CLICK)
カチ
TOPOPO
(POUR)
トポポ
ビー
BIIII
(BZZZ)
ビー
BIIII
CHI
(TINK)
チ
ビー
BIIII
THE COPS?
YES ...?
カチャ
KACHA
(KCHAK)
MEL?
YES...
IT'S ME...

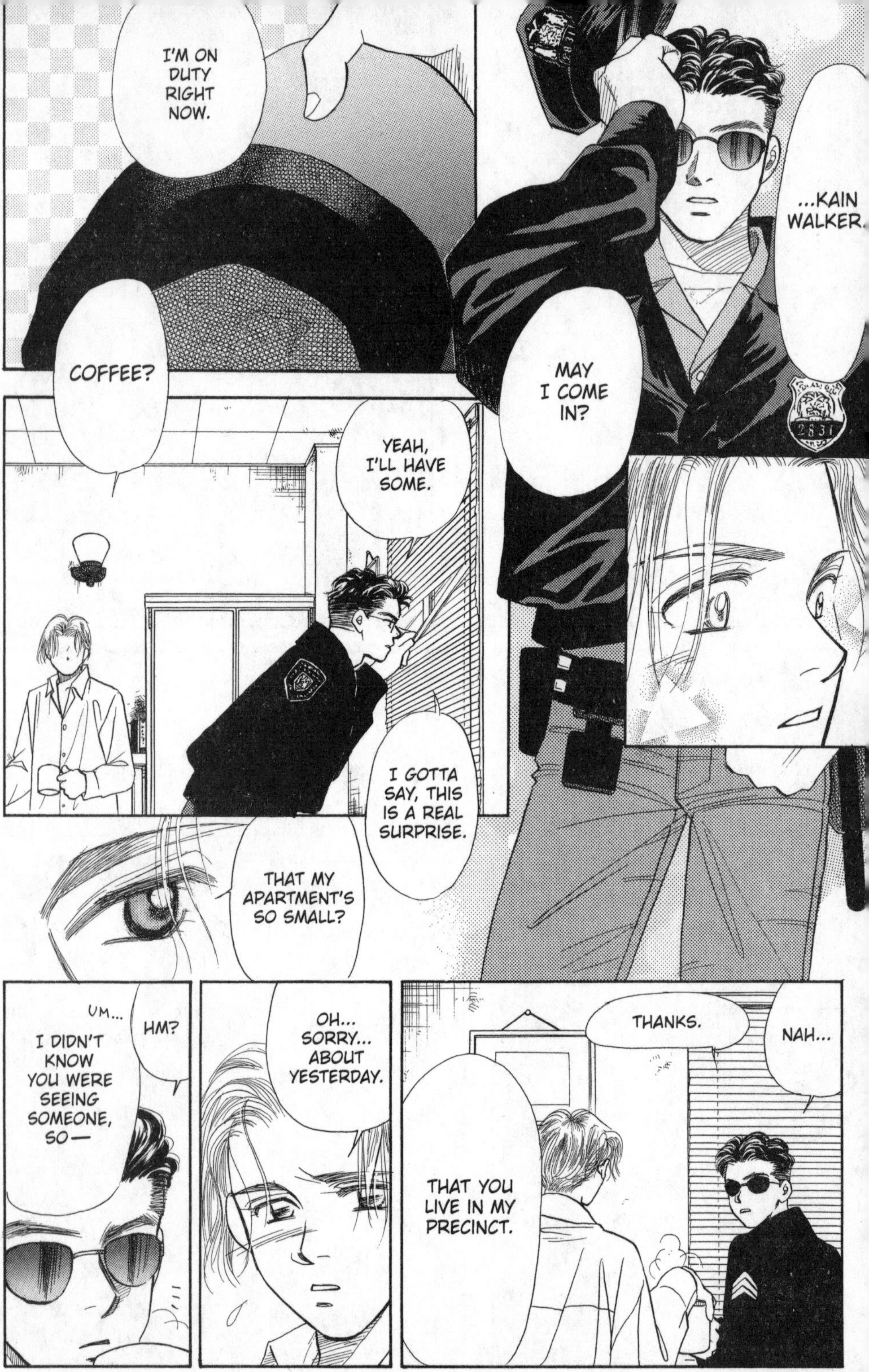
...KAIN WALKER.
MAY I COME IN?
I'M ON DUTY RIGHT NOW.
COFFEE?
YEAH, I'LL HAVE SOME.
I GOTTA SAY, THIS IS A REAL SURPRISE.
THAT MY APARTMENT'S SO SMALL?
NAH...
THANKS.
THAT YOU LIVE IN MY PRECINCT.
OH... SORRY... ABOUT YESTERDAY.
HM?
UM...
I DIDN'T KNOW YOU WERE SEEING SOMEONE, SO—

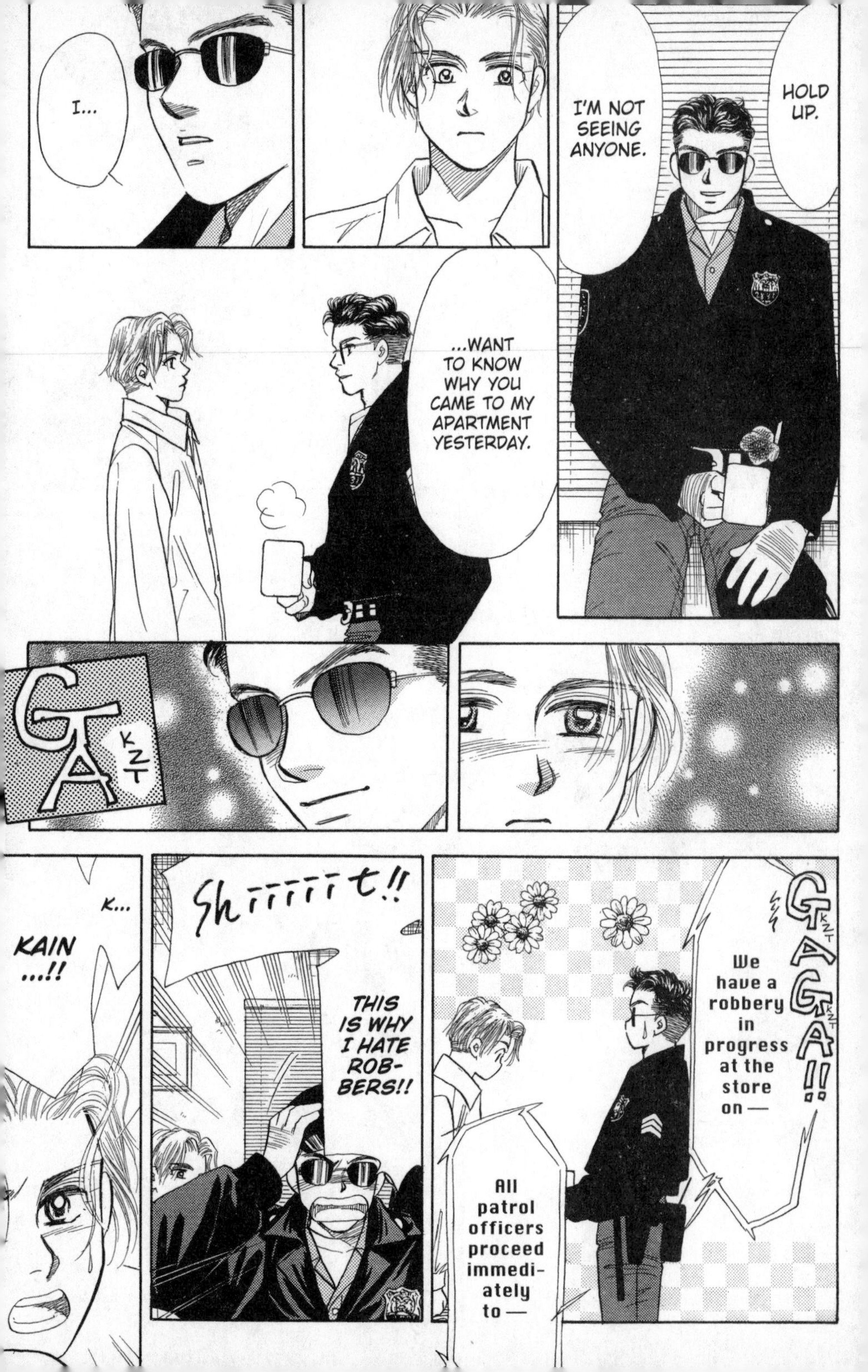
HOLD UP.
I'M NOT SEEING ANYONE.
I...
...WANT TO KNOW WHY YOU CAME TO MY APARTMENT YESTERDAY.
GA
KZT
GA
KZT
GA!!
KZT
We have a robbery in progress at the store on—
All patrol officers proceed immediately to—
Shiiiiit!!
THIS IS WHY I HATE ROB-BERS!!
K...
KAIN...!!

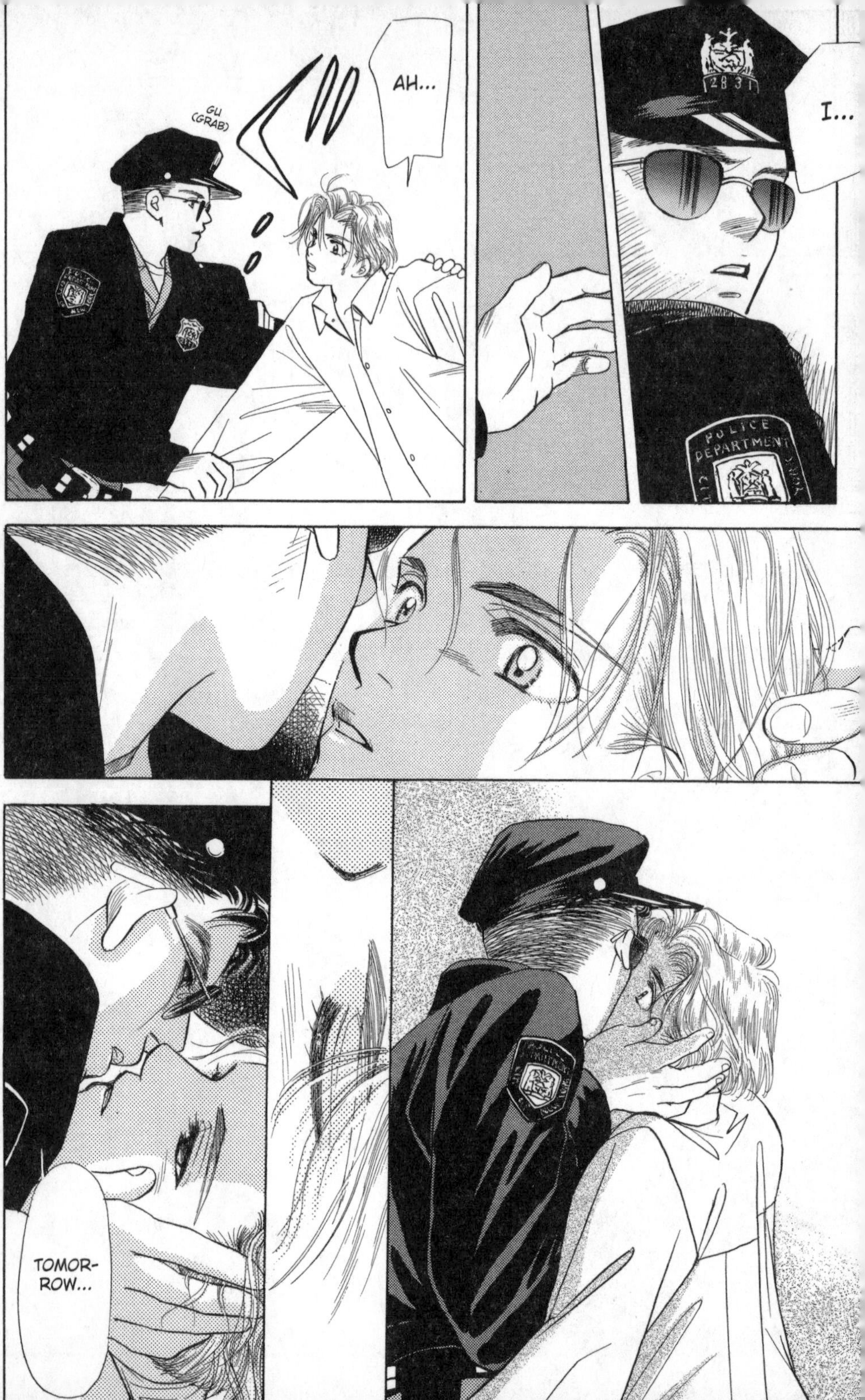
I...
AH...
GU
(GRAB)
TOMOR-
ROW...

KAIN!!

I'M TAKING A RISK HERE.

...I'M...

...OFF DUTY...

I THOUGHT IT WAS FATE...

SORRY.

HEY, DANNY.

I THOUGHT YOU WERE DYING IN THERE OR SOMETHING.

YOU'RE LATE!

......

IS IT JUST ME, OR IS THAT A SHIT-EATING GRIN YOU'VE GOT ON YOUR FACE?

IS THIS "FRIEND" A WOMAN?

......

IT WASN'T ANYTHING SERIOUS.

OH... UM...

WAS EVERYTHING ALL RIGHT? YOU SAID THEY WERE SICK IN BED, DIDN'T YOU?

HM?

HOW'S YOUR FRIEND?

IN THE APARTMENT JUST NOW.

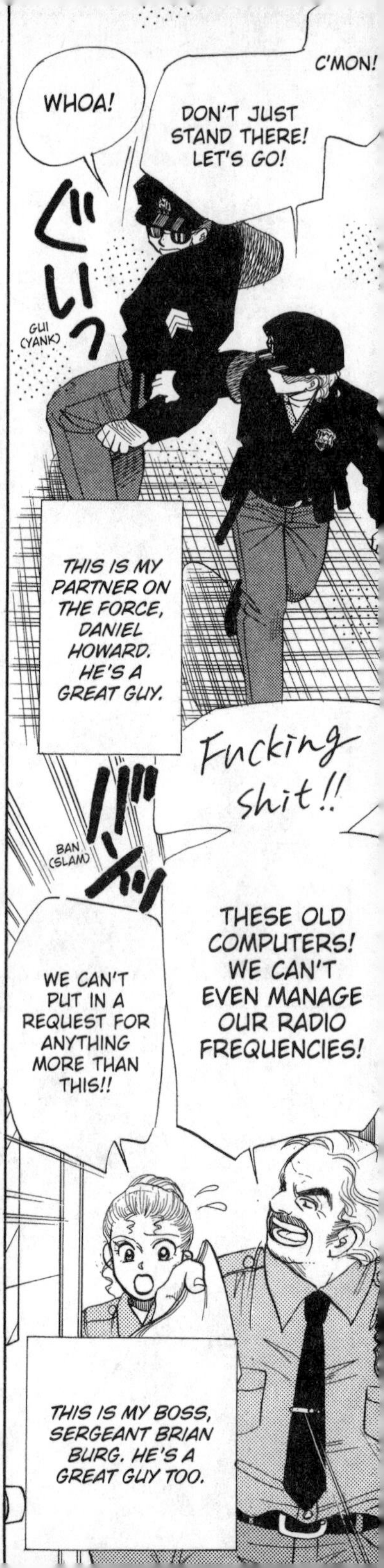
C'MON!
DON'T JUST STAND THERE! LET'S GO!
WHOA!
GUI (YANK)
THIS IS MY PARTNER ON THE FORCE, DANIEL HOWARD. HE'S A GREAT GUY.
Fucking shit!!
BAN (SLAM)
THESE OLD COMPUTERS! WE CAN'T EVEN MANAGE OUR RADIO FREQUENCIES!
WE CAN'T PUT IN A REQUEST FOR ANYTHING MORE THAN THIS!!
THIS IS MY BOSS, SERGEANT BRIAN BURG. HE'S A GREAT GUY TOO.

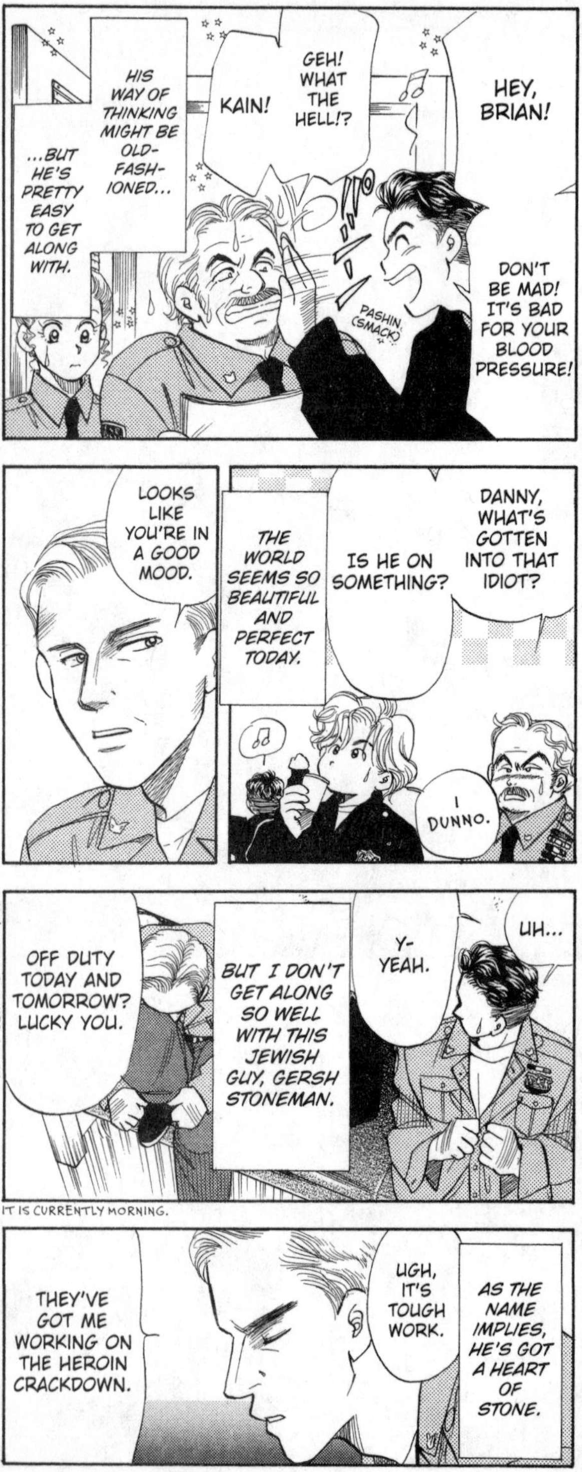
HEY, BRIAN!
DON'T BE MAD! IT'S BAD FOR YOUR BLOOD PRESSURE!
PASHIN (SMACK)
GEH! WHAT THE HELL!?
KAIN!
HIS WAY OF THINKING MIGHT BE OLD-FASHIONED...
...BUT HE'S PRETTY EASY TO GET ALONG WITH.
DANNY, WHAT'S GOTTEN INTO THAT IDIOT?
IS HE ON SOMETHING?
THE WORLD SEEMS SO BEAUTIFUL AND PERFECT TODAY.
I DUNNO.
LOOKS LIKE YOU'RE IN A GOOD MOOD.
UH...
Y-YEAH.
BUT I DON'T GET ALONG SO WELL WITH THIS JEWISH GUY, GERSH STONEMAN.
OFF DUTY TODAY AND TOMORROW? LUCKY YOU.
AS THE NAME IMPLIES, HE'S GOT A HEART OF STONE.
UGH, IT'S TOUGH WORK.
THEY'VE GOT ME WORKING ON THE HEROIN CRACKDOWN.

*KAIN'S JUST FINISHED A NIGHT SHIFT AND IS HEADING HOME.

IT IS CURRENTLY MORNING.

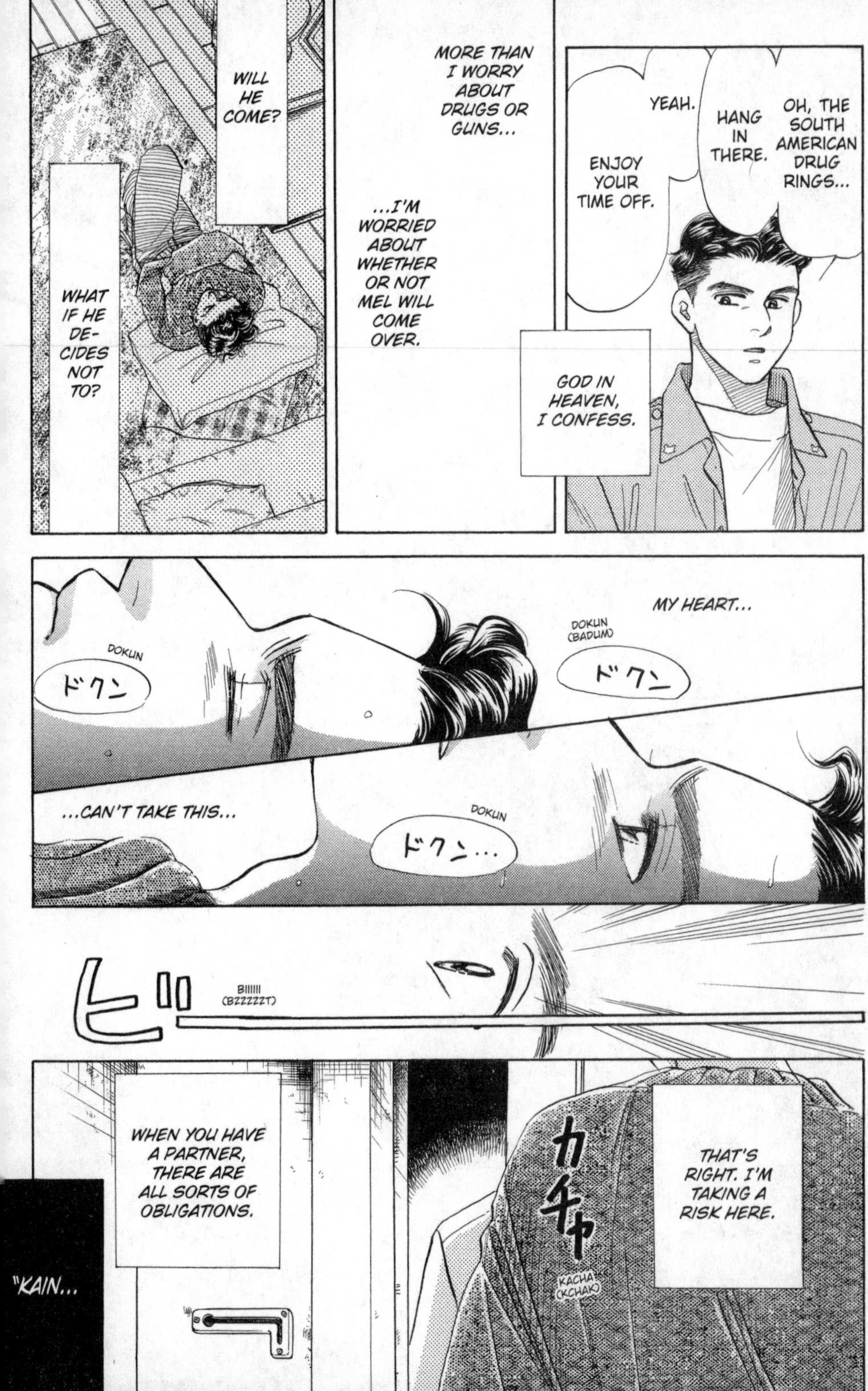
OH, THE SOUTH AMERICAN DRUG RINGS...
HANG IN THERE.
YEAH.
ENJOY YOUR TIME OFF.
GOD IN HEAVEN, I CONFESS.
MORE THAN I WORRY ABOUT DRUGS OR GUNS...
...I'M WORRIED ABOUT WHETHER OR NOT MEL WILL COME OVER.
WILL HE COME?
WHAT IF HE DE-CIDES NOT TO?
MY HEART...
ドクン
DOKUN (BADUM)
ドクン
DOKUN
...CAN'T TAKE THIS...
ドクン…
DOKUN
ビー
BIIIII (BZZZZZT)
THAT'S RIGHT. I'M TAKING A RISK HERE.
カチャ
KACHA (KCHAK)
WHEN YOU HAVE A PARTNER, THERE ARE ALL SORTS OF OBLIGATIONS.
"KAIN...

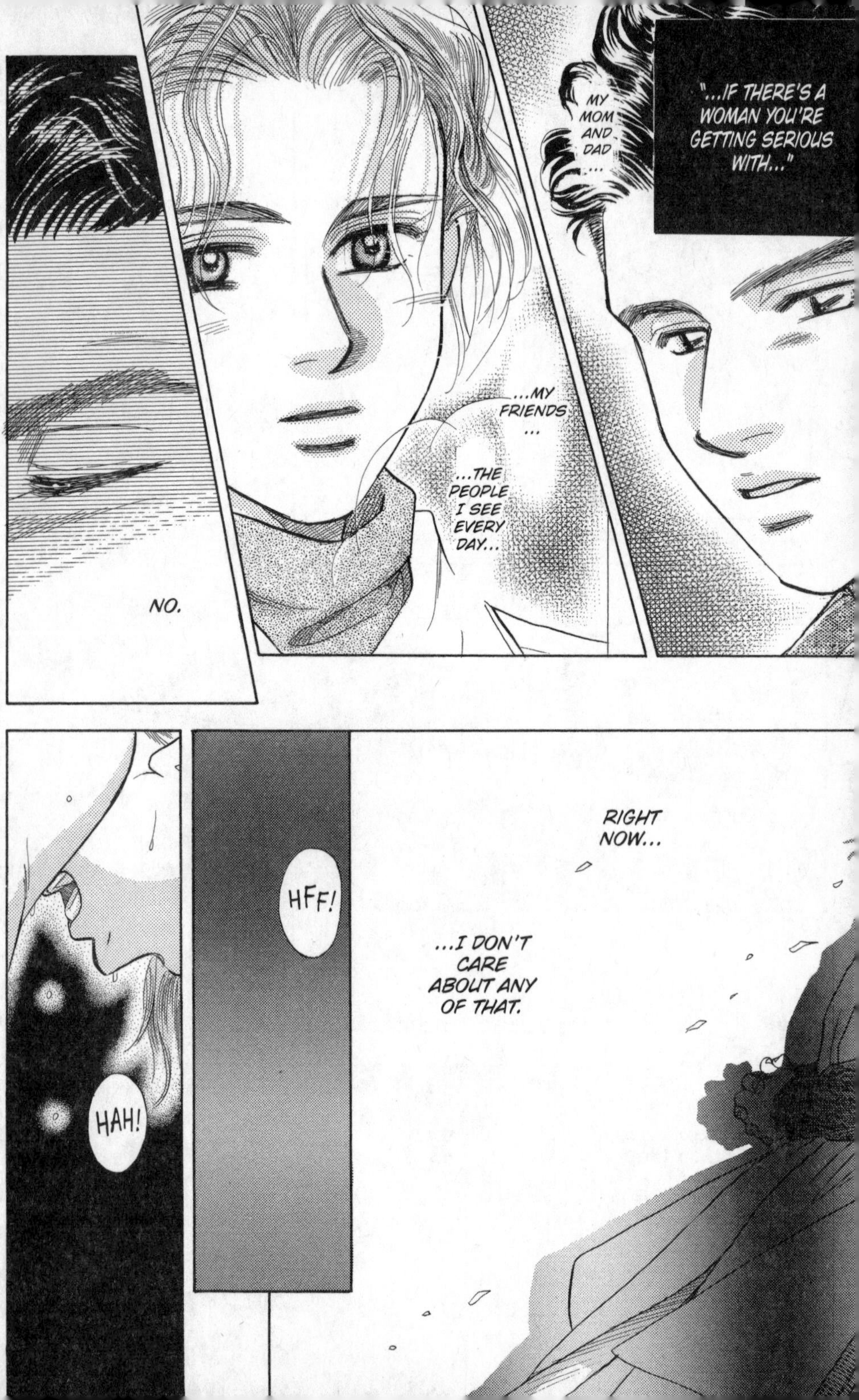
"...IF THERE'S A WOMAN YOU'RE GETTING SERIOUS WITH..."
MY MOM AND DAD...
...MY FRIENDS...
...THE PEOPLE I SEE EVERY DAY...
NO.
RIGHT NOW...
...I DON'T CARE ABOUT ANY OF THAT.
HFF!
HAH!

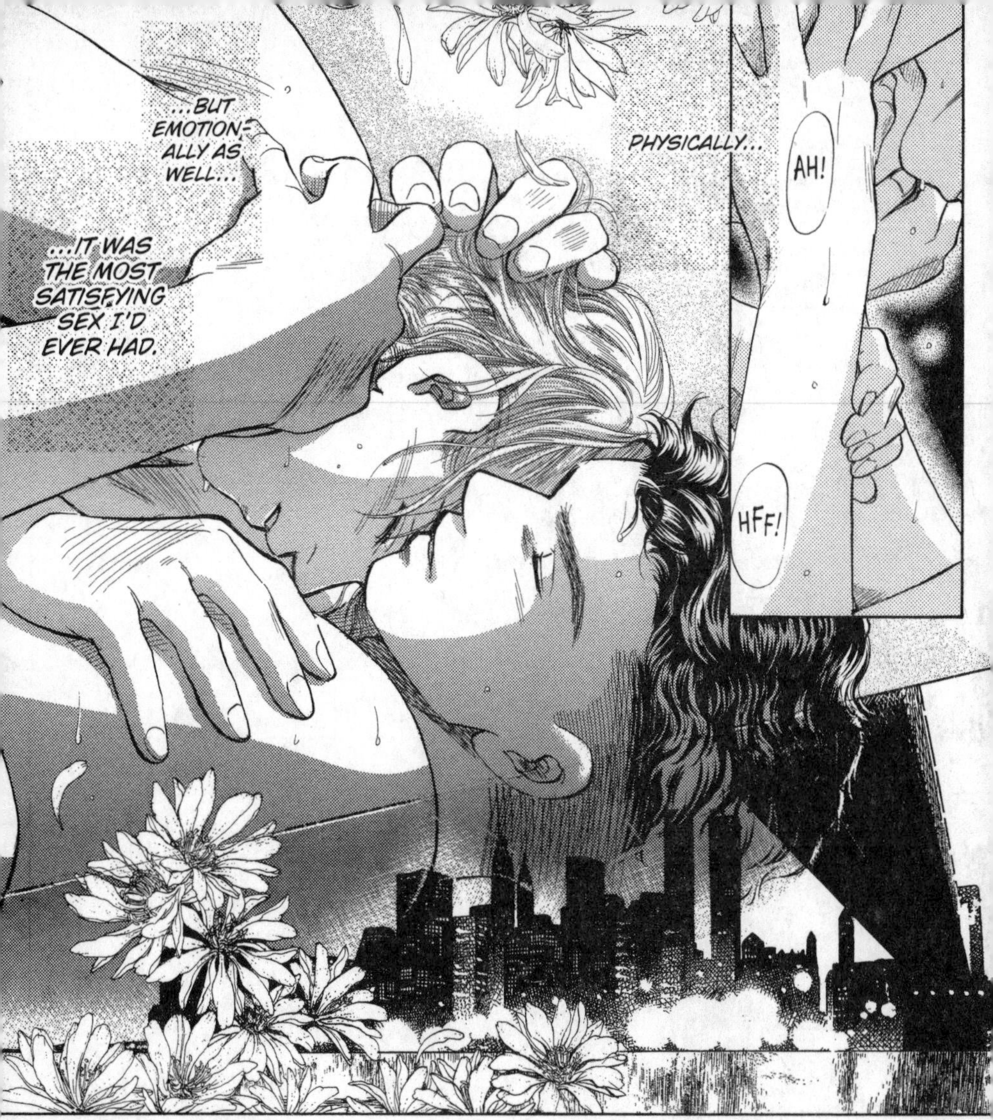
PHYSICALLY...
AH!
HFF!
...BUT EMOTIONALLY AS WELL...
...IT WAS THE MOST SATISFYING SEX I'D EVER HAD.
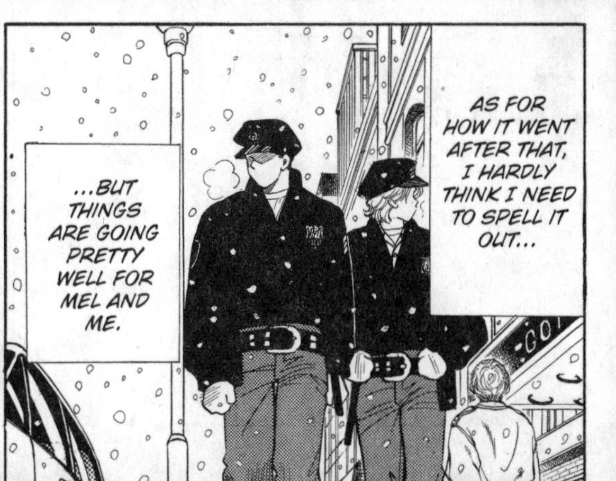
AS FOR HOW IT WENT AFTER THAT, I HARDLY THINK I NEED TO SPELL IT OUT...
...BUT THINGS ARE GOING PRETTY WELL FOR MEL AND ME.
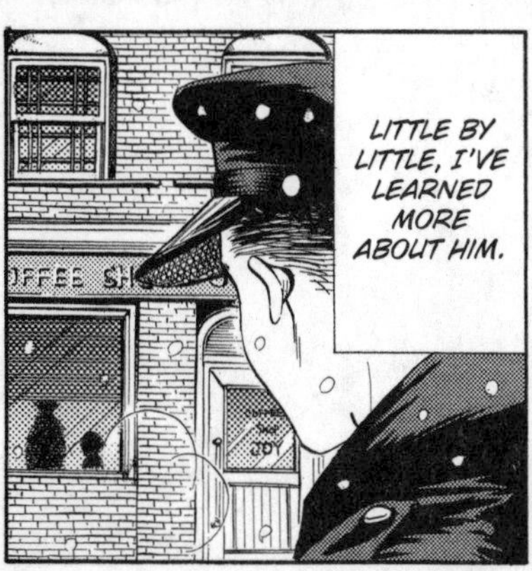
LITTLE BY LITTLE, I'VE LEARNED MORE ABOUT HIM.

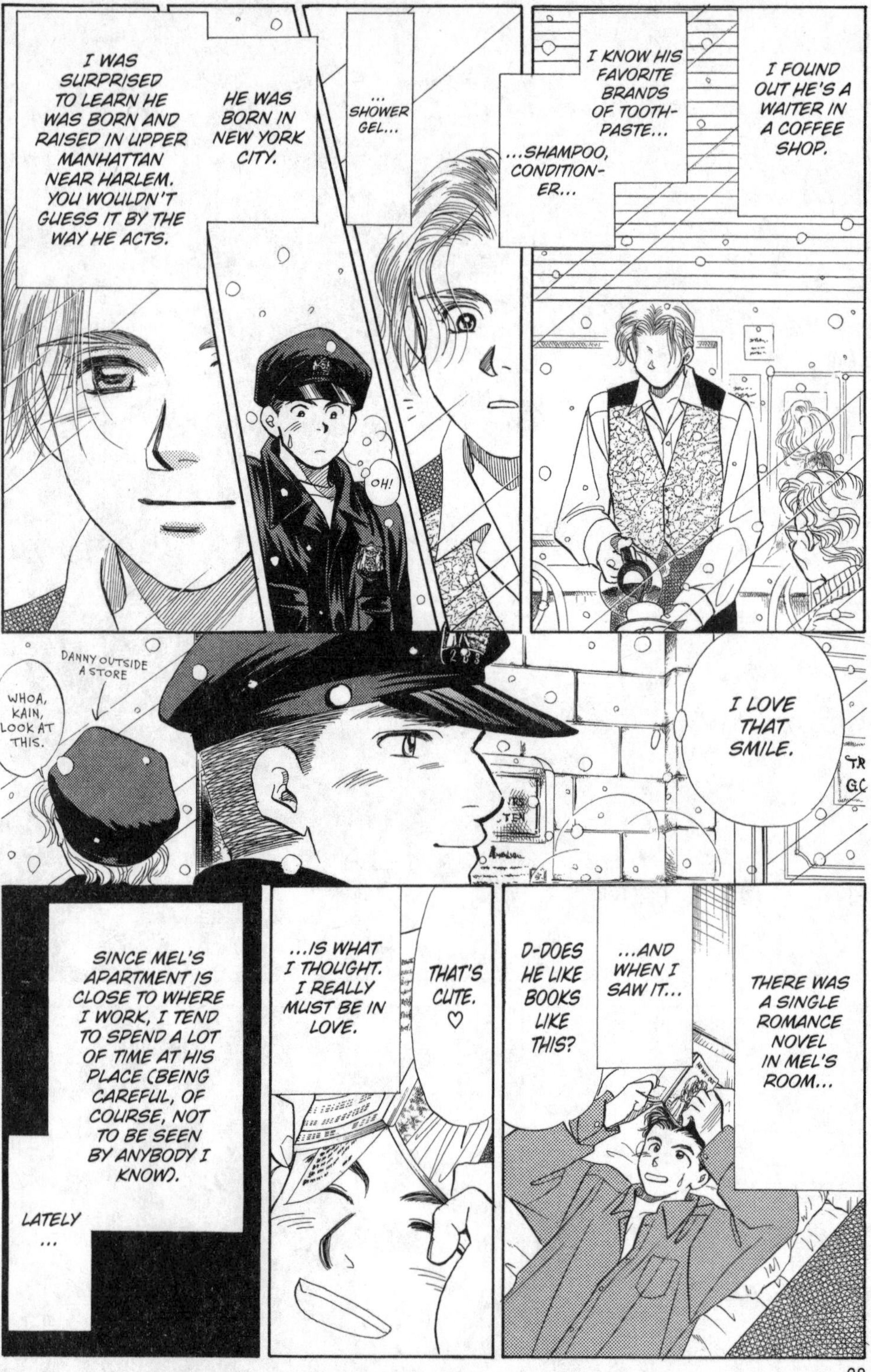
I FOUND OUT HE'S A WAITER IN A COFFEE SHOP.
I KNOW HIS FAVORITE BRANDS OF TOOTH-PASTE...
...SHAMPOO, CONDITION-ER...
...SHOWER GEL...
OH!
HE WAS BORN IN NEW YORK CITY.
I WAS SURPRISED TO LEARN HE WAS BORN AND RAISED IN UPPER MANHATTAN NEAR HARLEM. YOU WOULDN'T GUESS IT BY THE WAY HE ACTS.
I LOVE THAT SMILE.
DANNY OUTSIDE A STORE
WHOA, KAIN, LOOK AT THIS.
THERE WAS A SINGLE ROMANCE NOVEL IN MEL'S ROOM...
...AND WHEN I SAW IT...
D-DOES HE LIKE BOOKS LIKE THIS?
THAT'S CUTE. ♡
...IS WHAT I THOUGHT. I REALLY MUST BE IN LOVE.
SINCE MEL'S APARTMENT IS CLOSE TO WHERE I WORK, I TEND TO SPEND A LOT OF TIME AT HIS PLACE (BEING CAREFUL, OF COURSE, NOT TO BE SEEN BY ANYBODY I KNOW).
LATELY ...

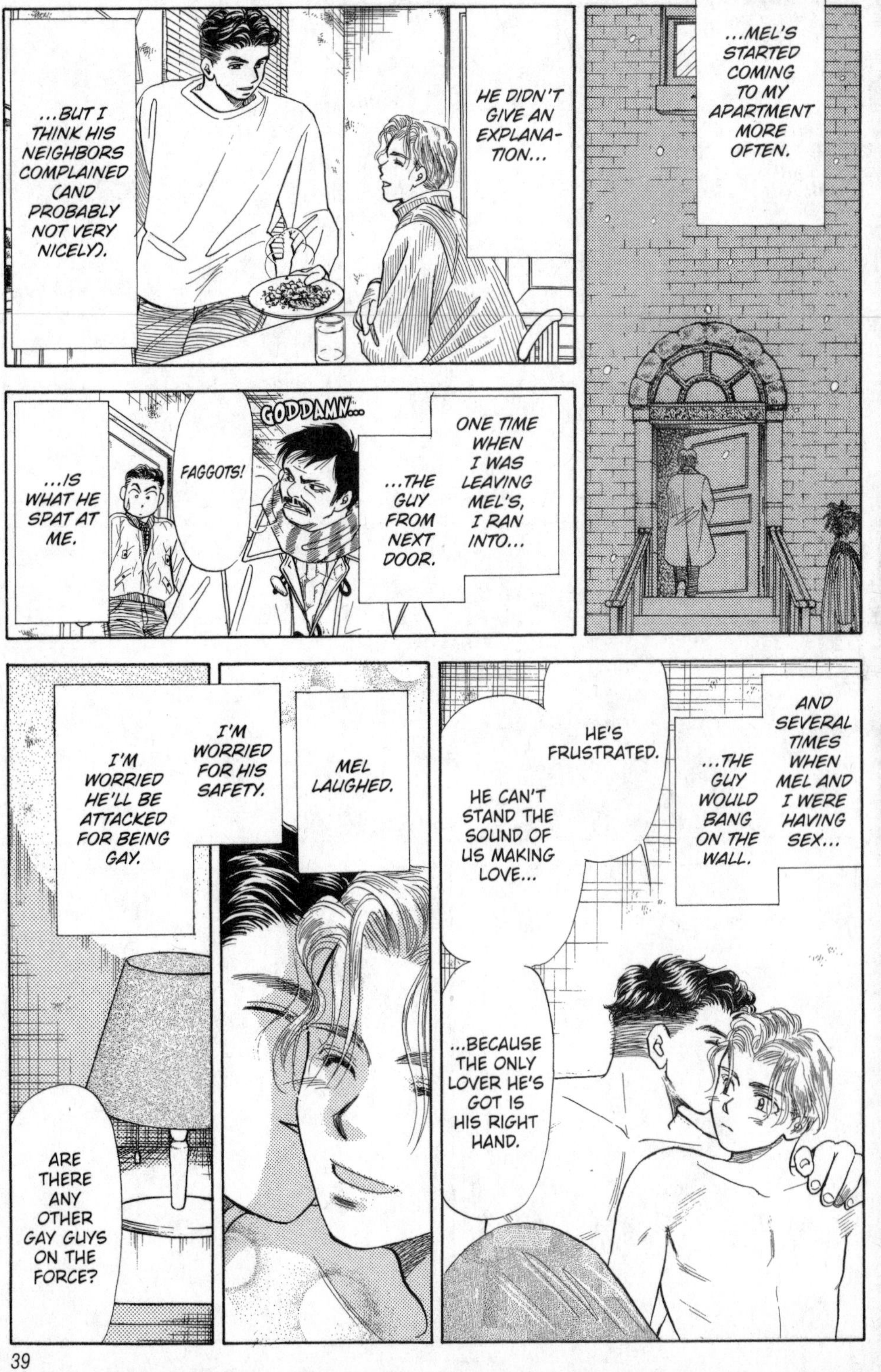
...MEL'S STARTED COMING TO MY APARTMENT MORE OFTEN.
HE DIDN'T GIVE AN EXPLANATION...
...BUT I THINK HIS NEIGHBORS COMPLAINED (AND PROBABLY NOT VERY NICELY).
ONE TIME WHEN I WAS LEAVING MEL'S, I RAN INTO...
...THE GUY FROM NEXT DOOR.
GODDAMN...
FAGGOTS!
...IS WHAT HE SPAT AT ME.
AND SEVERAL TIMES WHEN MEL AND I WERE HAVING SEX...
...THE GUY WOULD BANG ON THE WALL.
HE'S FRUSTRATED.
HE CAN'T STAND THE SOUND OF US MAKING LOVE...
...BECAUSE THE ONLY LOVER HE'S GOT IS HIS RIGHT HAND.
MEL LAUGHED.
I'M WORRIED FOR HIS SAFETY.
I'M WORRIED HE'LL BE ATTACKED FOR BEING GAY.
ARE THERE ANY OTHER GAY GUYS ON THE FORCE?

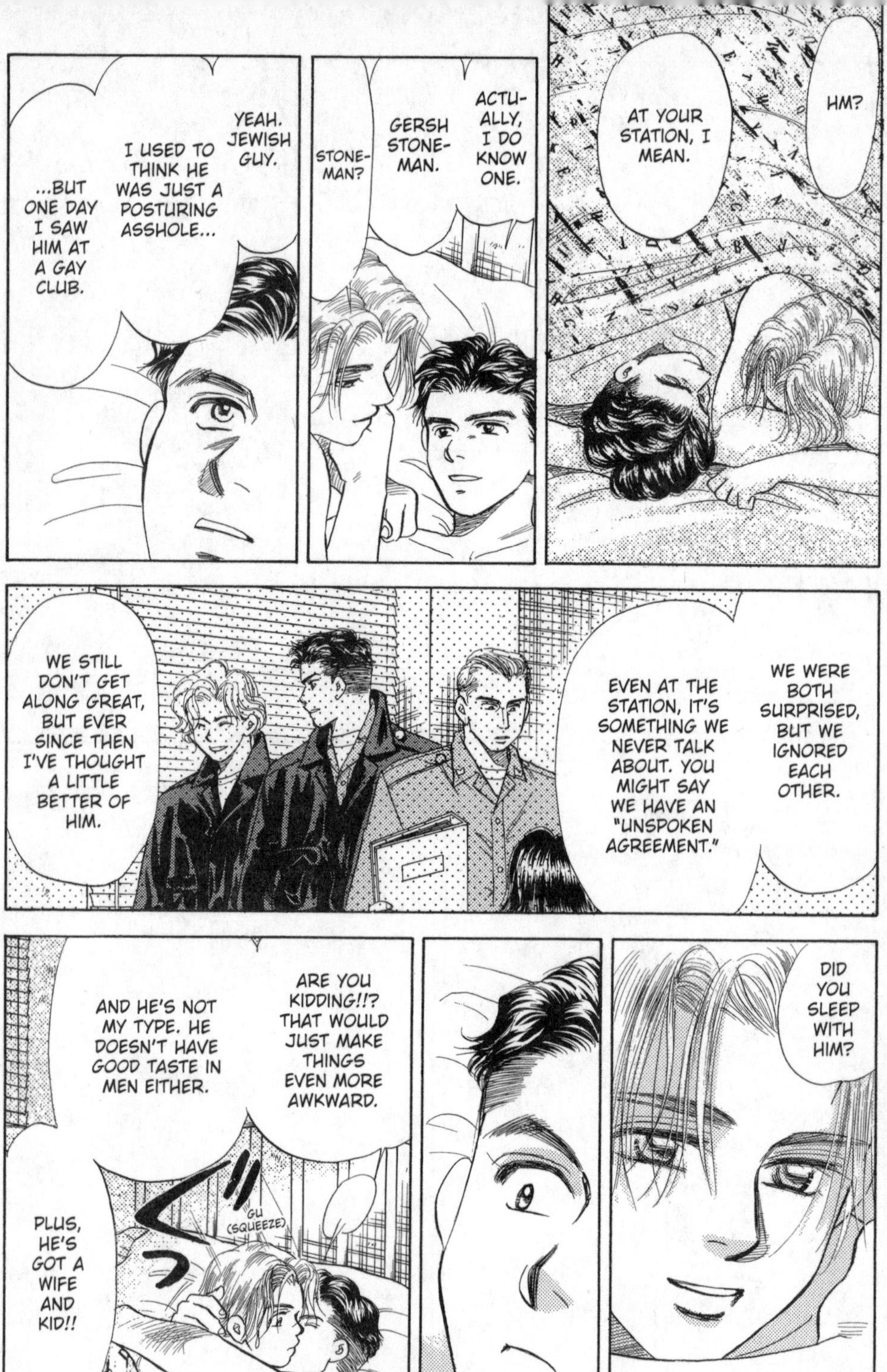
HM?
AT YOUR STATION, I MEAN.
ACTUALLY, I DO KNOW ONE.
GERSH STONEMAN.
STONEMAN?
YEAH. JEWISH GUY.
I USED TO THINK HE WAS JUST A POSTURING ASSHOLE...
...BUT ONE DAY I SAW HIM AT A GAY CLUB.
WE WERE BOTH SURPRISED, BUT WE IGNORED EACH OTHER.
EVEN AT THE STATION, IT'S SOMETHING WE NEVER TALK ABOUT. YOU MIGHT SAY WE HAVE AN "UNSPOKEN AGREEMENT."
WE STILL DON'T GET ALONG GREAT, BUT EVER SINCE THEN I'VE THOUGHT A LITTLE BETTER OF HIM.
DID YOU SLEEP WITH HIM?
ARE YOU KIDDING!!? THAT WOULD JUST MAKE THINGS EVEN MORE AWKWARD.
AND HE'S NOT MY TYPE. HE DOESN'T HAVE GOOD TASTE IN MEN EITHER.
GU (SQUEEZE)
PLUS, HE'S GOT A WIFE AND KID!!

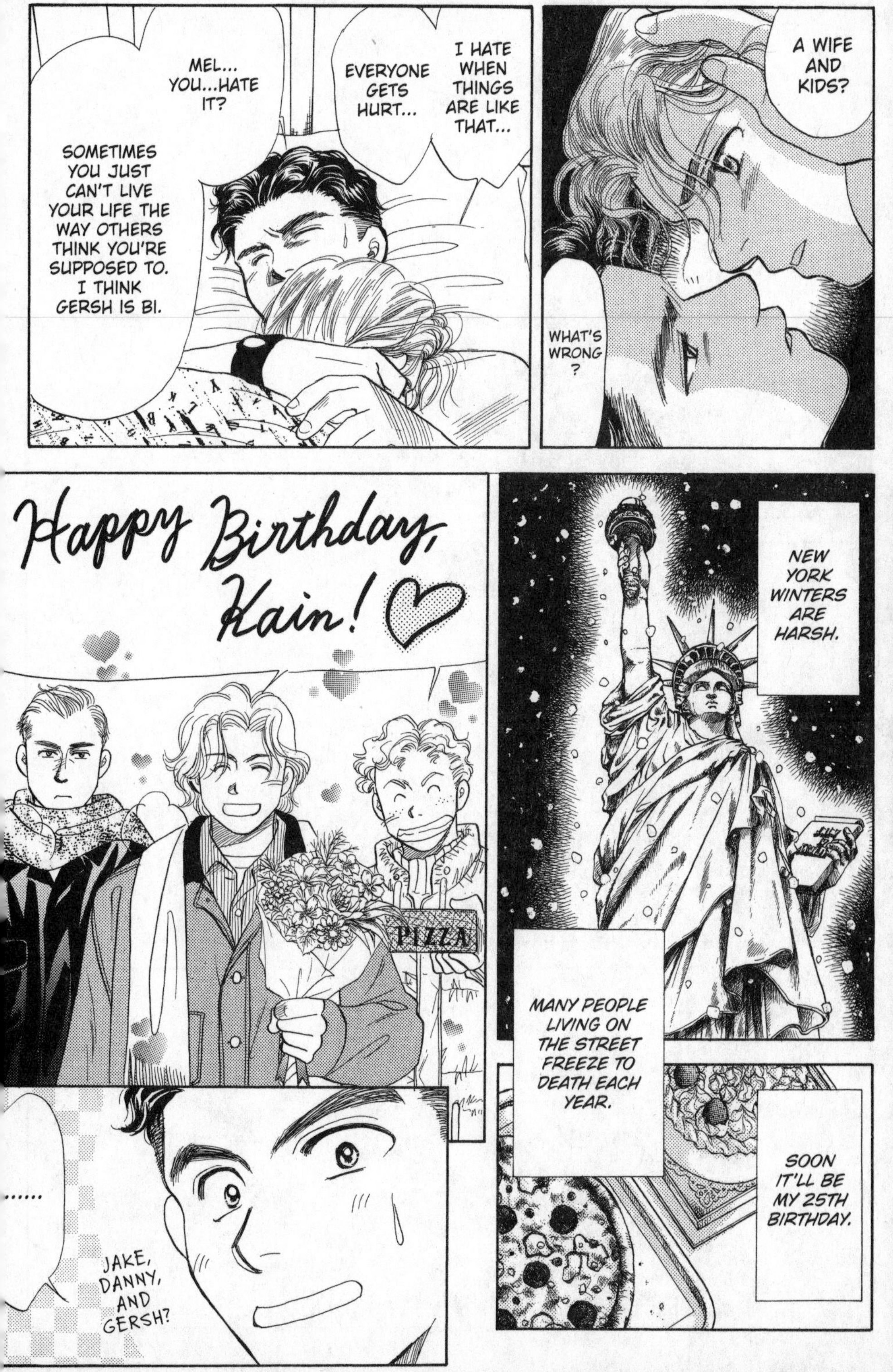
A WIFE AND KIDS?
WHAT'S WRONG?
I HATE WHEN THINGS ARE LIKE THAT...
EVERYONE GETS HURT...
MEL... YOU...HATE IT?
SOMETIMES YOU JUST CAN'T LIVE YOUR LIFE THE WAY OTHERS THINK YOU'RE SUPPOSED TO. I THINK GERSH IS BI.
NEW YORK WINTERS ARE HARSH.
MANY PEOPLE LIVING ON THE STREET FREEZE TO DEATH EACH YEAR.
SOON IT'LL BE MY 25TH BIRTHDAY.
Happy Birthday, Kain!
PIZZA
......
JAKE, DANNY, AND GERSH?

SHIT!!

MEL, IT'S THE GUYS FROM WORK!!

PYU (ZWOOM)

WAIT.

WAIT!

WAIT!!

W—

C'MON, MAN, LET US IN ALREADY.

IT'S FINE.

I...I'M SORRY... I REALLY WISH...

WHAT?

....

OKAY.

I'LL GO BACK TO MY APARTMENT FOR TODAY.

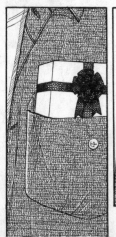

SU (SSK)

AND...

...HERE'S YOUR PRESENT.

MWA!

HAPPY BIRTH-DAY.

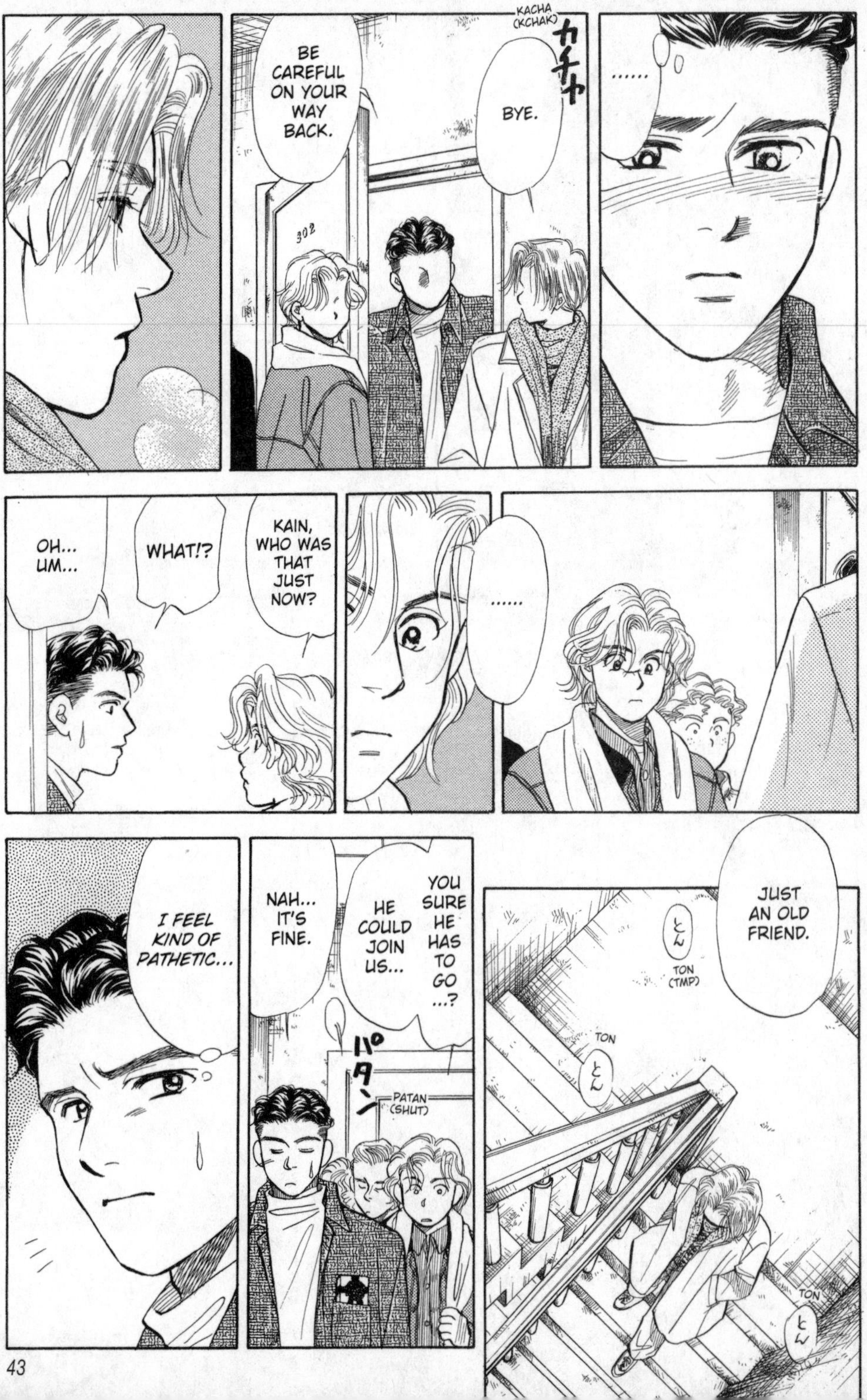
......
カチャ
KACHA (KCHAK)
BYE.
BE CAREFUL ON YOUR WAY BACK.
......
KAIN, WHO WAS THAT JUST NOW?
WHAT!?
OH... UM...
JUST AN OLD FRIEND.
とん
TON (TMP)
TON
とん
TON
とん
YOU SURE HE HAS TO GO ...?
HE COULD JOIN US...
NAH... IT'S FINE.
パタン
PATAN (SHUT)
I FEEL KIND OF PATHETIC...

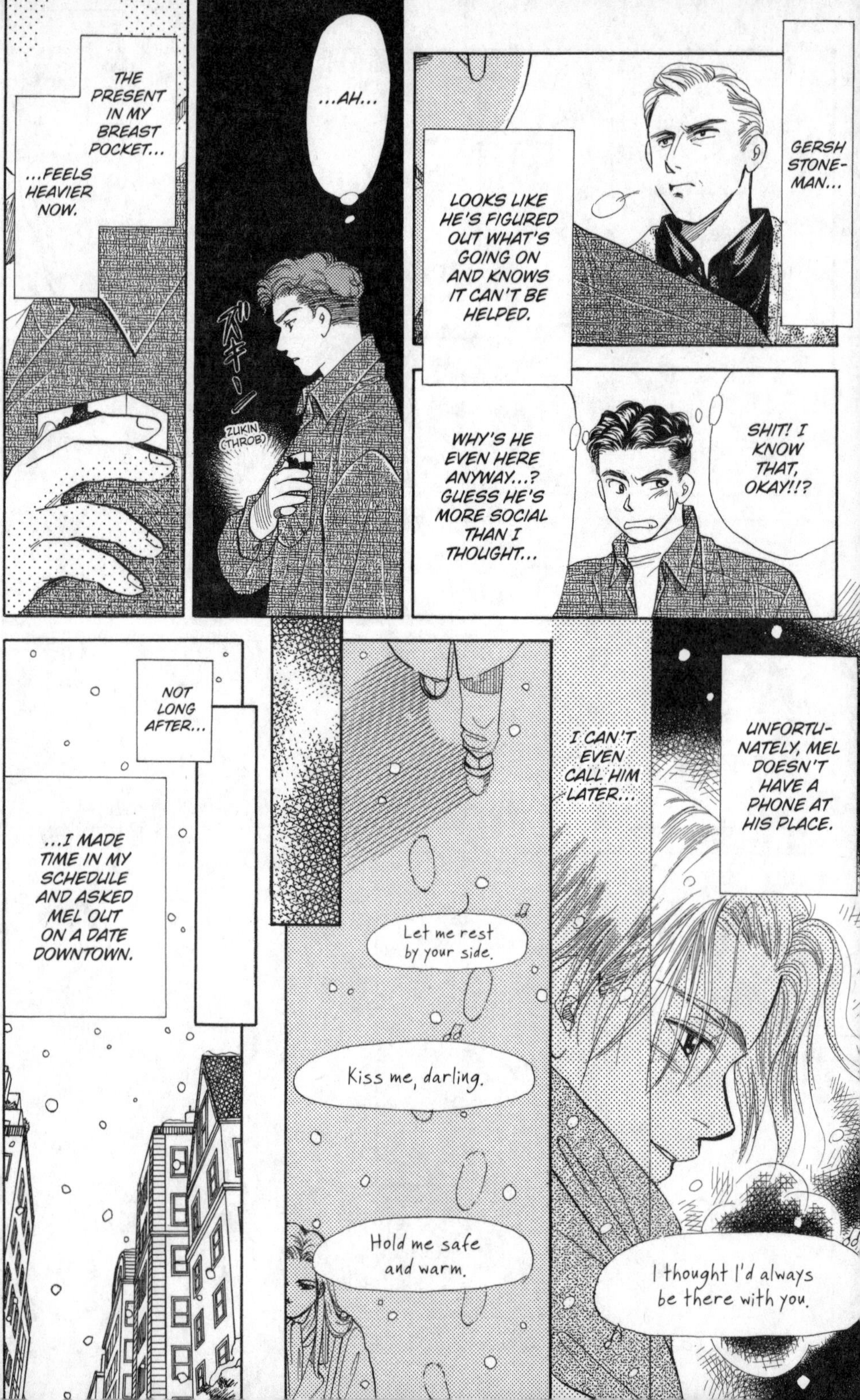
GERSH STONEMAN...
LOOKS LIKE HE'S FIGURED OUT WHAT'S GOING ON AND KNOWS IT CAN'T BE HELPED.
SHIT! I KNOW THAT, OKAY!!?
WHY'S HE EVEN HERE ANYWAY...? GUESS HE'S MORE SOCIAL THAN I THOUGHT...
...AH...
ズキーン
ZUKIN (THROB)
THE PRESENT IN MY BREAST POCKET...
...FEELS HEAVIER NOW.
UNFORTUNATELY, MEL DOESN'T HAVE A PHONE AT HIS PLACE.
I CAN'T EVEN CALL HIM LATER...
I thought I'd always be there with you.
Let me rest by your side.
Kiss me, darling.
Hold me safe and warm.
NOT LONG AFTER...
...I MADE TIME IN MY SCHEDULE AND ASKED MEL OUT ON A DATE DOWNTOWN.

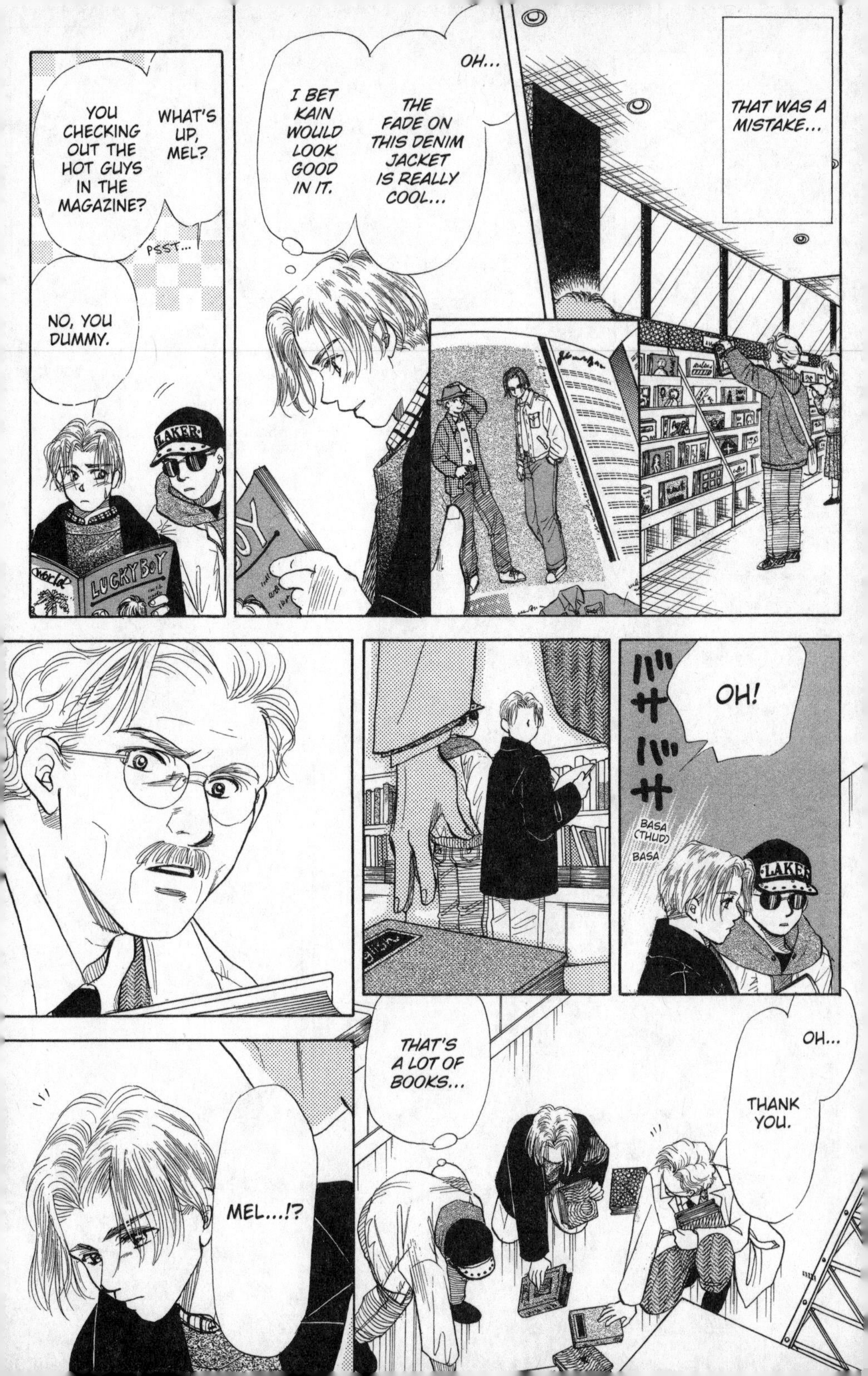
THAT WAS A MISTAKE...
OH...
THE FADE ON THIS DENIM JACKET IS REALLY COOL...
I BET KAIN WOULD LOOK GOOD IN IT.
WHAT'S UP, MEL?
YOU CHECKING OUT THE HOT GUYS IN THE MAGAZINE?
PSST...
NO, YOU DUMMY.
LUCKY BOY
バサバサ
OH!
BASA (THUD) BASA
OH...
THANK YOU.
THAT'S A LOT OF BOOKS...
MEL...!?

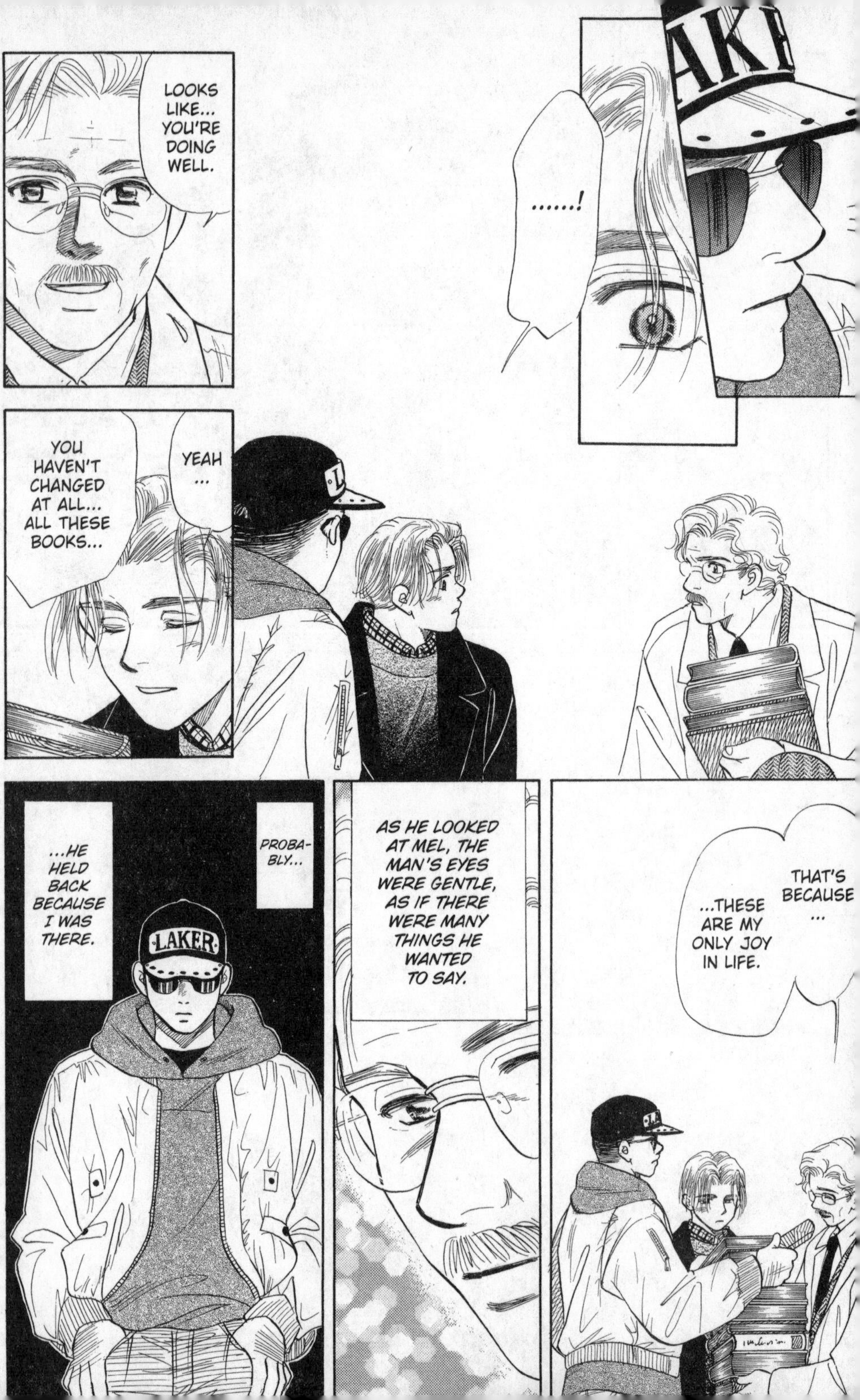
……!
LOOKS LIKE... YOU'RE DOING WELL.
YEAH ...
YOU HAVEN'T CHANGED AT ALL... ALL THESE BOOKS...
THAT'S BECAUSE ...
...THESE ARE MY ONLY JOY IN LIFE.
AS HE LOOKED AT MEL, THE MAN'S EYES WERE GENTLE, AS IF THERE WERE MANY THINGS HE WANTED TO SAY.
PROBA-BLY...
...HE HELD BACK BECAUSE I WAS THERE.

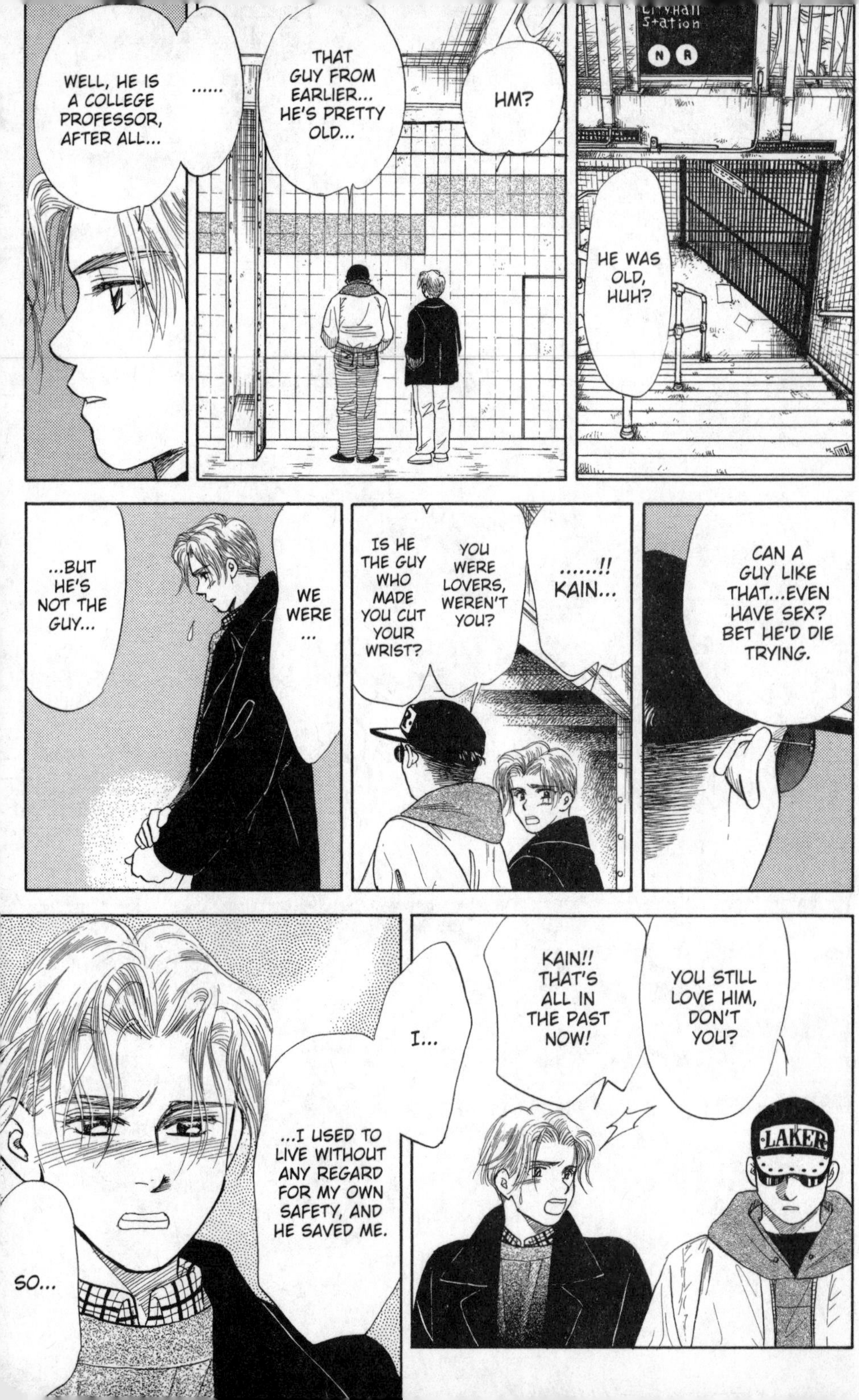
Station
N R
HE WAS OLD, HUH?
HM?
THAT GUY FROM EARLIER... HE'S PRETTY OLD...
......
WELL, HE IS A COLLEGE PROFESSOR, AFTER ALL...
CAN A GUY LIKE THAT...EVEN HAVE SEX? BET HE'D DIE TRYING.
......!! KAIN...
YOU WERE LOVERS, WEREN'T YOU?
IS HE THE GUY WHO MADE YOU CUT YOUR WRIST?
WE WERE ...
...BUT HE'S NOT THE GUY...
LAKER
YOU STILL LOVE HIM, DON'T YOU?
KAIN!! THAT'S ALL IN THE PAST NOW!
I...
...I USED TO LIVE WITHOUT ANY REGARD FOR MY OWN SAFETY, AND HE SAVED ME.
SO...

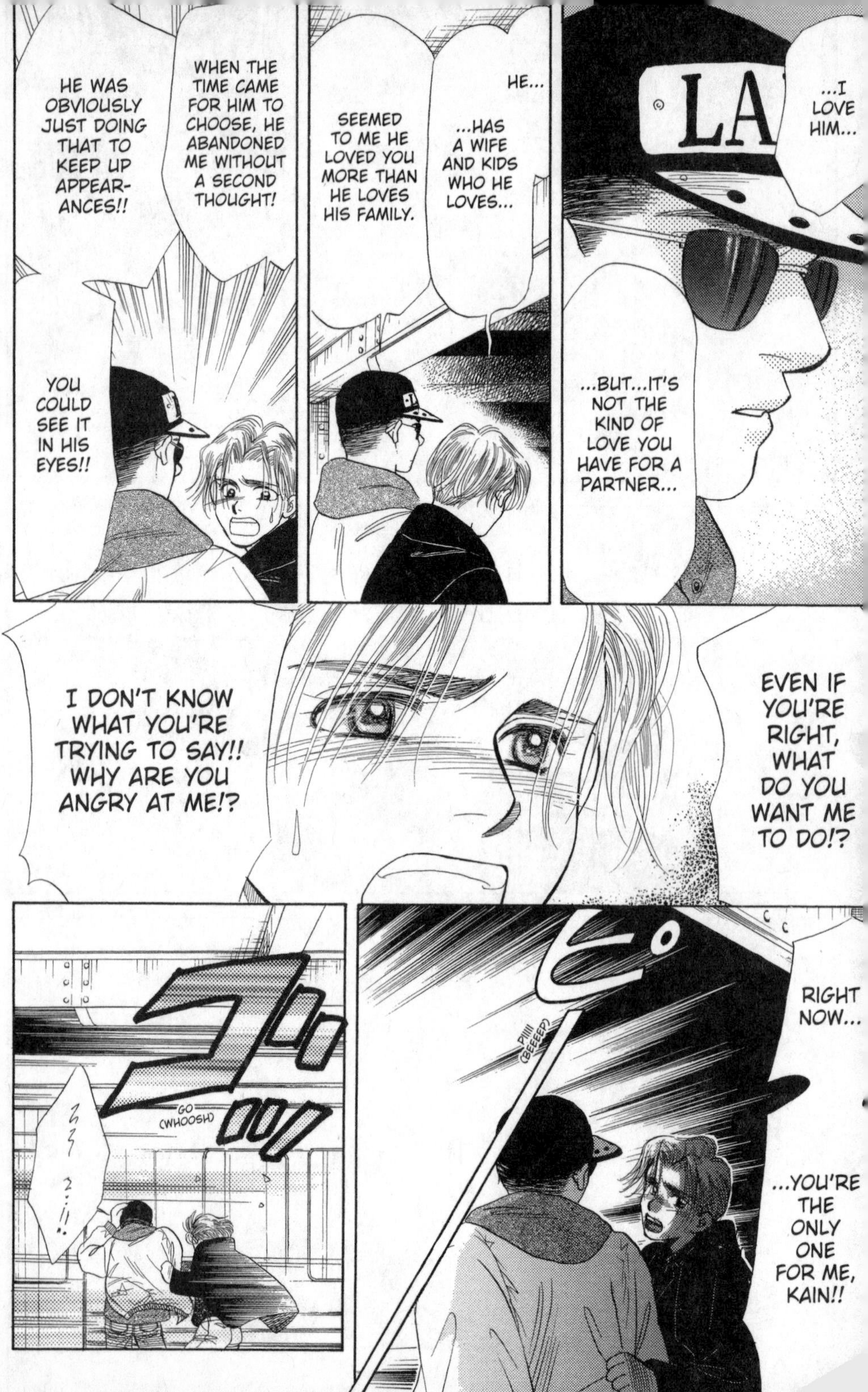
...I LOVE HIM...
...BUT...IT'S NOT THE KIND OF LOVE YOU HAVE FOR A PARTNER...
HE...
...HAS A WIFE AND KIDS WHO HE LOVES...
SEEMED TO ME HE LOVED YOU MORE THAN HE LOVES HIS FAMILY.
WHEN THE TIME CAME FOR HIM TO CHOOSE, HE ABANDONED ME WITHOUT A SECOND THOUGHT!
HE WAS OBVIOUSLY JUST DOING THAT TO KEEP UP APPEAR-ANCES!!
YOU COULD SEE IT IN HIS EYES!!
EVEN IF YOU'RE RIGHT, WHAT DO YOU WANT ME TO DO!?
I DON'T KNOW WHAT YOU'RE TRYING TO SAY!! WHY ARE YOU ANGRY AT ME!?
RIGHT NOW...
PIIII (BEEEEP)
...YOU'RE THE ONLY ONE FOR ME, KAIN!!
GO (WHOOSH)

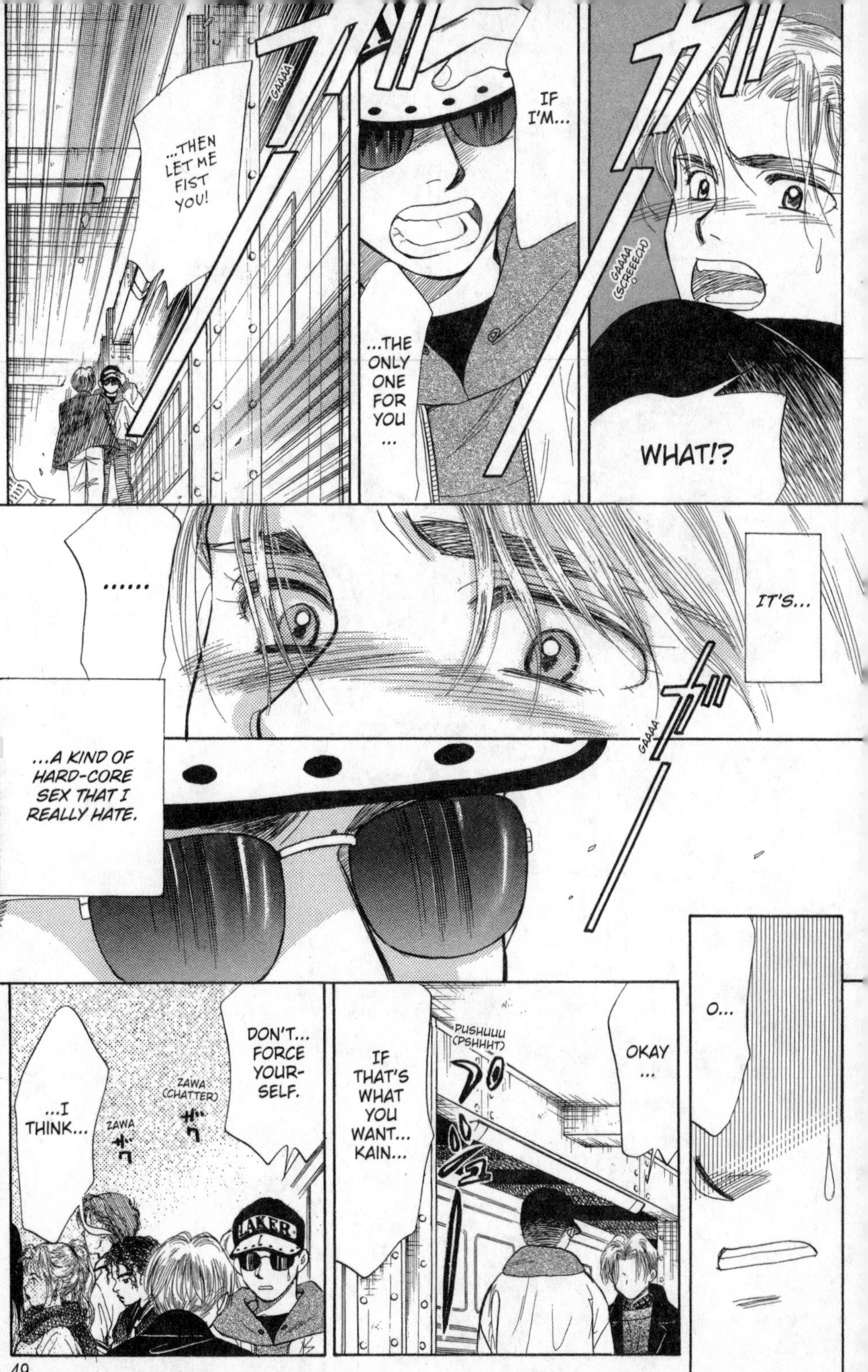
WHAT!?
GAAAA (SCREEECH)
IF I'M...
...THE ONLY ONE FOR YOU ...
GAAAA
...THEN LET ME FIST YOU!
IT'S...
......
GAAAA
...A KIND OF HARD-CORE SEX THAT I REALLY HATE.
O...
OKAY ...
PUSHUUU (PSHHHT)
IF THAT'S WHAT YOU WANT... KAIN...
DON'T... FORCE YOUR-SELF.
ZAWA (CHATTER)
ZAWA
...I THINK...

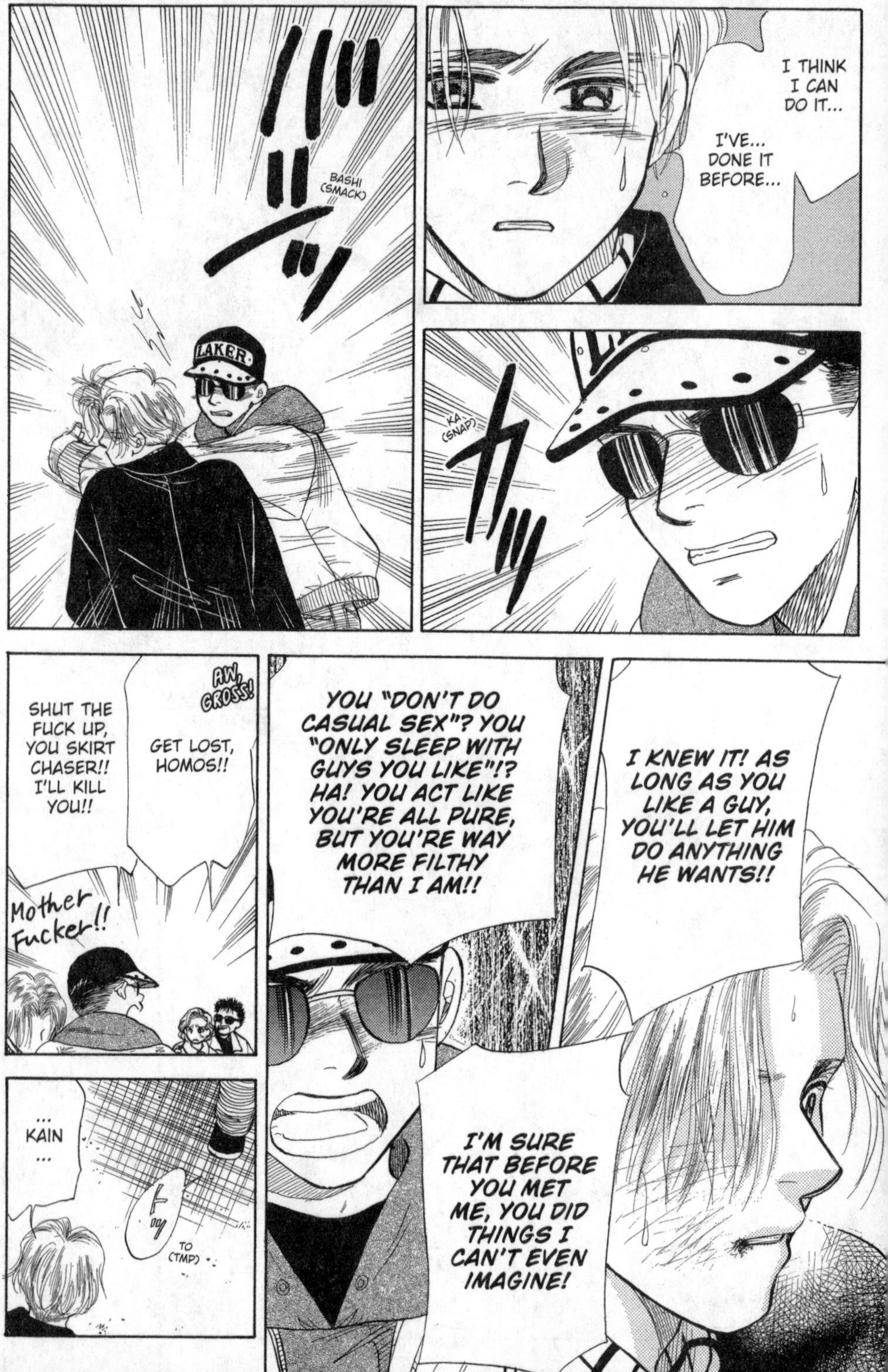
I THINK I CAN DO IT...
I'VE... DONE IT BEFORE...
KA (SNAP)
BASHI (SMACK)
I KNEW IT! AS LONG AS YOU LIKE A GUY, YOU'LL LET HIM DO ANYTHING HE WANTS!!
I'M SURE THAT BEFORE YOU MET ME, YOU DID THINGS I CAN'T EVEN IMAGINE!
YOU "DON'T DO CASUAL SEX"? YOU "ONLY SLEEP WITH GUYS YOU LIKE"!? HA! YOU ACT LIKE YOU'RE ALL PURE, BUT YOU'RE WAY MORE FILTHY THAN I AM!!
AW, GROSS!
GET LOST, HOMOS!!
SHUT THE FUCK UP, YOU SKIRT CHASER!! I'LL KILL YOU!!
Mother Fucker!!
... KAIN ...
TO (TMP)

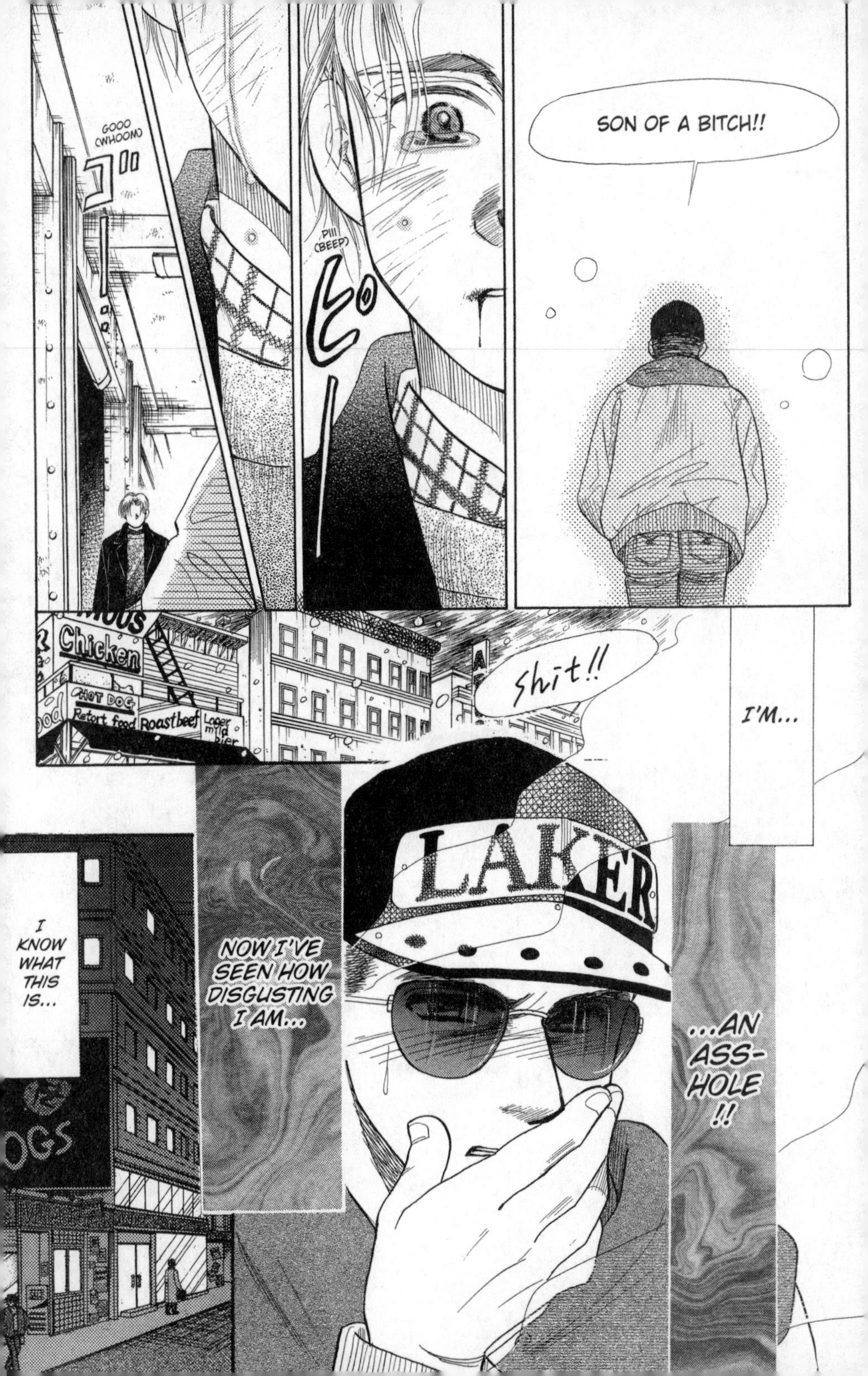
SON OF A BITCH!!
PIII
(BEEP)
GOOO
(WHOOM)
I'M...
shit!!
Chicken
HOT DOG
Retort food
Roastbeef
Lager
mild
LAKER
...AN ASS-HOLE!!
NOW I'VE SEEN HOW DISGUSTING I AM...
I KNOW WHAT THIS IS...

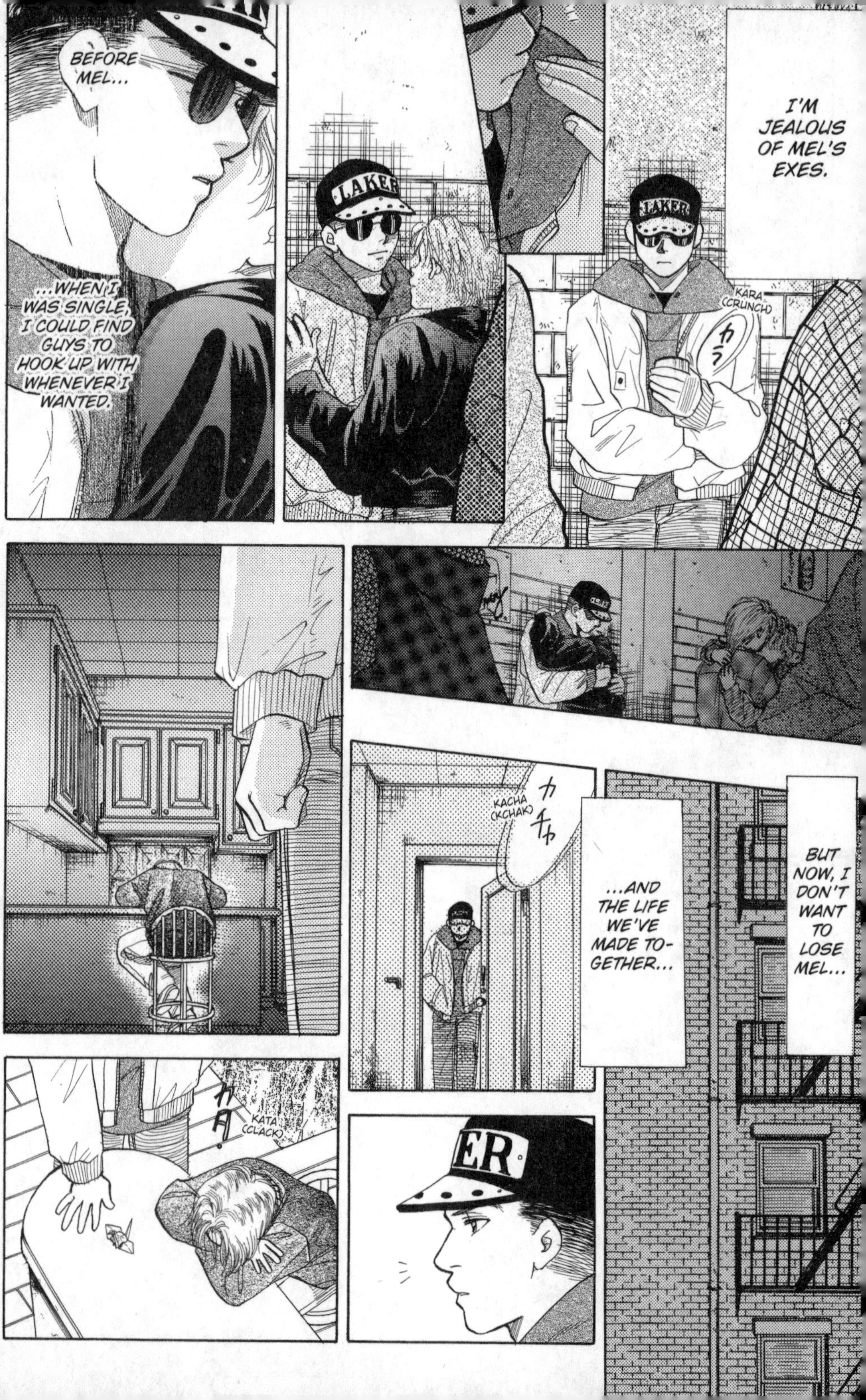
I'M JEALOUS OF MEL'S EXES.
KARA (CRUNCH)
カラ
BEFORE MEL...
...WHEN I WAS SINGLE, I COULD FIND GUYS TO HOOK UP WITH WHENEVER I WANTED.
BUT NOW, I DON'T WANT TO LOSE MEL...
KACHA (KCHAK)
カチャ
...AND THE LIFE WE'VE MADE TO-GETHER...
ER
KATA (CLACK)
カタ

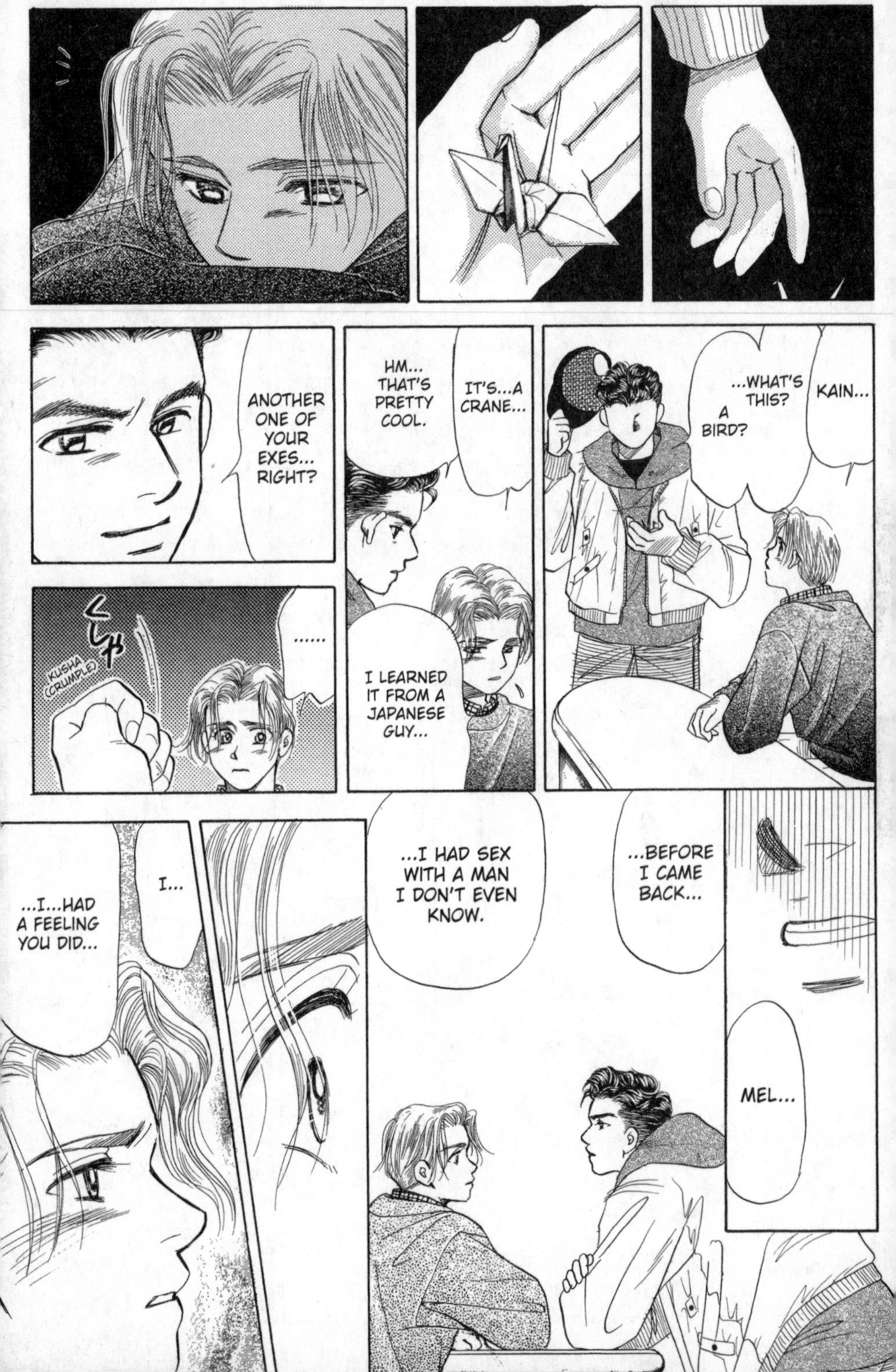

KAIN...
...WHAT'S THIS?
A BIRD?
IT'S...A CRANE...
HM... THAT'S PRETTY COOL.
I LEARNED IT FROM A JAPANESE GUY...
ANOTHER ONE OF YOUR EXES... RIGHT?
......
くしゃ
KUSHA (CRUMPLE)
MEL...
...BEFORE I CAME BACK...
...I HAD SEX WITH A MAN I DON'T EVEN KNOW.
I...
...I...HAD A FEELING YOU DID...

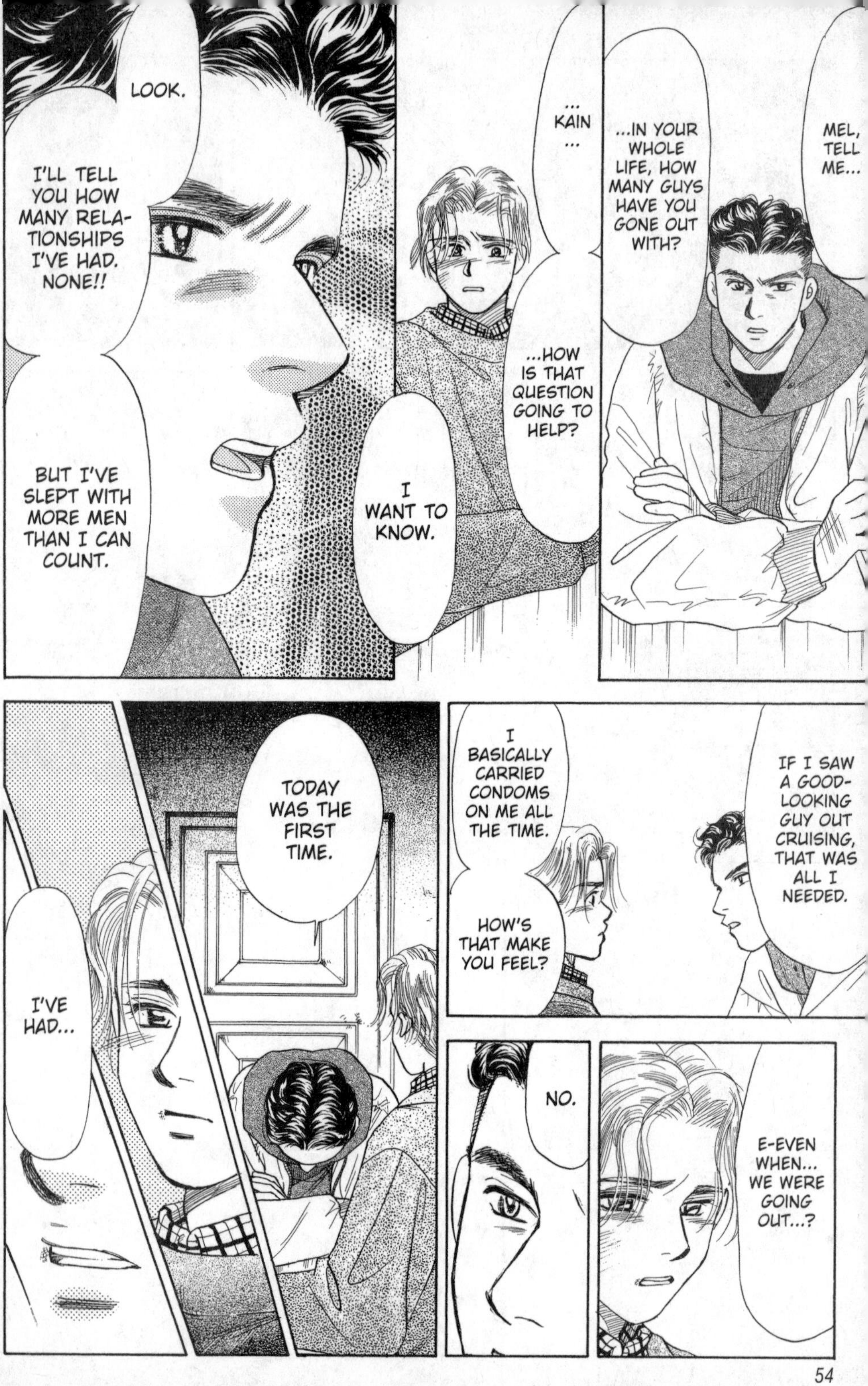
MEL, TELL ME...
...IN YOUR WHOLE LIFE, HOW MANY GUYS HAVE YOU GONE OUT WITH?
... KAIN ...
...HOW IS THAT QUESTION GOING TO HELP?
I WANT TO KNOW.
LOOK.
I'LL TELL YOU HOW MANY RELATIONSHIPS I'VE HAD. NONE!!
BUT I'VE SLEPT WITH MORE MEN THAN I CAN COUNT.
IF I SAW A GOOD-LOOKING GUY OUT CRUISING, THAT WAS ALL I NEEDED.
I BASICALLY CARRIED CONDOMS ON ME ALL THE TIME.
HOW'S THAT MAKE YOU FEEL?
E-EVEN WHEN... WE WERE GOING OUT...?
NO.
TODAY WAS THE FIRST TIME.
I'VE HAD...

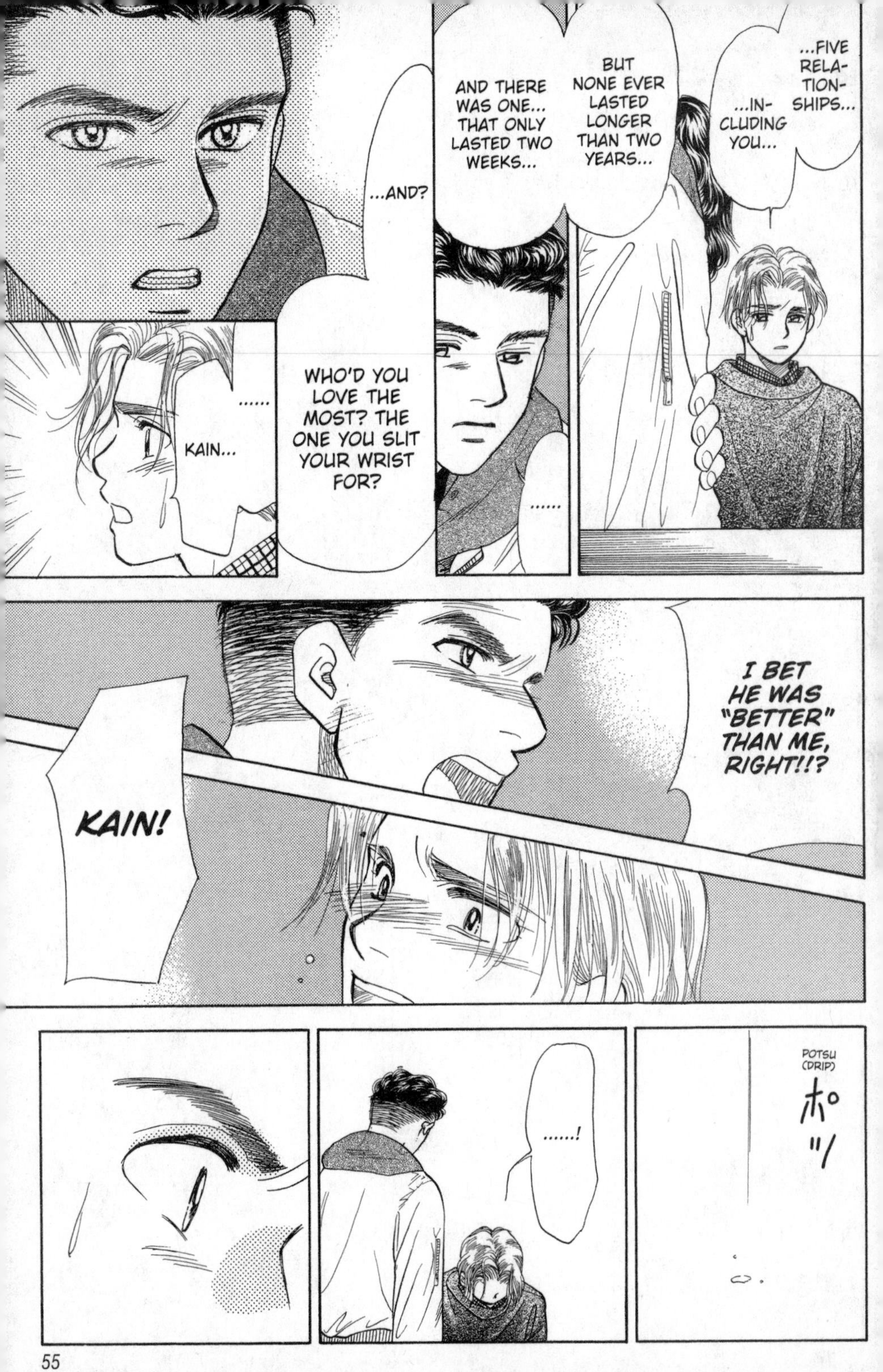

...FIVE RELA-TIONSHIPS...
...IN-CLUDING YOU...
BUT NONE EVER LASTED LONGER THAN TWO YEARS...
AND THERE WAS ONE... THAT ONLY LASTED TWO WEEKS...
......
...AND?
WHO'D YOU LOVE THE MOST? THE ONE YOU SLIT YOUR WRIST FOR?
......
KAIN...
I BET HE WAS "BETTER" THAN ME, RIGHT!!?
KAIN!
POTSU (DRIP)
ポッ
......!

...MEL...

I'M SORRY.

IT'S...

...SO I WON'T ASK YOU ABOUT ALL THIS AGAIN.

...FINDING OUT ABOUT YOUR EXES IS HARD FOR ME...

I JUST WANT YOU TO KNOW...

...NOT MY PLACE TO SAY THOSE THINGS.

THIS IS...

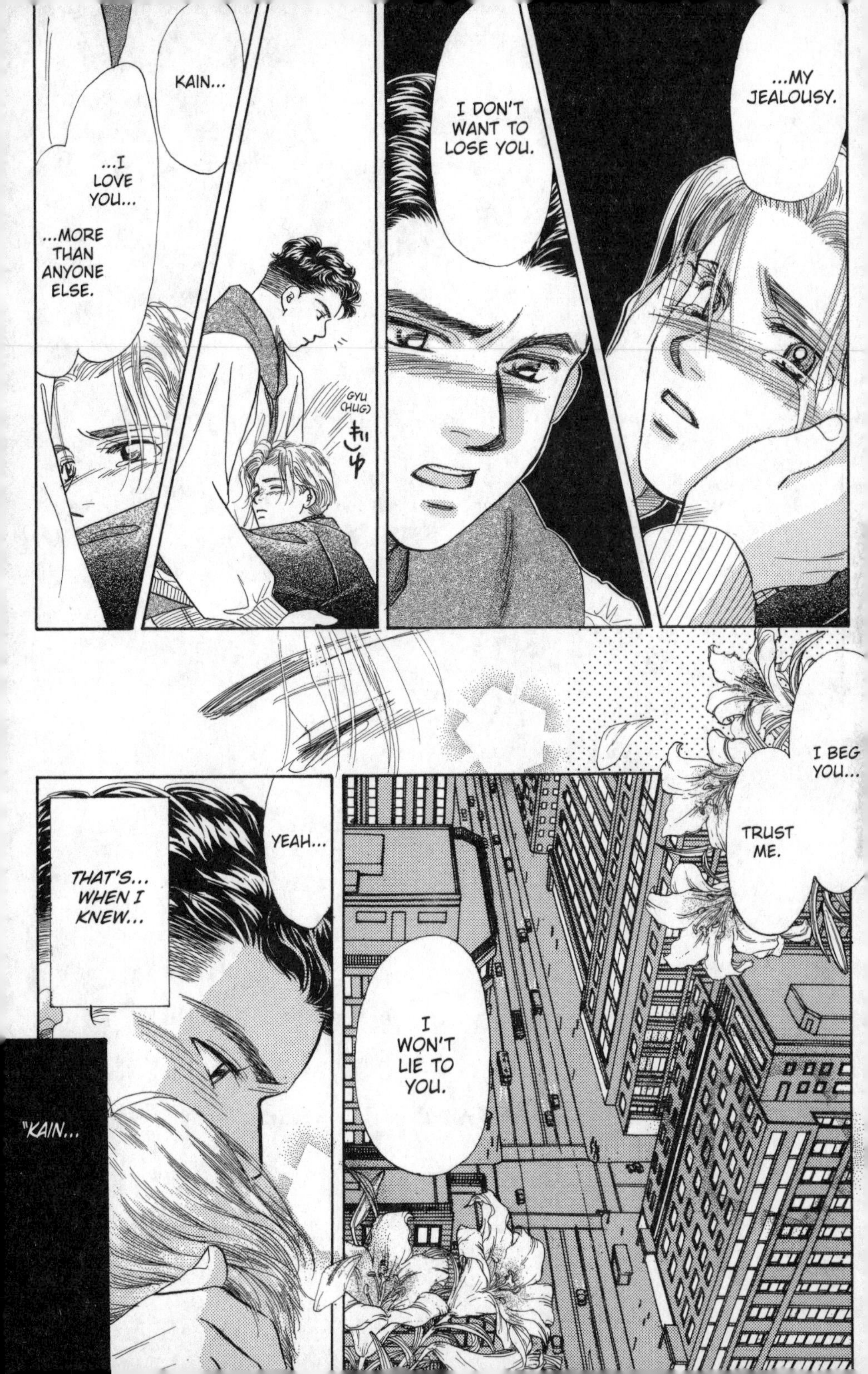
...MY JEALOUSY.
I DON'T WANT TO LOSE YOU.
KAIN...
GYU (HUG)
...I LOVE YOU...
...MORE THAN ANYONE ELSE.
I BEG YOU...
TRUST ME.
I WON'T LIE TO YOU.
YEAH...
THAT'S... WHEN I KNEW...
"KAIN...

CAN YOU BELIEVE IT?

IT'S BEEN LESS THAN TWO MONTHS, AND WE'RE ALREADY MOVING IN TOGETHER.

I CAN'T HELP BUT THINK...

...IT WAS FATE.

MEL...

"...I HOPE YOU'LL INTRODUCE HER TO ME."

"...IF THERE'S A WOMAN YOU'RE GETTING SERIOUS WITH..."

...LET'S MOVE IN TOGETHER...

THIS MOMENT...

...WOULD BE A TURNING POINT IN MY LIFE.

EPISODE I

SCENE 2

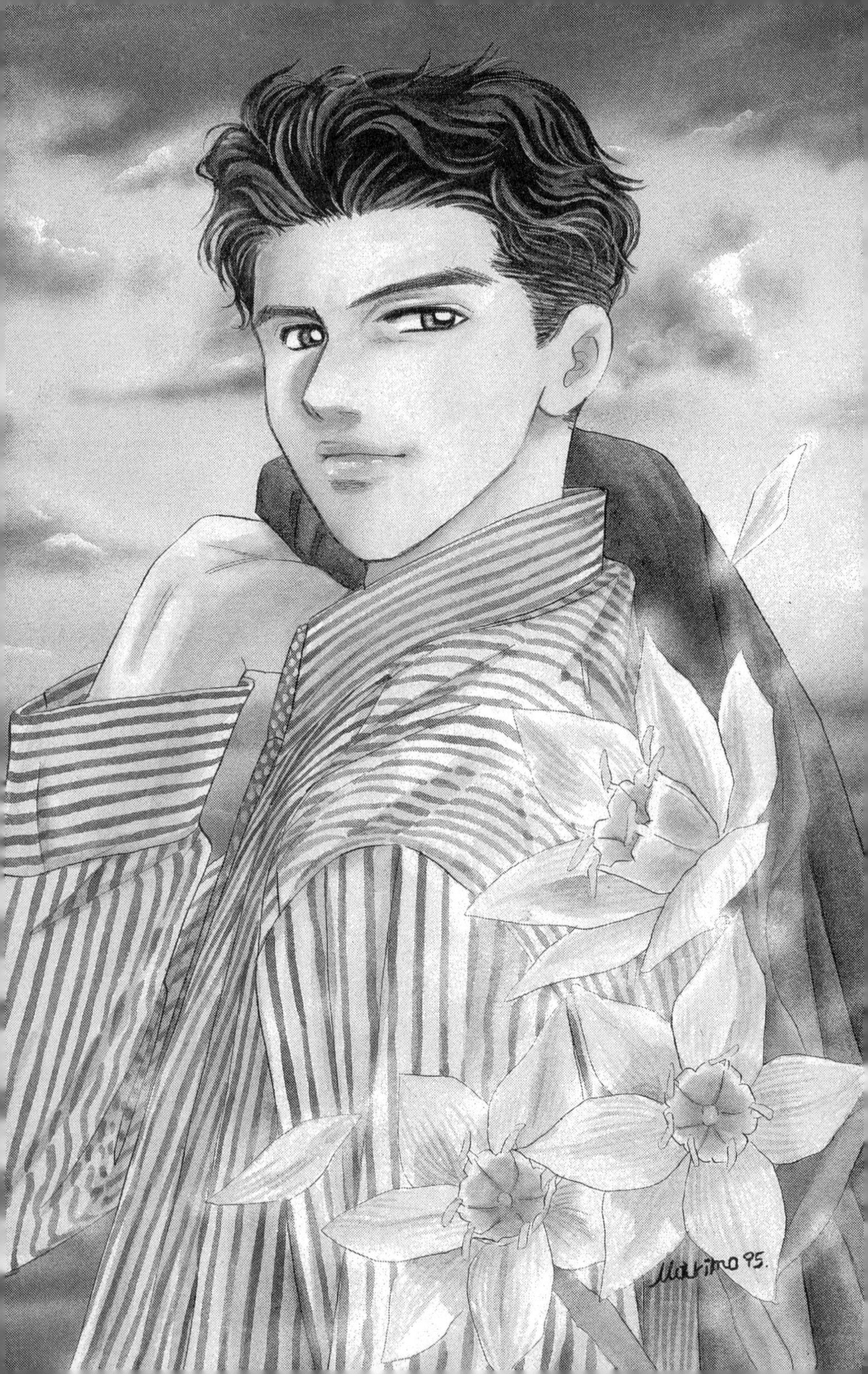

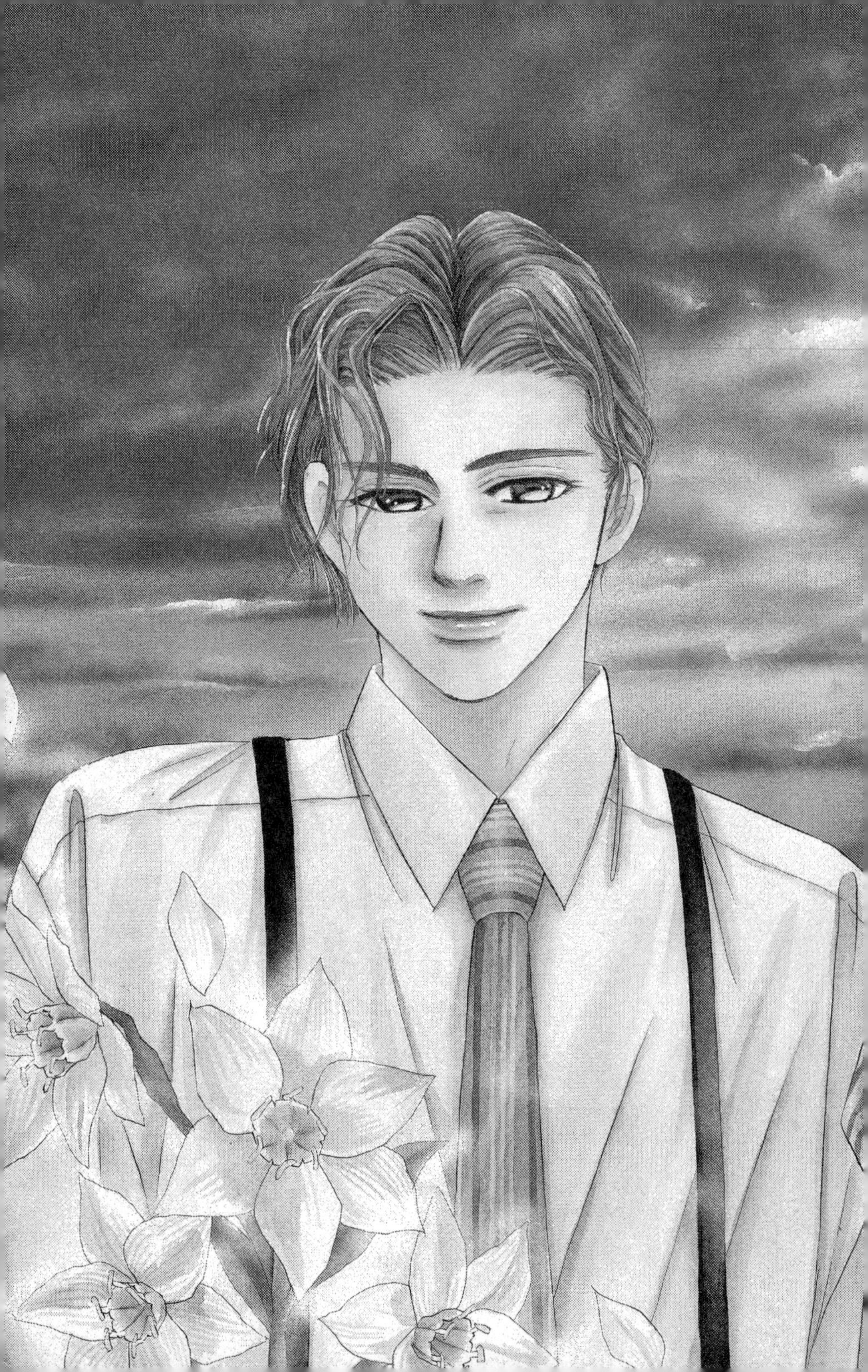

Bedroom
Porch
Bath-
room
Dining room
kitchen
Bathroom
Great room
Master bedroom
TV
Porch

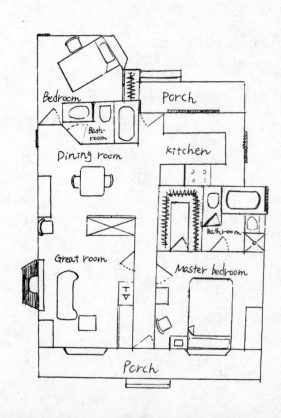

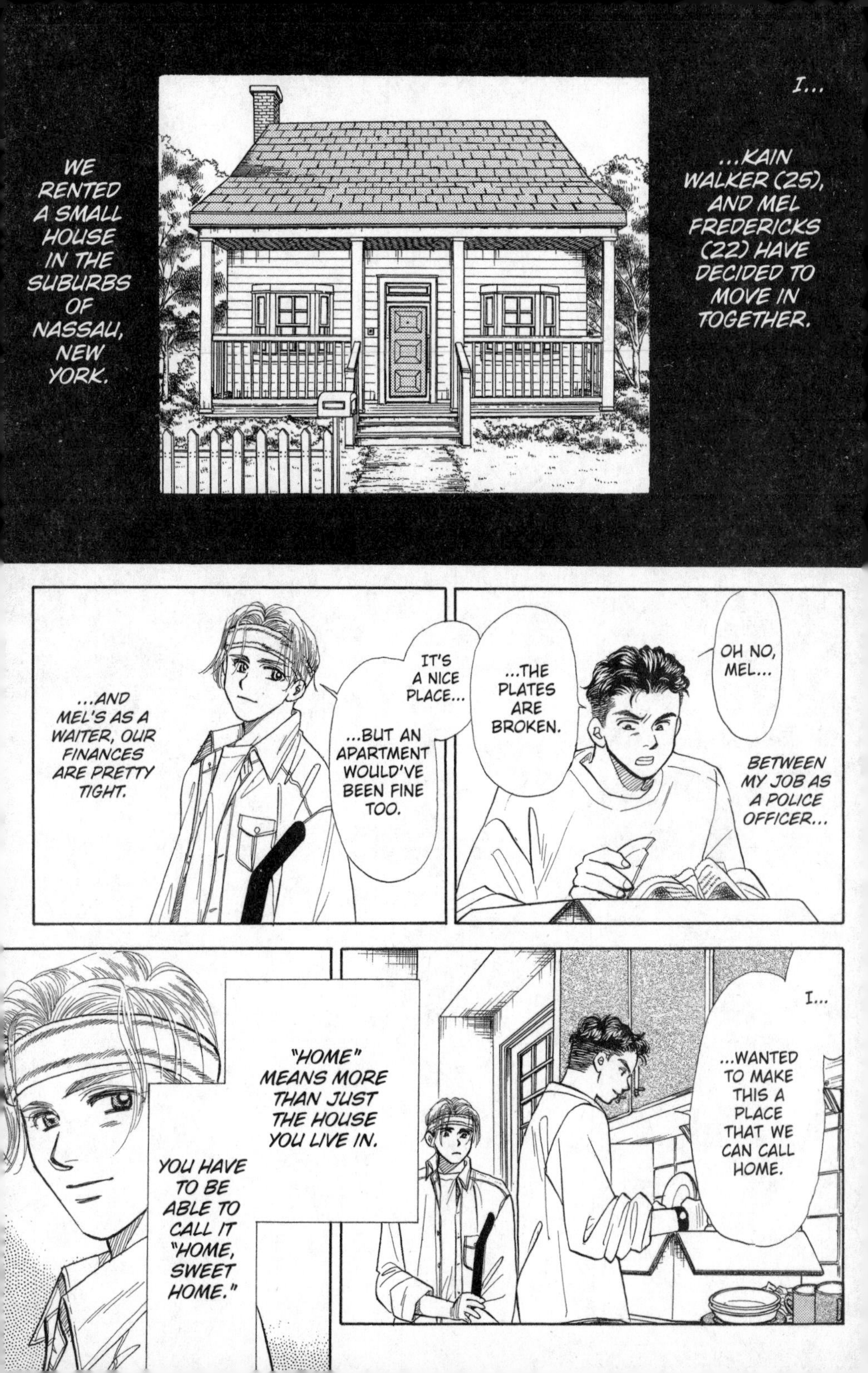
I...
...KAIN WALKER (25), AND MEL FREDERICKS (22) HAVE DECIDED TO MOVE IN TOGETHER.
WE RENTED A SMALL HOUSE IN THE SUBURBS OF NASSAU, NEW YORK.
OH NO, MEL...
...THE PLATES ARE BROKEN.
BETWEEN MY JOB AS A POLICE OFFICER...
IT'S A NICE PLACE...
...BUT AN APARTMENT WOULD'VE BEEN FINE TOO.
...AND MEL'S AS A WAITER, OUR FINANCES ARE PRETTY TIGHT.
I...
...WANTED TO MAKE THIS A PLACE THAT WE CAN CALL HOME.
"HOME" MEANS MORE THAN JUST THE HOUSE YOU LIVE IN.
YOU HAVE TO BE ABLE TO CALL IT "HOME, SWEET HOME."

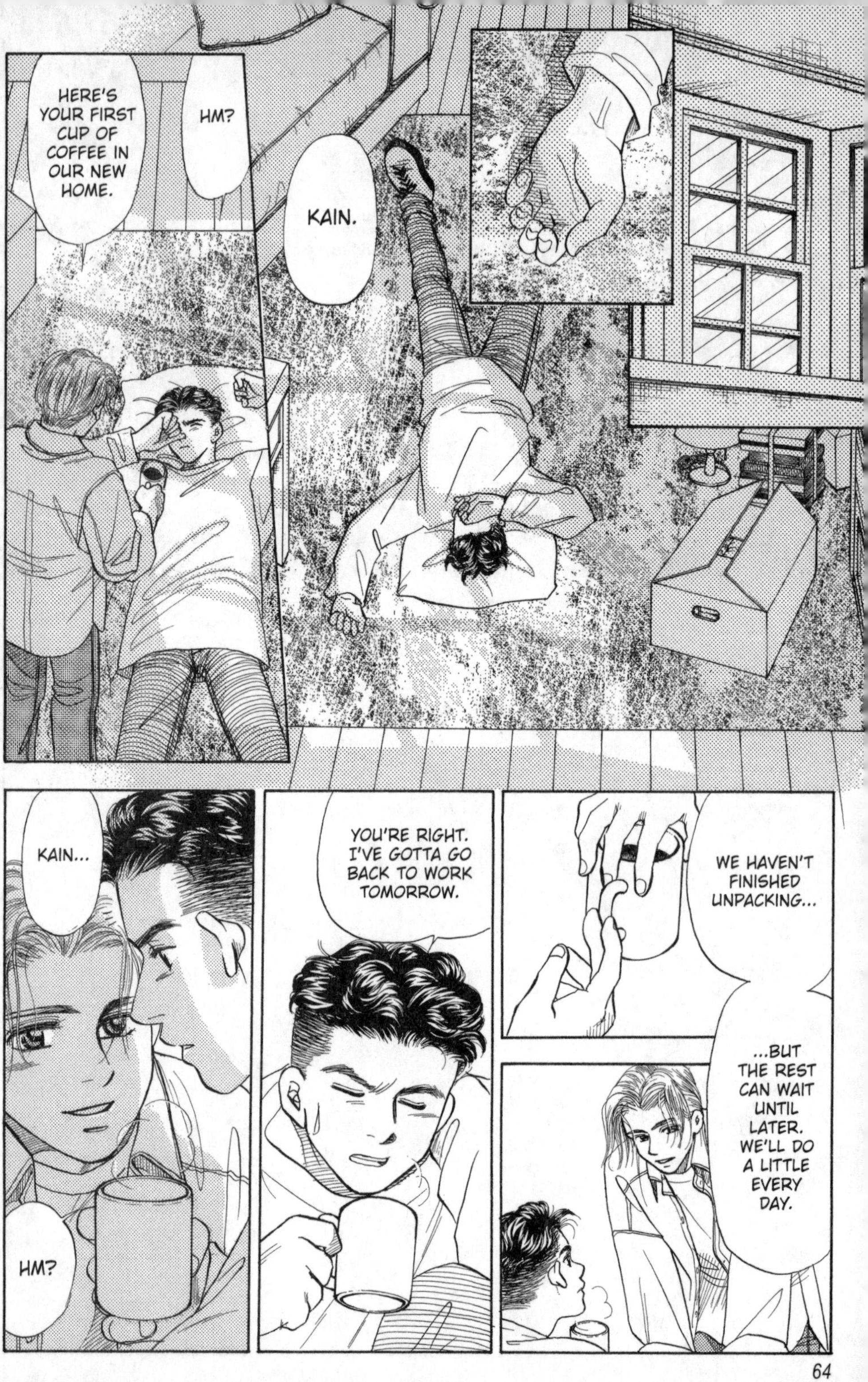
KAIN.
HM?
HERE'S YOUR FIRST CUP OF COFFEE IN OUR NEW HOME.
WE HAVEN'T FINISHED UNPACKING...
...BUT THE REST CAN WAIT UNTIL LATER. WE'LL DO A LITTLE EVERY DAY.
YOU'RE RIGHT. I'VE GOTTA GO BACK TO WORK TOMORROW.
KAIN...
HM?

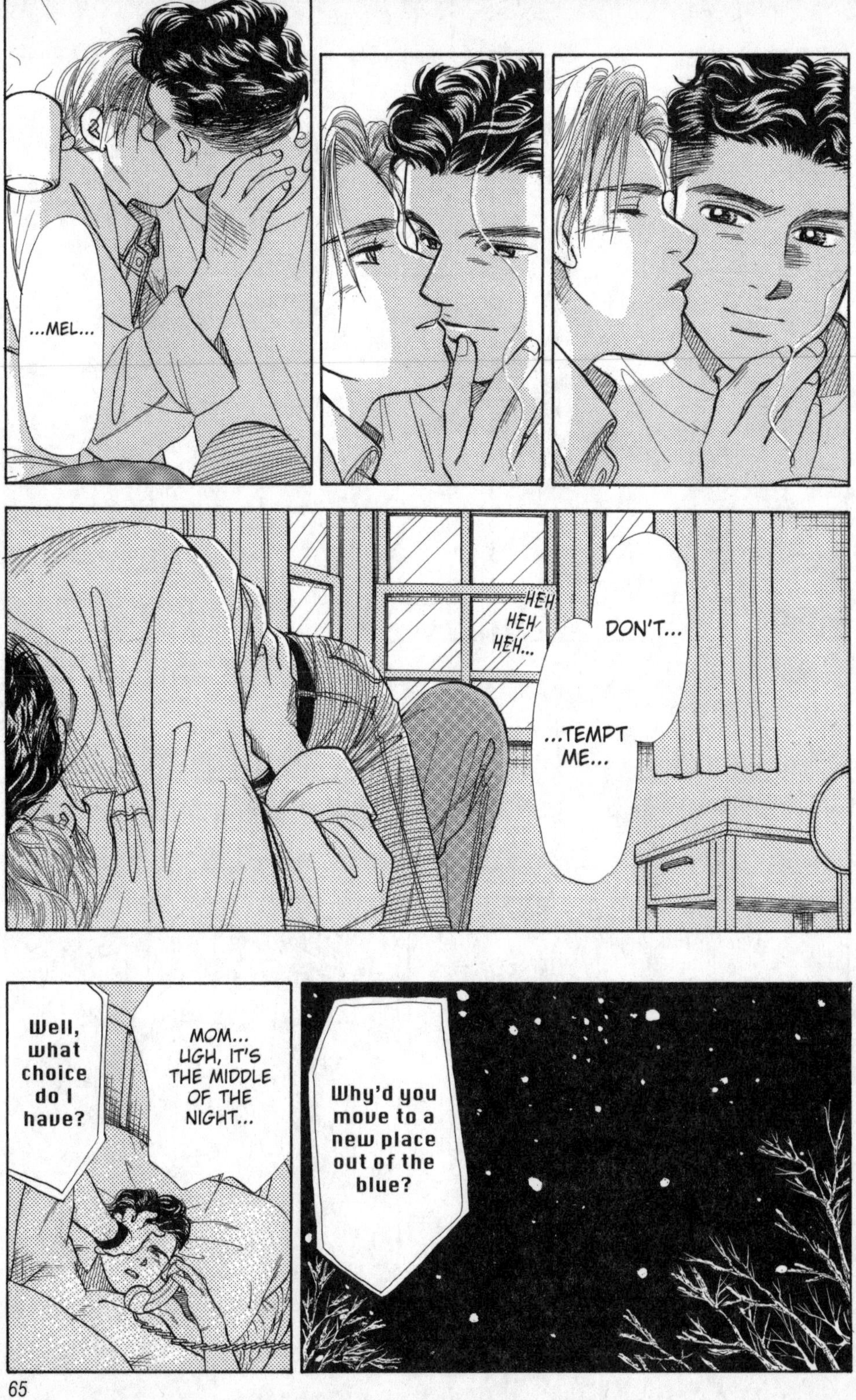
...MEL...
DON'T...
...TEMPT ME...
HEH HEH HEH...
Why'd you move to a new place out of the blue?
MOM... UGH, IT'S THE MIDDLE OF THE NIGHT...
Well, what choice do I have?

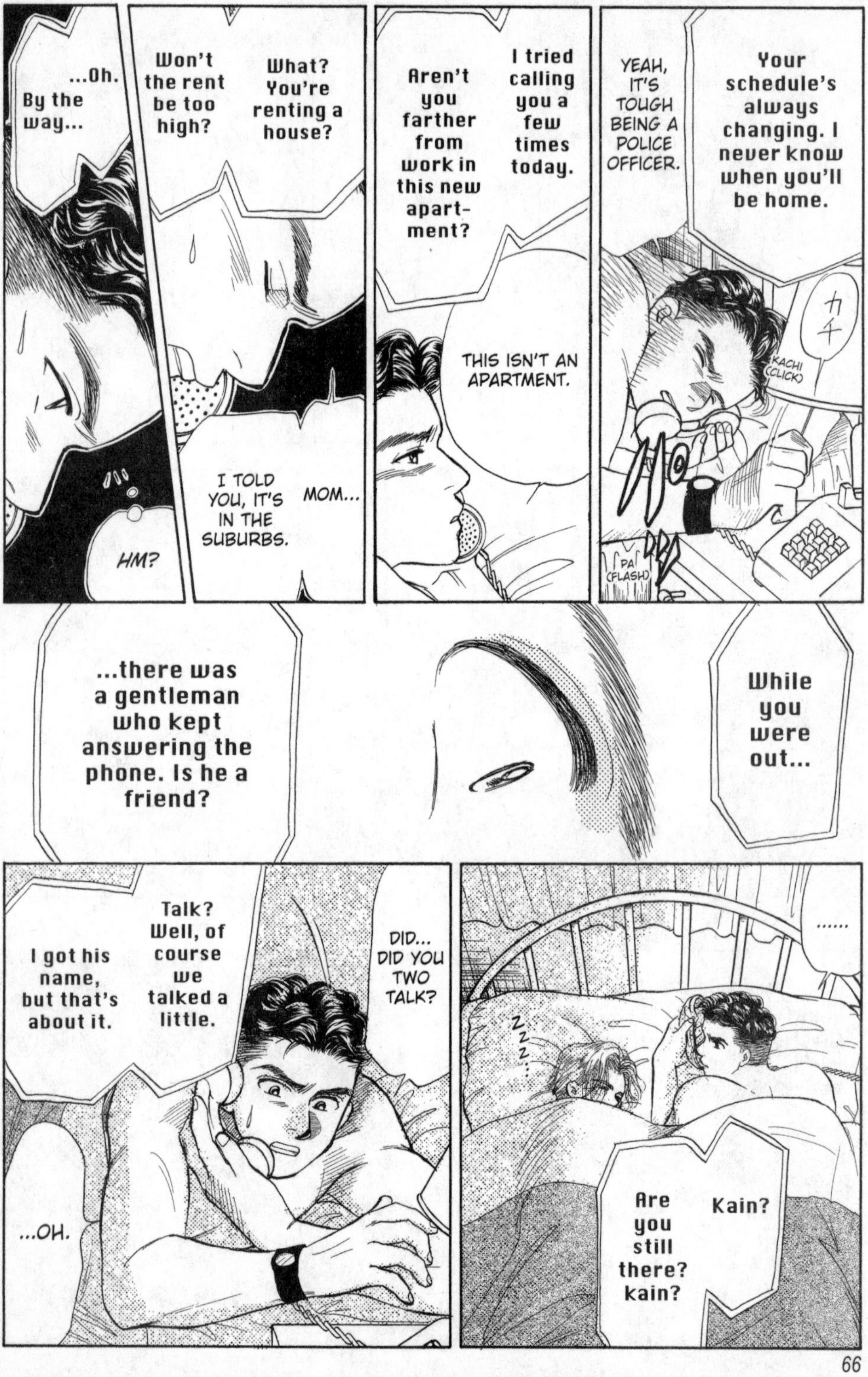
Your schedule's always changing. I never know when you'll be home.
YEAH, IT'S TOUGH BEING A POLICE OFFICER.
カチ
KACHI (CLICK)
PA (FLASH)
I tried calling you a few times today.
Aren't you farther from work in this new apartment?
THIS ISN'T AN APARTMENT.
What? You're renting a house?
Won't the rent be too high?
MOM...
I TOLD YOU, IT'S IN THE SUBURBS.
...Oh. By the way...
HM?
While you were out...
...there was a gentleman who kept answering the phone. Is he a friend?
......
Kain?
Are you still there? kain?
ZZZ...
DID... DID YOU TWO TALK?
Talk? Well, of course we talked a little.
I got his name, but that's about it.
...OH.

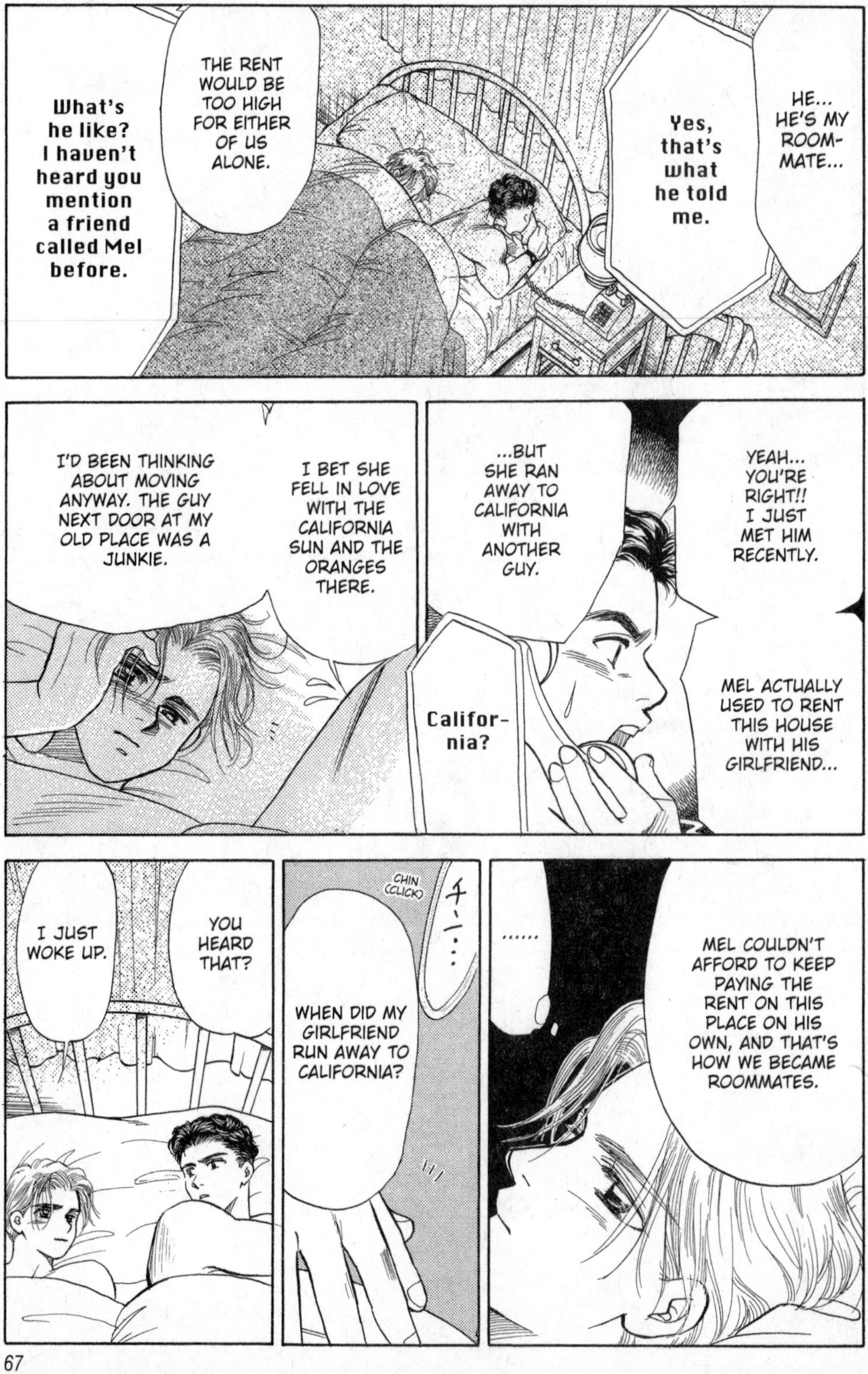
HE... HE'S MY ROOM-MATE...
Yes, that's what he told me.
THE RENT WOULD BE TOO HIGH FOR EITHER OF US ALONE.
What's he like? I haven't heard you mention a friend called Mel before.
YEAH... YOU'RE RIGHT!! I JUST MET HIM RECENTLY.
MEL ACTUALLY USED TO RENT THIS HOUSE WITH HIS GIRLFRIEND...
...BUT SHE RAN AWAY TO CALIFORNIA WITH ANOTHER GUY.
Califor-nia?
I BET SHE FELL IN LOVE WITH THE CALIFORNIA SUN AND THE ORANGES THERE.
I'D BEEN THINKING ABOUT MOVING ANYWAY. THE GUY NEXT DOOR AT MY OLD PLACE WAS A JUNKIE.
MEL COULDN'T AFFORD TO KEEP PAYING THE RENT ON THIS PLACE ON HIS OWN, AND THAT'S HOW WE BECAME ROOMMATES.
......
CHIN (CLICK)
チー...
WHEN DID MY GIRLFRIEND RUN AWAY TO CALIFORNIA?
YOU HEARD THAT?
I JUST WOKE UP.

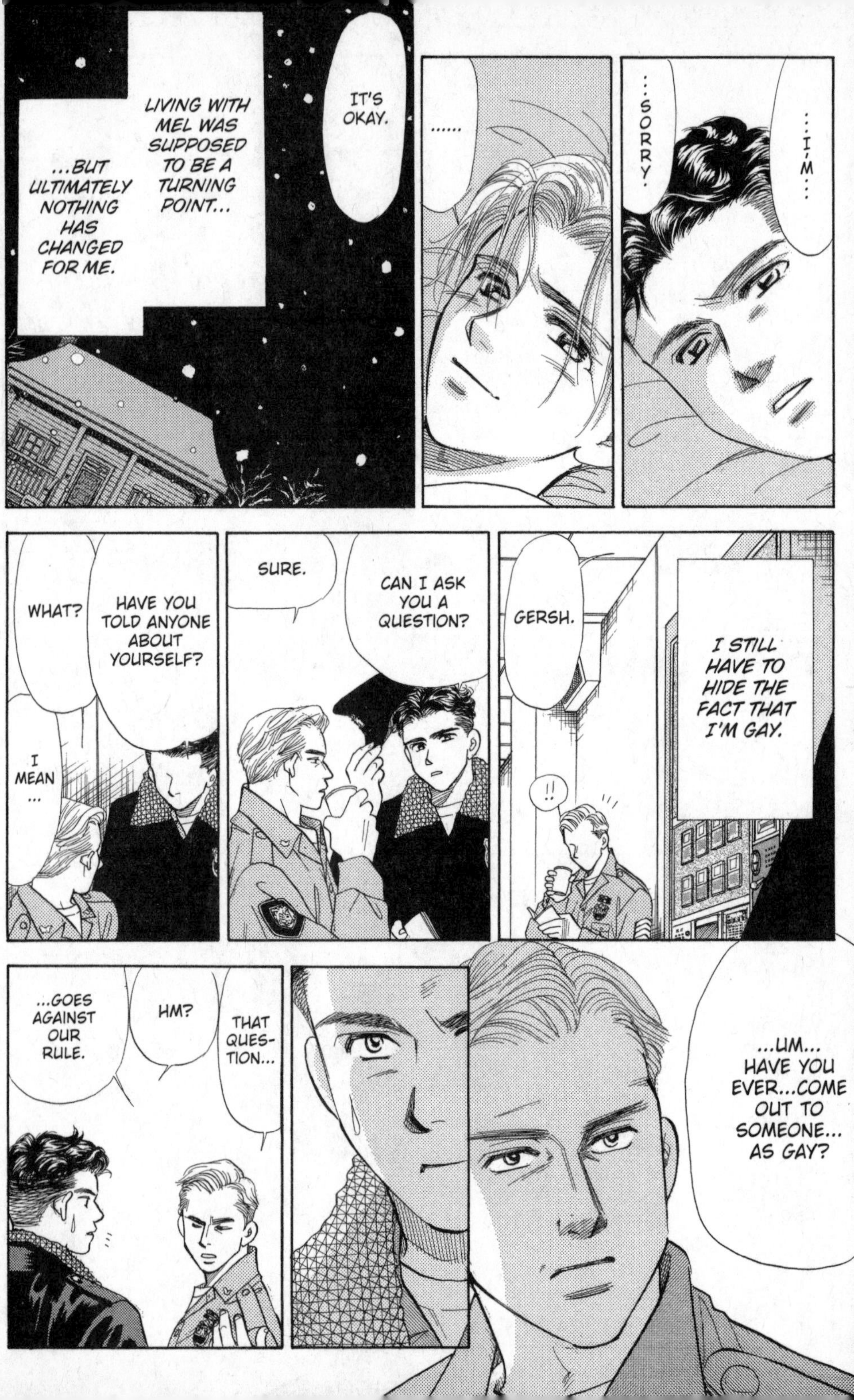
...I'M...
...SORRY.
......
IT'S OKAY.
LIVING WITH MEL WAS SUPPOSED TO BE A TURNING POINT...
...BUT ULTIMATELY NOTHING HAS CHANGED FOR ME.
I STILL HAVE TO HIDE THE FACT THAT I'M GAY.
GERSH.
!!
CAN I ASK YOU A QUESTION?
SURE.
HAVE YOU TOLD ANYONE ABOUT YOURSELF?
WHAT?
I MEAN ...
...UM... HAVE YOU EVER...COME OUT TO SOMEONE... AS GAY?
THAT QUES-TION...
HM?
...GOES AGAINST OUR RULE.

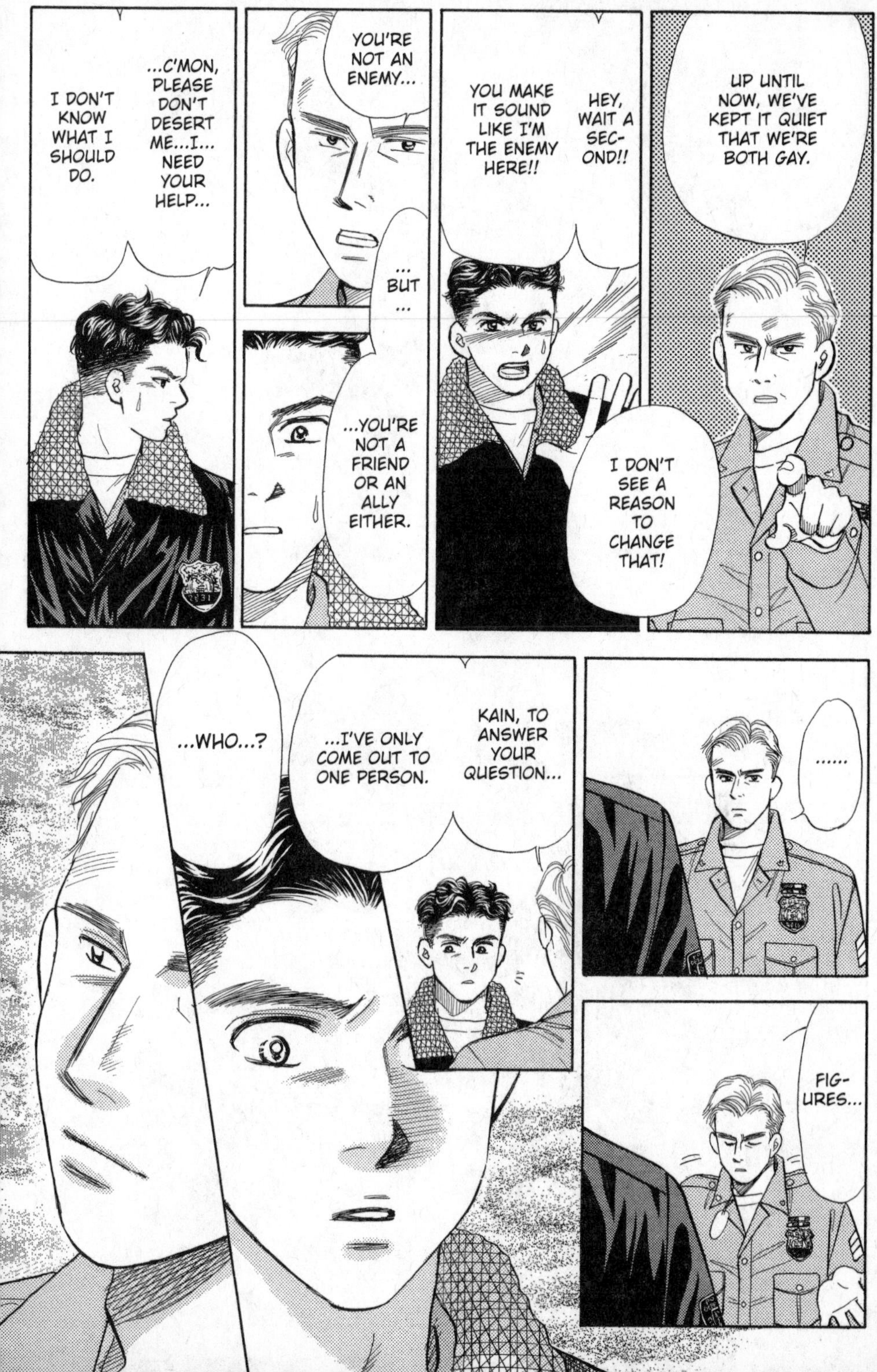
UP UNTIL NOW, WE'VE KEPT IT QUIET THAT WE'RE BOTH GAY.
I DON'T SEE A REASON TO CHANGE THAT!
HEY, WAIT A SEC-OND!!
YOU MAKE IT SOUND LIKE I'M THE ENEMY HERE!!
YOU'RE NOT AN ENEMY...
... BUT ...
...YOU'RE NOT A FRIEND OR AN ALLY EITHER.
...C'MON, PLEASE DON'T DESERT ME...I... NEED YOUR HELP...
I DON'T KNOW WHAT I SHOULD DO.
......
FIG-URES...
KAIN, TO ANSWER YOUR QUESTION...
...I'VE ONLY COME OUT TO ONE PERSON.
...WHO...?

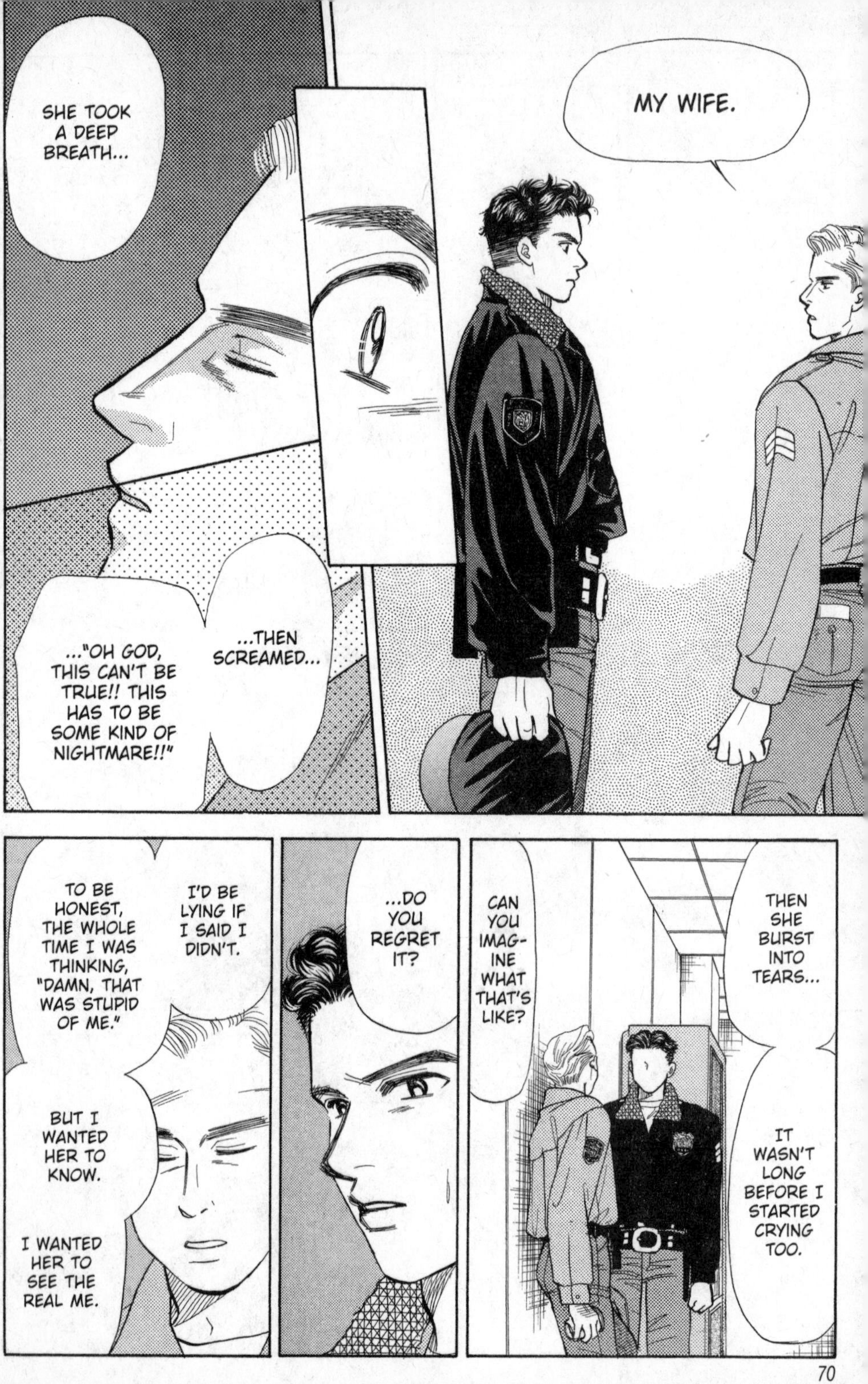
MY WIFE.
SHE TOOK A DEEP BREATH...
...THEN SCREAMED...
..."OH GOD, THIS CAN'T BE TRUE!! THIS HAS TO BE SOME KIND OF NIGHTMARE!!"
THEN SHE BURST INTO TEARS...
IT WASN'T LONG BEFORE I STARTED CRYING TOO.
CAN YOU IMAG-INE WHAT THAT'S LIKE?
...DO YOU REGRET IT?
I'D BE LYING IF I SAID I DIDN'T.
TO BE HONEST, THE WHOLE TIME I WAS THINKING, "DAMN, THAT WAS STUPID OF ME."
BUT I WANTED HER TO KNOW.
I WANTED HER TO SEE THE REAL ME.

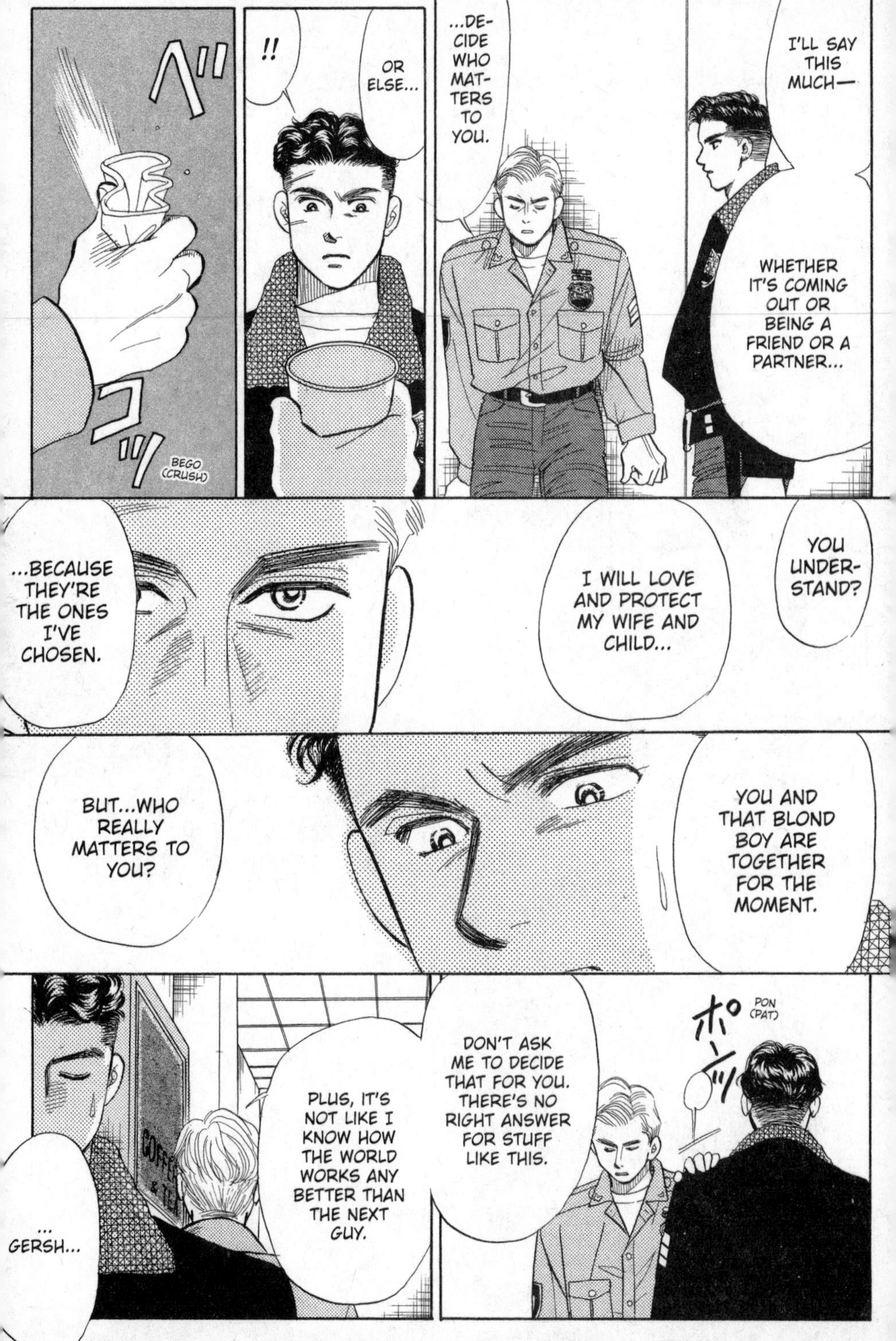
I'LL SAY THIS MUCH—
WHETHER IT'S COMING OUT OR BEING A FRIEND OR A PARTNER...
...DECIDE WHO MATTERS TO YOU.
OR ELSE...
!!
ベゴッ
BEGO (CRUSH)
YOU UNDERSTAND?
I WILL LOVE AND PROTECT MY WIFE AND CHILD...
...BECAUSE THEY'RE THE ONES I'VE CHOSEN.
YOU AND THAT BLOND BOY ARE TOGETHER FOR THE MOMENT.
BUT...WHO REALLY MATTERS TO YOU?
ポンッ
PON (PAT)
DON'T ASK ME TO DECIDE THAT FOR YOU. THERE'S NO RIGHT ANSWER FOR STUFF LIKE THIS.
PLUS, IT'S NOT LIKE I KNOW HOW THE WORLD WORKS ANY BETTER THAN THE NEXT GUY.
...GERSH...

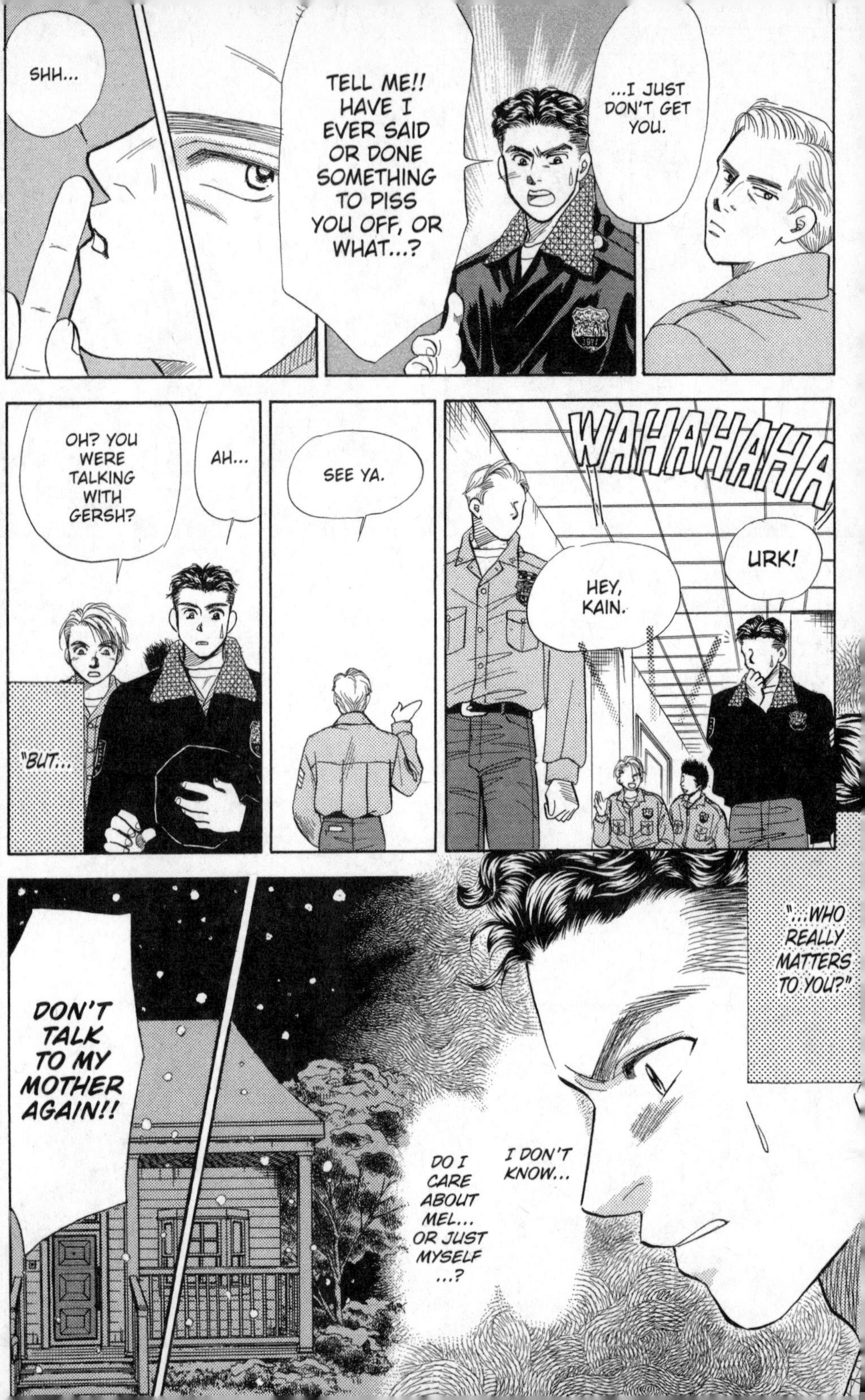
...I JUST DON'T GET YOU.
TELL ME!! HAVE I EVER SAID OR DONE SOMETHING TO PISS YOU OFF, OR WHAT...?
SHH...
WAHAHAHA
URK!
HEY, KAIN.
SEE YA.
AH...
OH? YOU WERE TALKING WITH GERSH?
"BUT...
"...WHO REALLY MATTERS TO YOU?"
I DON'T KNOW...
DO I CARE ABOUT MEL... OR JUST MYSELF ...?
DON'T TALK TO MY MOTHER AGAIN!!

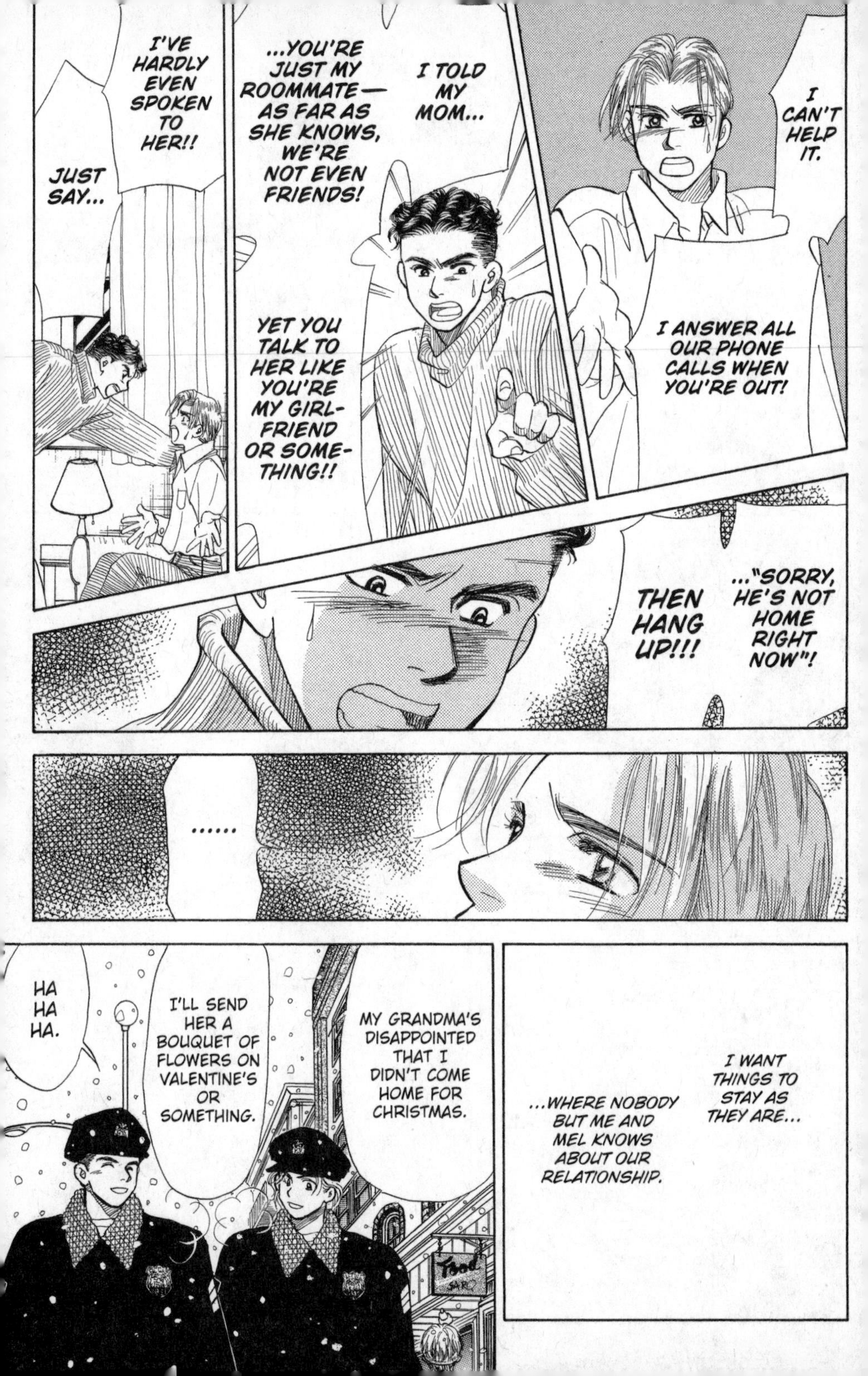
I CAN'T HELP IT.
I ANSWER ALL OUR PHONE CALLS WHEN YOU'RE OUT!
I TOLD MY MOM...
...YOU'RE JUST MY ROOMMATE— AS FAR AS SHE KNOWS, WE'RE NOT EVEN FRIENDS!
YET YOU TALK TO HER LIKE YOU'RE MY GIRL-FRIEND OR SOME-THING!!
I'VE HARDLY EVEN SPOKEN TO HER!!
JUST SAY...
..."SORRY, HE'S NOT HOME RIGHT NOW"!
THEN HANG UP!!!
......
I WANT THINGS TO STAY AS THEY ARE...
...WHERE NOBODY BUT ME AND MEL KNOWS ABOUT OUR RELATIONSHIP.
MY GRANDMA'S DISAPPOINTED THAT I DIDN'T COME HOME FOR CHRISTMAS.
I'LL SEND HER A BOUQUET OF FLOWERS ON VALENTINE'S OR SOMETHING.
HA HA HA.

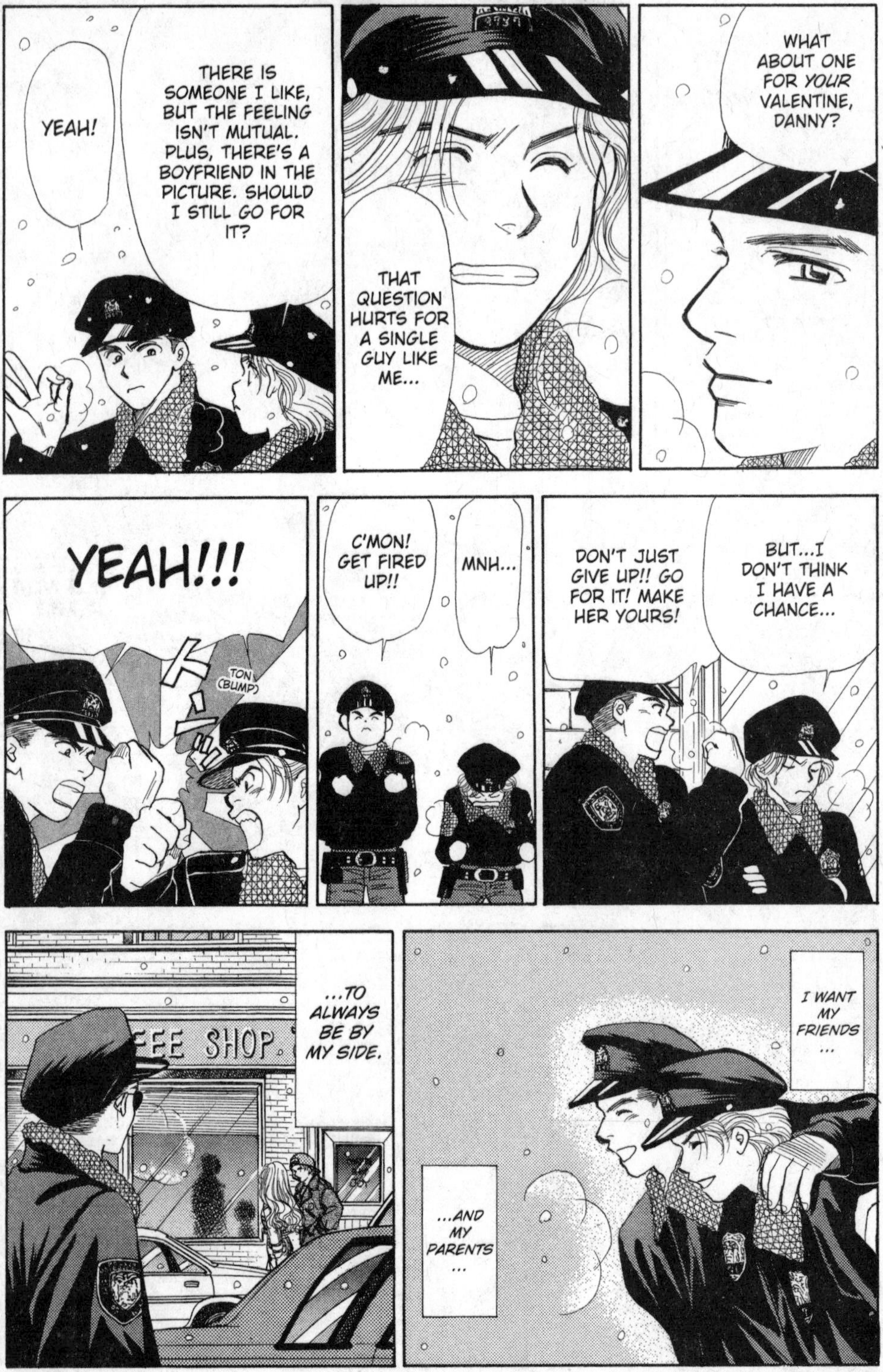
WHAT ABOUT ONE FOR *YOUR* VALENTINE, DANNY?
THAT QUESTION HURTS FOR A SINGLE GUY LIKE ME...
THERE IS SOMEONE I LIKE, BUT THE FEELING ISN'T MUTUAL. PLUS, THERE'S A BOYFRIEND IN THE PICTURE. SHOULD I STILL *GO* FOR IT?
YEAH!
BUT...I DON'T THINK I HAVE A CHANCE...
DON'T JUST GIVE UP!! GO FOR IT! MAKE HER YOURS!
MNH...
C'MON! GET FIRED UP!!
YEAH!!!
TON (BUMP)
I WANT MY FRIENDS ...
...AND MY PARENTS ...
...TO ALWAYS BE BY MY SIDE.

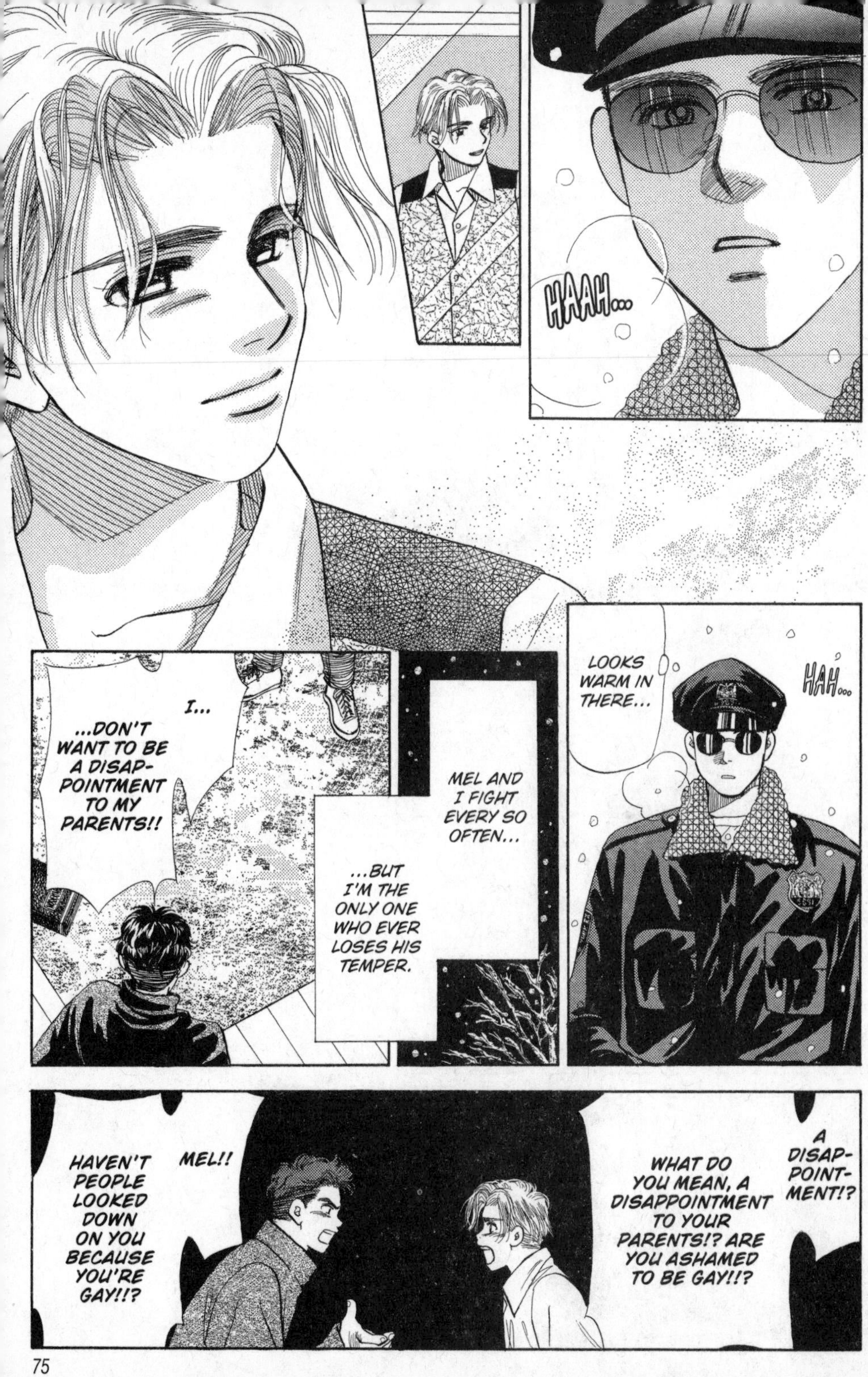
HAAH...
HAH...
LOOKS WARM IN THERE...
MEL AND I FIGHT EVERY SO OFTEN...
...BUT I'M THE ONLY ONE WHO EVER LOSES HIS TEMPER.
I...
...DON'T WANT TO BE A DISAPPOINTMENT TO MY PARENTS!!
A DISAPPOINTMENT!?
WHAT DO YOU MEAN, A DISAPPOINTMENT TO YOUR PARENTS!? ARE YOU ASHAMED TO BE GAY!!?
MEL!!
HAVEN'T PEOPLE LOOKED DOWN ON YOU BECAUSE YOU'RE GAY!!?

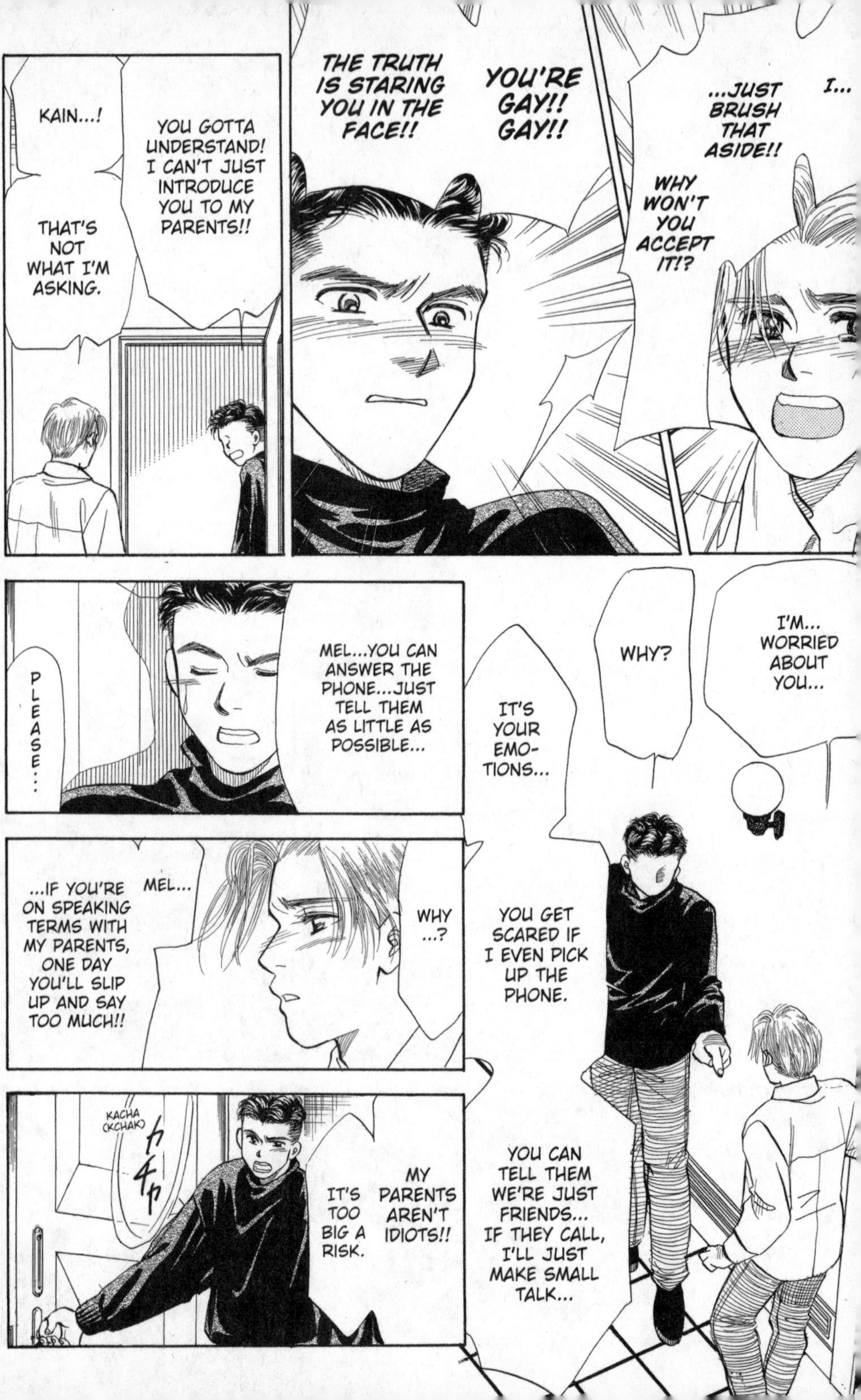
I...
...JUST BRUSH THAT ASIDE!!
WHY WON'T YOU ACCEPT IT!?
YOU'RE GAY!! GAY!!
THE TRUTH IS STARING YOU IN THE FACE!!
YOU GOTTA UNDERSTAND! I CAN'T JUST INTRODUCE YOU TO MY PARENTS!!
KAIN...!
THAT'S NOT WHAT I'M ASKING.
I'M... WORRIED ABOUT YOU...
WHY?
IT'S YOUR EMOTIONS...
YOU GET SCARED IF I EVEN PICK UP THE PHONE.
YOU CAN TELL THEM WE'RE JUST FRIENDS... IF THEY CALL, I'LL JUST MAKE SMALL TALK...
MEL...YOU CAN ANSWER THE PHONE...JUST TELL THEM AS LITTLE AS POSSIBLE...
PLEASE...
WHY ...?
MEL...
...IF YOU'RE ON SPEAKING TERMS WITH MY PARENTS, ONE DAY YOU'LL SLIP UP AND SAY TOO MUCH!!
MY PARENTS AREN'T IDIOTS!!
IT'S TOO BIG A RISK.
KACHA (KCHAK)

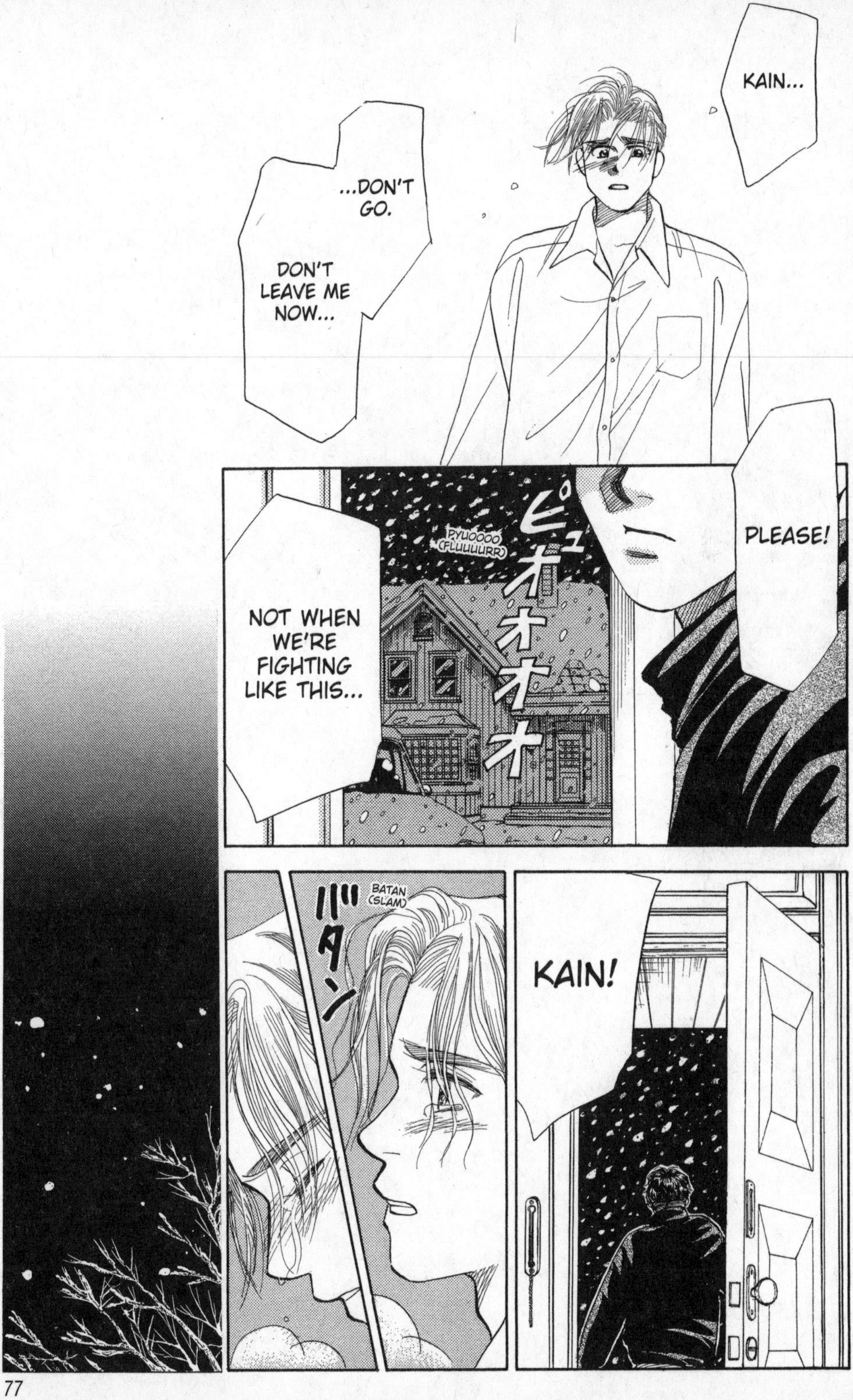
KAIN...
...DON'T GO.
DON'T LEAVE ME NOW...
PLEASE!
PYUOOOO (FLUUUURR)
NOT WHEN WE'RE FIGHTING LIKE THIS...
KAIN!
BATAN (SLAM)

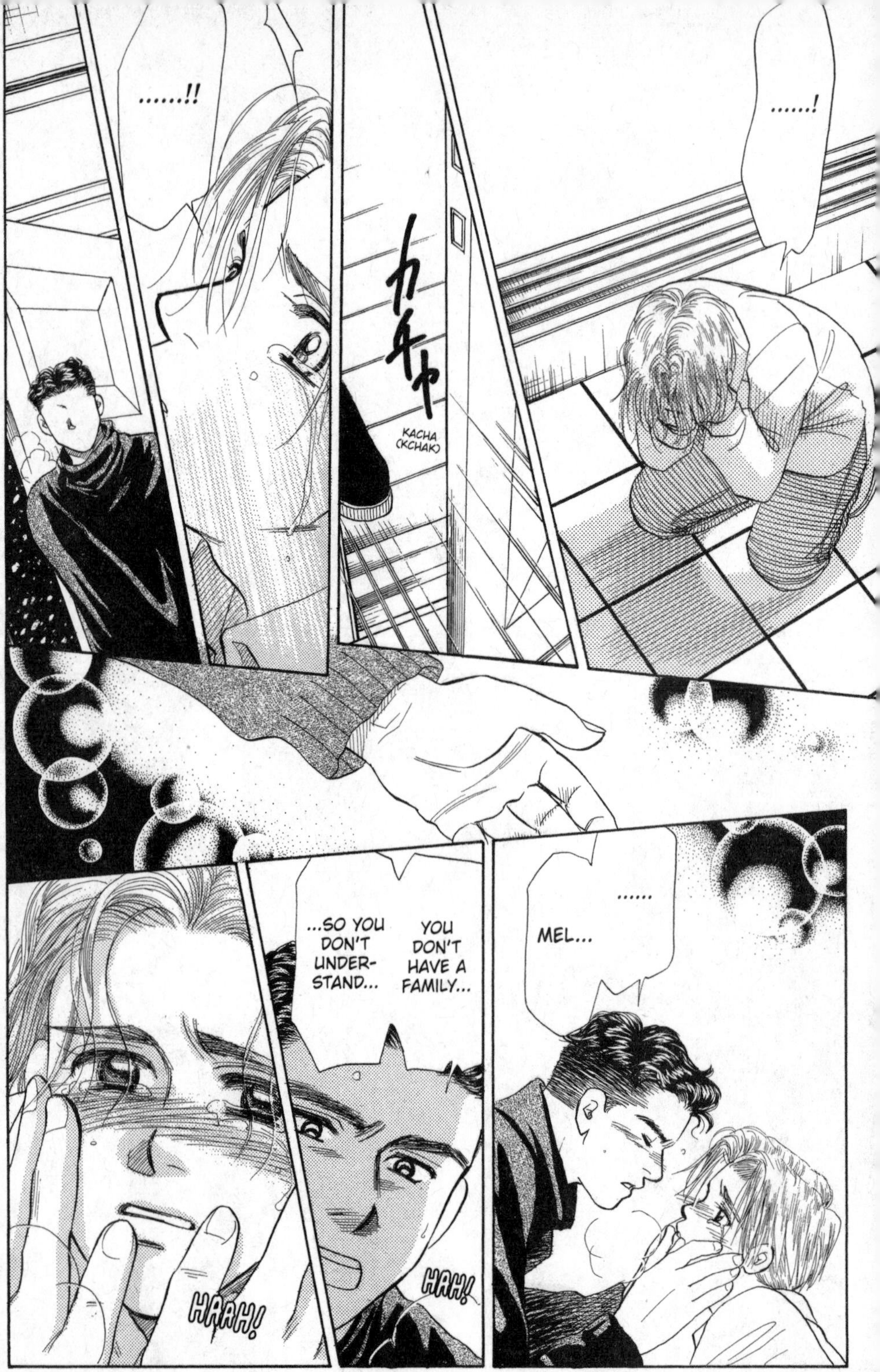
......!
カチャ
KACHA (KCHAK)
......!!
......
MEL...
YOU DON'T HAVE A FAMILY...
...SO YOU DON'T UNDERSTAND...
HAH!
HAAH!

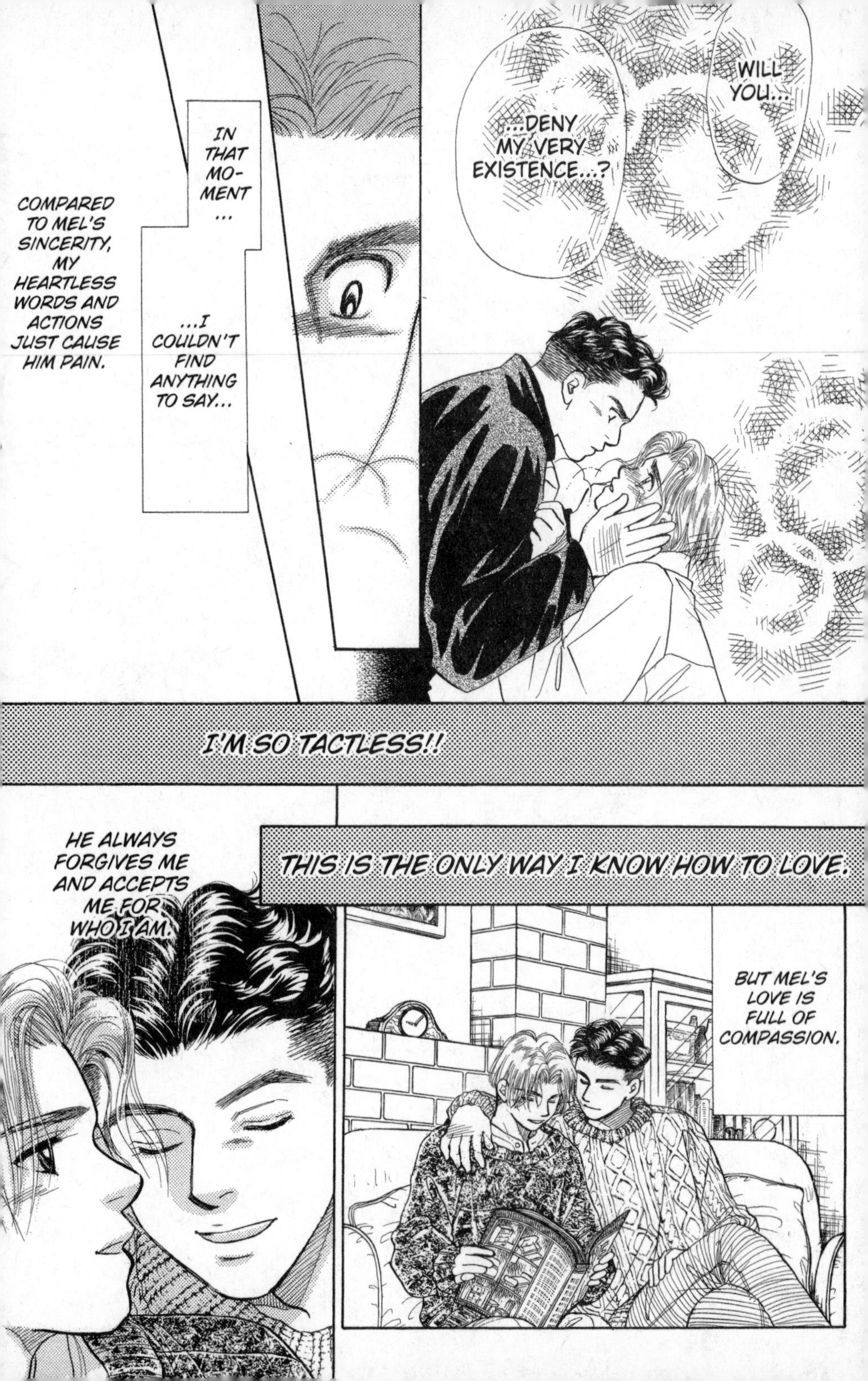
WILL YOU...
...DENY MY VERY EXISTENCE...?
IN THAT MO-MENT...
...I COULDN'T FIND ANYTHING TO SAY...
COMPARED TO MEL'S SINCERITY, MY HEARTLESS WORDS AND ACTIONS JUST CAUSE HIM PAIN.
I'M SO TACTLESS!!
THIS IS THE ONLY WAY I KNOW HOW TO LOVE.
BUT MEL'S LOVE IS FULL OF COMPASSION.
HE ALWAYS FORGIVES ME AND ACCEPTS ME FOR WHO I AM.

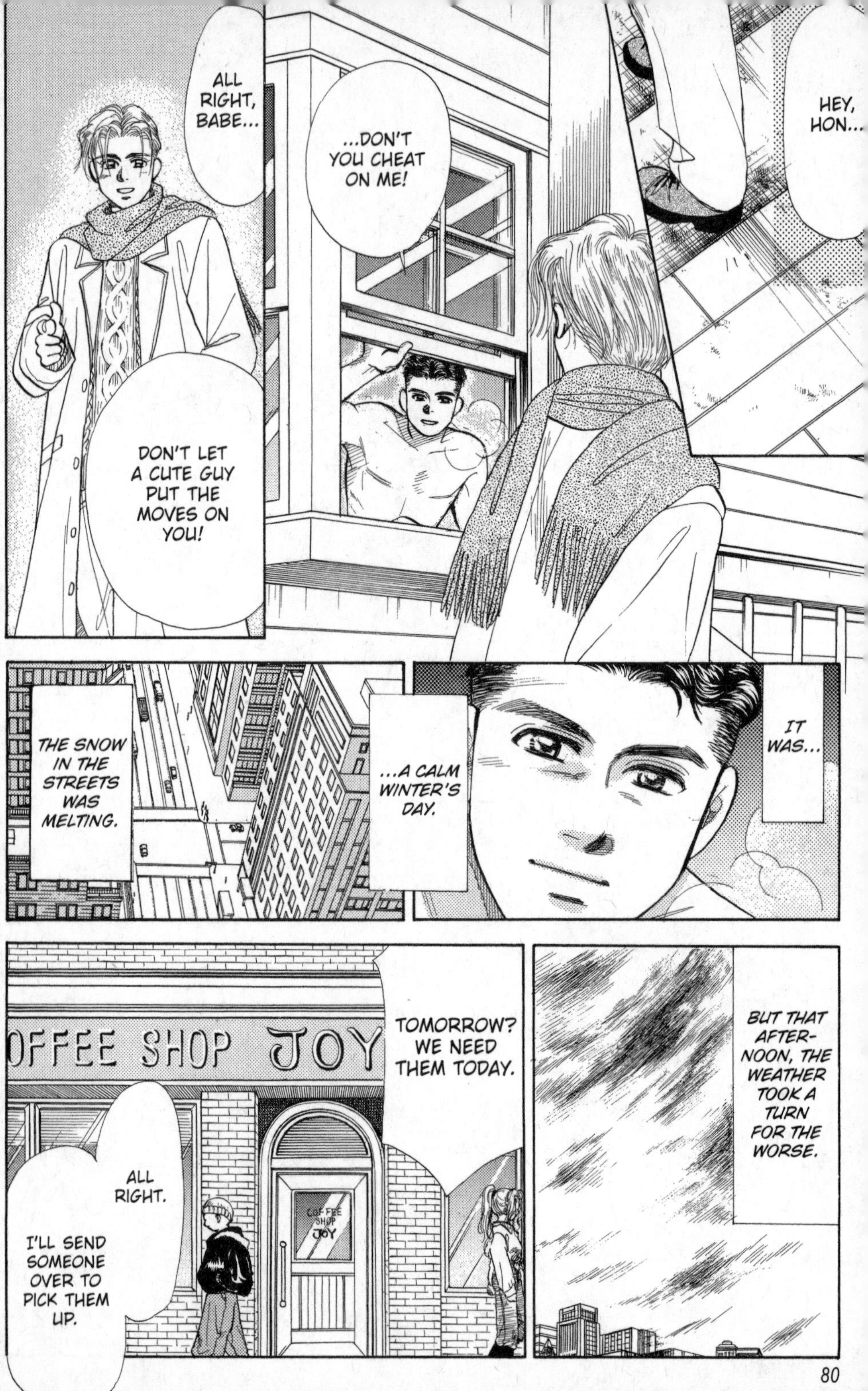
HEY, HON...
...DON'T YOU CHEAT ON ME!
ALL RIGHT, BABE...
DON'T LET A CUTE GUY PUT THE MOVES ON YOU!
IT WAS...
...A CALM WINTER'S DAY.
THE SNOW IN THE STREETS WAS MELTING.
BUT THAT AFTER-NOON, THE WEATHER TOOK A TURN FOR THE WORSE.
OFFEE SHOP JOY
TOMORROW? WE NEED THEM TODAY.
COFFEE SHOP JOY
ALL RIGHT.
I'LL SEND SOMEONE OVER TO PICK THEM UP.

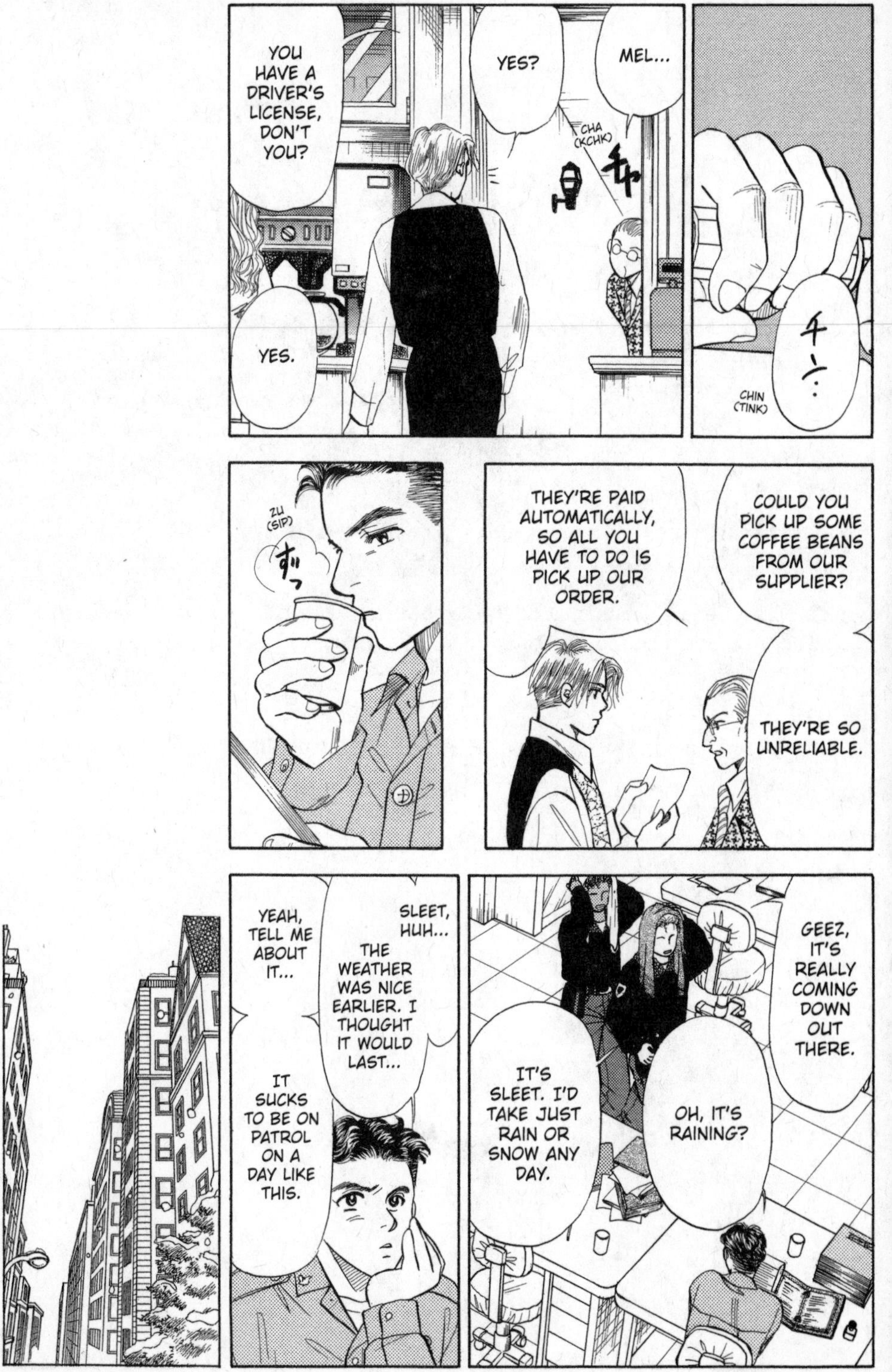
CHIN (TINK)
チーン…
MEL...
CHA (KCHK)
チャ
YES?
YOU HAVE A DRIVER'S LICENSE, DON'T YOU?
YES.
COULD YOU PICK UP SOME COFFEE BEANS FROM OUR SUPPLIER?
THEY'RE PAID AUTOMATICALLY, SO ALL YOU HAVE TO DO IS PICK UP OUR ORDER.
THEY'RE SO UNRELIABLE.
ZU (SIP)
ずっ
GEEZ, IT'S REALLY COMING DOWN OUT THERE.
OH, IT'S RAINING?
IT'S SLEET. I'D TAKE JUST RAIN OR SNOW ANY DAY.
SLEET, HUH...
THE WEATHER WAS NICE EARLIER. I THOUGHT IT WOULD LAST...
YEAH, TELL ME ABOUT IT...
IT SUCKS TO BE ON PATROL ON A DAY LIKE THIS.

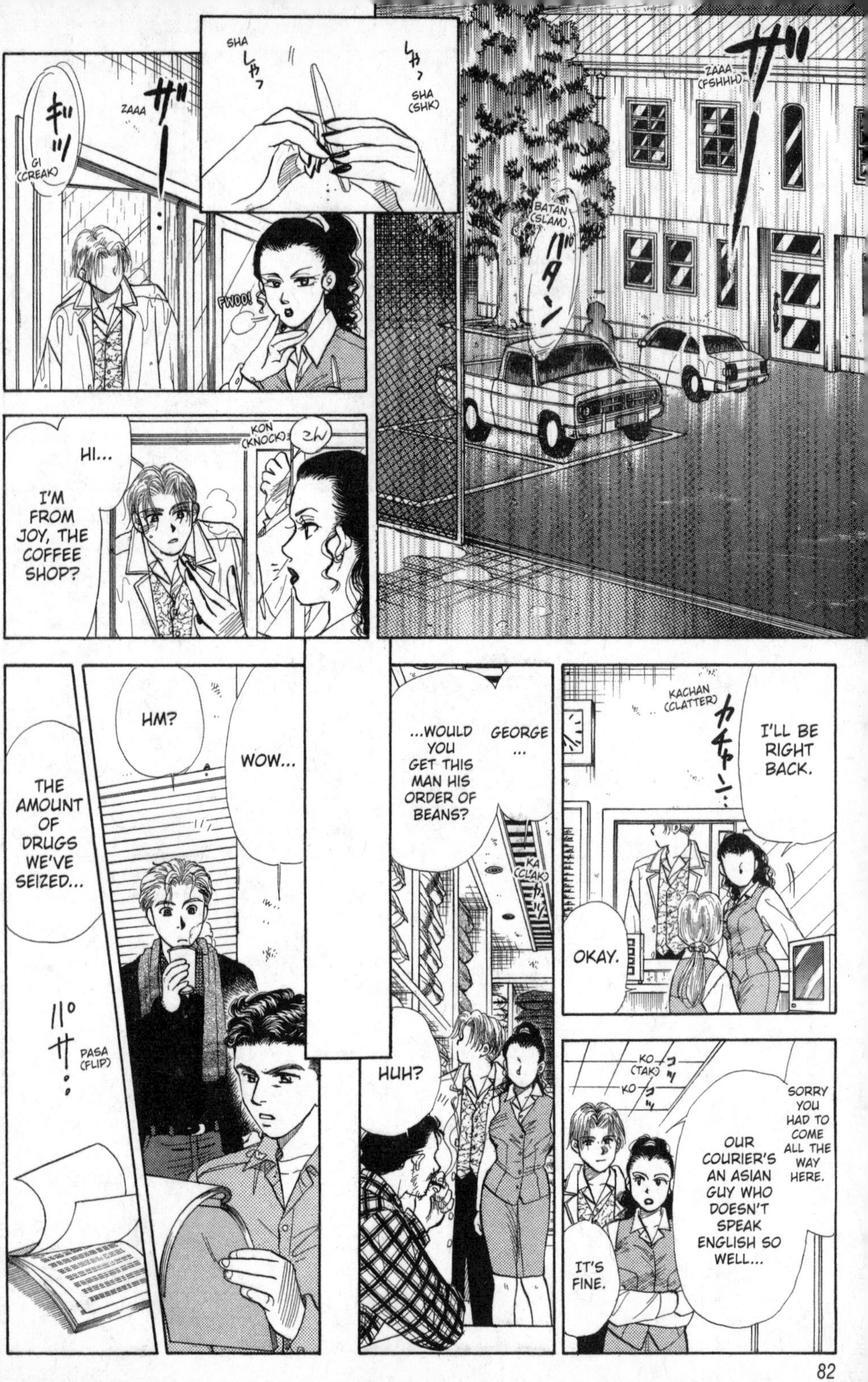
ZAAA (FSHHH)
ザー
BATAN (SLAM)
バタン
SHA
しゃっ
SHA (SHK)
しゃっ
ZAAA
ザー
GI (CREAK)
ギッ
FWOO!
KON (KNOCK)
こん
HI...
I'M FROM JOY, THE COFFEE SHOP?
KACHAN (CLATTER)
カチャーン
I'LL BE RIGHT BACK.
OKAY.
KO (TAK)
KO
SORRY YOU HAD TO COME ALL THE WAY HERE.
OUR COURIER'S AN ASIAN GUY WHO DOESN'T SPEAK ENGLISH SO WELL...
IT'S FINE.
GEORGE...
...WOULD YOU GET THIS MAN HIS ORDER OF BEANS?
KA (CLAK)
HUH?
HM?
WOW...
THE AMOUNT OF DRUGS WE'VE SEIZED...
PASA (FLIP)
パサ

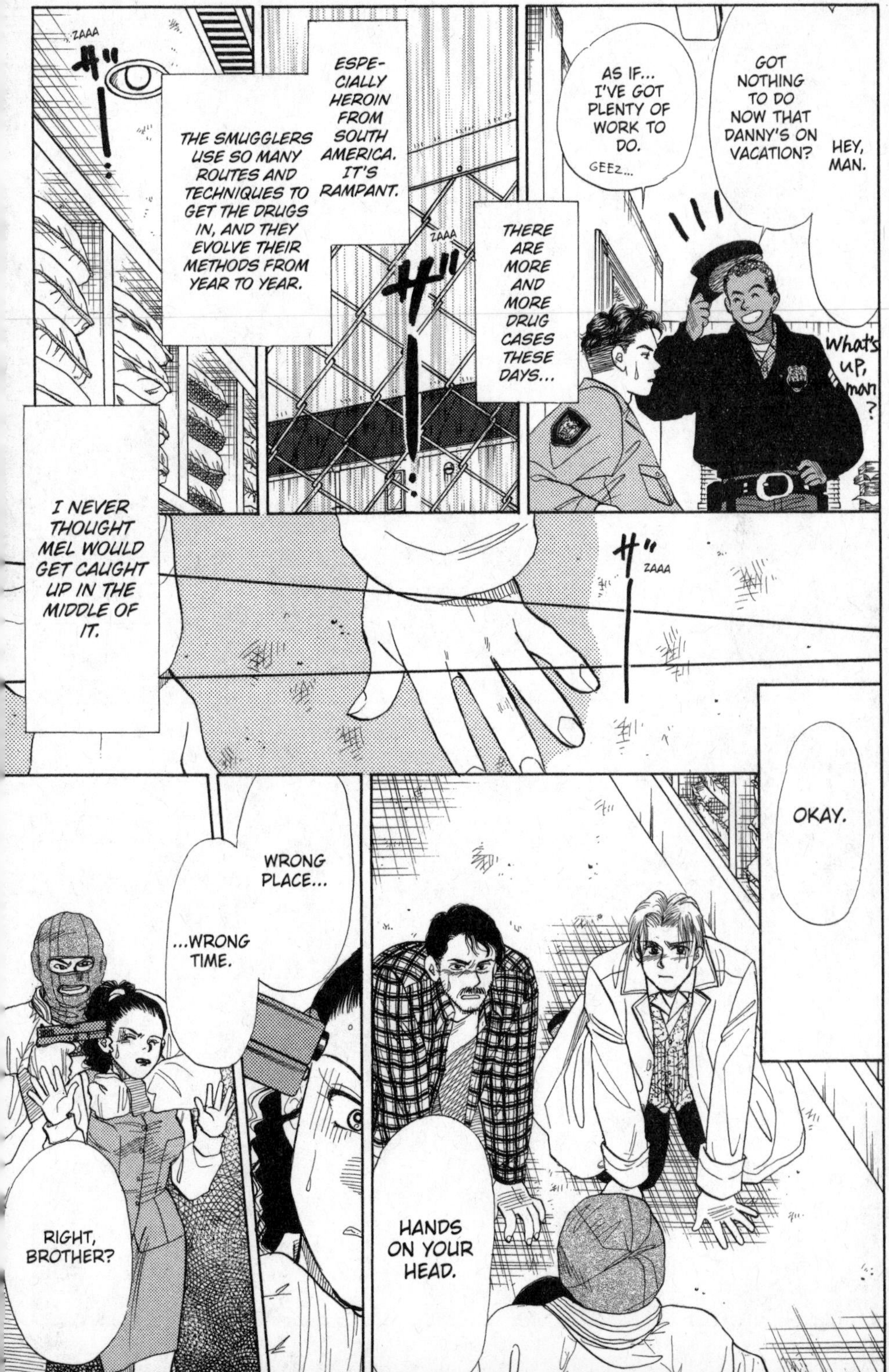
HEY, MAN.
GOT NOTHING TO DO NOW THAT DANNY'S ON VACATION?
What's up, man?
AS IF... I'VE GOT PLENTY OF WORK TO DO.
GEEZ...
THERE ARE MORE AND MORE DRUG CASES THESE DAYS...
ZAAA
ESPE-CIALLY HEROIN FROM SOUTH AMERICA. IT'S RAMPANT.
THE SMUGGLERS USE SO MANY ROUTES AND TECHNIQUES TO GET THE DRUGS IN, AND THEY EVOLVE THEIR METHODS FROM YEAR TO YEAR.
ZAAA
ZAAA
I NEVER THOUGHT MEL WOULD GET CAUGHT UP IN THE MIDDLE OF IT.
OKAY.
HANDS ON YOUR HEAD.
WRONG PLACE...
...WRONG TIME.
RIGHT, BROTHER?

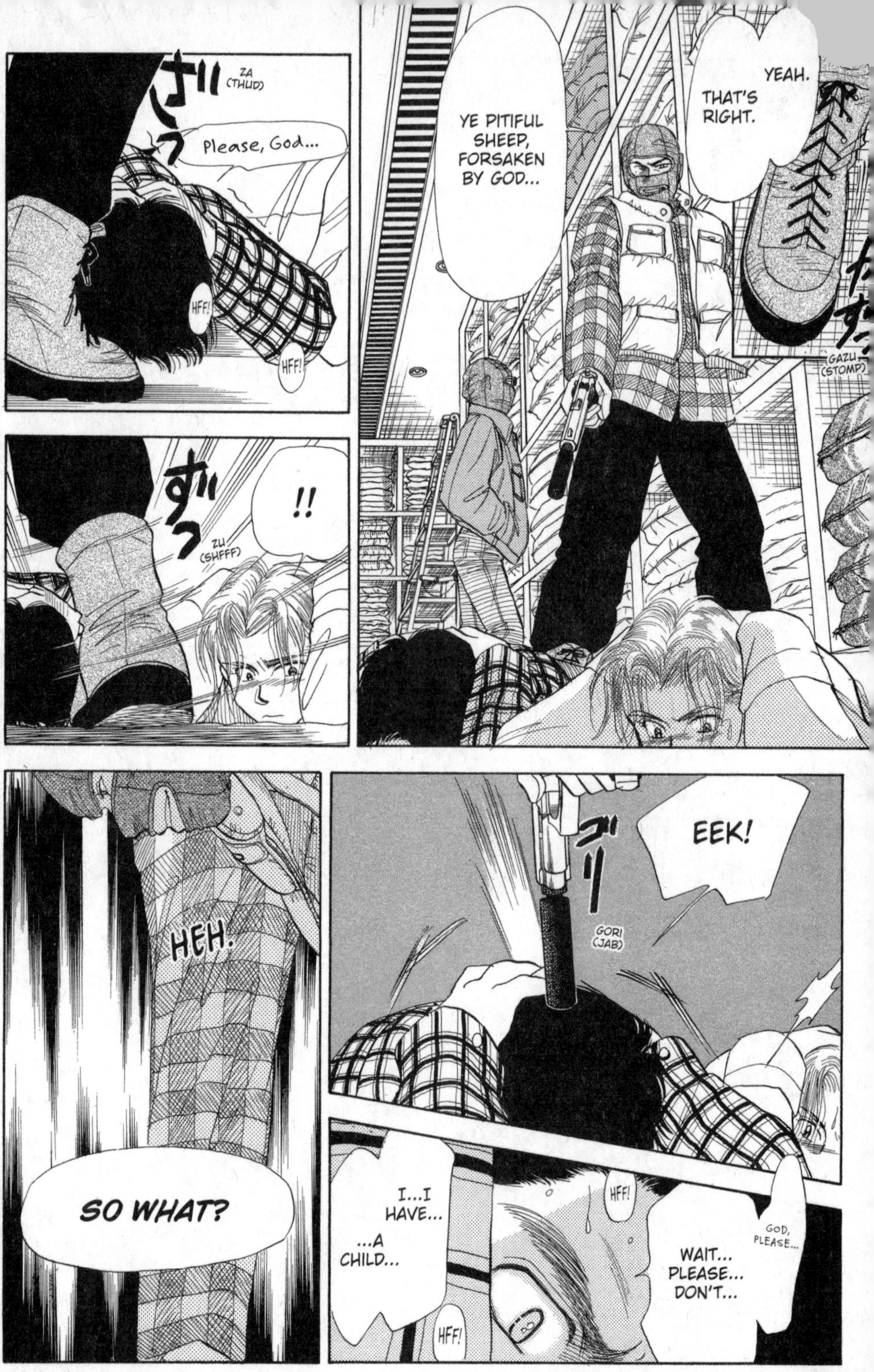
YEAH.
THAT'S RIGHT.
GAZU (STOMP)
YE PITIFUL SHEEP, FORSAKEN BY GOD...
ざっ
ZA (THUD)
Please, God...
HFF!
HFF!
ずっ
ZU (SHFFF)
!!
EEK!
ゴリ
GORI (JAB)
GOD, PLEASE...
WAIT... PLEASE... DON'T...
HFF!
I...I HAVE...
...A CHILD...
HFF!
HEH.
SO WHAT?

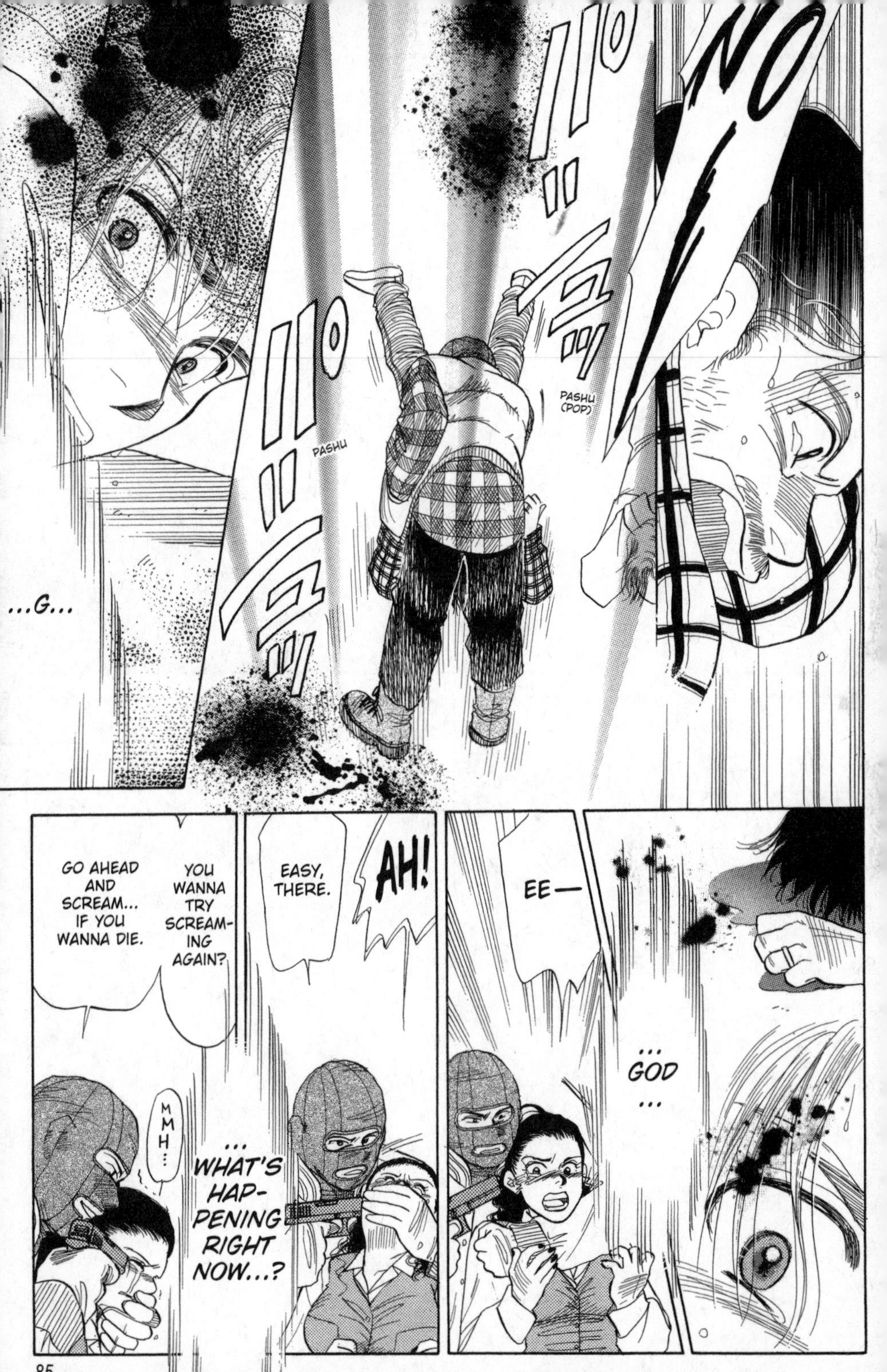
NO
PASHU (POP)
PASHU
...G...
... GOD ...
EE—
AH!
EASY, THERE.
... WHAT'S HAP-PENING RIGHT NOW...?
YOU WANNA TRY SCREAM-ING AGAIN?
GO AHEAD AND SCREAM... IF YOU WANNA DIE.
MMH...

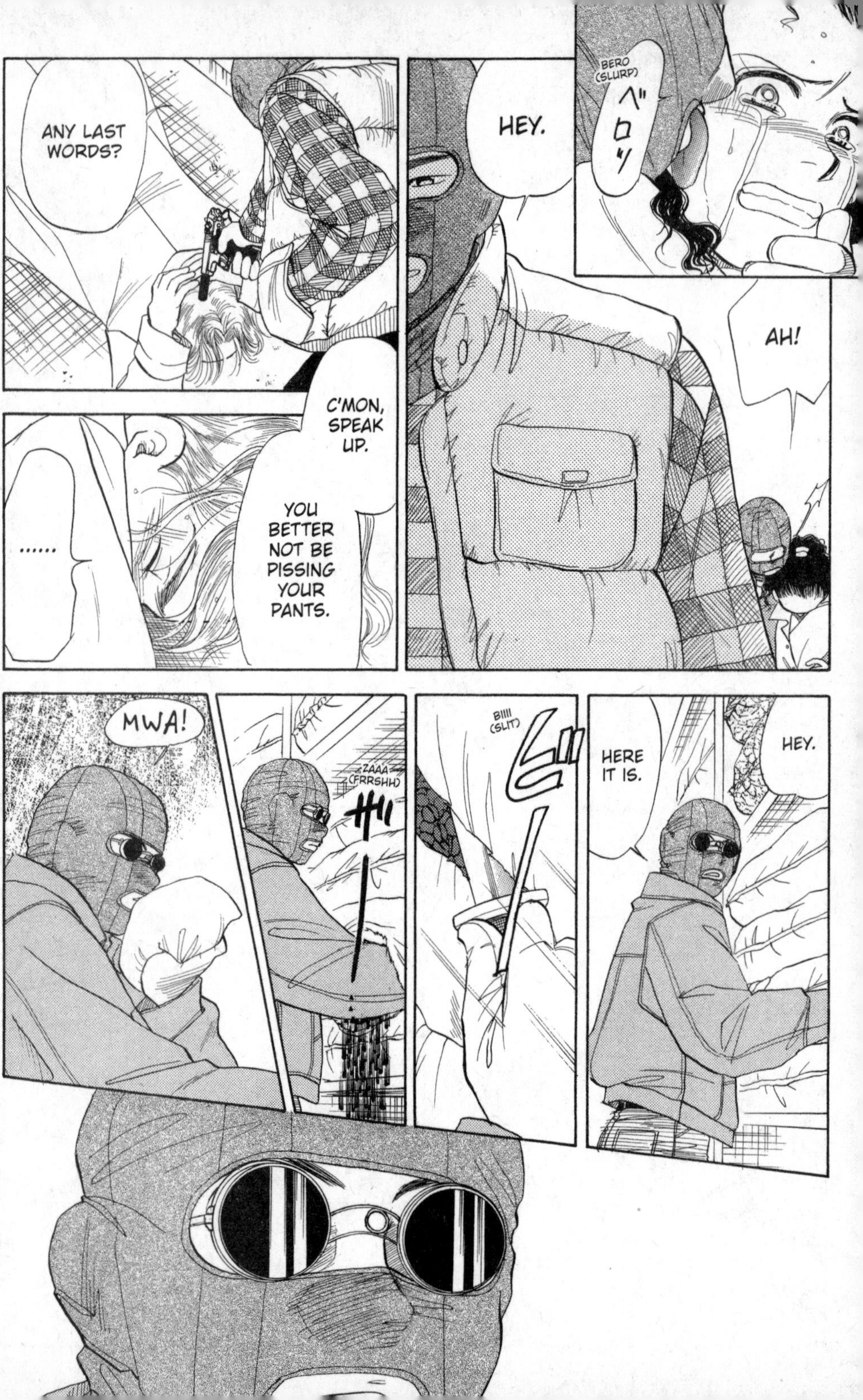
BERO (SLURP)
ベロッ
HEY.
AH!
ANY LAST WORDS?
C'MON, SPEAK UP.
YOU BETTER NOT BE PISSING YOUR PANTS.
......
HEY.
HERE IT IS.
BIIII (SLIT)
ビッ
ZAAA (FRRSHH)
ザッ
MWA!

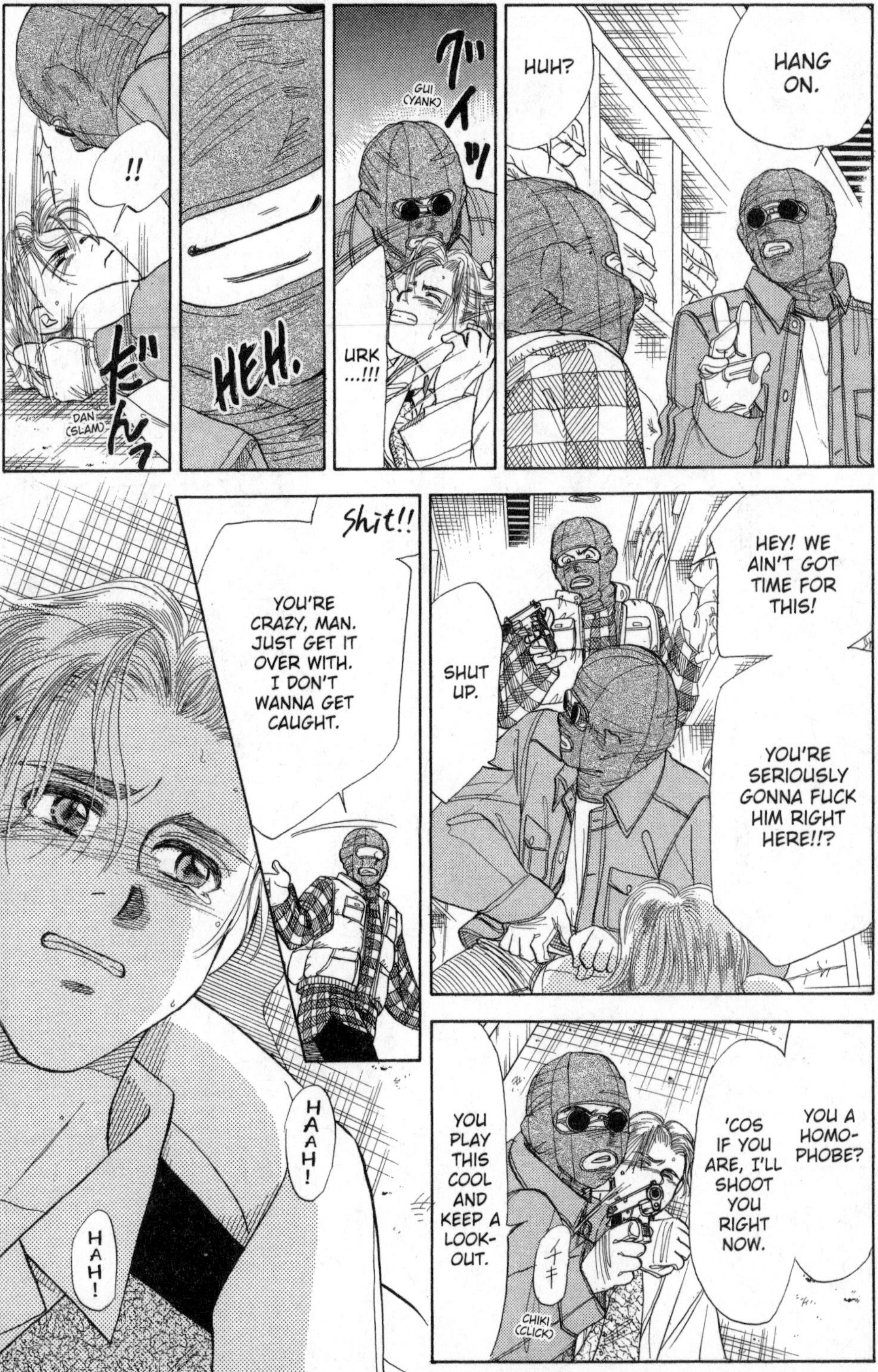
HANG ON.
HUH?
グイッ
GUI (YANK)
URK ...!!!
HEH.
!!
だんっ
DAN (SLAM)
HEY! WE AIN'T GOT TIME FOR THIS!
YOU'RE SERIOUSLY GONNA FUCK HIM RIGHT HERE!!?
SHUT UP.
YOU A HOMO-PHOBE?
'COS IF YOU ARE, I'LL SHOOT YOU RIGHT NOW.
YOU PLAY THIS COOL AND KEEP A LOOK-OUT.
チキ
CHIKI (CLICK)
Shit!!
YOU'RE CRAZY, MAN. JUST GET IT OVER WITH. I DON'T WANNA GET CAUGHT.
HAAAH!
HAH!

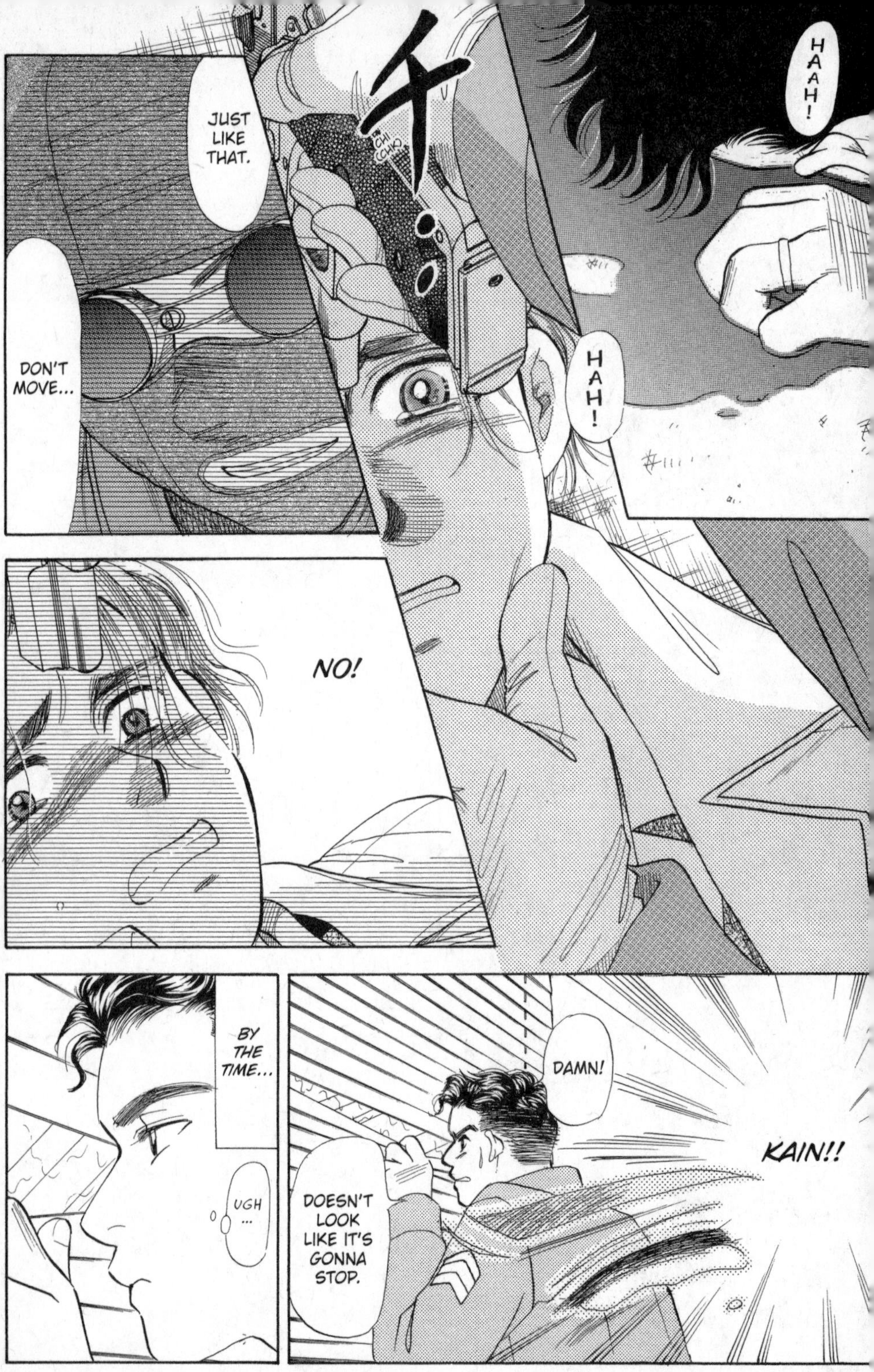
HAAH!
CHI CHK
HAH!
JUST LIKE THAT.
DON'T MOVE...
NO!
KAIN!!
DAMN!
DOESN'T LOOK LIKE IT'S GONNA STOP.
BY THE TIME...
UGH ...

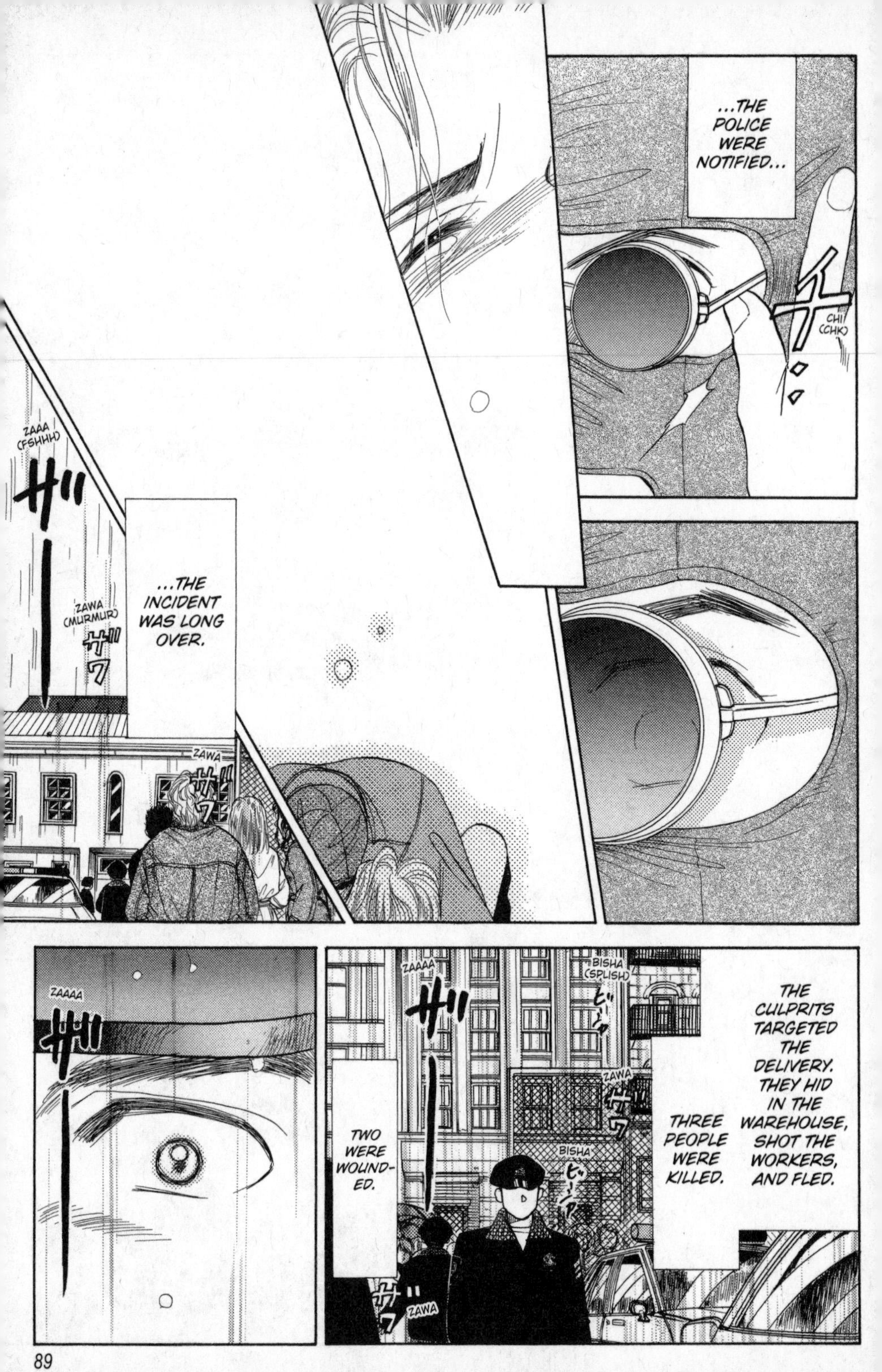
...THE POLICE WERE NOTIFIED...
CHI (CHK)
ZAAA (FSHHH)
ZAWA (MURMUR)
...THE INCIDENT WAS LONG OVER.
ZAWA
THE CULPRITS TARGETED THE DELIVERY. THEY HID IN THE WAREHOUSE, SHOT THE WORKERS, AND FLED.
THREE PEOPLE WERE KILLED.
BISHA (SPLISH)
ZAWA
BISHA
ZAAAA
TWO WERE WOUND-ED.
ZAWA
ZAAAA

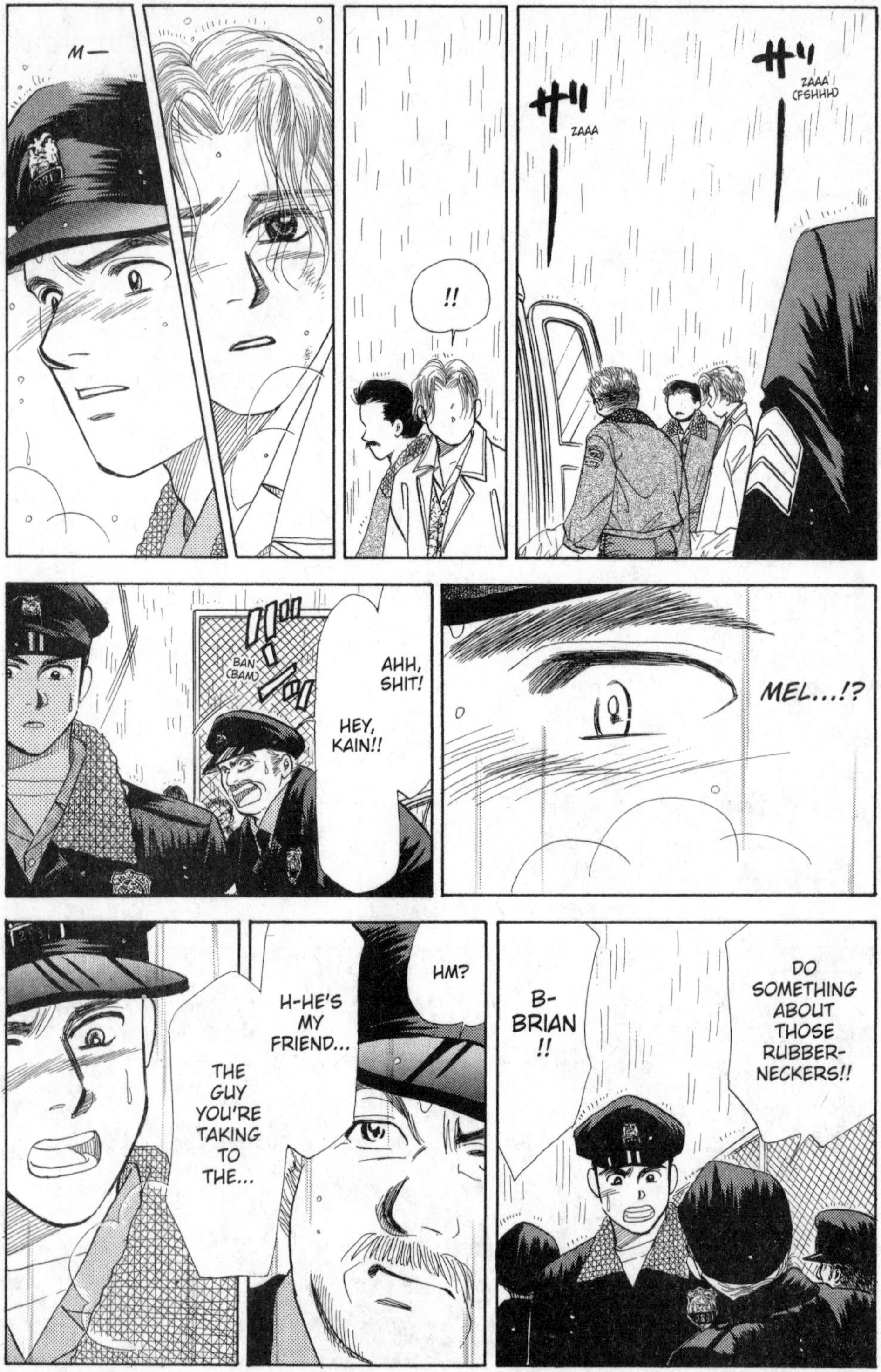
ザー
ZAAA (FSHHH)
ザー
ZAAA
!!
M—
MEL...!?
AHH, SHIT!
HEY, KAIN!!
BAN (BAM)
DO SOMETHING ABOUT THOSE RUBBER-NECKERS!!
B-BRIAN!!
HM?
H-HE'S MY FRIEND...
THE GUY YOU'RE TAKING TO THE...

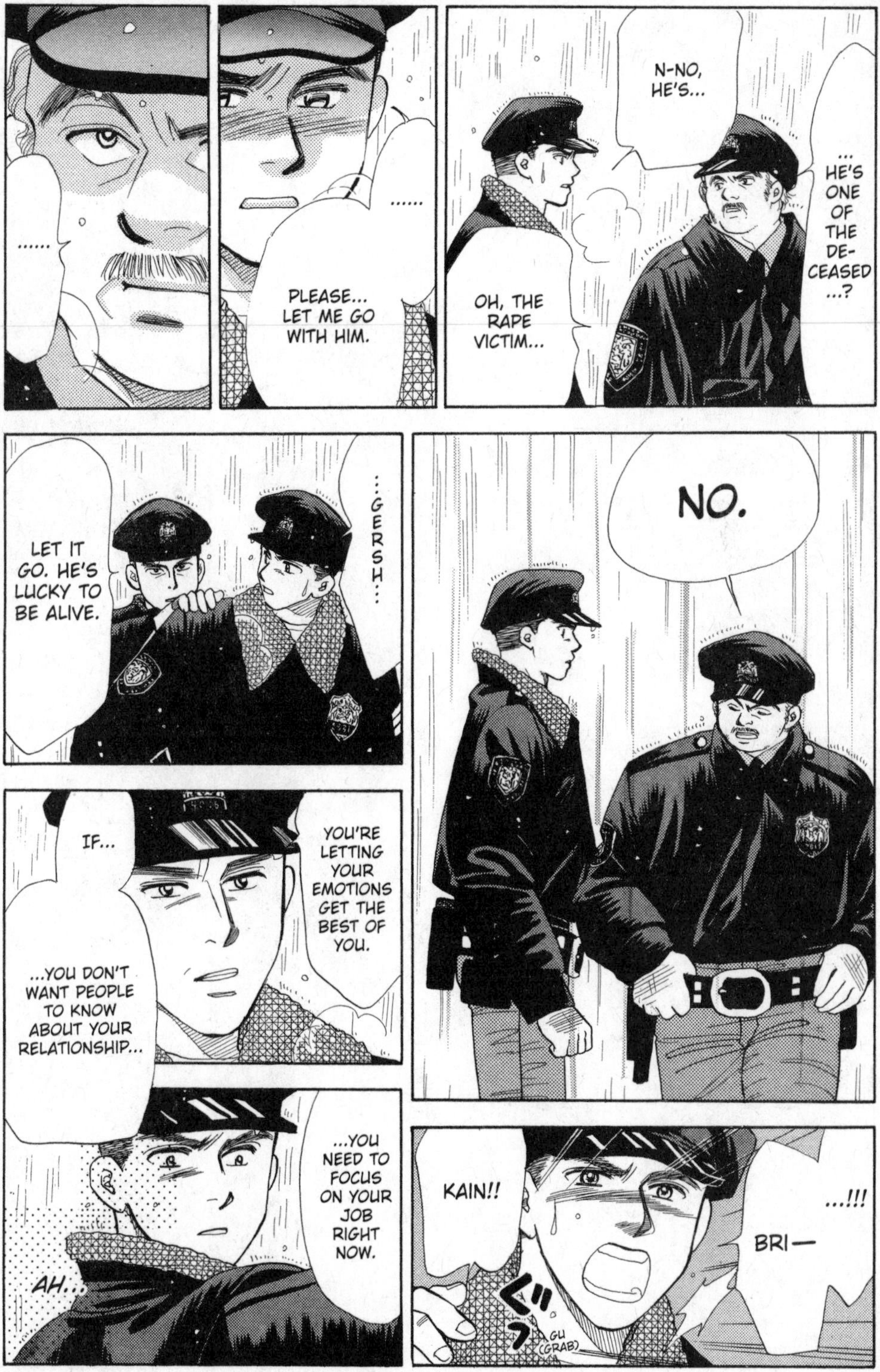
...HE'S ONE OF THE DE-CEASED...?
N-NO, HE'S...
OH, THE RAPE VICTIM...
......
PLEASE... LET ME GO WITH HIM.
......
NO.
...!!!
BRI—
KAIN!!
GU (GRAB)
...GERSH...
LET IT GO. HE'S LUCKY TO BE ALIVE.
YOU'RE LETTING YOUR EMOTIONS GET THE BEST OF YOU.
IF...
...YOU DON'T WANT PEOPLE TO KNOW ABOUT YOUR RELATIONSHIP...
...YOU NEED TO FOCUS ON YOUR JOB RIGHT NOW.
AH...

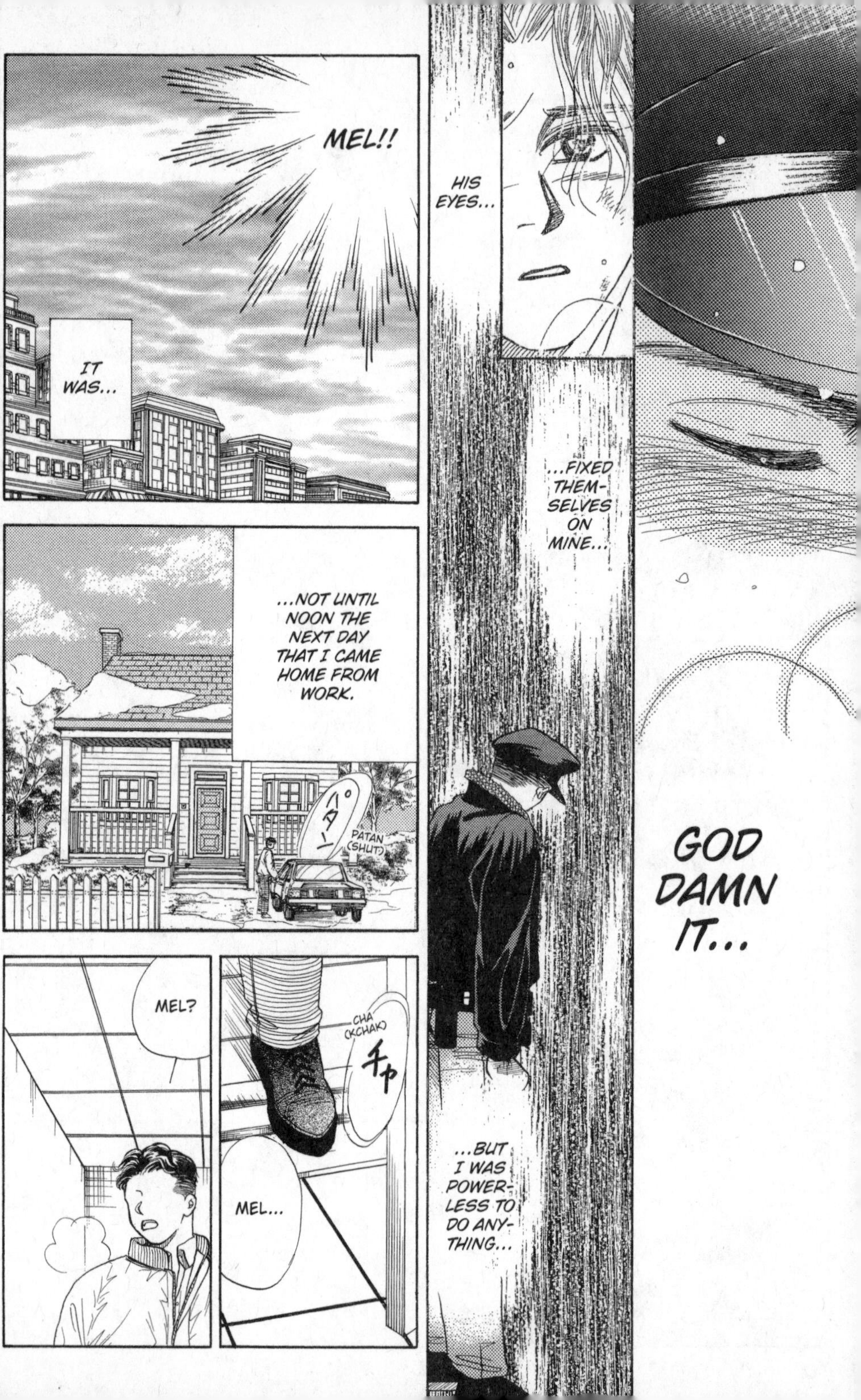
GOD DAMN IT...
HIS EYES...
...FIXED THEM-SELVES ON MINE...
...BUT I WAS POWER-LESS TO DO ANY-THING...
MEL!!
IT WAS...
...NOT UNTIL NOON THE NEXT DAY THAT I CAME HOME FROM WORK.
パタン
PATAN (SHUT)
CHA (KCHAK)
チャ
MEL...
MEL?

キ‼
GISH
(THMP)

......

キイ‥
KII
(CREAK)

MEL...

I...I'M
SORRY.

I...
WANTED
TO BE
WITH
YOU...

THE
HOSPITAL...
AND THE
POLICE
ASKED
WHERE I
LIVE...

HM?

OUR
AD-
DRESS
...

KAIN...

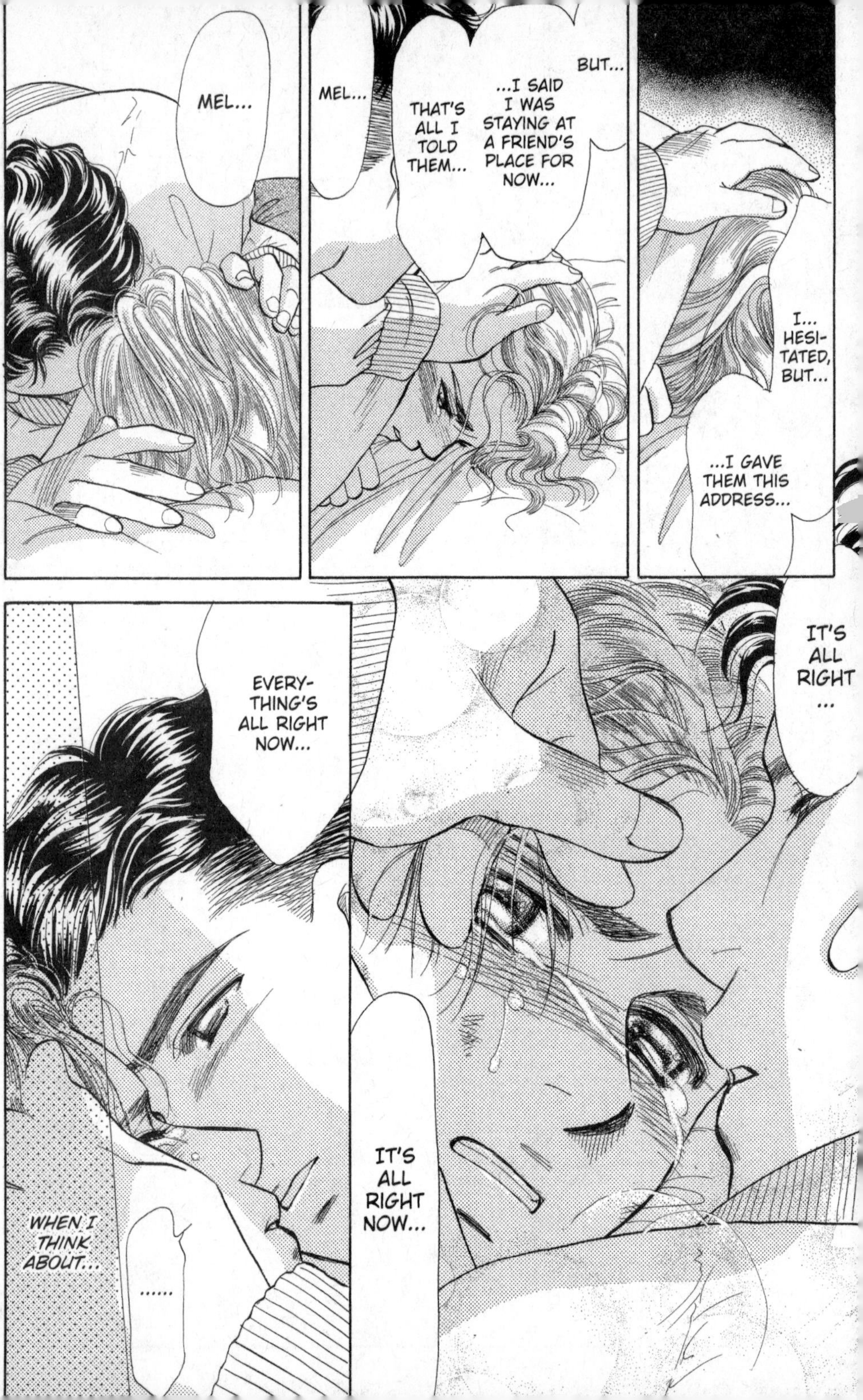

I... HESI-TATED, BUT...
...I GAVE THEM THIS ADDRESS...
BUT...
...I SAID I WAS STAYING AT A FRIEND'S PLACE FOR NOW...
THAT'S ALL I TOLD THEM...
MEL...
MEL...
IT'S ALL RIGHT ...
IT'S ALL RIGHT NOW...
EVERY-THING'S ALL RIGHT NOW...
WHEN I THINK ABOUT...
......

...A COLD-HEARTED GUY, AREN'T I...

I'M...

....MY HEART STARTS TO HURT.

HEY, DANNY...

...HOW MEL WAS THINKING ABOUT ME... EVEN IN A SITUATION LIKE THAT...

YES?

AND THERE'S ANOTHER PROBLEM.

DUNNO.

DID SOMETHING HAPPEN WHILE I WAS OUT?

BRIAN'S LOOKING KIND OF BLUE.

....

パタン (SHUT)

...SO...

I...I'M SORRY...

THE HOSPITAL'S RUNNING TESTS ON THAT GUY'S SEMEN...

MEL?

MEL DOESN'T WANT TO HAVE SEX.

......

I'M SORRY ...

......

DO YOU WANT ME TO...USE MY HAND...?

HE'S WORRIED ABOUT AIDS.

NO, IT'S FINE.

I CAN DEAL WITH THIS ON MY OWN.

I...I WAS SCARED...

HM?

KAIN...

SO SCARED ...

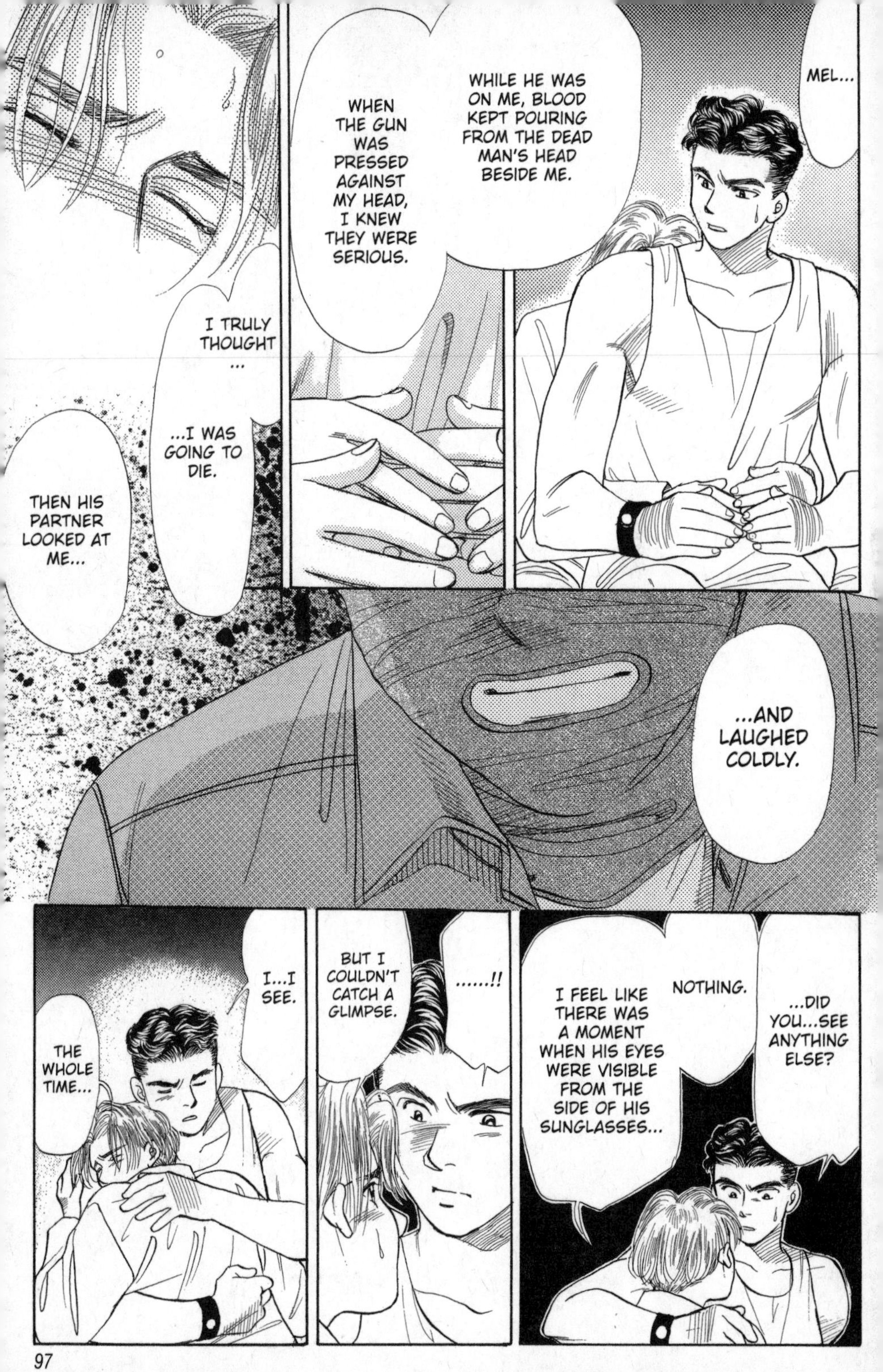
MEL...
WHILE HE WAS ON ME, BLOOD KEPT POURING FROM THE DEAD MAN'S HEAD BESIDE ME.
WHEN THE GUN WAS PRESSED AGAINST MY HEAD, I KNEW THEY WERE SERIOUS.
I TRULY THOUGHT ...
...I WAS GOING TO DIE.
THEN HIS PARTNER LOOKED AT ME...
...AND LAUGHED COLDLY.
...DID YOU...SEE ANYTHING ELSE?
NOTHING.
I FEEL LIKE THERE WAS A MOMENT WHEN HIS EYES WERE VISIBLE FROM THE SIDE OF HIS SUNGLASSES...
......!!
BUT I COULDN'T CATCH A GLIMPSE.
I...I SEE.
THE WHOLE TIME...

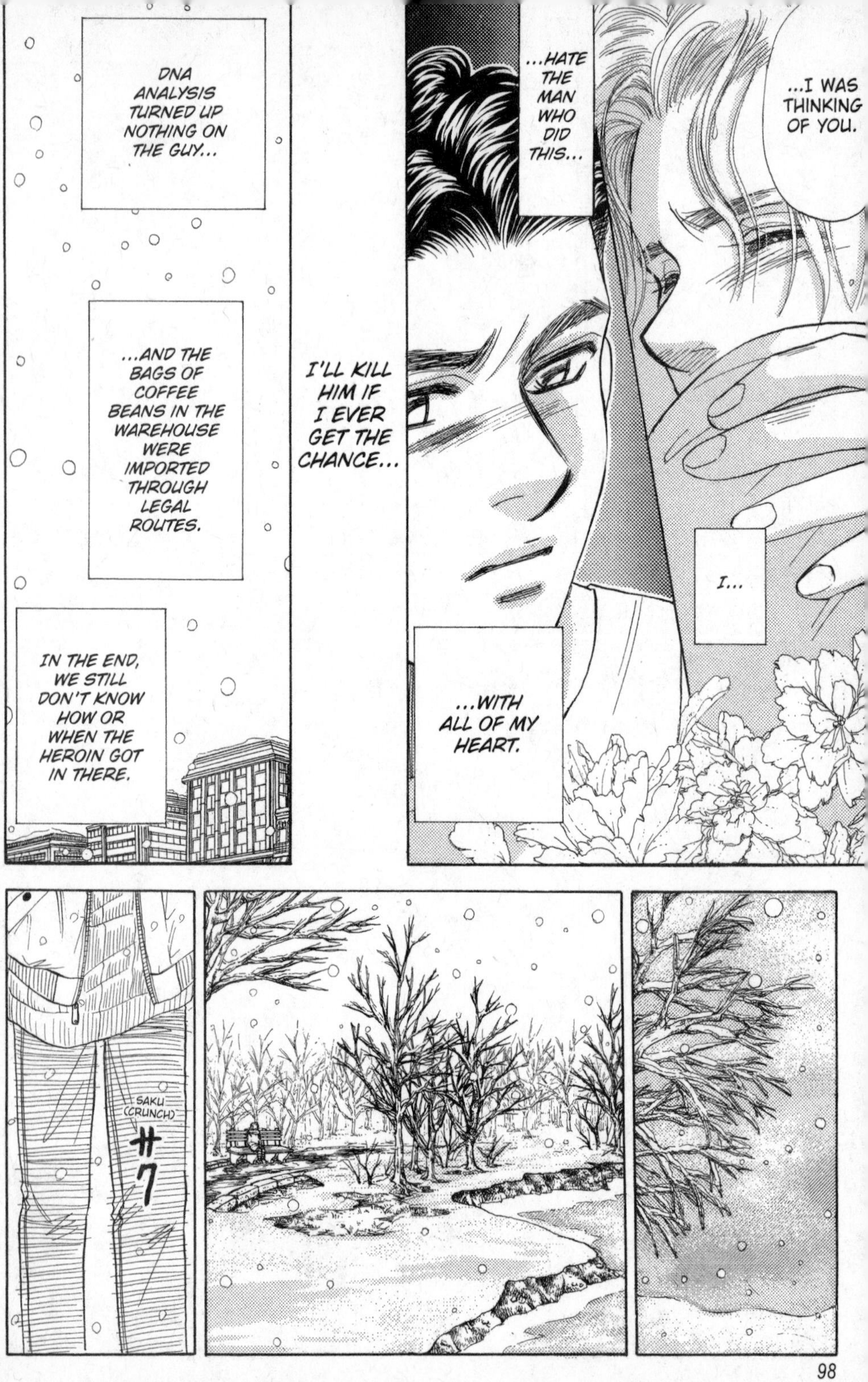
...I WAS THINKING OF YOU.
I...
...HATE THE MAN WHO DID THIS...
...WITH ALL OF MY HEART.
I'LL KILL HIM IF I EVER GET THE CHANCE...
DNA ANALYSIS TURNED UP NOTHING ON THE GUY...
...AND THE BAGS OF COFFEE BEANS IN THE WAREHOUSE WERE IMPORTED THROUGH LEGAL ROUTES.
IN THE END, WE STILL DON'T KNOW HOW OR WHEN THE HEROIN GOT IN THERE.
SAKU (CRUNCH)

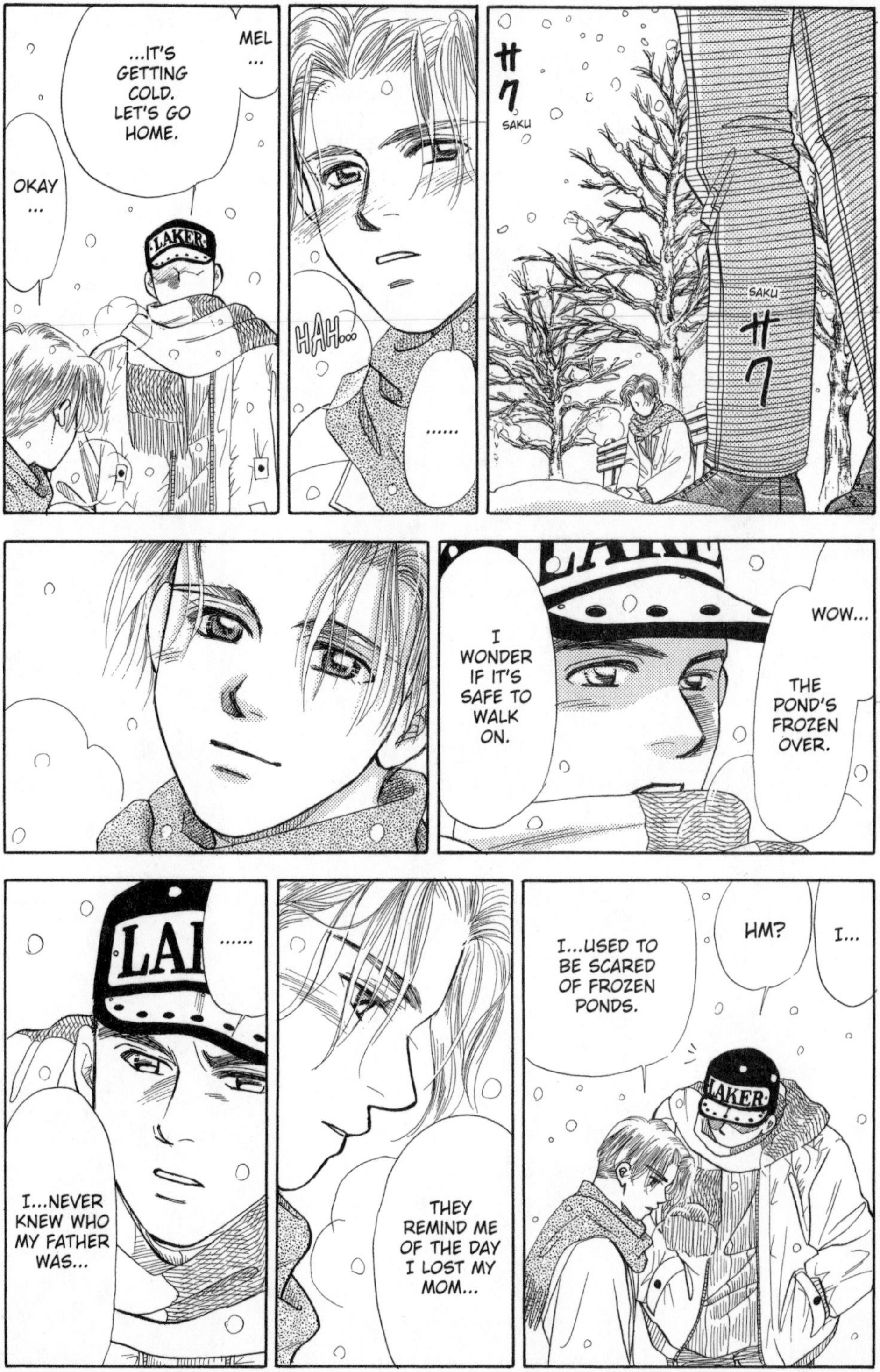
サク
SAKU
サク
SAKU
HAH...
......
MEL ...
...IT'S GETTING COLD. LET'S GO HOME.
OKAY ...
WOW...
THE POND'S FROZEN OVER.
I WONDER IF IT'S SAFE TO WALK ON.
I...
HM?
I...USED TO BE SCARED OF FROZEN PONDS.
THEY REMIND ME OF THE DAY I LOST MY MOM...
......
I...NEVER KNEW WHO MY FATHER WAS...

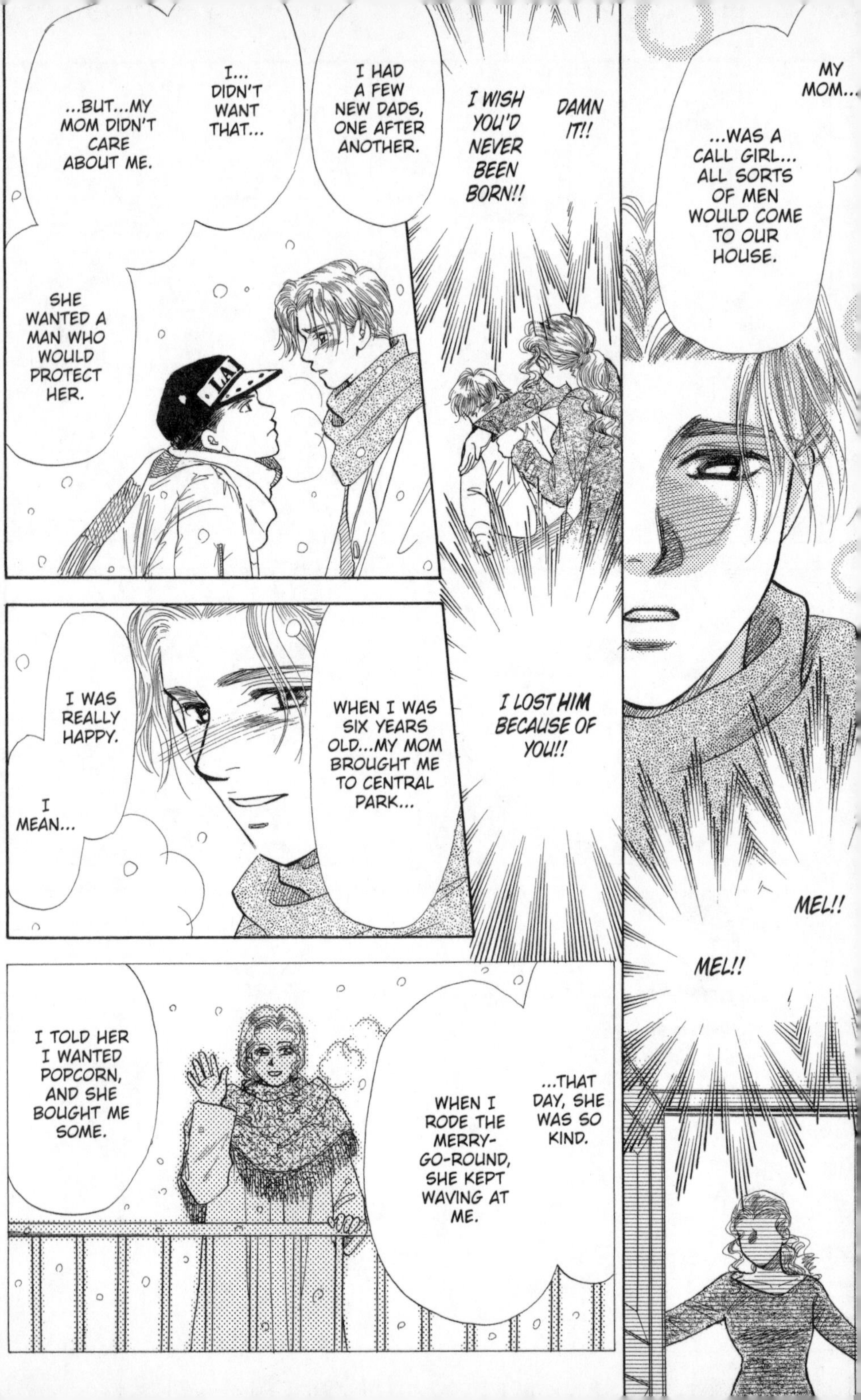
MY MOM...
...WAS A CALL GIRL... ALL SORTS OF MEN WOULD COME TO OUR HOUSE.
DAMN IT!!
I WISH YOU'D NEVER BEEN BORN!!
I LOST HIM BECAUSE OF YOU!!
MEL!!
MEL!!
I HAD A FEW NEW DADS, ONE AFTER ANOTHER.
I... DIDN'T WANT THAT...
...BUT...MY MOM DIDN'T CARE ABOUT ME.
SHE WANTED A MAN WHO WOULD PROTECT HER.
WHEN I WAS SIX YEARS OLD...MY MOM BROUGHT ME TO CENTRAL PARK...
I WAS REALLY HAPPY.
I MEAN...
...THAT DAY, SHE WAS SO KIND.
WHEN I RODE THE MERRY-GO-ROUND, SHE KEPT WAVING AT ME.
I TOLD HER I WANTED POPCORN, AND SHE BOUGHT ME SOME.

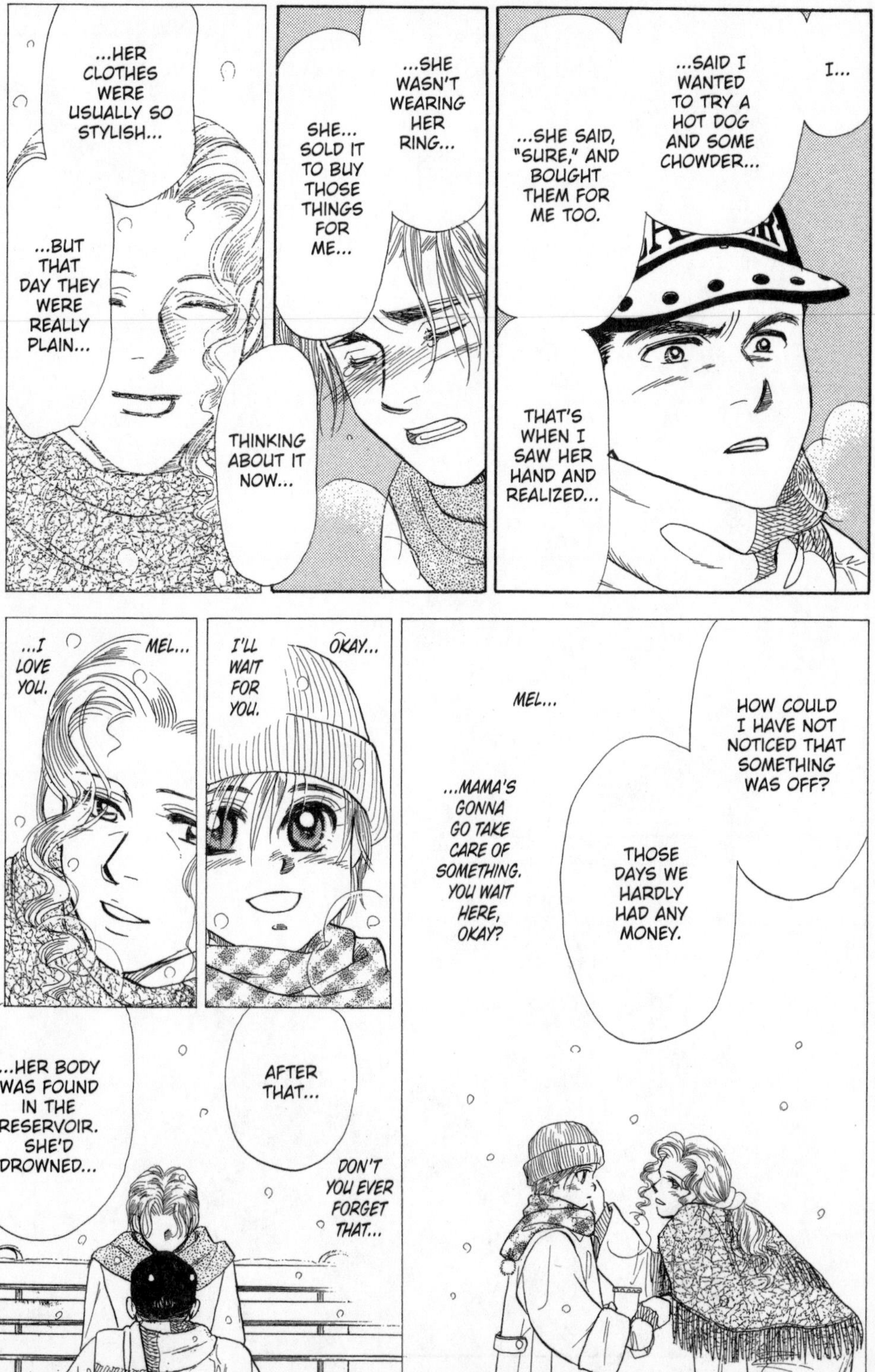
I...
...SAID I WANTED TO TRY A HOT DOG AND SOME CHOWDER...
...SHE SAID, "SURE," AND BOUGHT THEM FOR ME TOO.
THAT'S WHEN I SAW HER HAND AND REALIZED...
...SHE WASN'T WEARING HER RING...
SHE... SOLD IT TO BUY THOSE THINGS FOR ME...
THINKING ABOUT IT NOW...
...HER CLOTHES WERE USUALLY SO STYLISH...
...BUT THAT DAY THEY WERE REALLY PLAIN...
HOW COULD I HAVE NOT NOTICED THAT SOMETHING WAS OFF?
THOSE DAYS WE HARDLY HAD ANY MONEY.
MEL...
...MAMA'S GONNA GO TAKE CARE OF SOMETHING. YOU WAIT HERE, OKAY?
OKAY...
I'LL WAIT FOR YOU.
MEL...
...I LOVE YOU.
AFTER THAT...
...HER BODY WAS FOUND IN THE RESERVOIR. SHE'D DROWNED...
DON'T YOU EVER FORGET THAT...

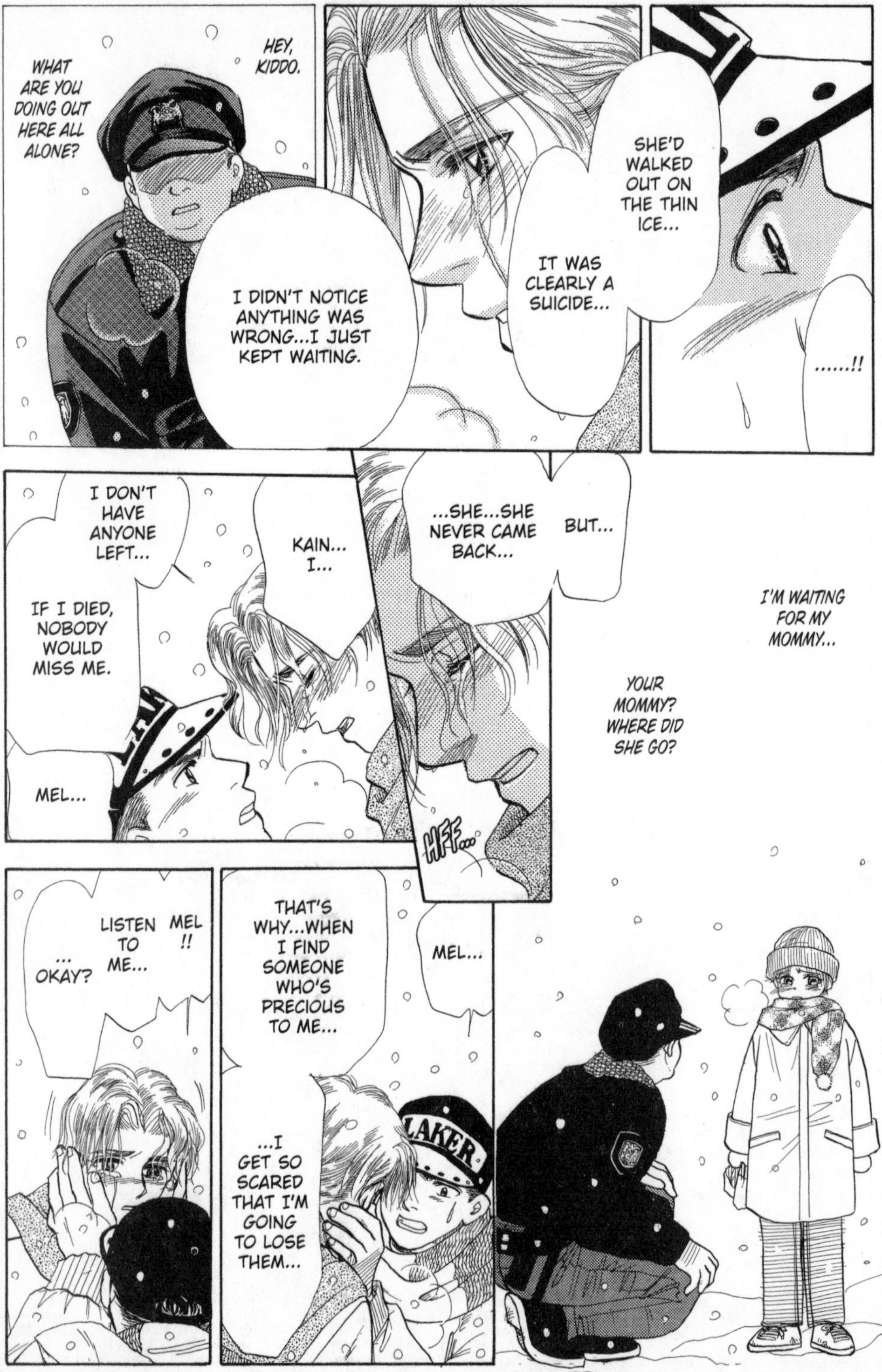
......!!
SHE'D WALKED OUT ON THE THIN ICE...
IT WAS CLEARLY A SUICIDE...
HEY, KIDDO.
WHAT ARE YOU DOING OUT HERE ALL ALONE?
I DIDN'T NOTICE ANYTHING WAS WRONG...I JUST KEPT WAITING.
I'M WAITING FOR MY MOMMY...
YOUR MOMMY? WHERE DID SHE GO?
BUT...
...SHE...SHE NEVER CAME BACK...
HFF...
KAIN... I...
I DON'T HAVE ANYONE LEFT...
IF I DIED, NOBODY WOULD MISS ME.
MEL...
MEL...
THAT'S WHY...WHEN I FIND SOMEONE WHO'S PRECIOUS TO ME...
...I GET SO SCARED THAT I'M GOING TO LOSE THEM...
LAKER
MEL !!
LISTEN TO ME...
... OKAY?

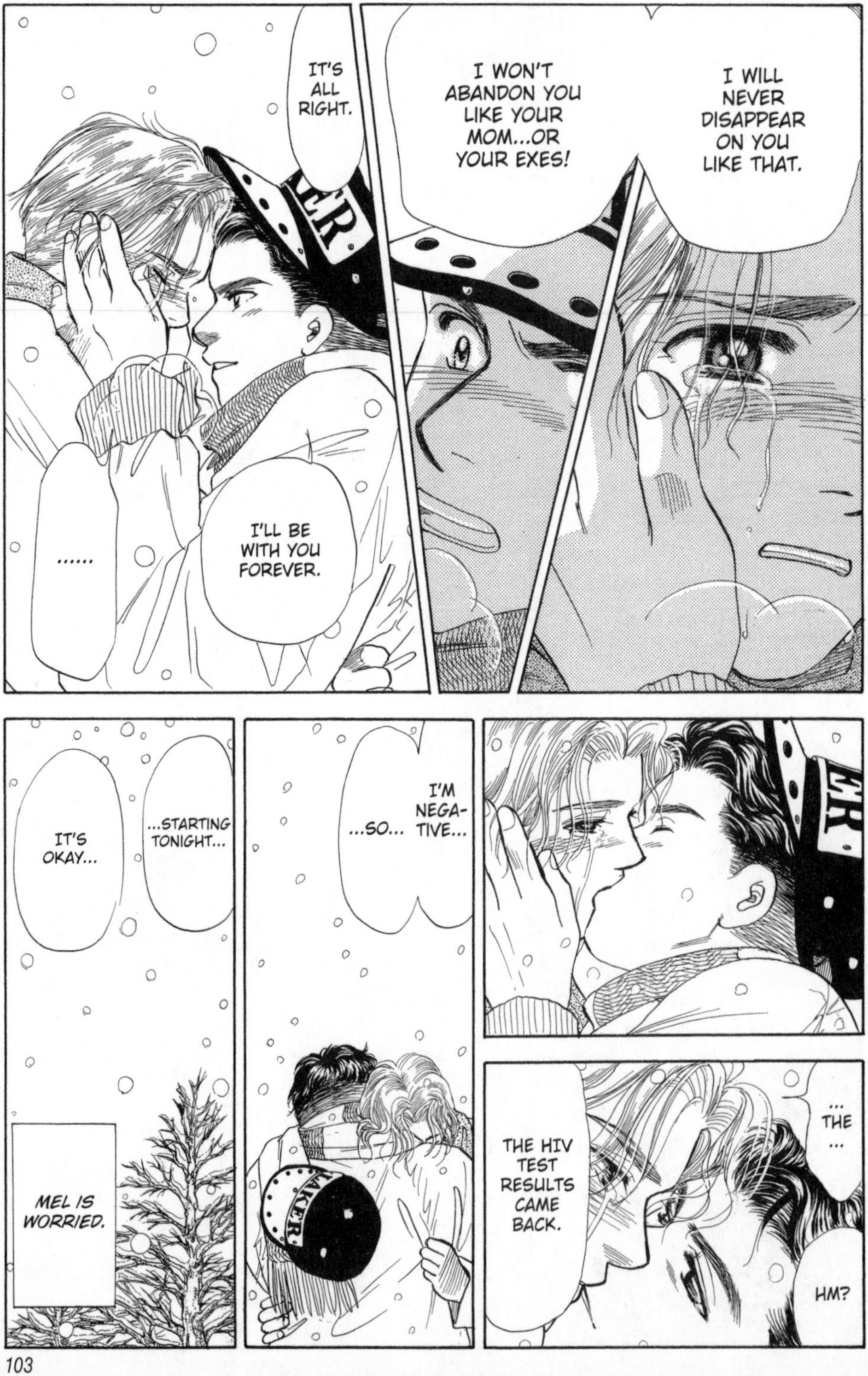
I WILL NEVER DISAPPEAR ON YOU LIKE THAT.
I WON'T ABANDON YOU LIKE YOUR MOM...OR YOUR EXES!
IT'S ALL RIGHT.
I'LL BE WITH YOU FOREVER.
......
... THE ...
HM?
THE HIV TEST RESULTS CAME BACK.
I'M NEGA-TIVE...
...SO...
...STARTING TONIGHT...
IT'S OKAY...
MEL IS WORRIED.

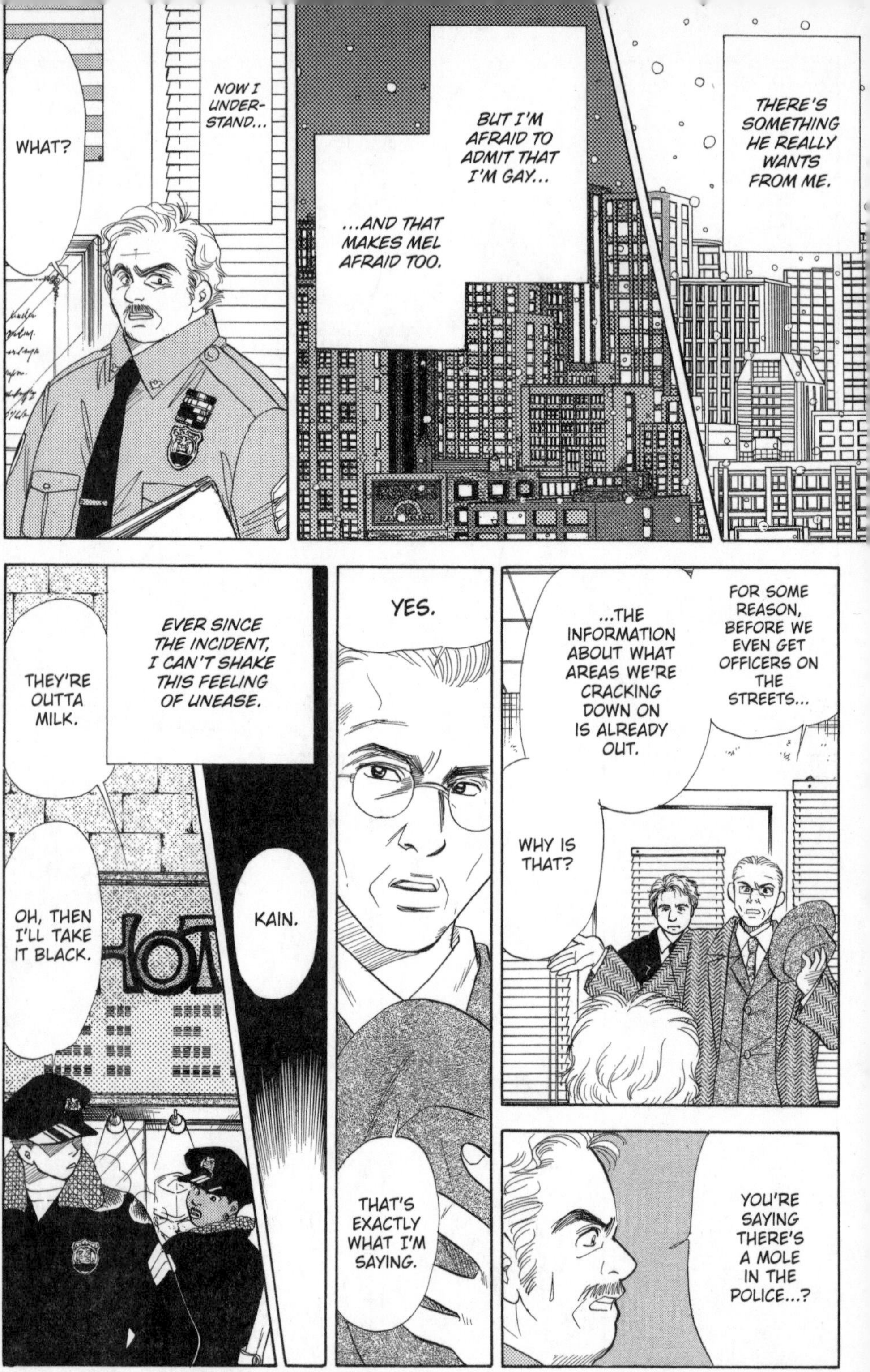
THERE'S SOMETHING HE REALLY WANTS FROM ME.
BUT I'M AFRAID TO ADMIT THAT I'M GAY...
...AND THAT MAKES MEL AFRAID TOO.
NOW I UNDER-STAND...
WHAT?
FOR SOME REASON, BEFORE WE EVEN GET OFFICERS ON THE STREETS...
...THE INFORMATION ABOUT WHAT AREAS WE'RE CRACKING DOWN ON IS ALREADY OUT.
WHY IS THAT?
YOU'RE SAYING THERE'S A MOLE IN THE POLICE...?
YES.
THAT'S EXACTLY WHAT I'M SAYING.
EVER SINCE THE INCIDENT, I CAN'T SHAKE THIS FEELING OF UNEASE.
THEY'RE OUTTA MILK.
KAIN.
OH, THEN I'LL TAKE IT BLACK.

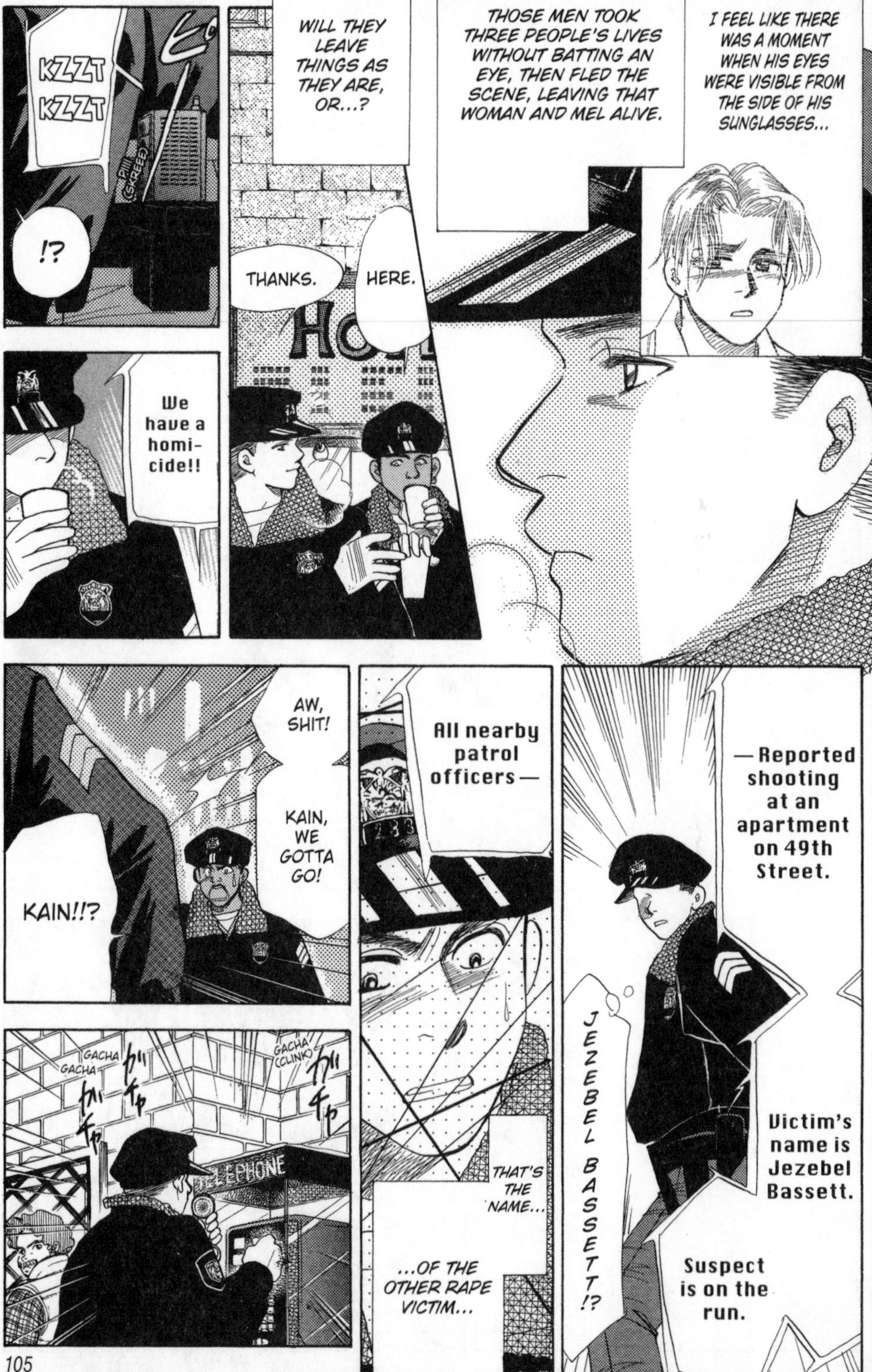
I FEEL LIKE THERE WAS A MOMENT WHEN HIS EYES WERE VISIBLE FROM THE SIDE OF HIS SUNGLASSES...
THOSE MEN TOOK THREE PEOPLE'S LIVES WITHOUT BATTING AN EYE, THEN FLED THE SCENE, LEAVING THAT WOMAN AND MEL ALIVE.
WILL THEY LEAVE THINGS AS THEY ARE, OR...?
HERE.
THANKS.
KZZZT KZZZT
P!!!! (SKREEE)
!?
We have a homicide!!
All nearby patrol officers—
—Reported shooting at an apartment on 49th Street.
Victim's name is Jezebel Bassett.
Suspect is on the run.
JEZEBEL BASSETT!?
THAT'S THE NAME...
...OF THE OTHER RAPE VICTIM...
AW, SHIT!
KAIN, WE GOTTA GO!
KAIN!!?
GACHA GACHA
GACHA (CLINK)
TELEPHONE

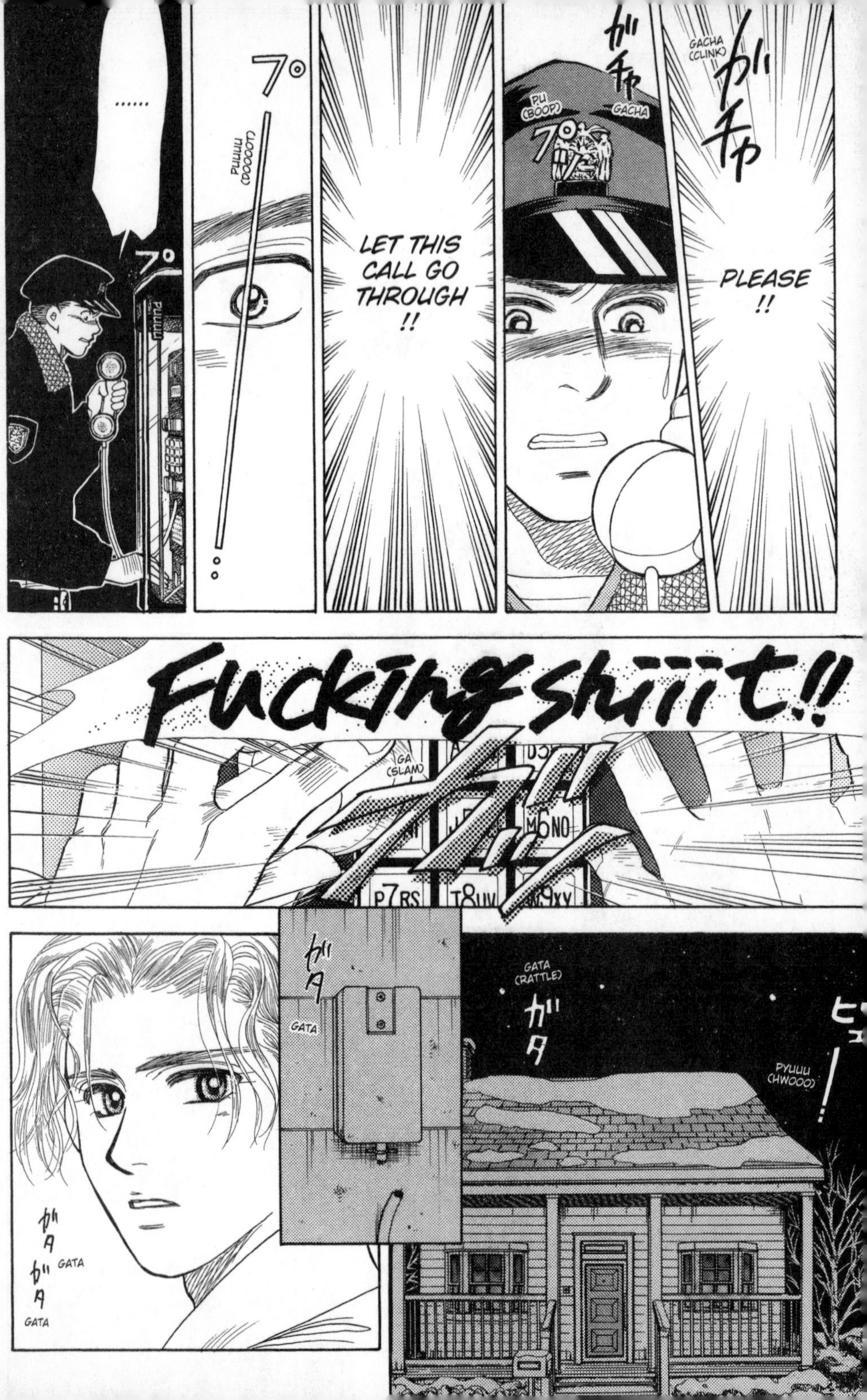

ガチャ
GACHA (CLINK)
PLEASE !!
ガチャ
PU (BOOP)
GACHA
LET THIS CALL GO THROUGH !!
プ
PUUUU (LOOOOO)
......
プ
PUUUU
Fucking shiiit!!
GA (SLAM)
ヒュ
PYUUU (HWOOO)
ガタ
GATA (RATTLE)
ガタ
GATA
ガタ
GATA
ガタ
GATA

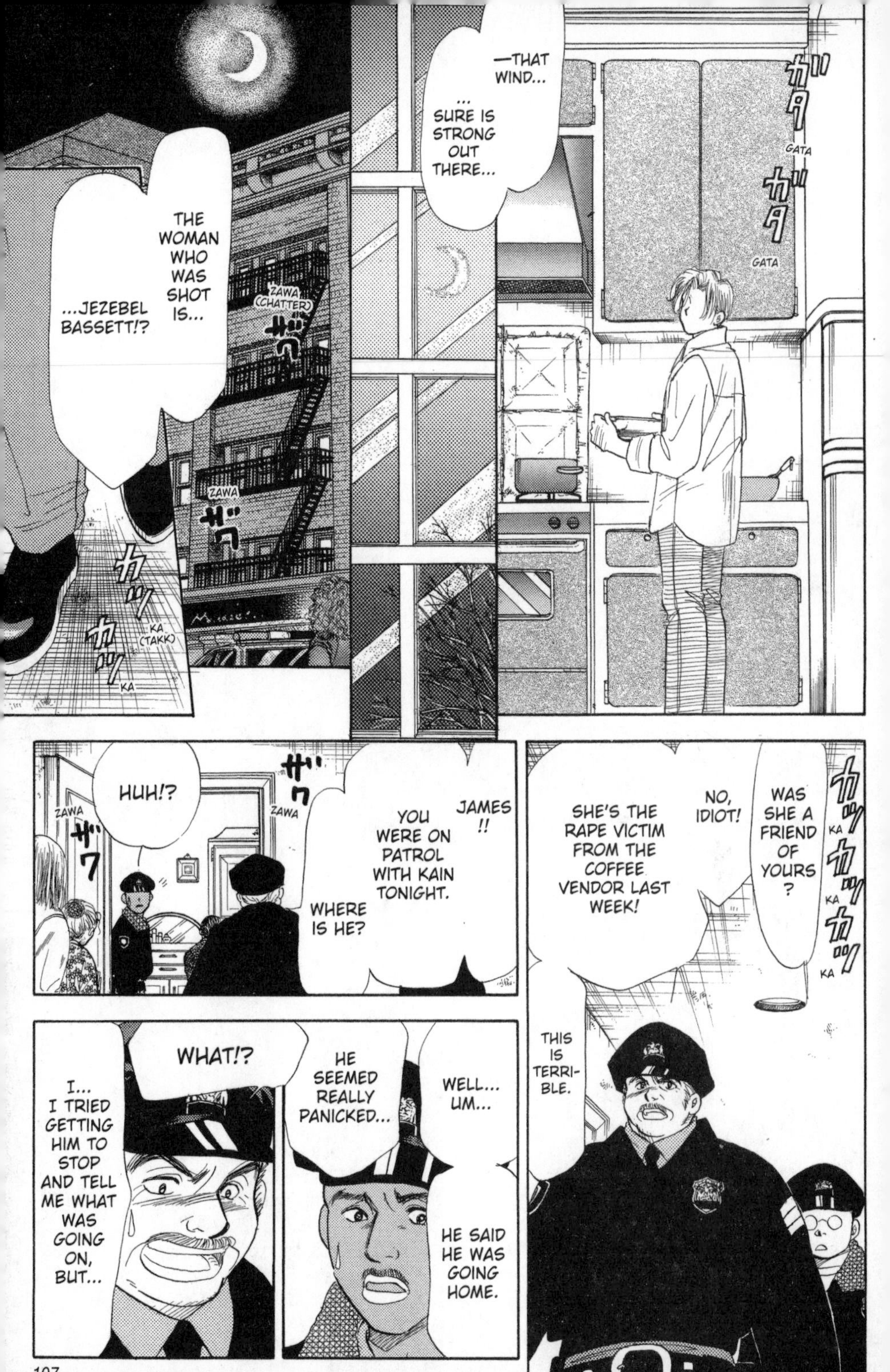
GATA
GATA
—THAT WIND...
...SURE IS STRONG OUT THERE...
THE WOMAN WHO WAS SHOT IS...
...JEZEBEL BASSETT!?
ZAWA (CHATTER)
ZAWA
KA (TAKK)
KA
WAS SHE A FRIEND OF YOURS?
NO, IDIOT!
SHE'S THE RAPE VICTIM FROM THE COFFEE VENDOR LAST WEEK!
KA
KA
KA
THIS IS TERRIBLE.
JAMES!!
YOU WERE ON PATROL WITH KAIN TONIGHT.
WHERE IS HE?
ZAWA
HUH!?
ZAWA
WELL... UM...
HE SEEMED REALLY PANICKED...
HE SAID HE WAS GOING HOME.
WHAT!?
I... I TRIED GETTING HIM TO STOP AND TELL ME WHAT WAS GOING ON, BUT...

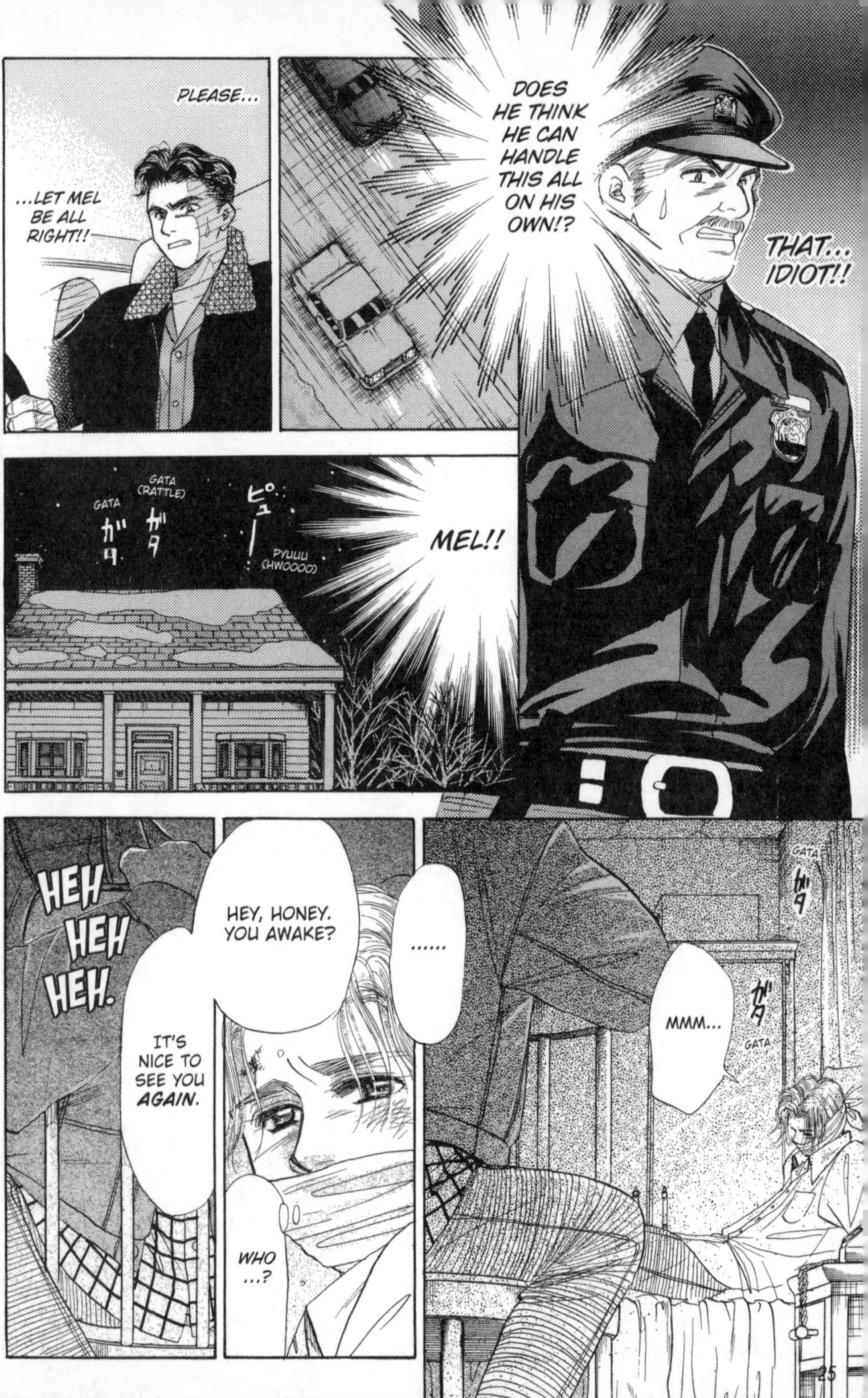
DOES HE THINK HE CAN HANDLE THIS ALL ON HIS OWN!?
THAT... IDIOT!!
PLEASE...
...LET MEL BE ALL RIGHT!!
MEL!!
ピュー
PYUUU (HWOOOO)
ガタ
GATA (RATTLE)
ガタ
GATA
GATA
ガタ
ガタ
GATA
MMM...
......
HEY, HONEY. YOU AWAKE?
IT'S NICE TO SEE YOU **AGAIN**.
WHO ...?
HEH HEH HEH.

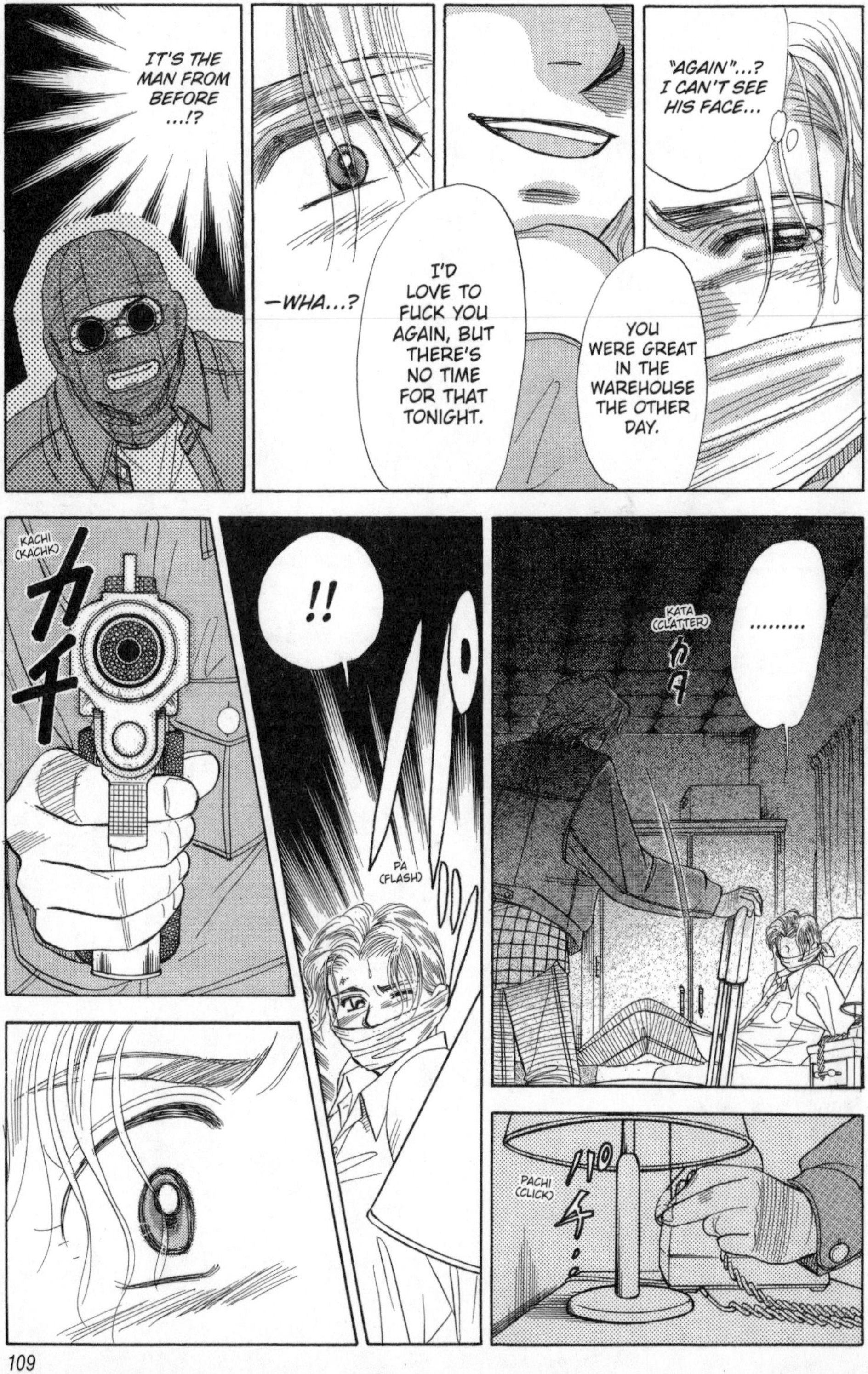
YOU WERE GREAT IN THE WAREHOUSE THE OTHER DAY.
I'D LOVE TO FUCK YOU AGAIN, BUT THERE'S NO TIME FOR THAT TONIGHT.
"AGAIN"...? I CAN'T SEE HIS FACE...
—WHA...?
IT'S THE MAN FROM BEFORE ...!?
KATA (CLATTER)
....
!!
PA (FLASH)
KACHI (KACHK)
PACHI (CLICK)

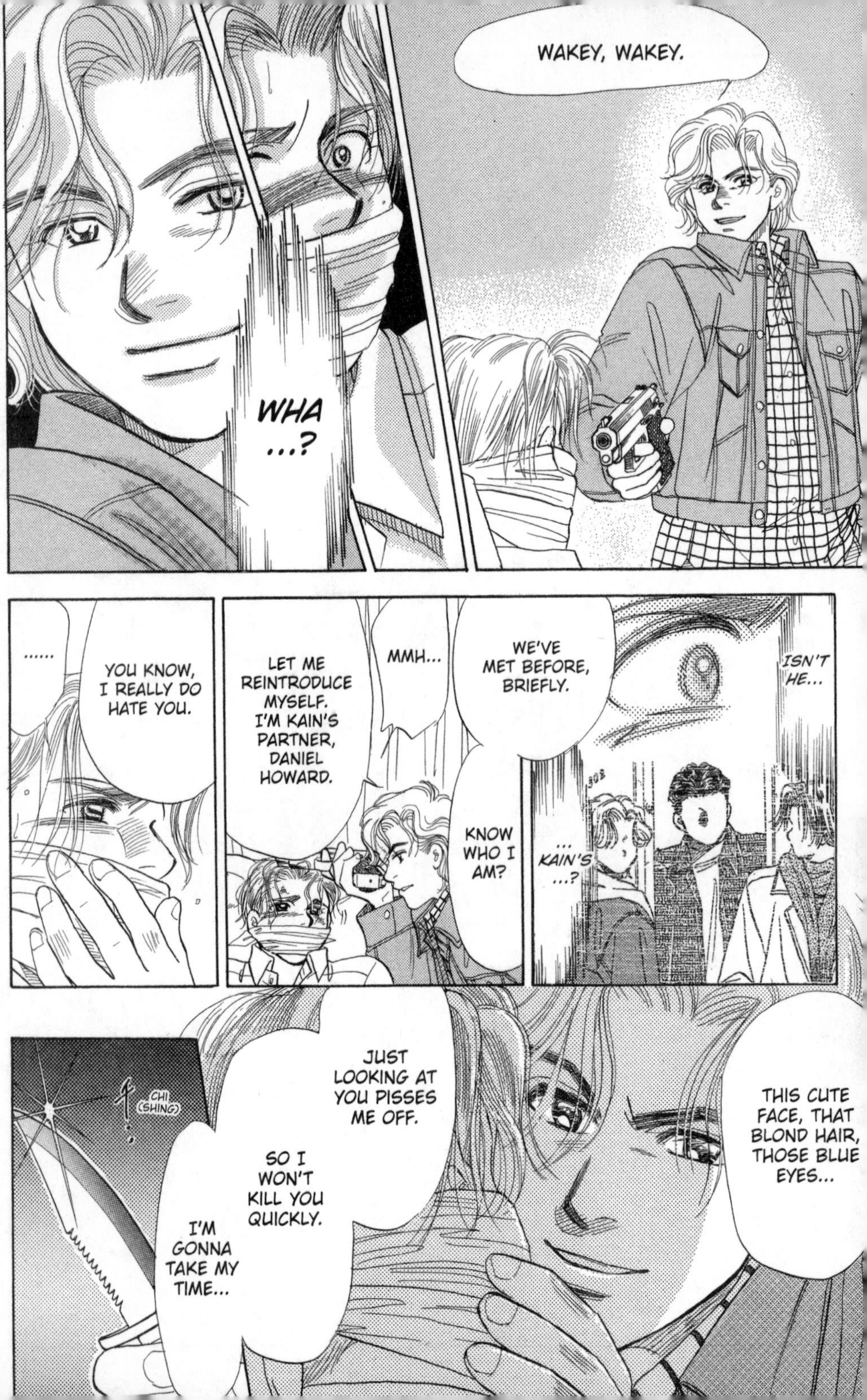
WAKEY, WAKEY.
WHA ...?
ISN'T HE...
... KAIN'S ...?
WE'VE MET BEFORE, BRIEFLY.
KNOW WHO I AM?
MMH...
LET ME REINTRODUCE MYSELF. I'M KAIN'S PARTNER, DANIEL HOWARD.
YOU KNOW, I REALLY DO HATE YOU.
......
THIS CUTE FACE, THAT BLOND HAIR, THOSE BLUE EYES...
JUST LOOKING AT YOU PISSES ME OFF.
SO I WON'T KILL YOU QUICKLY.
I'M GONNA TAKE MY TIME...
CHI (SHING)

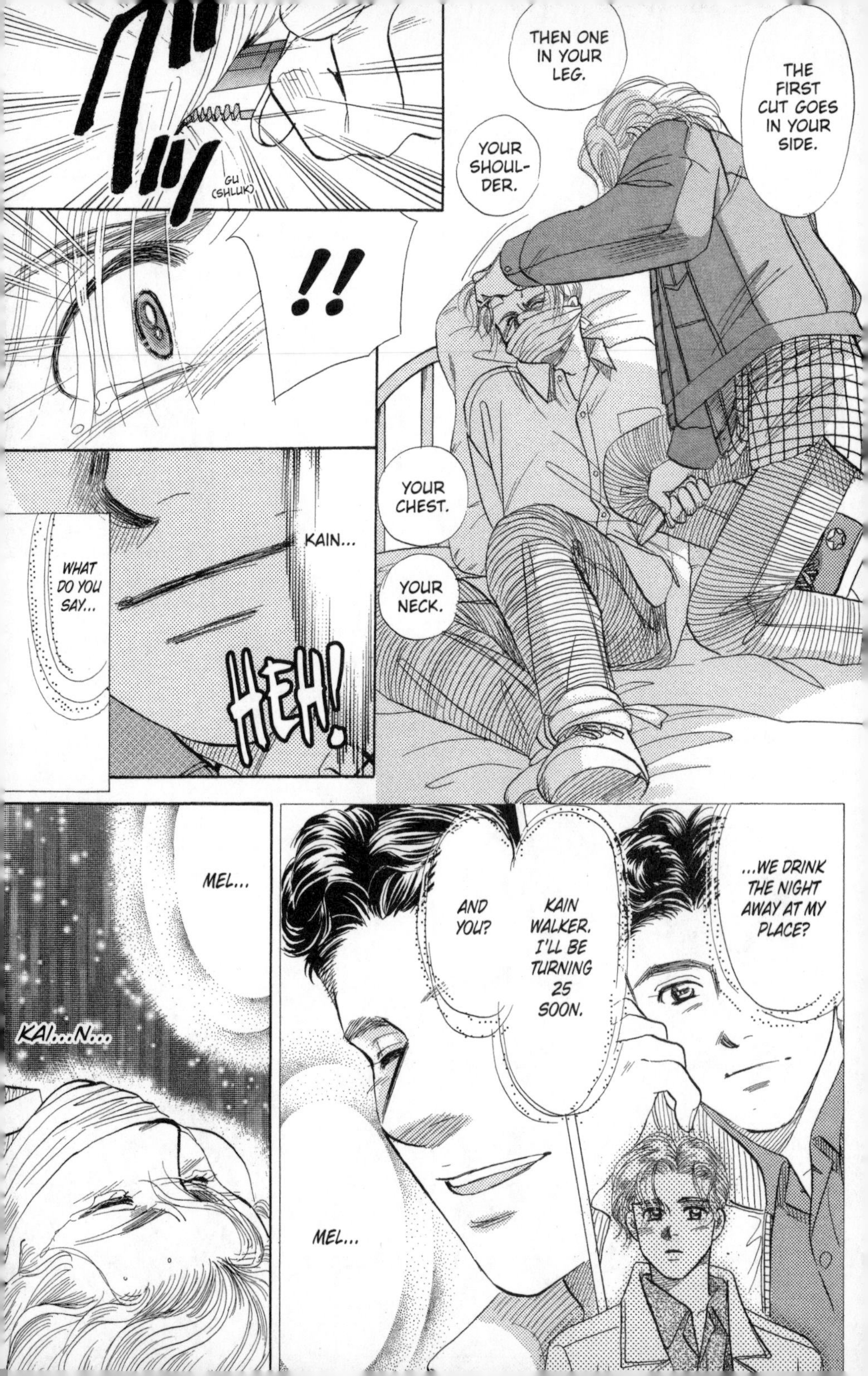
THE FIRST CUT GOES IN YOUR SIDE.
THEN ONE IN YOUR LEG.
YOUR SHOULDER.
YOUR CHEST.
YOUR NECK.
GU (SHLUK)
!!
KAIN...
HEH!
WHAT DO YOU SAY...
...WE DRINK THE NIGHT AWAY AT MY PLACE?
KAIN WALKER. I'LL BE TURNING 25 SOON.
AND YOU?
MEL...
MEL...
KAI...N...

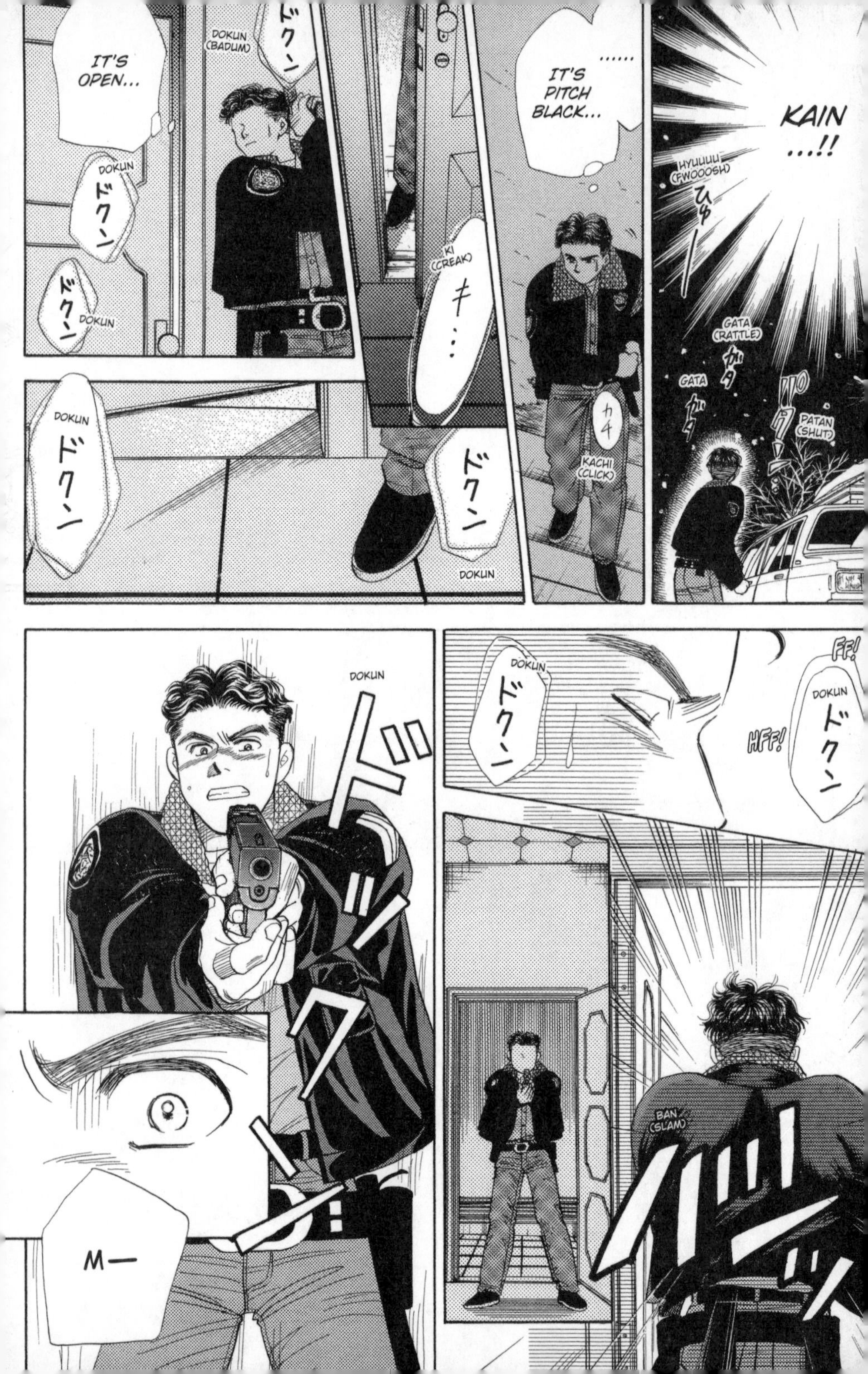
KAIN ...!!
HYUUUU (FWOOOSH)
ひゅー
GATA (RATTLE)
ガタ
GATA
ガタ
パタン
PATAN (SHUT)
......
IT'S PITCH BLACK...
カチ
KACHI (CLICK)
KI (CREAK)
キ・・・
ドクン
DOKUN
DOKUN (BADUM)
ドクン
IT'S OPEN...
DOKUN
ドクン
ドクン
DOKUN
DOKUN
ドクン
FF!
DOKUN
ドクン
HFF!
DOKUN
ドクン
BAN (SLAM)
DOKUN
ドクン
M—

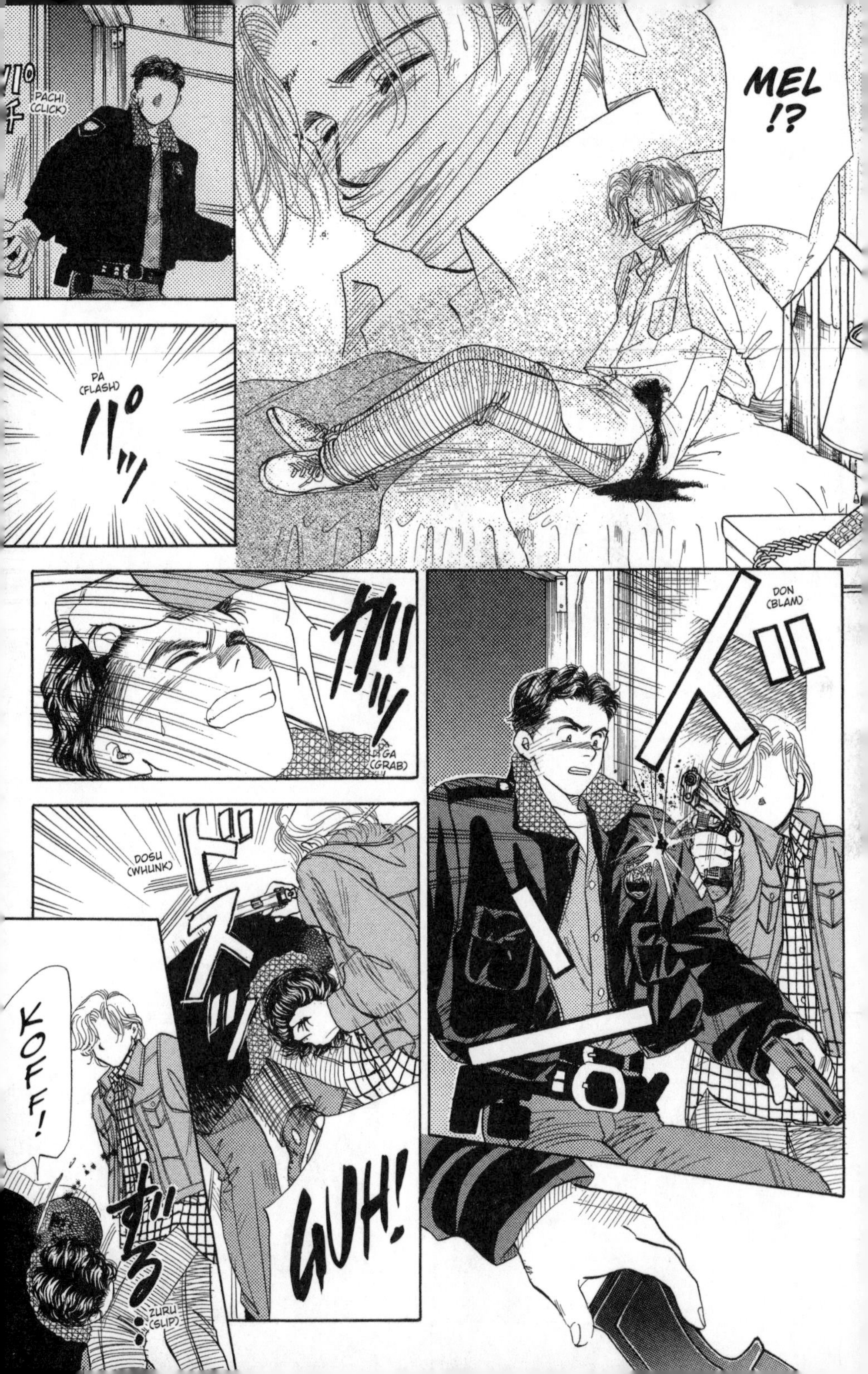
MEL !?
PACHI (CLICK)
PA (FLASH)
DON (BLAM)
GA (GRAB)
DOSU (WHUNK)
GUH!
KOFF!
ZURU (SLIP)

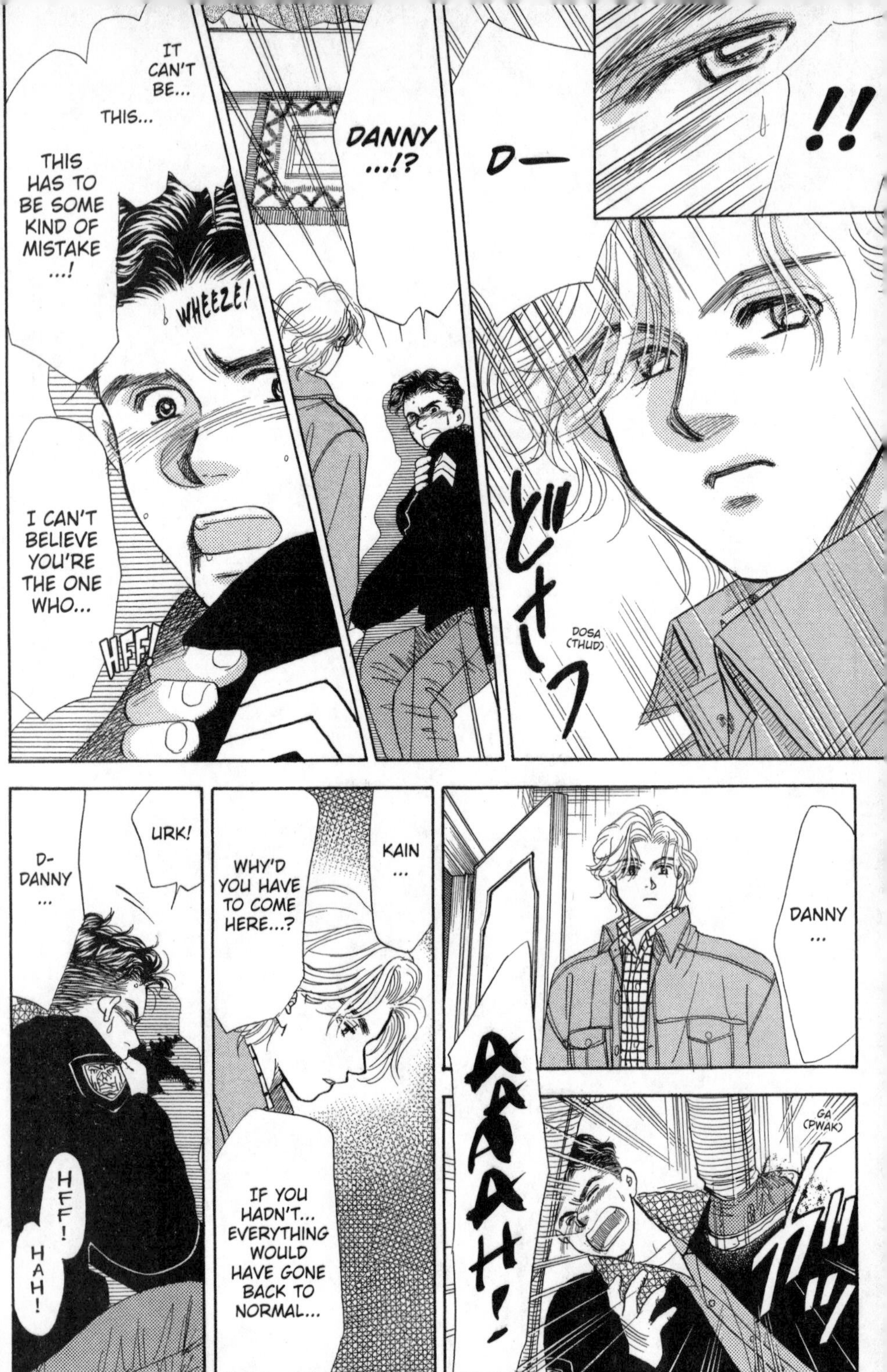

!!
D—
どさっ
DOSA (THUD)
DANNY ...!?
IT CAN'T BE...
THIS...
THIS HAS TO BE SOME KIND OF MISTAKE ...!
WHEEZE!
I CAN'T BELIEVE YOU'RE THE ONE WHO...
HFF!
DANNY ...
AAAAH!
ガッ
GA (PWAK)
KAIN ...
WHY'D YOU HAVE TO COME HERE...?
IF YOU HADN'T... EVERYTHING WOULD HAVE GONE BACK TO NORMAL...
URK!
D- DANNY ...
HFF! HAH!

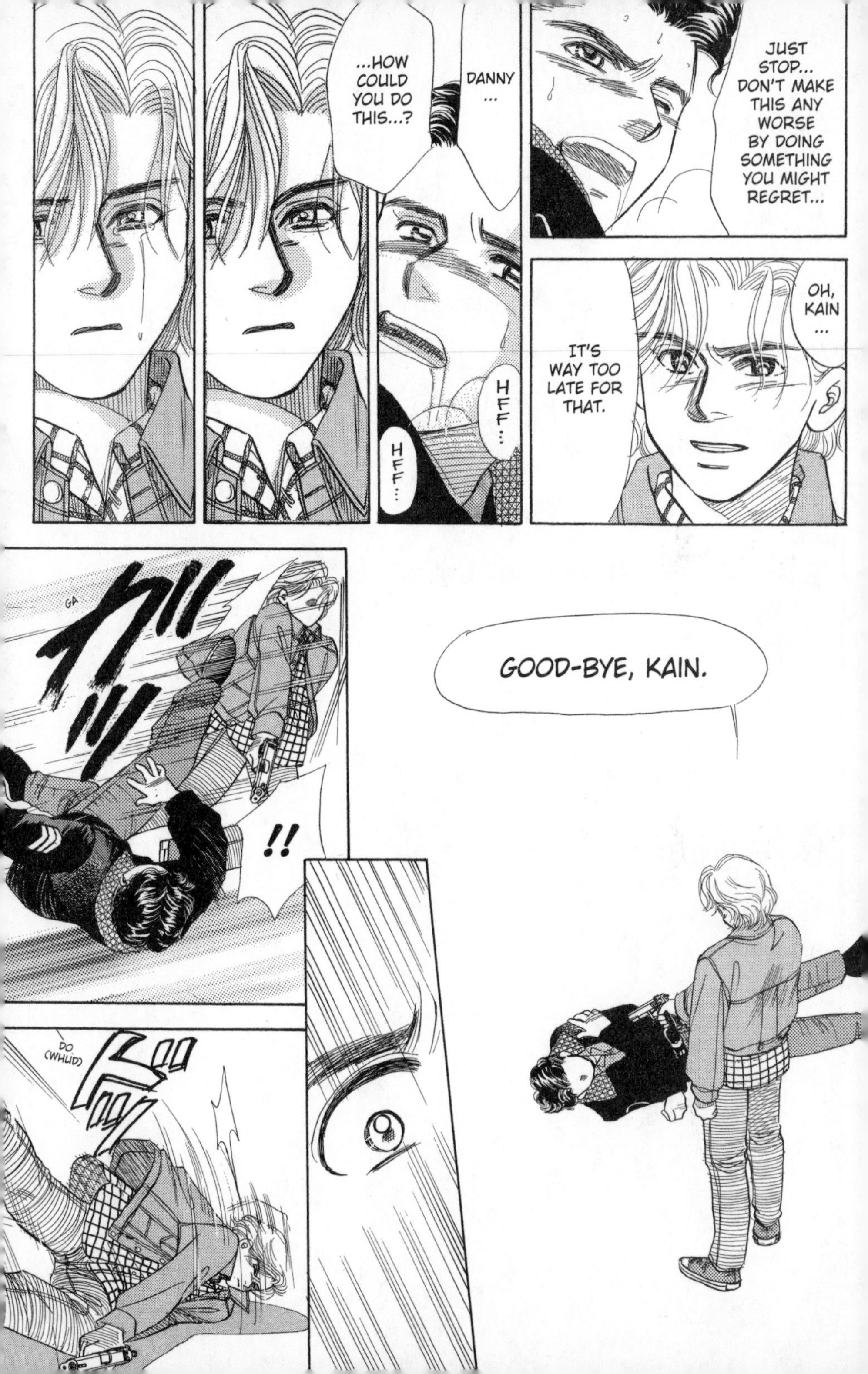
JUST STOP... DON'T MAKE THIS ANY WORSE BY DOING SOMETHING YOU MIGHT REGRET...
OH, KAIN...
IT'S WAY TOO LATE FOR THAT.
DANNY...
...HOW COULD YOU DO THIS...?
HFF...
HFF...
GOOD-BYE, KAIN.
GA
!!
DO (WHUD)

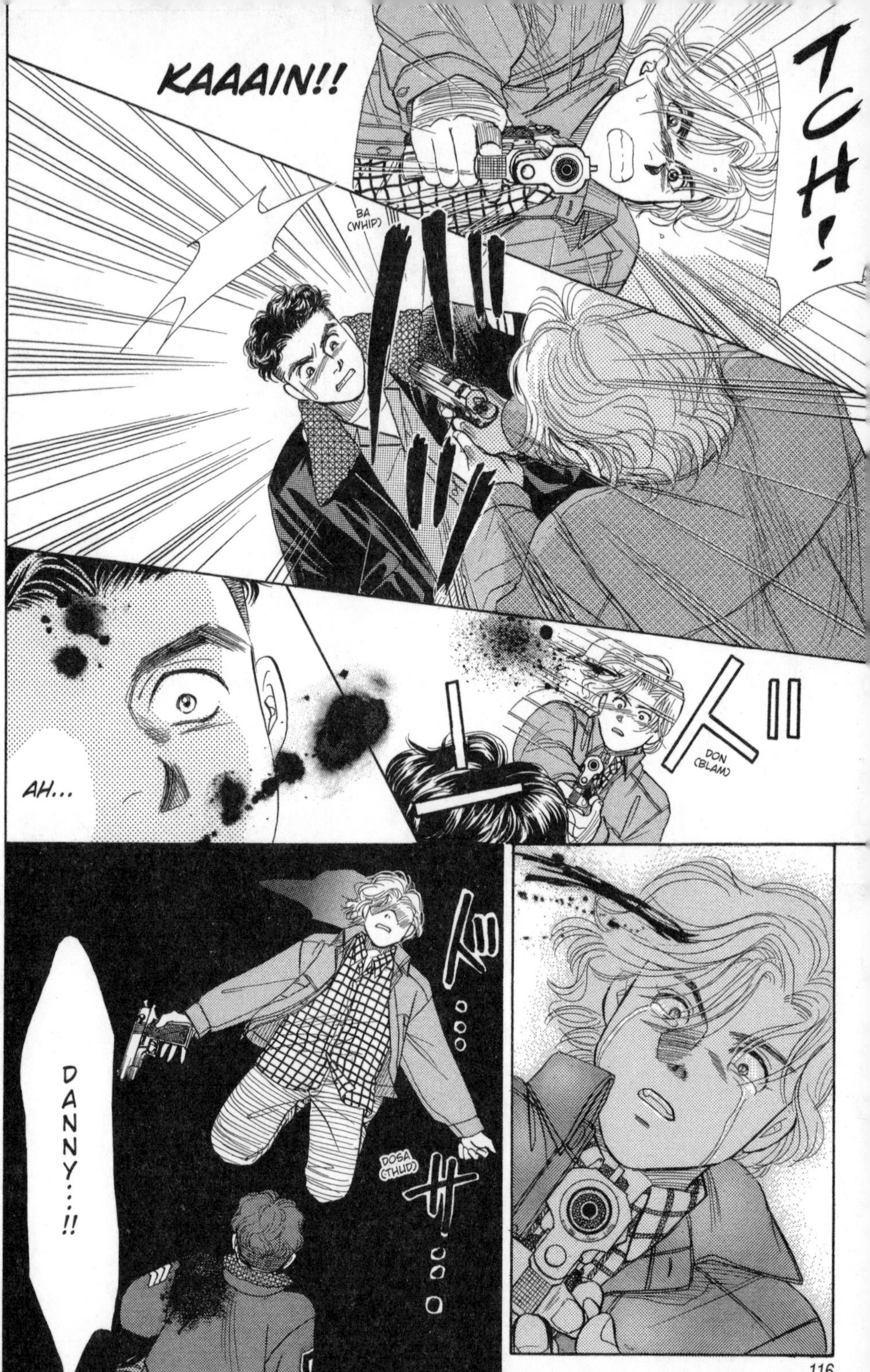
TCH!
KAAAIN!!
BA (WHIP)
DON (BLAM)
AH...
DANNY...!!
DOSA (THUD)

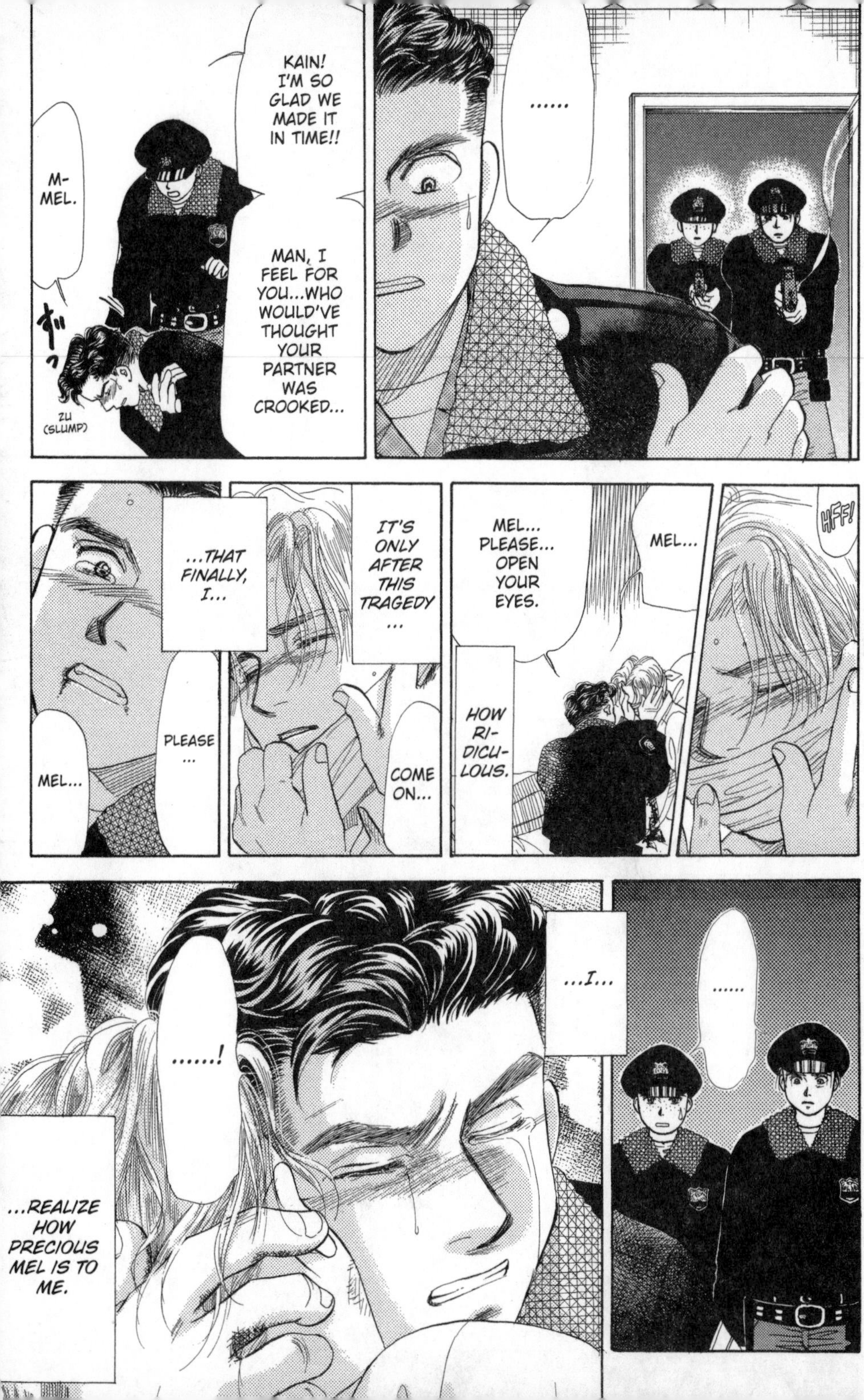
......
KAIN! I'M SO GLAD WE MADE IT IN TIME!!
MAN, I FEEL FOR YOU...WHO WOULD'VE THOUGHT YOUR PARTNER WAS CROOKED...
M-MEL.
ZU (SLUMP)
HFF!
MEL...
MEL... PLEASE... OPEN YOUR EYES.
HOW RI-DICU-LOUS.
IT'S ONLY AFTER THIS TRAGEDY...
COME ON...
...THAT FINALLY, I...
PLEASE...
MEL...
...I...
......
......!
...REALIZE HOW PRECIOUS MEL IS TO ME.

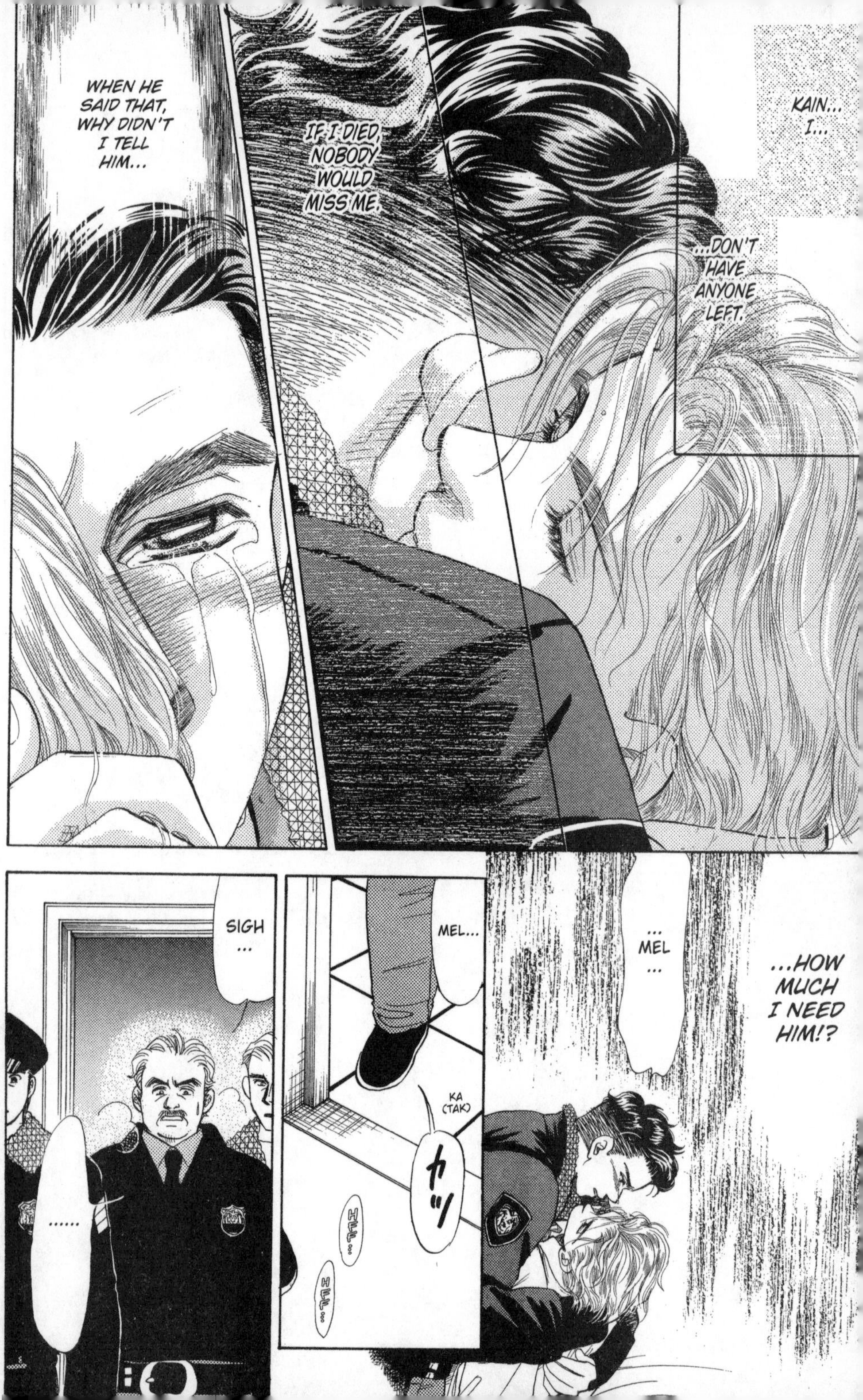
KAIN... I...
...DON'T HAVE ANYONE LEFT.
IF I DIED, NOBODY WOULD MISS ME.
WHEN HE SAID THAT, WHY DIDN'T I TELL HIM...
...MEL...
...HOW MUCH I NEED HIM!?
MEL...
KA (TAK)
カッ
HFF...
HFF...
SIGH...
......

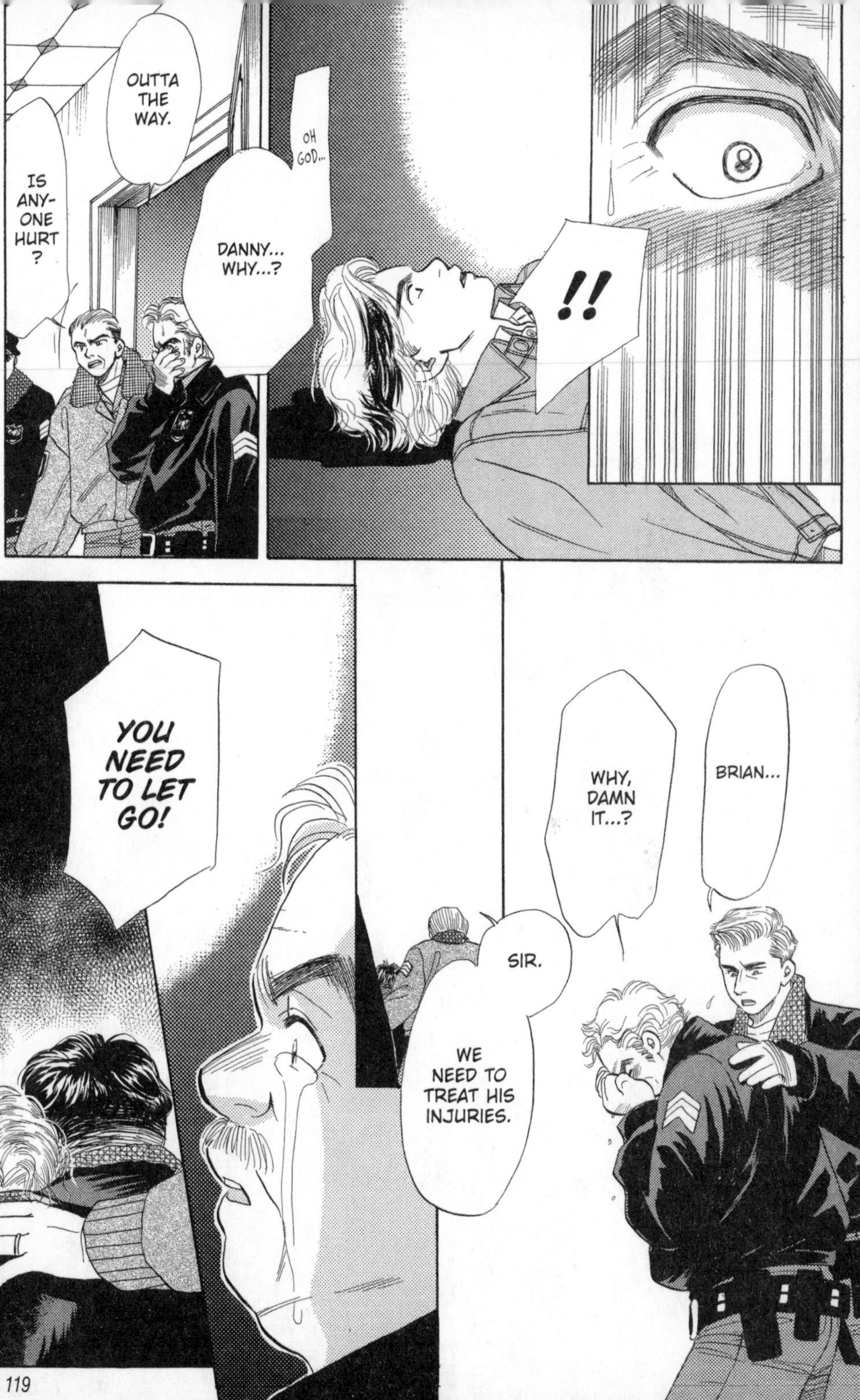
!!
OH GOD...
DANNY... WHY...?
OUTTA THE WAY.
IS ANY-ONE HURT?
BRIAN...
WHY, DAMN IT...?
SIR.
WE NEED TO TREAT HIS INJURIES.
YOU NEED TO LET GO!

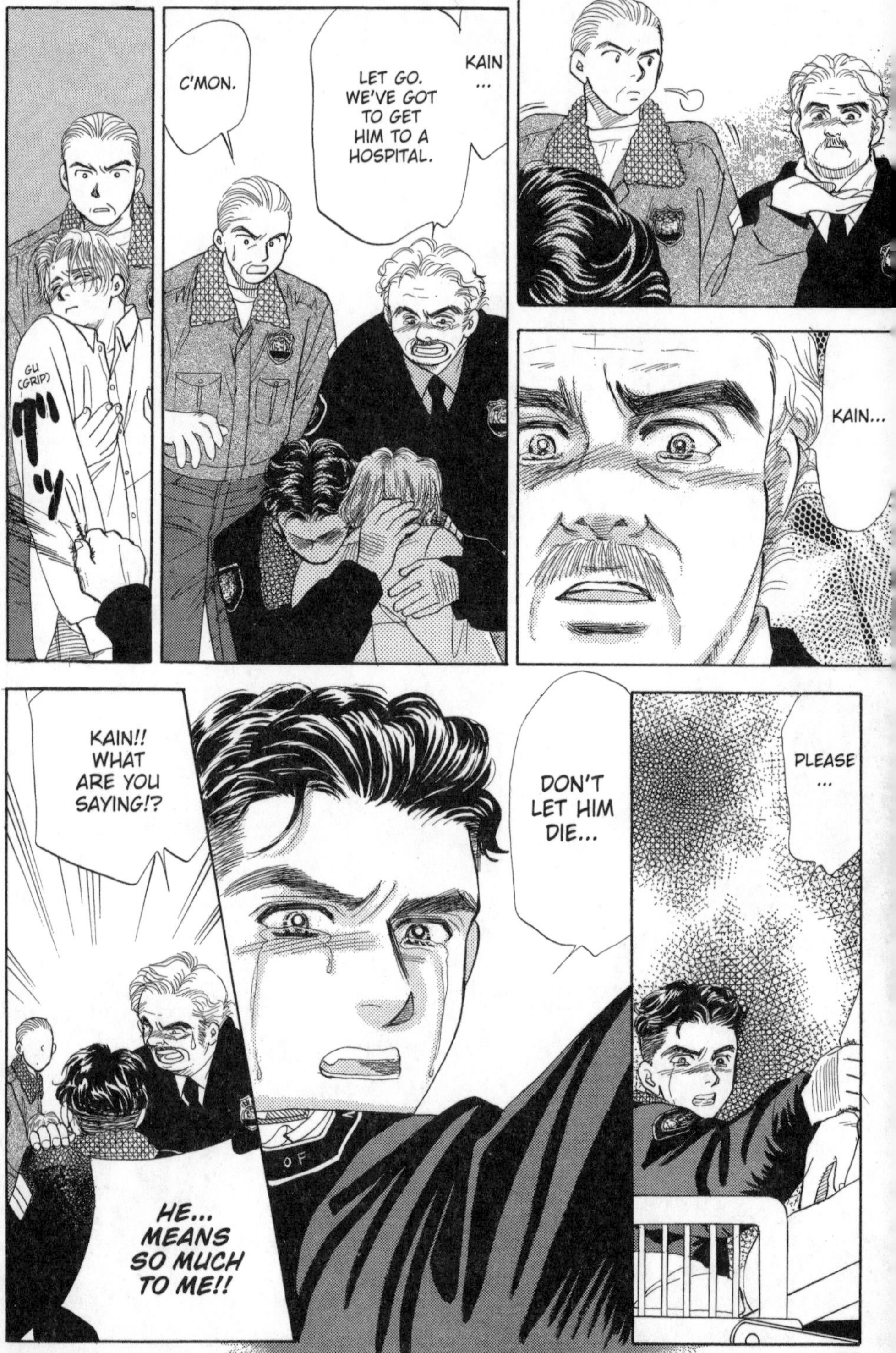
KAIN...
KAIN ...
LET GO. WE'VE GOT TO GET HIM TO A HOSPITAL.
C'MON.
GU (GRIP)
PLEASE ...
DON'T LET HIM DIE...
KAIN!! WHAT ARE YOU SAYING!?
HE... MEANS SO MUCH TO ME!!

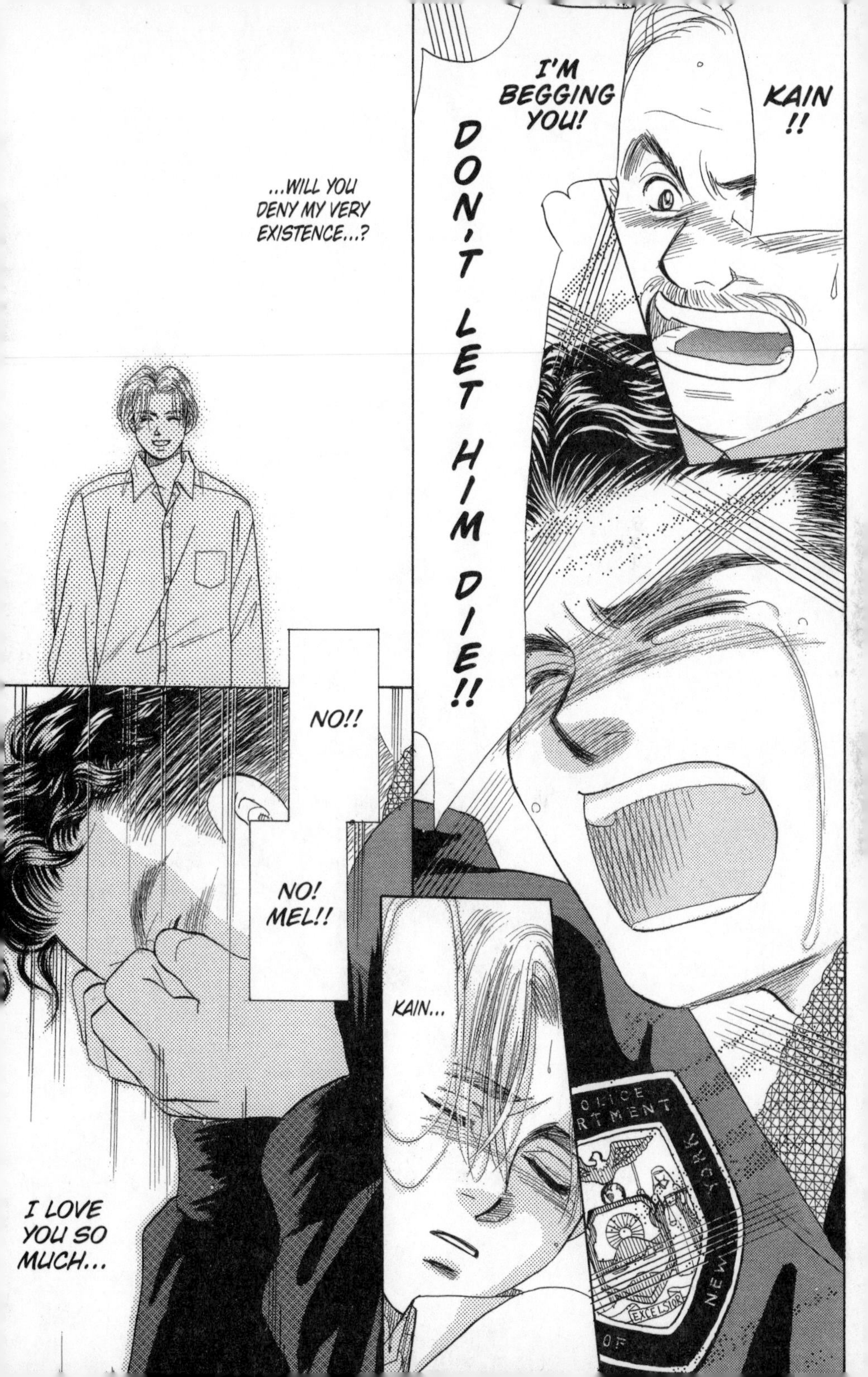
KAIN!!
I'M BEGGING YOU!
DON'T LET HIM DIE!!
KAIN...
...WILL YOU DENY MY VERY EXISTENCE...?
NO!!
NO! MEL!!
I LOVE YOU SO MUCH...

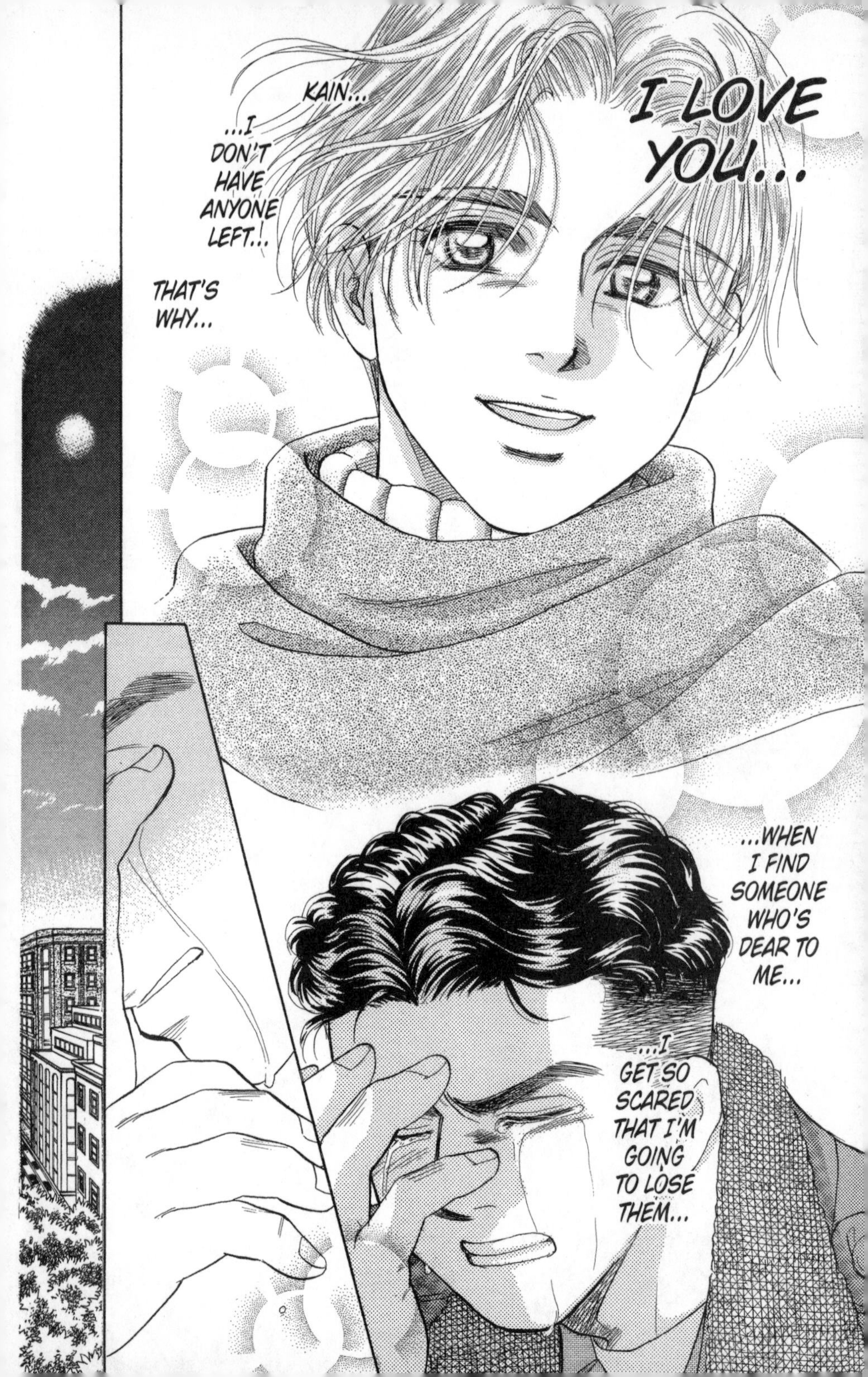
I LOVE YOU...
KAIN...
...I DON'T HAVE ANYONE LEFT...
THAT'S WHY...
...WHEN I FIND SOMEONE WHO'S DEAR TO ME...
...I GET SO SCARED THAT I'M GOING TO LOSE THEM...

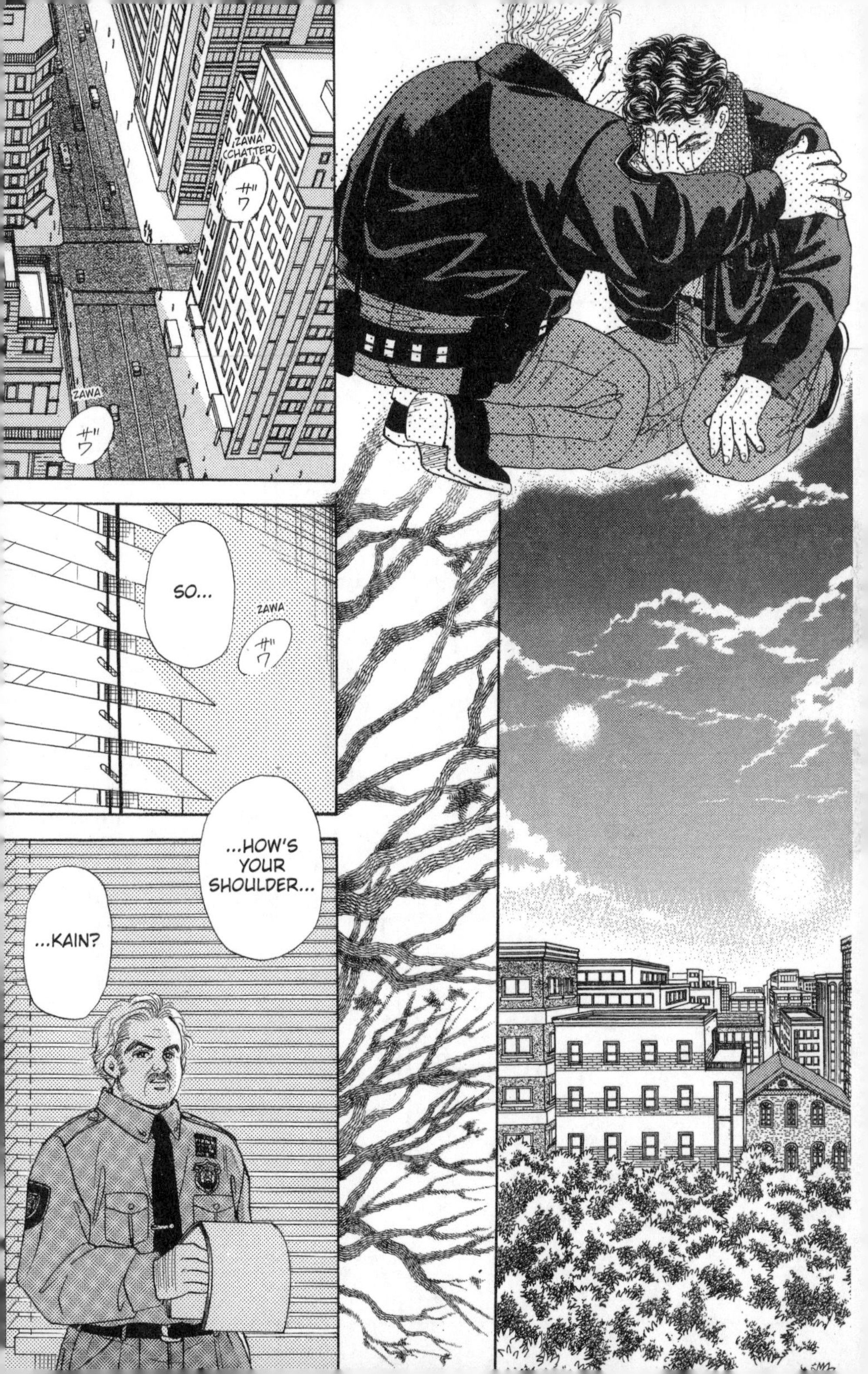
ZAWA (CHATTER)
ザワ
ZAWA
ザワ
SO...
ZAWA
ザワ
...HOW'S YOUR SHOULDER...
...KAIN?

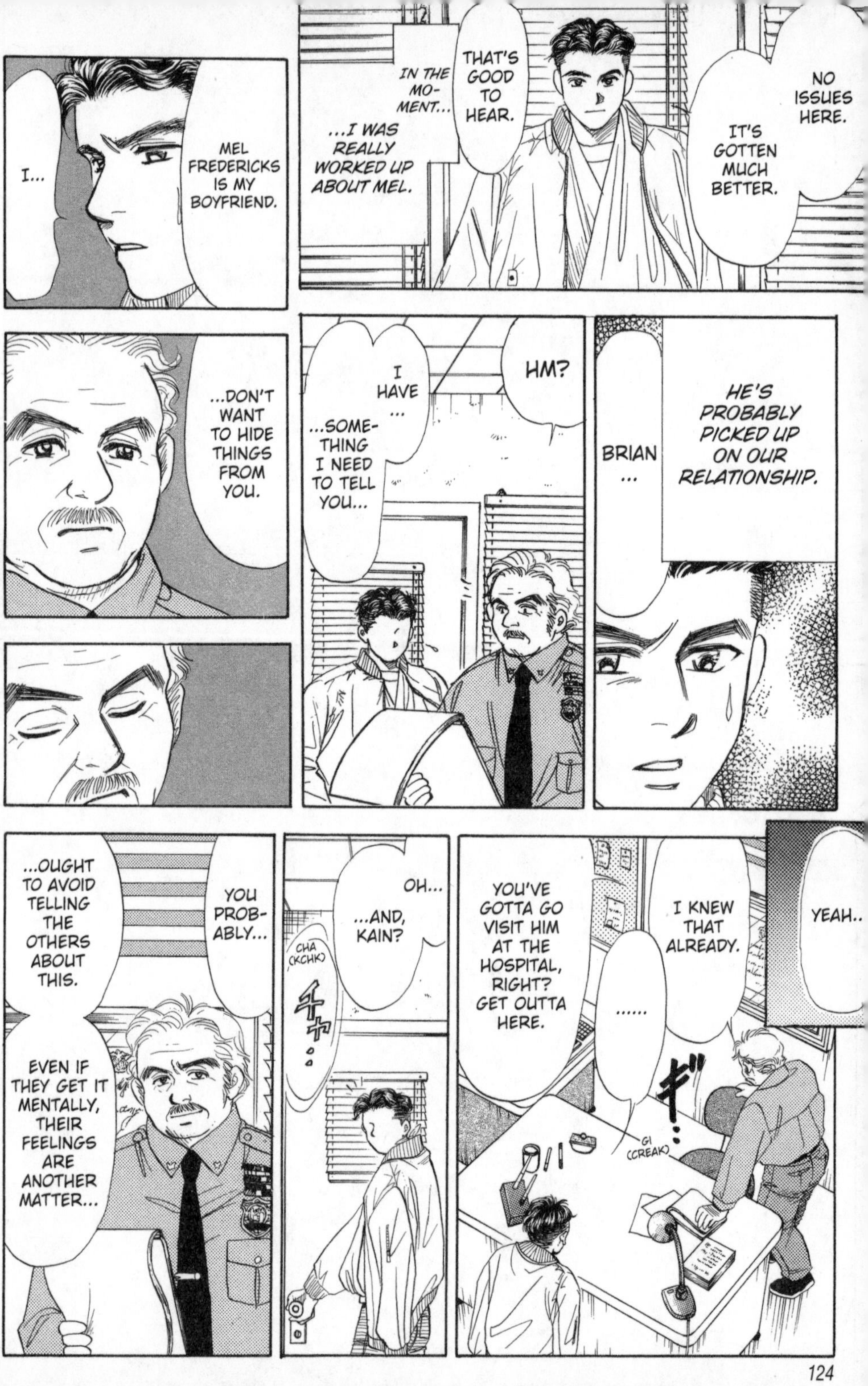
NO ISSUES HERE.
IT'S GOTTEN MUCH BETTER.
THAT'S GOOD TO HEAR.
IN THE MOMENT...
...I WAS REALLY WORKED UP ABOUT MEL.
MEL FREDERICKS IS MY BOYFRIEND.
I...
HE'S PROBABLY PICKED UP ON OUR RELATIONSHIP.
BRIAN...
HM?
I HAVE...
...SOMETHING I NEED TO TELL YOU...
...DON'T WANT TO HIDE THINGS FROM YOU.
YEAH..
I KNEW THAT ALREADY.
YOU'VE GOTTA GO VISIT HIM AT THE HOSPITAL, RIGHT? GET OUTTA HERE.
......
GI (CREAK)
OH...
...AND, KAIN?
CHA (KCHK)
YOU PROBABLY...
...OUGHT TO AVOID TELLING THE OTHERS ABOUT THIS.
EVEN IF THEY GET IT MENTALLY, THEIR FEELINGS ARE ANOTHER MATTER...

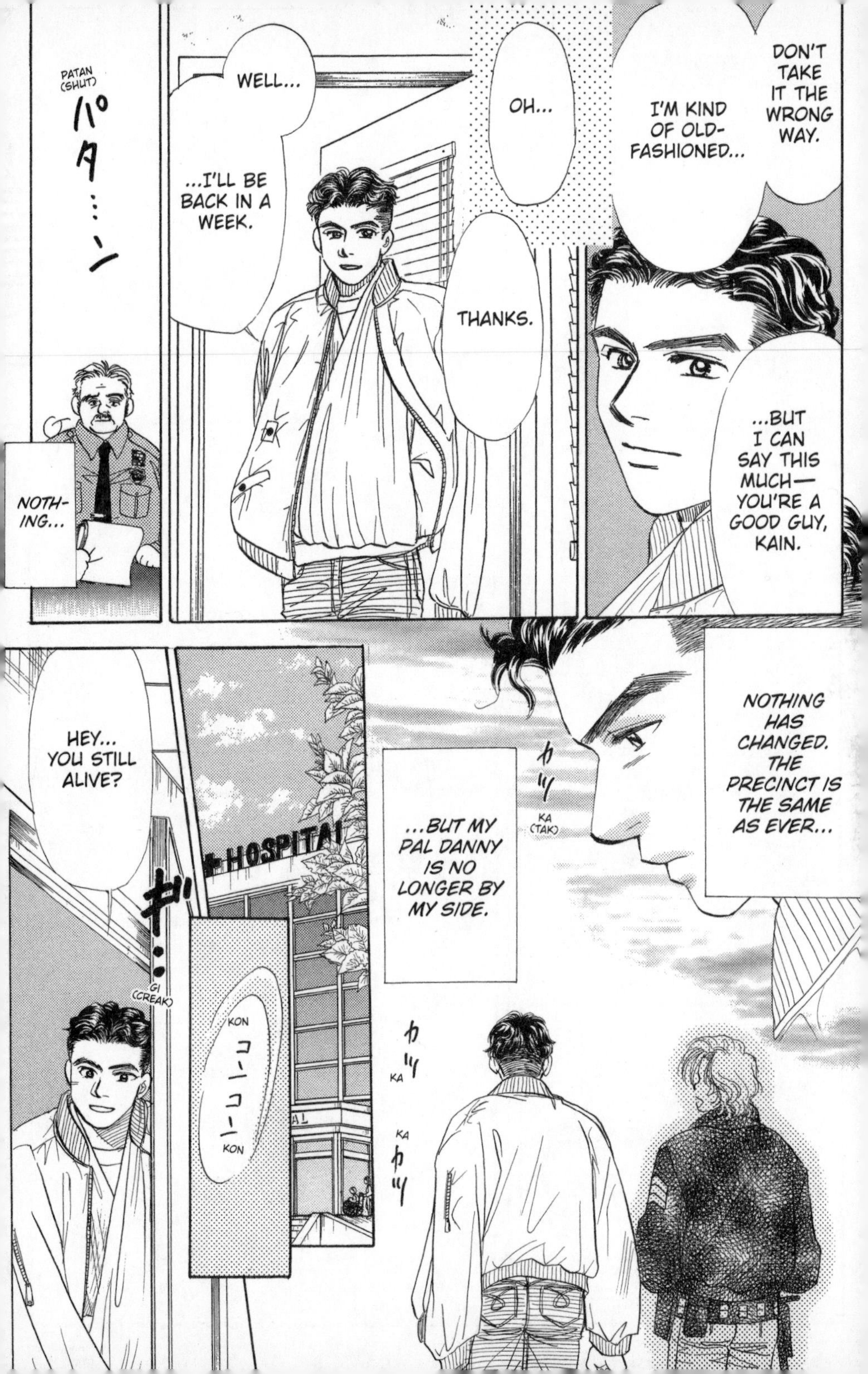
DON'T TAKE IT THE WRONG WAY.
I'M KIND OF OLD-FASHIONED...
...BUT I CAN SAY THIS MUCH—YOU'RE A GOOD GUY, KAIN.
OH...
THANKS.
WELL...
...I'LL BE BACK IN A WEEK.
PATAN (SHUT)
NOTHING...
NOTHING HAS CHANGED. THE PRECINCT IS THE SAME AS EVER...
KA (TAK)
...BUT MY PAL DANNY IS NO LONGER BY MY SIDE.
KA
KA
KON KON
GI (CREAK)
HEY... YOU STILL ALIVE?

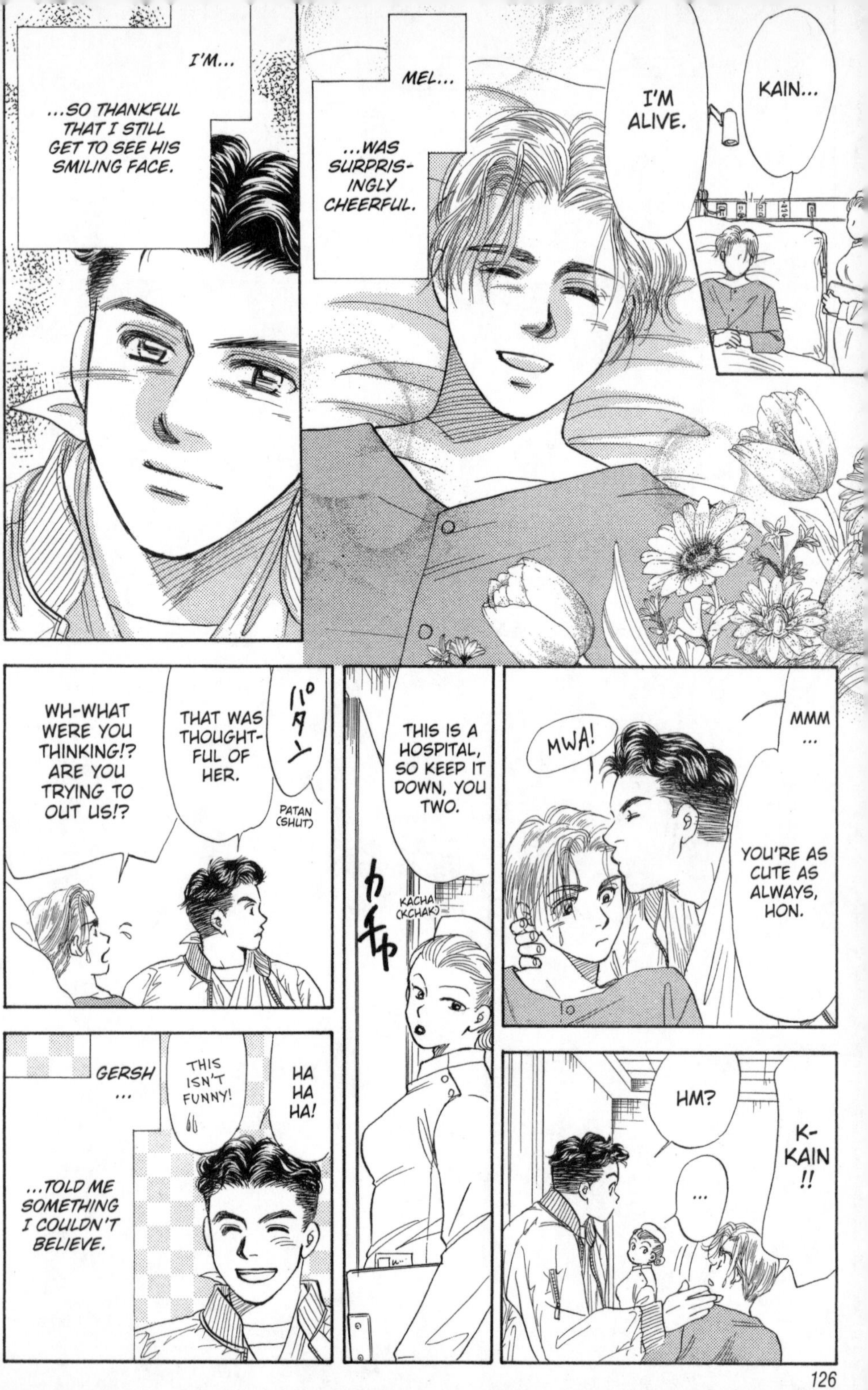
KAIN...
I'M ALIVE.
MEL...
...WAS SURPRISINGLY CHEERFUL.
I'M...
...SO THANKFUL THAT I STILL GET TO SEE HIS SMILING FACE.
MMM...
YOU'RE AS CUTE AS ALWAYS, HON.
MWA!
K-KAIN!!
HM?
...
KACHA (KCHAK)
THIS IS A HOSPITAL, SO KEEP IT DOWN, YOU TWO.
PATAN (SHUT)
THAT WAS THOUGHTFUL OF HER.
WH-WHAT WERE YOU THINKING!? ARE YOU TRYING TO OUT US!?
HA HA HA!
THIS ISN'T FUNNY!
GERSH...
...TOLD ME SOMETHING I COULDN'T BELIEVE.

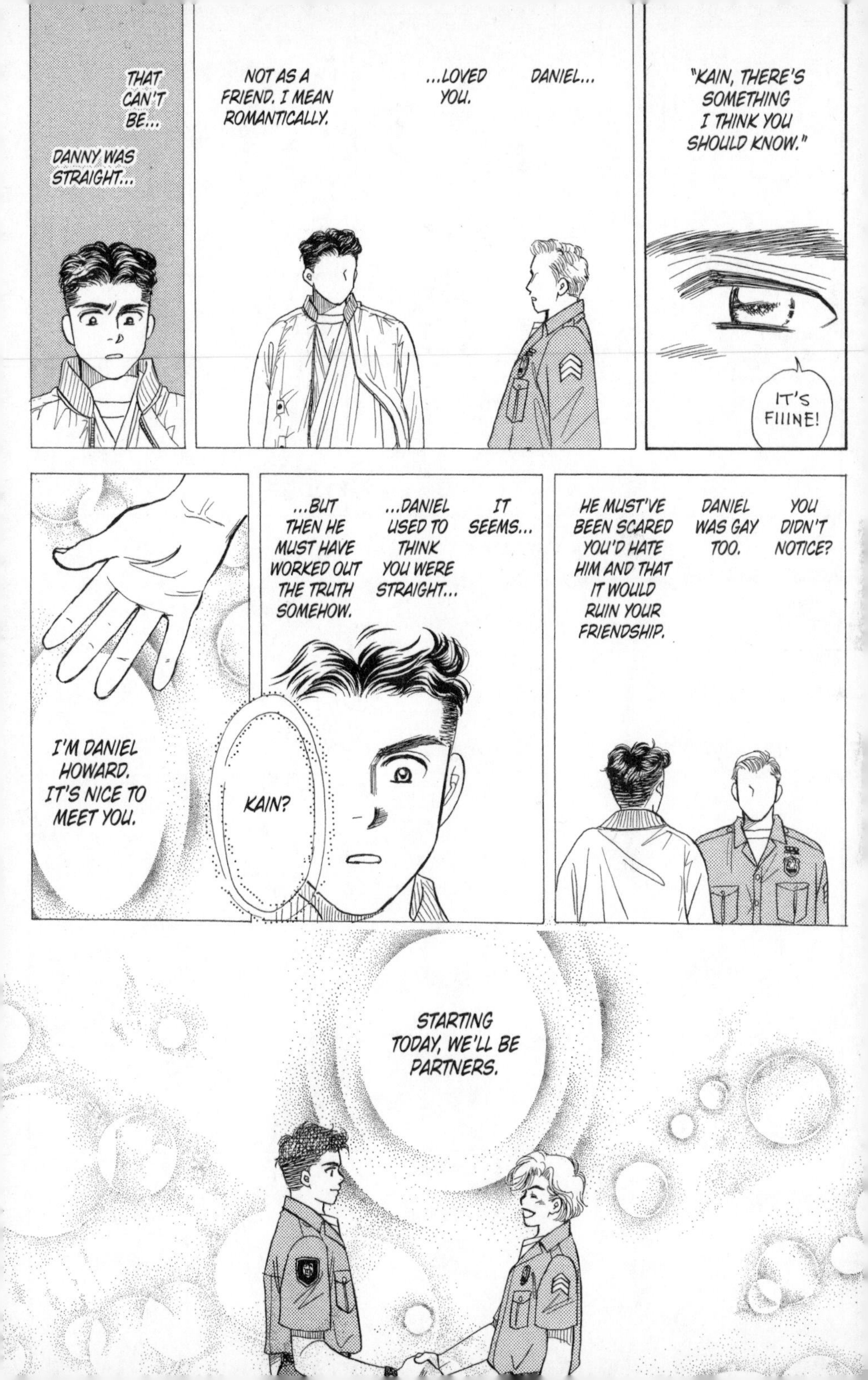
"KAIN, THERE'S SOMETHING I THINK YOU SHOULD KNOW."
IT'S FIIINE!
DANIEL...
...LOVED YOU.
NOT AS A FRIEND. I MEAN ROMANTICALLY.
THAT CAN'T BE...
DANNY WAS STRAIGHT...
YOU DIDN'T NOTICE?
DANIEL WAS GAY TOO.
HE MUST'VE BEEN SCARED YOU'D HATE HIM AND THAT IT WOULD RUIN YOUR FRIENDSHIP.
IT SEEMS...
...DANIEL USED TO THINK YOU WERE STRAIGHT...
...BUT THEN HE MUST HAVE WORKED OUT THE TRUTH SOMEHOW.
KAIN?
I'M DANIEL HOWARD. IT'S NICE TO MEET YOU.
STARTING TODAY, WE'LL BE PARTNERS.

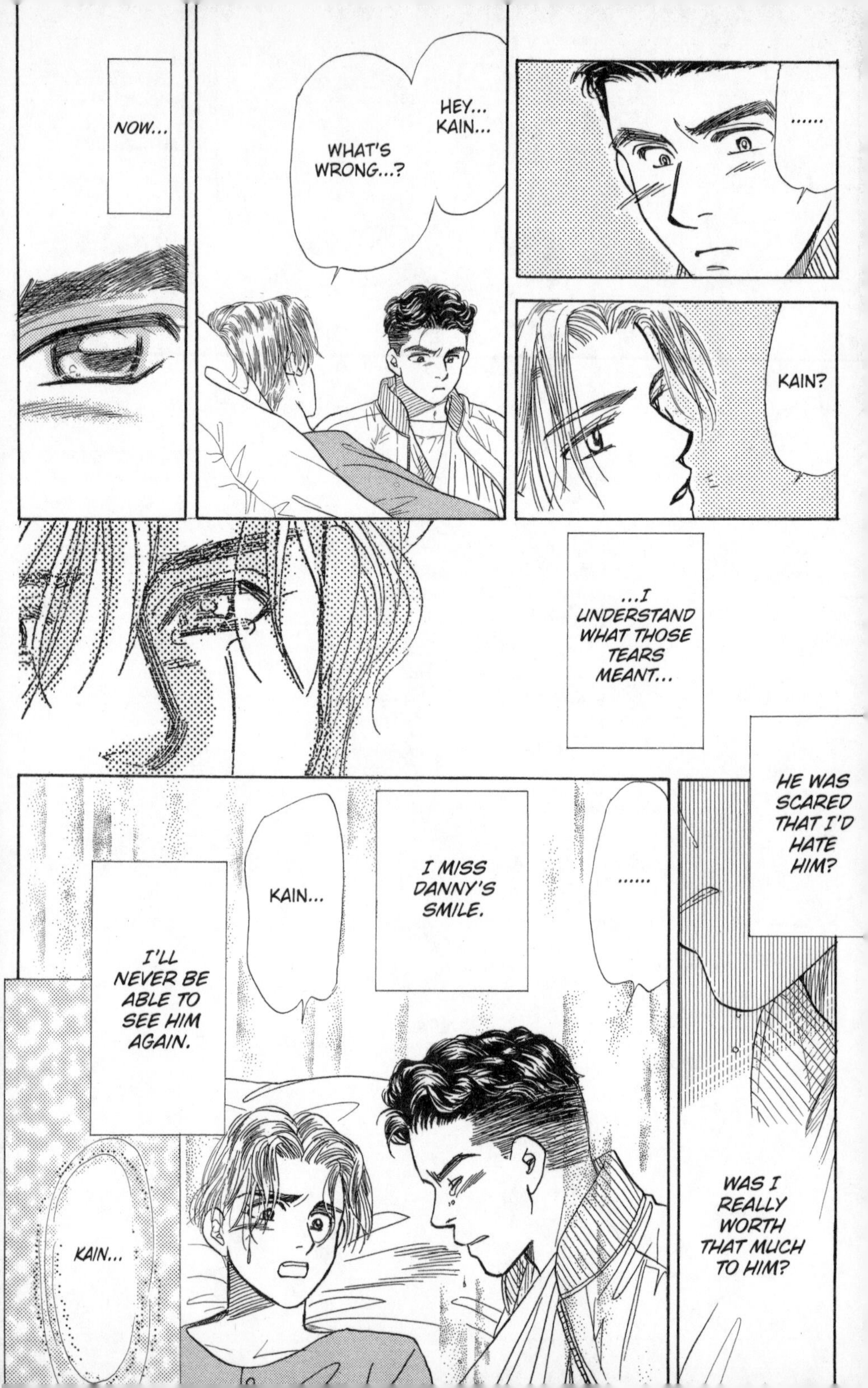
......
KAIN?
HEY... KAIN...
WHAT'S WRONG...?
NOW...
...I UNDERSTAND WHAT THOSE TEARS MEANT...
HE WAS SCARED THAT I'D HATE HIM?
WAS I REALLY WORTH THAT MUCH TO HIM?
......
I MISS DANNY'S SMILE.
KAIN...
I'LL NEVER BE ABLE TO SEE HIM AGAIN.
KAIN...

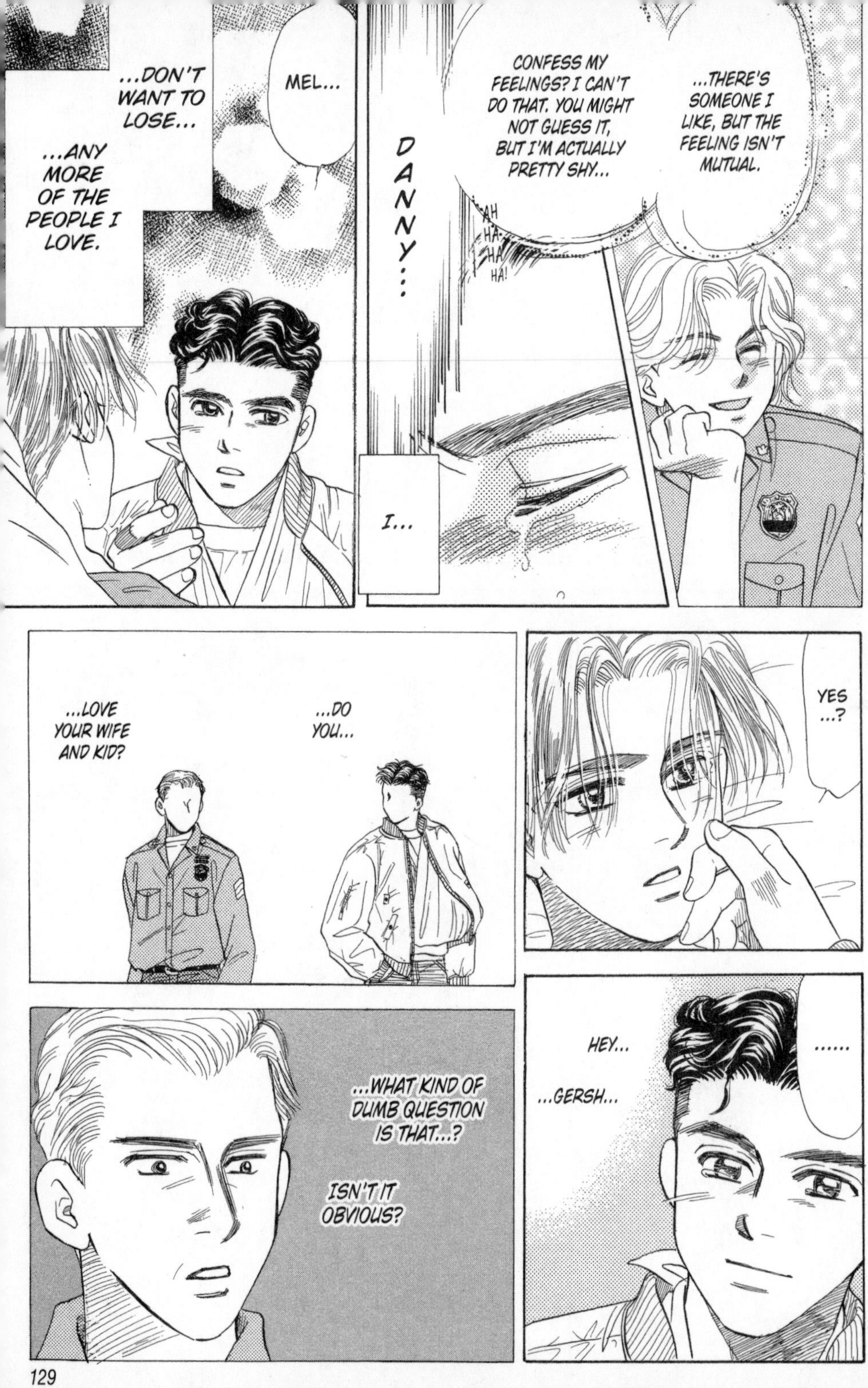
...THERE'S SOMEONE I LIKE, BUT THE FEELING ISN'T MUTUAL.
CONFESS MY FEELINGS? I CAN'T DO THAT. YOU MIGHT NOT GUESS IT, BUT I'M ACTUALLY PRETTY SHY...
AH HA HA HA!
DANNY...
I...
MEL...
...DON'T WANT TO LOSE...
...ANY MORE OF THE PEOPLE I LOVE.
YES ...?
...DO YOU...
...LOVE YOUR WIFE AND KID?
......
HEY...
...GERSH...
...WHAT KIND OF DUMB QUESTION IS THAT...?
ISN'T IT OBVIOUS?

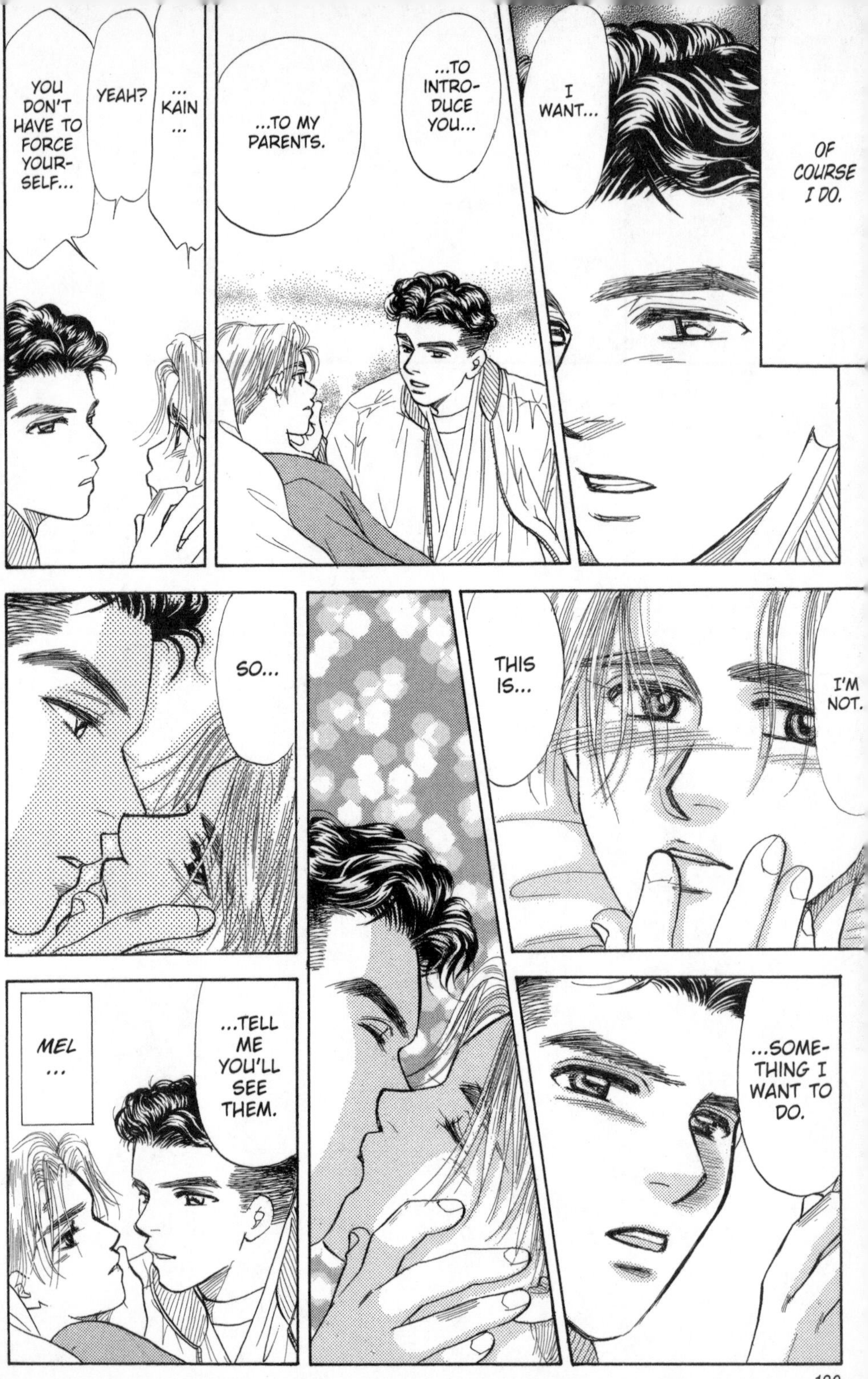
OF COURSE I DO.
I WANT...
...TO INTRODUCE YOU...
...TO MY PARENTS.
...KAIN...
YEAH?
YOU DON'T HAVE TO FORCE YOURSELF...
I'M NOT.
THIS IS...
...SOMETHING I WANT TO DO.
SO...
...TELL ME YOU'LL SEE THEM.
MEL...

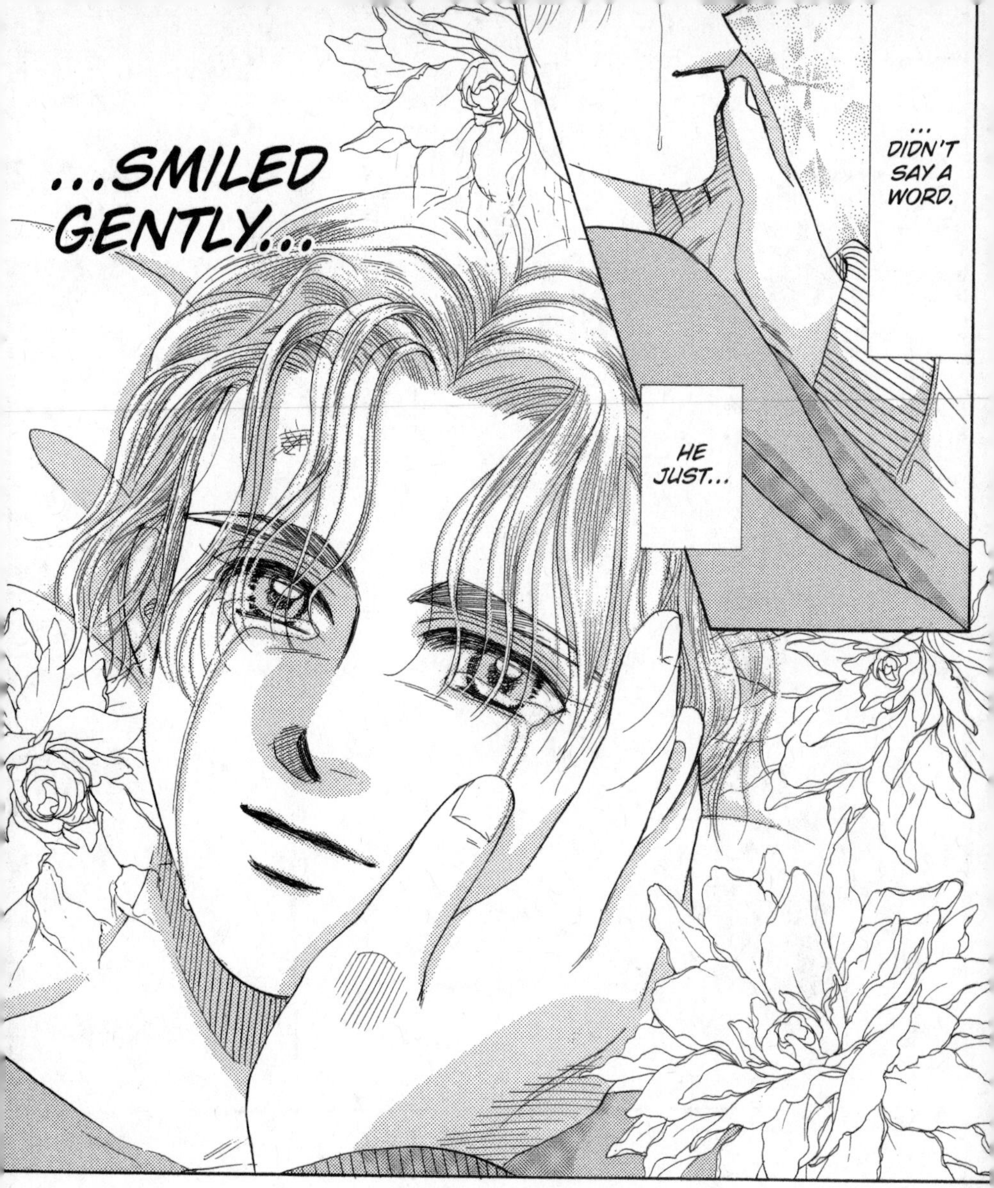
...DIDN'T SAY A WORD.
HE JUST...
...SMILED GENTLY...

THAT WAS HIS ANSWER.

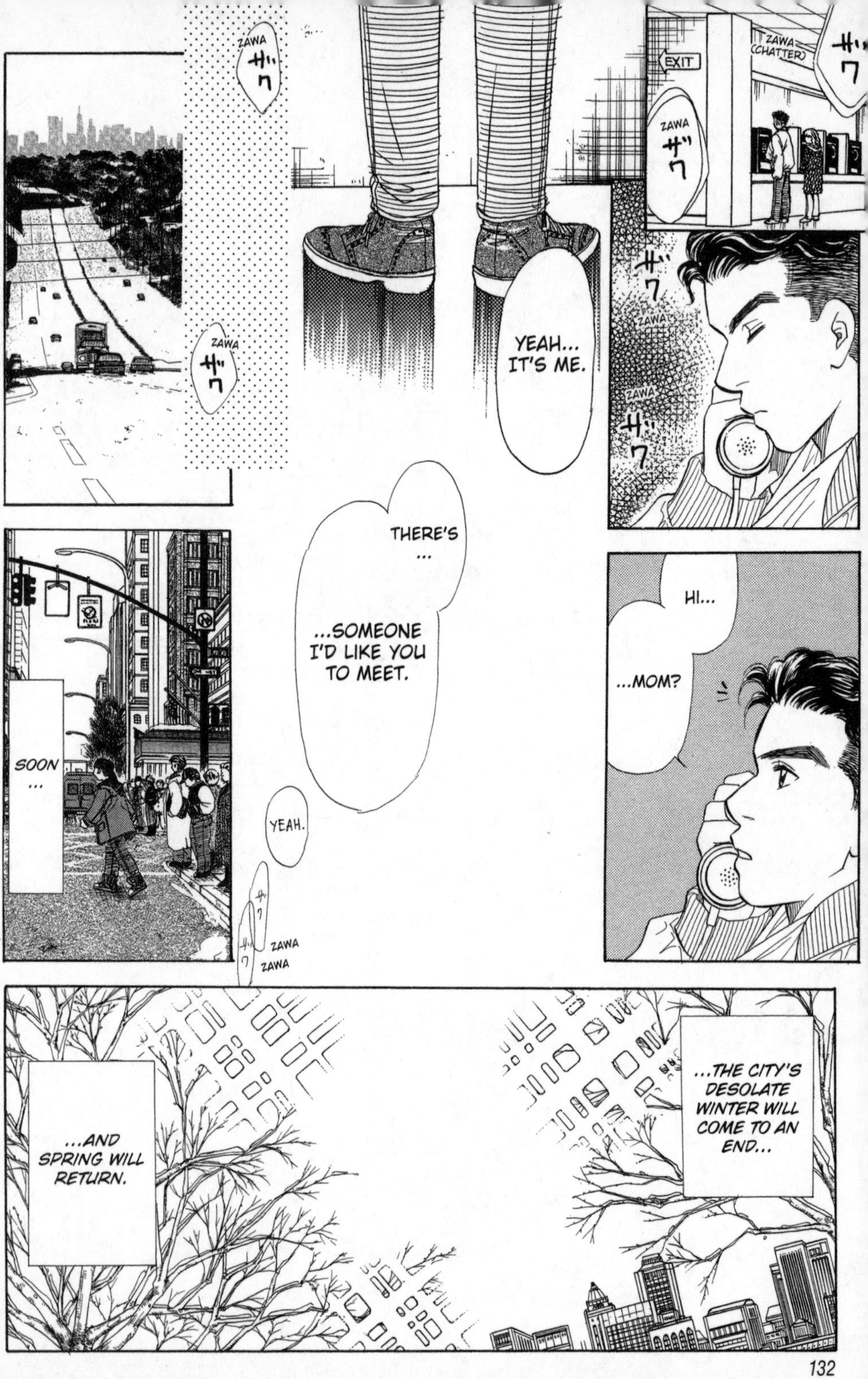
ZAWA (CHATTER)
ザワ
EXIT
ZAWA
ザワ
ザワ
ZAWA
ZAWA
ザワ
YEAH... IT'S ME.
ZAWA
ザワ
ZAWA
ザワ
HI...
...MOM?
THERE'S...
...SOMEONE I'D LIKE YOU TO MEET.
YEAH.
ザワ
ザワ
ZAWA
ZAWA
SOON...
...THE CITY'S DESOLATE WINTER WILL COME TO AN END...
...AND SPRING WILL RETURN.

EPISODE II

SCENE 1

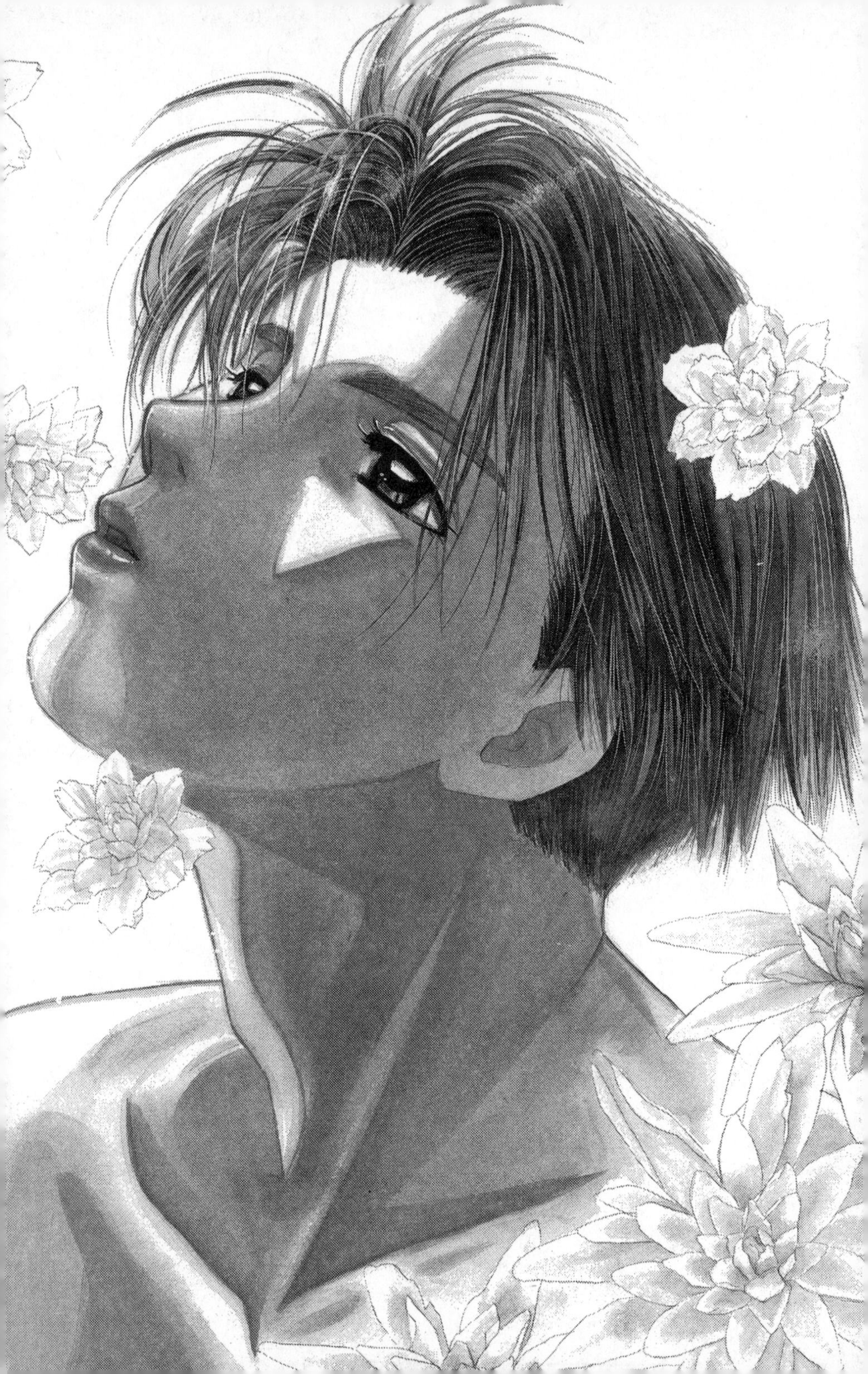

Marino

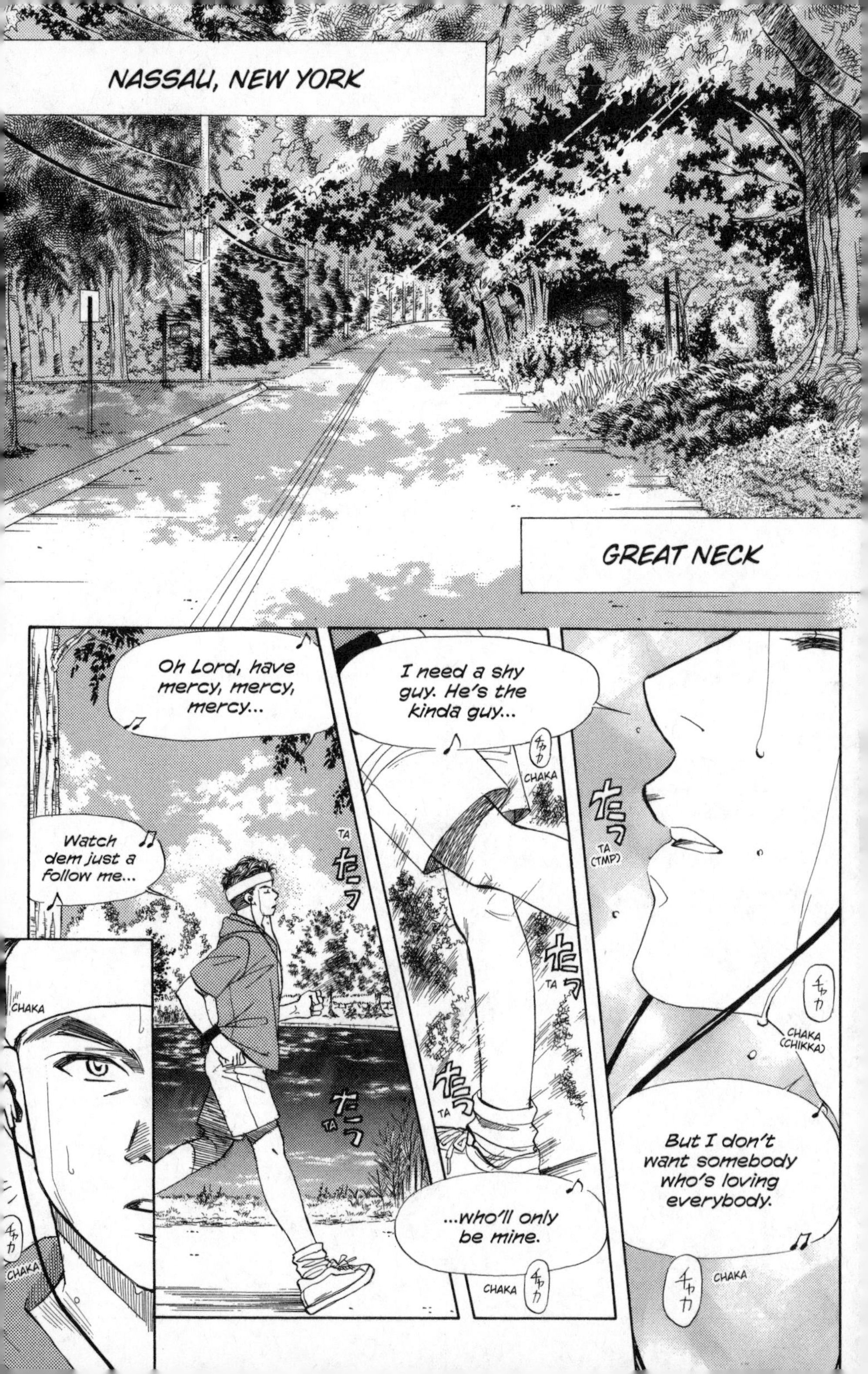
NASSAU, NEW YORK
GREAT NECK
たっ
TA (TMP)
チャカ
CHAKA (CHIKKA)
But I don't want somebody who's loving everybody.
チャカ
CHAKA
I need a shy guy. He's the kinda guy...
チャカ
CHAKA
たっ
TA
たっ
TA
...who'll only be mine.
チャカ
CHAKA
Oh Lord, have mercy, mercy, mercy...
Watch dem just a follow me...
たっ
TA
たっ
TA
CHAKA
チャカ
CHAKA

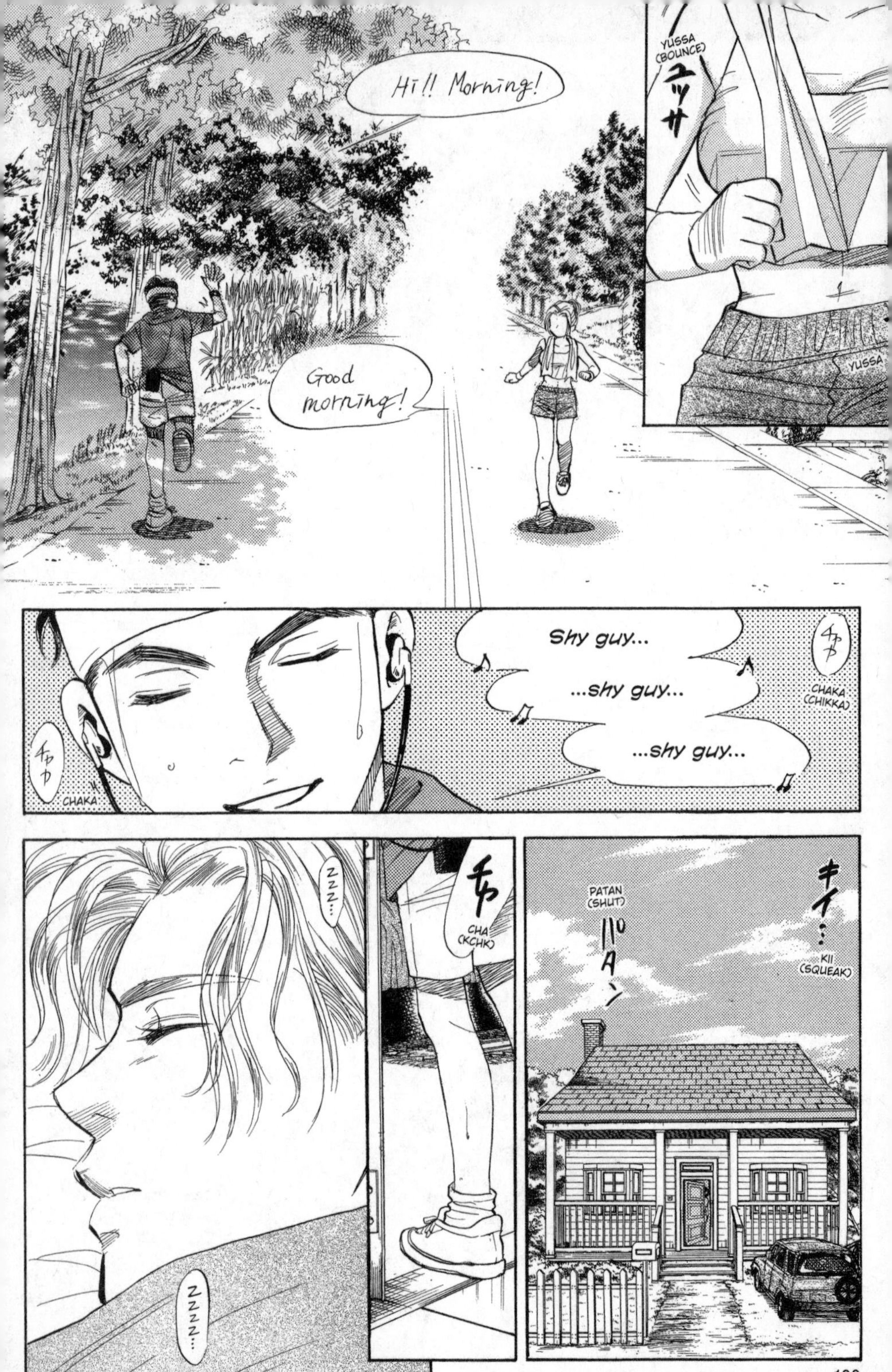

YUSSA (BOUNCE)
ユッサ
YUSSA
Hi!! Morning!
Good morning!
CHAKA (CHIKKA)
Shy guy...
...shy guy...
...shy guy...
CHAKA
KII (SQUEAK)
PATAN (SHUT)
CHA (KCHK)
Zzz...
Zzzz...

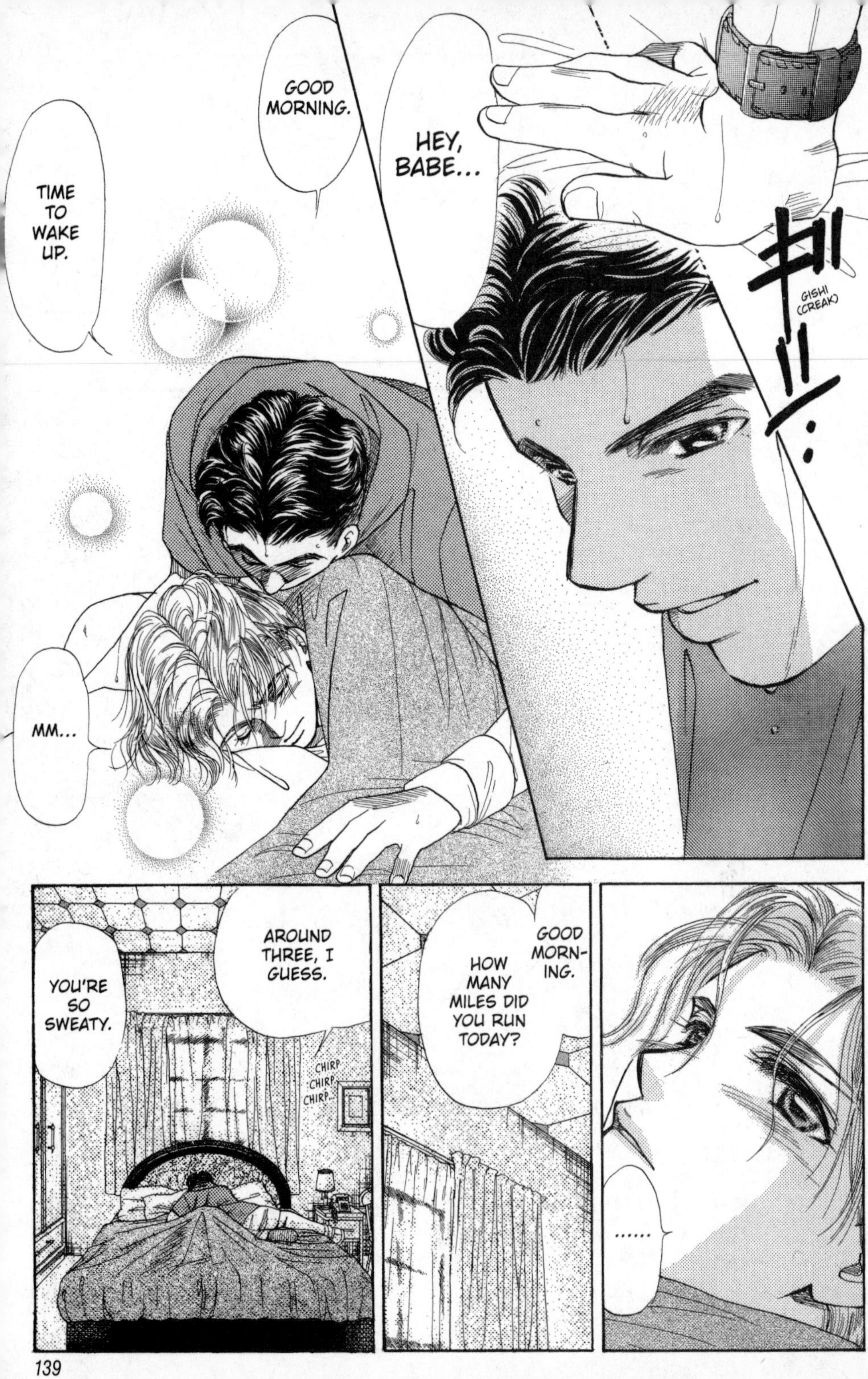
HEY, BABE...
GISHI (CREAK)
GOOD MORNING.
TIME TO WAKE UP.
MM...
......
GOOD MORN-ING.
HOW MANY MILES DID YOU RUN TODAY?
AROUND THREE, I GUESS.
YOU'RE SO SWEATY.
CHIRP CHIRP CHIRP...

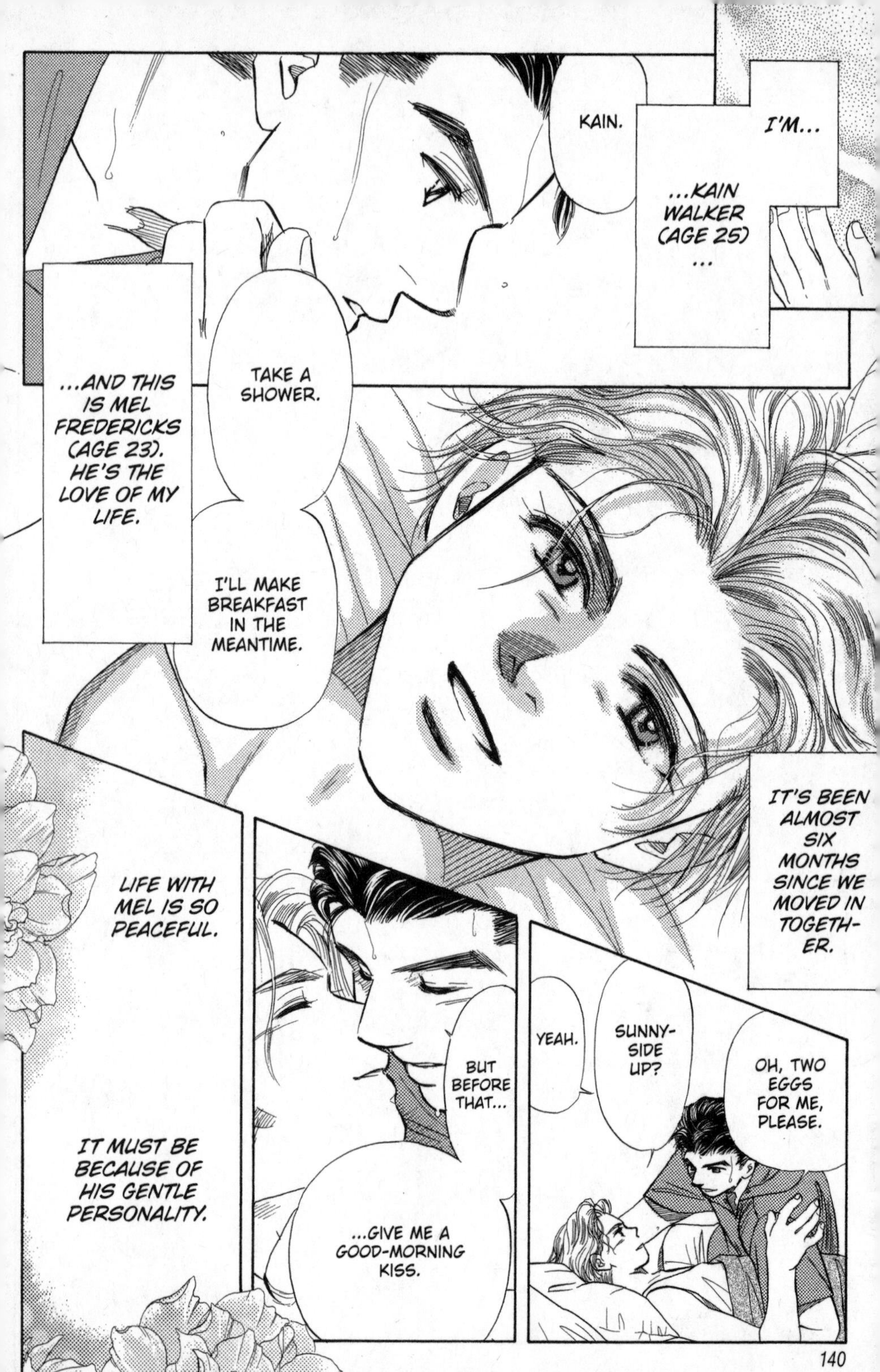
I'M... ...KAIN WALKER (AGE 25)...
KAIN.
...AND THIS IS MEL FREDERICKS (AGE 23). HE'S THE LOVE OF MY LIFE.
TAKE A SHOWER.
I'LL MAKE BREAKFAST IN THE MEANTIME.
IT'S BEEN ALMOST SIX MONTHS SINCE WE MOVED IN TOGETH-ER.
OH, TWO EGGS FOR ME, PLEASE.
SUNNY-SIDE UP?
YEAH.
BUT BEFORE THAT...
...GIVE ME A GOOD-MORNING KISS.
LIFE WITH MEL IS SO PEACEFUL.
IT MUST BE BECAUSE OF HIS GENTLE PERSONALITY.

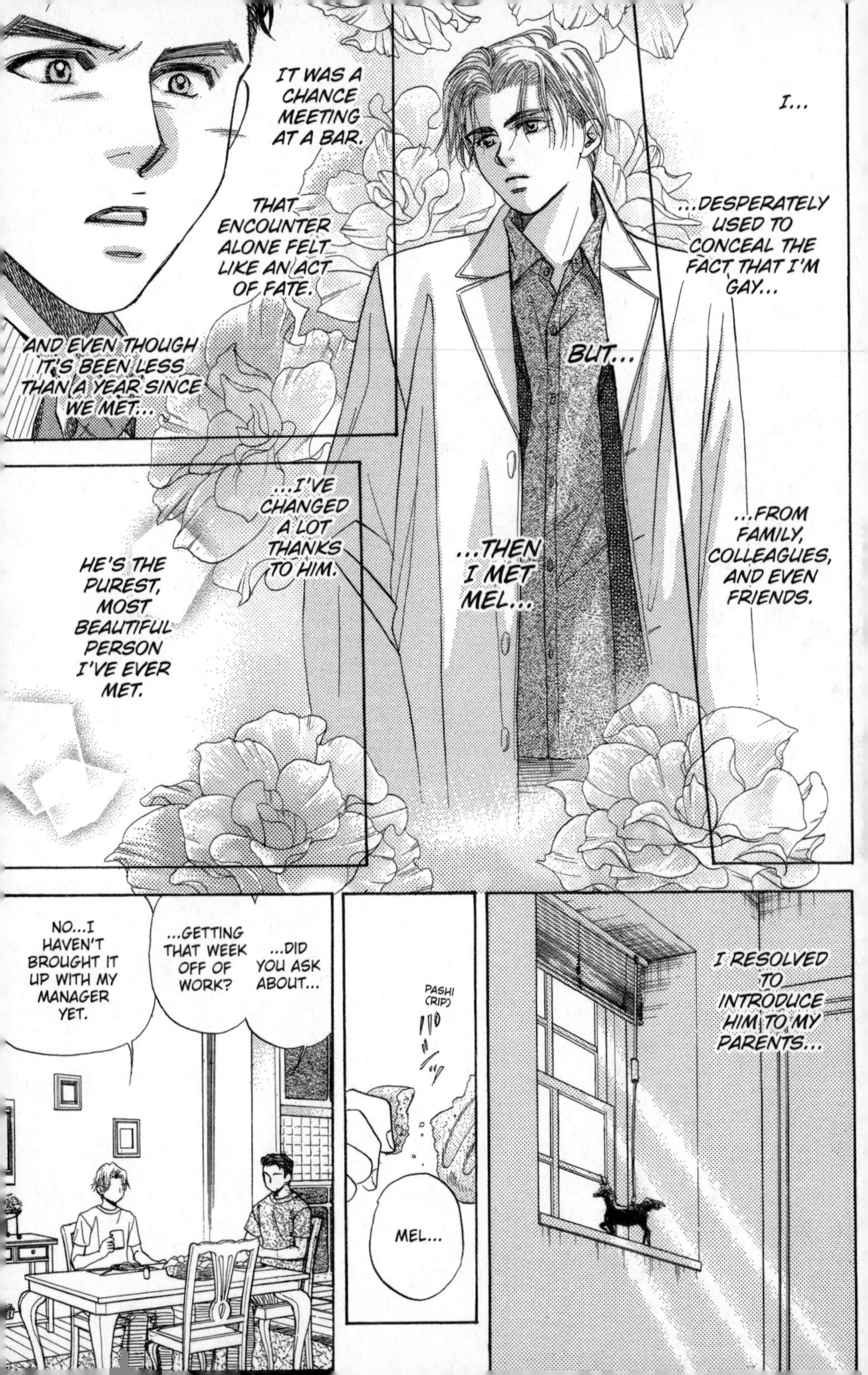
I...
...DESPERATELY USED TO CONCEAL THE FACT THAT I'M GAY...
...FROM FAMILY, COLLEAGUES, AND EVEN FRIENDS.
BUT...
...THEN I MET MEL...
IT WAS A CHANCE MEETING AT A BAR.
THAT ENCOUNTER ALONE FELT LIKE AN ACT OF FATE.
AND EVEN THOUGH IT'S BEEN LESS THAN A YEAR SINCE WE MET...
...I'VE CHANGED A LOT THANKS TO HIM.
HE'S THE PUREST, MOST BEAUTIFUL PERSON I'VE EVER MET.
I RESOLVED TO INTRODUCE HIM TO MY PARENTS...
PASHI (RIP)
MEL...
...DID YOU ASK ABOUT...
...GETTING THAT WEEK OFF OF WORK?
NO...I HAVEN'T BROUGHT IT UP WITH MY MANAGER YET.

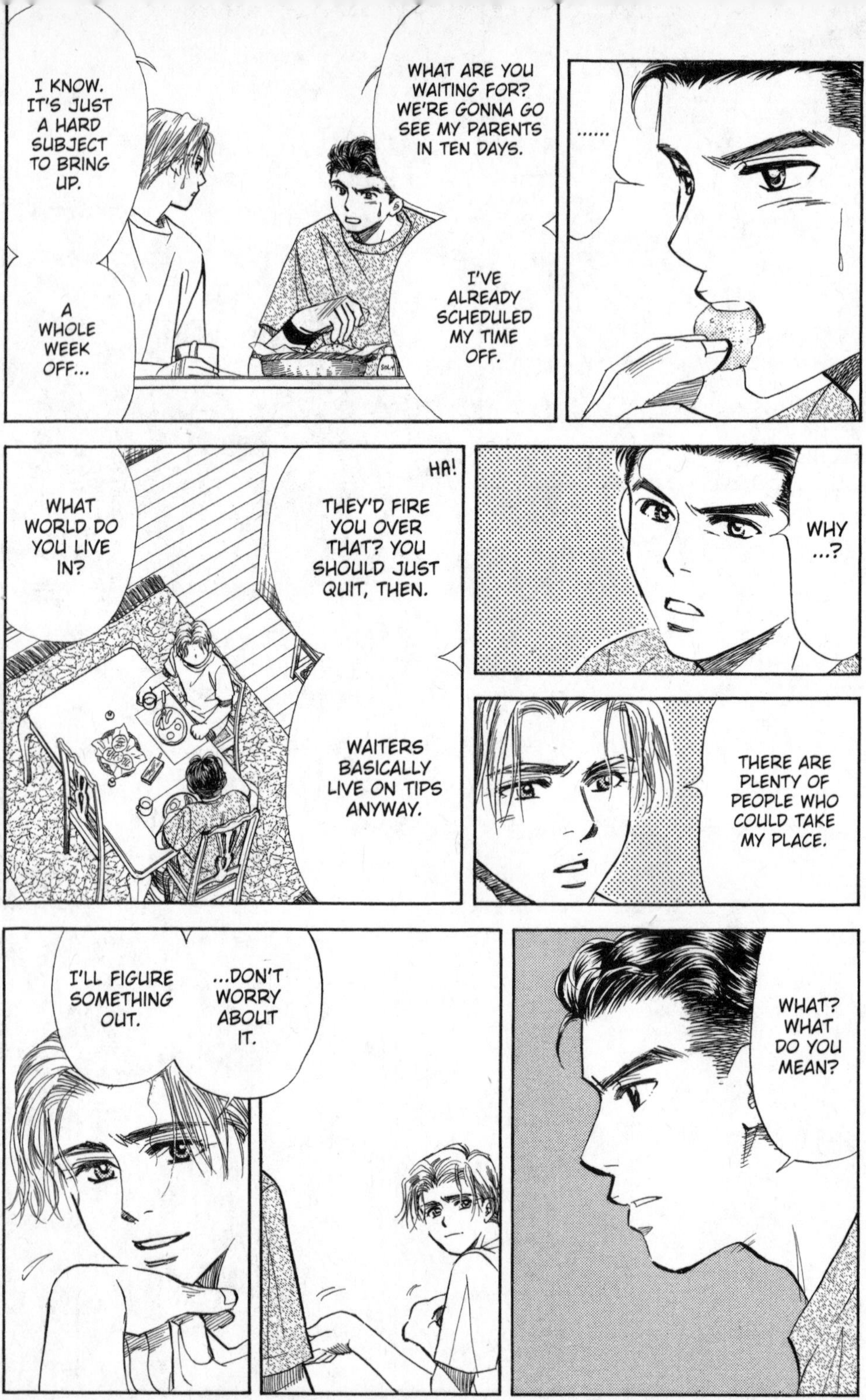
......
WHAT ARE YOU WAITING FOR? WE'RE GONNA GO SEE MY PARENTS IN TEN DAYS.
I KNOW. IT'S JUST A HARD SUBJECT TO BRING UP.
I'VE ALREADY SCHEDULED MY TIME OFF.
A WHOLE WEEK OFF...
WHY ...?
THERE ARE PLENTY OF PEOPLE WHO COULD TAKE MY PLACE.
HA!
THEY'D FIRE YOU OVER THAT? YOU SHOULD JUST QUIT, THEN.
WHAT WORLD DO YOU LIVE IN?
WAITERS BASICALLY LIVE ON TIPS ANYWAY.
WHAT? WHAT DO YOU MEAN?
...DON'T WORRY ABOUT IT.
I'LL FIGURE SOMETHING OUT.

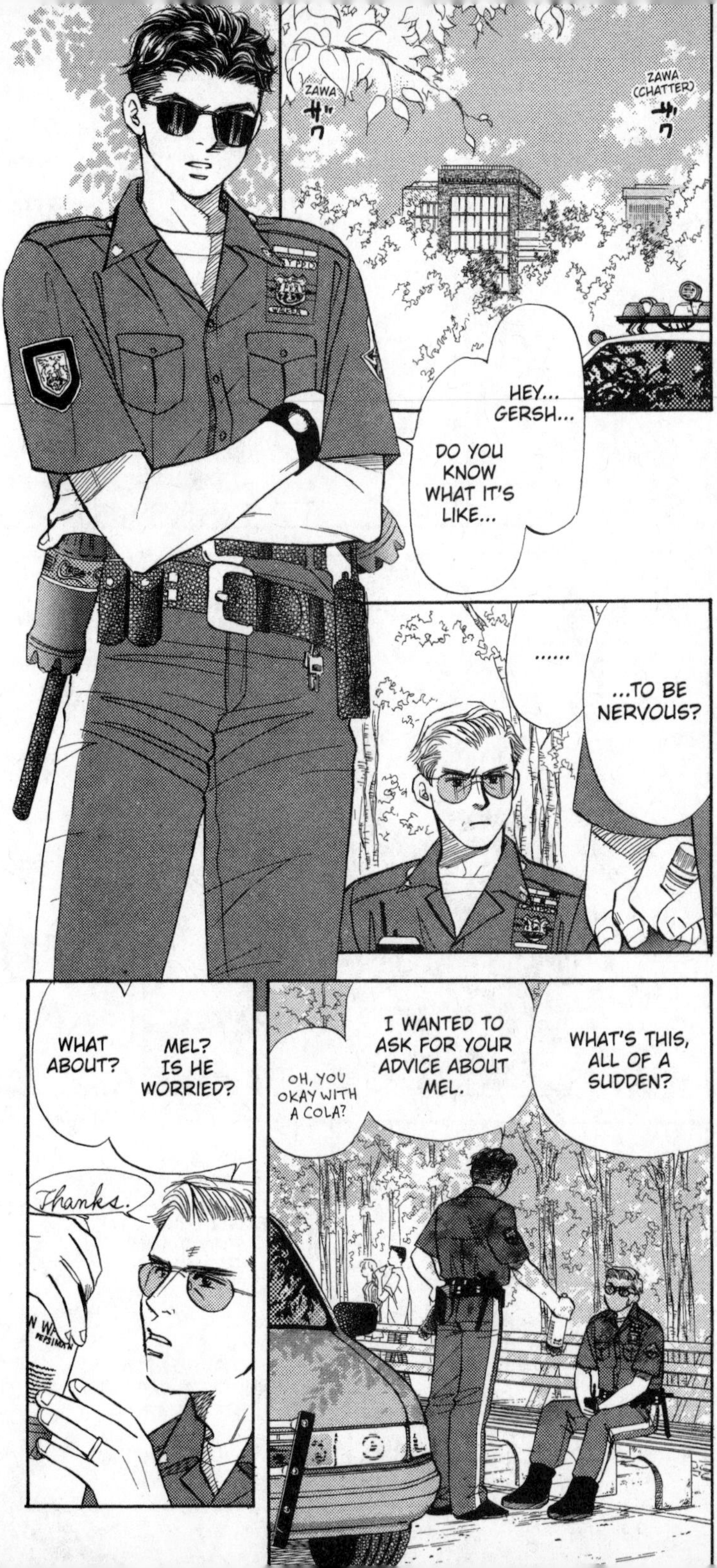
ZAWA (CHATTER)
ZAWA
HEY... GERSH...
DO YOU KNOW WHAT IT'S LIKE...
......
...TO BE NERVOUS?
WHAT'S THIS, ALL OF A SUDDEN?
I WANTED TO ASK FOR YOUR ADVICE ABOUT MEL.
OH, YOU OKAY WITH A COLA?
MEL? IS HE WORRIED?
WHAT ABOUT?
Thanks.

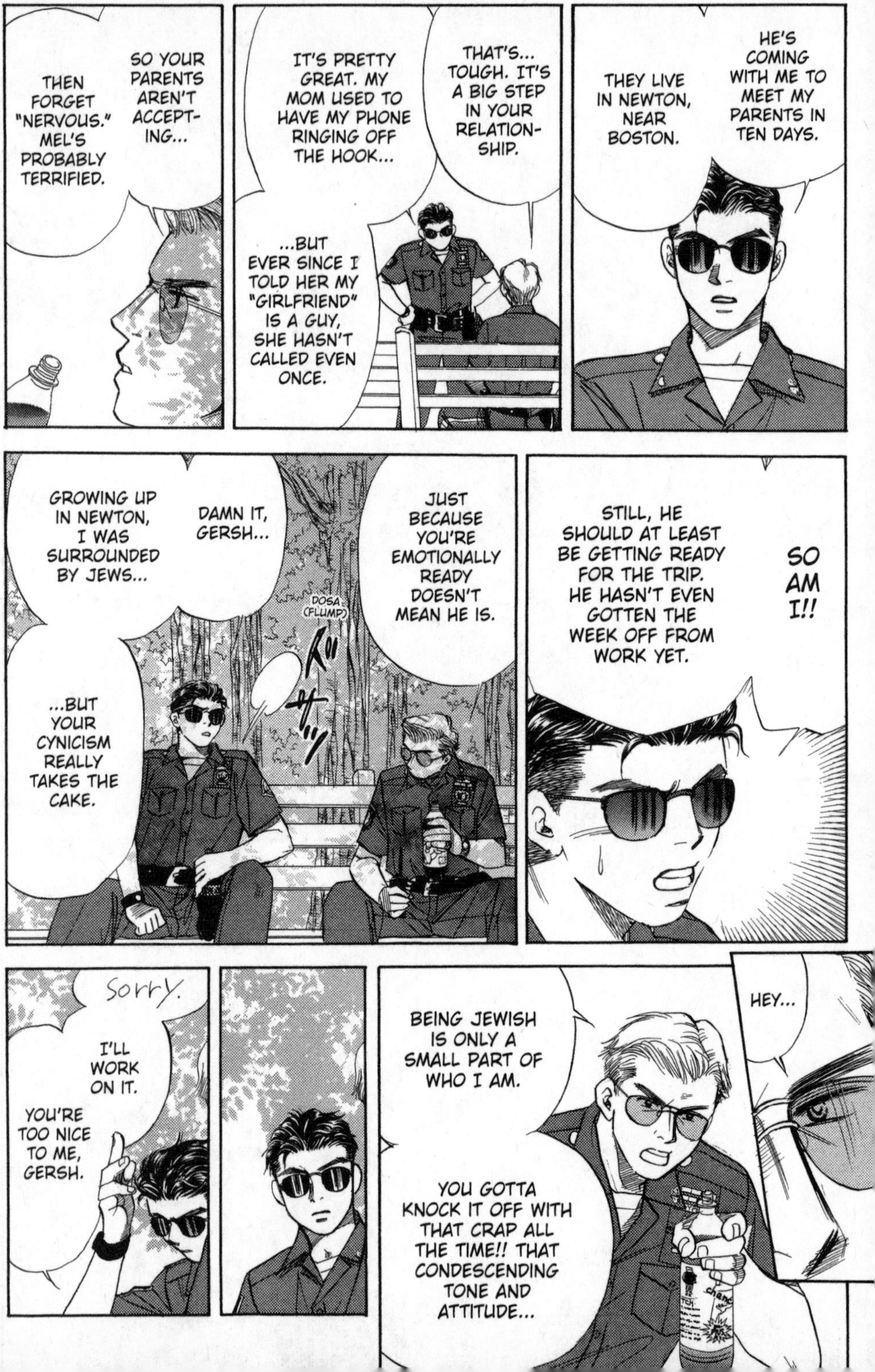
HE'S COMING WITH ME TO MEET MY PARENTS IN TEN DAYS.
THEY LIVE IN NEWTON, NEAR BOSTON.
THAT'S... TOUGH. IT'S A BIG STEP IN YOUR RELATIONSHIP.
IT'S PRETTY GREAT. MY MOM USED TO HAVE MY PHONE RINGING OFF THE HOOK...
...BUT EVER SINCE I TOLD HER MY "GIRLFRIEND" IS A GUY, SHE HASN'T CALLED EVEN ONCE.
SO YOUR PARENTS AREN'T ACCEPTING...
THEN FORGET "NERVOUS." MEL'S PROBABLY TERRIFIED.
SO AM I!!
STILL, HE SHOULD AT LEAST BE GETTING READY FOR THE TRIP. HE HASN'T EVEN GOTTEN THE WEEK OFF FROM WORK YET.
JUST BECAUSE YOU'RE EMOTIONALLY READY DOESN'T MEAN HE IS.
DOSA (FLUMP)
DAMN IT, GERSH...
GROWING UP IN NEWTON, I WAS SURROUNDED BY JEWS...
...BUT YOUR CYNICISM REALLY TAKES THE CAKE.
HEY...
BEING JEWISH IS ONLY A SMALL PART OF WHO I AM.
YOU GOTTA KNOCK IT OFF WITH THAT CRAP ALL THE TIME!! THAT CONDESCENDING TONE AND ATTITUDE...
Sorry.
I'LL WORK ON IT.
YOU'RE TOO NICE TO ME, GERSH.

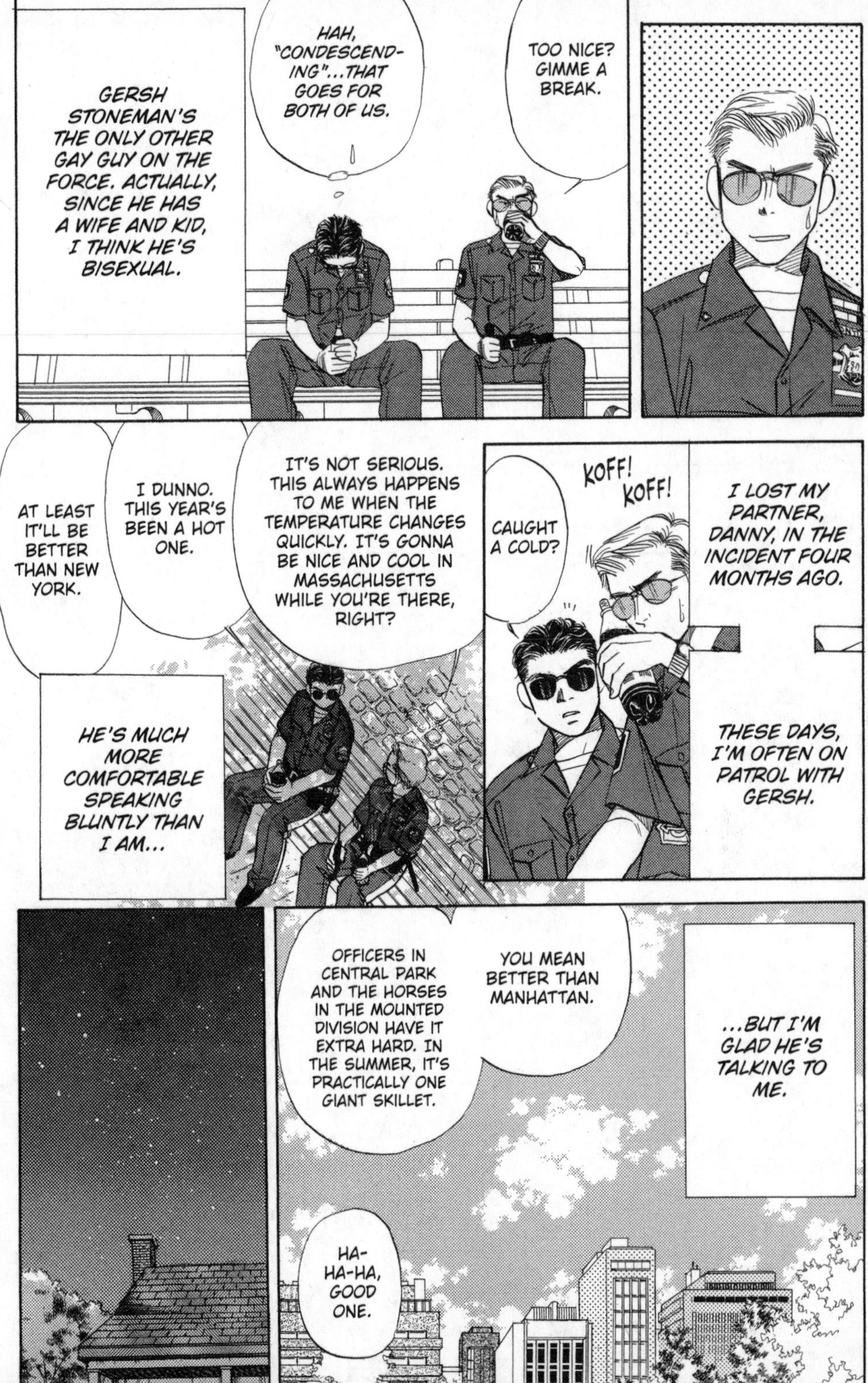
TOO NICE? GIMME A BREAK.
HAH, "CONDESCEND-ING"...THAT GOES FOR BOTH OF US.
GERSH STONEMAN'S THE ONLY OTHER GAY GUY ON THE FORCE. ACTUALLY, SINCE HE HAS A WIFE AND KID, I THINK HE'S BISEXUAL.
I LOST MY PARTNER, DANNY, IN THE INCIDENT FOUR MONTHS AGO.
KOFF! KOFF!
CAUGHT A COLD?
THESE DAYS, I'M OFTEN ON PATROL WITH GERSH.
IT'S NOT SERIOUS. THIS ALWAYS HAPPENS TO ME WHEN THE TEMPERATURE CHANGES QUICKLY. IT'S GONNA BE NICE AND COOL IN MASSACHUSETTS WHILE YOU'RE THERE, RIGHT?
I DUNNO. THIS YEAR'S BEEN A HOT ONE.
AT LEAST IT'LL BE BETTER THAN NEW YORK.
HE'S MUCH MORE COMFORTABLE SPEAKING BLUNTLY THAN I AM...
...BUT I'M GLAD HE'S TALKING TO ME.
YOU MEAN BETTER THAN MANHATTAN.
OFFICERS IN CENTRAL PARK AND THE HORSES IN THE MOUNTED DIVISION HAVE IT EXTRA HARD. IN THE SUMMER, IT'S PRACTICALLY ONE GIANT SKILLET.
HA-HA-HA, GOOD ONE.

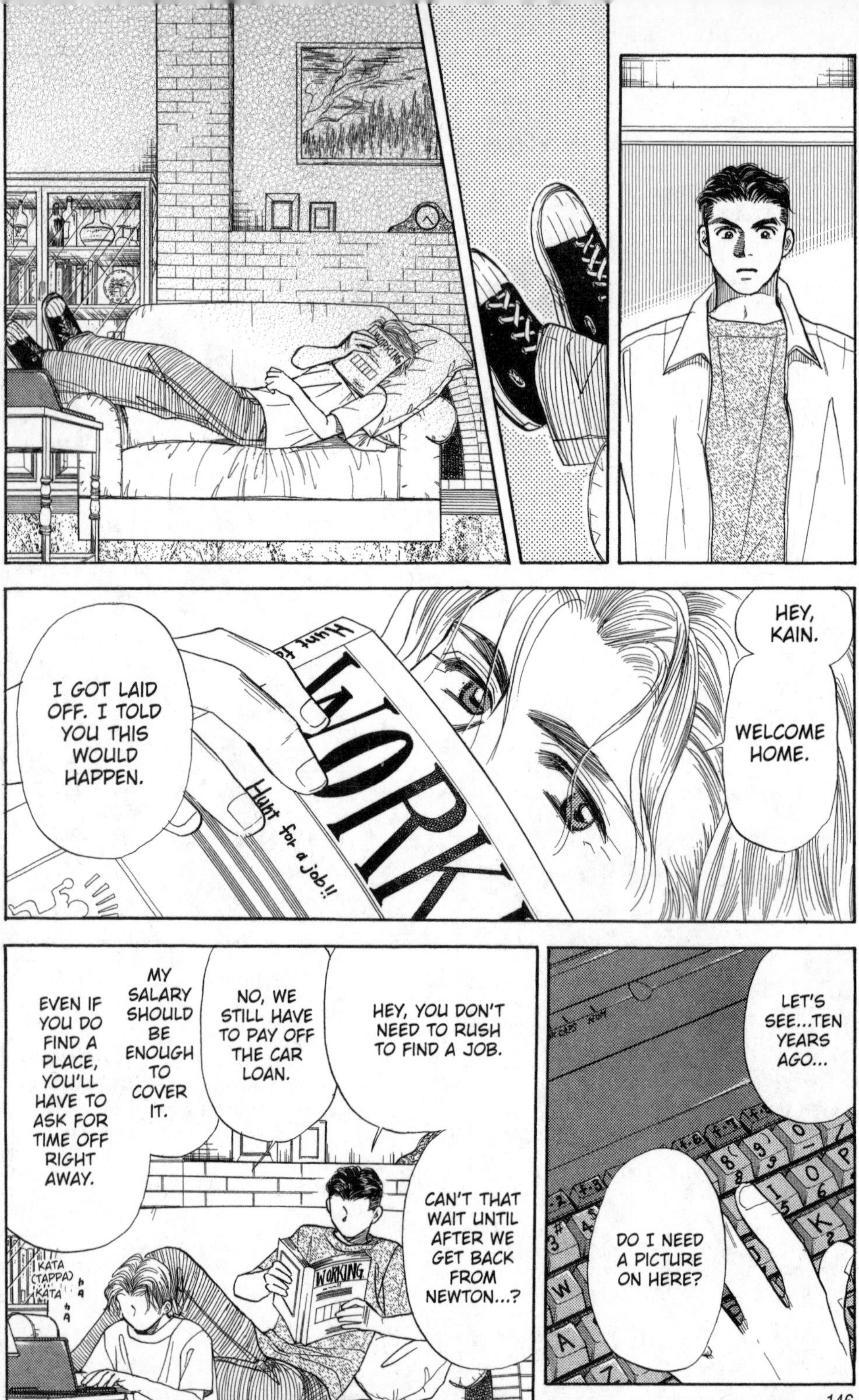
HEY, KAIN.
WELCOME HOME.
I GOT LAID OFF. I TOLD YOU THIS WOULD HAPPEN.
WORKING
Hunt for a job!!
LET'S SEE...TEN YEARS AGO...
DO I NEED A PICTURE ON HERE?
HEY, YOU DON'T NEED TO RUSH TO FIND A JOB.
NO, WE STILL HAVE TO PAY OFF THE CAR LOAN.
MY SALARY SHOULD BE ENOUGH TO COVER IT.
EVEN IF YOU DO FIND A PLACE, YOU'LL HAVE TO ASK FOR TIME OFF RIGHT AWAY.
CAN'T THAT WAIT UNTIL AFTER WE GET BACK FROM NEWTON...?
WORKING
KATA (TAPPA) KATA

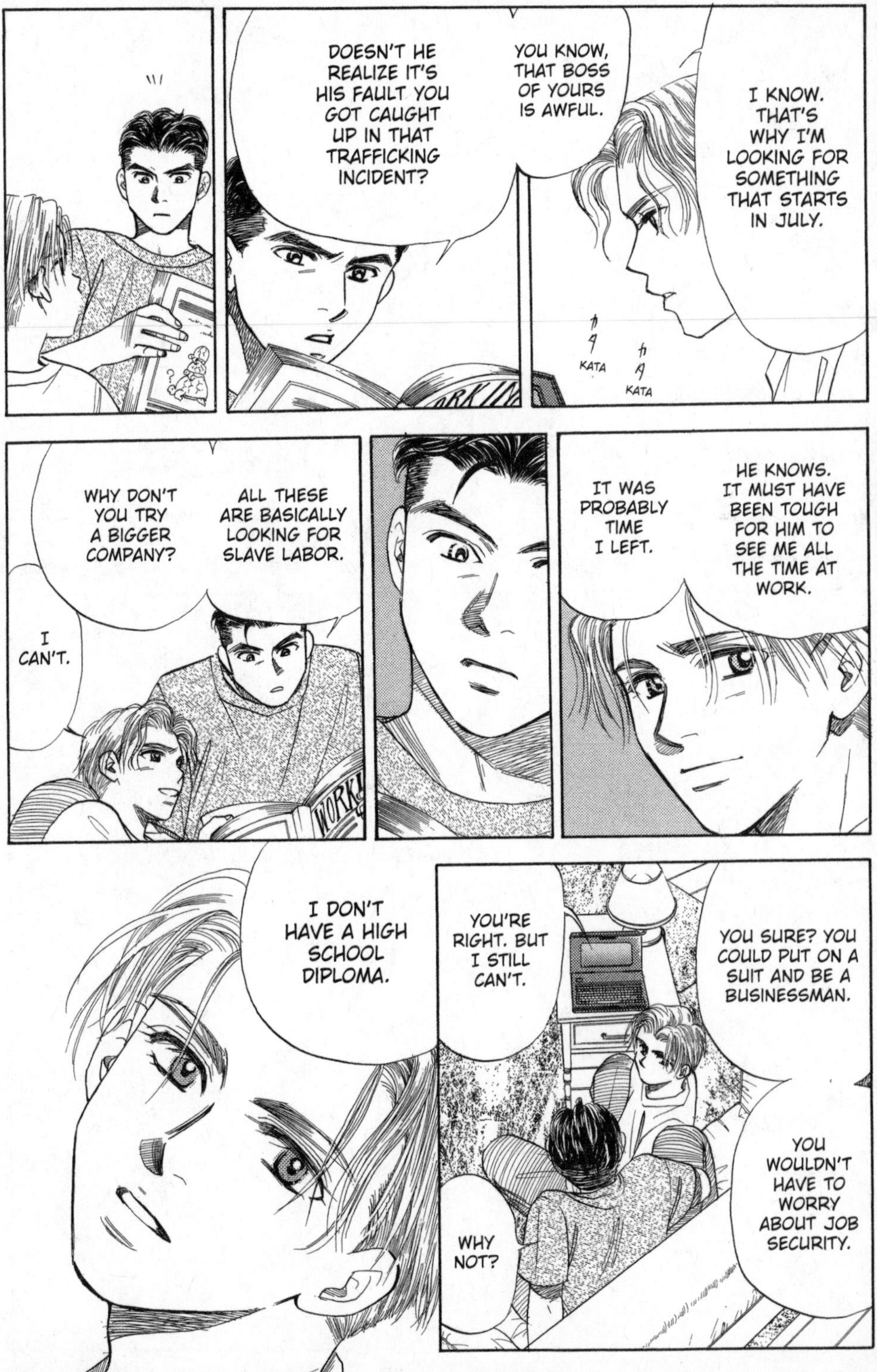
I KNOW. THAT'S WHY I'M LOOKING FOR SOMETHING THAT STARTS IN JULY.
カタ
KATA
カタ
KATA
YOU KNOW, THAT BOSS OF YOURS IS AWFUL.
DOESN'T HE REALIZE IT'S HIS FAULT YOU GOT CAUGHT UP IN THAT TRAFFICKING INCIDENT?
HE KNOWS. IT MUST HAVE BEEN TOUGH FOR HIM TO SEE ME ALL THE TIME AT WORK.
IT WAS PROBABLY TIME I LEFT.
ALL THESE ARE BASICALLY LOOKING FOR SLAVE LABOR.
WHY DON'T YOU TRY A BIGGER COMPANY?
I CAN'T.
YOU SURE? YOU COULD PUT ON A SUIT AND BE A BUSINESSMAN.
YOU'RE RIGHT. BUT I STILL CAN'T.
YOU WOULDN'T HAVE TO WORRY ABOUT JOB SECURITY.
WHY NOT?
I DON'T HAVE A HIGH SCHOOL DIPLOMA.

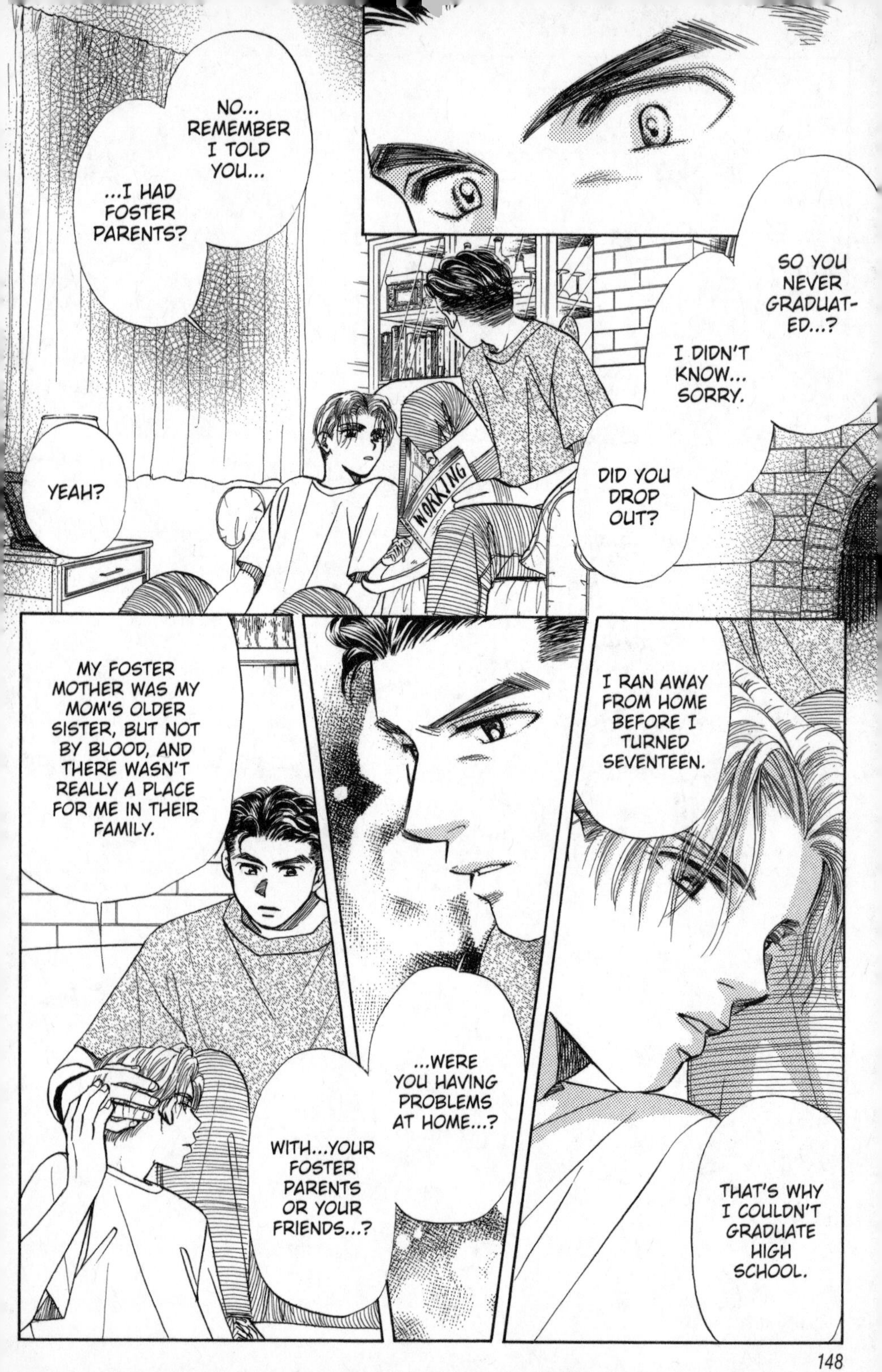
SO YOU NEVER GRADUAT-ED...?
I DIDN'T KNOW... SORRY.
DID YOU DROP OUT?
WORKING
NO... REMEMBER I TOLD YOU...
...I HAD FOSTER PARENTS?
YEAH?
I RAN AWAY FROM HOME BEFORE I TURNED SEVENTEEN.
THAT'S WHY I COULDN'T GRADUATE HIGH SCHOOL.
...WERE YOU HAVING PROBLEMS AT HOME...?
WITH...YOUR FOSTER PARENTS OR YOUR FRIENDS...?
MY FOSTER MOTHER WAS MY MOM'S OLDER SISTER, BUT NOT BY BLOOD, AND THERE WASN'T REALLY A PLACE FOR ME IN THEIR FAMILY.

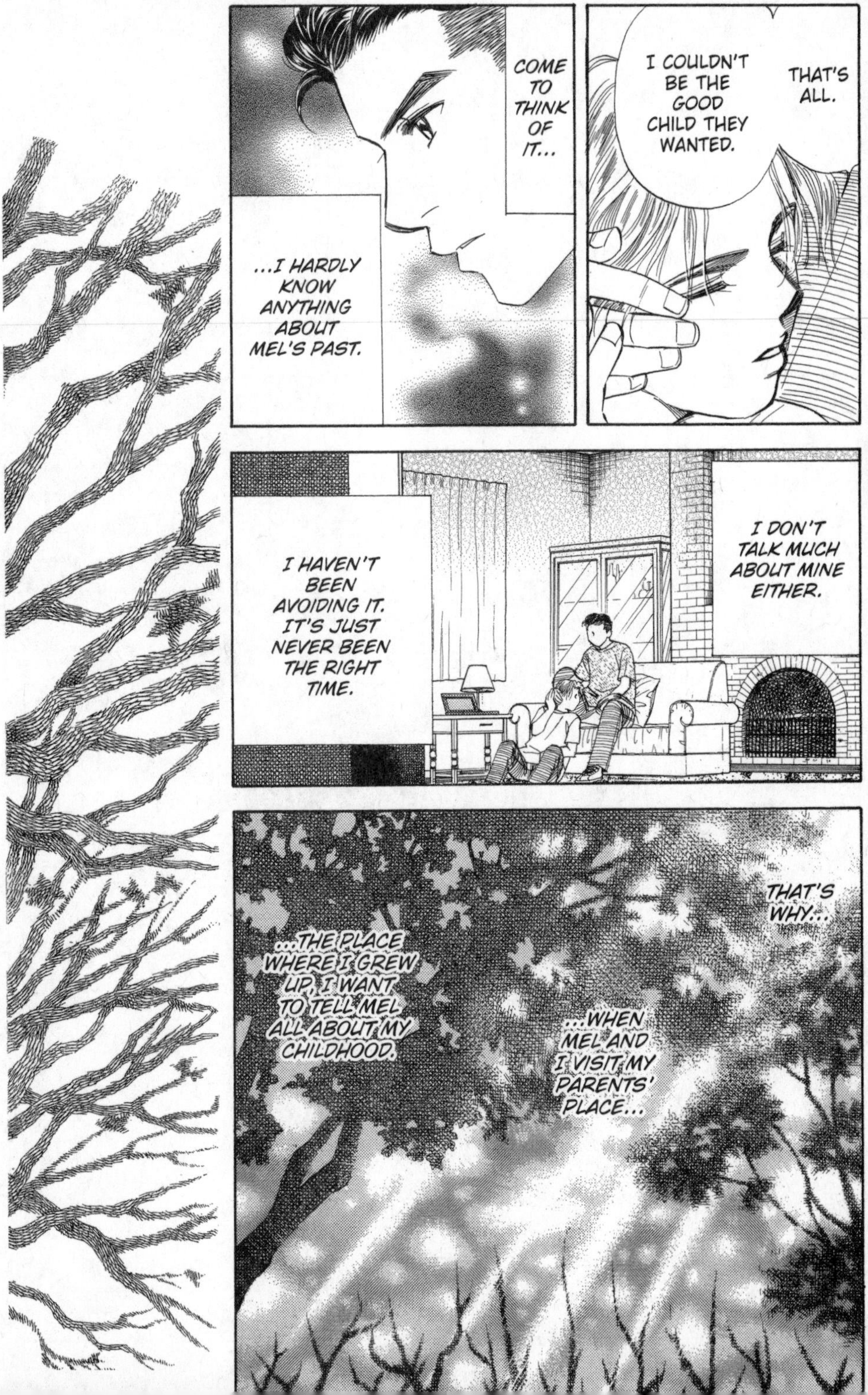
I COULDN'T BE THE GOOD CHILD THEY WANTED.
THAT'S ALL.
COME TO THINK OF IT...
...I HARDLY KNOW ANYTHING ABOUT MEL'S PAST.
I DON'T TALK MUCH ABOUT MINE EITHER.
I HAVEN'T BEEN AVOIDING IT. IT'S JUST NEVER BEEN THE RIGHT TIME.
THAT'S WHY...
...WHEN MEL AND I VISIT MY PARENTS' PLACE...
...THE PLACE WHERE I GREW UP, I WANT TO TELL MEL ALL ABOUT MY CHILDHOOD.

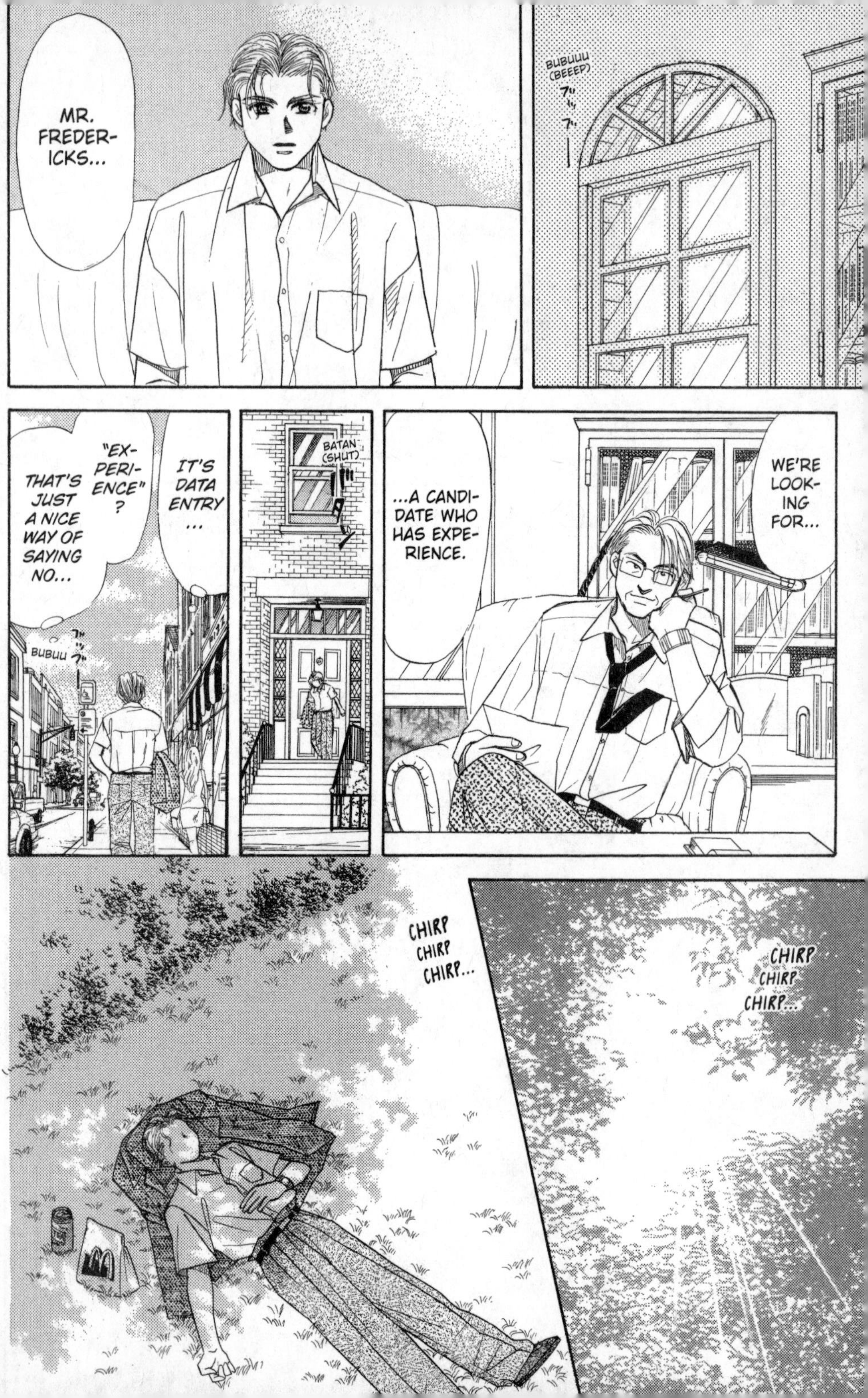
BUBUUU (BEEEP)
MR. FREDER-ICKS...
WE'RE LOOKING FOR...
...A CANDIDATE WHO HAS EXPERIENCE.
BATAN (SHUT)
IT'S DATA ENTRY...
"EXPERIENCE"?
THAT'S JUST A NICE WAY OF SAYING NO...
BUBUU
CHIRP CHIRP CHIRP...
CHIRP CHIRP CHIRP...

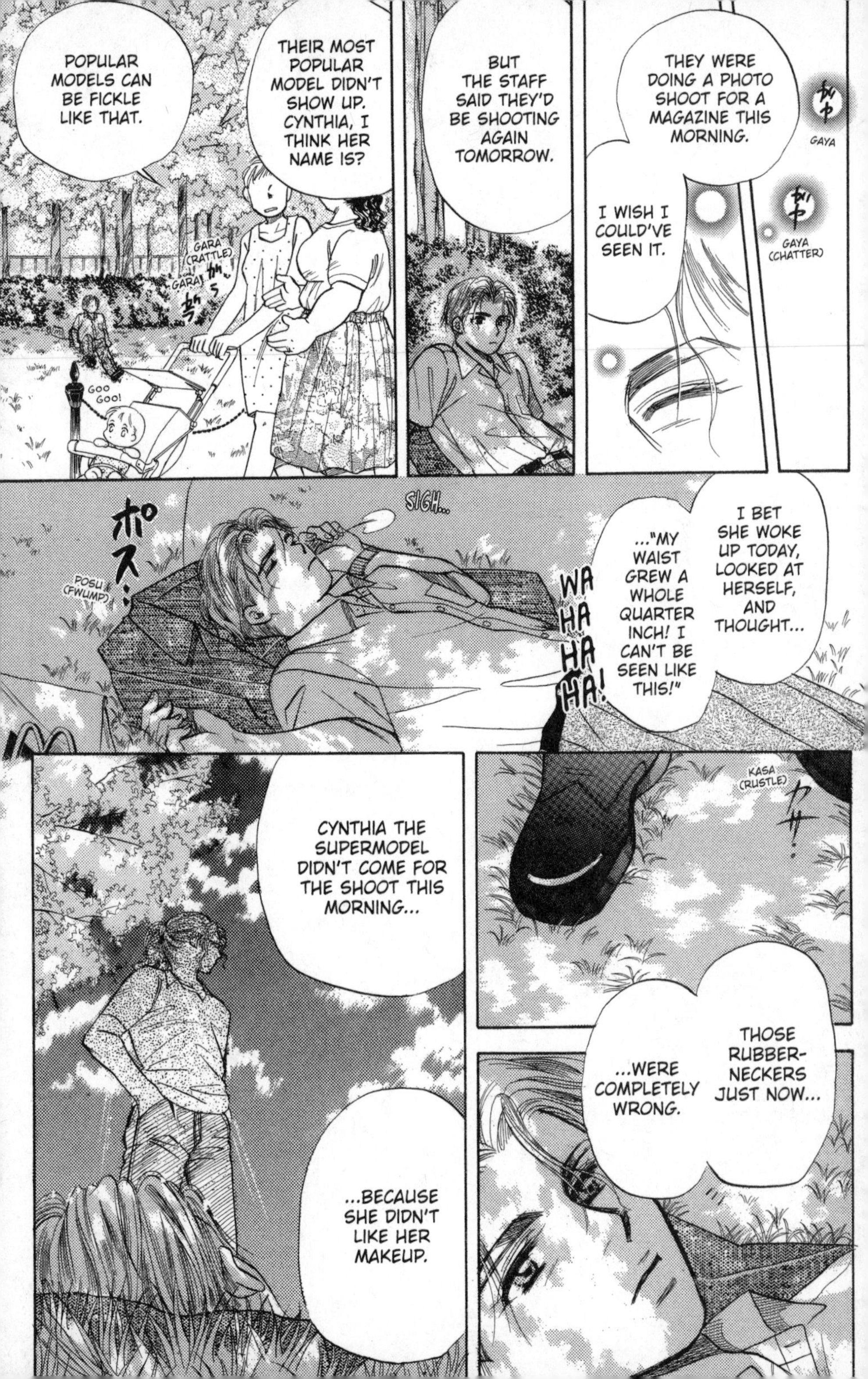
THEY WERE DOING A PHOTO SHOOT FOR A MAGAZINE THIS MORNING.
GAYA
GAYA (CHATTER)
I WISH I COULD'VE SEEN IT.
BUT THE STAFF SAID THEY'D BE SHOOTING AGAIN TOMORROW.
THEIR MOST POPULAR MODEL DIDN'T SHOW UP. CYNTHIA, I THINK HER NAME IS?
POPULAR MODELS CAN BE FICKLE LIKE THAT.
GARA (RATTLE)
GARA
GOO GOO!
I BET SHE WOKE UP TODAY, LOOKED AT HERSELF, AND THOUGHT...
..."MY WAIST GREW A WHOLE QUARTER INCH! I CAN'T BE SEEN LIKE THIS!"
WA HA HA HA!
SIGH...
POSU (FWUMP)
KASA (RUSTLE)
THOSE RUBBERNECKERS JUST NOW...
...WERE COMPLETELY WRONG.
CYNTHIA THE SUPERMODEL DIDN'T COME FOR THE SHOOT THIS MORNING...
...BECAUSE SHE DIDN'T LIKE HER MAKEUP.

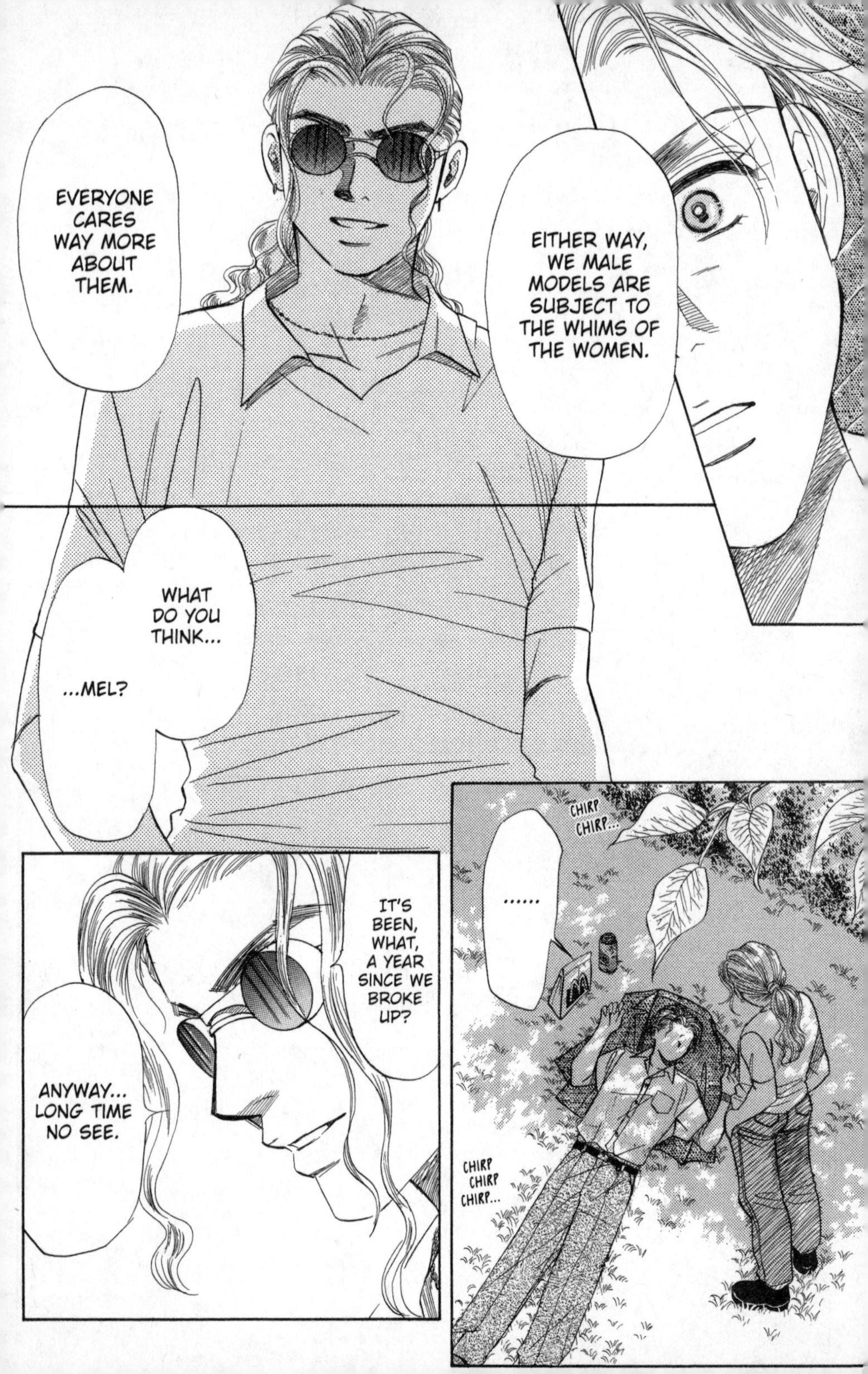
EITHER WAY, WE MALE MODELS ARE SUBJECT TO THE WHIMS OF THE WOMEN.
EVERYONE CARES WAY MORE ABOUT THEM.
WHAT DO YOU THINK...
...MEL?
CHIRP CHIRP...
......
CHIRP CHIRP CHIRP...
IT'S BEEN, WHAT, A YEAR SINCE WE BROKE UP?
ANYWAY... LONG TIME NO SEE.

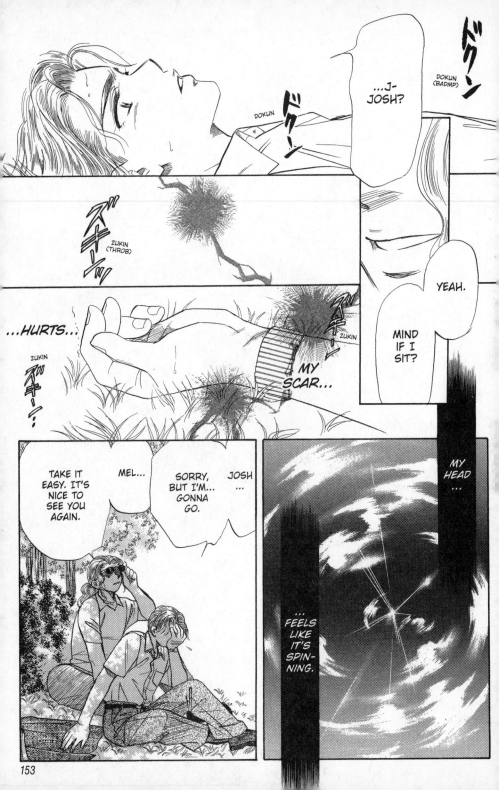

...J-
JOSH?

DOKUN

DOKUN
(BADMP)

DOKUN

ZUKIN
(THROB)

...HURTS...

ZUKIN

ZUKIN

ZUKIN

MY
SCAR...

YEAH.

MIND
IF I
SIT?

TAKE IT
EASY. IT'S
NICE TO
SEE YOU
AGAIN.

MEL...

SORRY,
BUT I'M...
GONNA
GO.

JOSH
...

MY
HEAD
...

...
FEELS
LIKE
IT'S
SPIN-
NING.

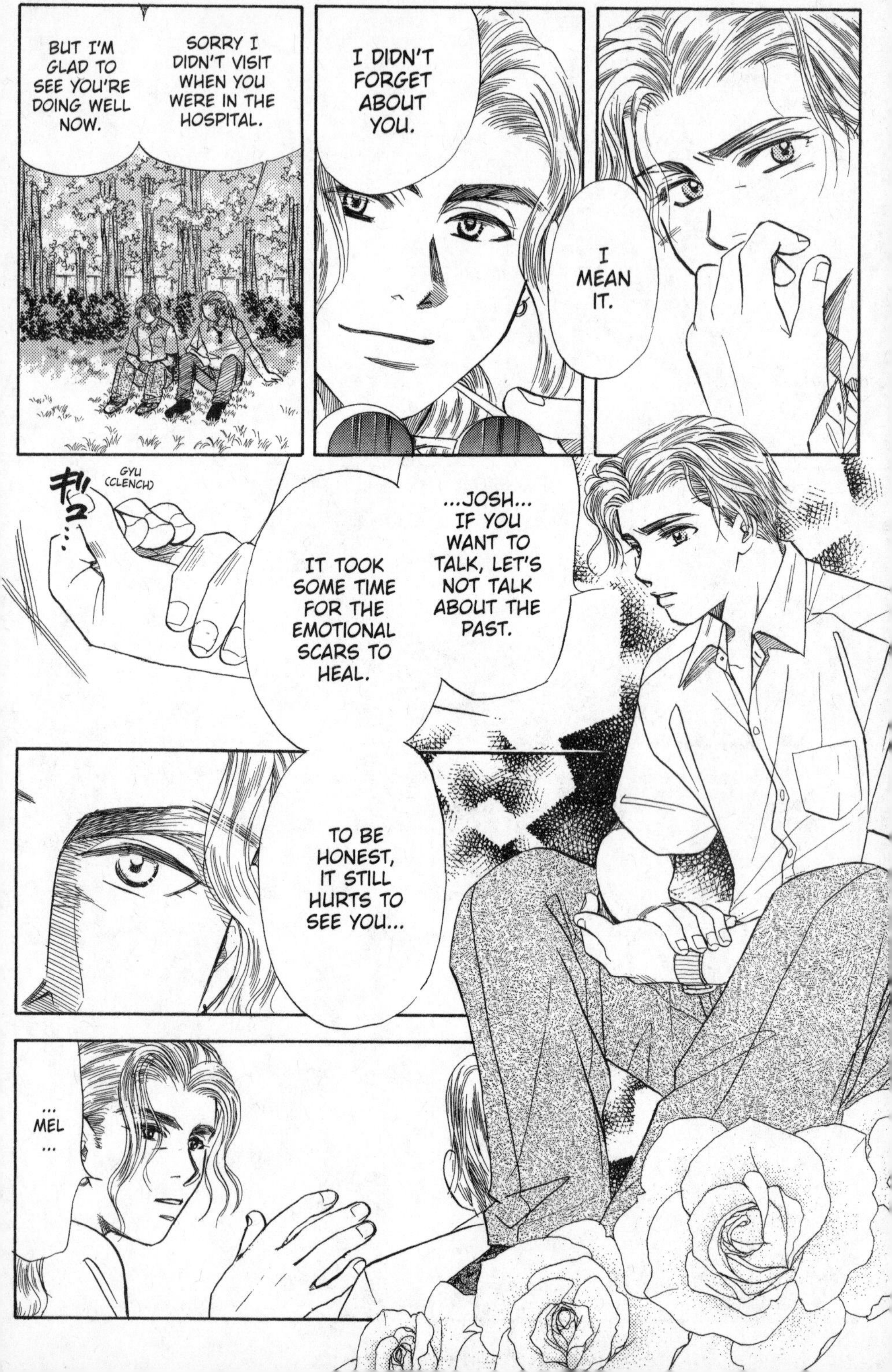
I MEAN IT.
I DIDN'T FORGET ABOUT YOU.
SORRY I DIDN'T VISIT WHEN YOU WERE IN THE HOSPITAL.
BUT I'M GLAD TO SEE YOU'RE DOING WELL NOW.
...JOSH... IF YOU WANT TO TALK, LET'S NOT TALK ABOUT THE PAST.
IT TOOK SOME TIME FOR THE EMOTIONAL SCARS TO HEAL.
GYU (CLENCH)
TO BE HONEST, IT STILL HURTS TO SEE YOU...
... MEL ...

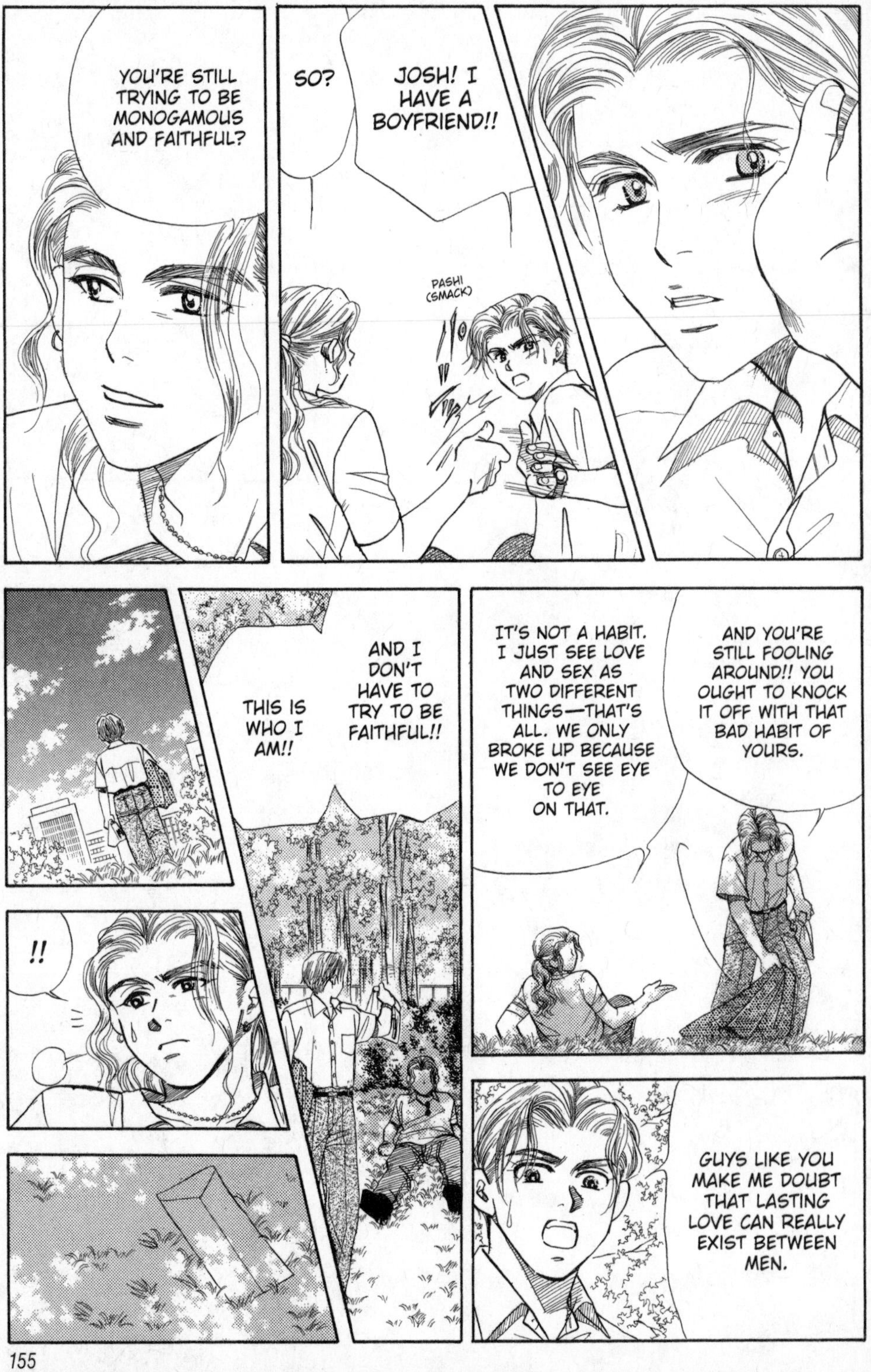
JOSH! I HAVE A BOYFRIEND!!
SO?
PASHI (SMACK)
YOU'RE STILL TRYING TO BE MONOGAMOUS AND FAITHFUL?
AND YOU'RE STILL FOOLING AROUND!! YOU OUGHT TO KNOCK IT OFF WITH THAT BAD HABIT OF YOURS.
IT'S NOT A HABIT. I JUST SEE LOVE AND SEX AS TWO DIFFERENT THINGS—THAT'S ALL. WE ONLY BROKE UP BECAUSE WE DON'T SEE EYE TO EYE ON THAT.
GUYS LIKE YOU MAKE ME DOUBT THAT LASTING LOVE CAN REALLY EXIST BETWEEN MEN.
AND I DON'T HAVE TO TRY TO BE FAITHFUL!!
THIS IS WHO I AM!!
!!

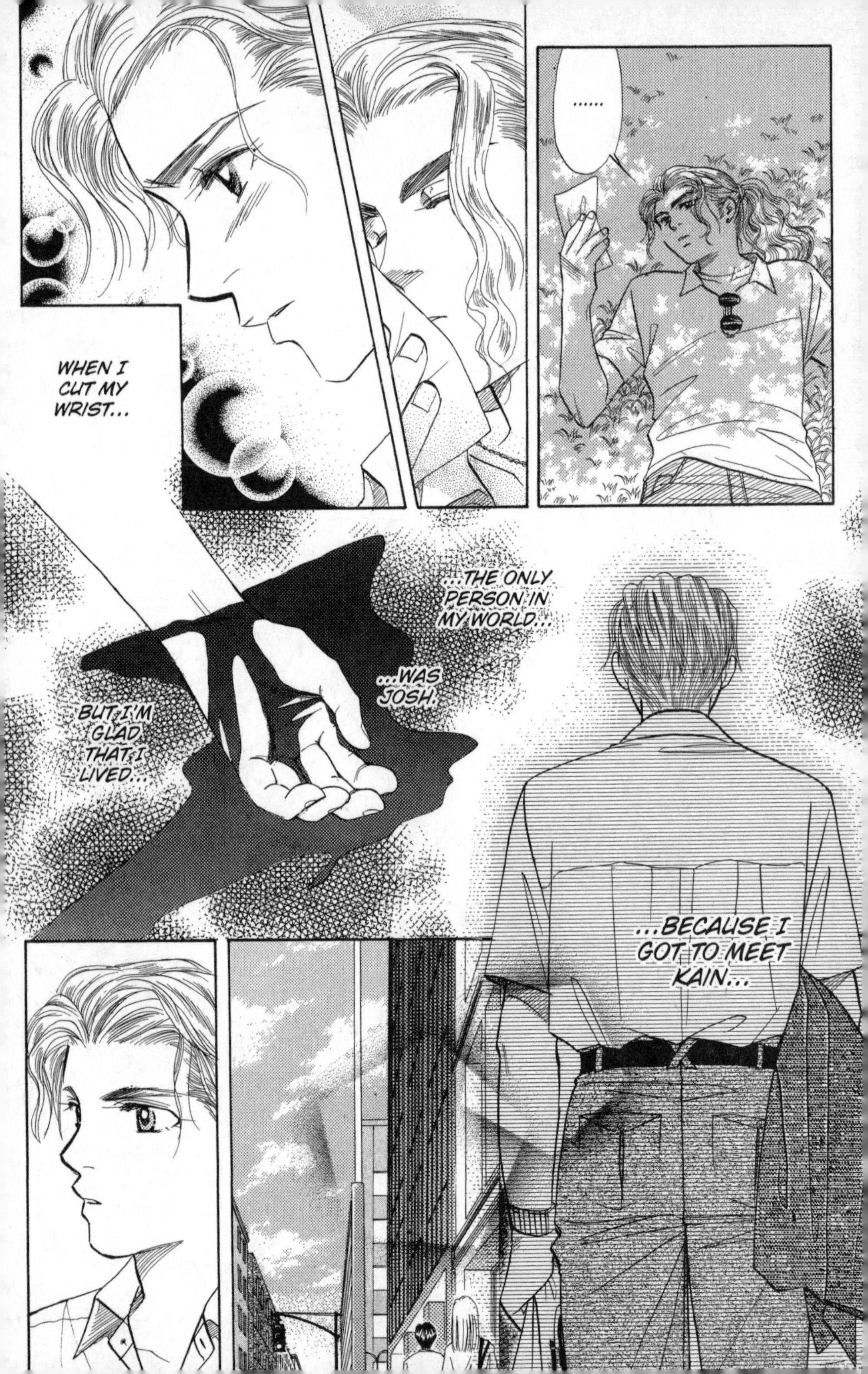
......
WHEN I CUT MY WRIST...
...THE ONLY PERSON IN MY WORLD...
...WAS JOSH.
BUT I'M GLAD THAT I LIVED...
...BECAUSE I GOT TO MEET KAIN...

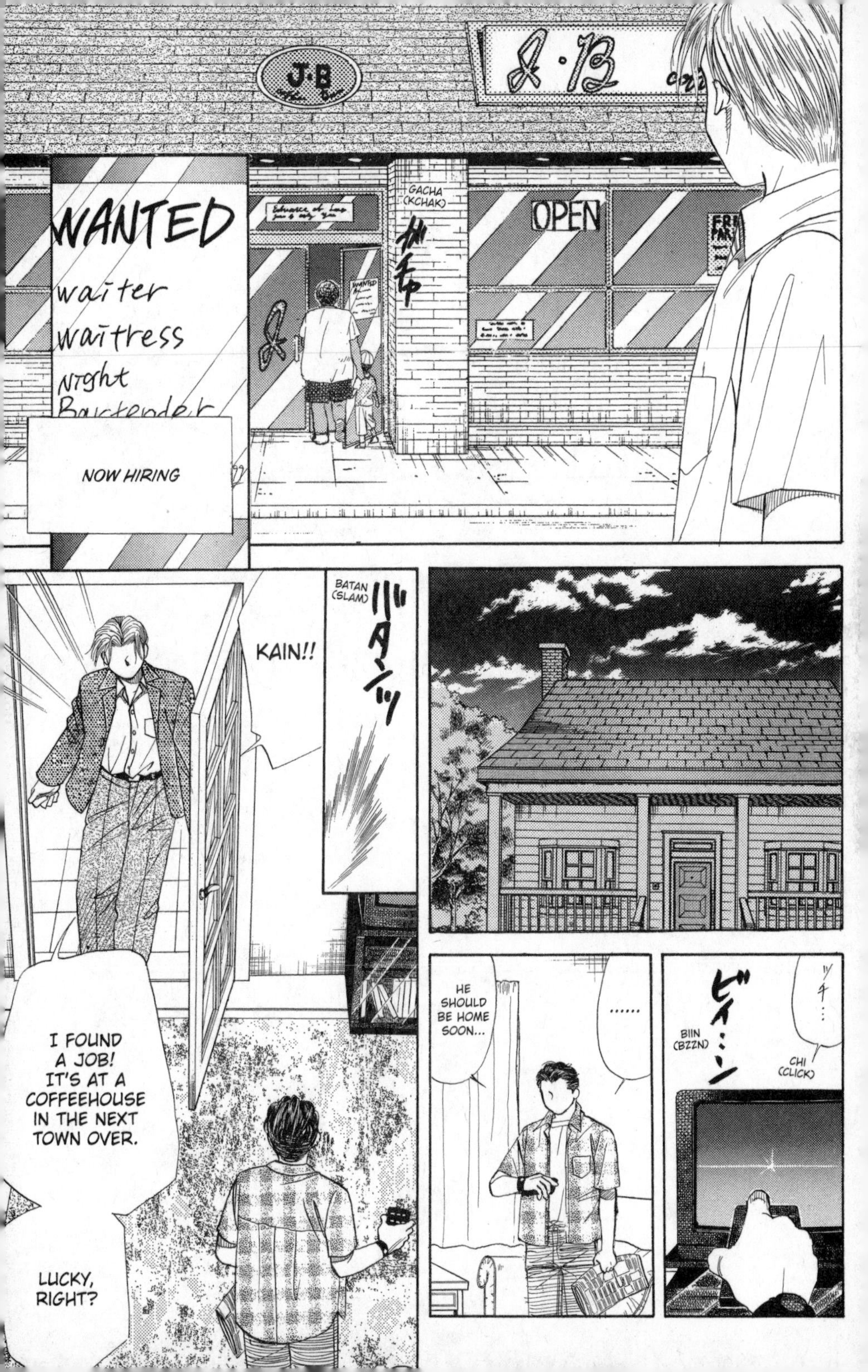
J·B
WANTED
waiter
waitress
Night
Bartender
NOW HIRING
GACHA (KCHAK)
ガチャ
OPEN
BIIN (BZZN)
ビイ～ン
ッチ…
CHI (CLICK)
HE SHOULD BE HOME SOON...
......
BATAN (SLAM)
バタンッ
KAIN!!
I FOUND A JOB! IT'S AT A COFFEEHOUSE IN THE NEXT TOWN OVER.
LUCKY, RIGHT?

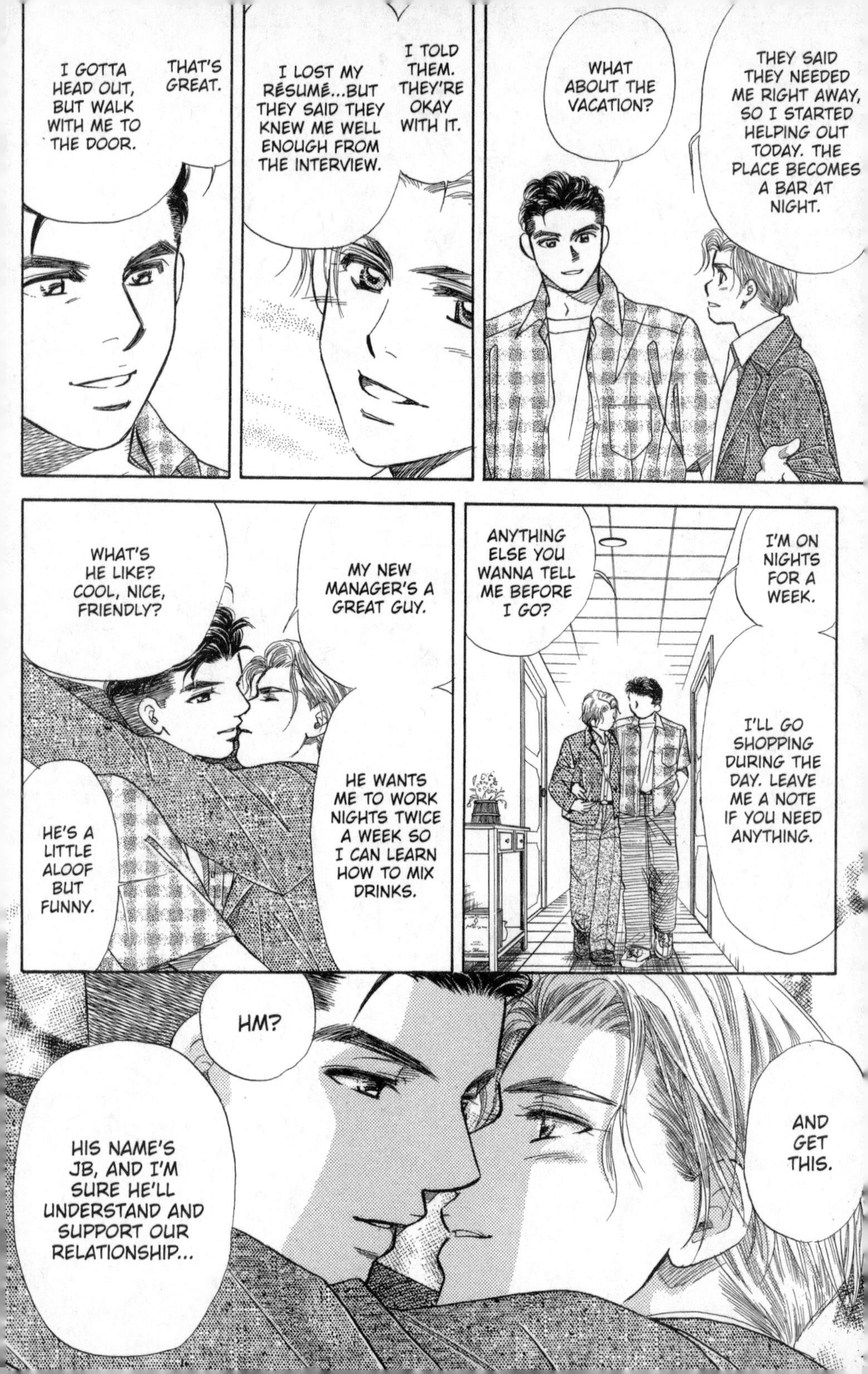
THEY SAID THEY NEEDED ME RIGHT AWAY, SO I STARTED HELPING OUT TODAY. THE PLACE BECOMES A BAR AT NIGHT.
WHAT ABOUT THE VACATION?
I TOLD THEM. THEY'RE OKAY WITH IT.
I LOST MY RÉSUMÉ...BUT THEY SAID THEY KNEW ME WELL ENOUGH FROM THE INTERVIEW.
THAT'S GREAT.
I GOTTA HEAD OUT, BUT WALK WITH ME TO THE DOOR.
I'M ON NIGHTS FOR A WEEK.
I'LL GO SHOPPING DURING THE DAY. LEAVE ME A NOTE IF YOU NEED ANYTHING.
ANYTHING ELSE YOU WANNA TELL ME BEFORE I GO?
MY NEW MANAGER'S A GREAT GUY.
WHAT'S HE LIKE? COOL, NICE, FRIENDLY?
HE WANTS ME TO WORK NIGHTS TWICE A WEEK SO I CAN LEARN HOW TO MIX DRINKS.
HE'S A LITTLE ALOOF BUT FUNNY.
AND GET THIS.
HM?
HIS NAME'S JB, AND I'M SURE HE'LL UNDERSTAND AND SUPPORT OUR RELATIONSHIP...

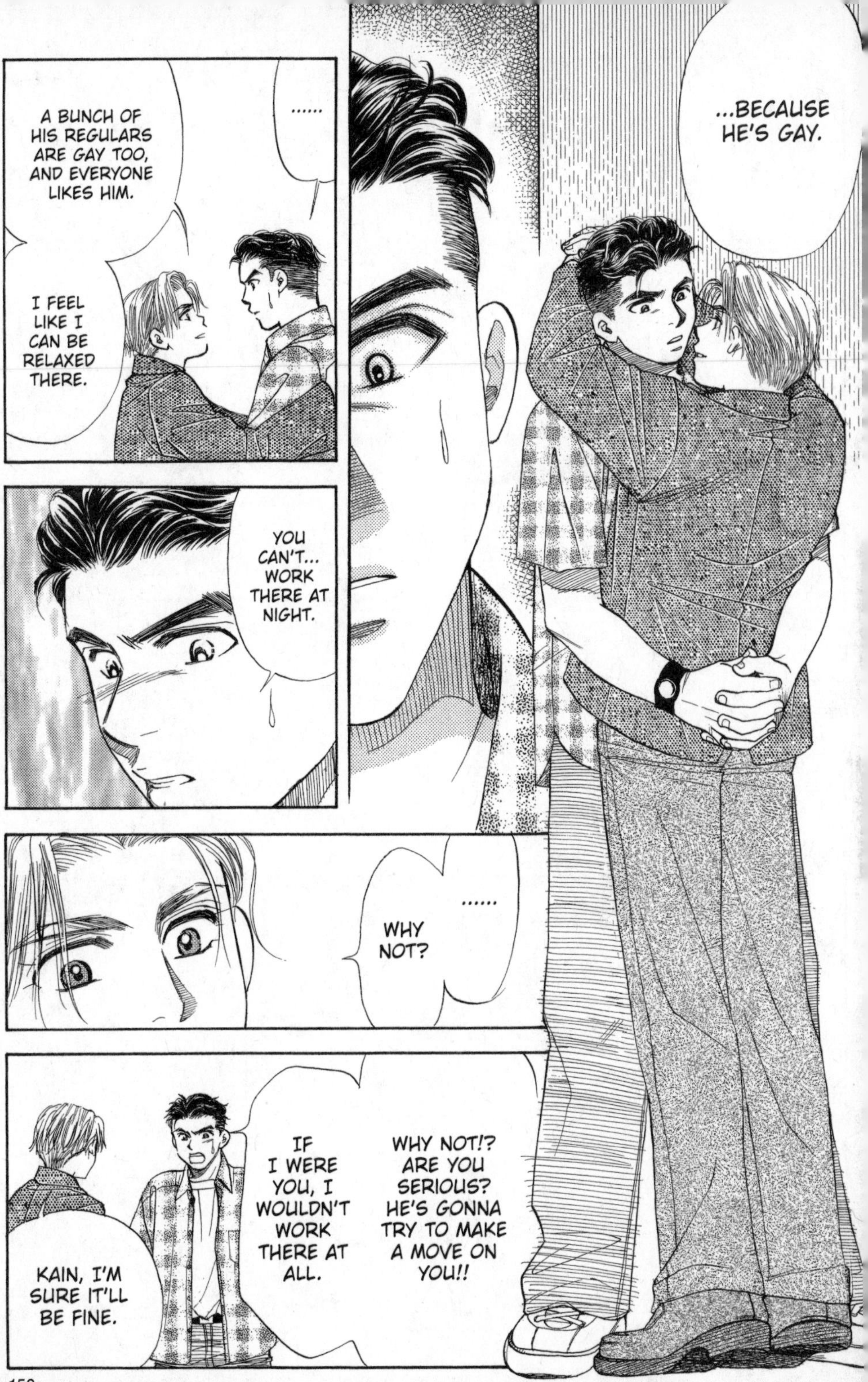
...BECAUSE HE'S GAY.
......
A BUNCH OF HIS REGULARS ARE GAY TOO, AND EVERYONE LIKES HIM.
I FEEL LIKE I CAN BE RELAXED THERE.
YOU CAN'T... WORK THERE AT NIGHT.
......
WHY NOT?
WHY NOT!? ARE YOU SERIOUS? HE'S GONNA TRY TO MAKE A MOVE ON YOU!!
IF I WERE YOU, I WOULDN'T WORK THERE AT ALL.
KAIN, I'M SURE IT'LL BE FINE.

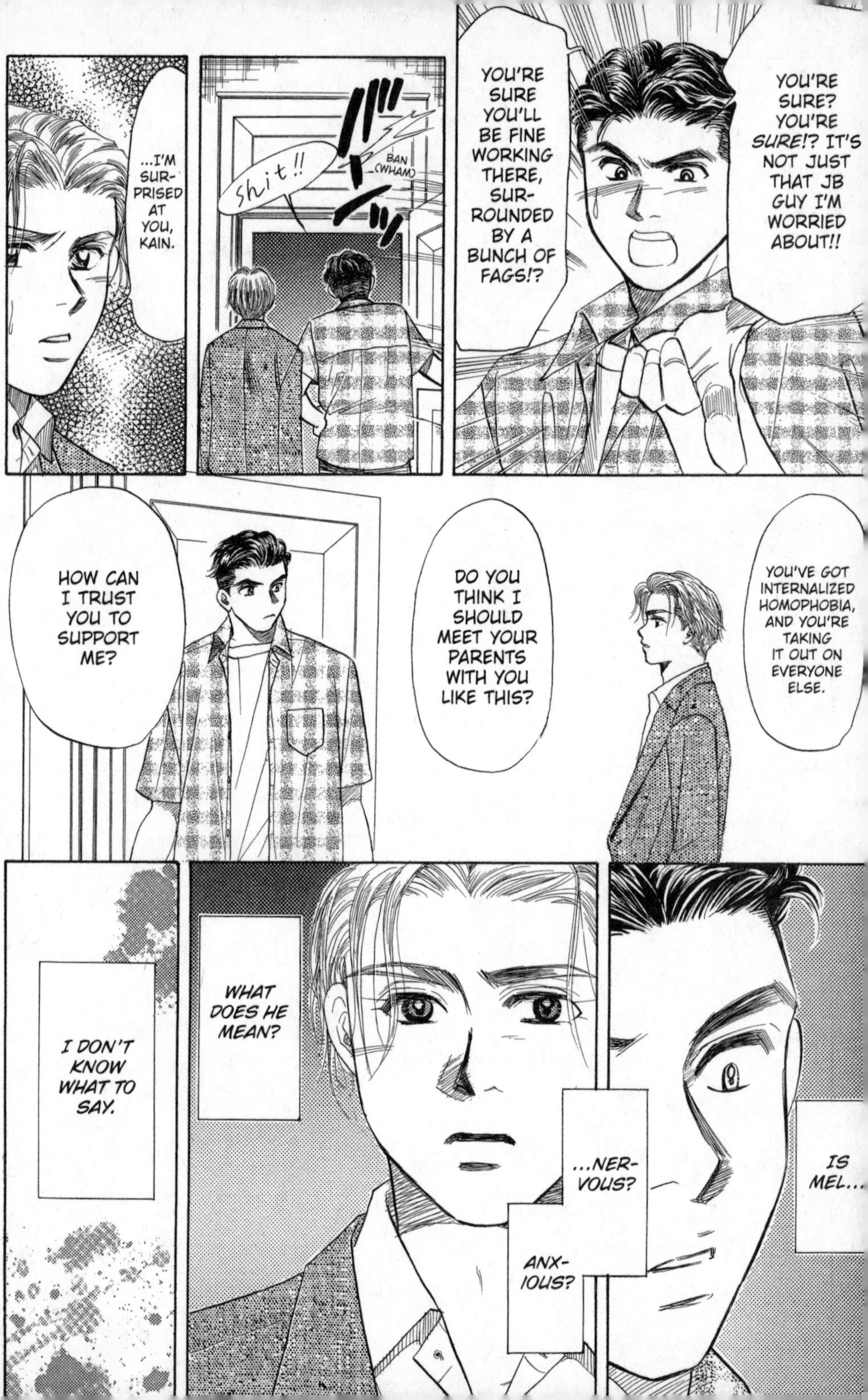
YOU'RE SURE? YOU'RE SURE!? IT'S NOT JUST THAT JB GUY I'M WORRIED ABOUT!!
YOU'RE SURE YOU'LL BE FINE WORKING THERE, SURROUNDED BY A BUNCH OF FAGS!?
BAN (WHAM)
Shit!!
...I'M SURPRISED AT YOU, KAIN.
YOU'VE GOT INTERNALIZED HOMOPHOBIA, AND YOU'RE TAKING IT OUT ON EVERYONE ELSE.
DO YOU THINK I SHOULD MEET YOUR PARENTS WITH YOU LIKE THIS?
HOW CAN I TRUST YOU TO SUPPORT ME?
IS MEL...
...NERVOUS?
ANXIOUS?
WHAT DOES HE MEAN?
I DON'T KNOW WHAT TO SAY.

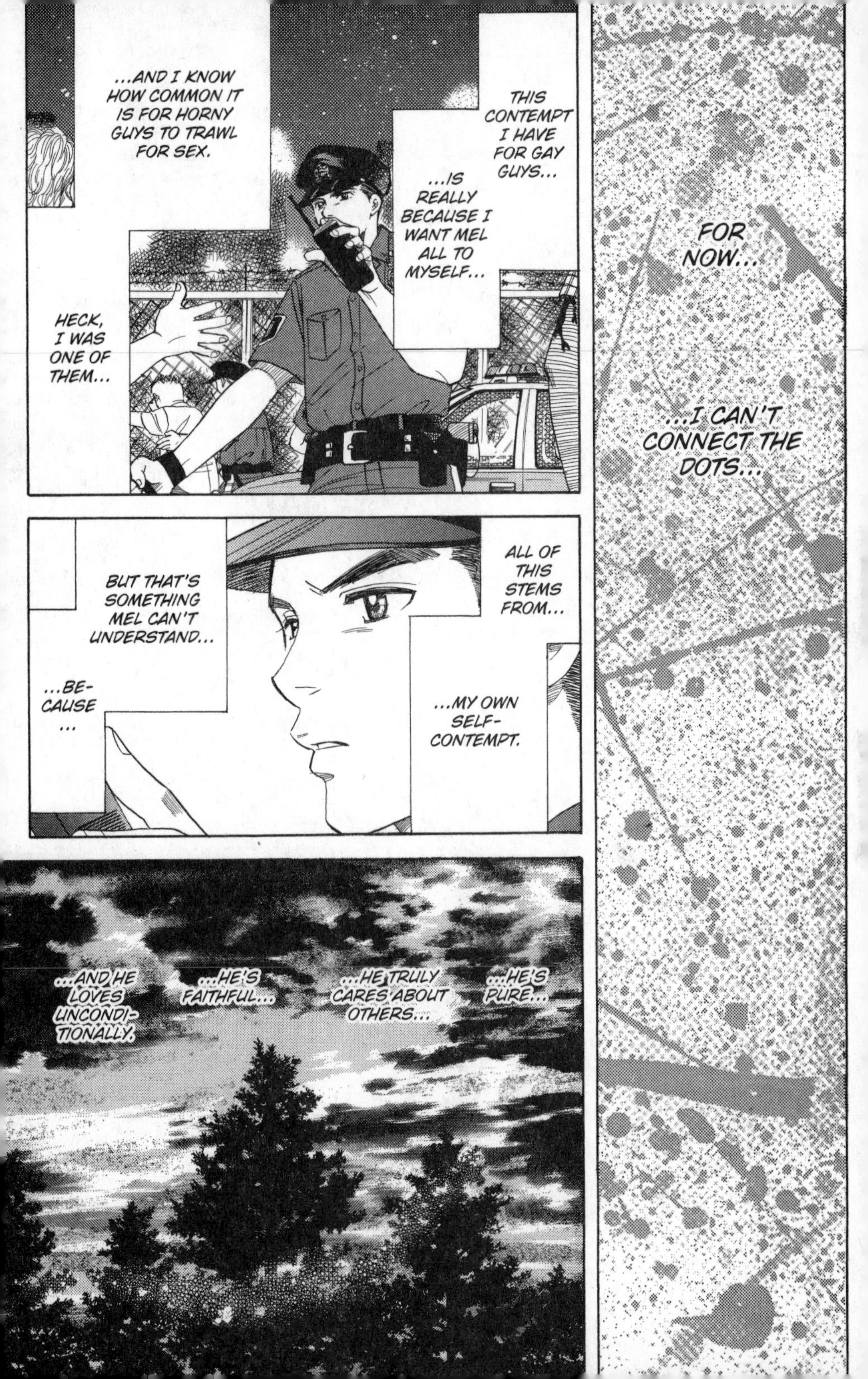
FOR NOW...
...I CAN'T CONNECT THE DOTS...
THIS CONTEMPT I HAVE FOR GAY GUYS...
...IS REALLY BECAUSE I WANT MEL ALL TO MYSELF...
...AND I KNOW HOW COMMON IT IS FOR HORNY GUYS TO TRAWL FOR SEX.
HECK, I WAS ONE OF THEM...
ALL OF THIS STEMS FROM...
...MY OWN SELF-CONTEMPT.
BUT THAT'S SOMETHING MEL CAN'T UNDERSTAND...
...BE-CAUSE...
...HE'S PURE...
...HE TRULY CARES ABOUT OTHERS...
...HE'S FAITHFUL...
...AND HE LOVES UNCONDI-TIONALLY.

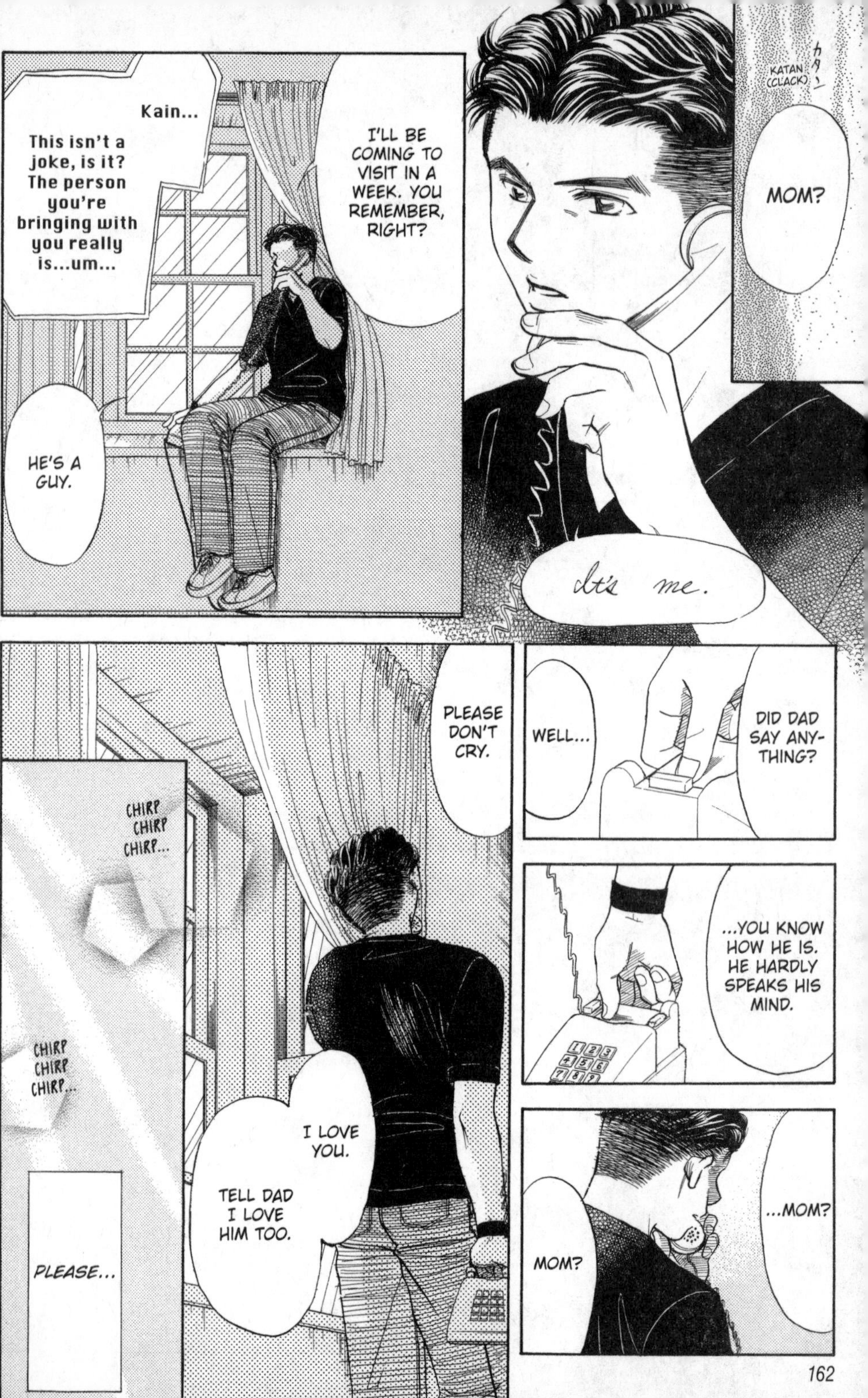
カタン
KATAN (CLACK)
MOM?
It's me.
I'LL BE COMING TO VISIT IN A WEEK. YOU REMEMBER, RIGHT?
Kain...
This isn't a joke, is it? The person you're bringing with you really is...um...
HE'S A GUY.
DID DAD SAY ANYTHING?
WELL...
...YOU KNOW HOW HE IS. HE HARDLY SPEAKS HIS MIND.
...MOM?
MOM?
PLEASE DON'T CRY.
CHIRP CHIRP CHIRP...
I LOVE YOU.
TELL DAD I LOVE HIM TOO.
CHIRP CHIRP CHIRP...
PLEASE...

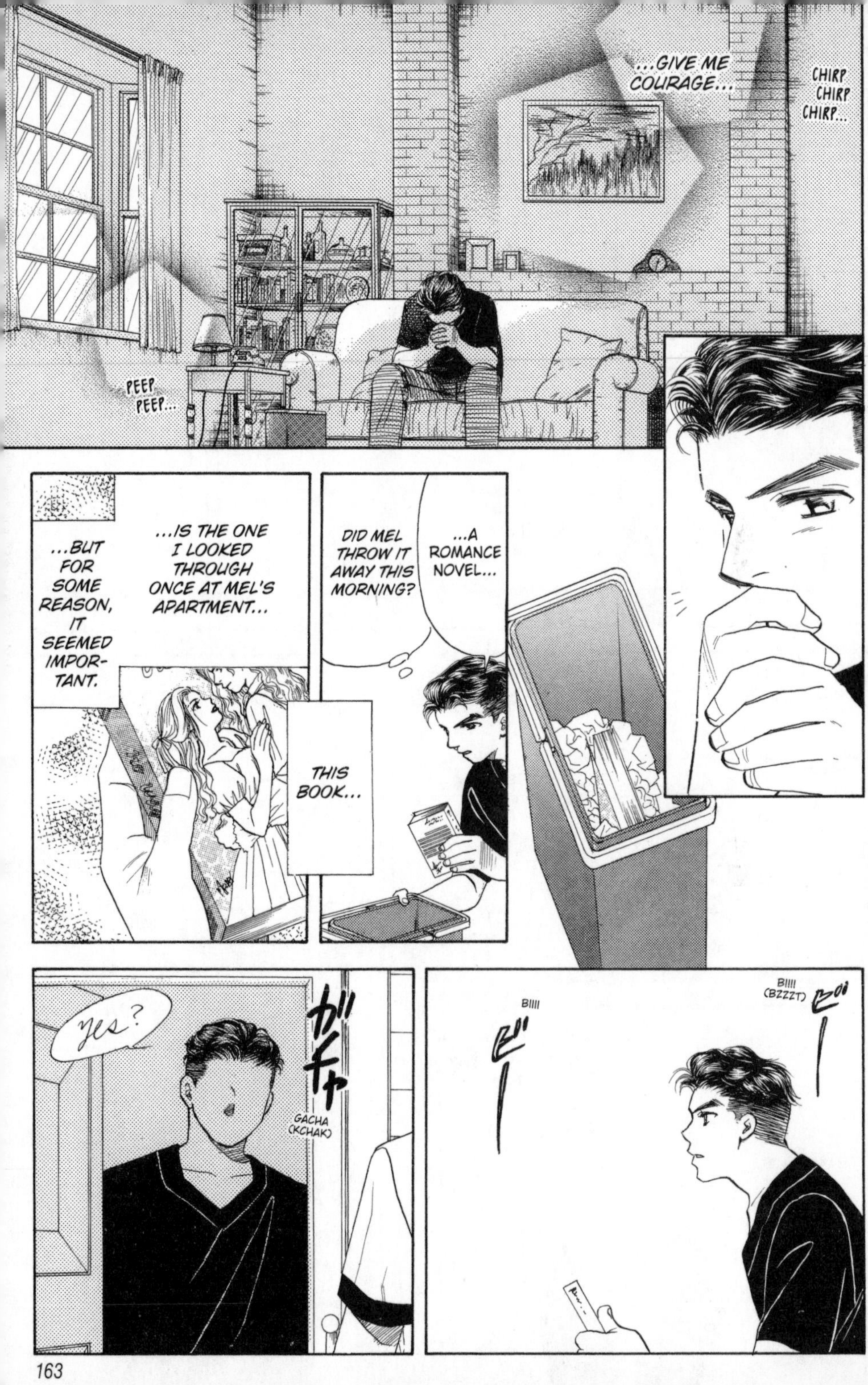
...GIVE ME COURAGE...
CHIRP CHIRP CHIRP...
PEEP PEEP...
...A ROMANCE NOVEL...
DID MEL THROW IT AWAY THIS MORNING?
THIS BOOK...
...IS THE ONE I LOOKED THROUGH ONCE AT MEL'S APARTMENT...
...BUT FOR SOME REASON, IT SEEMED IMPORTANT.
BIIII (BZZZT)
BIIII
GACHA (KCHAK)
Yes?

OH...

SORRY, I LOOKED INSIDE.

I BELIEVE THIS BELONGS TO MR. FREDER- ICKS.

HI!!

THAT'S HOW I GOT THIS ADDRESS.

WELL...

THANK YOU.

YOU'RE BEING KINDA WEIRD.

SORRY, BUT I'M GONNA HAVE TO ASK YOU TO LEAVE.

OH...

TOO FOR- WARD?

IT'S NICE TO MEET YOU!!

MY NAME'S JOSHUA BRONSON...

...BUT YOU CAN CALL ME JOSH.

NO PROBLEM.

I JUST WANTED TO SEE WHAT KIND OF GUY MEL'S NEW LOVER IS, THAT'S ALL.

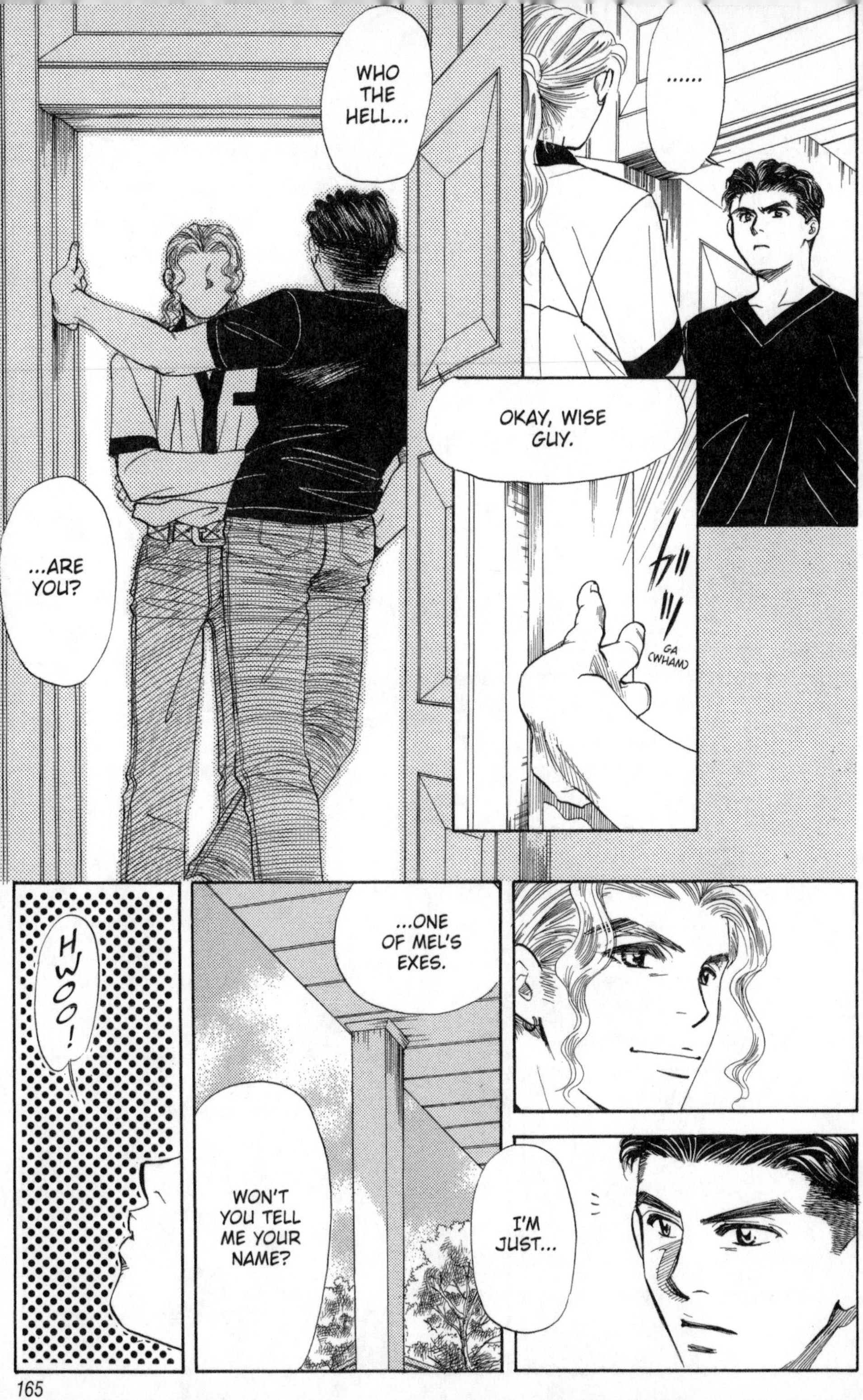
......
OKAY, WISE GUY.
GA (WHAM)
WHO THE HELL...
...ARE YOU?
I'M JUST...
...ONE OF MEL'S EXES.
WON'T YOU TELL ME YOUR NAME?
HWOO!

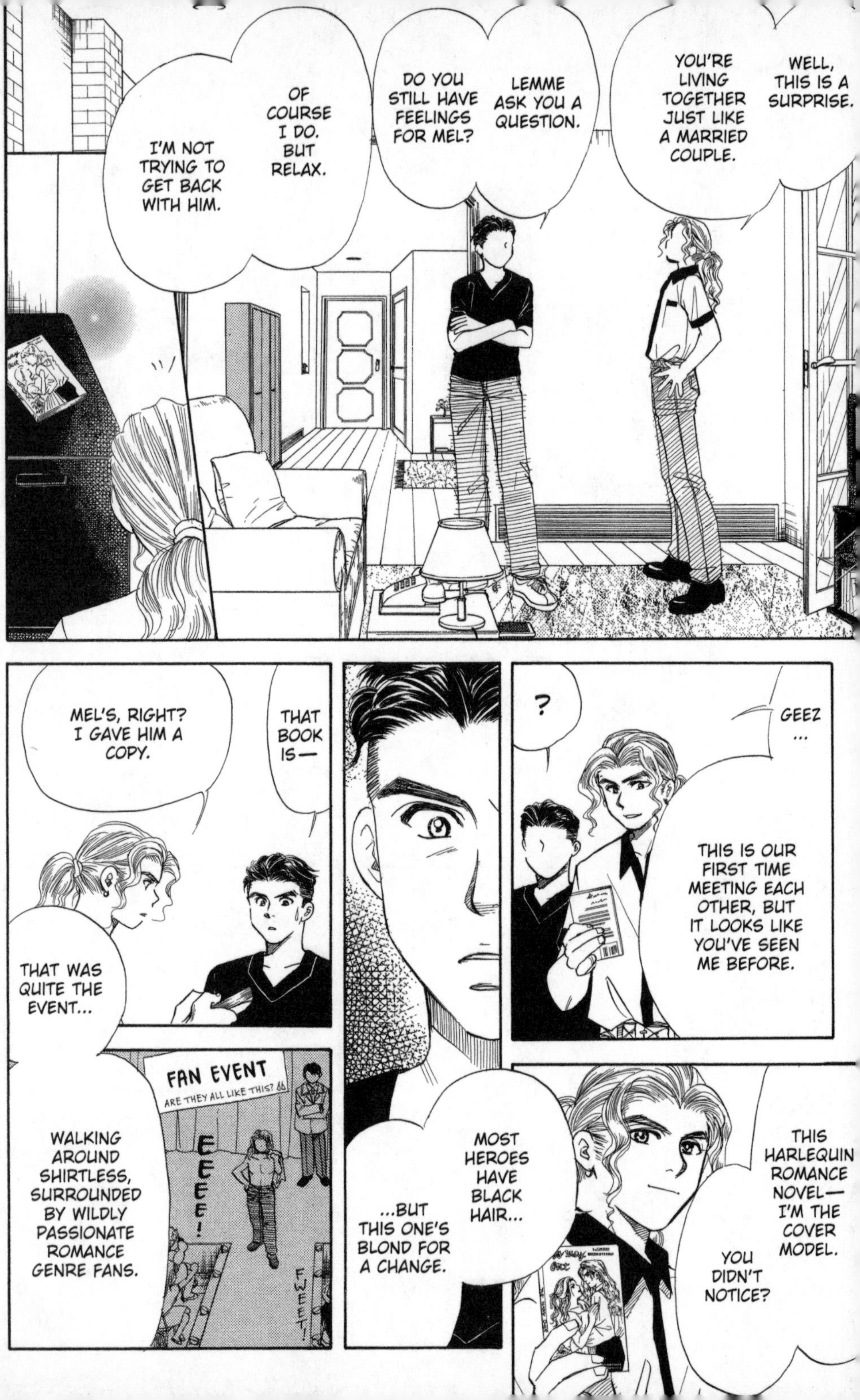
WELL, THIS IS A SURPRISE.
YOU'RE LIVING TOGETHER JUST LIKE A MARRIED COUPLE.
LEMME ASK YOU A QUESTION.
DO YOU STILL HAVE FEELINGS FOR MEL?
OF COURSE I DO. BUT RELAX.
I'M NOT TRYING TO GET BACK WITH HIM.
GEEZ ...
?
THIS IS OUR FIRST TIME MEETING EACH OTHER, BUT IT LOOKS LIKE YOU'VE SEEN ME BEFORE.
THIS HARLEQUIN ROMANCE NOVEL— I'M THE COVER MODEL.
YOU DIDN'T NOTICE?
MOST HEROES HAVE BLACK HAIR...
...BUT THIS ONE'S BLOND FOR A CHANGE.
THAT BOOK IS—
MEL'S, RIGHT? I GAVE HIM A COPY.
THAT WAS QUITE THE EVENT...
FAN EVENT
ARE THEY ALL LIKE THIS?
EEEE!
FWEET!
WALKING AROUND SHIRTLESS, SURROUNDED BY WILDLY PASSIONATE ROMANCE GENRE FANS.

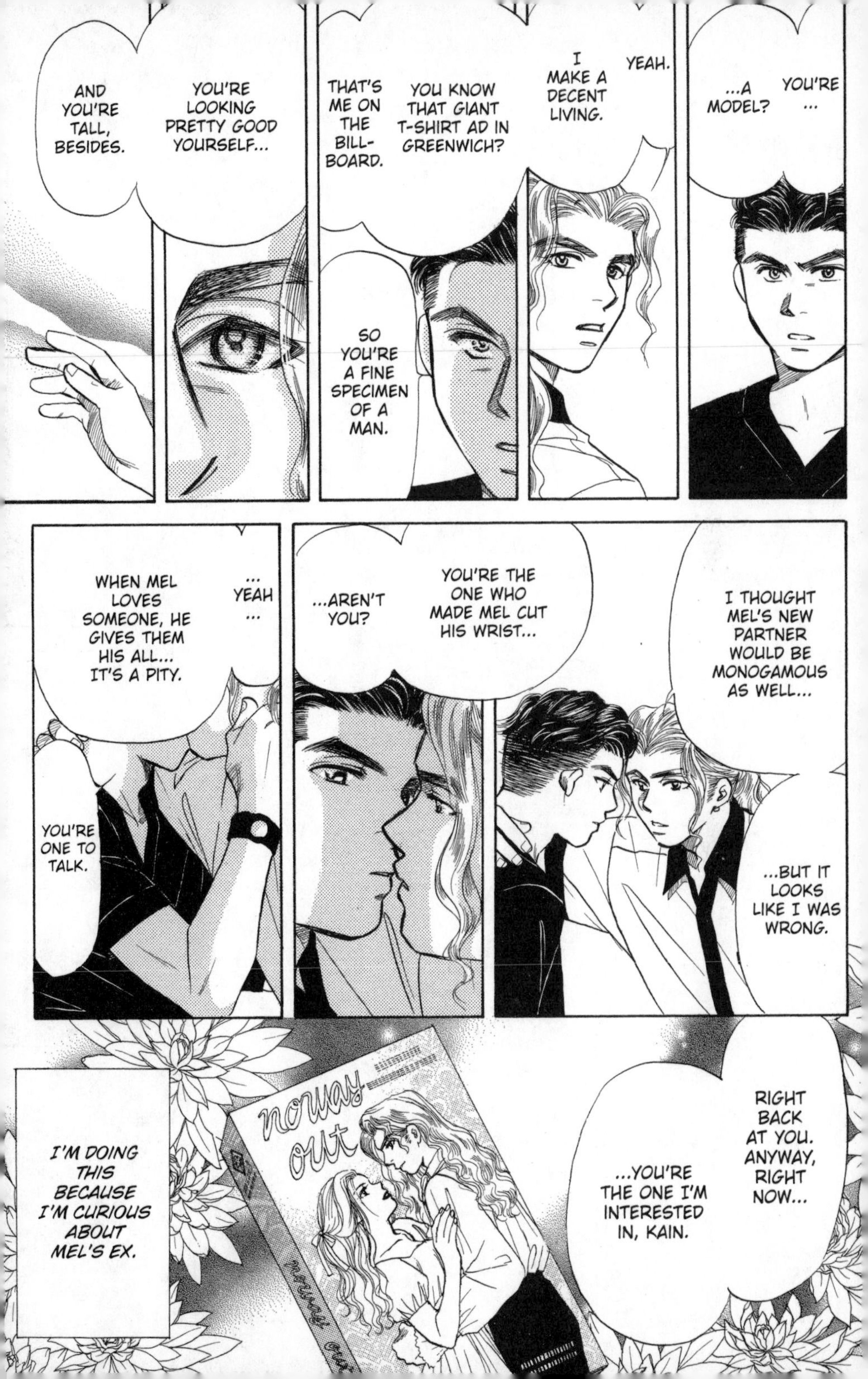
YOU'RE ...
...A MODEL?
YEAH.
I MAKE A DECENT LIVING.
YOU KNOW THAT GIANT T-SHIRT AD IN GREENWICH?
THAT'S ME ON THE BILL-BOARD.
SO YOU'RE A FINE SPECIMEN OF A MAN.
YOU'RE LOOKING PRETTY GOOD YOURSELF...
AND YOU'RE TALL, BESIDES.
I THOUGHT MEL'S NEW PARTNER WOULD BE MONOGAMOUS AS WELL...
...BUT IT LOOKS LIKE I WAS WRONG.
YOU'RE THE ONE WHO MADE MEL CUT HIS WRIST...
...AREN'T YOU?
... YEAH ...
WHEN MEL LOVES SOMEONE, HE GIVES THEM HIS ALL... IT'S A PITY.
YOU'RE ONE TO TALK.
RIGHT BACK AT YOU. ANYWAY, RIGHT NOW...
...YOU'RE THE ONE I'M INTERESTED IN, KAIN.
norway out
I'M DOING THIS BECAUSE I'M CURIOUS ABOUT MEL'S EX.

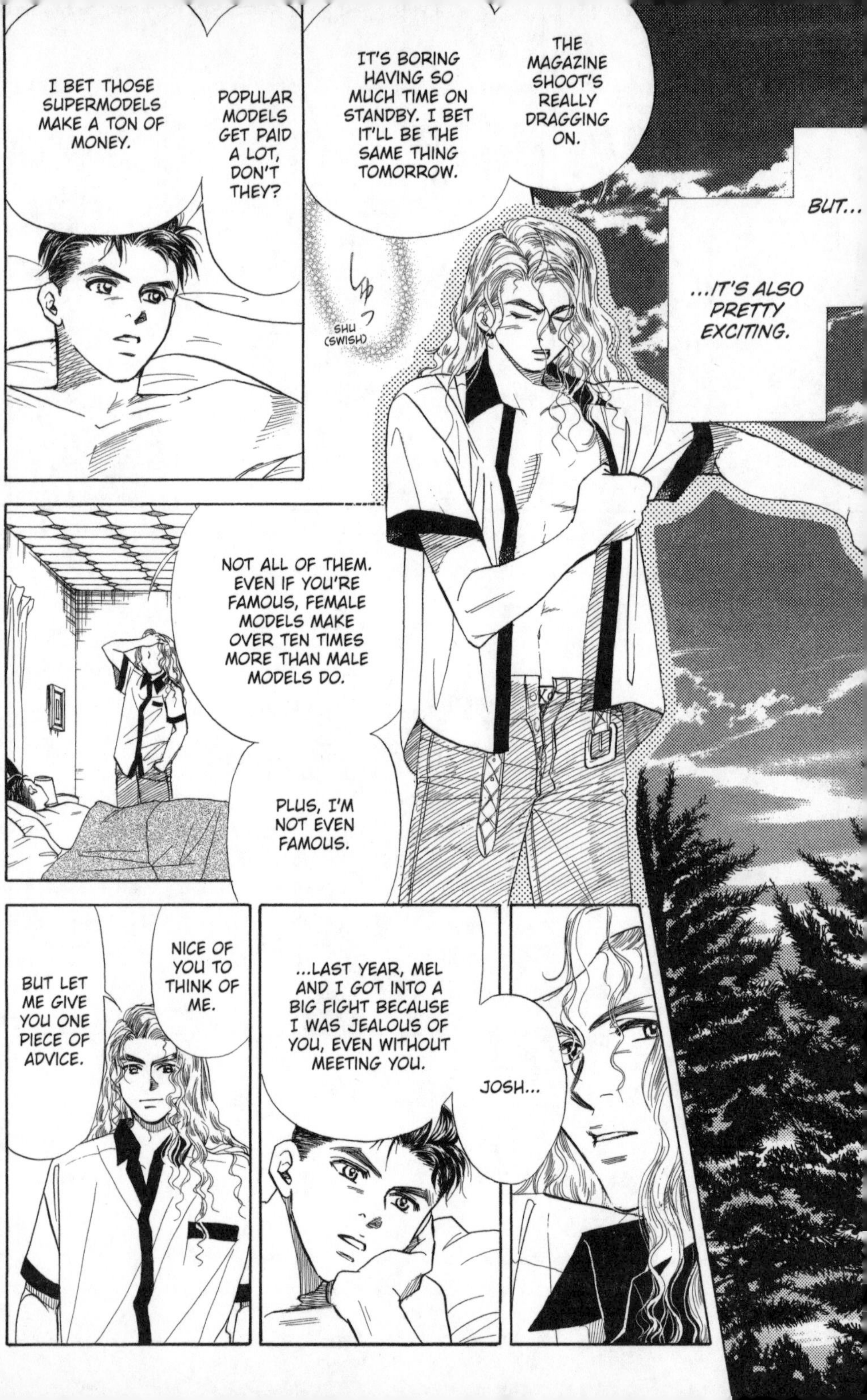
THE MAGAZINE SHOOT'S REALLY DRAGGING ON.
IT'S BORING HAVING SO MUCH TIME ON STANDBY. I BET IT'LL BE THE SAME THING TOMORROW.
SHU (SWISH)
BUT...
...IT'S ALSO PRETTY EXCITING.
POPULAR MODELS GET PAID A LOT, DON'T THEY?
I BET THOSE SUPERMODELS MAKE A TON OF MONEY.
NOT ALL OF THEM. EVEN IF YOU'RE FAMOUS, FEMALE MODELS MAKE OVER TEN TIMES MORE THAN MALE MODELS DO.
PLUS, I'M NOT EVEN FAMOUS.
JOSH...
...LAST YEAR, MEL AND I GOT INTO A BIG FIGHT BECAUSE I WAS JEALOUS OF YOU, EVEN WITHOUT MEETING YOU.
NICE OF YOU TO THINK OF ME.
BUT LET ME GIVE YOU ONE PIECE OF ADVICE.

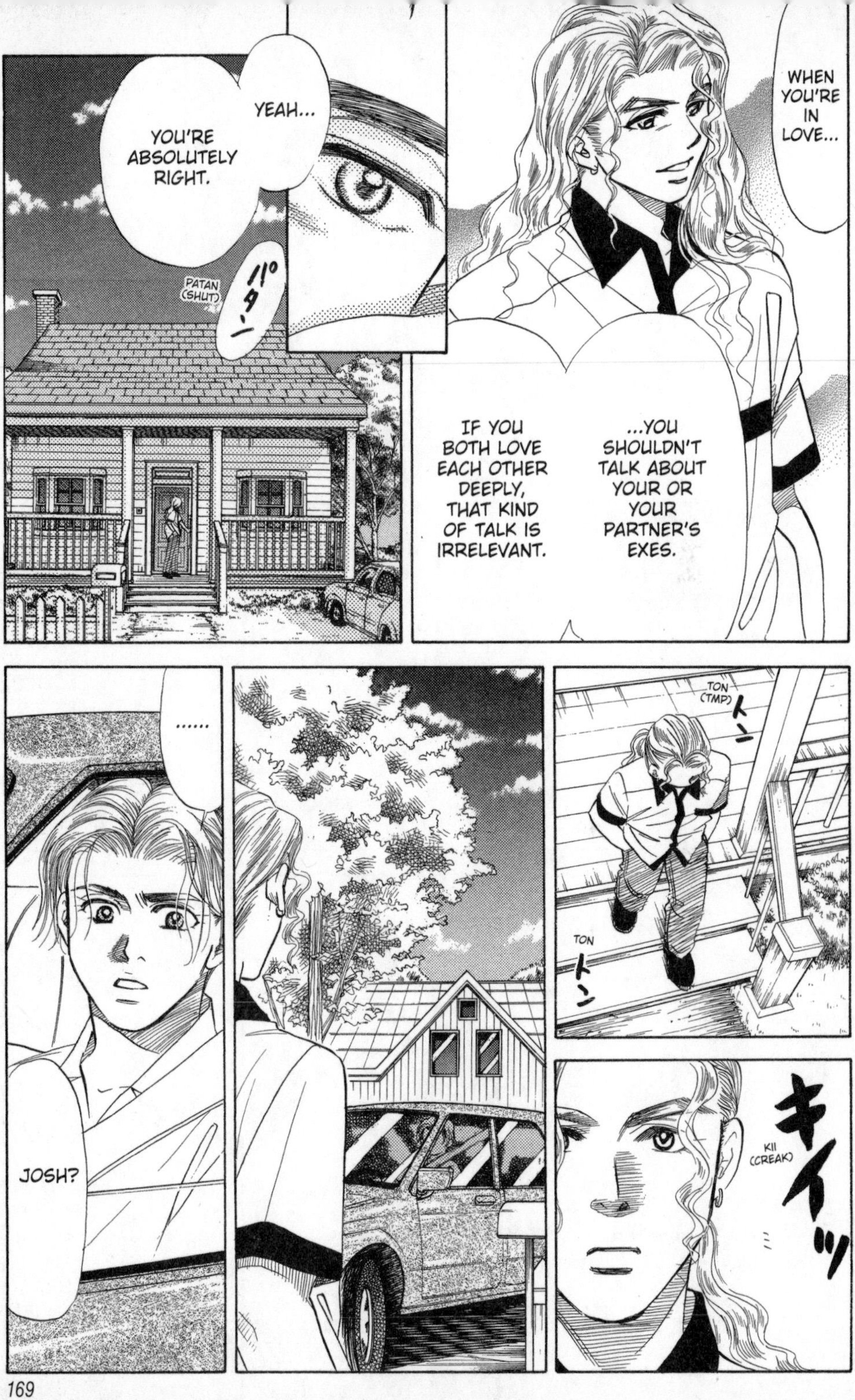
WHEN YOU'RE IN LOVE...
...YOU SHOULDN'T TALK ABOUT YOUR OR YOUR PARTNER'S EXES.
IF YOU BOTH LOVE EACH OTHER DEEPLY, THAT KIND OF TALK IS IRRELEVANT.
YEAH...
YOU'RE ABSOLUTELY RIGHT.
パタン
PATAN (SHUT)
トン
TON (TMP)
トン
TON
キイッ
KII (CREAK)
......
JOSH?

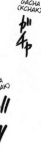

GACHA
(KCHAK)

GA
(CHAK)

GACHA

BAN
(BAM)

OH GOD...

I CAN'T
BELIEVE
IT...!!

......

170

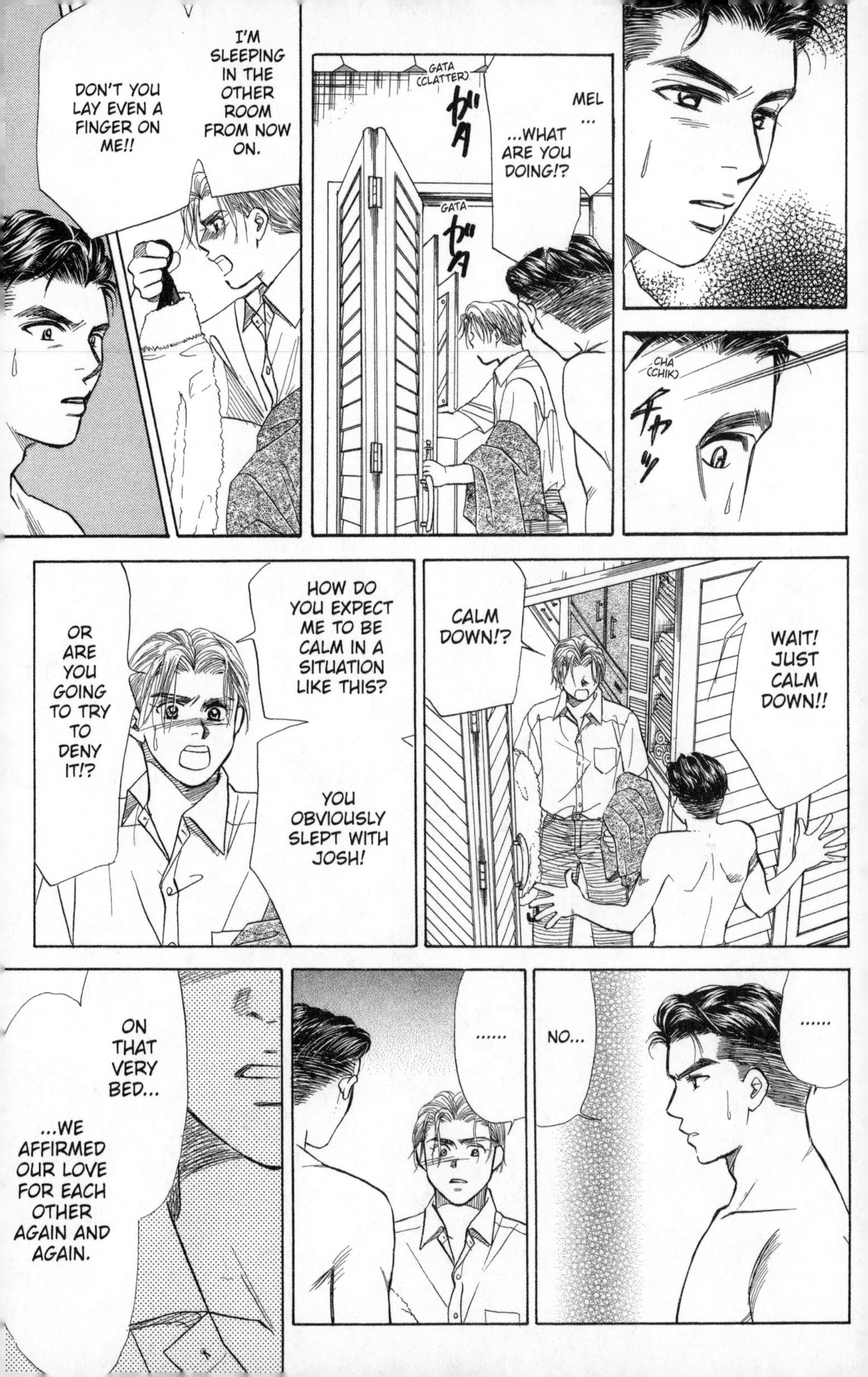
CHA (CHIK)
チャッ
GATA (CLATTER)
ガタ
MEL ...
...WHAT ARE YOU DOING!?
GATA
ガタ
I'M SLEEPING IN THE OTHER ROOM FROM NOW ON.
DON'T YOU LAY EVEN A FINGER ON ME!!
WAIT! JUST CALM DOWN!!
CALM DOWN!?
HOW DO YOU EXPECT ME TO BE CALM IN A SITUATION LIKE THIS?
YOU OBVIOUSLY SLEPT WITH JOSH!
OR ARE YOU GOING TO TRY TO DENY IT!?
......
NO...
......
ON THAT VERY BED...
...WE AFFIRMED OUR LOVE FOR EACH OTHER AGAIN AND AGAIN.

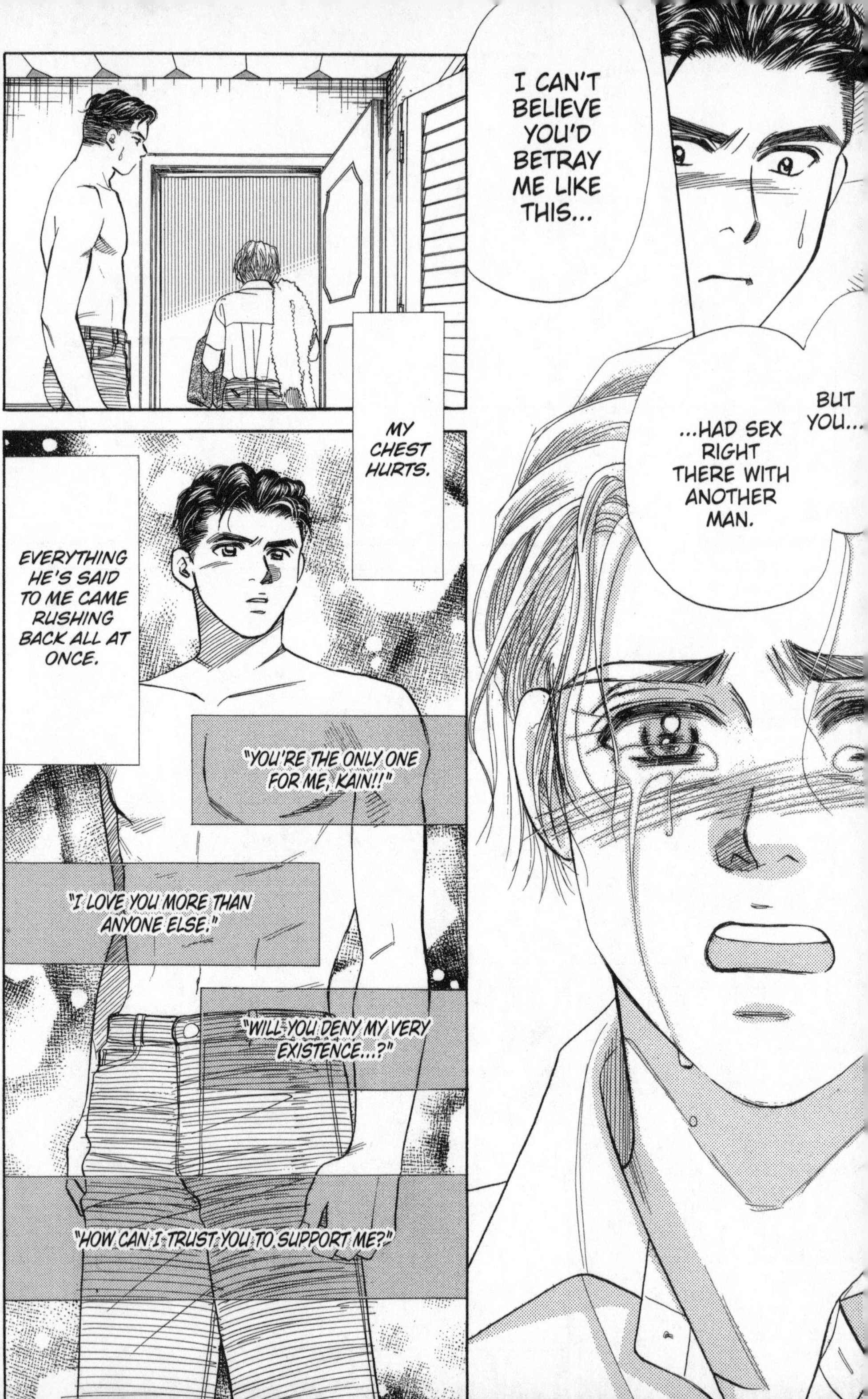
I CAN'T BELIEVE YOU'D BETRAY ME LIKE THIS...
BUT YOU...
...HAD SEX RIGHT THERE WITH ANOTHER MAN.
MY CHEST HURTS.
EVERYTHING HE'S SAID TO ME CAME RUSHING BACK ALL AT ONCE.
"YOU'RE THE ONLY ONE FOR ME, KAIN!!"
"I LOVE YOU MORE THAN ANYONE ELSE."
"WILL YOU DENY MY VERY EXISTENCE...?"
"HOW CAN I TRUST YOU TO SUPPORT ME?"

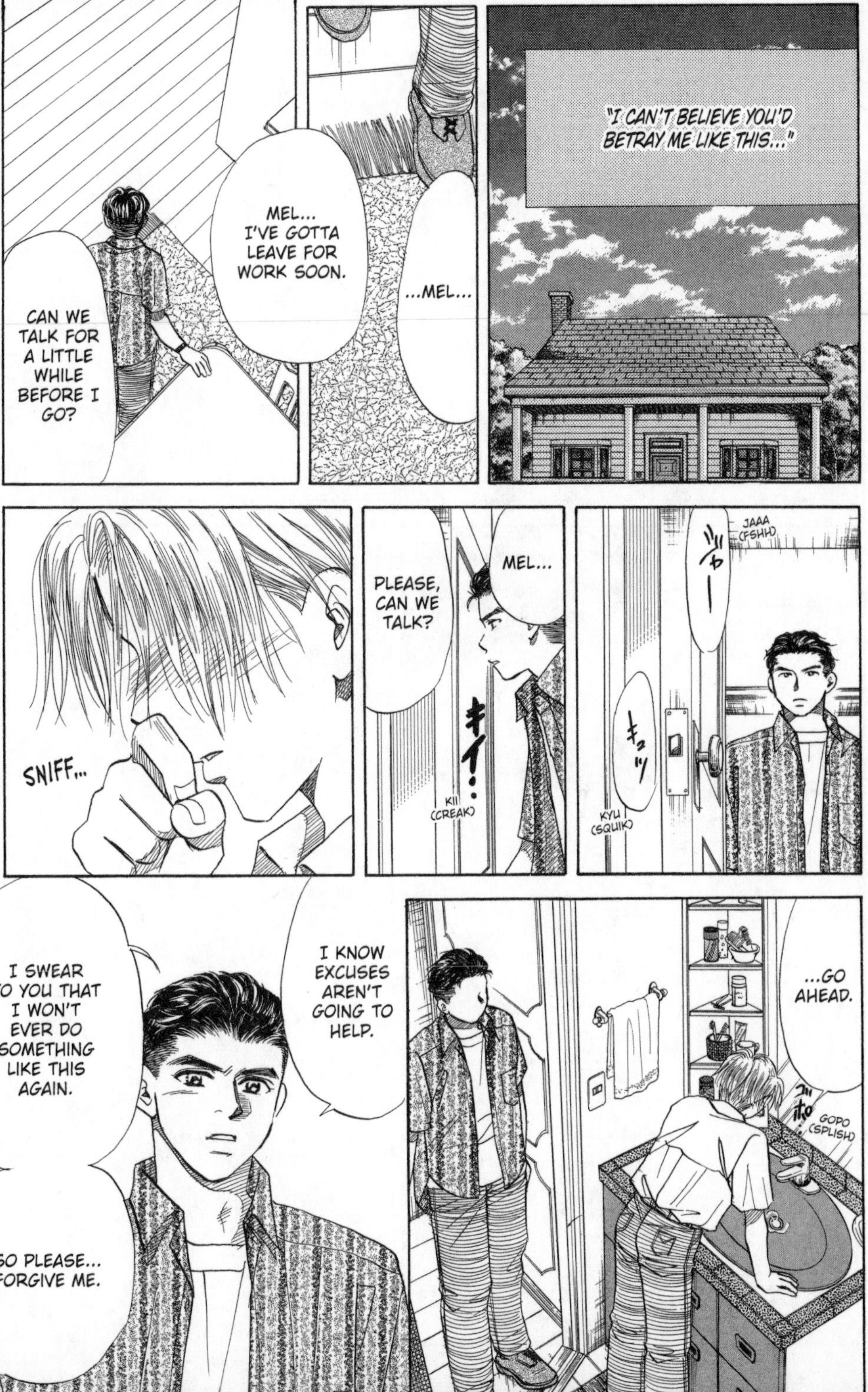
"I CAN'T BELIEVE YOU'D BETRAY ME LIKE THIS..."
...MEL...
MEL... I'VE GOTTA LEAVE FOR WORK SOON.
CAN WE TALK FOR A LITTLE WHILE BEFORE I GO?
ジャー
JAAA (FSHH)
キュッ
KYU (SQUIK)
MEL...
PLEASE, CAN WE TALK?
キイ!!
KII (CREAK)
SNIFF...
...GO AHEAD.
ゴポ
GOPO (SPLISH)
I KNOW EXCUSES AREN'T GOING TO HELP.
I SWEAR TO YOU THAT I WON'T EVER DO SOMETHING LIKE THIS AGAIN.
SO PLEASE... FORGIVE ME.

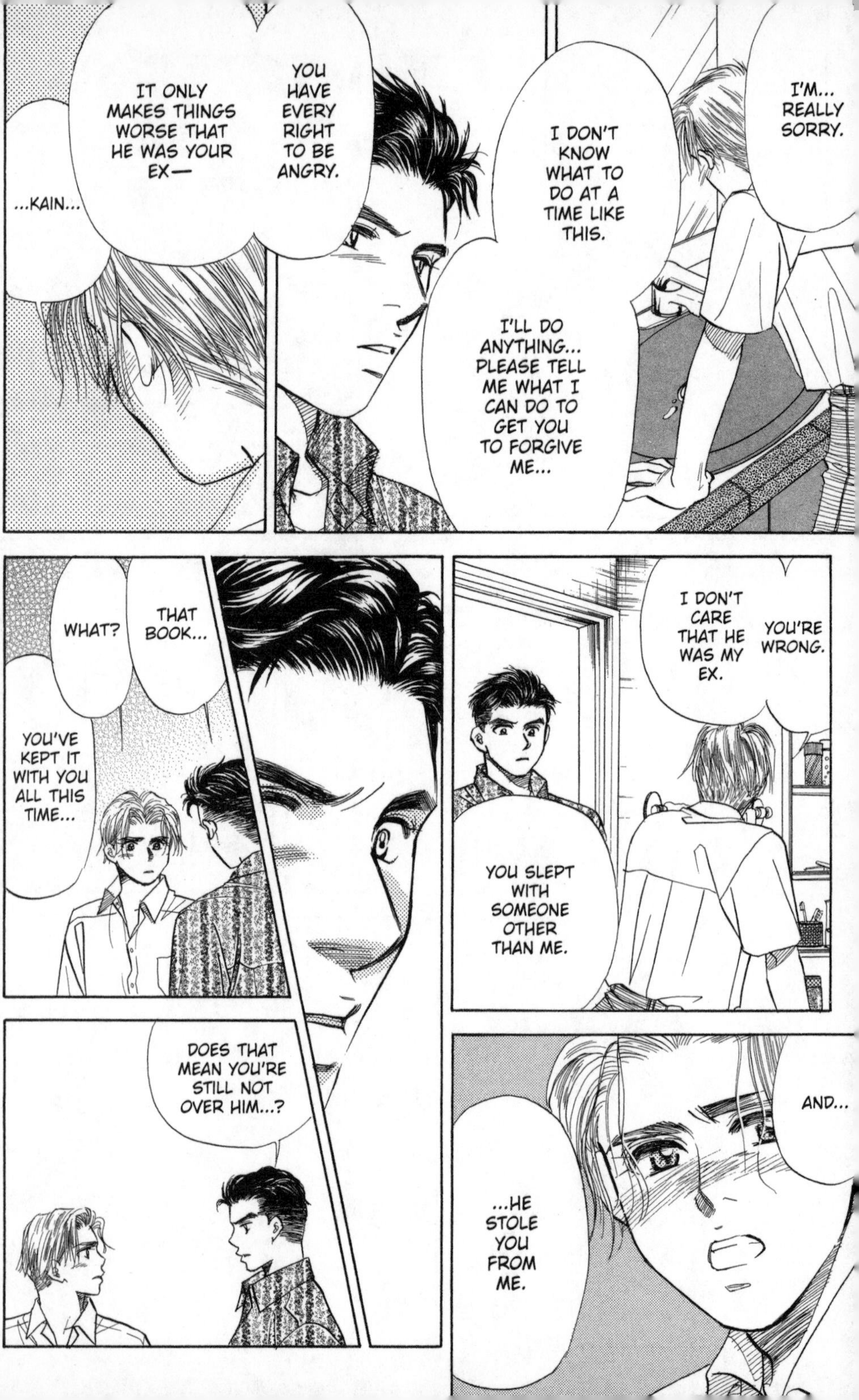
I'M... REALLY SORRY.
I DON'T KNOW WHAT TO DO AT A TIME LIKE THIS.
I'LL DO ANYTHING... PLEASE TELL ME WHAT I CAN DO TO GET YOU TO FORGIVE ME...
YOU HAVE EVERY RIGHT TO BE ANGRY.
IT ONLY MAKES THINGS WORSE THAT HE WAS YOUR EX—
...KAIN...
YOU'RE WRONG.
I DON'T CARE THAT HE WAS MY EX.
YOU SLEPT WITH SOMEONE OTHER THAN ME.
AND...
...HE STOLE YOU FROM ME.
THAT BOOK...
WHAT?
YOU'VE KEPT IT WITH YOU ALL THIS TIME...
DOES THAT MEAN YOU'RE STILL NOT OVER HIM...?

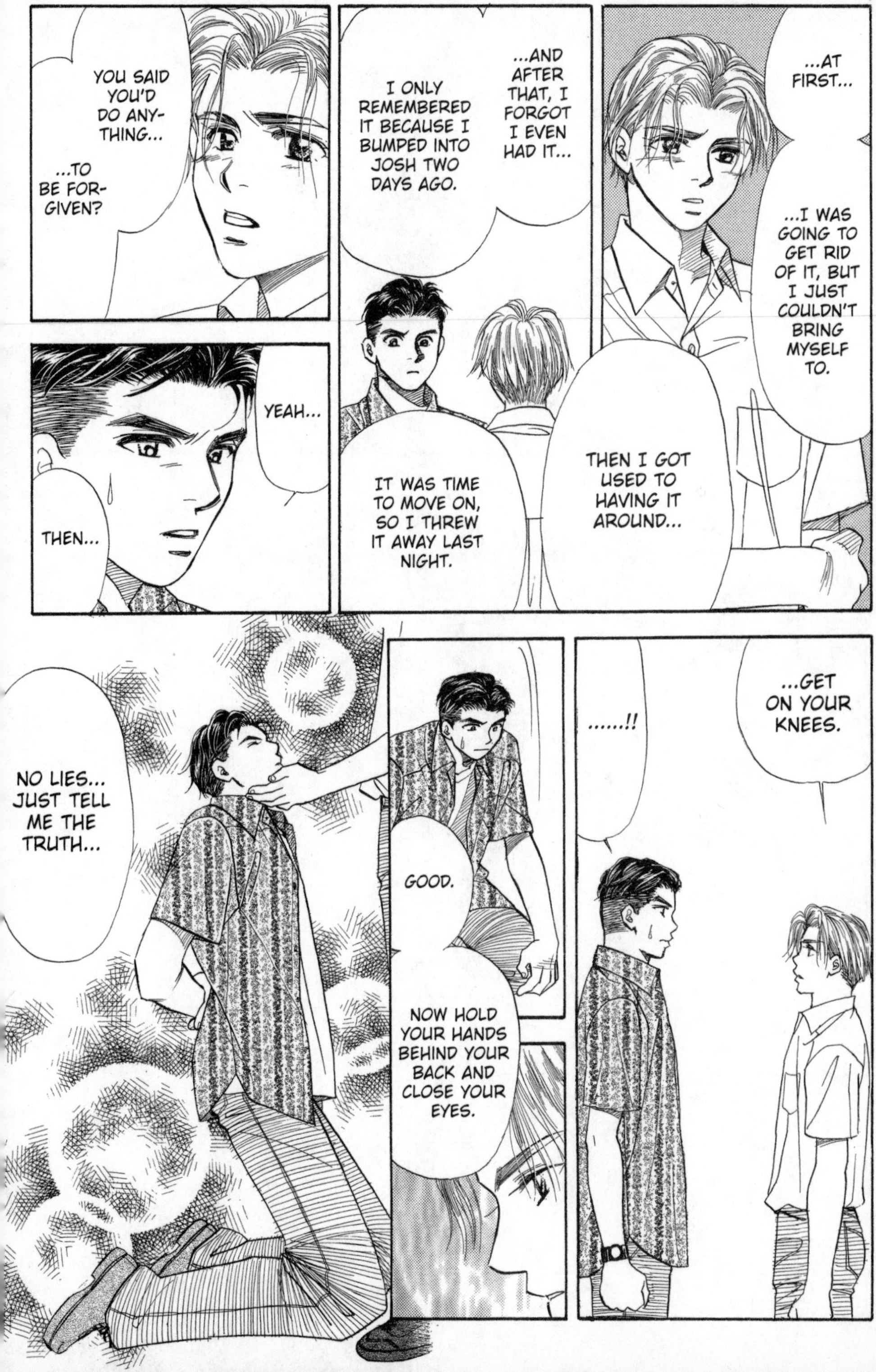
...AT FIRST...
...I WAS GOING TO GET RID OF IT, BUT I JUST COULDN'T BRING MYSELF TO.
THEN I GOT USED TO HAVING IT AROUND...
...AND AFTER THAT, I FORGOT I EVEN HAD IT...
I ONLY REMEMBERED IT BECAUSE I BUMPED INTO JOSH TWO DAYS AGO.
IT WAS TIME TO MOVE ON, SO I THREW IT AWAY LAST NIGHT.
YOU SAID YOU'D DO ANY-THING...
...TO BE FOR-GIVEN?
YEAH...
THEN...
...GET ON YOUR KNEES.
......!!
GOOD.
NOW HOLD YOUR HANDS BEHIND YOUR BACK AND CLOSE YOUR EYES.
NO LIES... JUST TELL ME THE TRUTH...

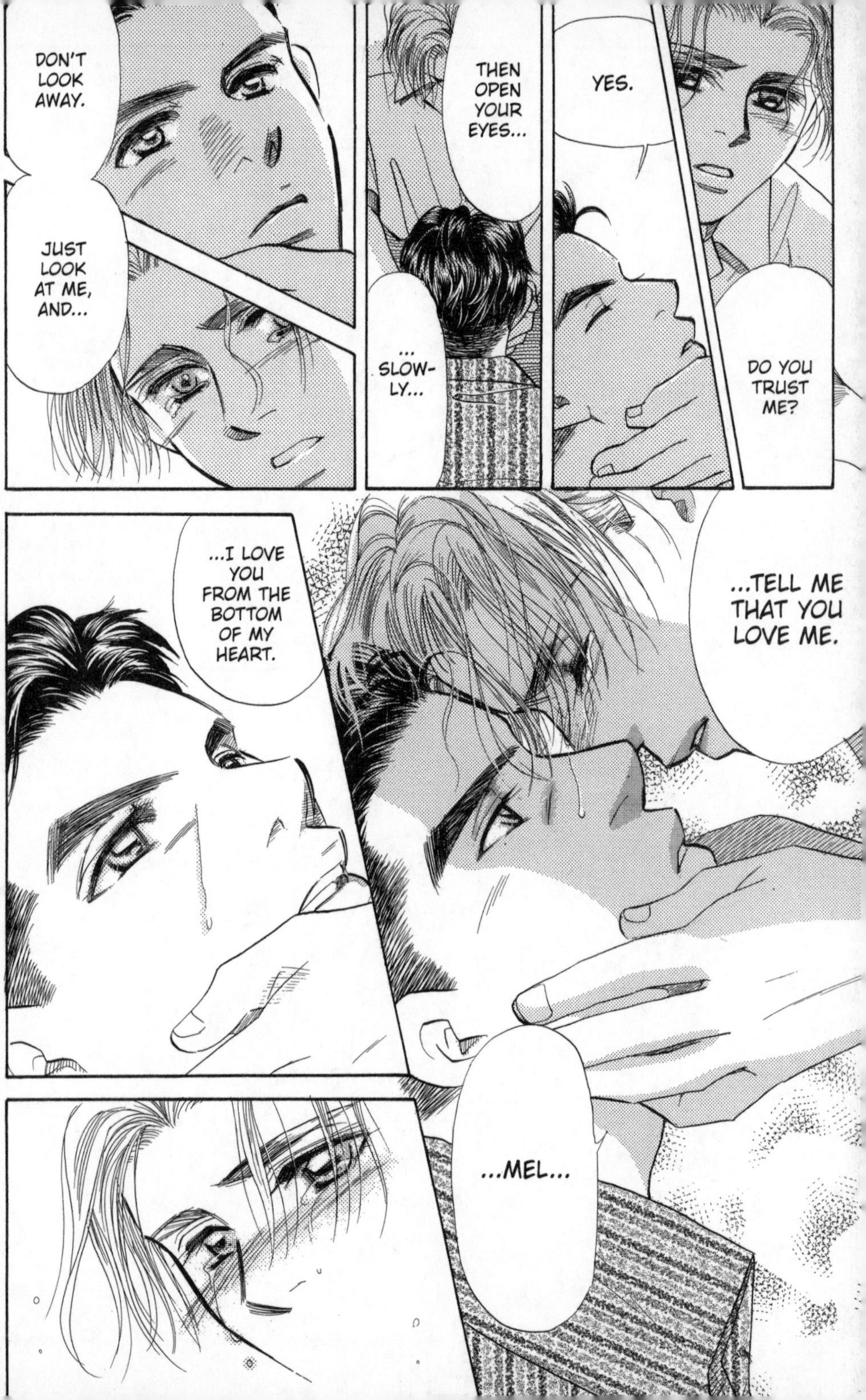
DO YOU TRUST ME?
YES.
THEN OPEN YOUR EYES...
...SLOWLY...
DON'T LOOK AWAY.
JUST LOOK AT ME, AND...
...TELL ME THAT YOU LOVE ME.
...I LOVE YOU FROM THE BOTTOM OF MY HEART.
...MEL...

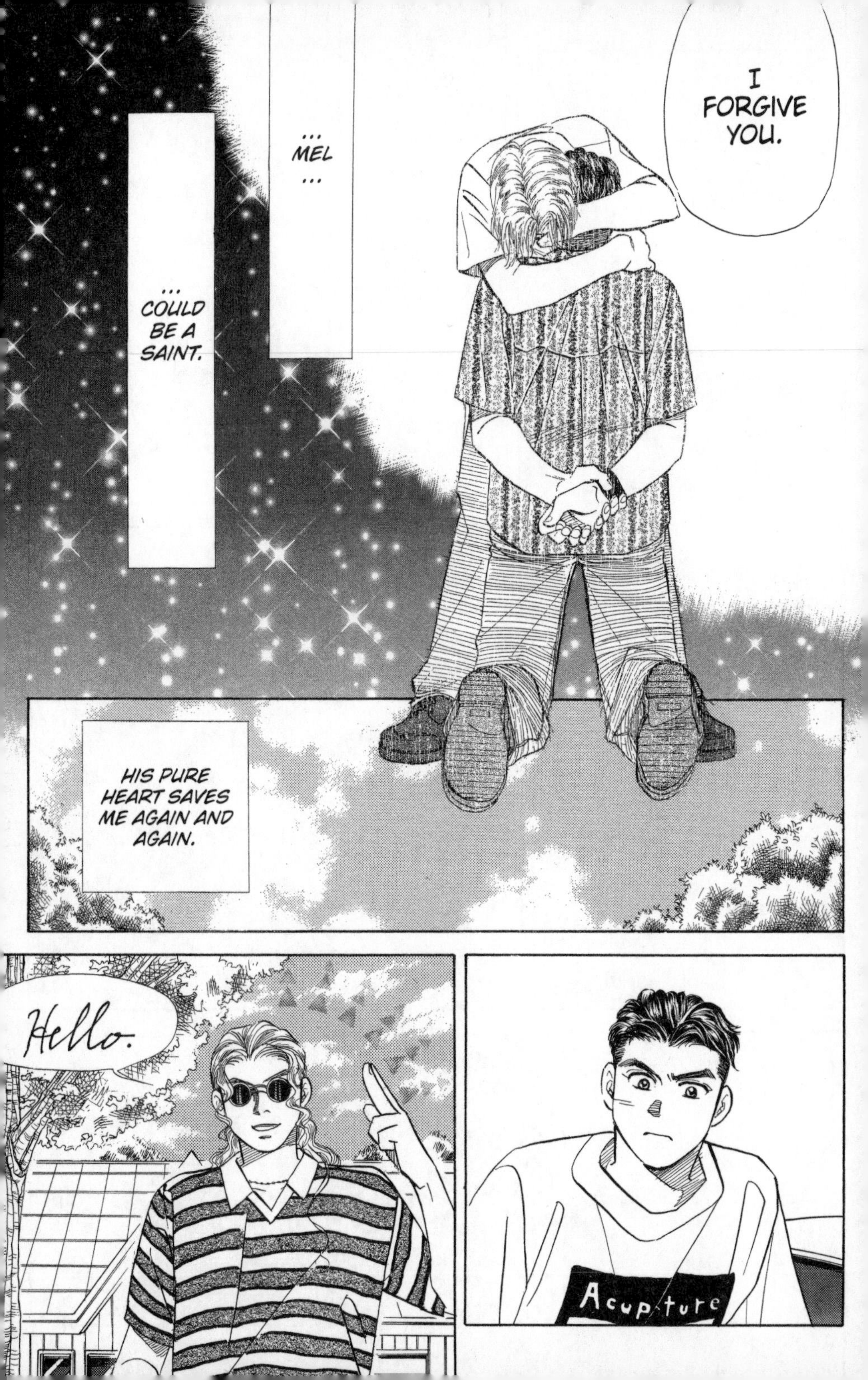
I FORGIVE YOU.
...MEL...
...COULD BE A SAINT.
HIS PURE HEART SAVES ME AGAIN AND AGAIN.
Acupture
Hello.

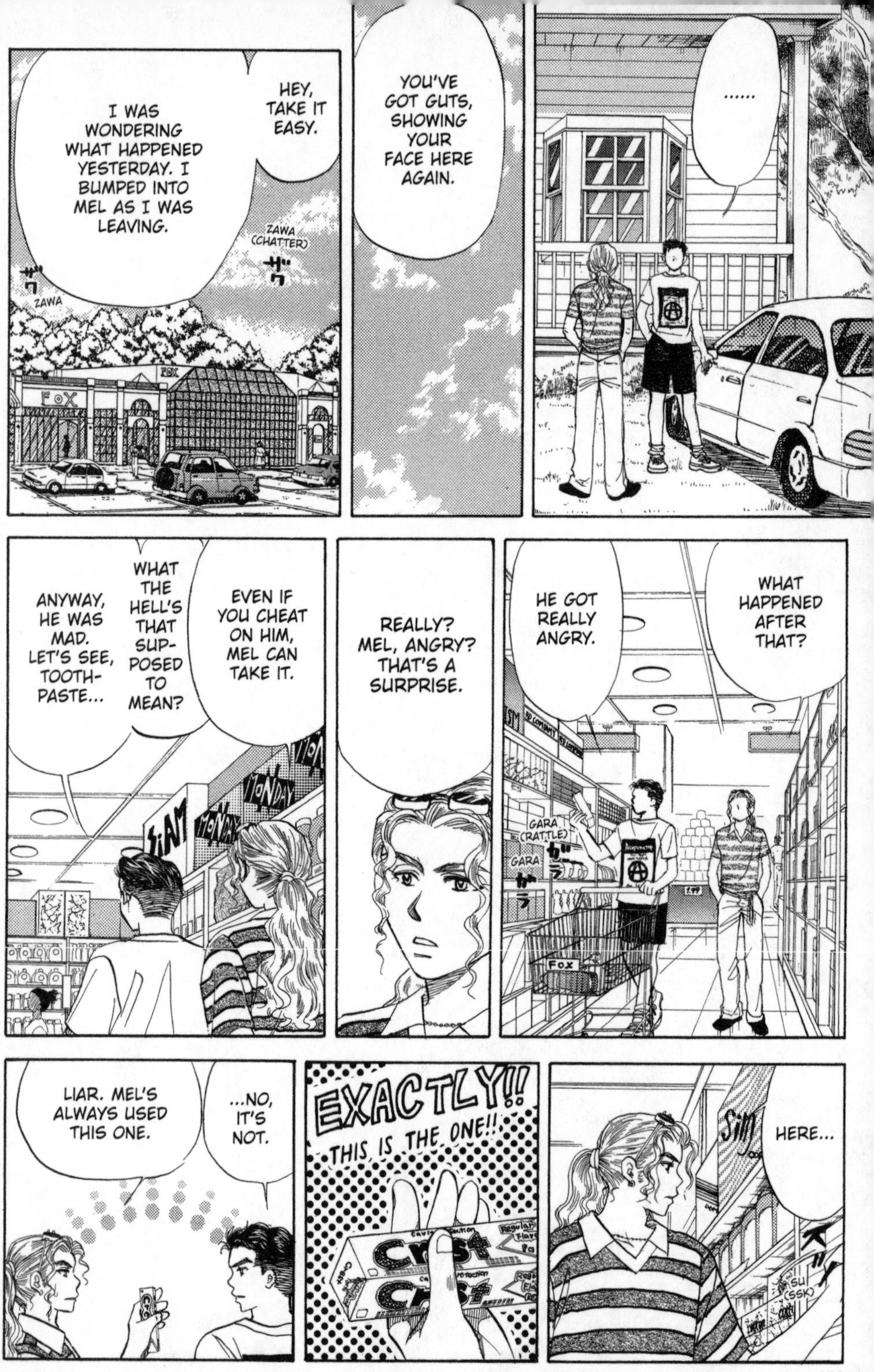
......
YOU'VE GOT GUTS, SHOWING YOUR FACE HERE AGAIN.
HEY, TAKE IT EASY.
I WAS WONDERING WHAT HAPPENED YESTERDAY. I BUMPED INTO MEL AS I WAS LEAVING.
ZAWA (CHATTER)
ZAWA
WHAT HAPPENED AFTER THAT?
HE GOT REALLY ANGRY.
GARA (RATTLE)
GARA
REALLY? MEL, ANGRY? THAT'S A SURPRISE.
EVEN IF YOU CHEAT ON HIM, MEL CAN TAKE IT.
WHAT THE HELL'S THAT SUP-POSED TO MEAN?
ANYWAY, HE WAS MAD. LET'S SEE, TOOTH-PASTE...
HERE...
SU (SSK)
EXACTLY!!
THIS IS THE ONE!!
...NO, IT'S NOT.
LIAR. MEL'S ALWAYS USED THIS ONE.

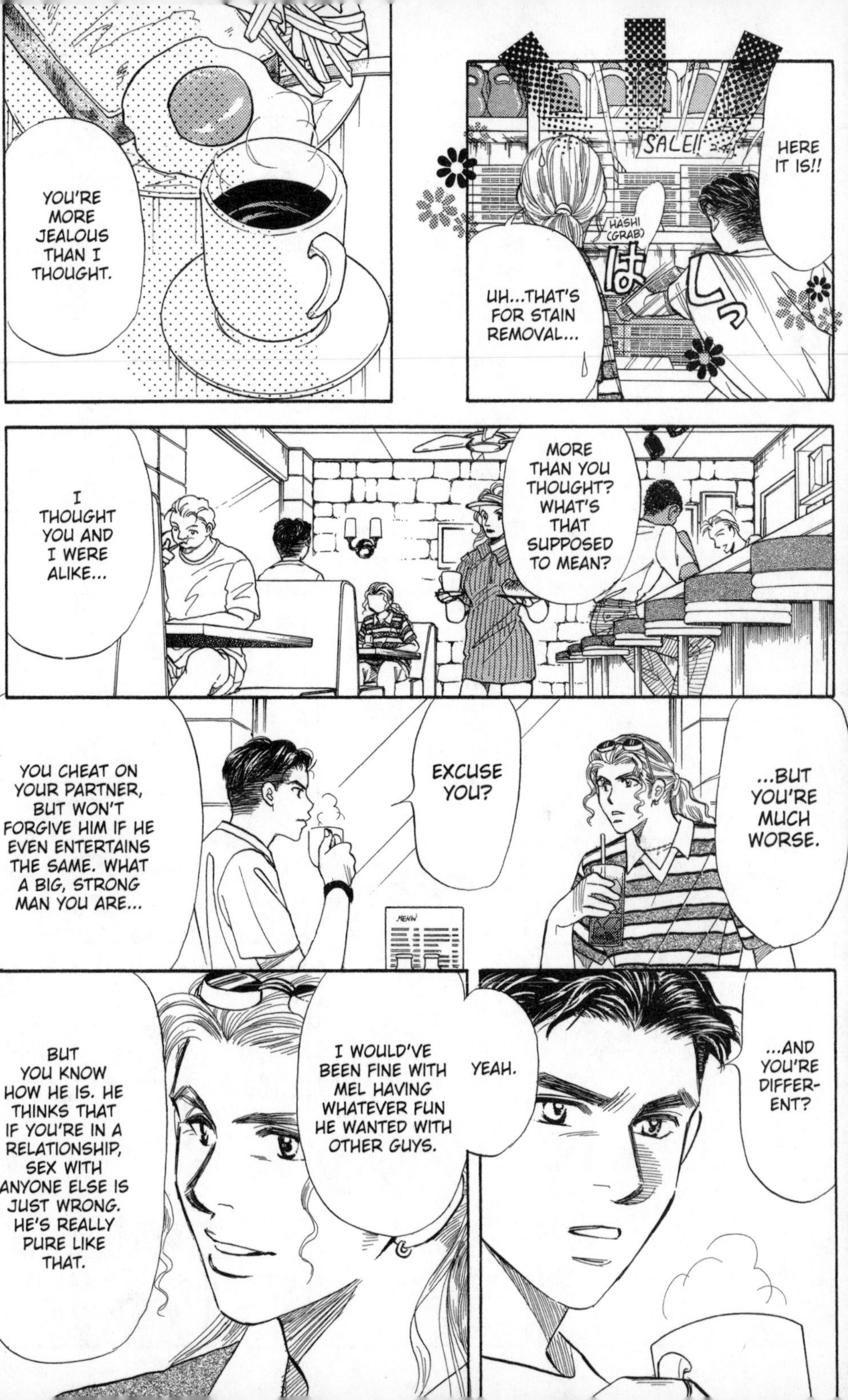
SALE!!
HERE IT IS!!
HASHI (GRAB)
はしっ
UH...THAT'S FOR STAIN REMOVAL...
YOU'RE MORE JEALOUS THAN I THOUGHT.
MORE THAN YOU THOUGHT? WHAT'S THAT SUPPOSED TO MEAN?
I THOUGHT YOU AND I WERE ALIKE...
...BUT YOU'RE MUCH WORSE.
EXCUSE YOU?
YOU CHEAT ON YOUR PARTNER, BUT WON'T FORGIVE HIM IF HE EVEN ENTERTAINS THE SAME. WHAT A BIG, STRONG MAN YOU ARE...
...AND YOU'RE DIFFERENT?
YEAH.
I WOULD'VE BEEN FINE WITH MEL HAVING WHATEVER FUN HE WANTED WITH OTHER GUYS.
BUT YOU KNOW HOW HE IS. HE THINKS THAT IF YOU'RE IN A RELATIONSHIP, SEX WITH ANYONE ELSE IS JUST WRONG. HE'S REALLY PURE LIKE THAT.

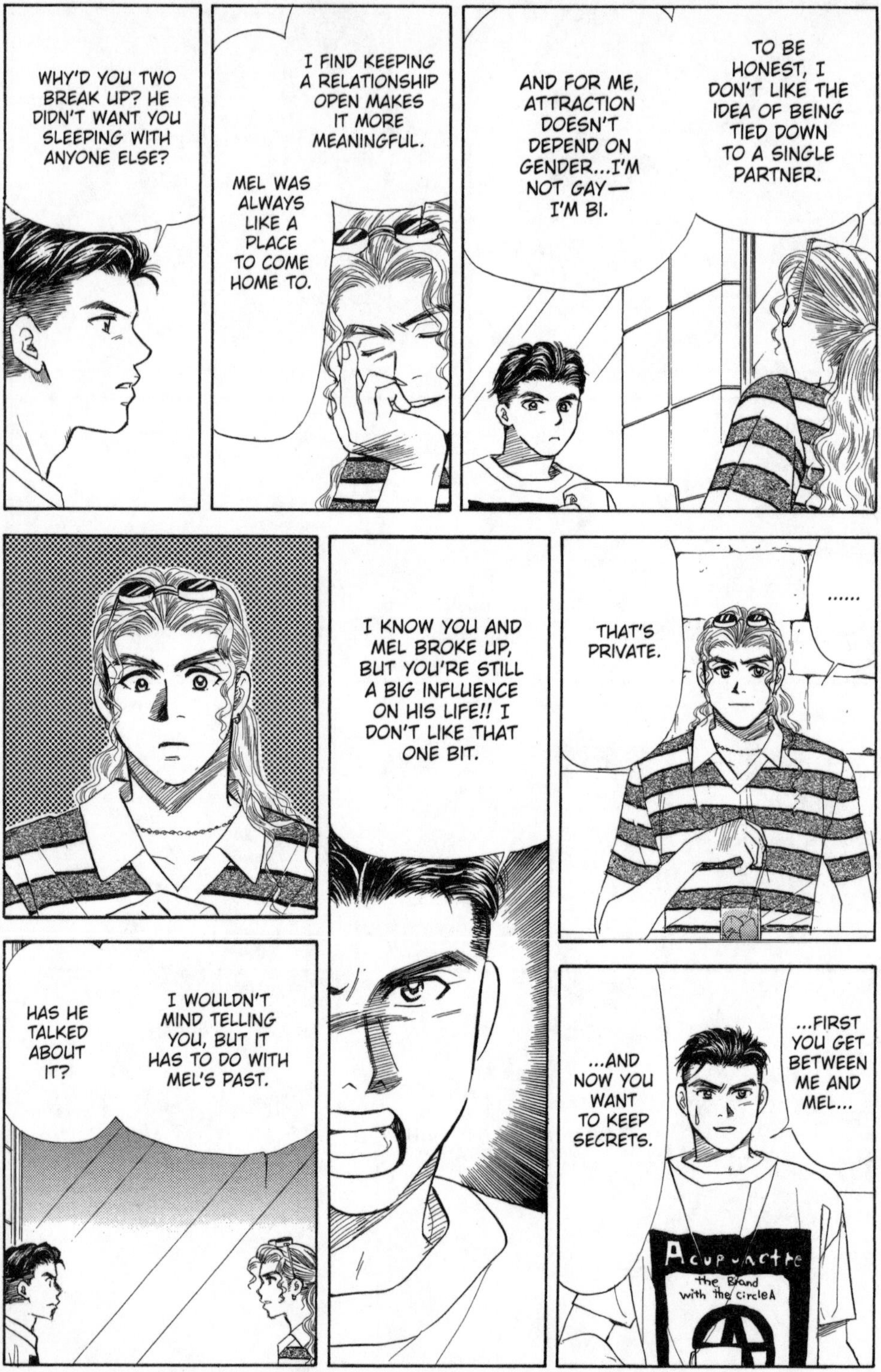
TO BE HONEST, I DON'T LIKE THE IDEA OF BEING TIED DOWN TO A SINGLE PARTNER.
AND FOR ME, ATTRACTION DOESN'T DEPEND ON GENDER...I'M NOT GAY— I'M BI.
I FIND KEEPING A RELATIONSHIP OPEN MAKES IT MORE MEANINGFUL.
MEL WAS ALWAYS LIKE A PLACE TO COME HOME TO.
WHY'D YOU TWO BREAK UP? HE DIDN'T WANT YOU SLEEPING WITH ANYONE ELSE?
......
THAT'S PRIVATE.
...FIRST YOU GET BETWEEN ME AND MEL...
...AND NOW YOU WANT TO KEEP SECRETS.
Acupunctre
the Brand with the circleA
I KNOW YOU AND MEL BROKE UP, BUT YOU'RE STILL A BIG INFLUENCE ON HIS LIFE!! I DON'T LIKE THAT ONE BIT.
I WOULDN'T MIND TELLING YOU, BUT IT HAS TO DO WITH MEL'S PAST.
HAS HE TALKED ABOUT IT?

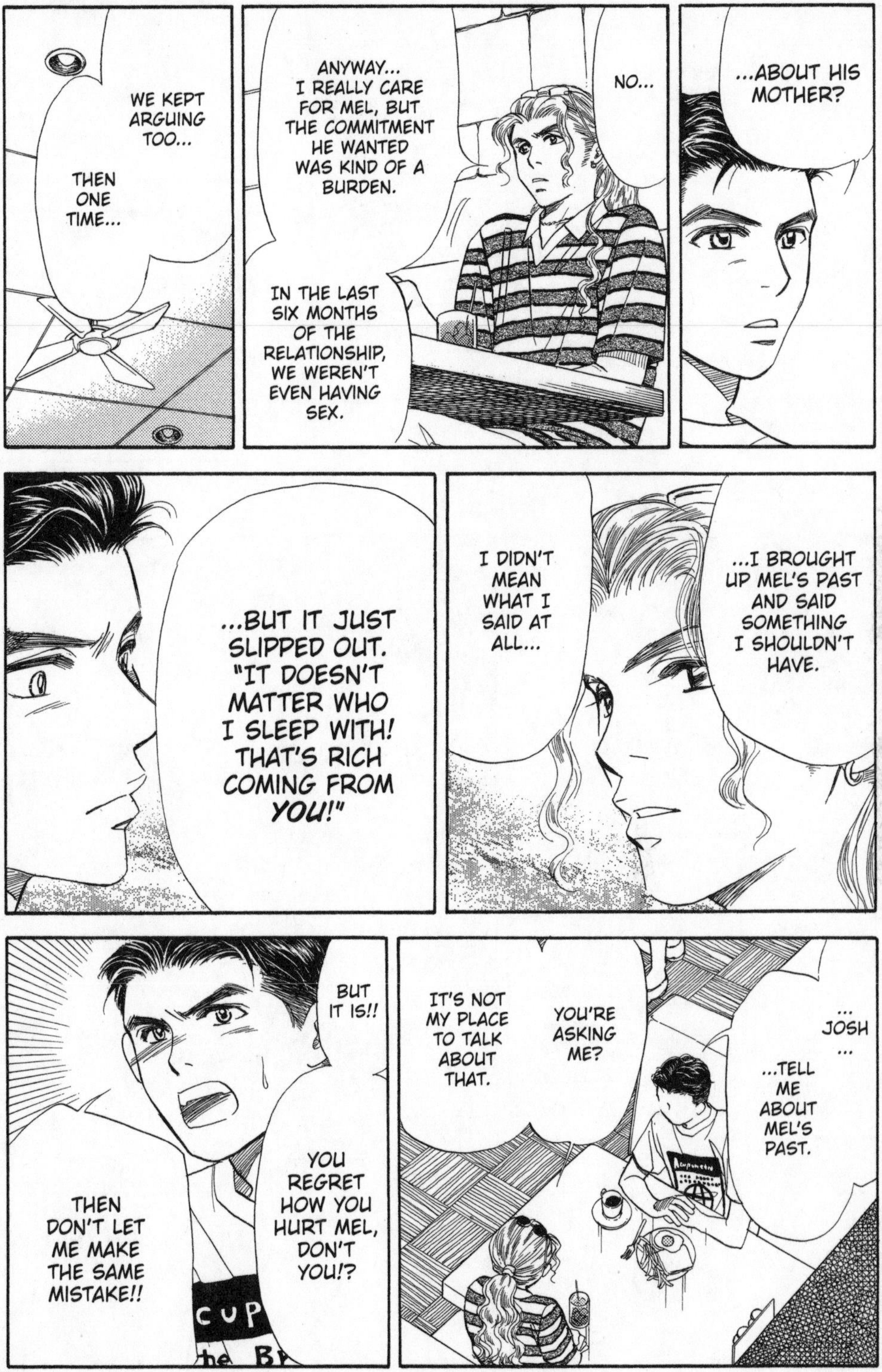
...ABOUT HIS MOTHER?
NO...
ANYWAY... I REALLY CARE FOR MEL, BUT THE COMMITMENT HE WANTED WAS KIND OF A BURDEN.
IN THE LAST SIX MONTHS OF THE RELATIONSHIP, WE WEREN'T EVEN HAVING SEX.
WE KEPT ARGUING TOO...
THEN ONE TIME...
...I BROUGHT UP MEL'S PAST AND SAID SOMETHING I SHOULDN'T HAVE.
I DIDN'T MEAN WHAT I SAID AT ALL...
...BUT IT JUST SLIPPED OUT. "IT DOESN'T MATTER WHO I SLEEP WITH! THAT'S RICH COMING FROM *YOU*!"
... JOSH ...
...TELL ME ABOUT MEL'S PAST.
YOU'RE ASKING ME?
IT'S NOT MY PLACE TO TALK ABOUT THAT.
BUT IT IS!!
YOU REGRET HOW YOU HURT MEL, DON'T YOU!?
THEN DON'T LET ME MAKE THE SAME MISTAKE!!

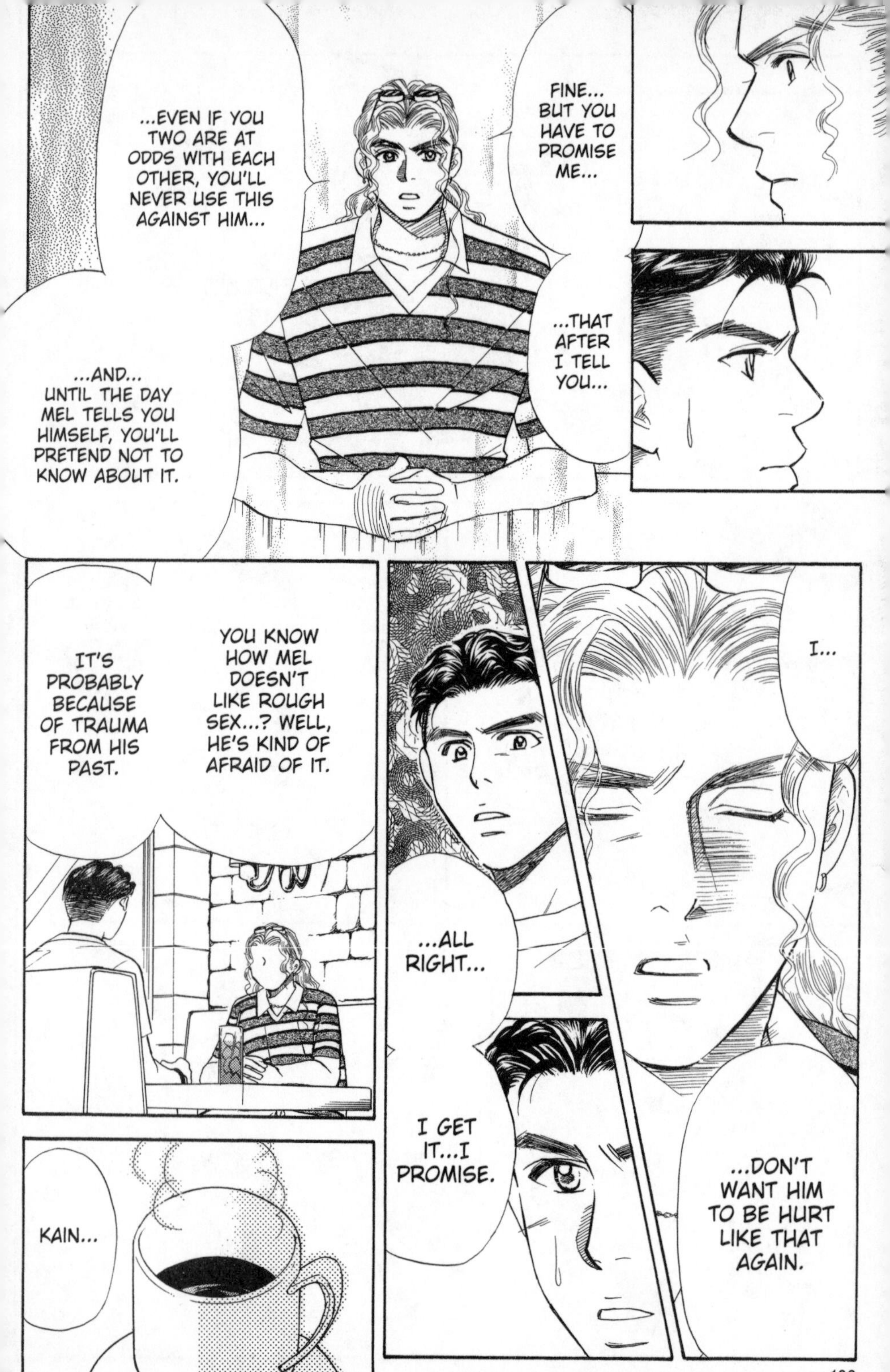
FINE... BUT YOU HAVE TO PROMISE ME...
...THAT AFTER I TELL YOU...
...EVEN IF YOU TWO ARE AT ODDS WITH EACH OTHER, YOU'LL NEVER USE THIS AGAINST HIM...
...AND... UNTIL THE DAY MEL TELLS YOU HIMSELF, YOU'LL PRETEND NOT TO KNOW ABOUT IT.
I...
...DON'T WANT HIM TO BE HURT LIKE THAT AGAIN.
...ALL RIGHT...
I GET IT...I PROMISE.
YOU KNOW HOW MEL DOESN'T LIKE ROUGH SEX...? WELL, HE'S KIND OF AFRAID OF IT.
IT'S PROBABLY BECAUSE OF TRAUMA FROM HIS PAST.
KAIN...

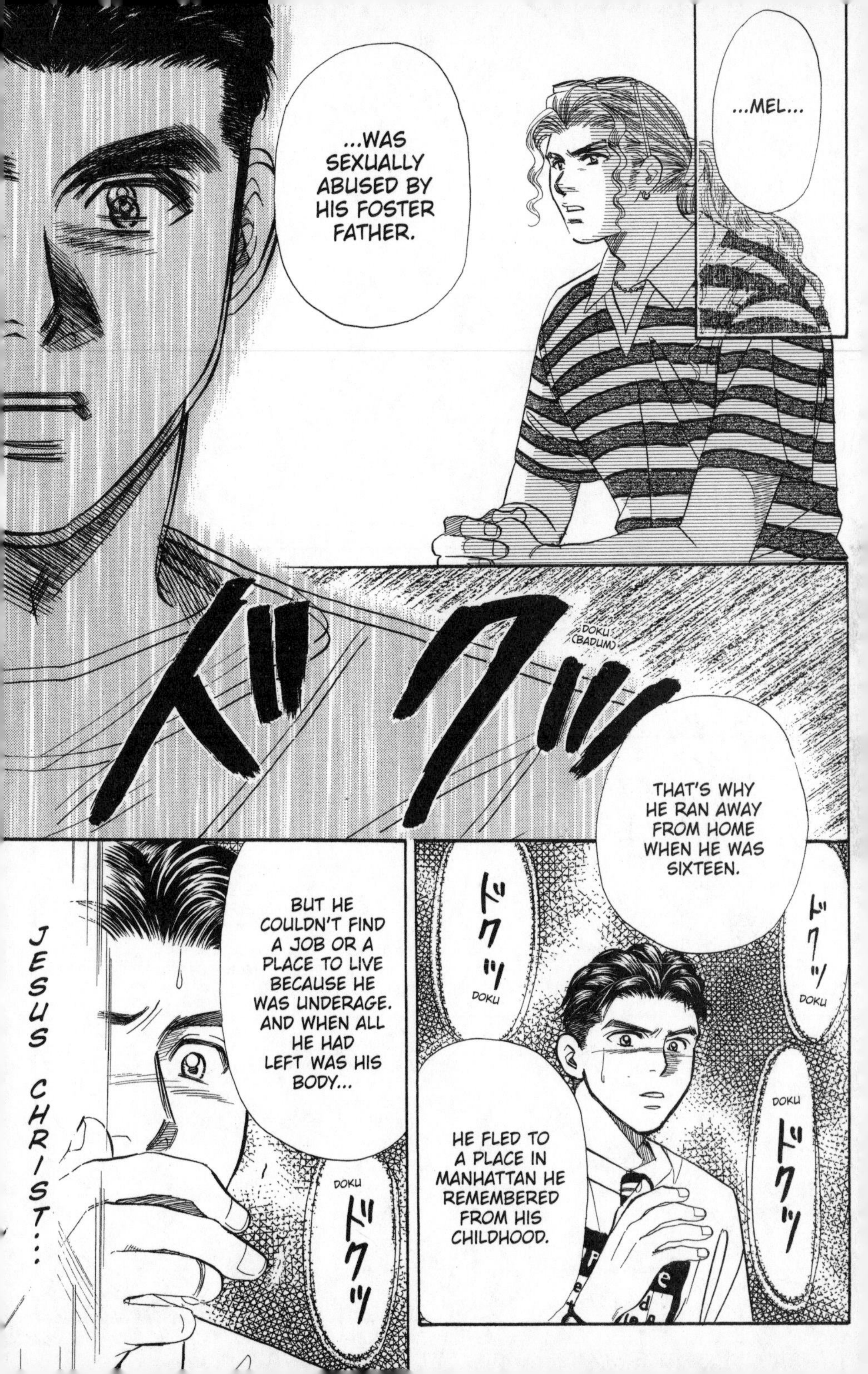
...MEL...
...WAS SEXUALLY ABUSED BY HIS FOSTER FATHER.
ドクッ
DOKU (BADUM)
THAT'S WHY HE RAN AWAY FROM HOME WHEN HE WAS SIXTEEN.
ドクッ
DOKU
DOKU
ドクッ
HE FLED TO A PLACE IN MANHATTAN HE REMEMBERED FROM HIS CHILDHOOD.
ドクッ
DOKU
BUT HE COULDN'T FIND A JOB OR A PLACE TO LIVE BECAUSE HE WAS UNDERAGE. AND WHEN ALL HE HAD LEFT WAS HIS BODY...
DOKU
ドクッ
JESUS CHRIST...

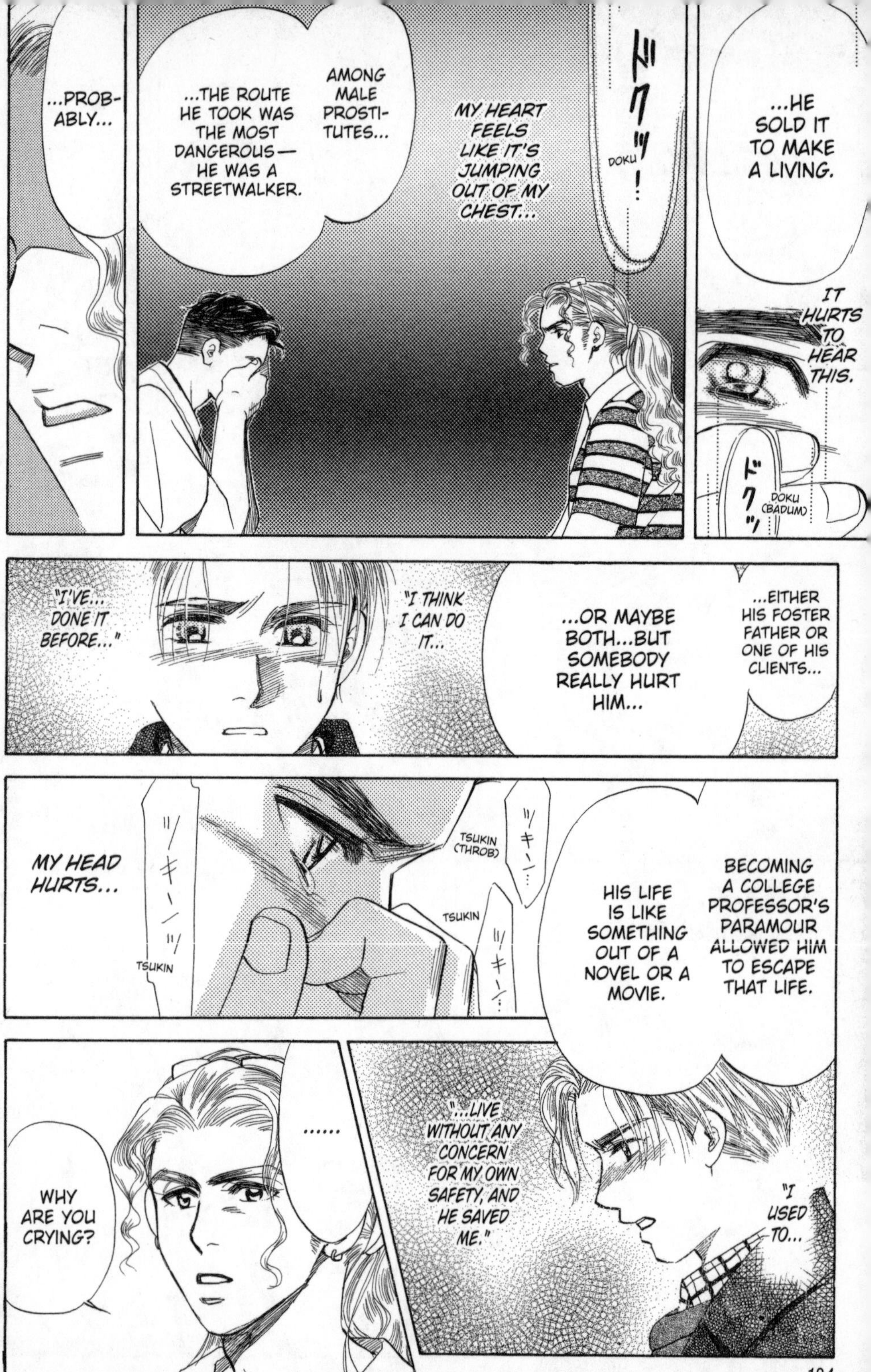
...HE SOLD IT TO MAKE A LIVING.
IT HURTS TO HEAR THIS.
ドクッ
DOKU (BADUM)
ドクッ!
DOKU
MY HEART FEELS LIKE IT'S JUMPING OUT OF MY CHEST...
AMONG MALE PROSTITUTES...
...THE ROUTE HE TOOK WAS THE MOST DANGEROUS—HE WAS A STREETWALKER.
...PROBABLY...
...EITHER HIS FOSTER FATHER OR ONE OF HIS CLIENTS...
...OR MAYBE BOTH...BUT SOMEBODY REALLY HURT HIM...
"I THINK I CAN DO IT...
"I'VE... DONE IT BEFORE..."
BECOMING A COLLEGE PROFESSOR'S PARAMOUR ALLOWED HIM TO ESCAPE THAT LIFE.
HIS LIFE IS LIKE SOMETHING OUT OF A NOVEL OR A MOVIE.
TSUKIN (THROB)
TSUKIN
TSUKIN
MY HEAD HURTS...
"I USED TO...
"...LIVE WITHOUT ANY CONCERN FOR MY OWN SAFETY, AND HE SAVED ME."
......
WHY ARE YOU CRYING?

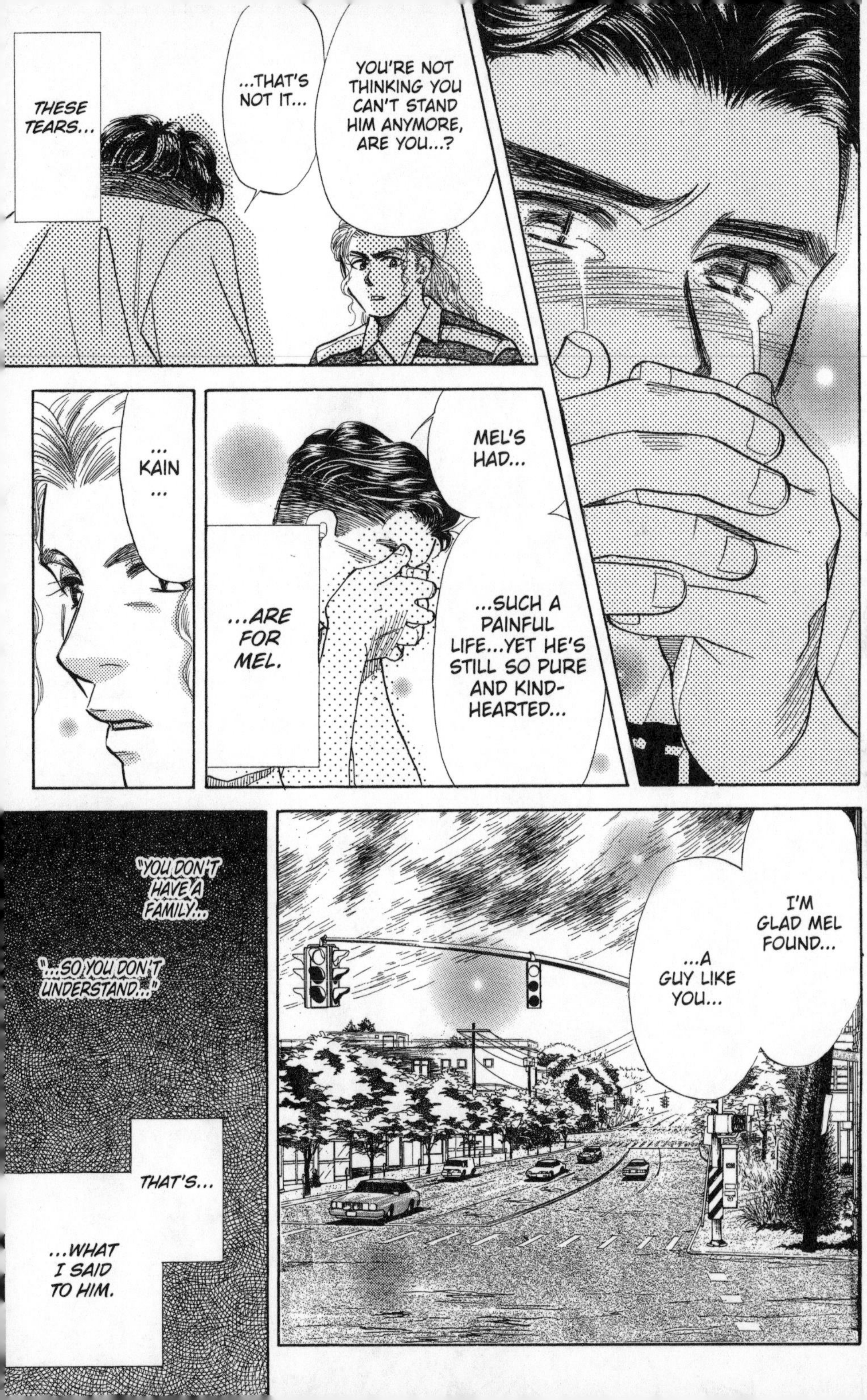
YOU'RE NOT THINKING YOU CAN'T STAND HIM ANYMORE, ARE YOU...?
...THAT'S NOT IT...
THESE TEARS...
MEL'S HAD...
...ARE FOR MEL.
...SUCH A PAINFUL LIFE...YET HE'S STILL SO PURE AND KIND-HEARTED...
...KAIN...
I'M GLAD MEL FOUND...
...A GUY LIKE YOU...
"YOU DON'T HAVE A FAMILY...
"...SO YOU DON'T UNDERSTAND..."
THAT'S...
...WHAT I SAID TO HIM.

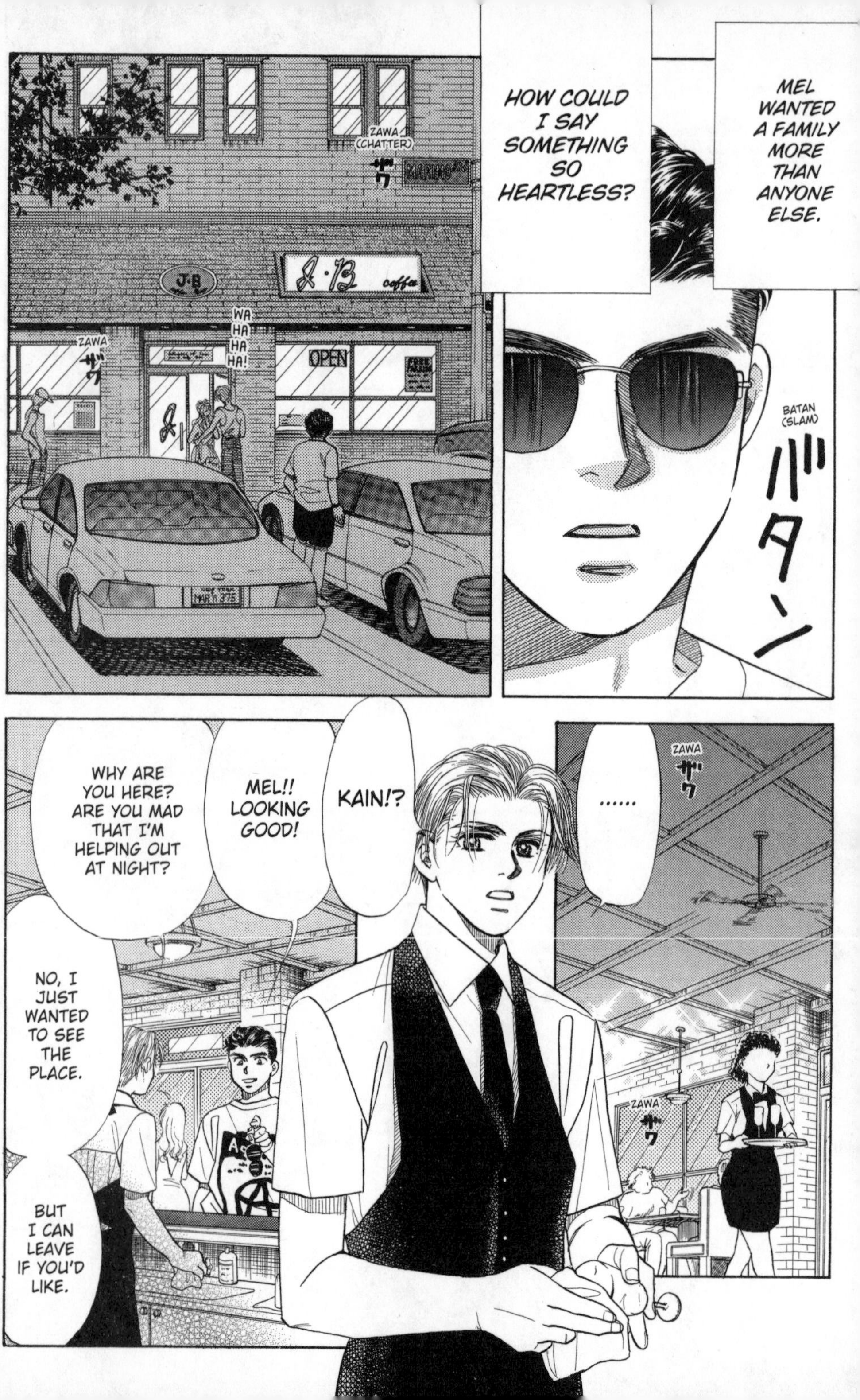
MEL WANTED A FAMILY MORE THAN ANYONE ELSE.
HOW COULD I SAY SOMETHING SO HEARTLESS?
BATAN (SLAM)
ZAWA (CHATTER)
J·B coffee
WA HA HA HA!
OPEN
ZAWA
......
ZAWA
KAIN!?
MEL!! LOOKING GOOD!
WHY ARE YOU HERE? ARE YOU MAD THAT I'M HELPING OUT AT NIGHT?
ZAWA
NO, I JUST WANTED TO SEE THE PLACE.
BUT I CAN LEAVE IF YOU'D LIKE.

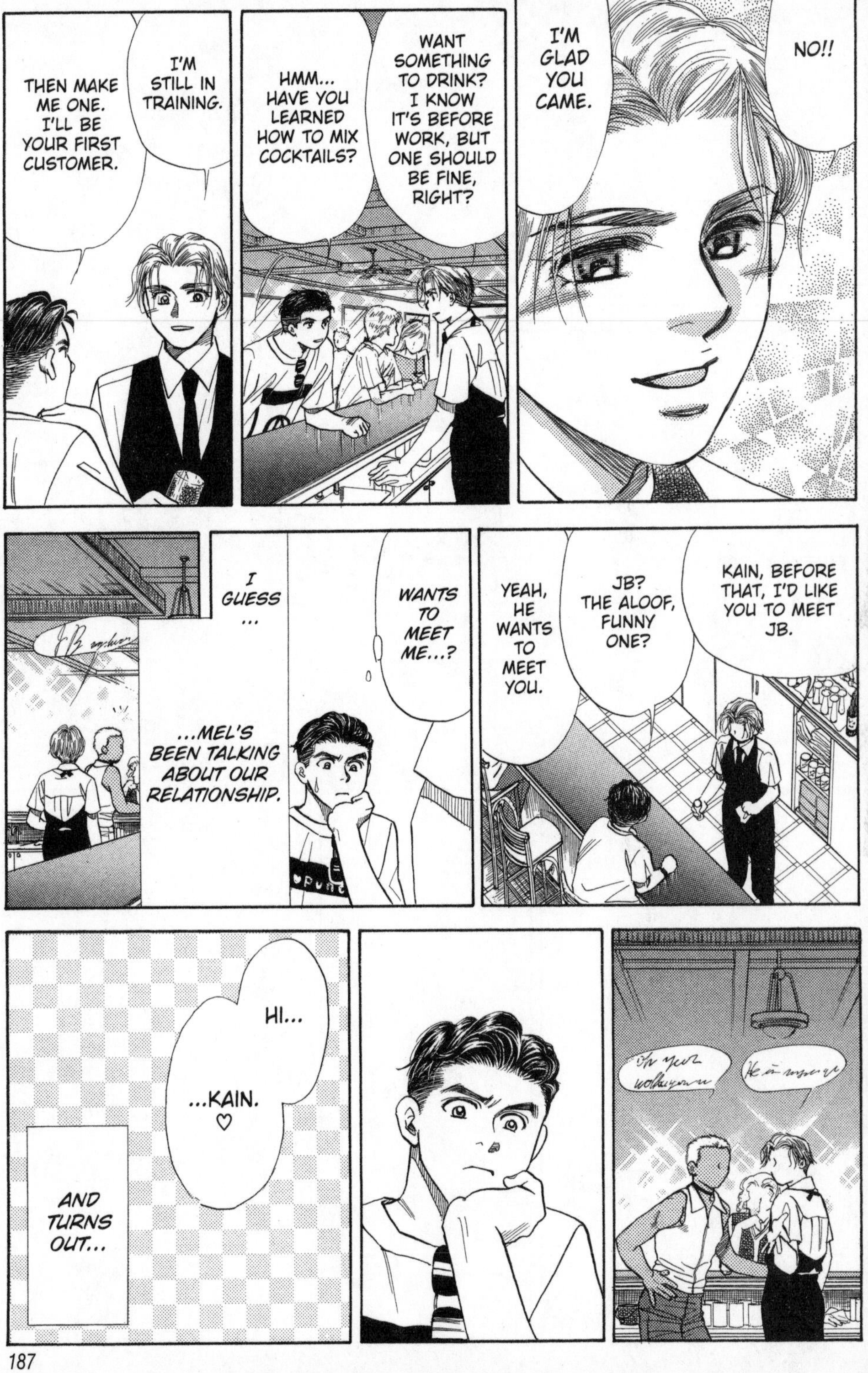
NO!!
I'M GLAD YOU CAME.
WANT SOMETHING TO DRINK? I KNOW IT'S BEFORE WORK, BUT ONE SHOULD BE FINE, RIGHT?
HMM... HAVE YOU LEARNED HOW TO MIX COCKTAILS?
I'M STILL IN TRAINING.
THEN MAKE ME ONE. I'LL BE YOUR FIRST CUSTOMER.
KAIN, BEFORE THAT, I'D LIKE YOU TO MEET JB.
JB? THE ALOOF, FUNNY ONE?
YEAH, HE WANTS TO MEET YOU.
WANTS TO MEET ME...?
I GUESS...
...MEL'S BEEN TALKING ABOUT OUR RELATIONSHIP.
HI...
...KAIN. ♡
AND TURNS OUT...

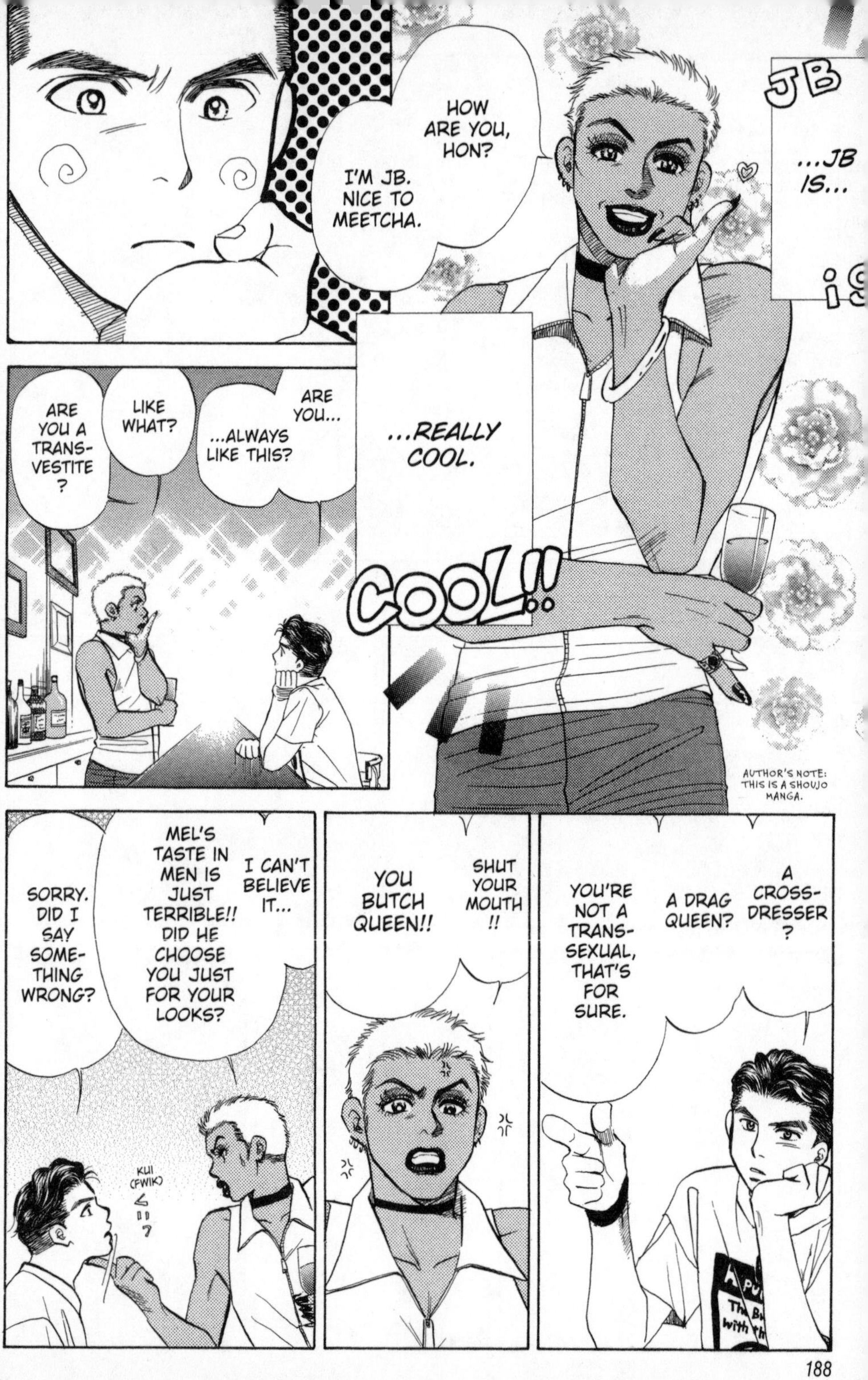
JB
...JB IS...
iS
HOW ARE YOU, HON?
I'M JB. NICE TO MEETCHA.
...REALLY COOL.
COOL!!
ARE YOU...
...ALWAYS LIKE THIS?
LIKE WHAT?
ARE YOU A TRANS-VESTITE?
AUTHOR'S NOTE: THIS IS A SHOUJO MANGA.
A CROSS-DRESSER?
A DRAG QUEEN?
YOU'RE NOT A TRANS-SEXUAL, THAT'S FOR SURE.
SHUT YOUR MOUTH!!
YOU BUTCH QUEEN!!
I CAN'T BELIEVE IT...
MEL'S TASTE IN MEN IS JUST TERRIBLE!! DID HE CHOOSE YOU JUST FOR YOUR LOOKS?
KUI (FWIK)
SORRY. DID I SAY SOME-THING WRONG?

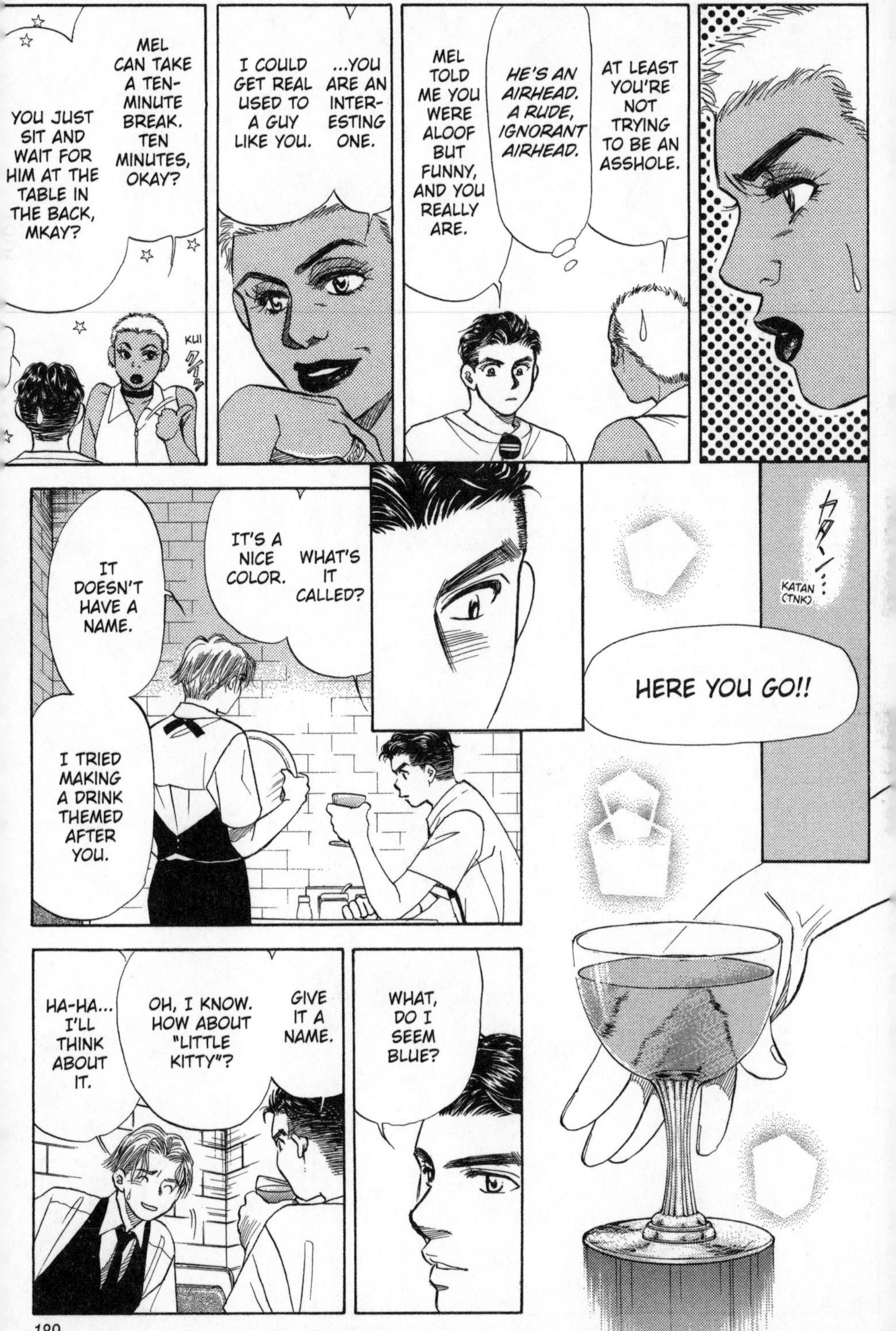
AT LEAST YOU'RE NOT TRYING TO BE AN ASSHOLE.
HE'S AN AIRHEAD. A RUDE, IGNORANT AIRHEAD.
MEL TOLD ME YOU WERE ALOOF BUT FUNNY, AND YOU REALLY ARE.
...YOU ARE AN INTERESTING ONE.
I COULD GET REAL USED TO A GUY LIKE YOU.
MEL CAN TAKE A TEN-MINUTE BREAK. TEN MINUTES, OKAY?
YOU JUST SIT AND WAIT FOR HIM AT THE TABLE IN THE BACK, MKAY?
クイッ
KUI
カタン…
KATAN (TNK)
HERE YOU GO!!
WHAT'S IT CALLED?
IT'S A NICE COLOR.
IT DOESN'T HAVE A NAME.
I TRIED MAKING A DRINK THEMED AFTER YOU.
WHAT, DO I SEEM BLUE?
GIVE IT A NAME.
OH, I KNOW. HOW ABOUT "LITTLE KITTY"?
HA-HA... I'LL THINK ABOUT IT.

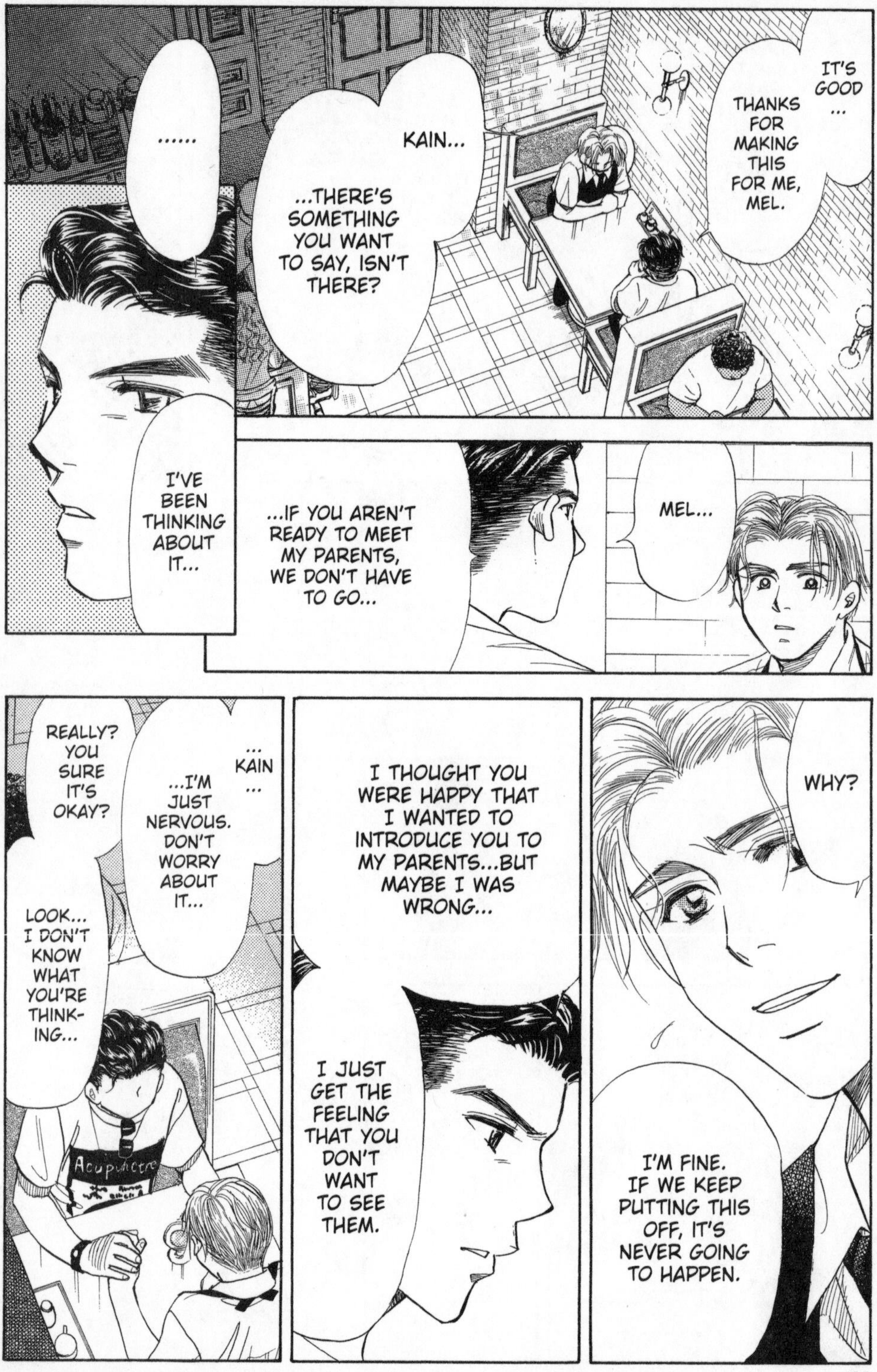
IT'S GOOD...
THANKS FOR MAKING THIS FOR ME, MEL.
KAIN...
...THERE'S SOMETHING YOU WANT TO SAY, ISN'T THERE?
MEL...
...IF YOU AREN'T READY TO MEET MY PARENTS, WE DON'T HAVE TO GO...
......
I'VE BEEN THINKING ABOUT IT...
WHY?
I'M FINE. IF WE KEEP PUTTING THIS OFF, IT'S NEVER GOING TO HAPPEN.
I THOUGHT YOU WERE HAPPY THAT I WANTED TO INTRODUCE YOU TO MY PARENTS...BUT MAYBE I WAS WRONG...
I JUST GET THE FEELING THAT YOU DON'T WANT TO SEE THEM.
...KAIN...
...I'M JUST NERVOUS. DON'T WORRY ABOUT IT...
REALLY? YOU SURE IT'S OKAY?
LOOK... I DON'T KNOW WHAT YOU'RE THINK-ING...

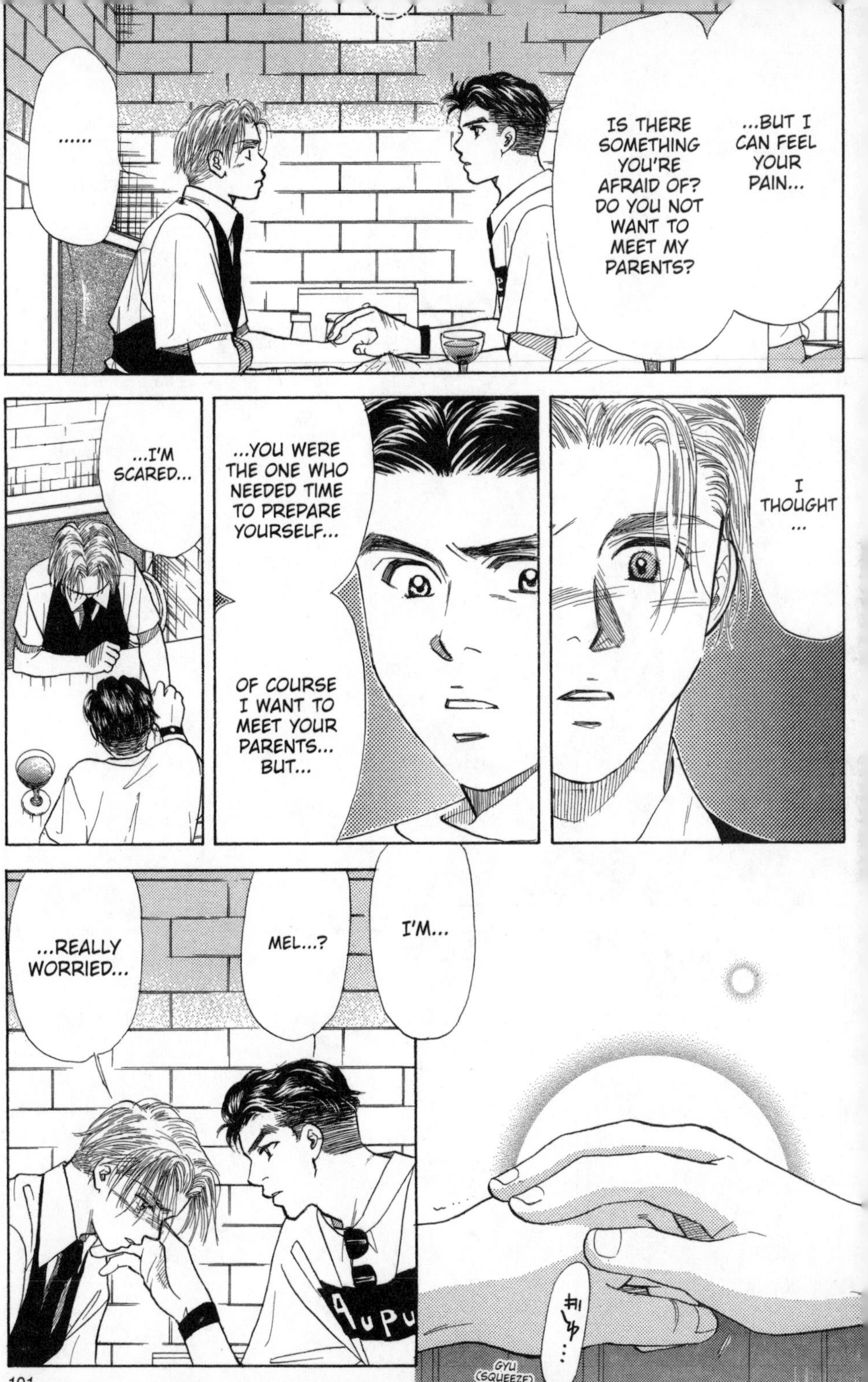
...BUT I CAN FEEL YOUR PAIN...
IS THERE SOMETHING YOU'RE AFRAID OF? DO YOU NOT WANT TO MEET MY PARENTS?
......
I THOUGHT ...
...YOU WERE THE ONE WHO NEEDED TIME TO PREPARE YOURSELF...
OF COURSE I WANT TO MEET YOUR PARENTS... BUT...
...I'M SCARED...
ギュ…
GYU (SQUEEZE)
I'M...
MEL...?
...REALLY WORRIED...

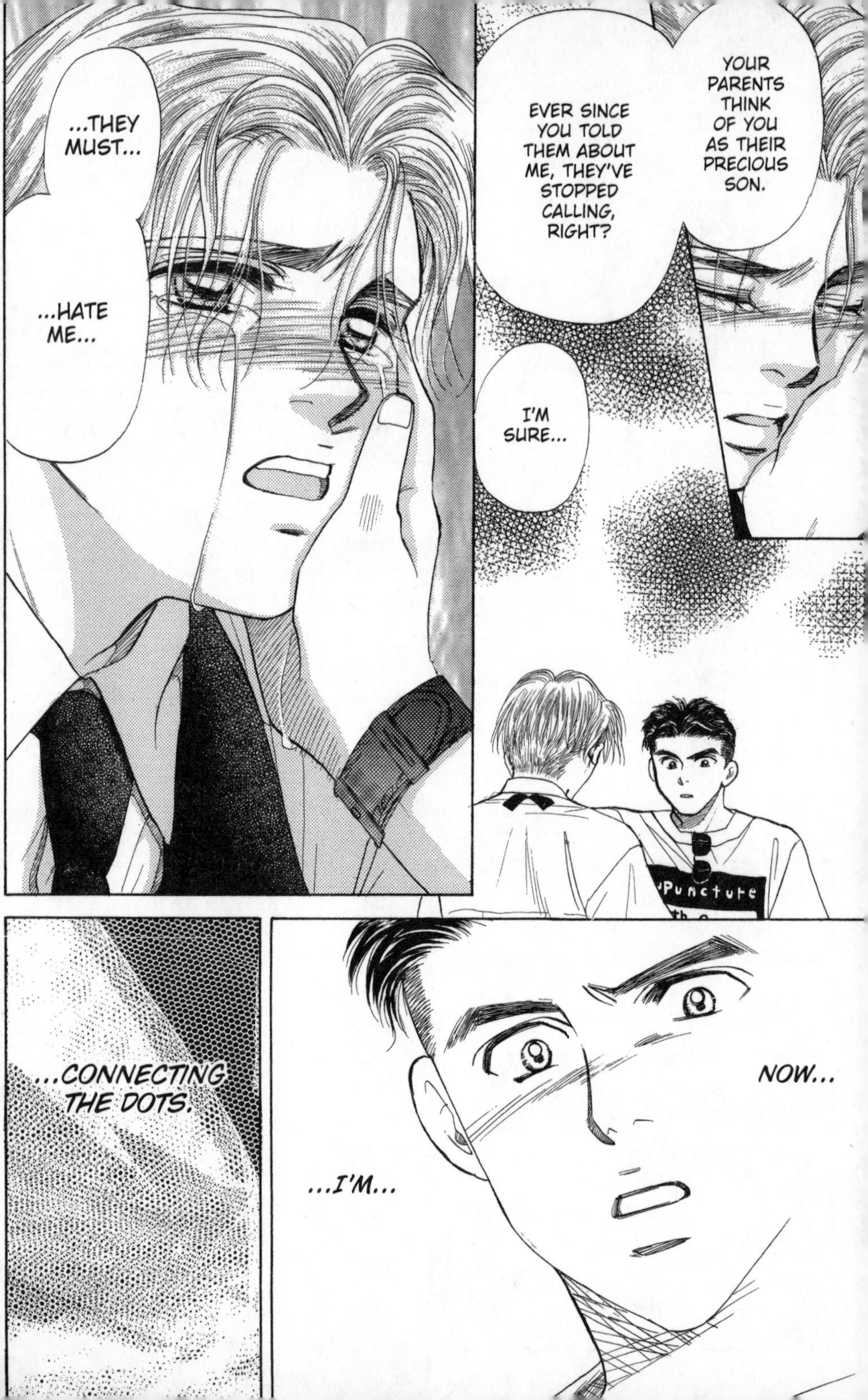
YOUR PARENTS THINK OF YOU AS THEIR PRECIOUS SON.
EVER SINCE YOU TOLD THEM ABOUT ME, THEY'VE STOPPED CALLING, RIGHT?
I'M SURE...
...THEY MUST...
...HATE ME...
NOW...
...I'M...
...CONNECTING THE DOTS.

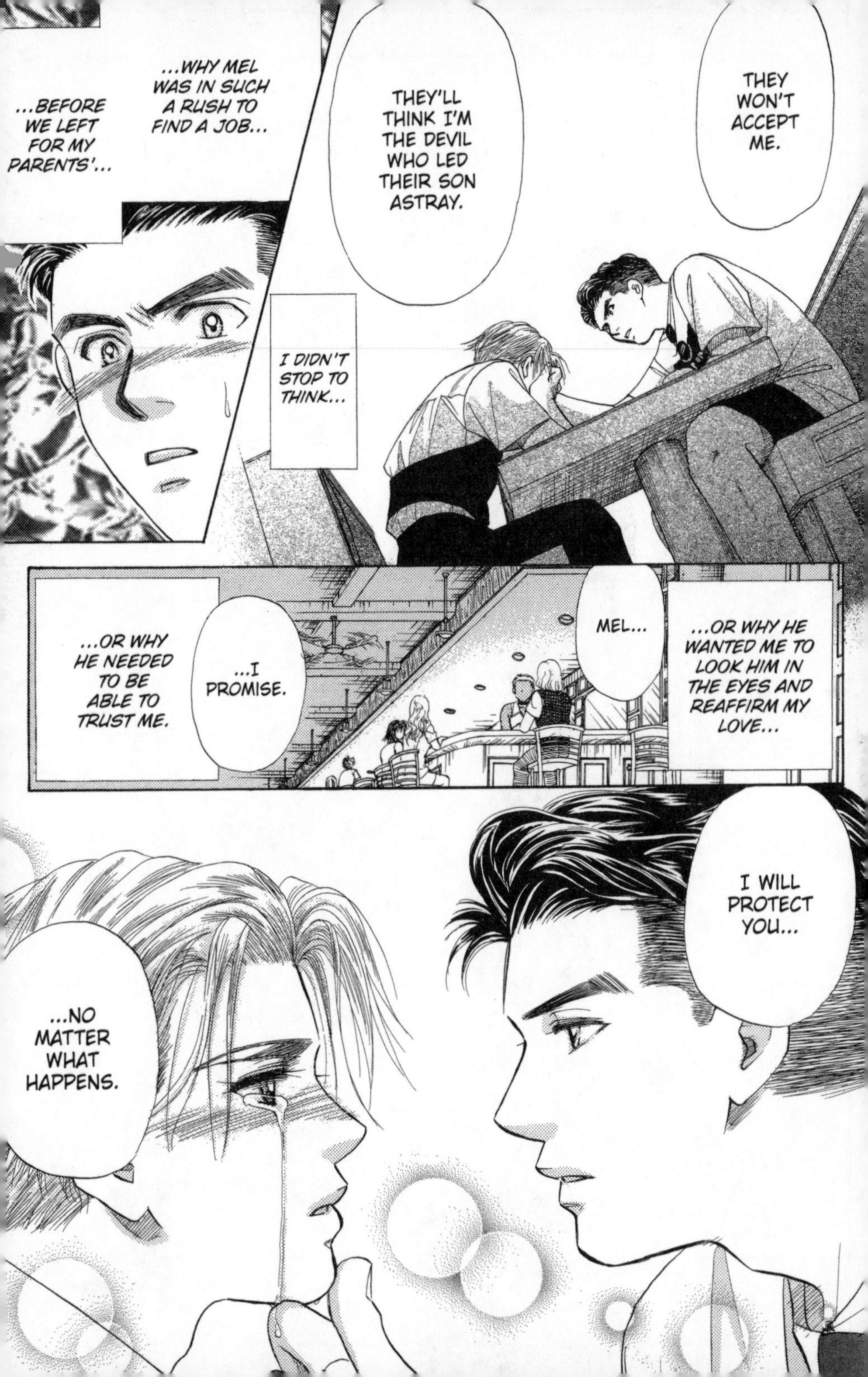
THEY WON'T ACCEPT ME.
THEY'LL THINK I'M THE DEVIL WHO LED THEIR SON ASTRAY.
I DIDN'T STOP TO THINK...
...WHY MEL WAS IN SUCH A RUSH TO FIND A JOB...
...BEFORE WE LEFT FOR MY PARENTS'...
...OR WHY HE WANTED ME TO LOOK HIM IN THE EYES AND REAFFIRM MY LOVE...
MEL...
...I PROMISE.
...OR WHY HE NEEDED TO BE ABLE TO TRUST ME.
I WILL PROTECT YOU...
...NO MATTER WHAT HAPPENS.

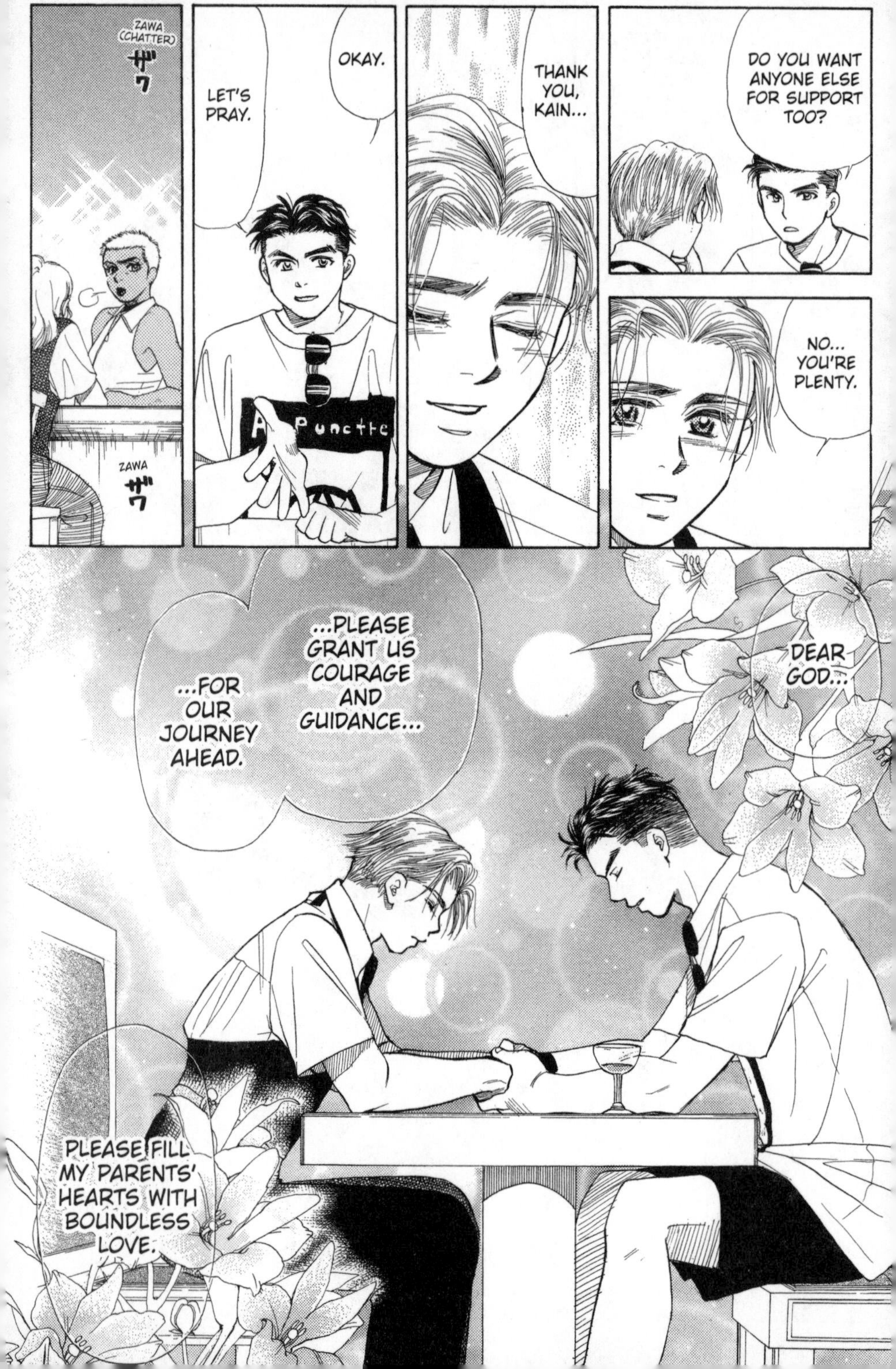
DO YOU WANT ANYONE ELSE FOR SUPPORT TOO?
NO... YOU'RE PLENTY.
THANK YOU, KAIN...
OKAY.
LET'S PRAY.
ZAWA (CHATTER)
ザワ
ZAWA
ザワ
DEAR GOD...
...PLEASE GRANT US COURAGE AND GUIDANCE...
...FOR OUR JOURNEY AHEAD.
PLEASE FILL MY PARENTS' HEARTS WITH BOUNDLESS LOVE.

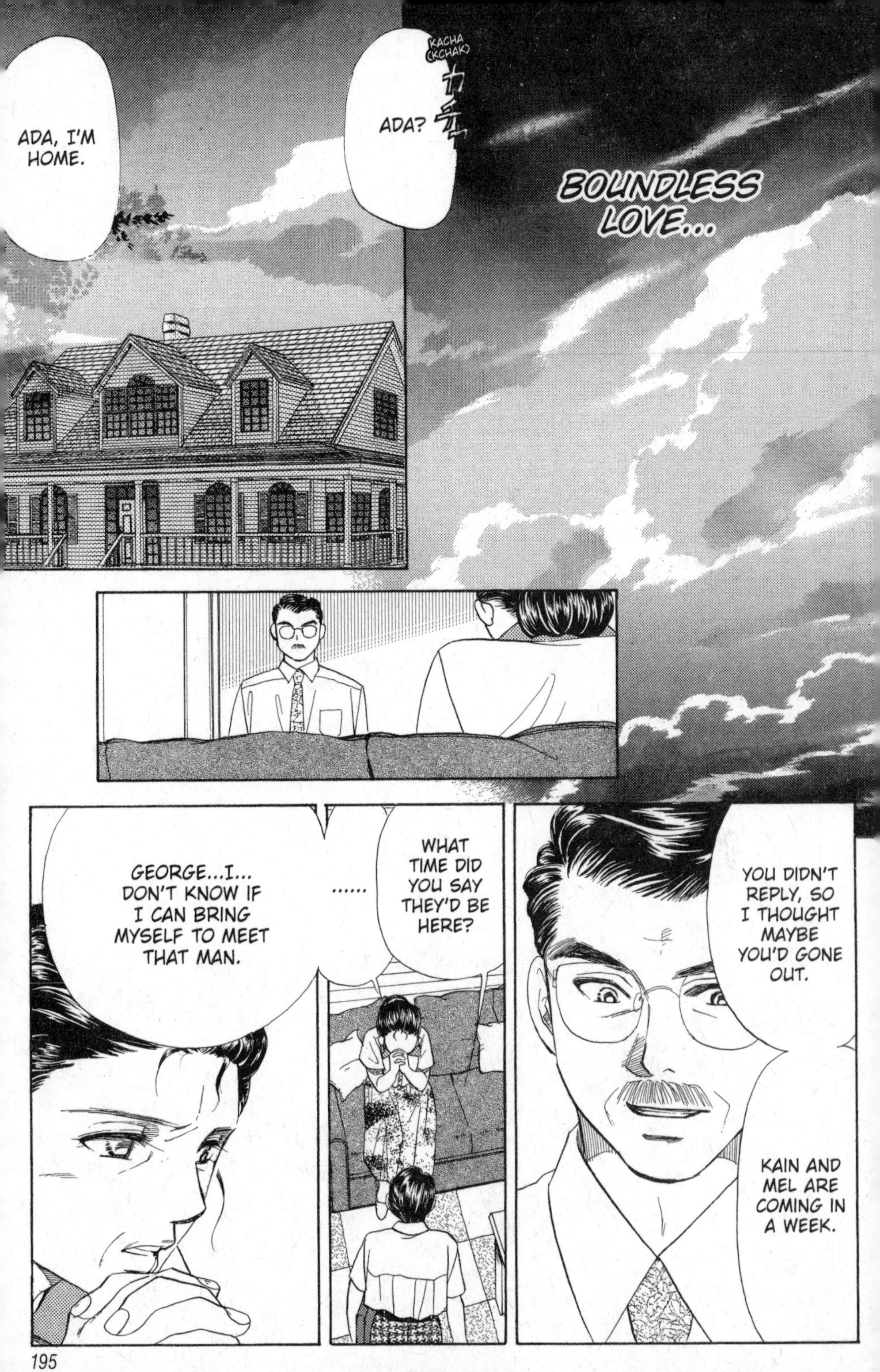
BOUNDLESS LOVE...
ADA, I'M HOME.
KACHA (KCHAK)
ADA?
YOU DIDN'T REPLY, SO I THOUGHT MAYBE YOU'D GONE OUT.
KAIN AND MEL ARE COMING IN A WEEK.
WHAT TIME DID YOU SAY THEY'D BE HERE?
......
GEORGE...I... DON'T KNOW IF I CAN BRING MYSELF TO MEET THAT MAN.

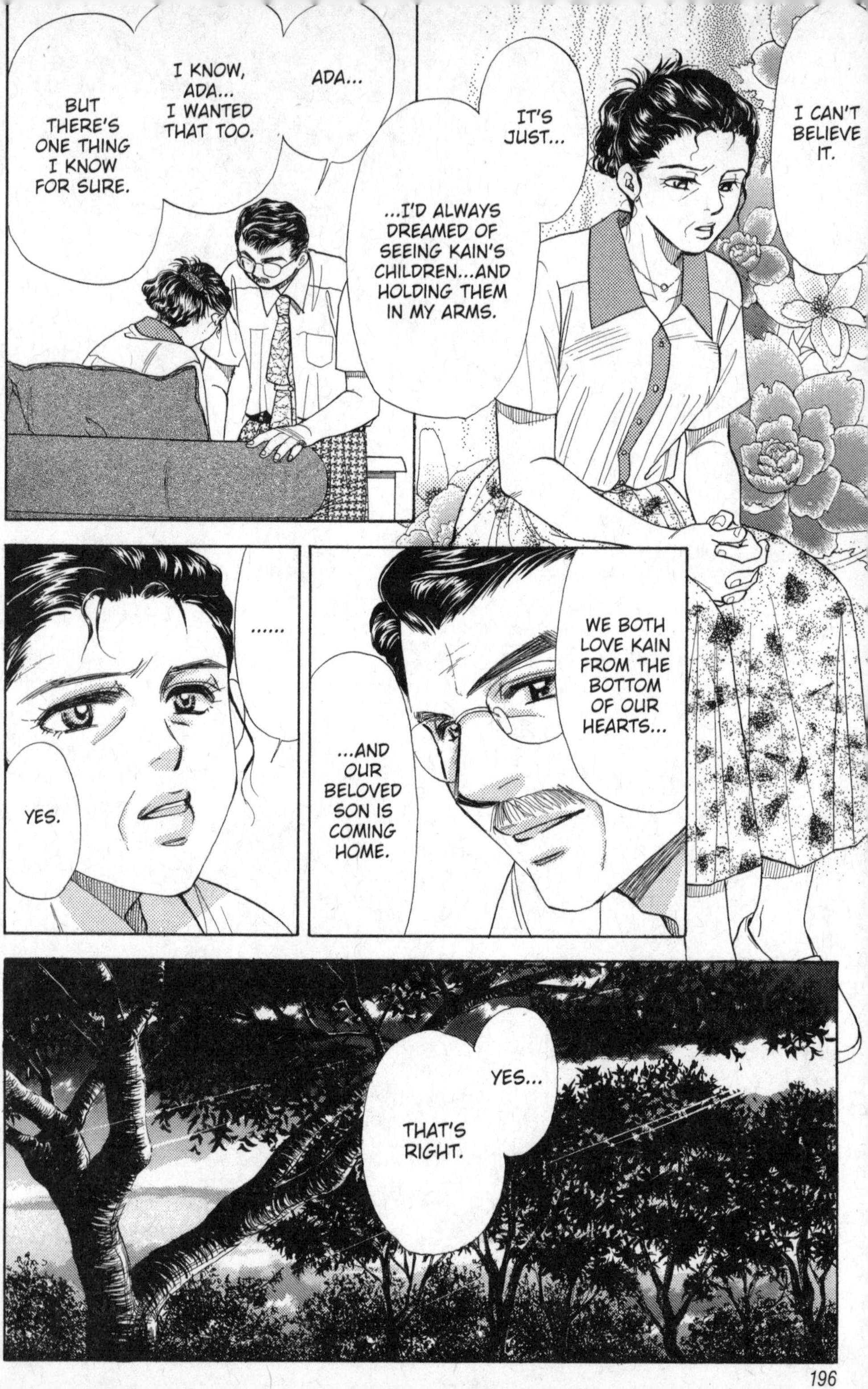
I CAN'T BELIEVE IT.
IT'S JUST...
...I'D ALWAYS DREAMED OF SEEING KAIN'S CHILDREN...AND HOLDING THEM IN MY ARMS.
ADA...
I KNOW, ADA... I WANTED THAT TOO.
BUT THERE'S ONE THING I KNOW FOR SURE.
WE BOTH LOVE KAIN FROM THE BOTTOM OF OUR HEARTS...
...AND OUR BELOVED SON IS COMING HOME.
......
YES.
YES...
THAT'S RIGHT.

EPISODE II

SCENE 2

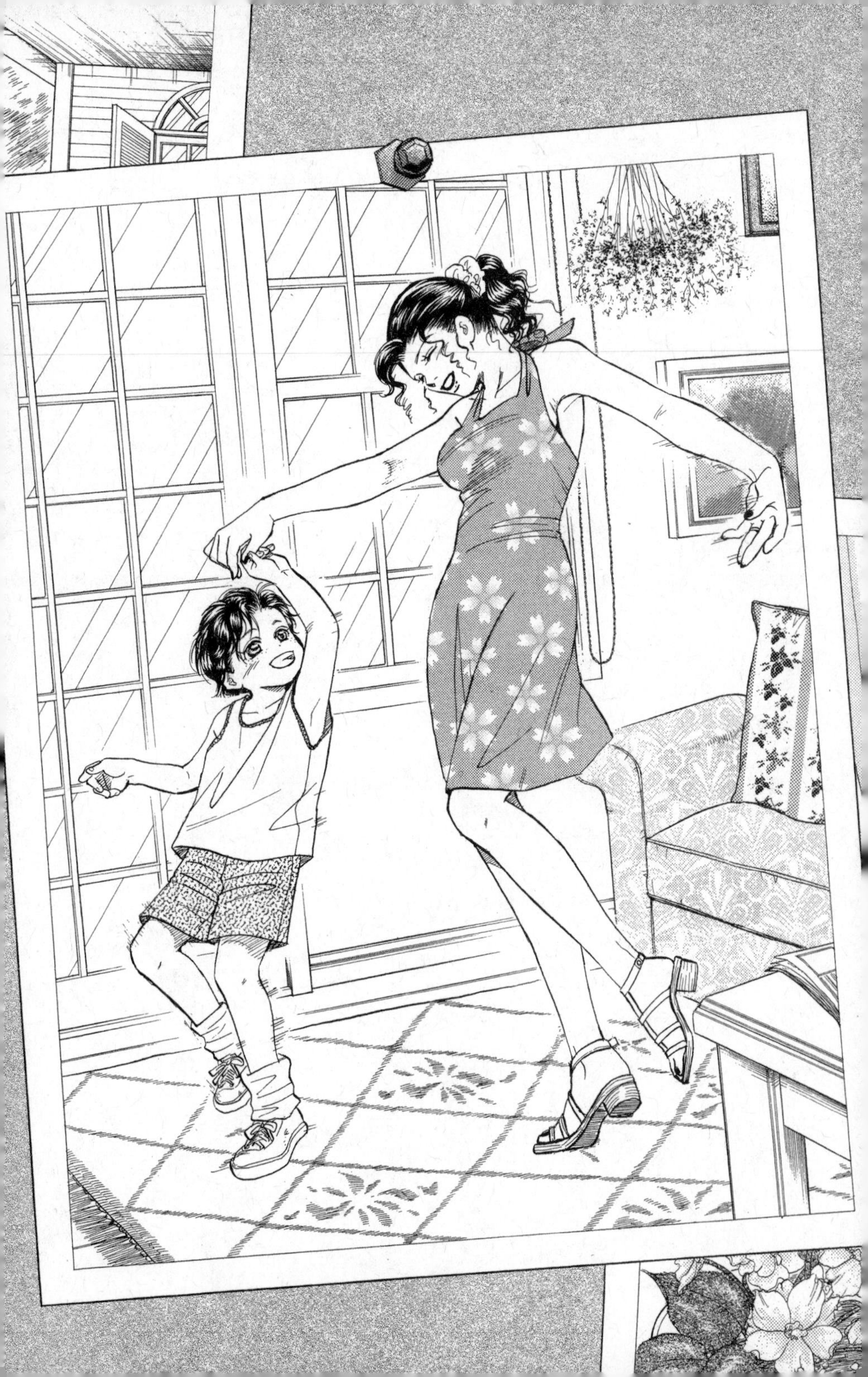

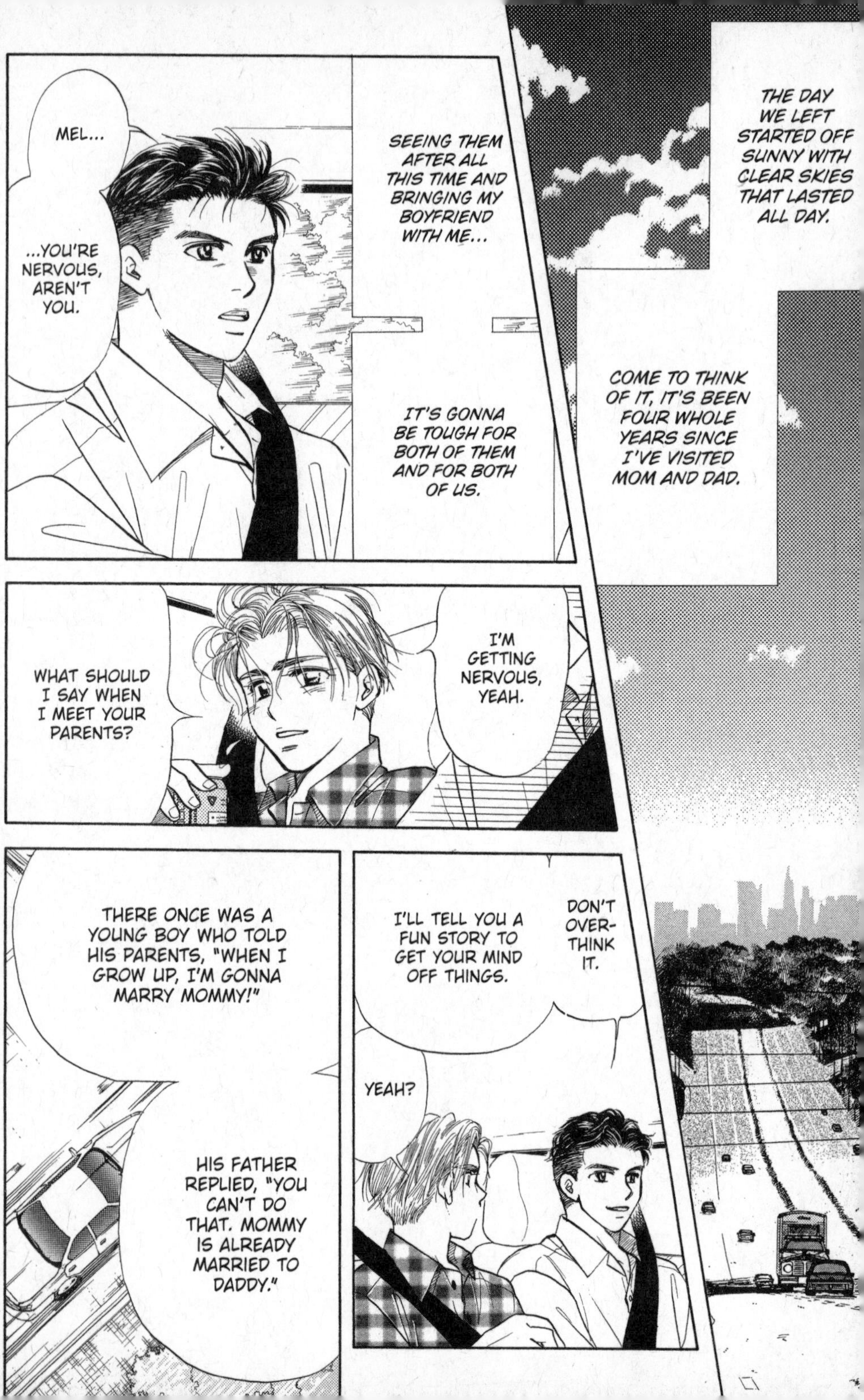
THE DAY WE LEFT STARTED OFF SUNNY WITH CLEAR SKIES THAT LASTED ALL DAY.
COME TO THINK OF IT, IT'S BEEN FOUR WHOLE YEARS SINCE I'VE VISITED MOM AND DAD.
SEEING THEM AFTER ALL THIS TIME AND BRINGING MY BOYFRIEND WITH ME...
IT'S GONNA BE TOUGH FOR BOTH OF THEM AND FOR BOTH OF US.
MEL...
...YOU'RE NERVOUS, AREN'T YOU.
I'M GETTING NERVOUS, YEAH.
WHAT SHOULD I SAY WHEN I MEET YOUR PARENTS?
DON'T OVER-THINK IT.
I'LL TELL YOU A FUN STORY TO GET YOUR MIND OFF THINGS.
YEAH?
THERE ONCE WAS A YOUNG BOY WHO TOLD HIS PARENTS, "WHEN I GROW UP, I'M GONNA MARRY MOMMY!"
HIS FATHER REPLIED, "YOU CAN'T DO THAT. MOMMY IS ALREADY MARRIED TO DADDY."

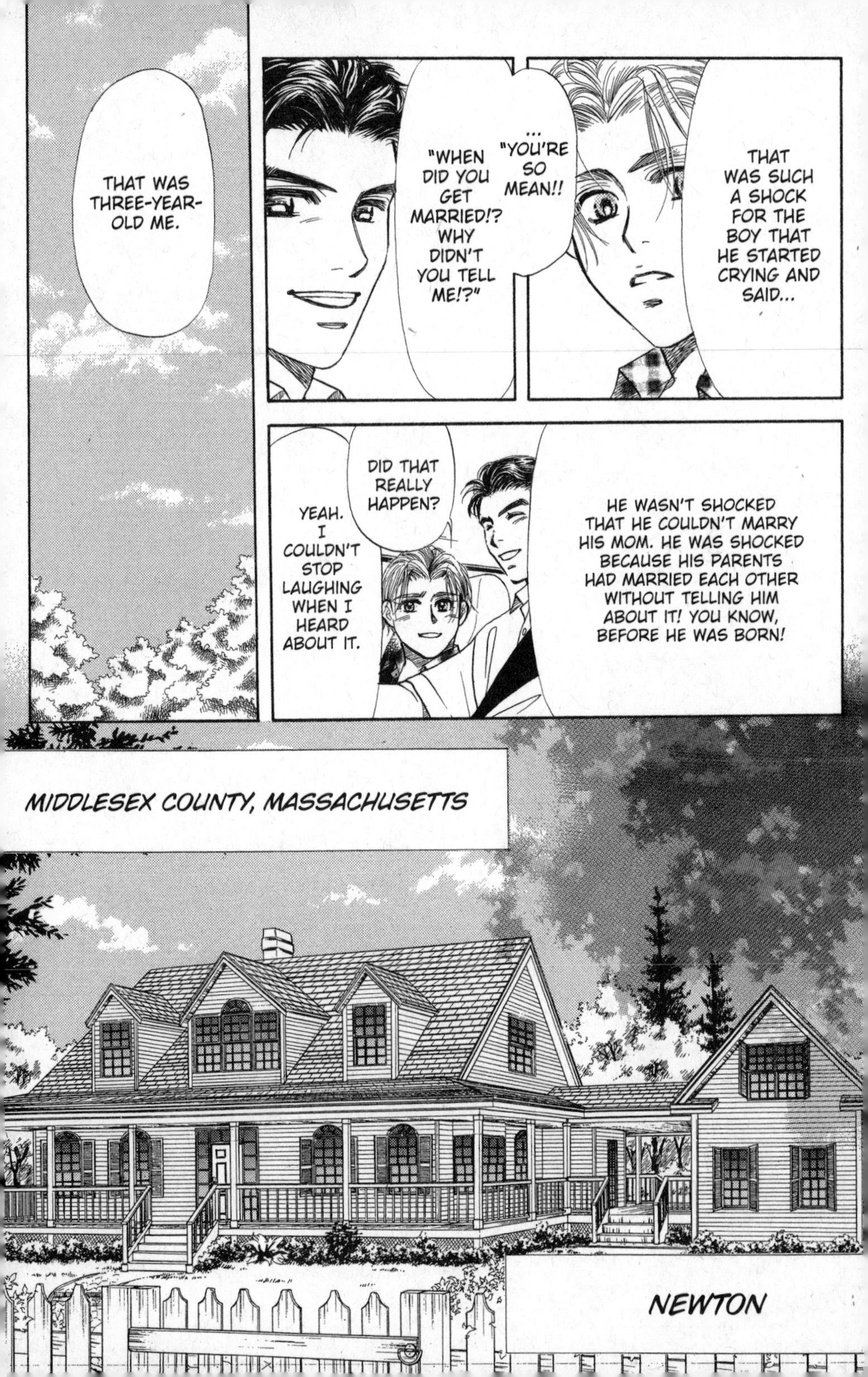
THAT WAS SUCH A SHOCK FOR THE BOY THAT HE STARTED CRYING AND SAID...
... "YOU'RE SO MEAN!!
"WHEN DID YOU GET MARRIED!? WHY DIDN'T YOU TELL ME!?"
HE WASN'T SHOCKED THAT HE COULDN'T MARRY HIS MOM. HE WAS SHOCKED BECAUSE HIS PARENTS HAD MARRIED EACH OTHER WITHOUT TELLING HIM ABOUT IT! YOU KNOW, BEFORE HE WAS BORN!
DID THAT REALLY HAPPEN?
YEAH. I COULDN'T STOP LAUGHING WHEN I HEARD ABOUT IT.
THAT WAS THREE-YEAR-OLD ME.
MIDDLESEX COUNTY, MASSACHUSETTS
NEWTON

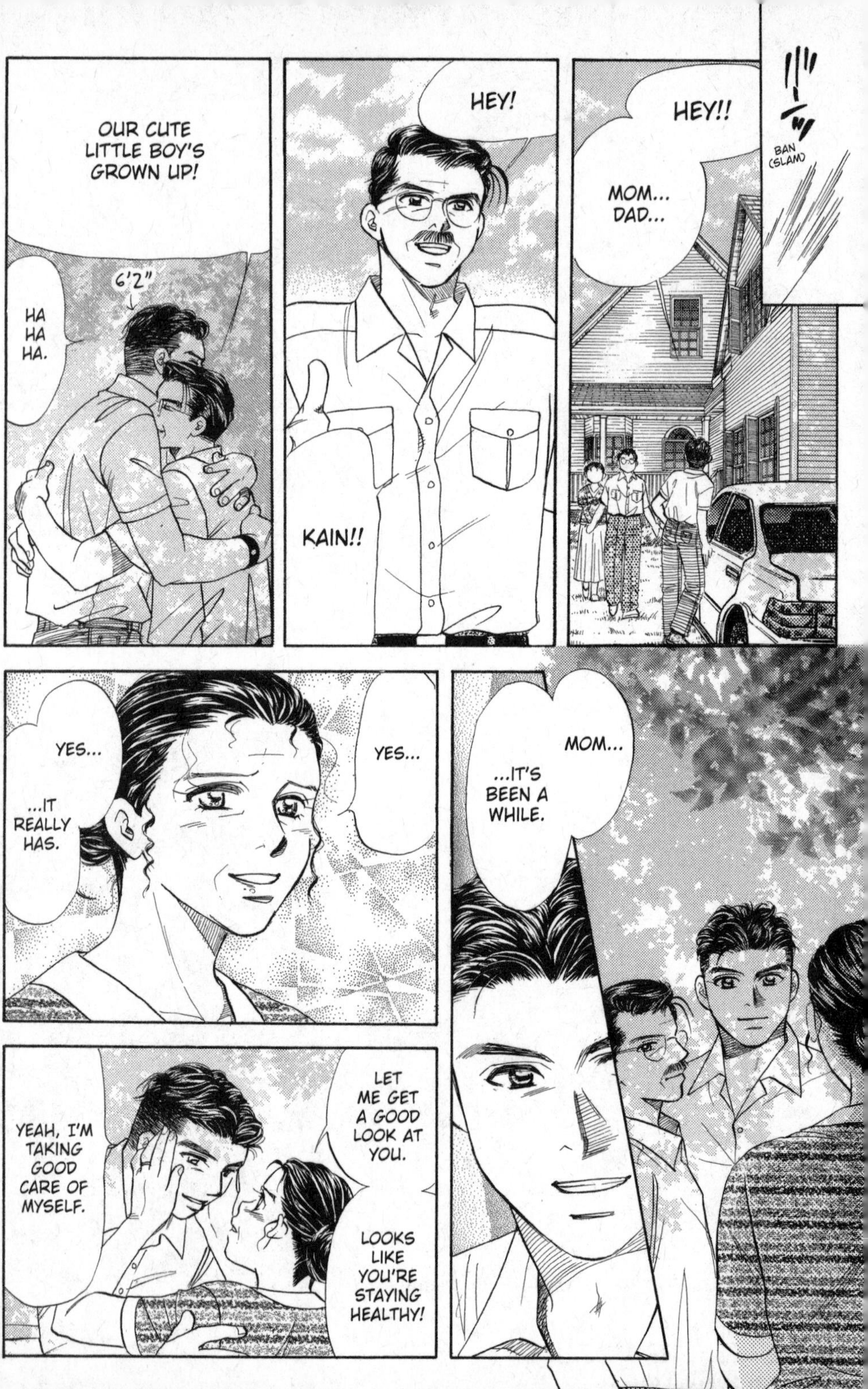
BAN (SLAM)
HEY!!
MOM... DAD...
HEY!
KAIN!!
OUR CUTE LITTLE BOY'S GROWN UP!
6'2"
HA HA HA.
MOM...
...IT'S BEEN A WHILE.
YES...
YES...
...IT REALLY HAS.
LET ME GET A GOOD LOOK AT YOU.
LOOKS LIKE YOU'RE STAYING HEALTHY!
YEAH, I'M TAKING GOOD CARE OF MYSELF.

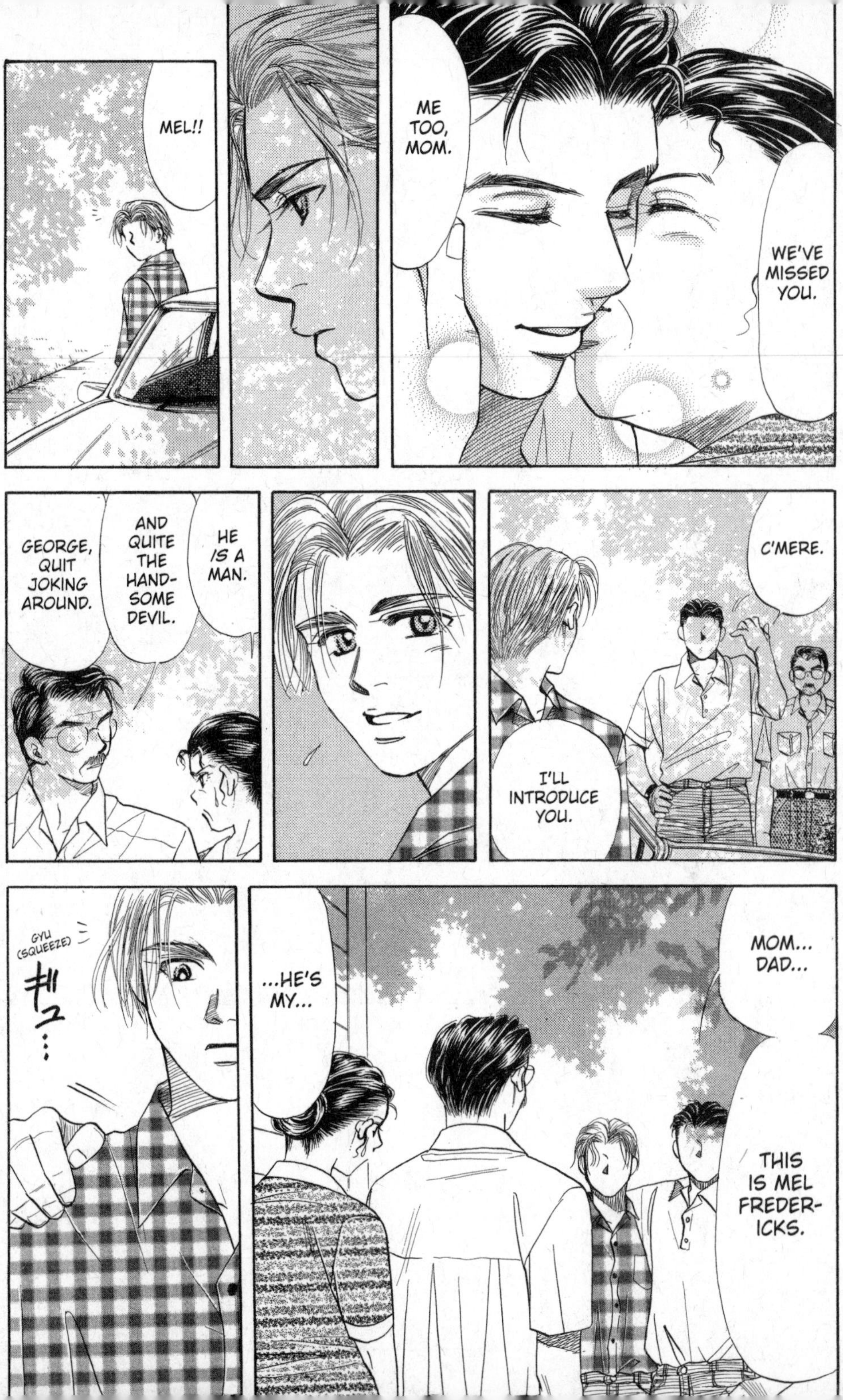
WE'VE MISSED YOU.
ME TOO, MOM.
MEL!!
C'MERE.
I'LL INTRODUCE YOU.
HE IS A MAN.
AND QUITE THE HAND-SOME DEVIL.
GEORGE, QUIT JOKING AROUND.
MOM... DAD...
THIS IS MEL FREDER-ICKS.
...HE'S MY...
GYU (SQUEEZE)
ギュ…

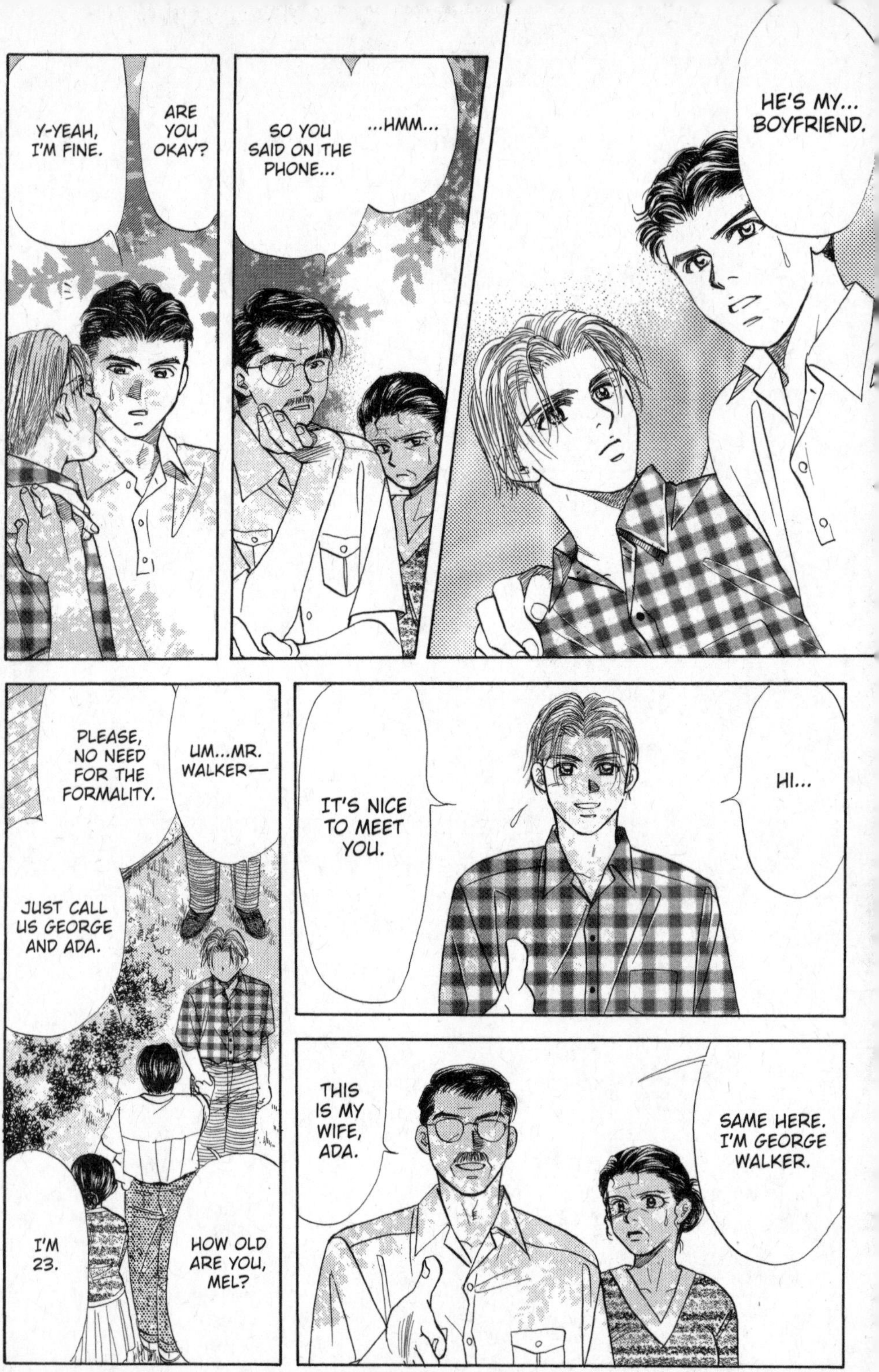
HE'S MY... BOYFRIEND.
...HMM...
SO YOU SAID ON THE PHONE...
ARE YOU OKAY?
Y-YEAH, I'M FINE.
HI...
IT'S NICE TO MEET YOU.
SAME HERE. I'M GEORGE WALKER.
THIS IS MY WIFE, ADA.
UM...MR. WALKER—
PLEASE, NO NEED FOR THE FORMALITY.
JUST CALL US GEORGE AND ADA.
HOW OLD ARE YOU, MEL?
I'M 23.

......

...ADA.

IT'S NICE TO MEET YOU...

MOM...

......

OH?

YES...OF COURSE...

WE'RE TIRED FROM THE LONG DRIVE. WOULD YOU MIND LETTING US REST UP A BIT?

I JUST CAN'T!!

I TOLD YOU...

...I CAN'T!!

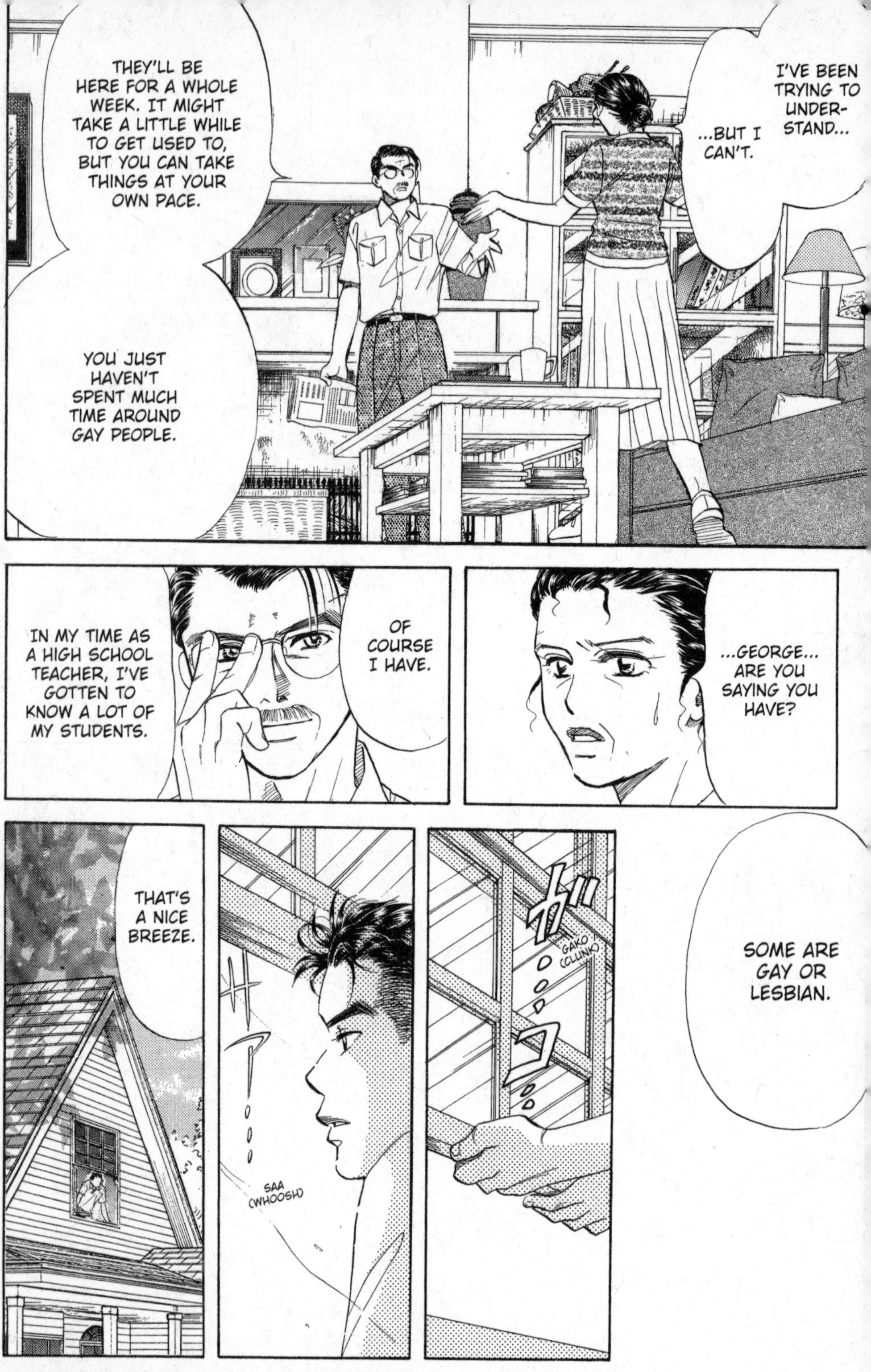
I'VE BEEN TRYING TO UNDER-STAND...
...BUT I CAN'T.
THEY'LL BE HERE FOR A WHOLE WEEK. IT MIGHT TAKE A LITTLE WHILE TO GET USED TO, BUT YOU CAN TAKE THINGS AT YOUR OWN PACE.
YOU JUST HAVEN'T SPENT MUCH TIME AROUND GAY PEOPLE.
...GEORGE... ARE YOU SAYING YOU HAVE?
OF COURSE I HAVE.
IN MY TIME AS A HIGH SCHOOL TEACHER, I'VE GOTTEN TO KNOW A LOT OF MY STUDENTS.
SOME ARE GAY OR LESBIAN.
GAKO (CLUNK)
SAA (WHOOSH)
THAT'S A NICE BREEZE.

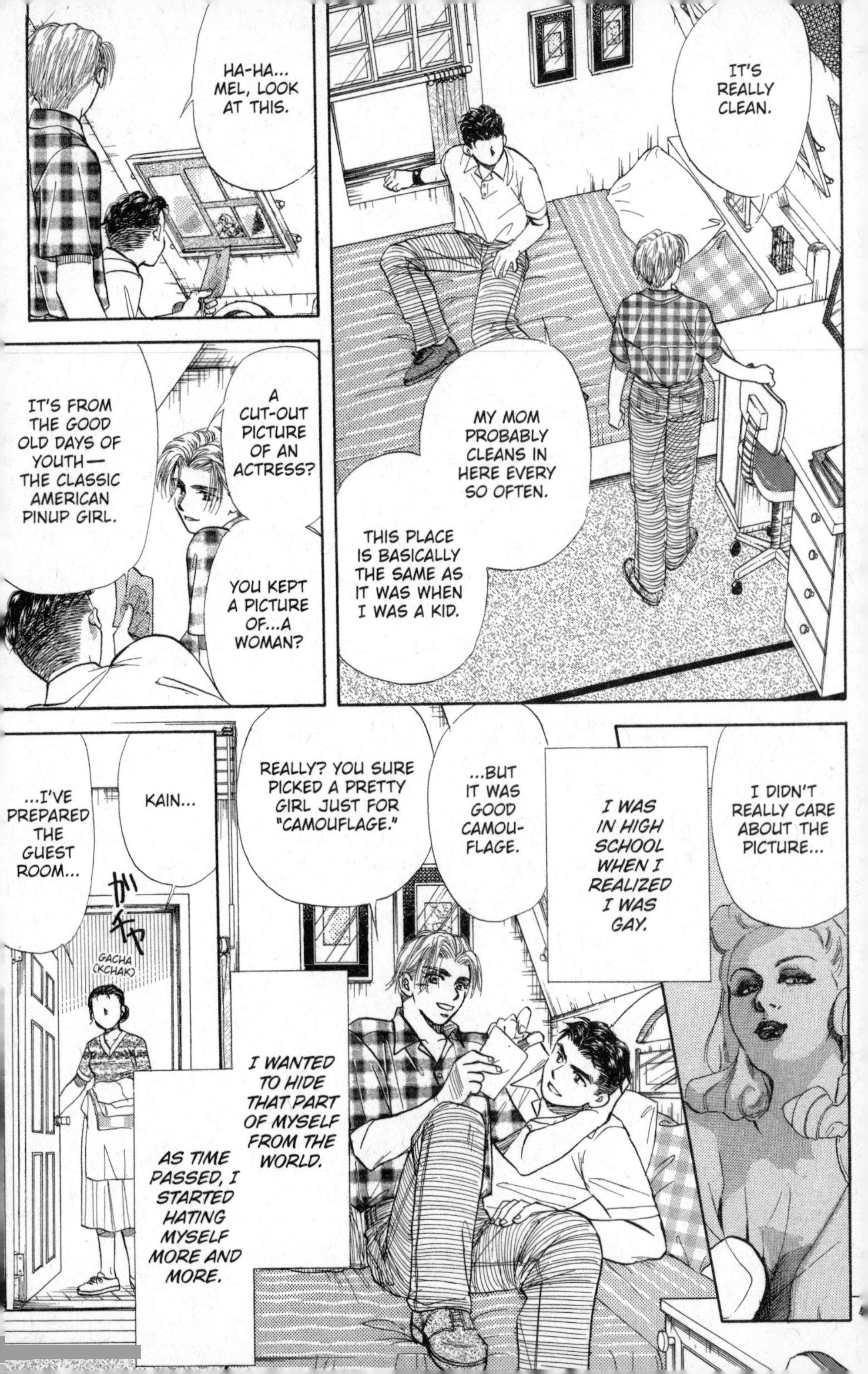
IT'S REALLY CLEAN.
MY MOM PROBABLY CLEANS IN HERE EVERY SO OFTEN.
THIS PLACE IS BASICALLY THE SAME AS IT WAS WHEN I WAS A KID.
HA-HA... MEL, LOOK AT THIS.
A CUT-OUT PICTURE OF AN ACTRESS?
YOU KEPT A PICTURE OF...A WOMAN?
IT'S FROM THE GOOD OLD DAYS OF YOUTH—THE CLASSIC AMERICAN PINUP GIRL.
I DIDN'T REALLY CARE ABOUT THE PICTURE...
I WAS IN HIGH SCHOOL WHEN I REALIZED I WAS GAY.
...BUT IT WAS GOOD CAMOUFLAGE.
REALLY? YOU SURE PICKED A PRETTY GIRL JUST FOR "CAMOUFLAGE."
I WANTED TO HIDE THAT PART OF MYSELF FROM THE WORLD.
AS TIME PASSED, I STARTED HATING MYSELF MORE AND MORE.
ガチャ
GACHA (KCHAK)
KAIN...
...I'VE PREPARED THE GUEST ROOM...

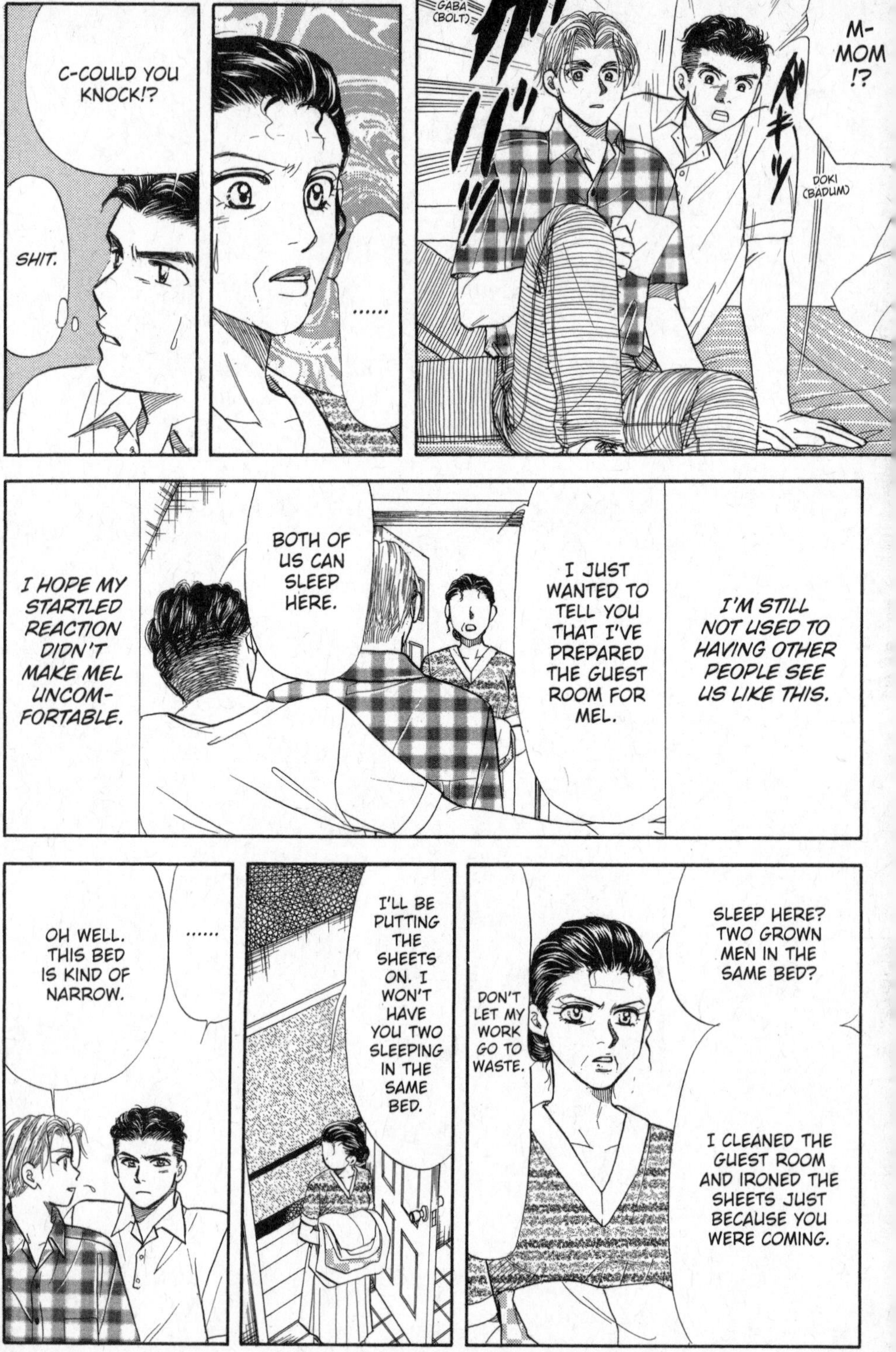
M-MOM!?
GABA (BOLT)
DOKI (BADUM)
......
C-COULD YOU KNOCK!?
SHIT.
I'M STILL NOT USED TO HAVING OTHER PEOPLE SEE US LIKE THIS.
I JUST WANTED TO TELL YOU THAT I'VE PREPARED THE GUEST ROOM FOR MEL.
BOTH OF US CAN SLEEP HERE.
I HOPE MY STARTLED REACTION DIDN'T MAKE MEL UNCOM-FORTABLE.
SLEEP HERE? TWO GROWN MEN IN THE SAME BED?
I CLEANED THE GUEST ROOM AND IRONED THE SHEETS JUST BECAUSE YOU WERE COMING.
DON'T LET MY WORK GO TO WASTE.
I'LL BE PUTTING THE SHEETS ON. I WON'T HAVE YOU TWO SLEEPING IN THE SAME BED.
......
OH WELL. THIS BED IS KIND OF NARROW.

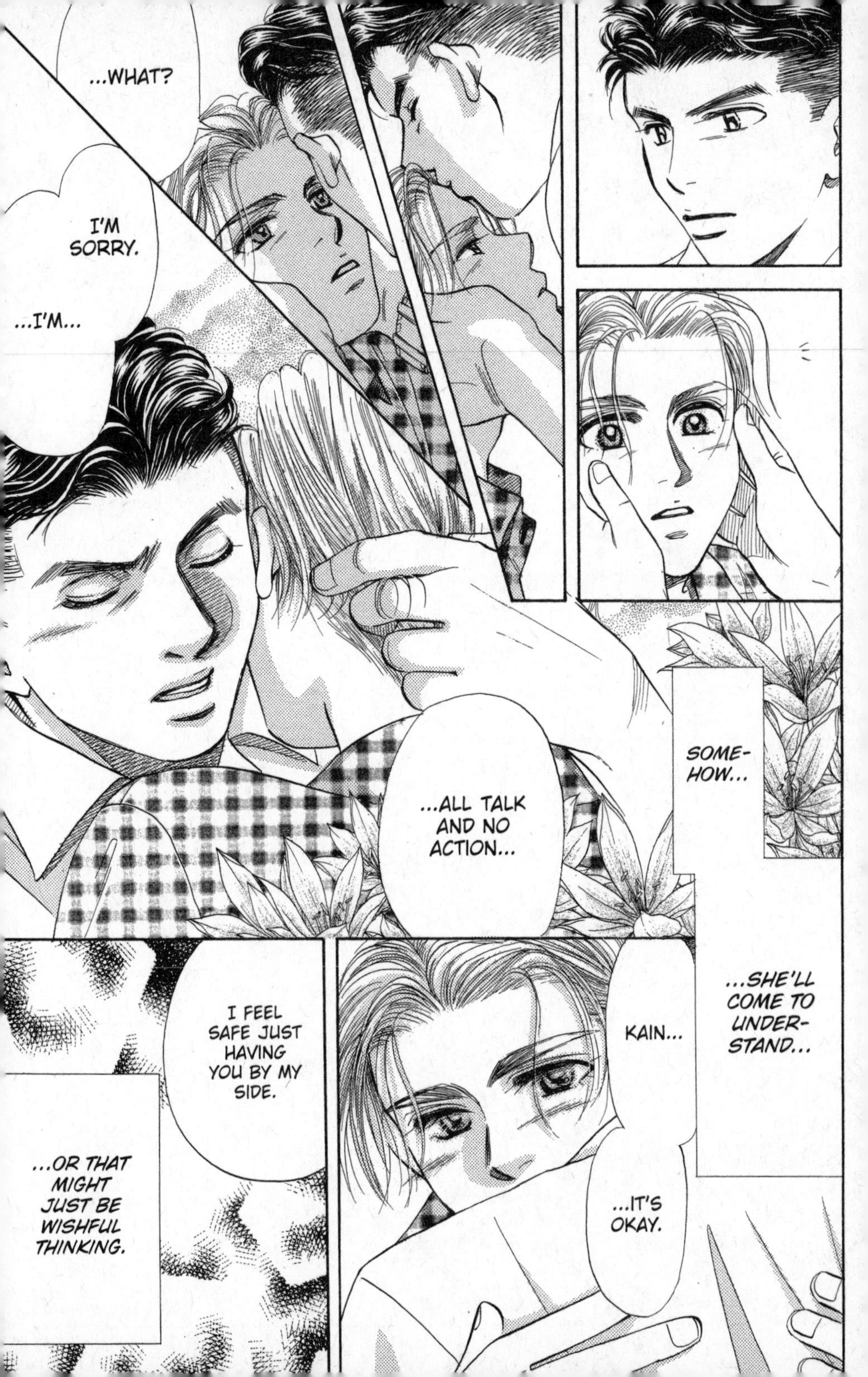
...WHAT?
I'M SORRY.
...I'M...
...ALL TALK AND NO ACTION...
SOME-HOW...
...SHE'LL COME TO UNDER-STAND...
KAIN...
...IT'S OKAY.
I FEEL SAFE JUST HAVING YOU BY MY SIDE.
...OR THAT MIGHT JUST BE WISHFUL THINKING.

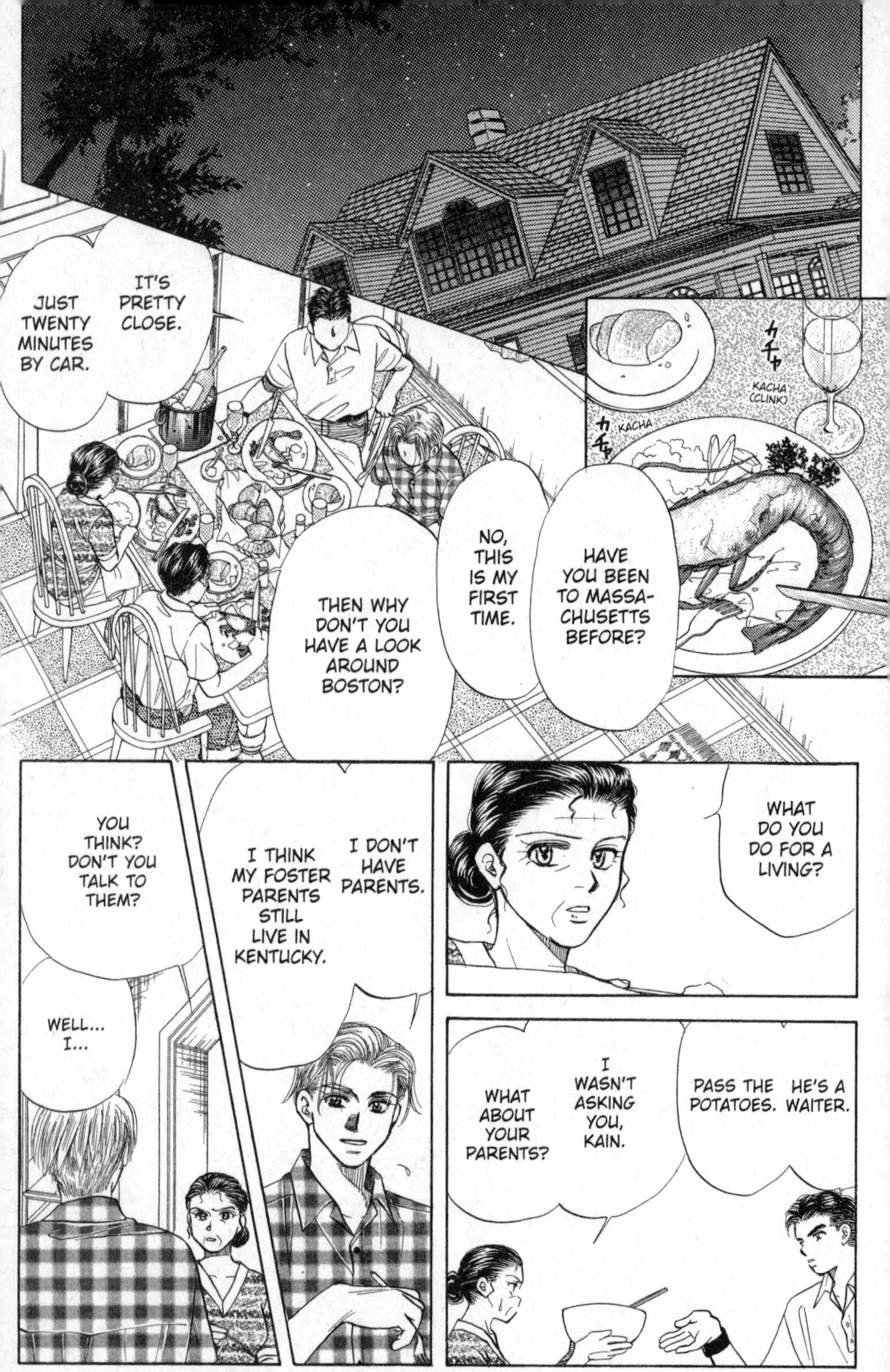
カチャ
KACHA (CLINK)
カチャ
KACHA
HAVE YOU BEEN TO MASSA-CHUSETTS BEFORE?
NO, THIS IS MY FIRST TIME.
THEN WHY DON'T YOU HAVE A LOOK AROUND BOSTON?
IT'S PRETTY CLOSE.
JUST TWENTY MINUTES BY CAR.
WHAT DO YOU DO FOR A LIVING?
HE'S A WAITER.
PASS THE POTATOES.
I WASN'T ASKING YOU, KAIN.
WHAT ABOUT YOUR PARENTS?
I DON'T HAVE PARENTS.
I THINK MY FOSTER PARENTS STILL LIVE IN KENTUCKY.
YOU THINK? DON'T YOU TALK TO THEM?
WELL... I...

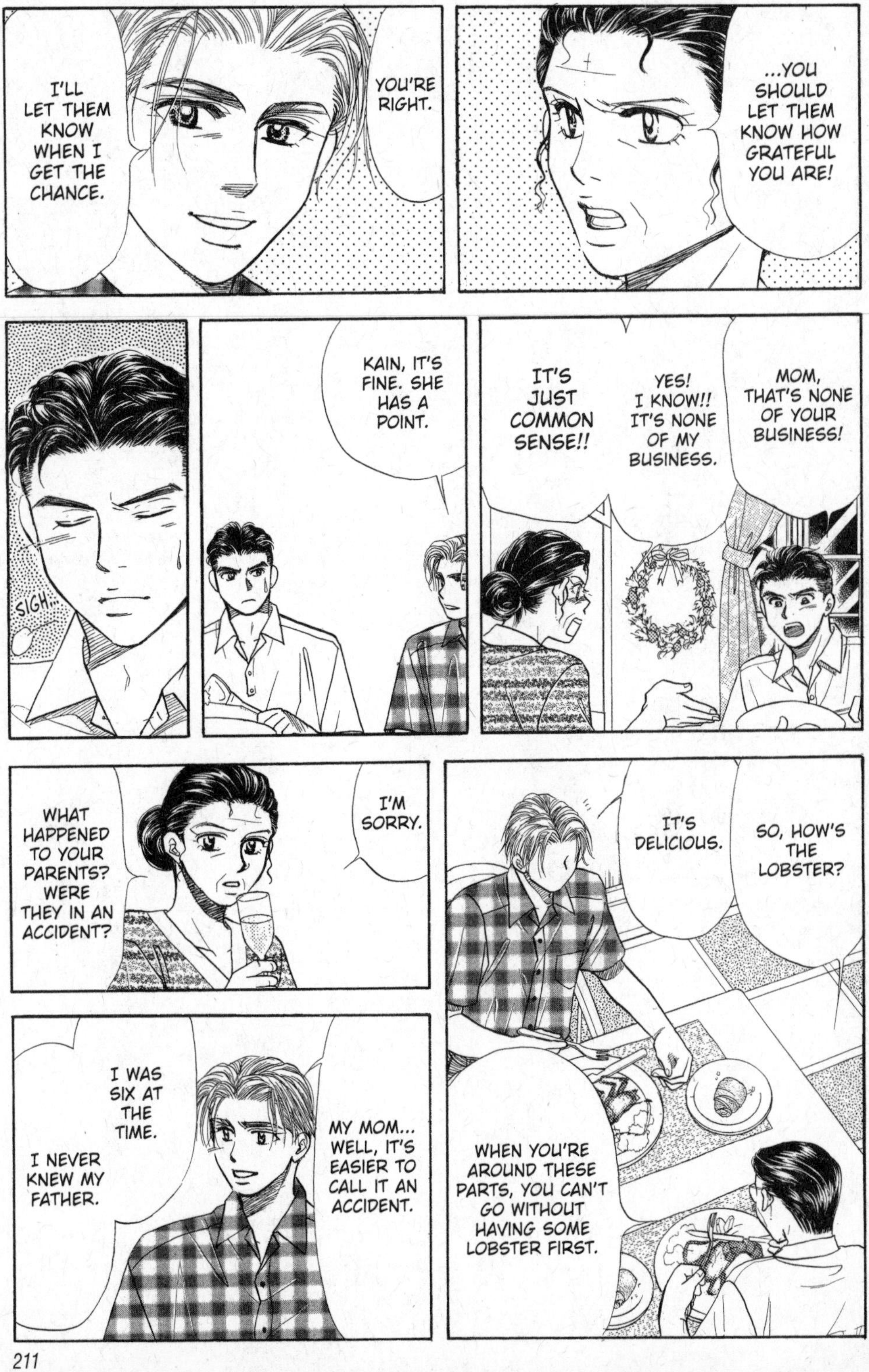
...YOU SHOULD LET THEM KNOW HOW GRATEFUL YOU ARE!
YOU'RE RIGHT.
I'LL LET THEM KNOW WHEN I GET THE CHANCE.
MOM, THAT'S NONE OF YOUR BUSINESS!
YES! I KNOW!! IT'S NONE OF MY BUSINESS.
IT'S JUST COMMON SENSE!!
KAIN, IT'S FINE. SHE HAS A POINT.
SIGH...
SO, HOW'S THE LOBSTER?
IT'S DELICIOUS.
WHEN YOU'RE AROUND THESE PARTS, YOU CAN'T GO WITHOUT HAVING SOME LOBSTER FIRST.
I'M SORRY.
WHAT HAPPENED TO YOUR PARENTS? WERE THEY IN AN ACCIDENT?
MY MOM... WELL, IT'S EASIER TO CALL IT AN ACCIDENT.
I WAS SIX AT THE TIME.
I NEVER KNEW MY FATHER.

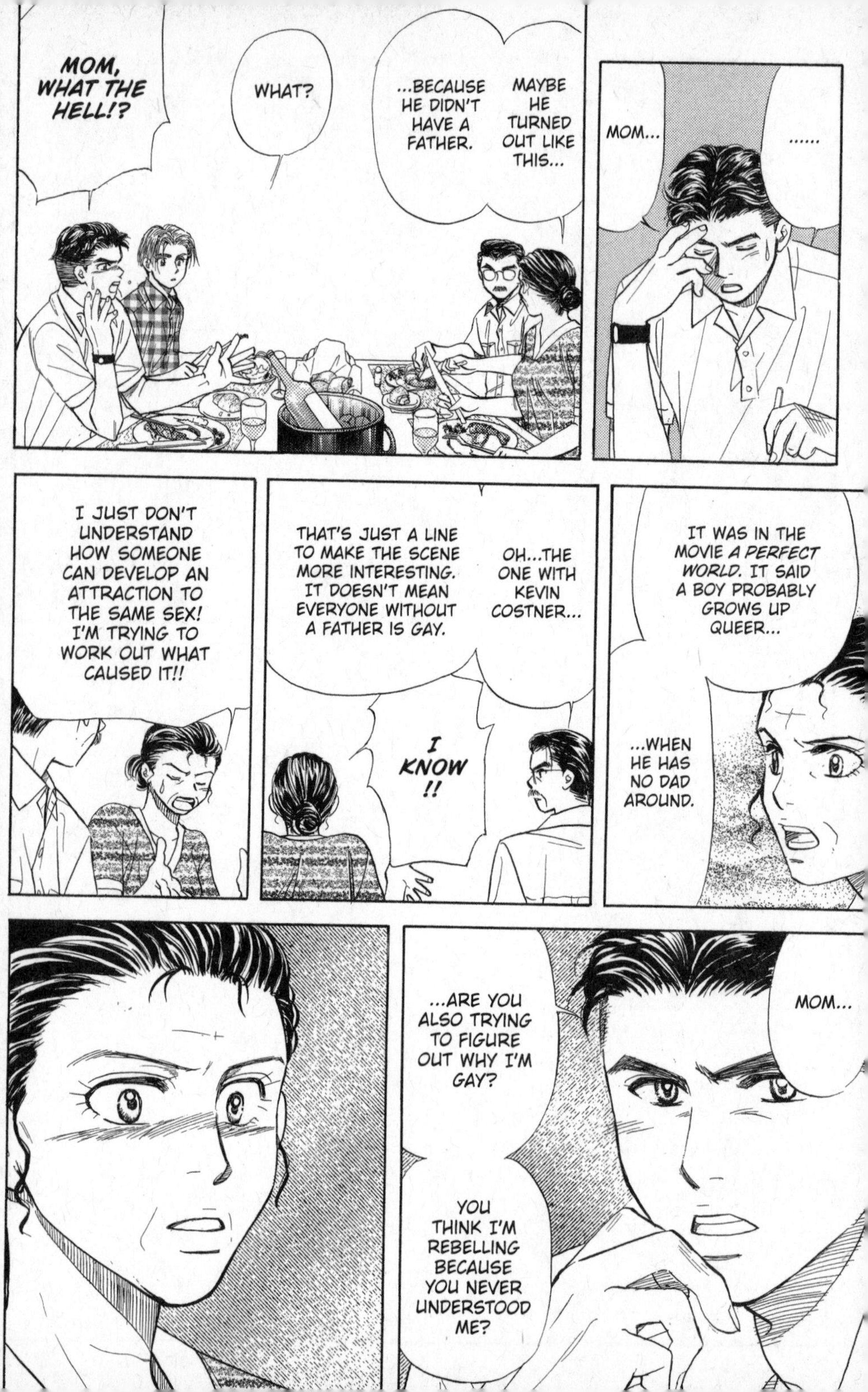
......
MOM...
MAYBE HE TURNED OUT LIKE THIS...
...BECAUSE HE DIDN'T HAVE A FATHER.
WHAT?
MOM, WHAT THE HELL!?
IT WAS IN THE MOVIE *A PERFECT WORLD*. IT SAID A BOY PROBABLY GROWS UP QUEER...
...WHEN HE HAS NO DAD AROUND.
OH...THE ONE WITH KEVIN COSTNER...
THAT'S JUST A LINE TO MAKE THE SCENE MORE INTERESTING. IT DOESN'T MEAN EVERYONE WITHOUT A FATHER IS GAY.
I KNOW!!
I JUST DON'T UNDERSTAND HOW SOMEONE CAN DEVELOP AN ATTRACTION TO THE SAME SEX! I'M TRYING TO WORK OUT WHAT CAUSED IT!!
MOM...
...ARE YOU ALSO TRYING TO FIGURE OUT WHY I'M GAY?
YOU THINK I'M REBELLING BECAUSE YOU NEVER UNDERSTOOD ME?

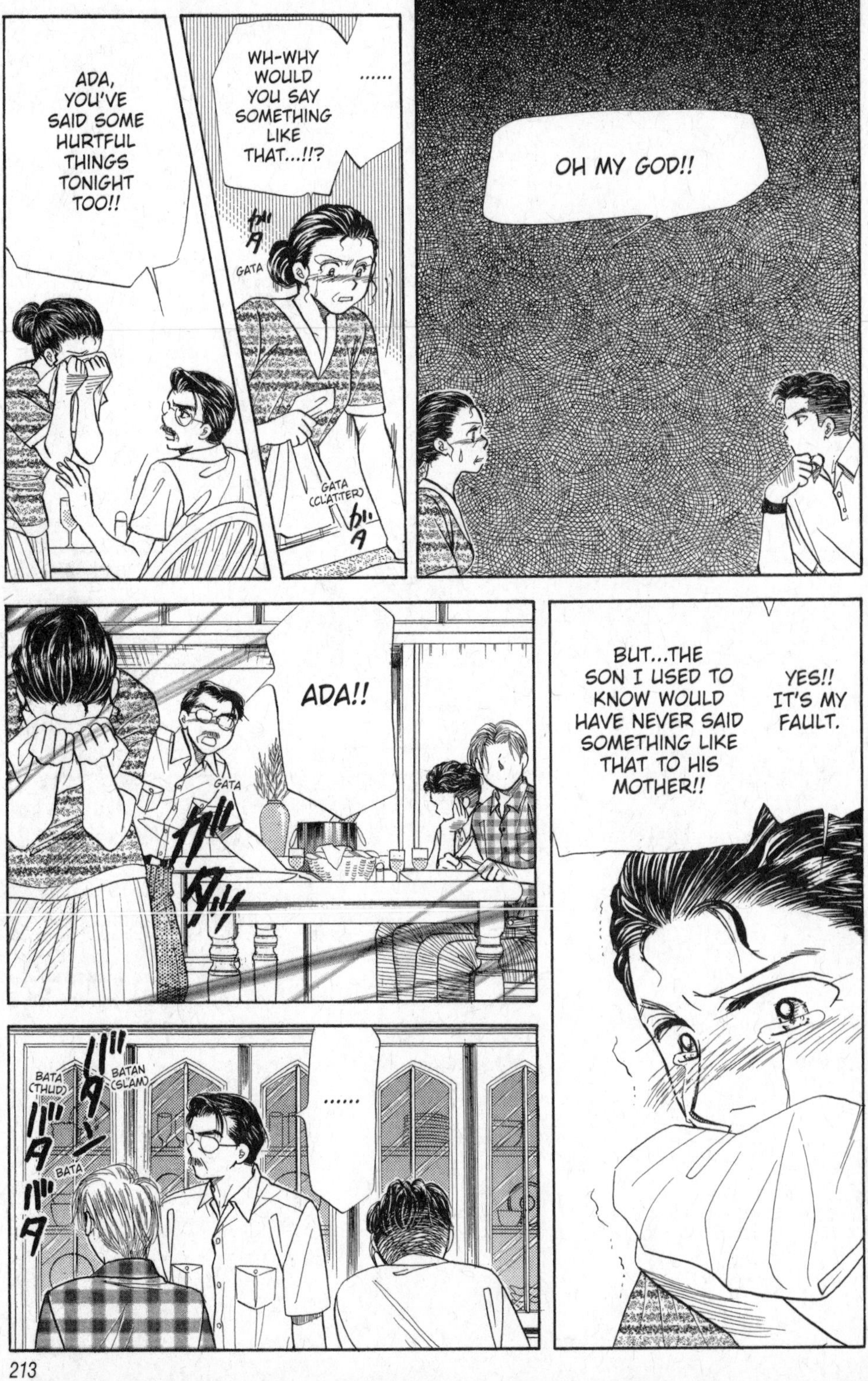
OH MY GOD!!
WH-WHY WOULD YOU SAY SOMETHING LIKE THAT...!!?
......
GATA
GATA (CLATTER)
ADA, YOU'VE SAID SOME HURTFUL THINGS TONIGHT TOO!!
YES!! IT'S MY FAULT.
BUT...THE SON I USED TO KNOW WOULD HAVE NEVER SAID SOMETHING LIKE THAT TO HIS MOTHER!!
ADA!!
GATA
BATAN (SLAM)
BATA (THUD)
BATA
......

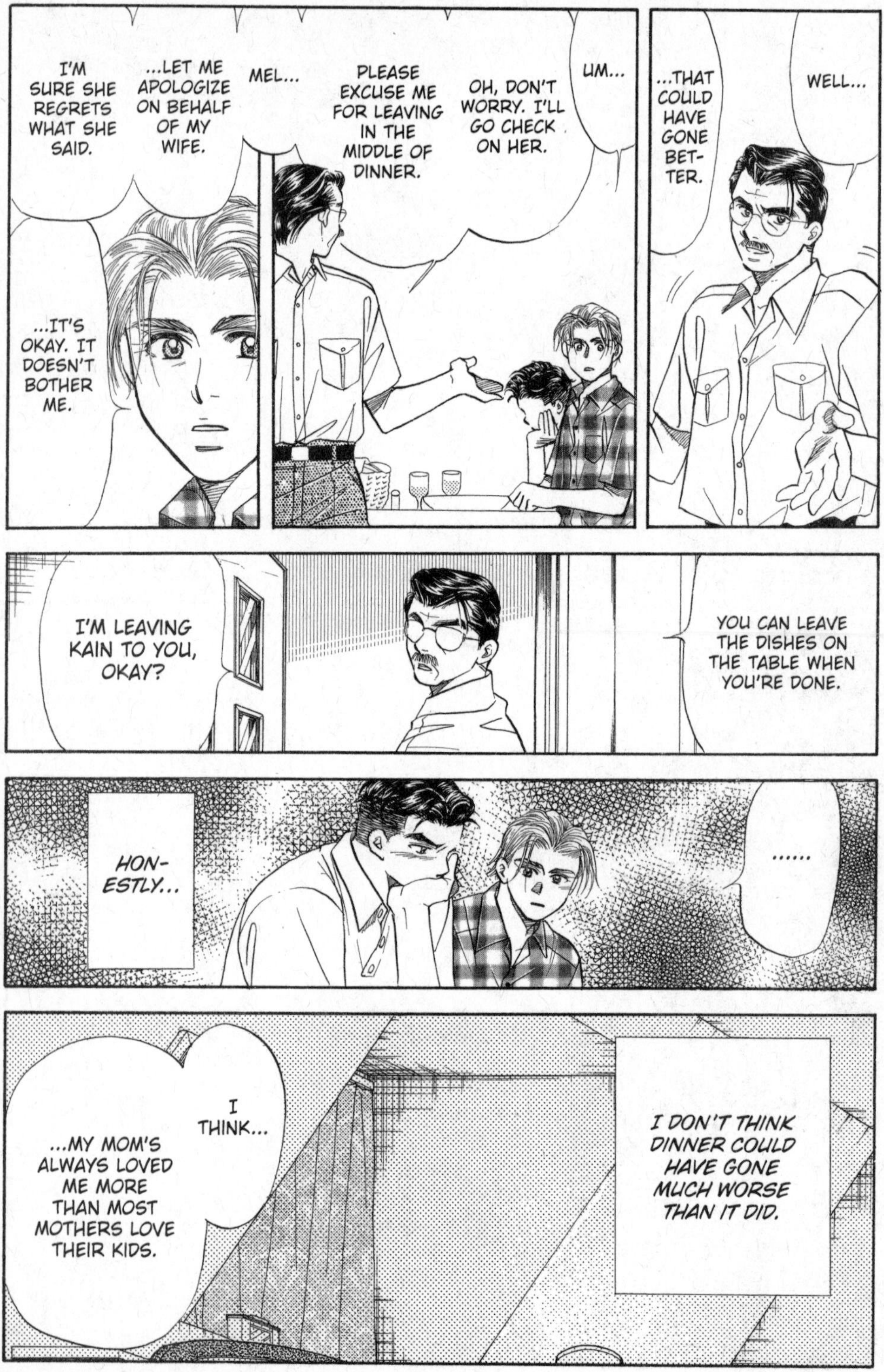
WELL...
...THAT COULD HAVE GONE BET-TER.
UM...
OH, DON'T WORRY. I'LL GO CHECK ON HER.
PLEASE EXCUSE ME FOR LEAVING IN THE MIDDLE OF DINNER.
MEL...
...LET ME APOLOGIZE ON BEHALF OF MY WIFE.
I'M SURE SHE REGRETS WHAT SHE SAID.
...IT'S OKAY. IT DOESN'T BOTHER ME.
YOU CAN LEAVE THE DISHES ON THE TABLE WHEN YOU'RE DONE.
I'M LEAVING KAIN TO YOU, OKAY?
......
HON-ESTLY...
I DON'T THINK DINNER COULD HAVE GONE MUCH WORSE THAN IT DID.
I THINK...
...MY MOM'S ALWAYS LOVED ME MORE THAN MOST MOTHERS LOVE THEIR KIDS.

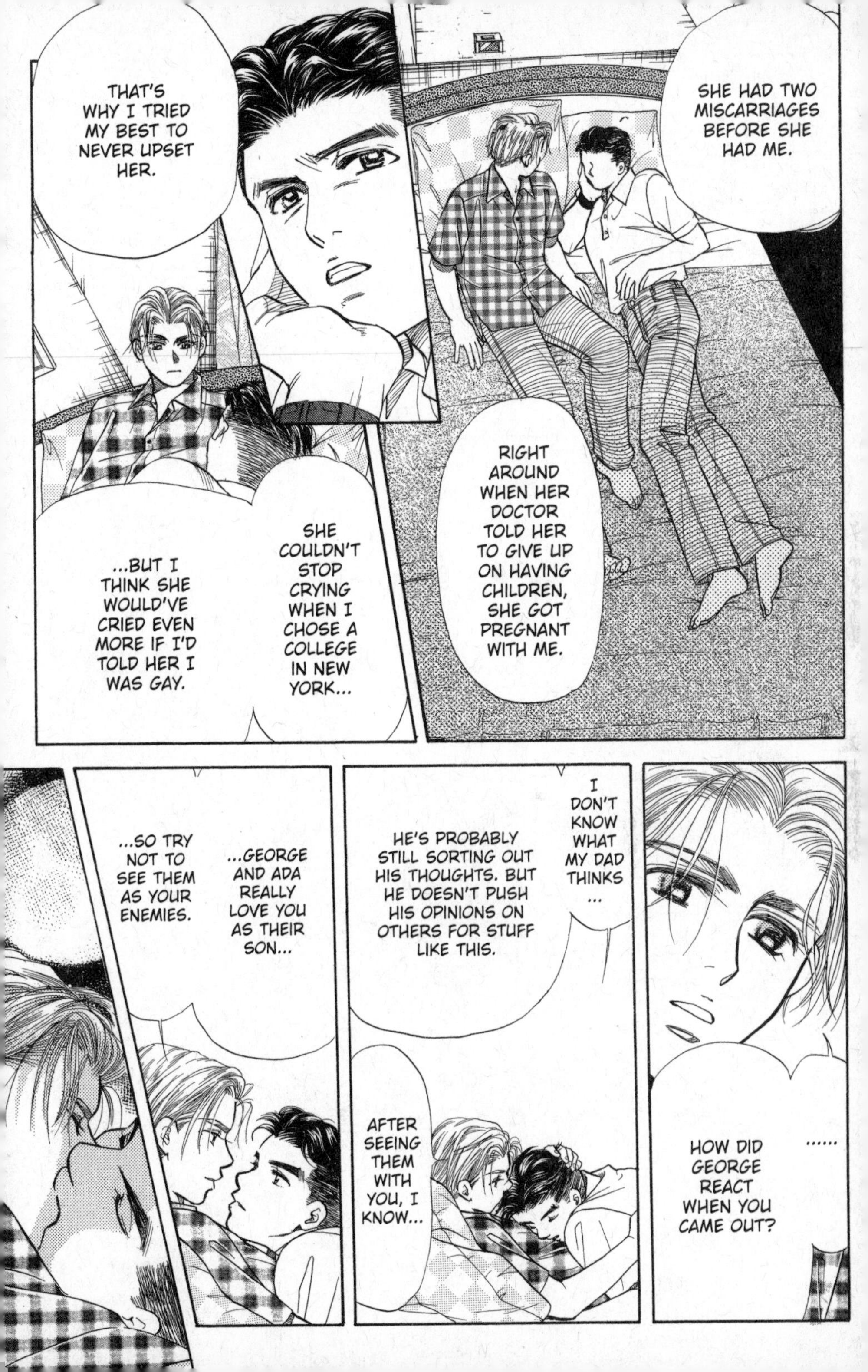
SHE HAD TWO MISCARRIAGES BEFORE SHE HAD ME.
RIGHT AROUND WHEN HER DOCTOR TOLD HER TO GIVE UP ON HAVING CHILDREN, SHE GOT PREGNANT WITH ME.
THAT'S WHY I TRIED MY BEST TO NEVER UPSET HER.
SHE COULDN'T STOP CRYING WHEN I CHOSE A COLLEGE IN NEW YORK...
...BUT I THINK SHE WOULD'VE CRIED EVEN MORE IF I'D TOLD HER I WAS GAY.
HOW DID GEORGE REACT WHEN YOU CAME OUT?
......
I DON'T KNOW WHAT MY DAD THINKS ...
HE'S PROBABLY STILL SORTING OUT HIS THOUGHTS. BUT HE DOESN'T PUSH HIS OPINIONS ON OTHERS FOR STUFF LIKE THIS.
AFTER SEEING THEM WITH YOU, I KNOW...
...GEORGE AND ADA REALLY LOVE YOU AS THEIR SON...
...SO TRY NOT TO SEE THEM AS YOUR ENEMIES.

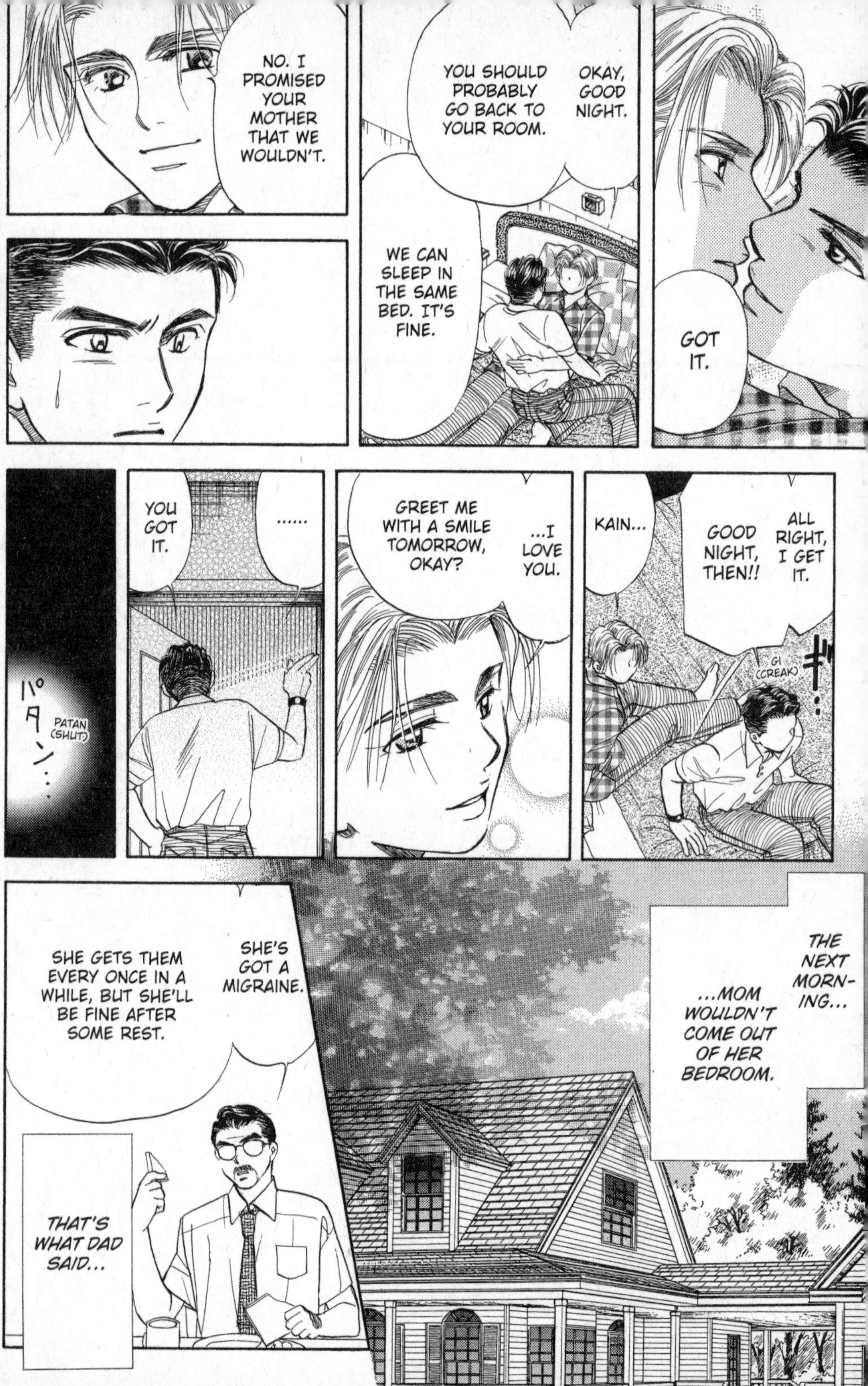
GOT IT.
OKAY, GOOD NIGHT.
YOU SHOULD PROBABLY GO BACK TO YOUR ROOM.
WE CAN SLEEP IN THE SAME BED. IT'S FINE.
NO. I PROMISED YOUR MOTHER THAT WE WOULDN'T.
ALL RIGHT, I GET IT.
GOOD NIGHT, THEN!!
ギ…
GI (CREAK)
KAIN...
...I LOVE YOU.
GREET ME WITH A SMILE TOMORROW, OKAY?
......
YOU GOT IT.
パタン…
PATAN (SHUT)
THE NEXT MORNING...
...MOM WOULDN'T COME OUT OF HER BEDROOM.
SHE'S GOT A MIGRAINE.
SHE GETS THEM EVERY ONCE IN A WHILE, BUT SHE'LL BE FINE AFTER SOME REST.
THAT'S WHAT DAD SAID...

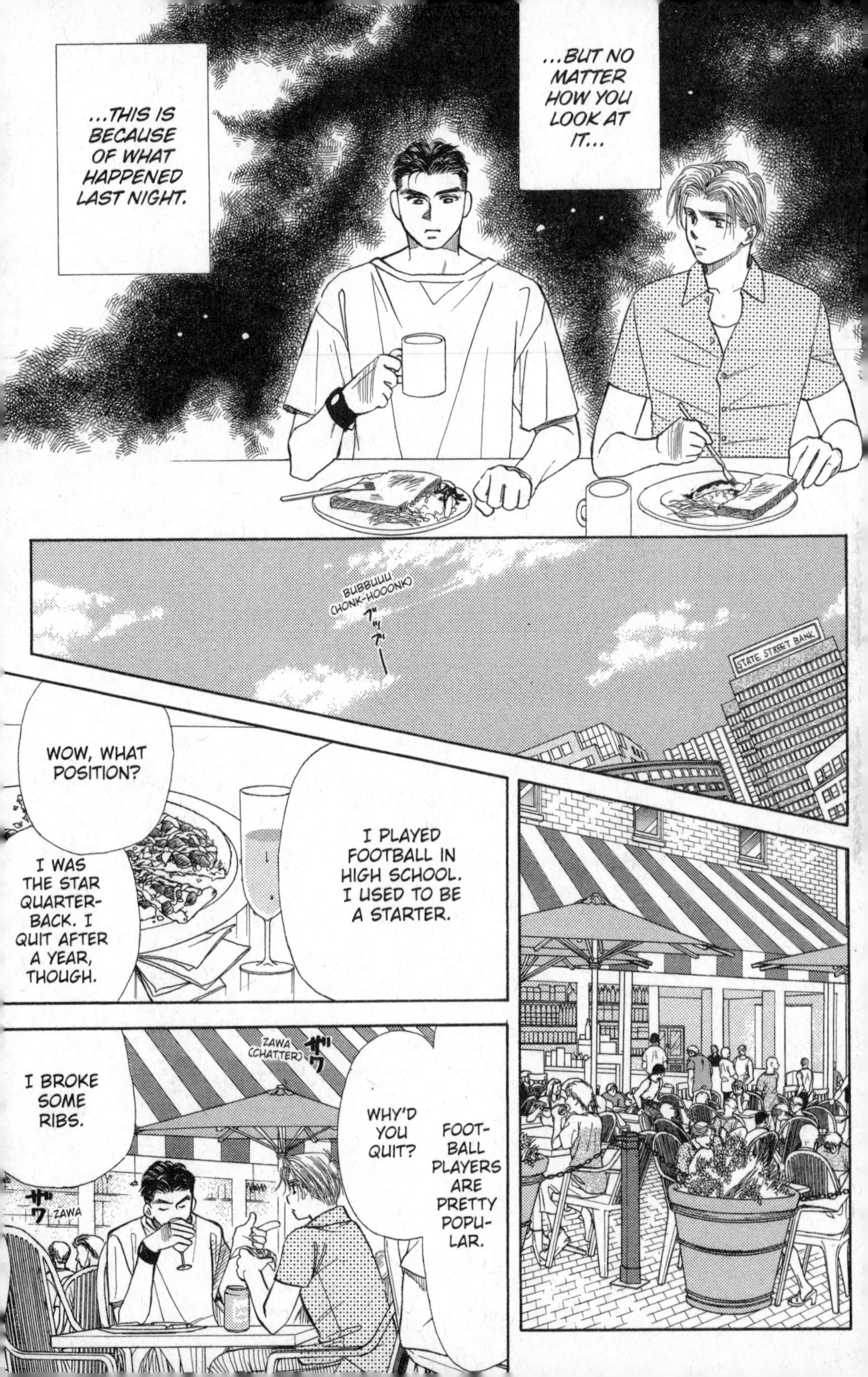
...BUT NO MATTER HOW YOU LOOK AT IT...
...THIS IS BECAUSE OF WHAT HAPPENED LAST NIGHT.
BUBBUUU (HONK-HOOONK)
STATE STREET BANK
I PLAYED FOOTBALL IN HIGH SCHOOL. I USED TO BE A STARTER.
WOW, WHAT POSITION?
I WAS THE STAR QUARTER-BACK. I QUIT AFTER A YEAR, THOUGH.
ZAWA (CHATTER)
FOOT-BALL PLAYERS ARE PRETTY POPU-LAR.
WHY'D YOU QUIT?
I BROKE SOME RIBS.
ZAWA

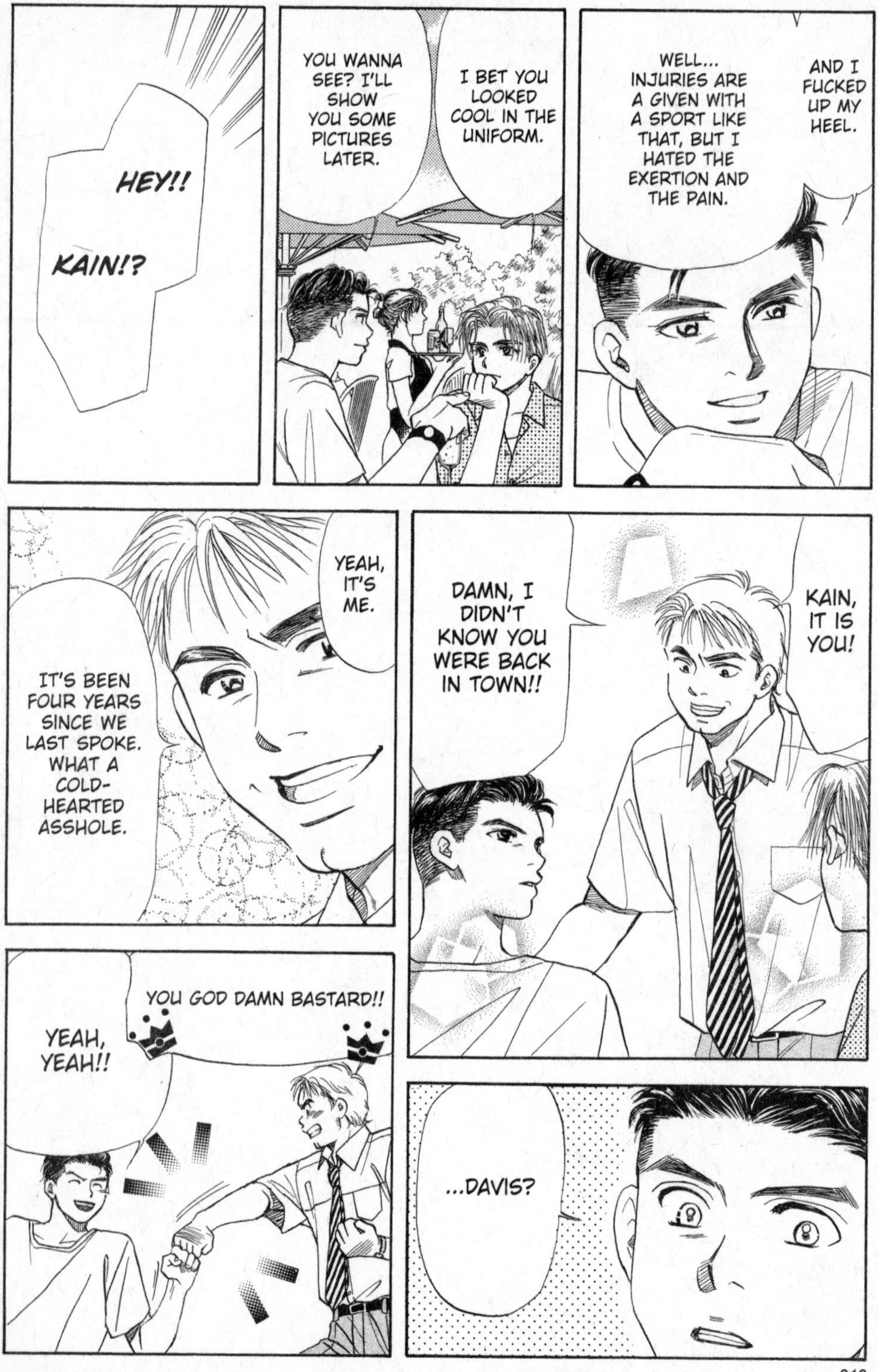
AND I FUCKED UP MY HEEL.
WELL... INJURIES ARE A GIVEN WITH A SPORT LIKE THAT, BUT I HATED THE EXERTION AND THE PAIN.
I BET YOU LOOKED COOL IN THE UNIFORM.
YOU WANNA SEE? I'LL SHOW YOU SOME PICTURES LATER.
HEY!!
KAIN!?
KAIN, IT IS YOU!
DAMN, I DIDN'T KNOW YOU WERE BACK IN TOWN!!
YEAH, IT'S ME.
IT'S BEEN FOUR YEARS SINCE WE LAST SPOKE. WHAT A COLD-HEARTED ASSHOLE.
...DAVIS?
YOU GOD DAMN BASTARD!!
YEAH, YEAH!!

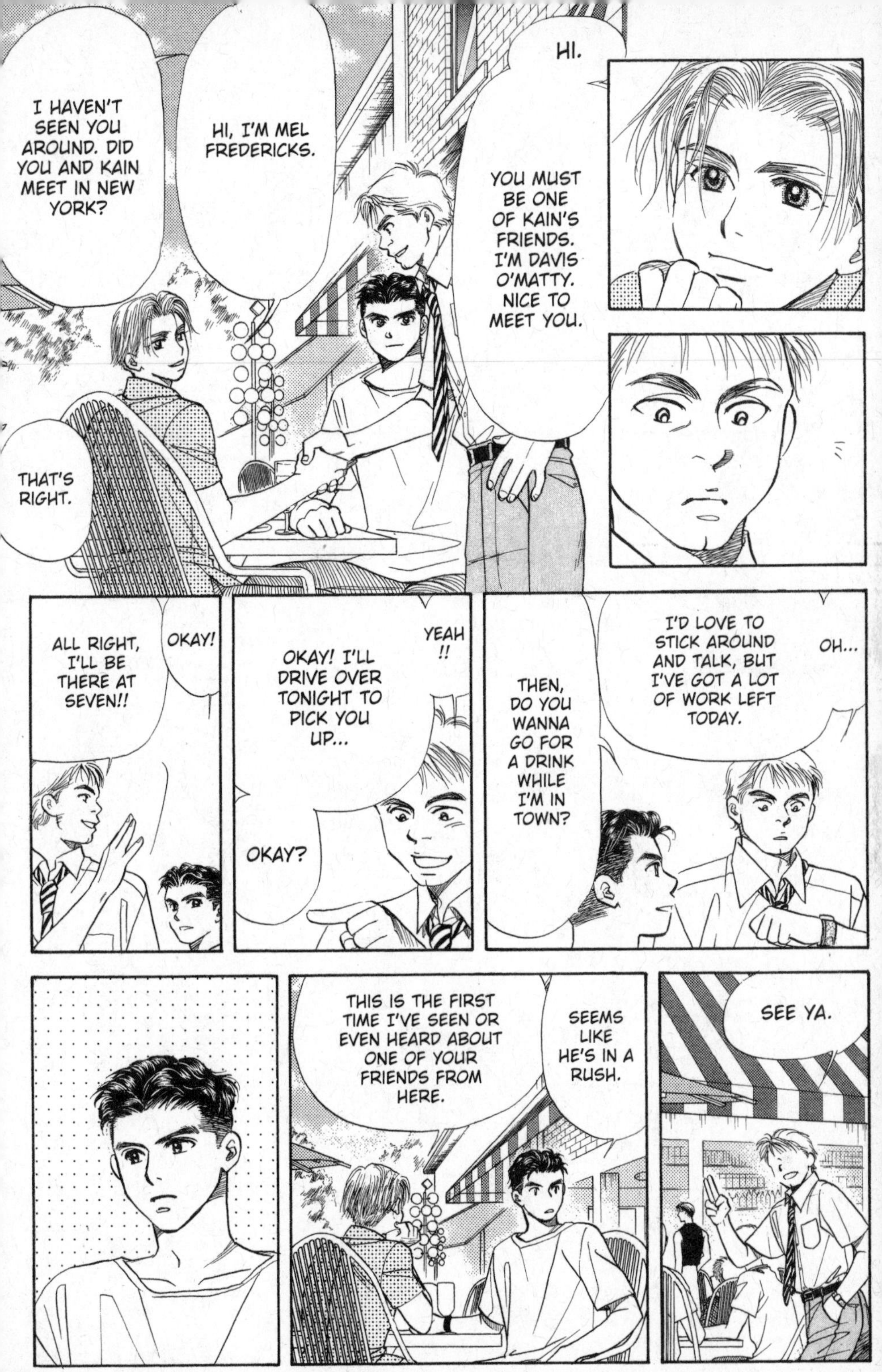
HI.
YOU MUST BE ONE OF KAIN'S FRIENDS. I'M DAVIS O'MATTY. NICE TO MEET YOU.
HI, I'M MEL FREDERICKS.
I HAVEN'T SEEN YOU AROUND. DID YOU AND KAIN MEET IN NEW YORK?
THAT'S RIGHT.
OH...
I'D LOVE TO STICK AROUND AND TALK, BUT I'VE GOT A LOT OF WORK LEFT TODAY.
THEN, DO YOU WANNA GO FOR A DRINK WHILE I'M IN TOWN?
YEAH!!
OKAY! I'LL DRIVE OVER TONIGHT TO PICK YOU UP...
OKAY?
OKAY!
ALL RIGHT, I'LL BE THERE AT SEVEN!!
SEE YA.
SEEMS LIKE HE'S IN A RUSH.
THIS IS THE FIRST TIME I'VE SEEN OR EVEN HEARD ABOUT ONE OF YOUR FRIENDS FROM HERE.

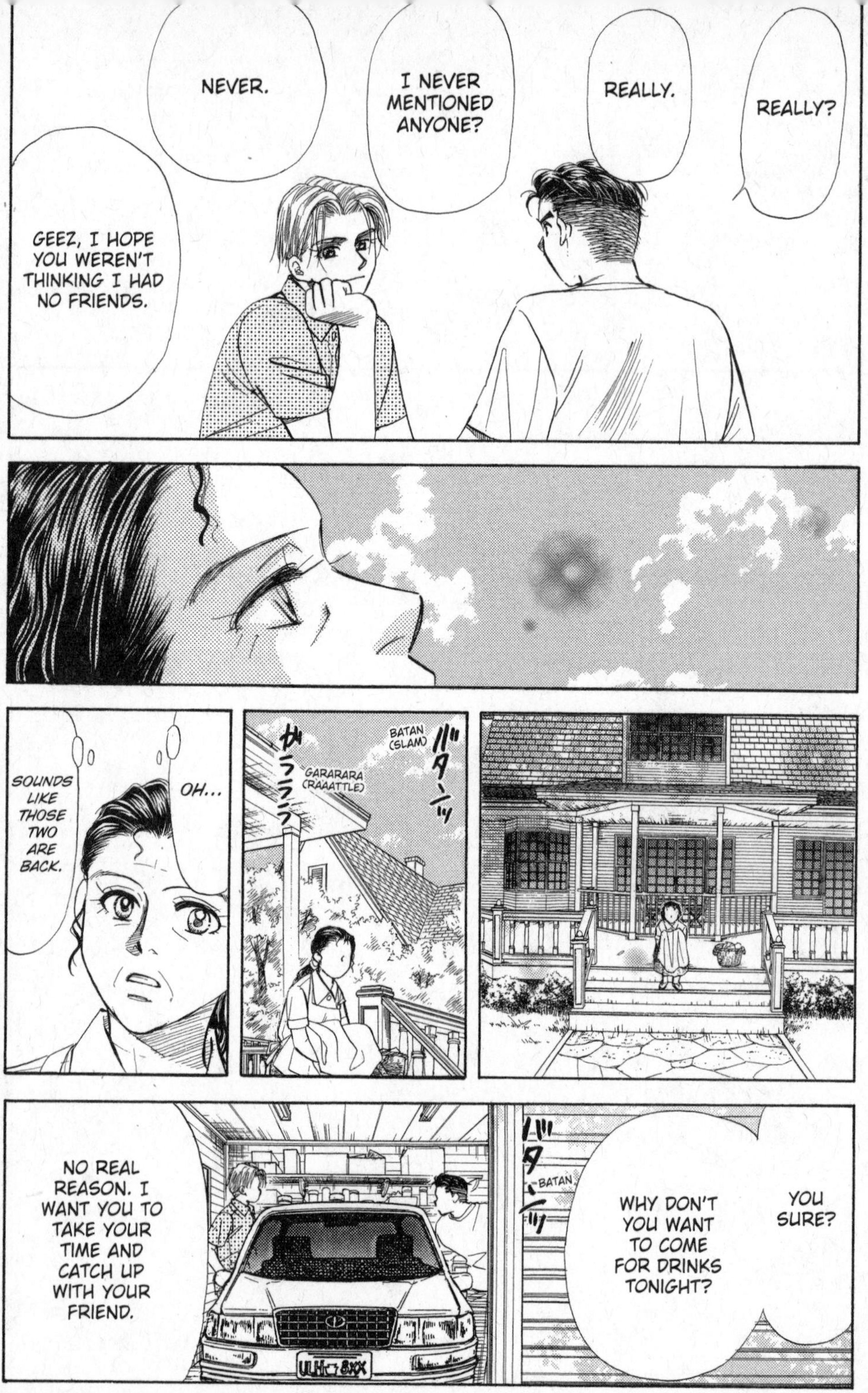
REALLY?
REALLY.
I NEVER MENTIONED ANYONE?
NEVER.
GEEZ, I HOPE YOU WEREN'T THINKING I HAD NO FRIENDS.
BATAN (SLAM)
GARARARA (RAAATTLE)
OH...
SOUNDS LIKE THOSE TWO ARE BACK.
YOU SURE?
WHY DON'T YOU WANT TO COME FOR DRINKS TONIGHT?
BATAN
NO REAL REASON. I WANT YOU TO TAKE YOUR TIME AND CATCH UP WITH YOUR FRIEND.

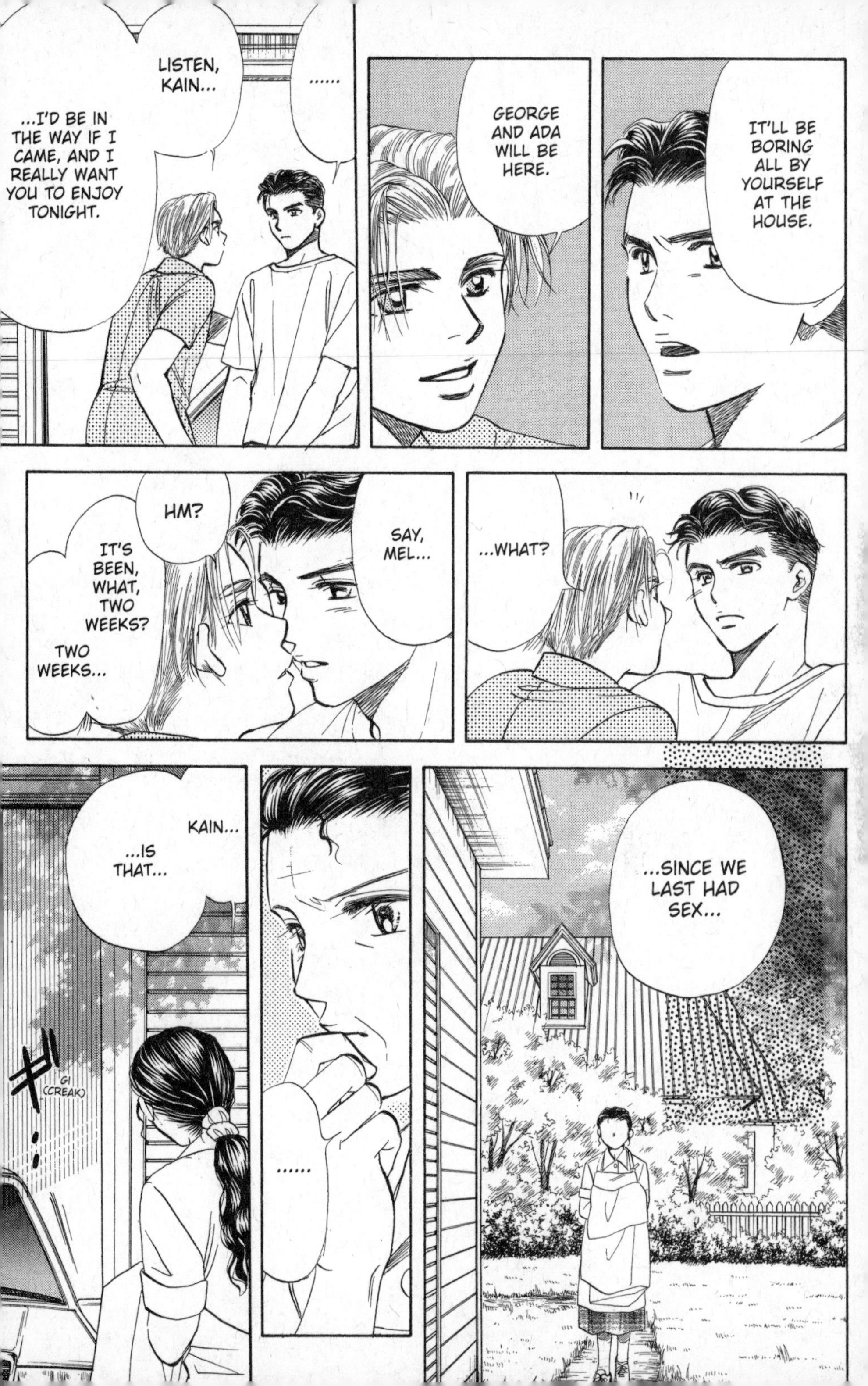
IT'LL BE BORING ALL BY YOURSELF AT THE HOUSE.
GEORGE AND ADA WILL BE HERE.
......
LISTEN, KAIN...
...I'D BE IN THE WAY IF I CAME, AND I REALLY WANT YOU TO ENJOY TONIGHT.
...WHAT?
SAY, MEL...
HM?
IT'S BEEN, WHAT, TWO WEEKS?
TWO WEEKS...
...SINCE WE LAST HAD SEX...
......
KAIN...
...IS THAT...
GI (CREAK)

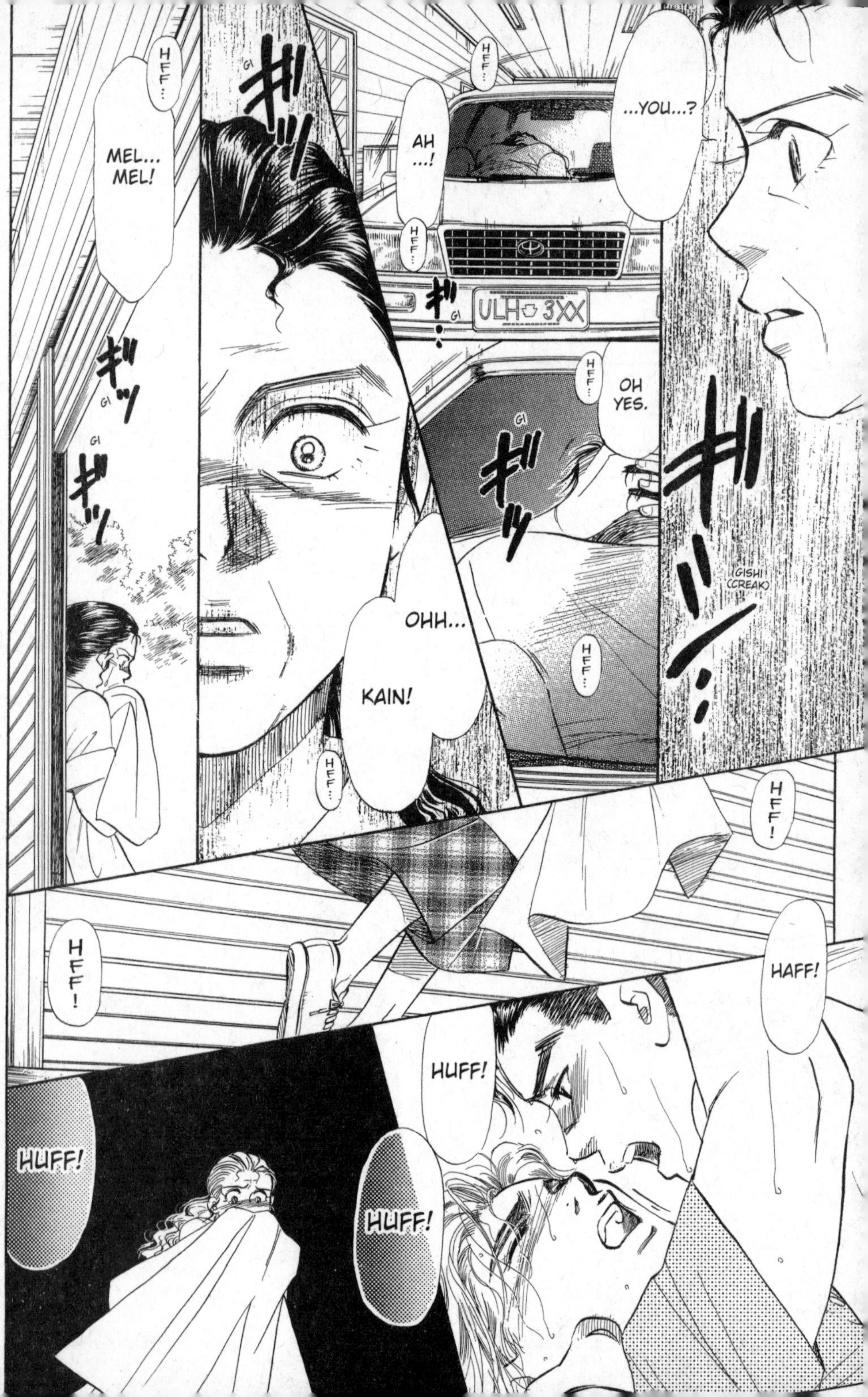
...YOU...?
GISHI (CREAK)
HFF...
AH ...!
HFF...
GI
HFF...
OH YES.
GI
HFF...
GI
OHH...
KAIN!
HFF...
HFF...
MEL... MEL!
GI
GI
HFF!
HAFF!
HFF!
HUFF!
HUFF!
HUFF!

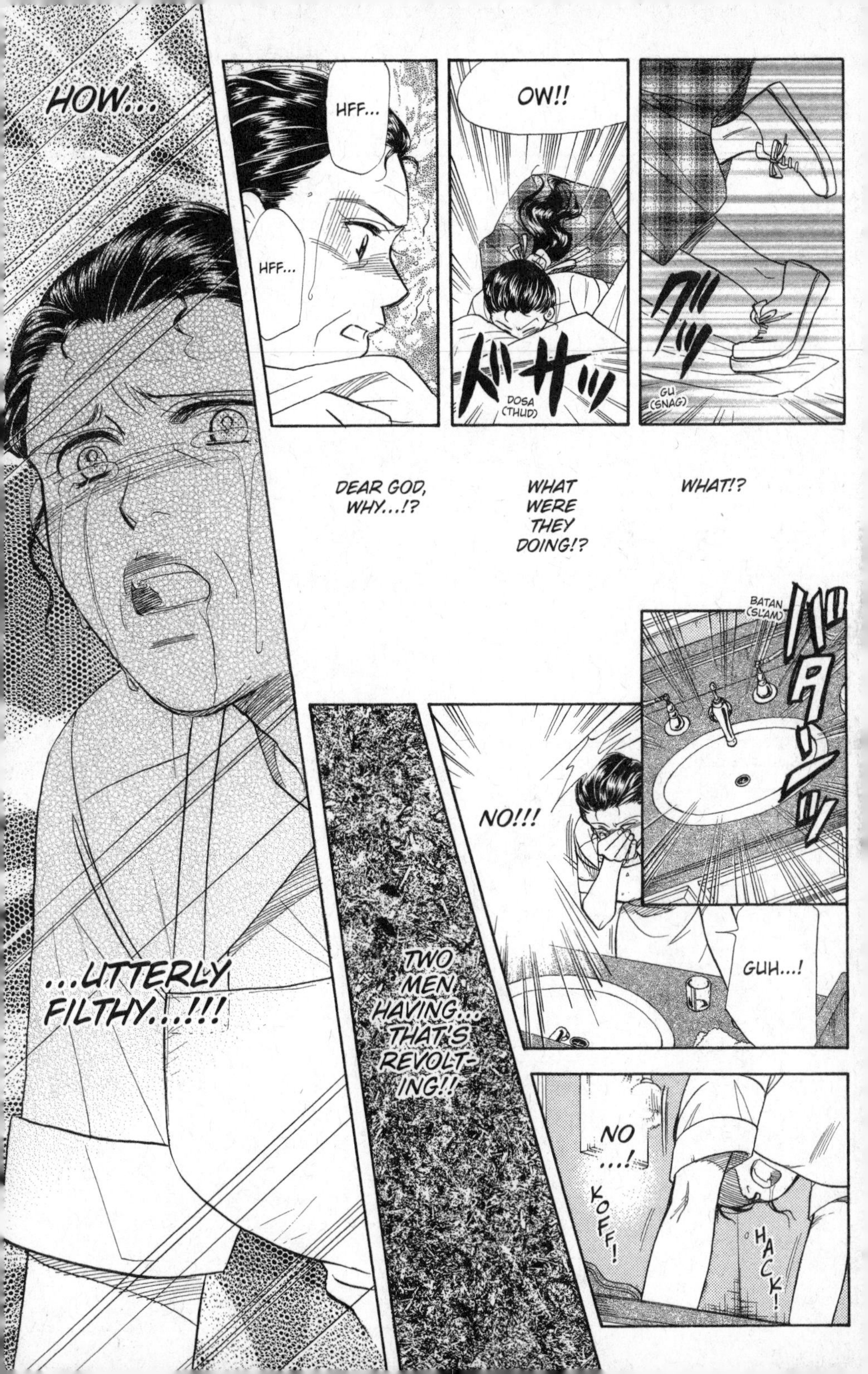
グッ
GU (SNAG)
OW!!
ドサッ
DOSA (THUD)
HFF...
HFF...
WHAT!?
WHAT WERE THEY DOING!?
DEAR GOD, WHY...!?
バタンッ
BATAN (SLAM)
NO!!!
GUH...!
TWO MEN HAVING... THAT'S REVOLTING!!
NO ...!
KOFF!
HACK!
HOW...
...UTTERLY FILTHY...!!!

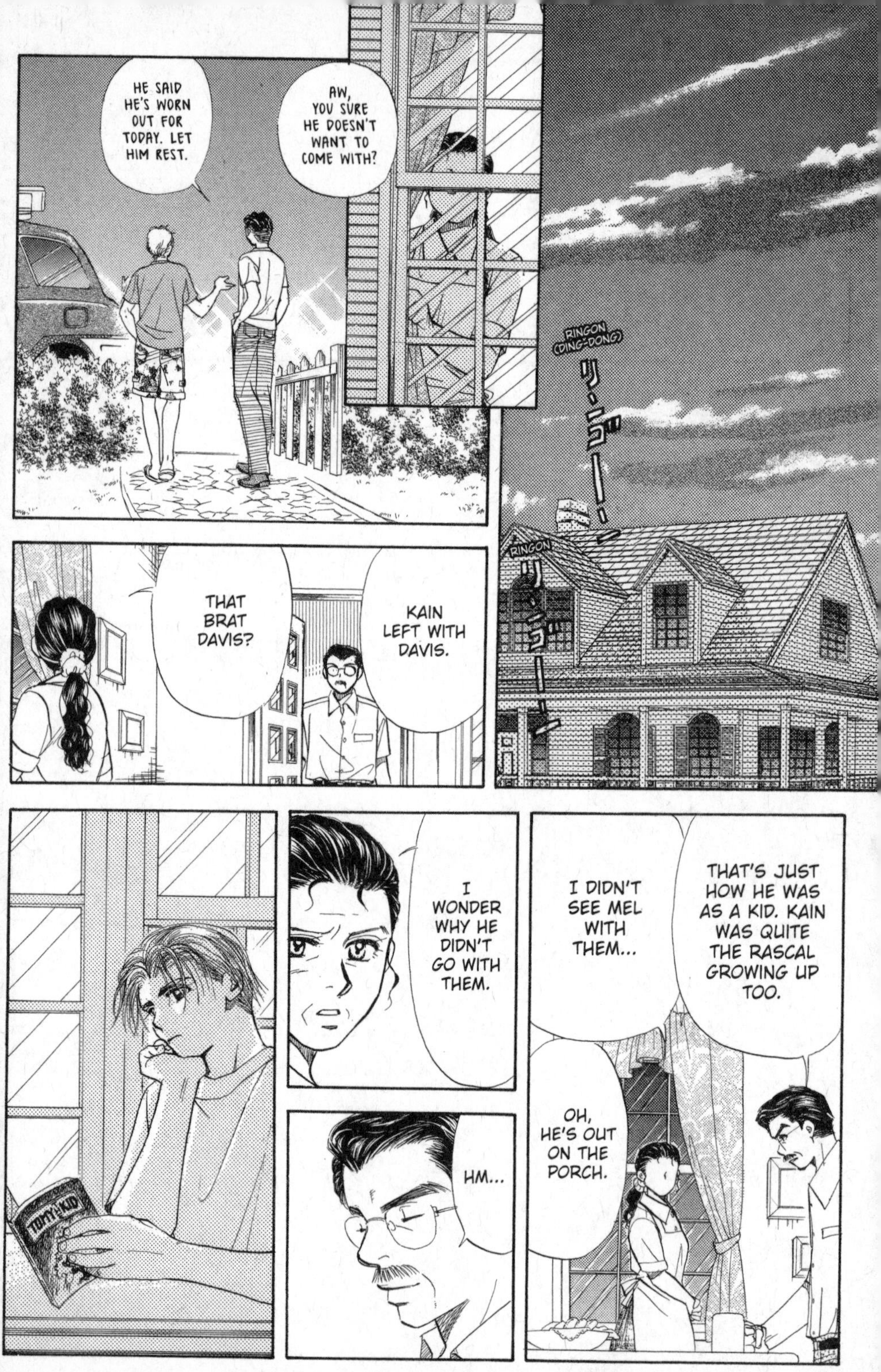
RINGON (DING-DONG)
RINGON
AW, YOU SURE HE DOESN'T WANT TO COME WITH?
HE SAID HE'S WORN OUT FOR TODAY. LET HIM REST.
KAIN LEFT WITH DAVIS.
THAT BRAT DAVIS?
THAT'S JUST HOW HE WAS AS A KID. KAIN WAS QUITE THE RASCAL GROWING UP TOO.
I DIDN'T SEE MEL WITH THEM...
OH, HE'S OUT ON THE PORCH.
I WONDER WHY HE DIDN'T GO WITH THEM.
HM...

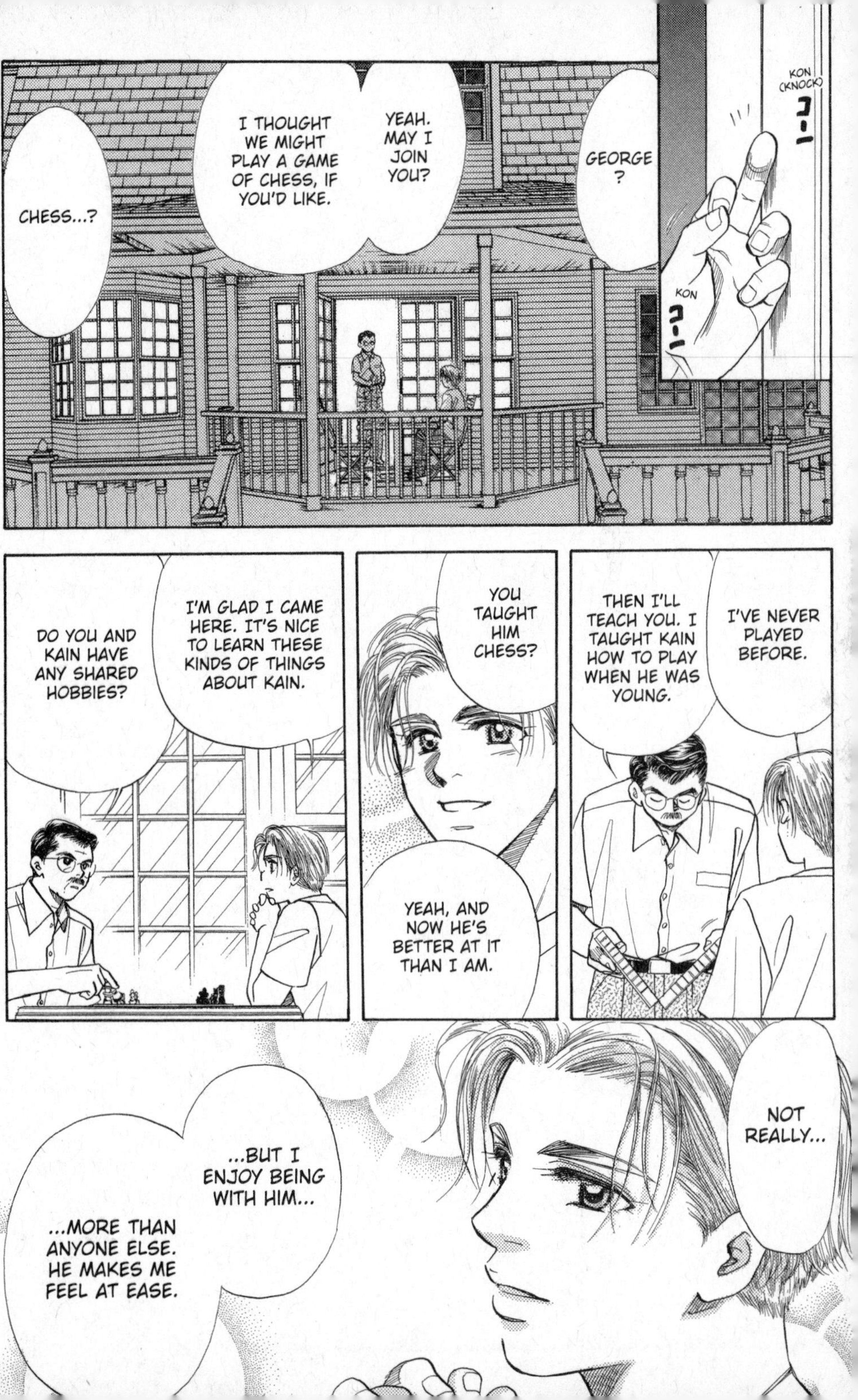
KON (KNOCK)
KON
GEORGE?
YEAH. MAY I JOIN YOU?
I THOUGHT WE MIGHT PLAY A GAME OF CHESS, IF YOU'D LIKE.
CHESS...?
I'VE NEVER PLAYED BEFORE.
THEN I'LL TEACH YOU. I TAUGHT KAIN HOW TO PLAY WHEN HE WAS YOUNG.
YOU TAUGHT HIM CHESS?
YEAH, AND NOW HE'S BETTER AT IT THAN I AM.
I'M GLAD I CAME HERE. IT'S NICE TO LEARN THESE KINDS OF THINGS ABOUT KAIN.
DO YOU AND KAIN HAVE ANY SHARED HOBBIES?
NOT REALLY...
...BUT I ENJOY BEING WITH HIM...
...MORE THAN ANYONE ELSE. HE MAKES ME FEEL AT EASE.

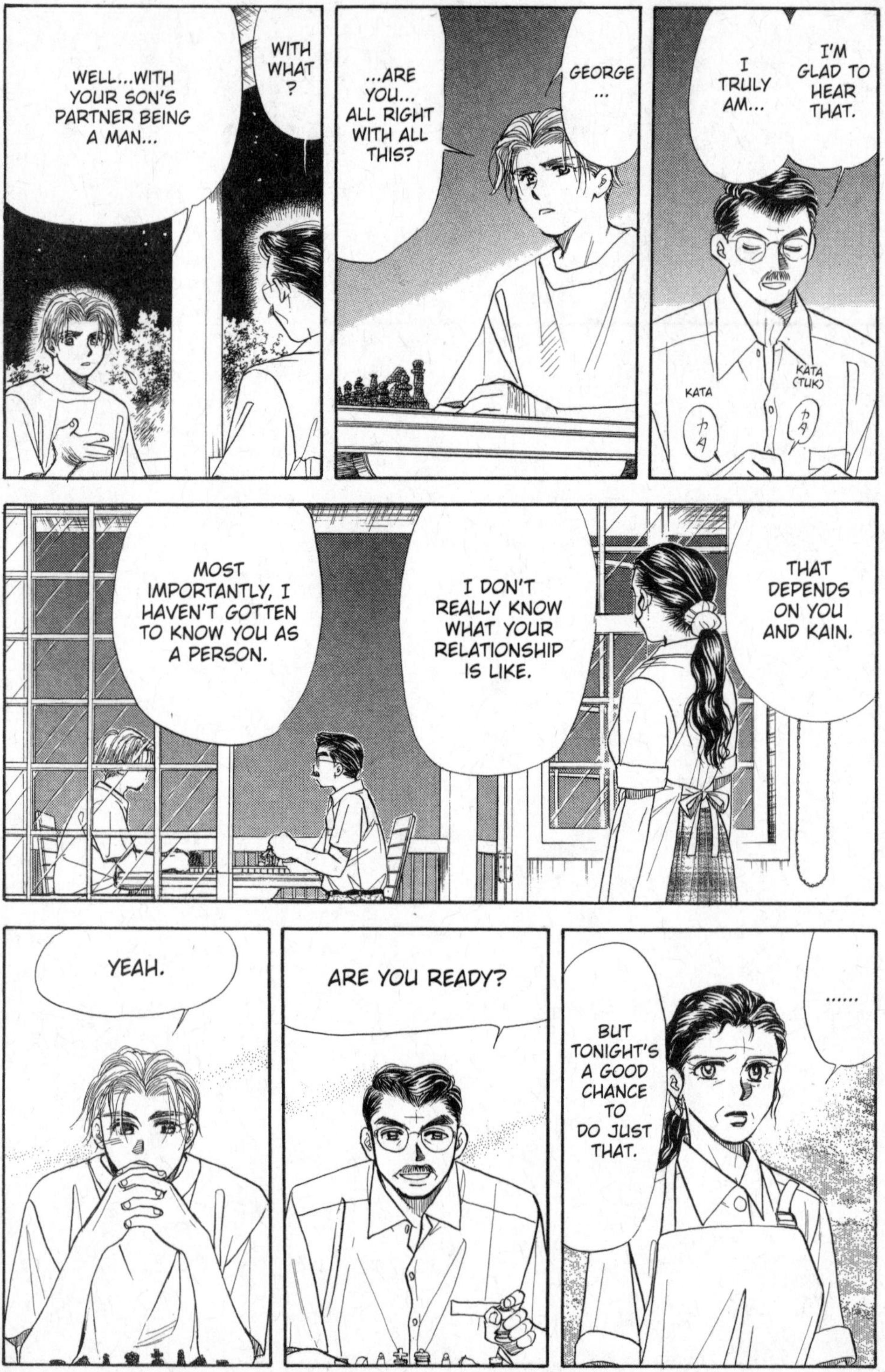
I'M GLAD TO HEAR THAT.
I TRULY AM...
KATA (TUK) カタ
KATA カタ
GEORGE...
...ARE YOU... ALL RIGHT WITH ALL THIS?
WITH WHAT?
WELL...WITH YOUR SON'S PARTNER BEING A MAN...
THAT DEPENDS ON YOU AND KAIN.
I DON'T REALLY KNOW WHAT YOUR RELATIONSHIP IS LIKE.
MOST IMPORTANTLY, I HAVEN'T GOTTEN TO KNOW YOU AS A PERSON.
......
BUT TONIGHT'S A GOOD CHANCE TO DO JUST THAT.
ARE YOU READY?
YEAH.

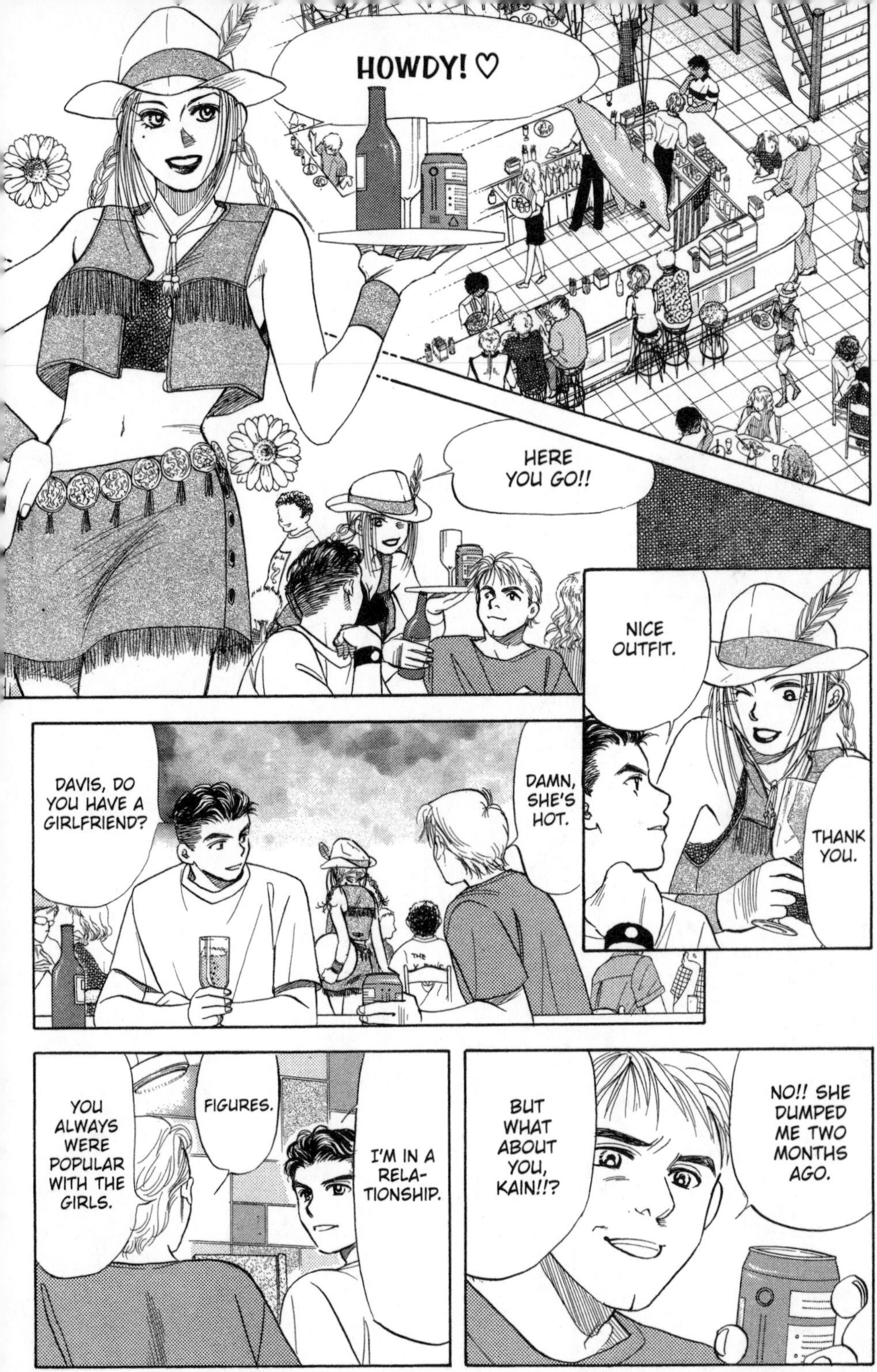
HOWDY! ♡
HERE YOU GO!!
NICE OUTFIT.
THANK YOU.
DAMN, SHE'S HOT.
DAVIS, DO YOU HAVE A GIRLFRIEND?
NO!! SHE DUMPED ME TWO MONTHS AGO.
BUT WHAT ABOUT YOU, KAIN!!?
I'M IN A RELATIONSHIP.
FIGURES.
YOU ALWAYS WERE POPULAR WITH THE GIRLS.

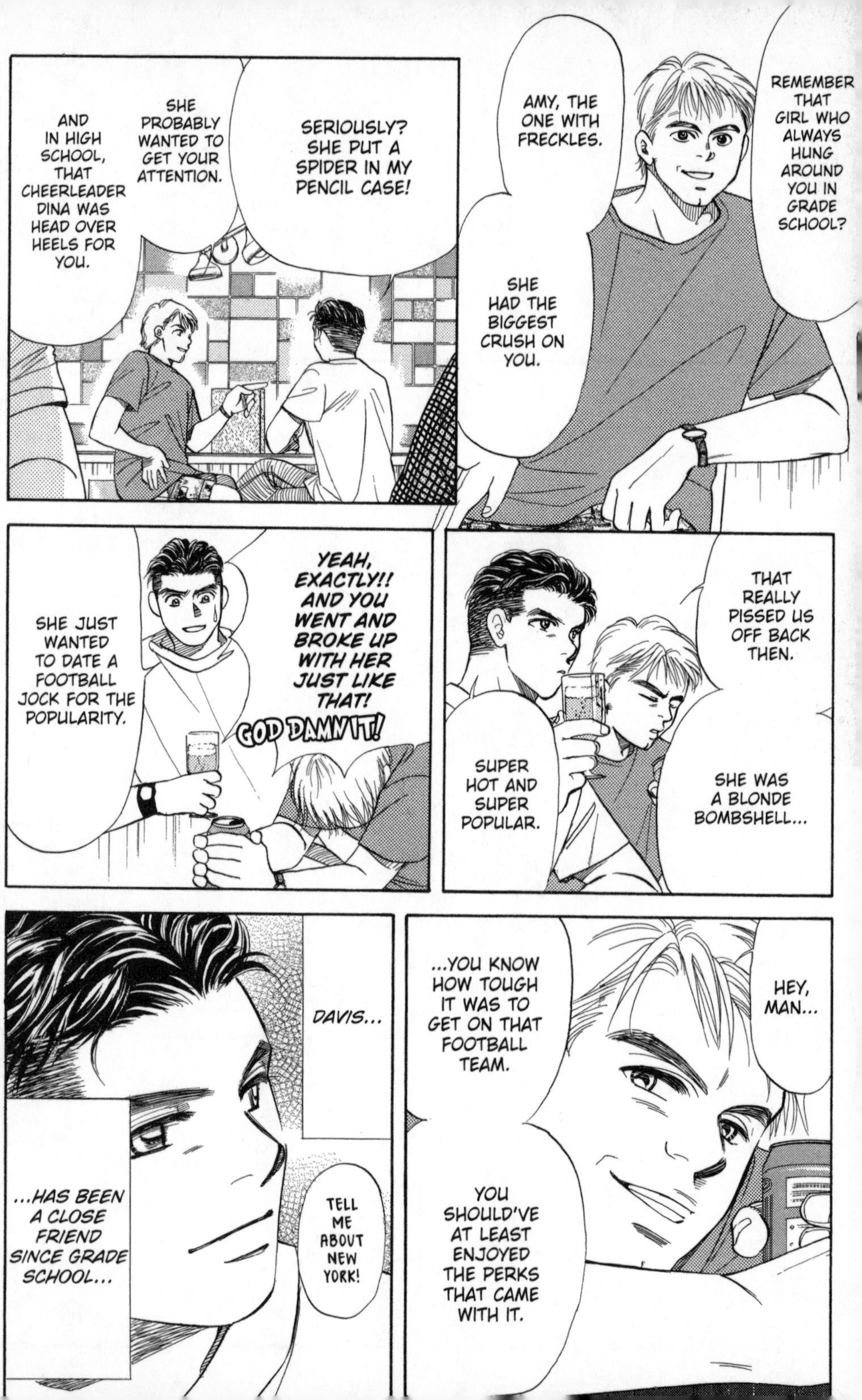
REMEMBER THAT GIRL WHO ALWAYS HUNG AROUND YOU IN GRADE SCHOOL?
AMY, THE ONE WITH FRECKLES.
SHE HAD THE BIGGEST CRUSH ON YOU.
SERIOUSLY? SHE PUT A SPIDER IN MY PENCIL CASE!
SHE PROBABLY WANTED TO GET YOUR ATTENTION.
AND IN HIGH SCHOOL, THAT CHEERLEADER DINA WAS HEAD OVER HEELS FOR YOU.
THAT REALLY PISSED US OFF BACK THEN.
SHE WAS A BLONDE BOMBSHELL...
SUPER HOT AND SUPER POPULAR.
YEAH, EXACTLY!! AND YOU WENT AND BROKE UP WITH HER JUST LIKE THAT!
GOD DAMN IT!
SHE JUST WANTED TO DATE A FOOTBALL JOCK FOR THE POPULARITY.
HEY, MAN...
...YOU KNOW HOW TOUGH IT WAS TO GET ON THAT FOOTBALL TEAM.
YOU SHOULD'VE AT LEAST ENJOYED THE PERKS THAT CAME WITH IT.
DAVIS...
TELL ME ABOUT NEW YORK!
...HAS BEEN A CLOSE FRIEND SINCE GRADE SCHOOL...

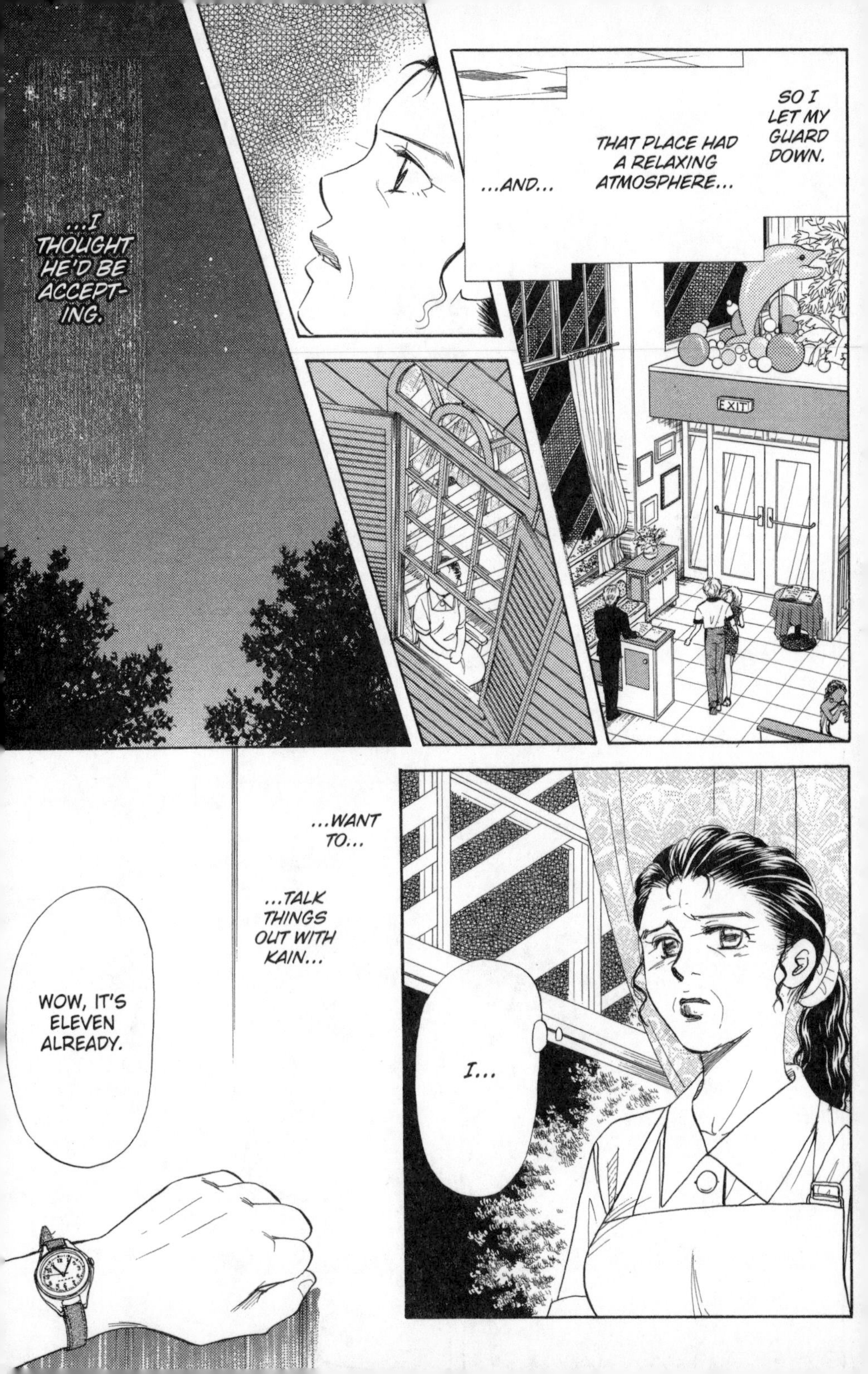
SO I LET MY GUARD DOWN.
THAT PLACE HAD A RELAXING ATMOSPHERE...
...AND...
EXIT
...I THOUGHT HE'D BE ACCEPTING.
I...
...WANT TO...
...TALK THINGS OUT WITH KAIN...
WOW, IT'S ELEVEN ALREADY.

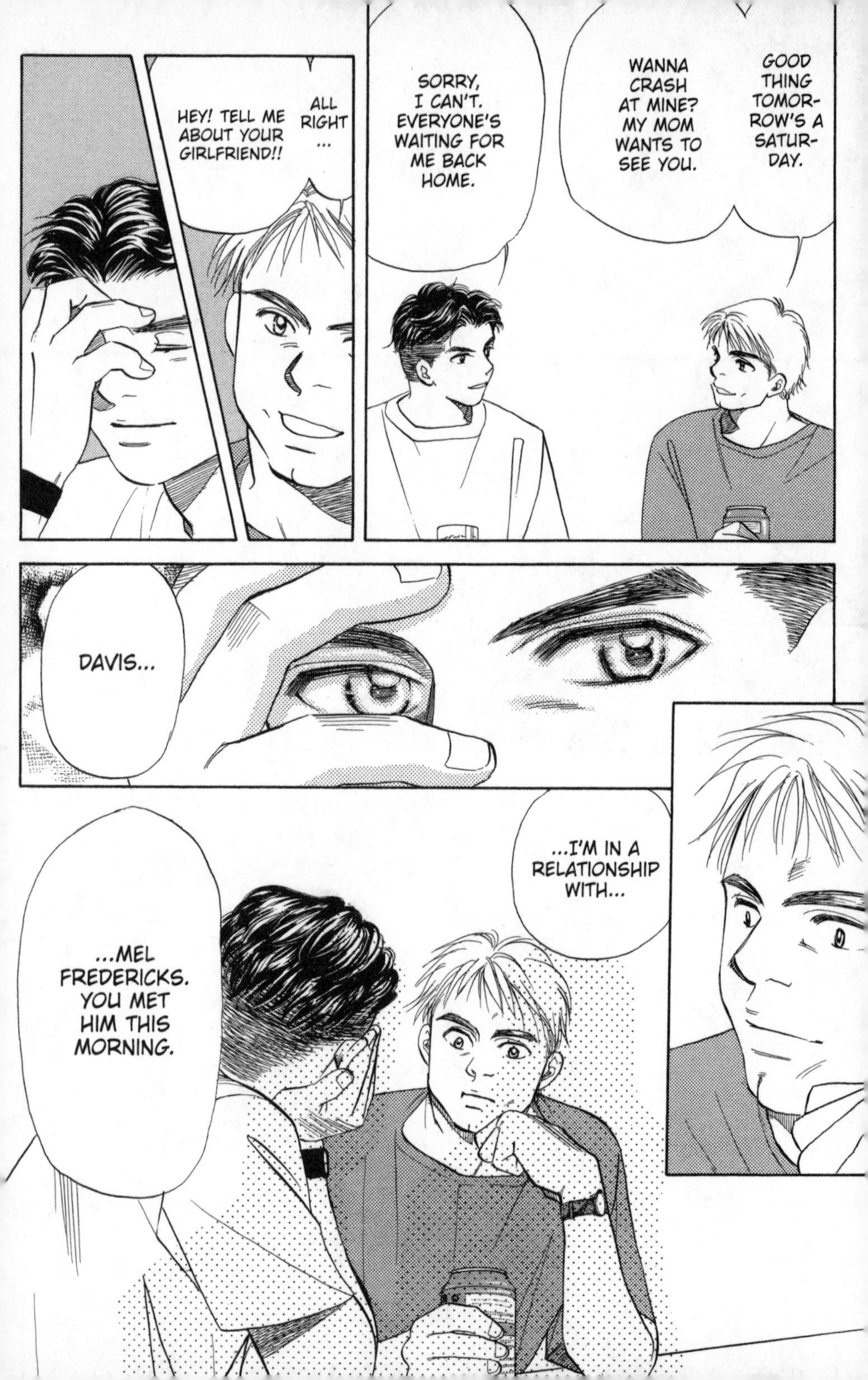
GOOD THING TOMORROW'S A SATURDAY.
WANNA CRASH AT MINE? MY MOM WANTS TO SEE YOU.
SORRY, I CAN'T. EVERYONE'S WAITING FOR ME BACK HOME.
ALL RIGHT...
HEY! TELL ME ABOUT YOUR GIRLFRIEND!!
DAVIS...
...I'M IN A RELATIONSHIP WITH...
...MEL FREDERICKS. YOU MET HIM THIS MORNING.

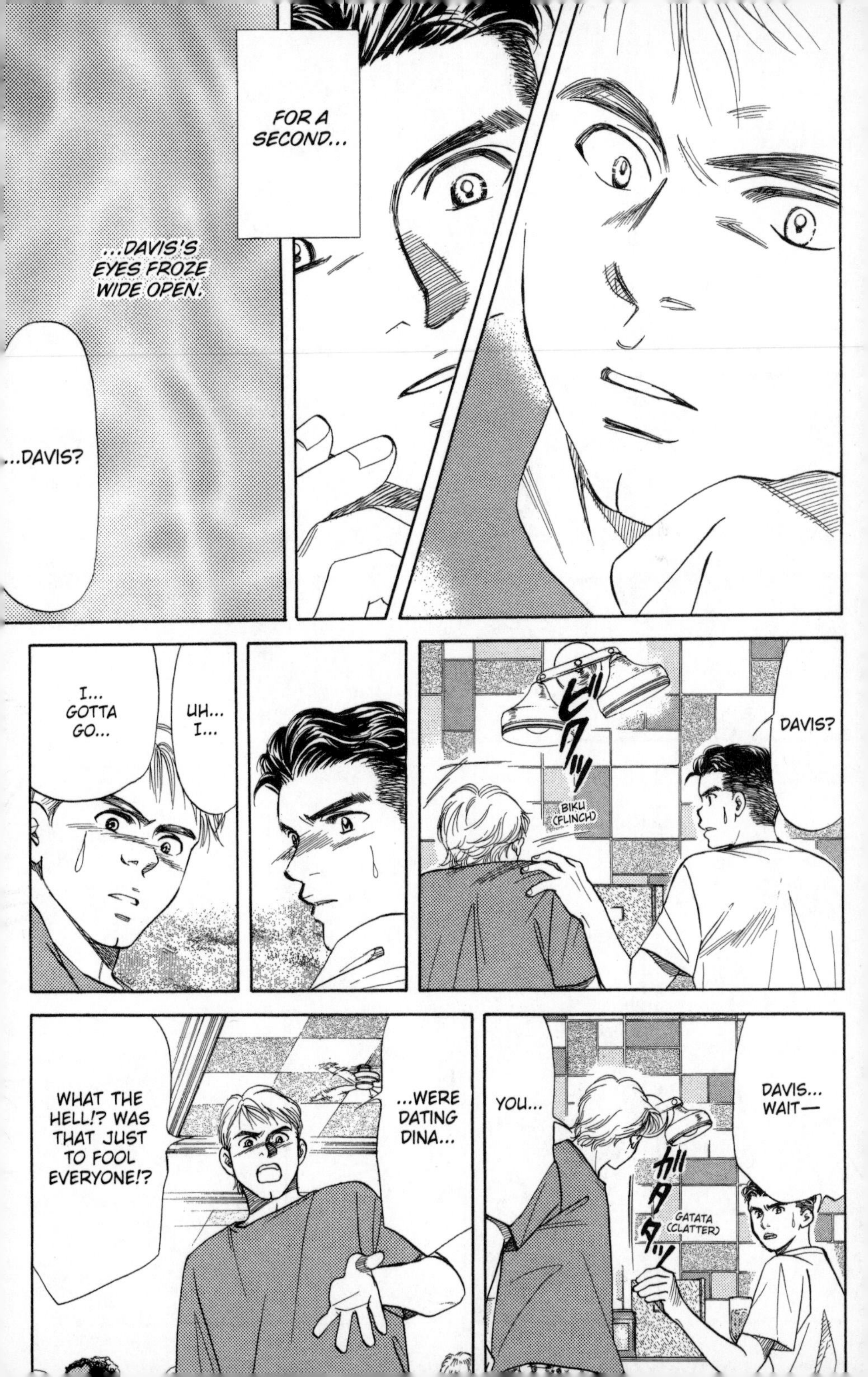
FOR A SECOND...
...DAVIS'S EYES FROZE WIDE OPEN.
...DAVIS?
DAVIS?
BIKU (FLINCH)
UH... I...
I... GOTTA GO...
DAVIS... WAIT—
GATATA (CLATTER)
YOU...
...WERE DATING DINA...
WHAT THE HELL!? WAS THAT JUST TO FOOL EVERYONE!?

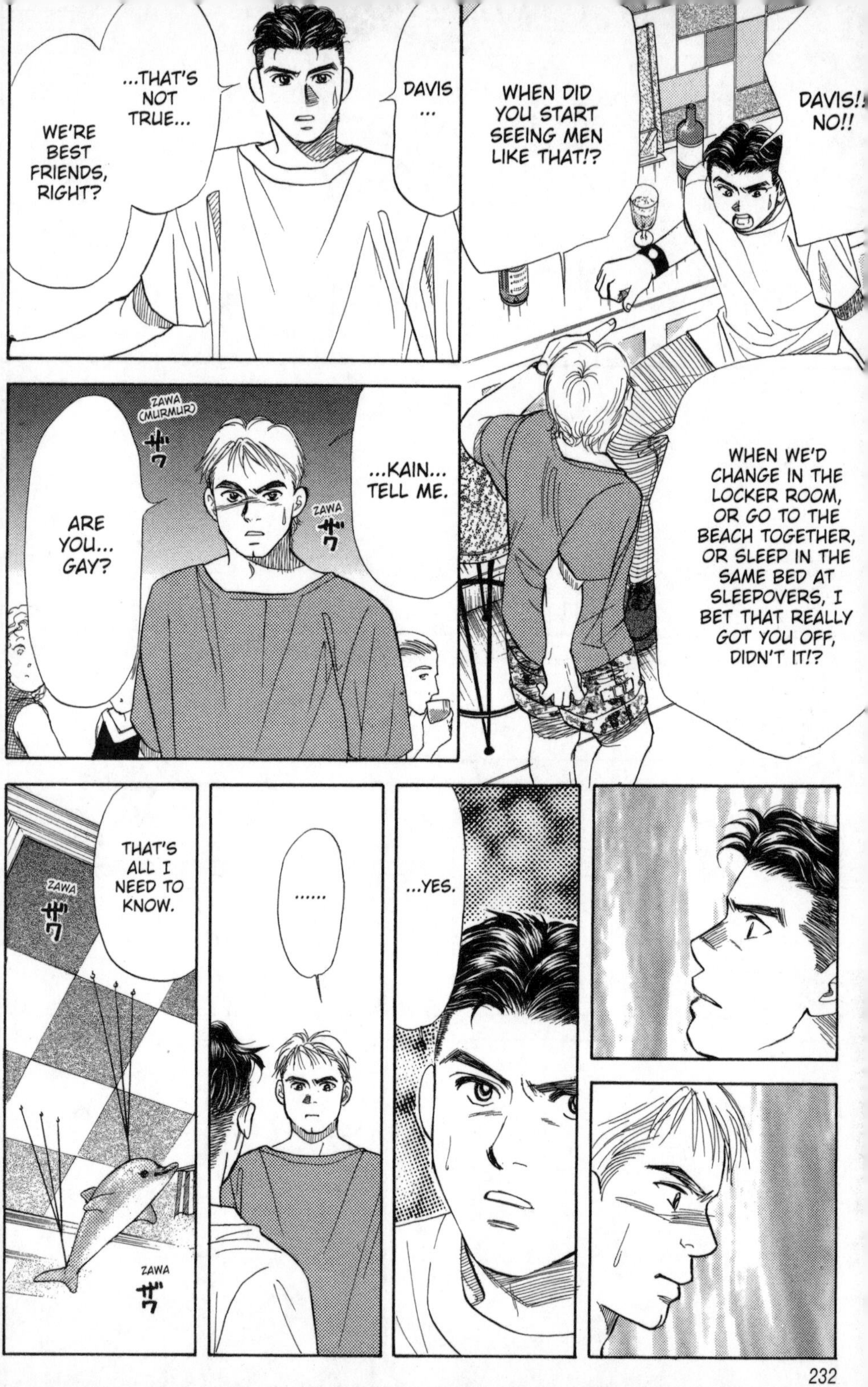
DAVIS!! NO!!
WHEN DID YOU START SEEING MEN LIKE THAT!?
WHEN WE'D CHANGE IN THE LOCKER ROOM, OR GO TO THE BEACH TOGETHER, OR SLEEP IN THE SAME BED AT SLEEPOVERS, I BET THAT REALLY GOT YOU OFF, DIDN'T IT!?
DAVIS ...
...THAT'S NOT TRUE...
WE'RE BEST FRIENDS, RIGHT?
...KAIN... TELL ME.
ZAWA
ザワ
ARE YOU... GAY?
ZAWA (MURMUR)
ザワ
...YES.
......
THAT'S ALL I NEED TO KNOW.
ZAWA
ザワ
ZAWA
ザワ

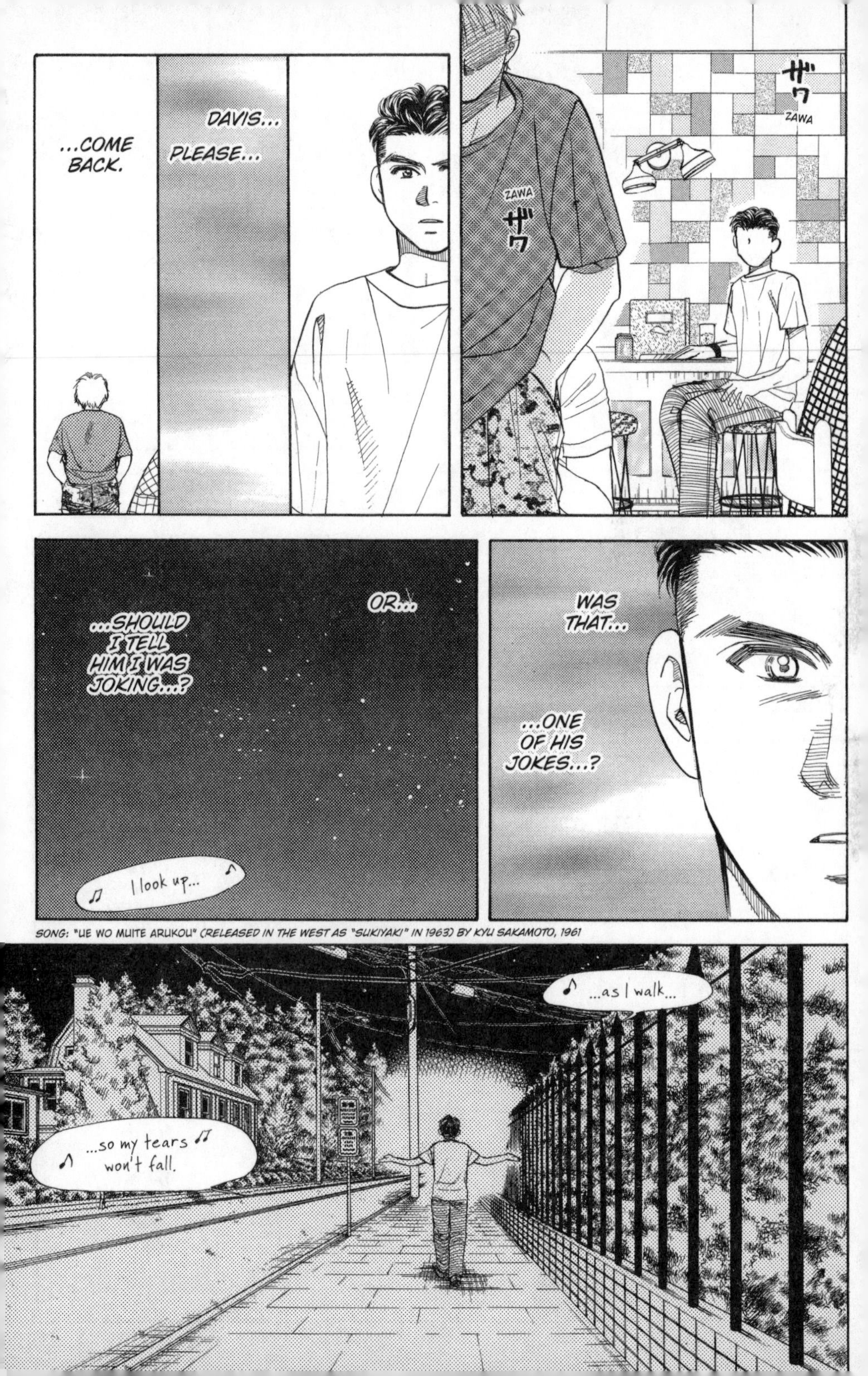
ザワ
ZAWA
ZAWA
ザワ
DAVIS...
PLEASE...
...COME BACK.
WAS THAT...
...ONE OF HIS JOKES...?
OR...
...SHOULD I TELL HIM I WAS JOKING...?
♫ I look up... ♪
♪ ...as I walk...
♪ ...so my tears ♫ won't fall.

SONG: "UE WO MUITE ARUKOU" (RELEASED IN THE WEST AS "SUKIYAKI" IN 1963) BY KYU SAKAMOTO, 1961

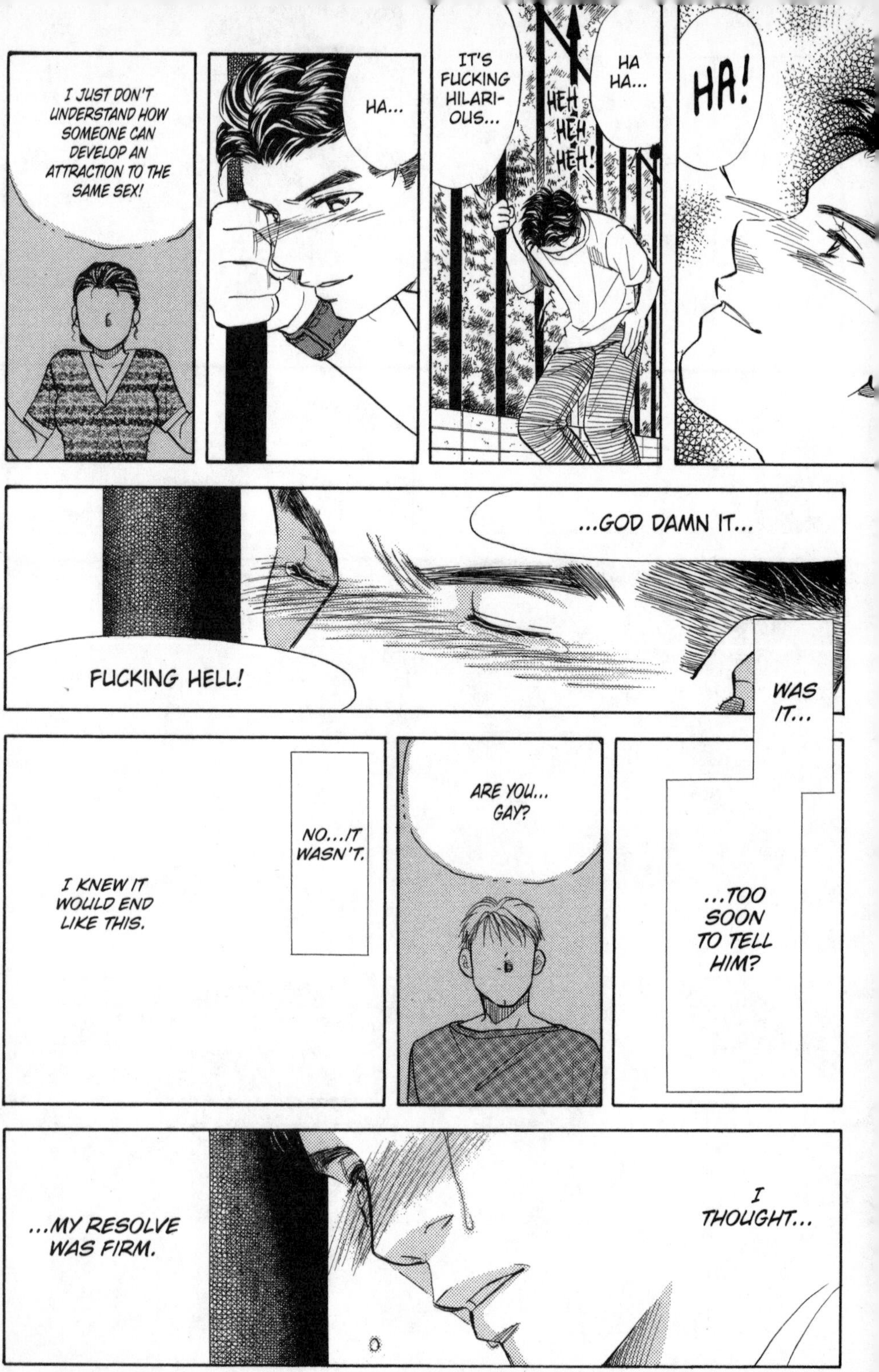
HA!
HA HA...
IT'S FUCKING HILARI-OUS...
HEH HEH HEH!
HA...
I JUST DON'T UNDERSTAND HOW SOMEONE CAN DEVELOP AN ATTRACTION TO THE SAME SEX!
...GOD DAMN IT...
FUCKING HELL!
WAS IT...
...TOO SOON TO TELL HIM?
ARE YOU... GAY?
NO...IT WASN'T.
I KNEW IT WOULD END LIKE THIS.
I THOUGHT...
...MY RESOLVE WAS FIRM.

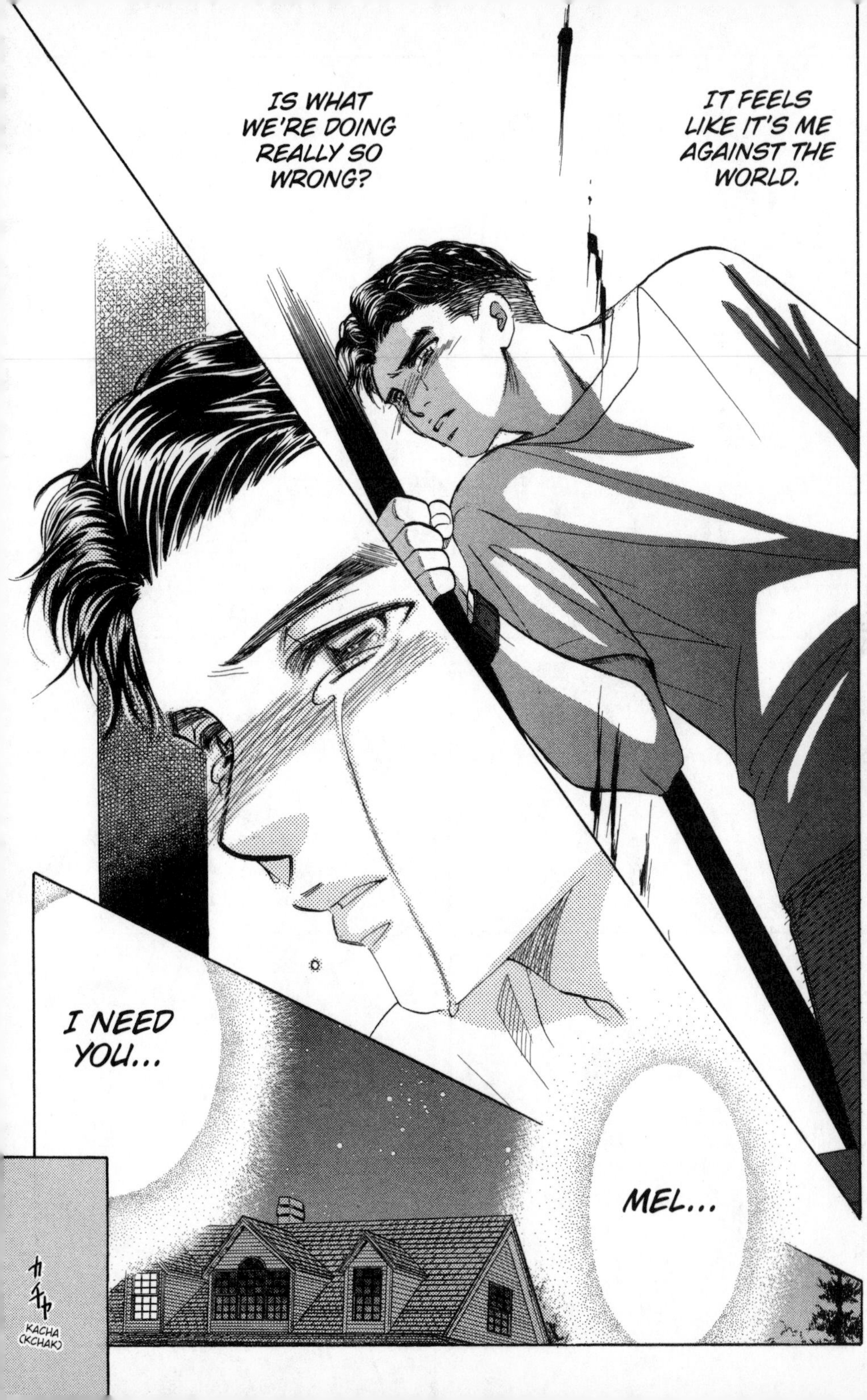
IT FEELS LIKE IT'S ME AGAINST THE WORLD.
IS WHAT WE'RE DOING REALLY SO WRONG?
I NEED YOU...
MEL...
カチャ
KACHA (KCHAK)

WELL... GOOD NIGHT.

KAIN... WAIT.

I DIDN'T HEAR DAVIS'S CAR...

OH... YOU'RE STILL AWAKE.

IS THAT YOU?

KAIN?

I WALKED HOME TO SOBER UP.

OH...

トン
TON
(TMP)
トン

I'M REALLY TIRED...

... SORRY.

...WANT US TO TALK.

I REALLY ...

......

トン
TON
トン

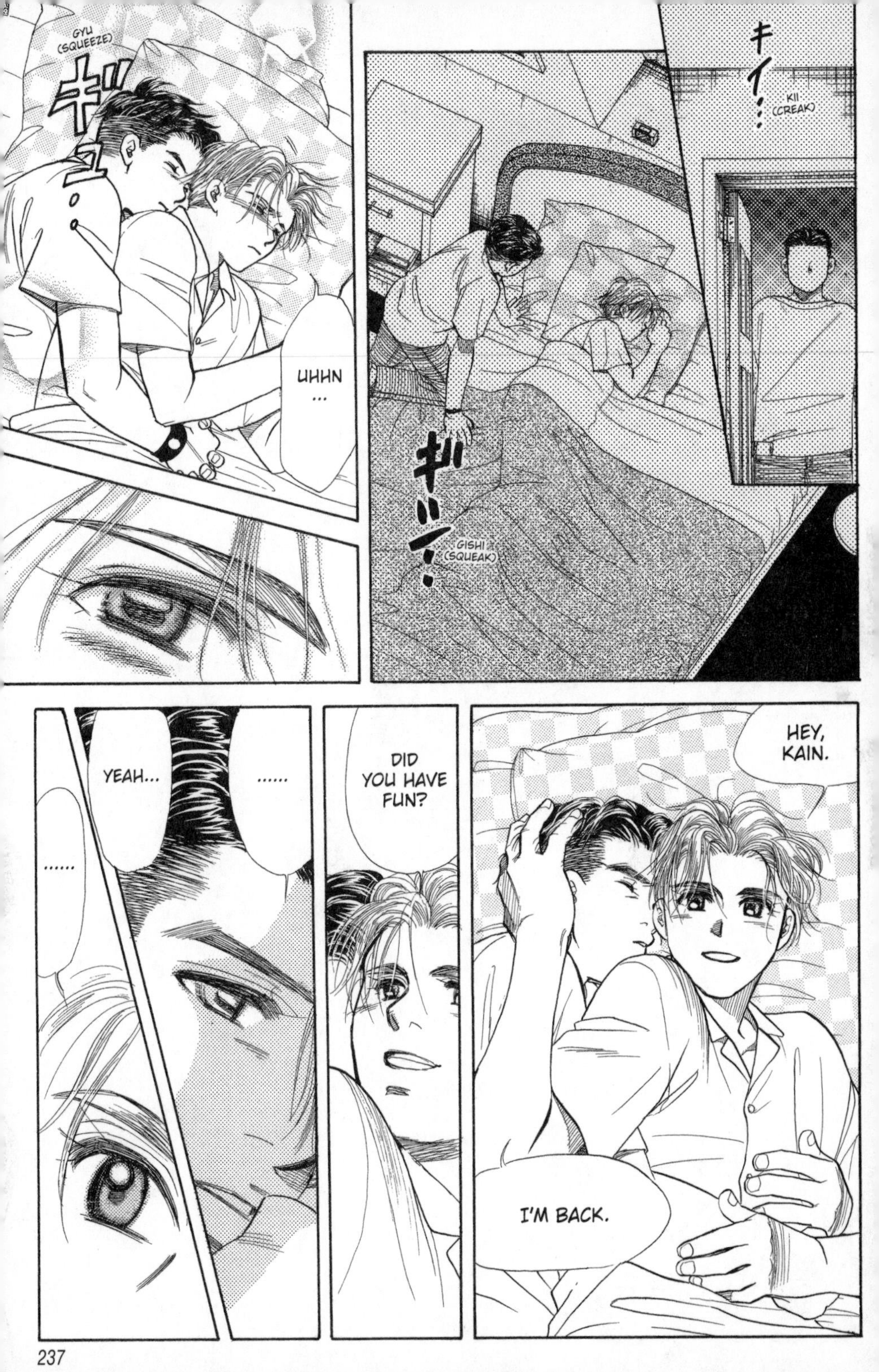
KII (CREAK)
GISHI (SQUEAK)
GYU (SQUEEZE)
UHHN ...
HEY, KAIN.
I'M BACK.
DID YOU HAVE FUN?
......
YEAH...
......

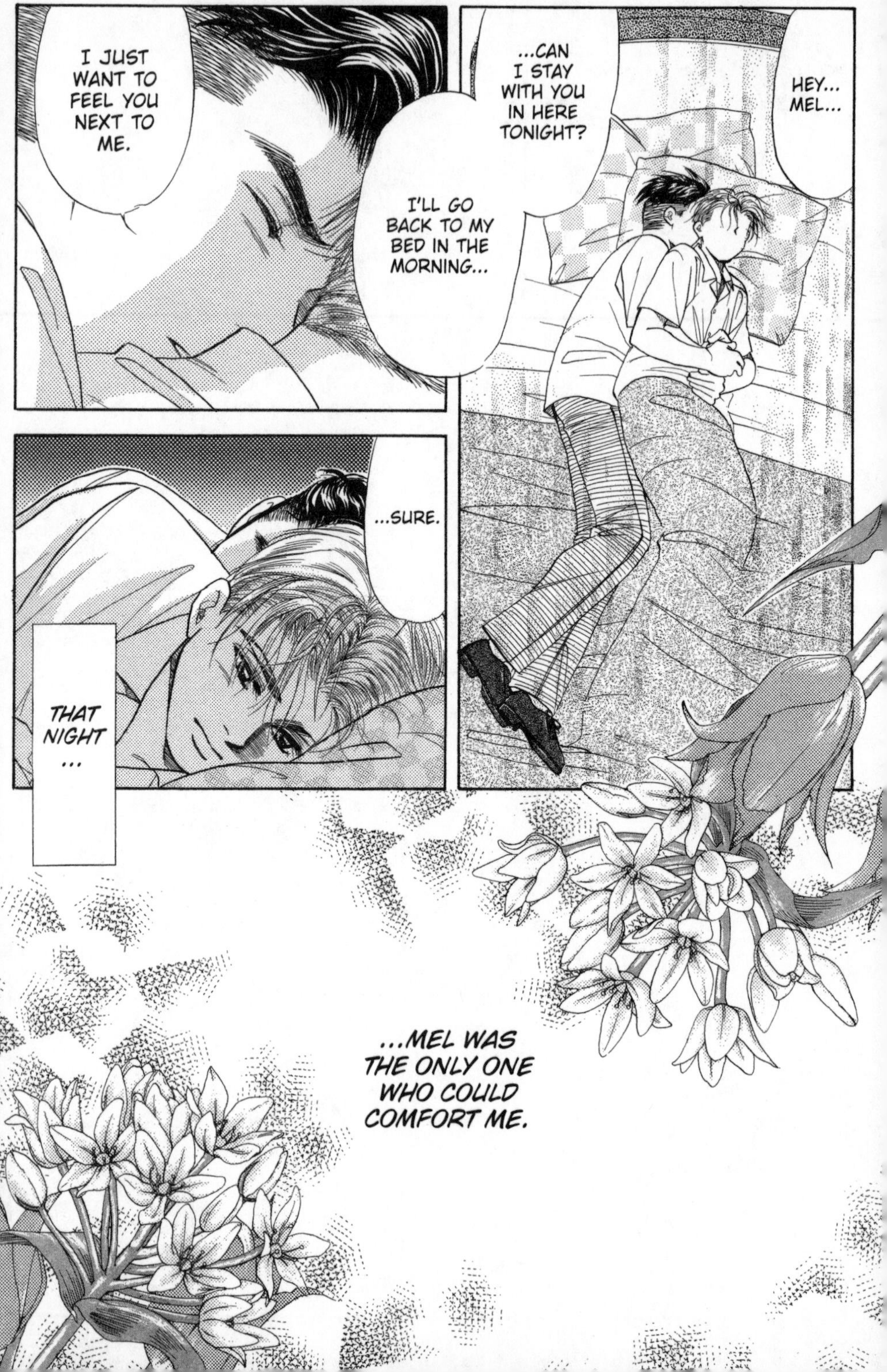
HEY... MEL...
...CAN I STAY WITH YOU IN HERE TONIGHT?
I'LL GO BACK TO MY BED IN THE MORNING...
I JUST WANT TO FEEL YOU NEXT TO ME.
...SURE.
THAT NIGHT...
...MEL WAS THE ONLY ONE WHO COULD COMFORT ME.

EPISODE II

SCENE 3

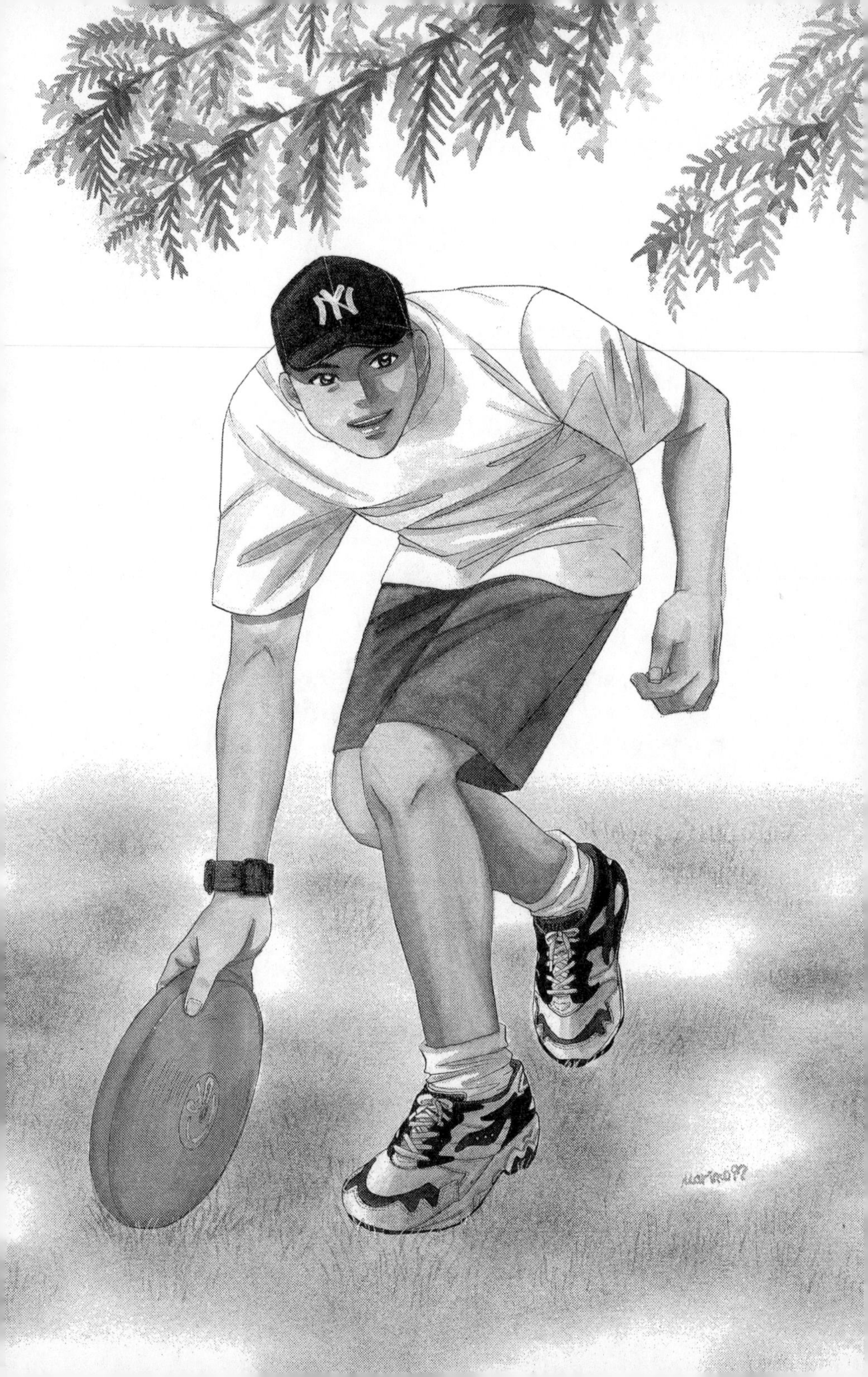
NY
marimo97

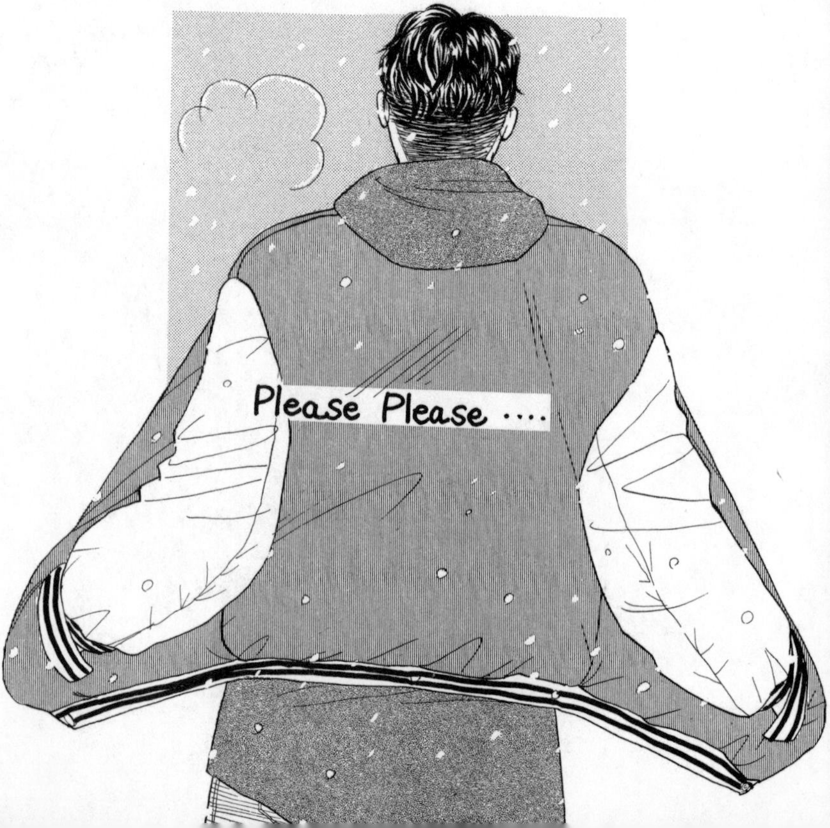
Please Please ....

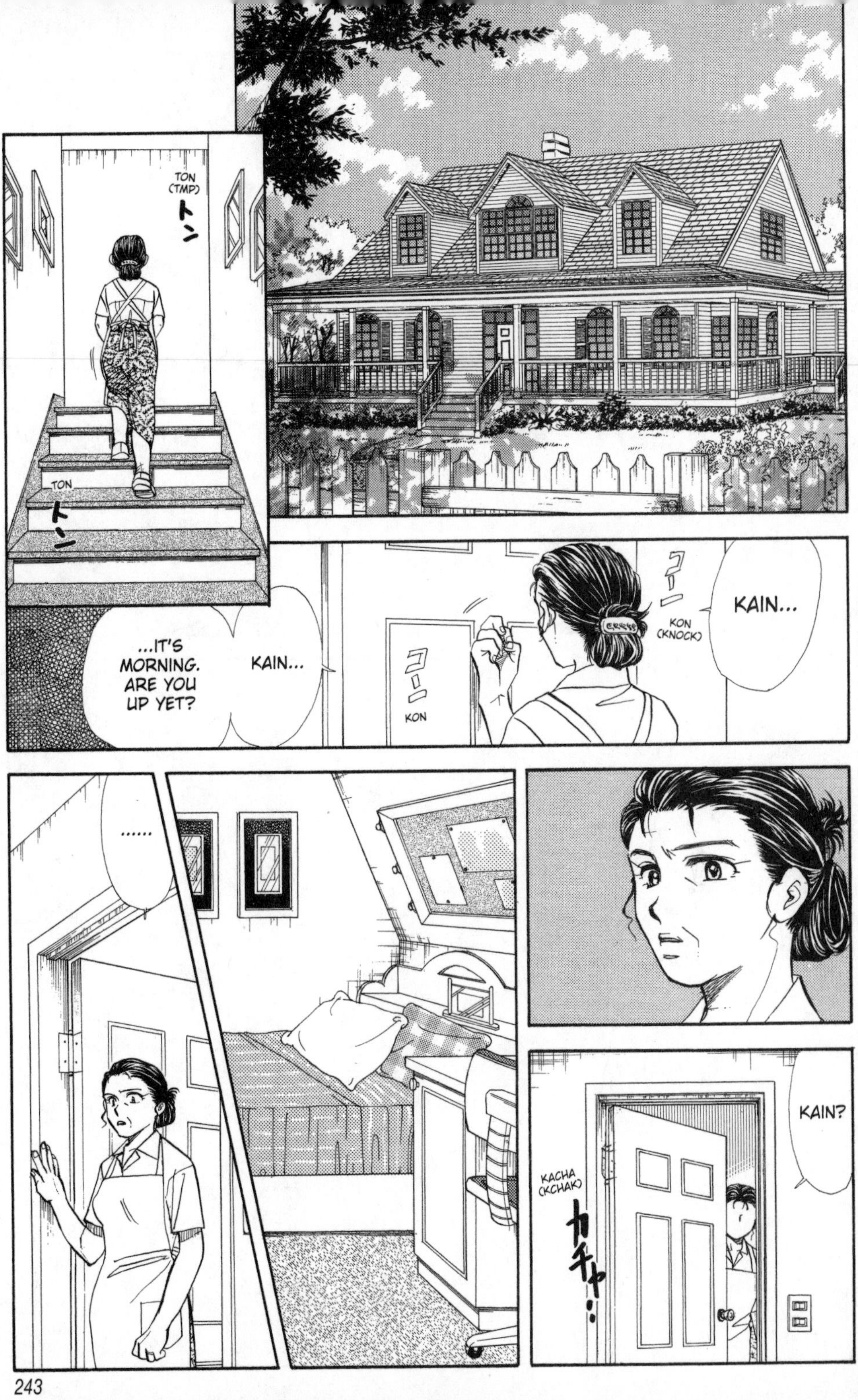
TON (TMP)
トン
TON
トン
KAIN...
KON (KNOCK)
コー
KON
コー
KAIN...
...IT'S MORNING. ARE YOU UP YET?
KAIN?
KACHA (KCHAK)
カチャ!!
......

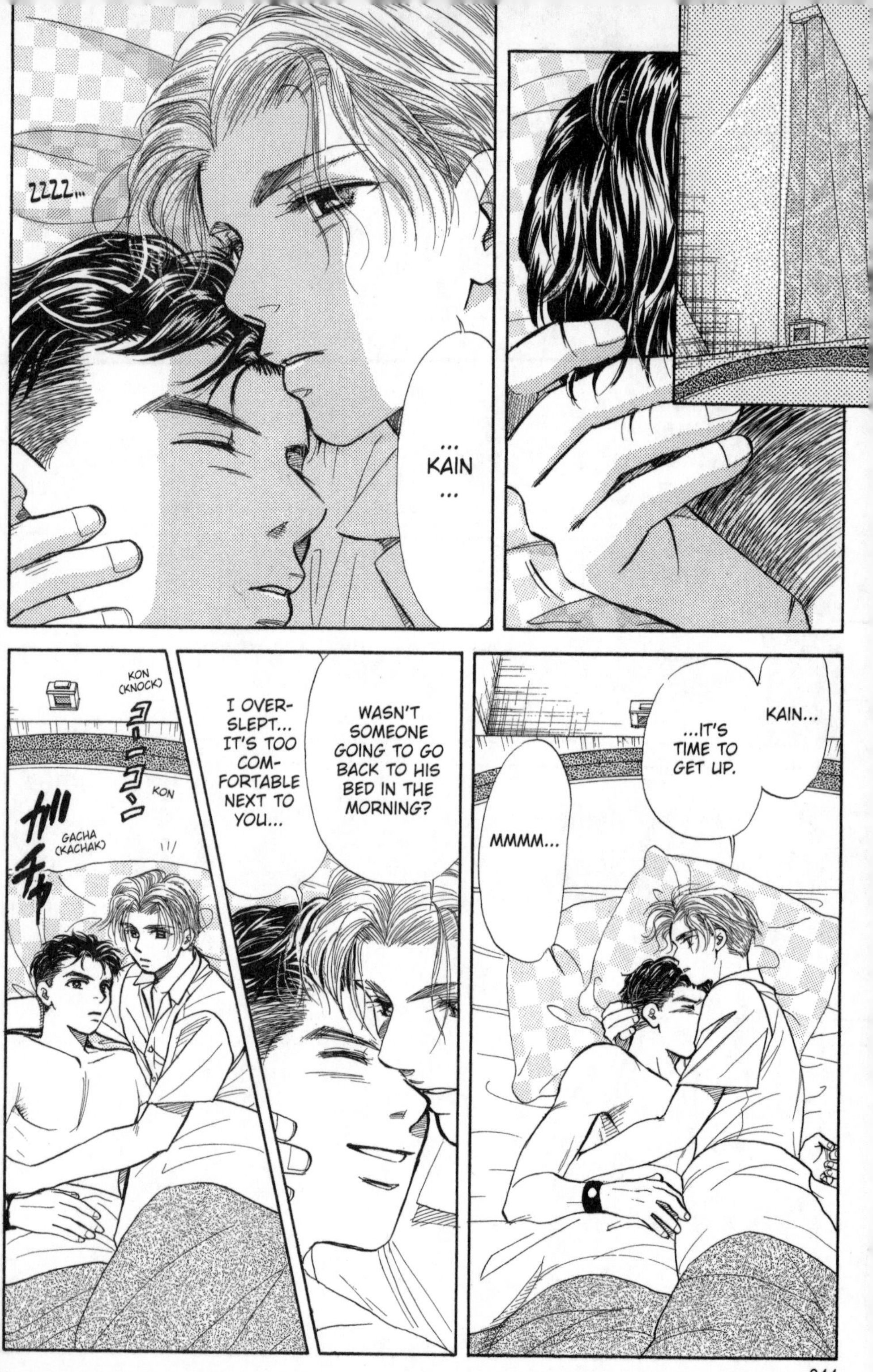
ZZZZ...
...KAIN...
KAIN...
...IT'S TIME TO GET UP.
MMMM...
WASN'T SOMEONE GOING TO GO BACK TO HIS BED IN THE MORNING?
I OVER-SLEPT... IT'S TOO COM-FORTABLE NEXT TO YOU...
KON (KNOCK)
コンコン
KON
GACHA (KACHAK)
ガチャ

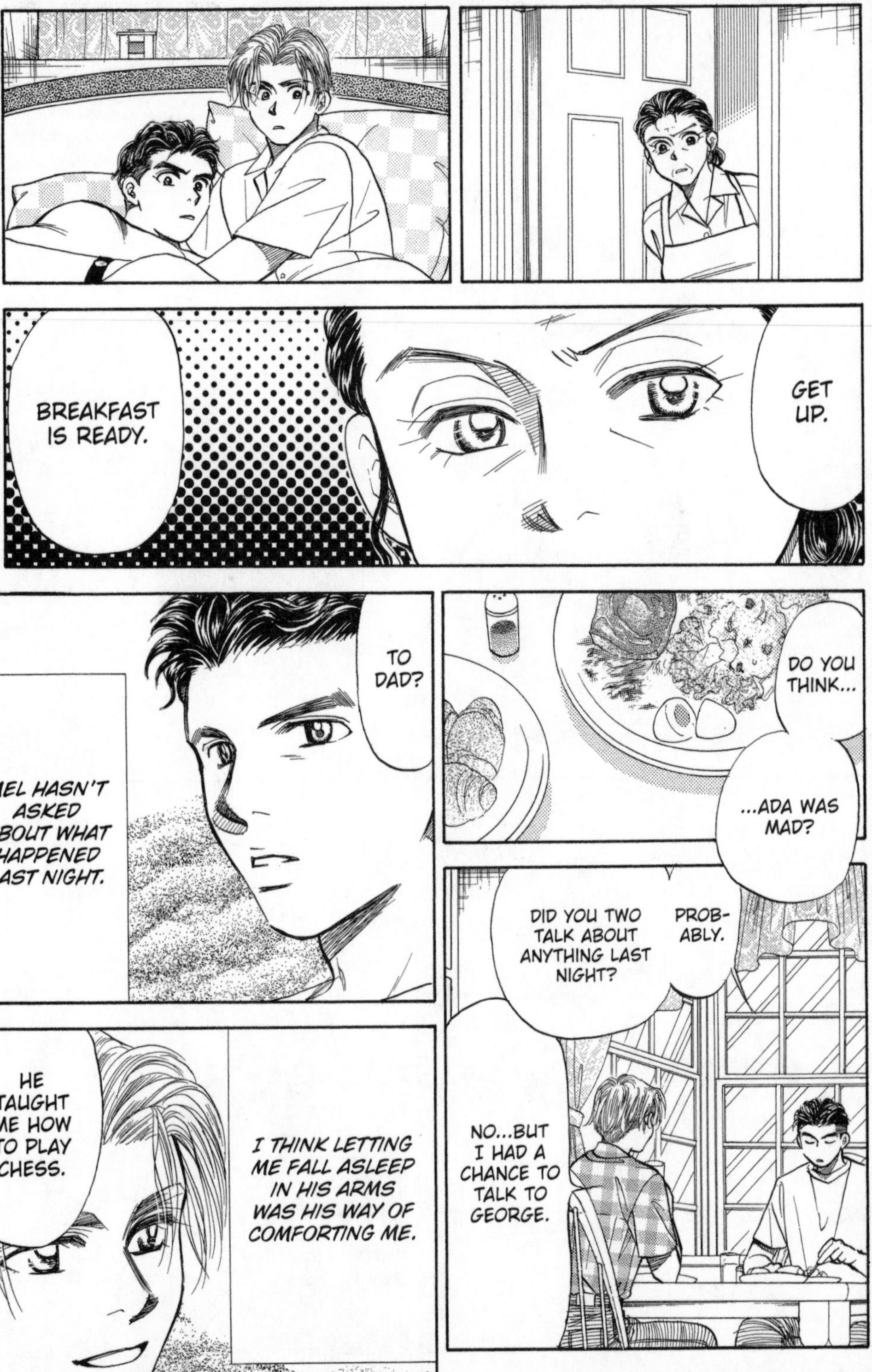
GET UP.
BREAKFAST IS READY.
DO YOU THINK...
...ADA WAS MAD?
PROB-ABLY.
DID YOU TWO TALK ABOUT ANYTHING LAST NIGHT?
NO...BUT I HAD A CHANCE TO TALK TO GEORGE.
TO DAD?
MEL HASN'T ASKED ABOUT WHAT HAPPENED LAST NIGHT.
HE TAUGHT ME HOW TO PLAY CHESS.
I THINK LETTING ME FALL ASLEEP IN HIS ARMS WAS HIS WAY OF COMFORTING ME.

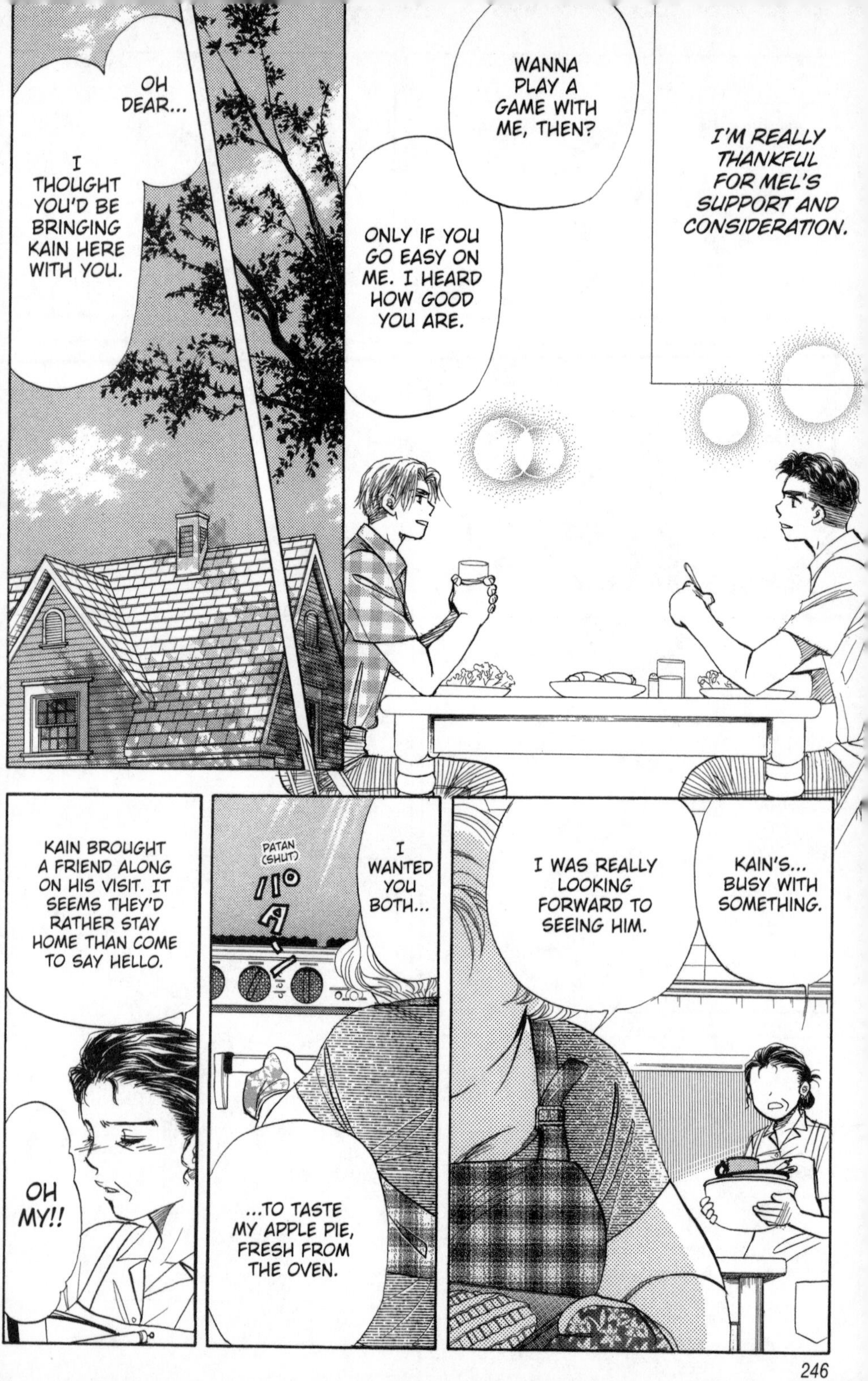
I'M REALLY THANKFUL FOR MEL'S SUPPORT AND CONSIDERATION.
WANNA PLAY A GAME WITH ME, THEN?
ONLY IF YOU GO EASY ON ME. I HEARD HOW GOOD YOU ARE.
OH DEAR...
I THOUGHT YOU'D BE BRINGING KAIN HERE WITH YOU.
KAIN'S... BUSY WITH SOMETHING.
I WAS REALLY LOOKING FORWARD TO SEEING HIM.
PATAN (SHUT)
I WANTED YOU BOTH...
...TO TASTE MY APPLE PIE, FRESH FROM THE OVEN.
KAIN BROUGHT A FRIEND ALONG ON HIS VISIT. IT SEEMS THEY'D RATHER STAY HOME THAN COME TO SAY HELLO.
OH MY!!

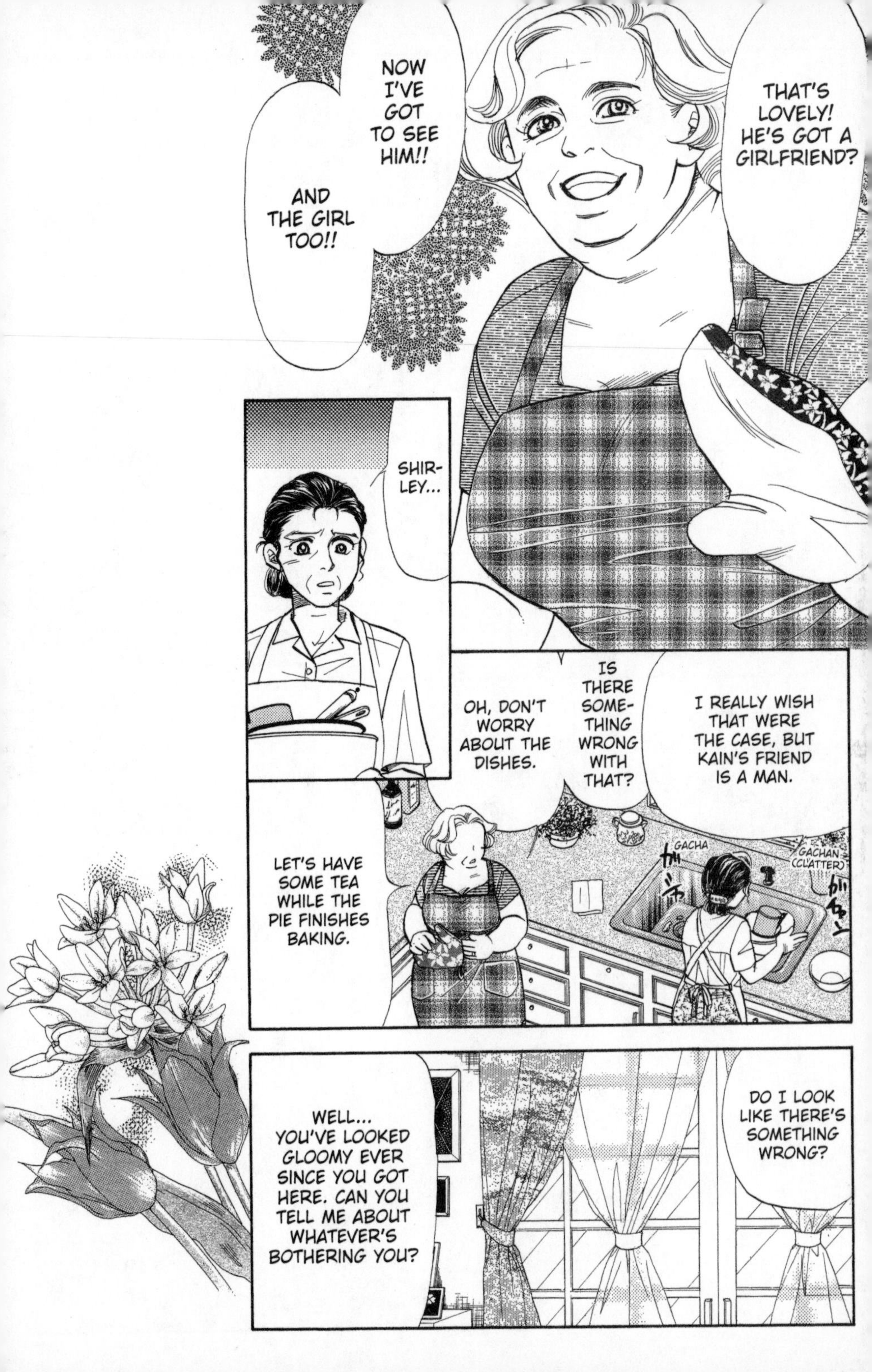
THAT'S LOVELY! HE'S GOT A GIRLFRIEND?
NOW I'VE GOT TO SEE HIM!!
AND THE GIRL TOO!!
SHIR-LEY...
I REALLY WISH THAT WERE THE CASE, BUT KAIN'S FRIEND IS A MAN.
IS THERE SOME-THING WRONG WITH THAT?
OH, DON'T WORRY ABOUT THE DISHES.
GACHAN (CLATTER)
GACHA
LET'S HAVE SOME TEA WHILE THE PIE FINISHES BAKING.
DO I LOOK LIKE THERE'S SOMETHING WRONG?
WELL... YOU'VE LOOKED GLOOMY EVER SINCE YOU GOT HERE. CAN YOU TELL ME ABOUT WHATEVER'S BOTHERING YOU?

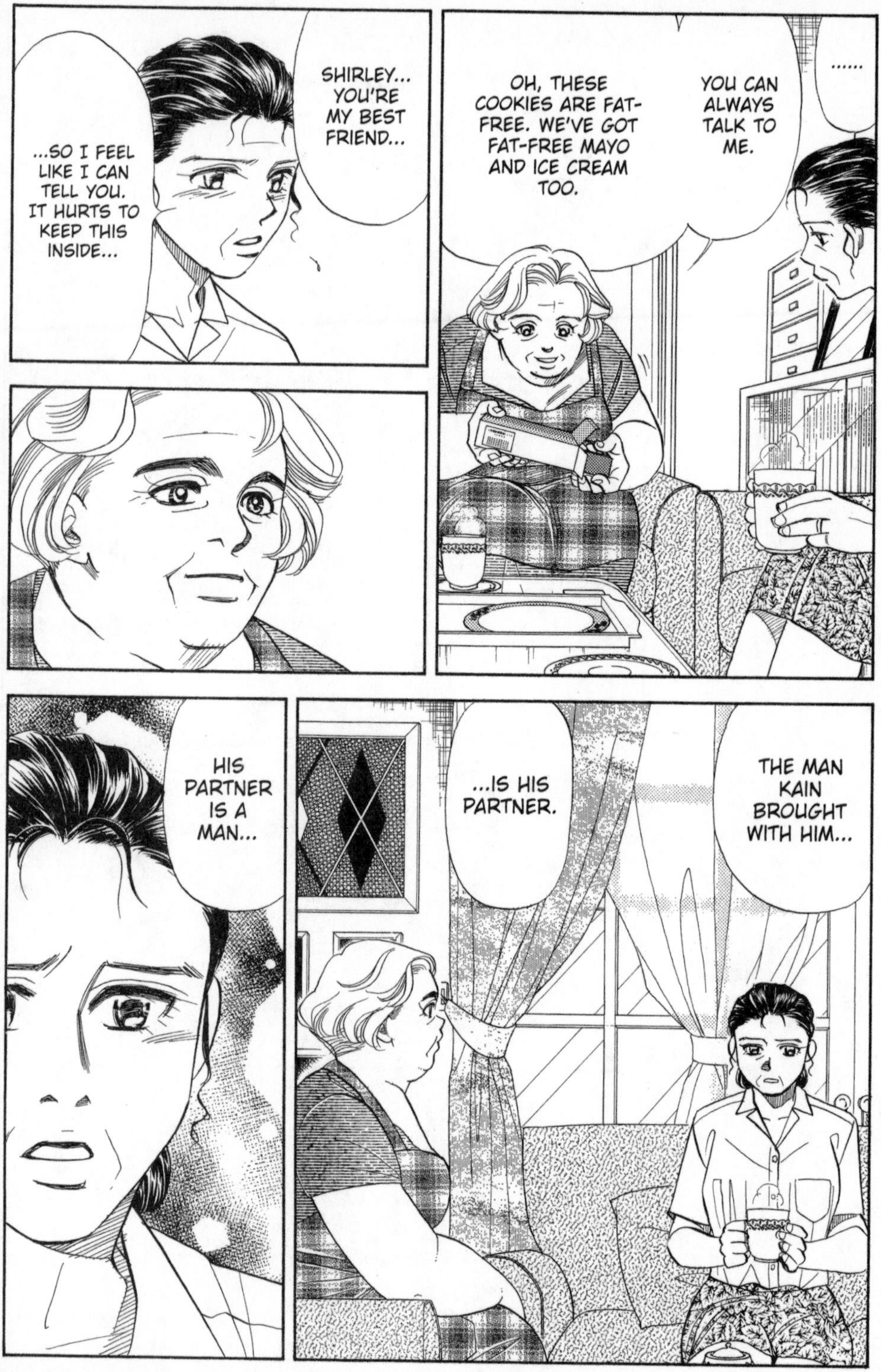
......
YOU CAN ALWAYS TALK TO ME.
OH, THESE COOKIES ARE FAT-FREE. WE'VE GOT FAT-FREE MAYO AND ICE CREAM TOO.
SHIRLEY... YOU'RE MY BEST FRIEND...
...SO I FEEL LIKE I CAN TELL YOU. IT HURTS TO KEEP THIS INSIDE...
THE MAN KAIN BROUGHT WITH HIM...
...IS HIS PARTNER.
HIS PARTNER IS A MAN...

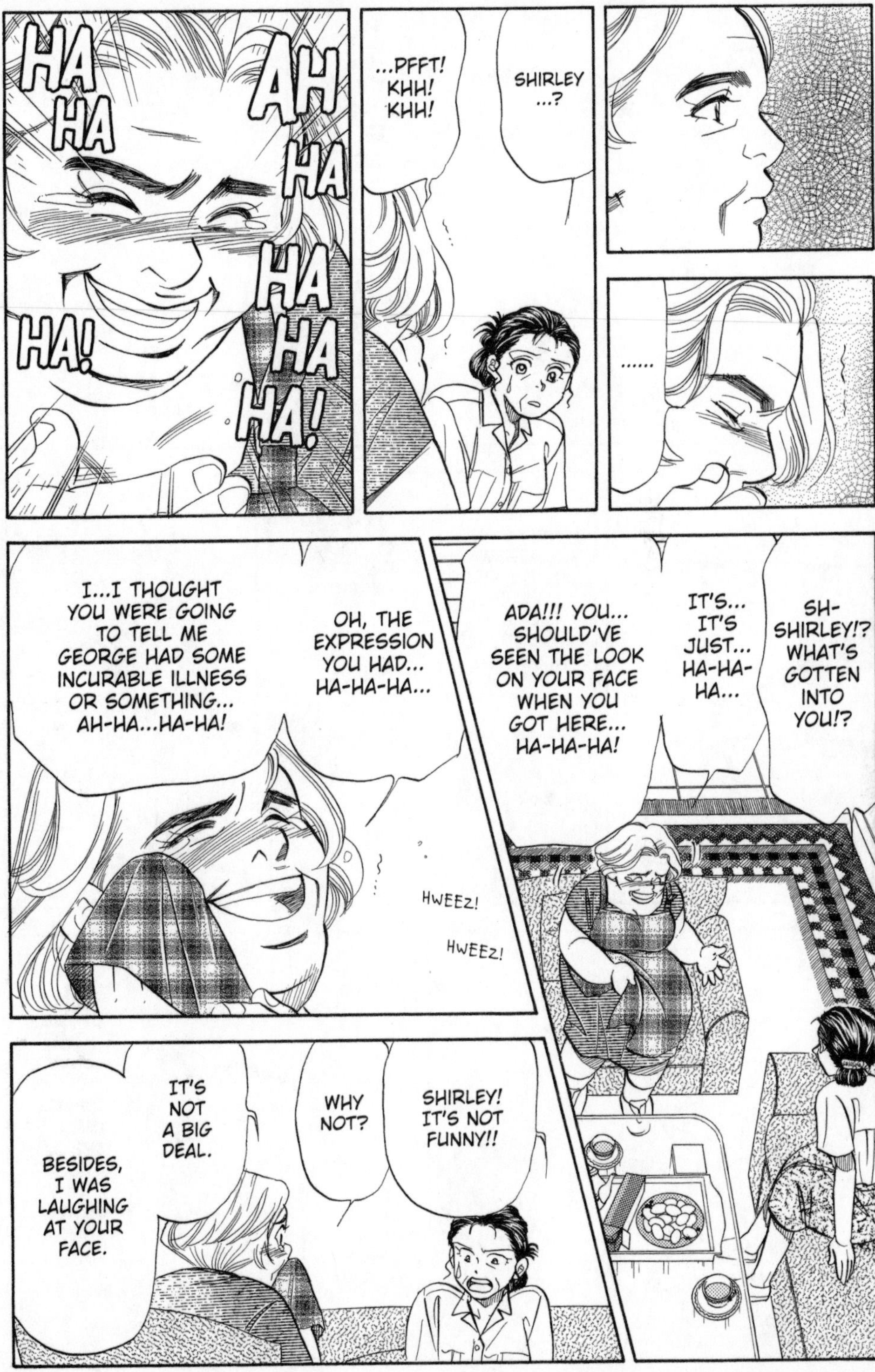
......
SHIRLEY ...?
...PFFT! KHH! KHH!
AH HA HA HA HA HA!
HA HA HA!
SH-SHIRLEY!? WHAT'S GOTTEN INTO YOU!?
IT'S... IT'S JUST... HA-HA-HA...
ADA!!! YOU... SHOULD'VE SEEN THE LOOK ON YOUR FACE WHEN YOU GOT HERE... HA-HA-HA!
OH, THE EXPRESSION YOU HAD... HA-HA-HA...
I...I THOUGHT YOU WERE GOING TO TELL ME GEORGE HAD SOME INCURABLE ILLNESS OR SOMETHING... AH-HA...HA-HA!
HWEEZ!
HWEEZ!
SHIRLEY! IT'S NOT FUNNY!!
WHY NOT?
IT'S NOT A BIG DEAL.
BESIDES, I WAS LAUGHING AT YOUR FACE.

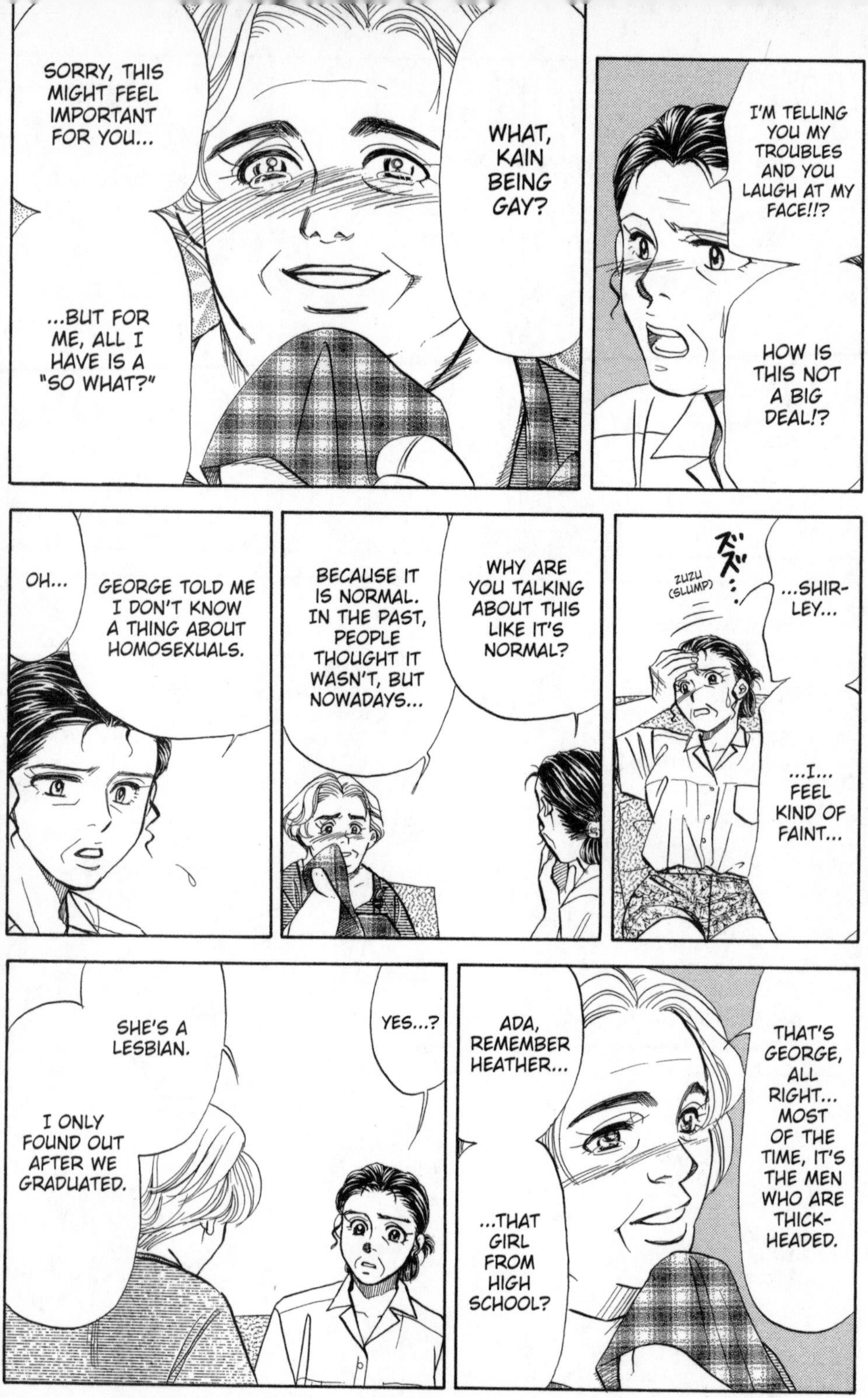
I'M TELLING YOU MY TROUBLES AND YOU LAUGH AT MY FACE!!?
HOW IS THIS NOT A BIG DEAL!?
WHAT, KAIN BEING GAY?
SORRY, THIS MIGHT FEEL IMPORTANT FOR YOU...
...BUT FOR ME, ALL I HAVE IS A "SO WHAT?"
ズズ…
ZUZU (SLUMP)
...SHIR-LEY...
...I... FEEL KIND OF FAINT...
WHY ARE YOU TALKING ABOUT THIS LIKE IT'S NORMAL?
BECAUSE IT IS NORMAL. IN THE PAST, PEOPLE THOUGHT IT WASN'T, BUT NOWADAYS...
GEORGE TOLD ME I DON'T KNOW A THING ABOUT HOMOSEXUALS.
OH...
THAT'S GEORGE, ALL RIGHT... MOST OF THE TIME, IT'S THE MEN WHO ARE THICK-HEADED.
ADA, REMEMBER HEATHER...
...THAT GIRL FROM HIGH SCHOOL?
YES...?
SHE'S A LESBIAN.
I ONLY FOUND OUT AFTER WE GRADUATED.

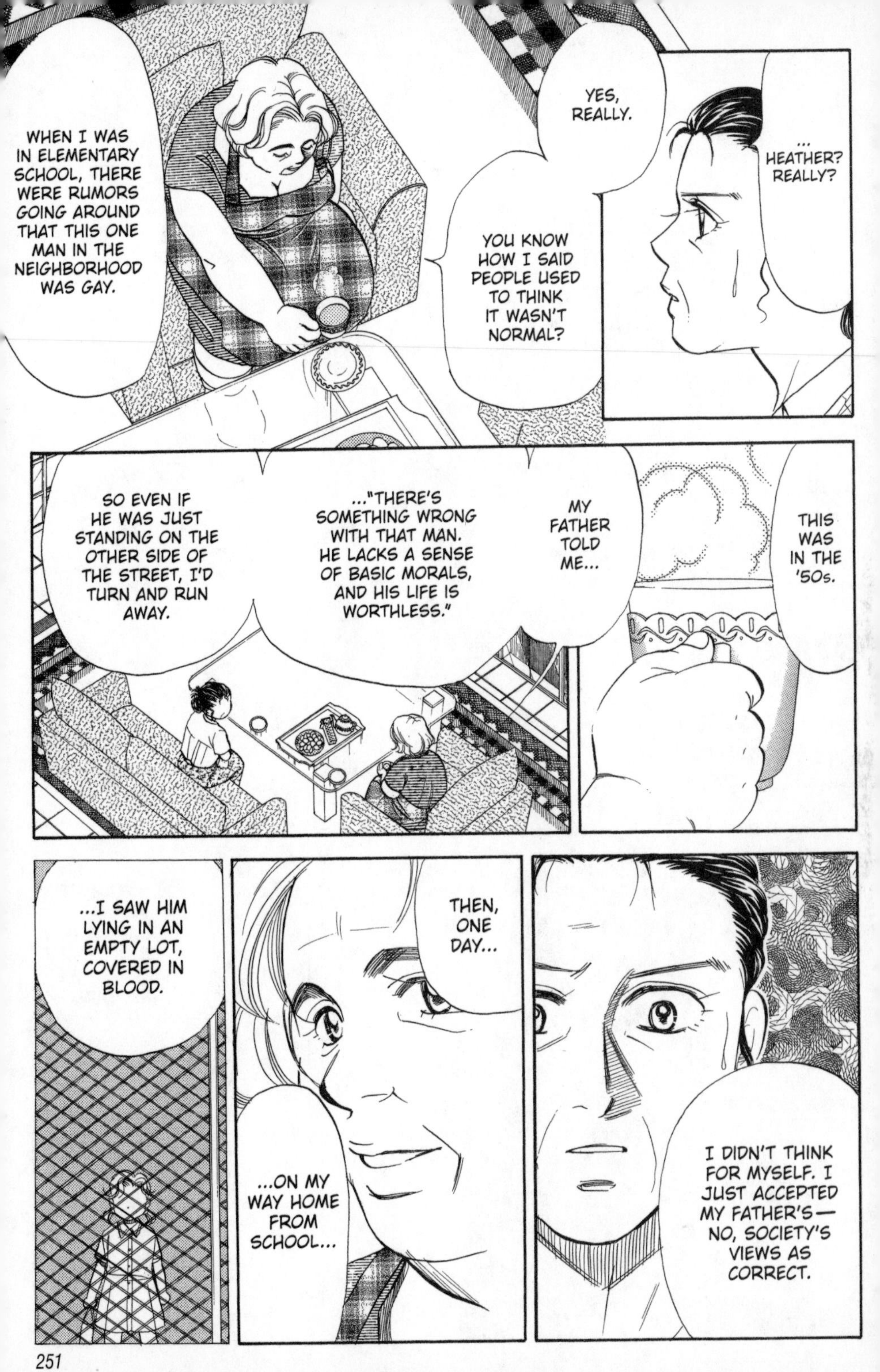
...HEATHER? REALLY?
YES, REALLY.
YOU KNOW HOW I SAID PEOPLE USED TO THINK IT WASN'T NORMAL?
WHEN I WAS IN ELEMENTARY SCHOOL, THERE WERE RUMORS GOING AROUND THAT THIS ONE MAN IN THE NEIGHBORHOOD WAS GAY.
THIS WAS IN THE '50s.
MY FATHER TOLD ME...
..."THERE'S SOMETHING WRONG WITH THAT MAN. HE LACKS A SENSE OF BASIC MORALS, AND HIS LIFE IS WORTHLESS."
SO EVEN IF HE WAS JUST STANDING ON THE OTHER SIDE OF THE STREET, I'D TURN AND RUN AWAY.
I DIDN'T THINK FOR MYSELF. I JUST ACCEPTED MY FATHER'S—NO, SOCIETY'S VIEWS AS CORRECT.
THEN, ONE DAY...
...ON MY WAY HOME FROM SCHOOL...
...I SAW HIM LYING IN AN EMPTY LOT, COVERED IN BLOOD.

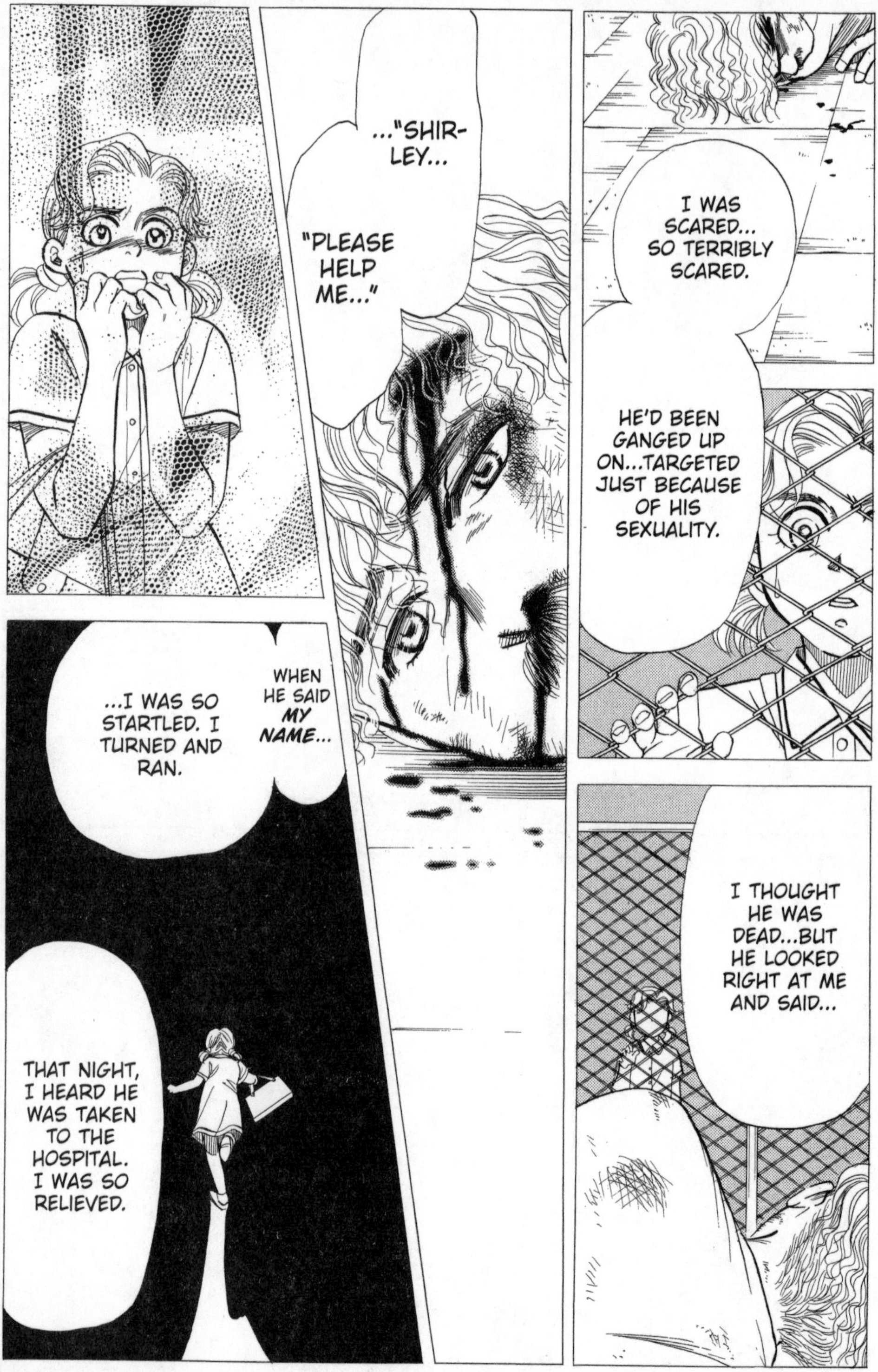
I WAS SCARED... SO TERRIBLY SCARED.
HE'D BEEN GANGED UP ON...TARGETED JUST BECAUSE OF HIS SEXUALITY.
I THOUGHT HE WAS DEAD...BUT HE LOOKED RIGHT AT ME AND SAID...
..."SHIRLEY...
"PLEASE HELP ME..."
WHEN HE SAID *MY NAME*...
...I WAS SO STARTLED. I TURNED AND RAN.
THAT NIGHT, I HEARD HE WAS TAKEN TO THE HOSPITAL. I WAS SO RELIEVED.

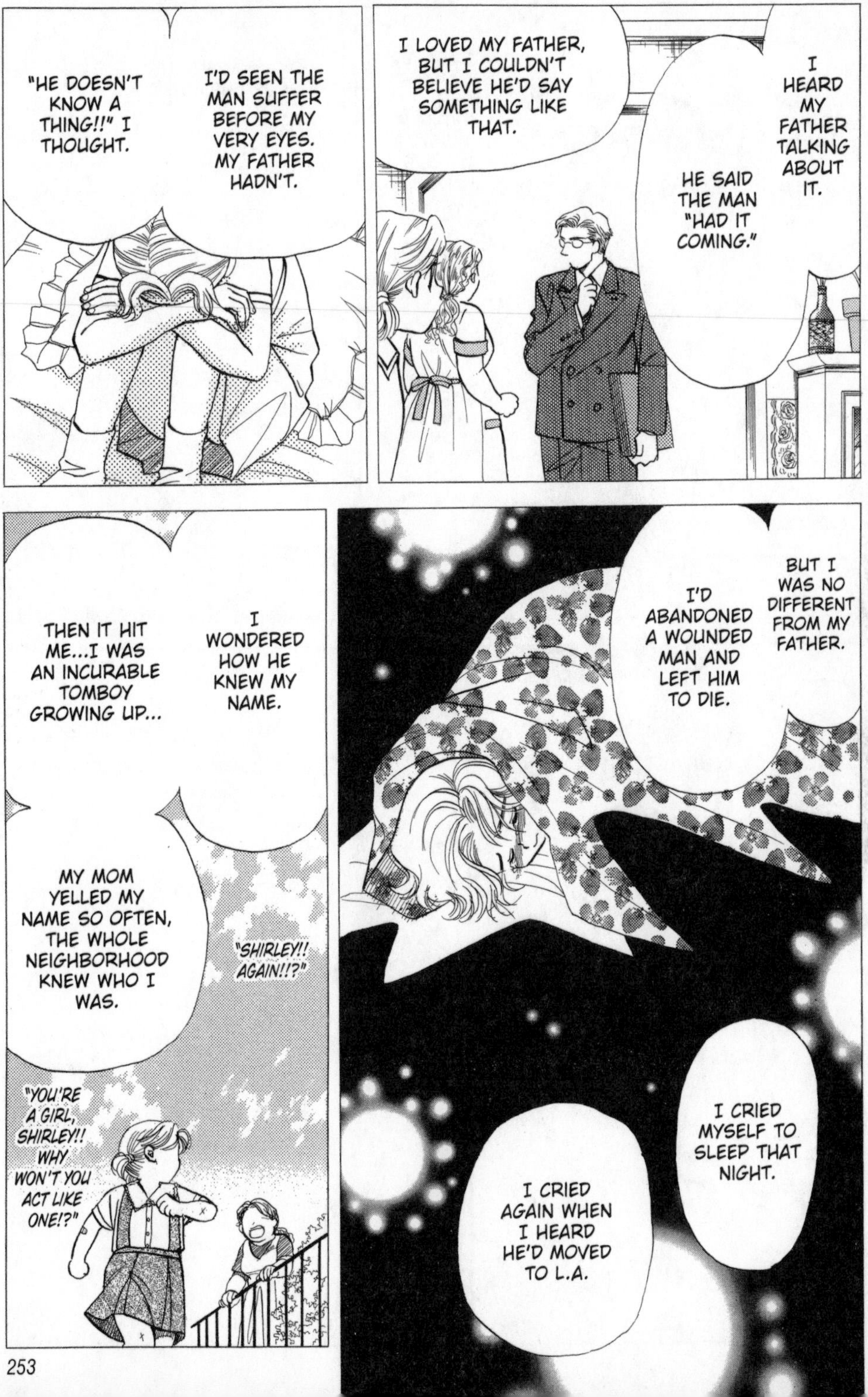
I HEARD MY FATHER TALKING ABOUT IT.
HE SAID THE MAN "HAD IT COMING."
I LOVED MY FATHER, BUT I COULDN'T BELIEVE HE'D SAY SOMETHING LIKE THAT.
I'D SEEN THE MAN SUFFER BEFORE MY VERY EYES. MY FATHER HADN'T.
"HE DOESN'T KNOW A THING!!" I THOUGHT.
BUT I WAS NO DIFFERENT FROM MY FATHER.
I'D ABANDONED A WOUNDED MAN AND LEFT HIM TO DIE.
I CRIED MYSELF TO SLEEP THAT NIGHT.
I CRIED AGAIN WHEN I HEARD HE'D MOVED TO L.A.
I WONDERED HOW HE KNEW MY NAME.
THEN IT HIT ME...I WAS AN INCURABLE TOMBOY GROWING UP...
MY MOM YELLED MY NAME SO OFTEN, THE WHOLE NEIGHBORHOOD KNEW WHO I WAS.
"SHIRLEY!! AGAIN!!?"
"YOU'RE A GIRL, SHIRLEY!! WHY WON'T YOU ACT LIKE ONE!?"

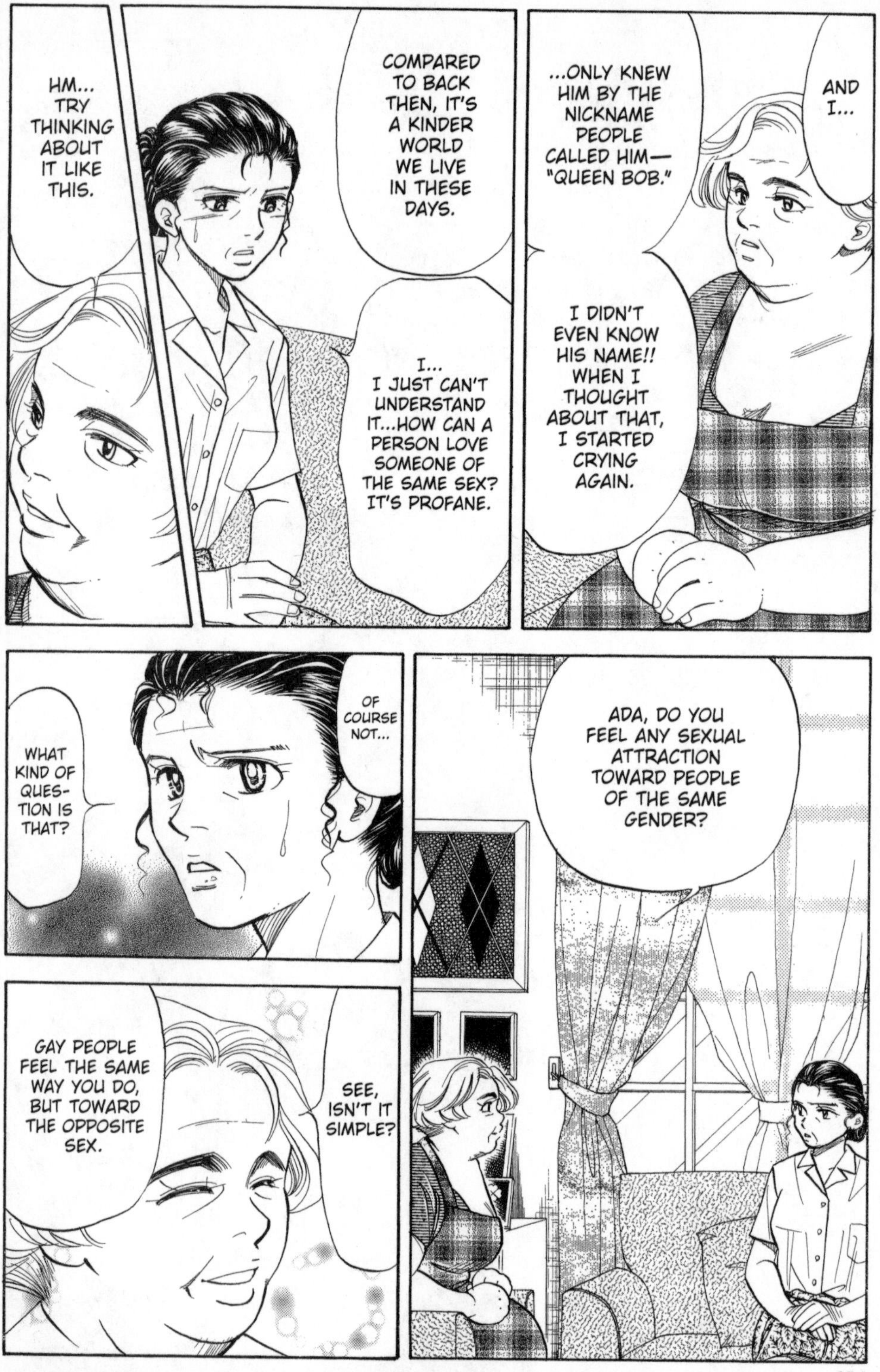
AND I...
...ONLY KNEW HIM BY THE NICKNAME PEOPLE CALLED HIM—"QUEEN BOB."
I DIDN'T EVEN KNOW HIS NAME!! WHEN I THOUGHT ABOUT THAT, I STARTED CRYING AGAIN.
COMPARED TO BACK THEN, IT'S A KINDER WORLD WE LIVE IN THESE DAYS.
I... I JUST CAN'T UNDERSTAND IT...HOW CAN A PERSON LOVE SOMEONE OF THE SAME SEX? IT'S PROFANE.
HM... TRY THINKING ABOUT IT LIKE THIS.
ADA, DO YOU FEEL ANY SEXUAL ATTRACTION TOWARD PEOPLE OF THE SAME GENDER?
OF COURSE NOT...
WHAT KIND OF QUES-TION IS THAT?
GAY PEOPLE FEEL THE SAME WAY YOU DO, BUT TOWARD THE OPPOSITE SEX.
SEE, ISN'T IT SIMPLE?

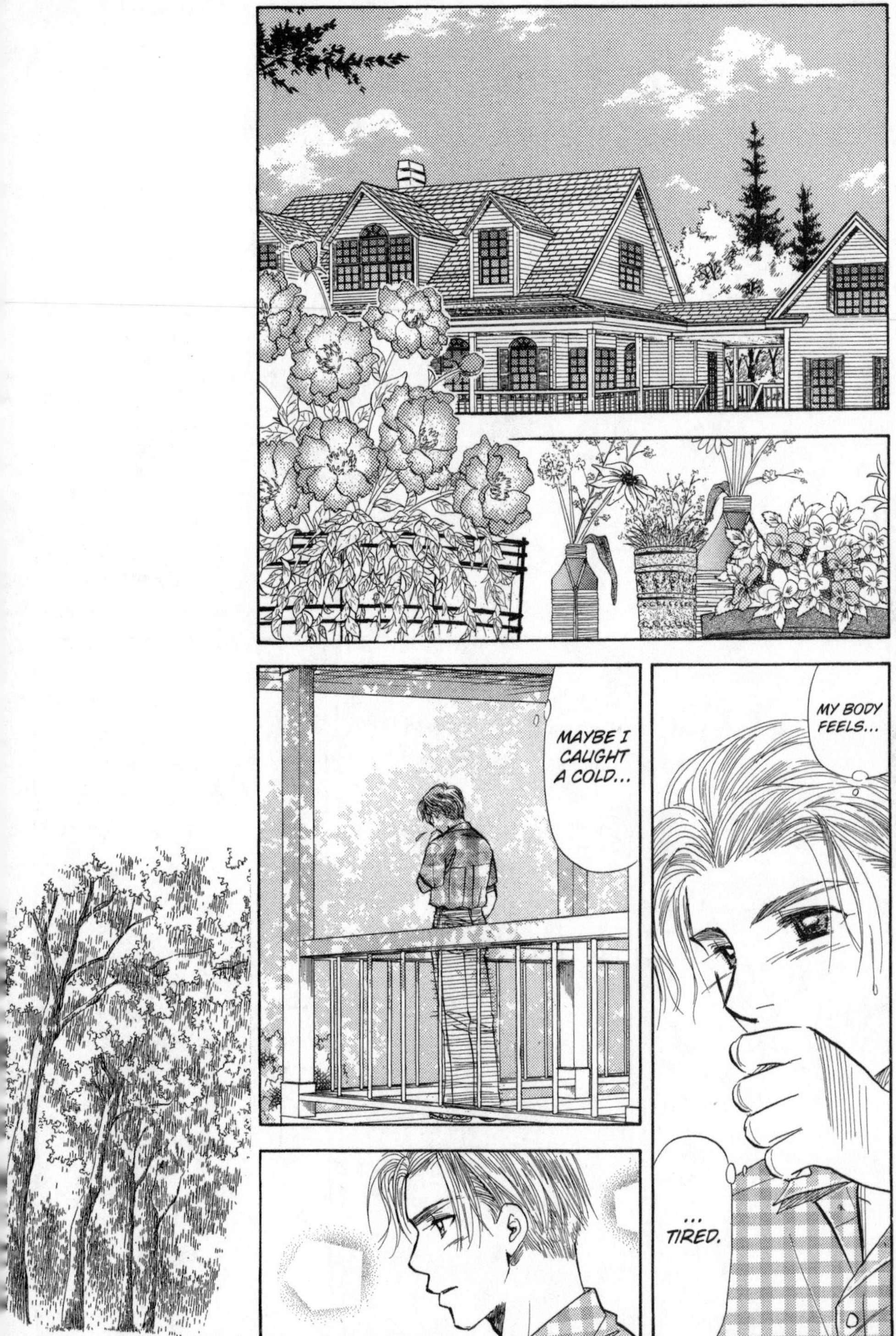
MY BODY FEELS...
... TIRED.
MAYBE I CAUGHT A COLD...

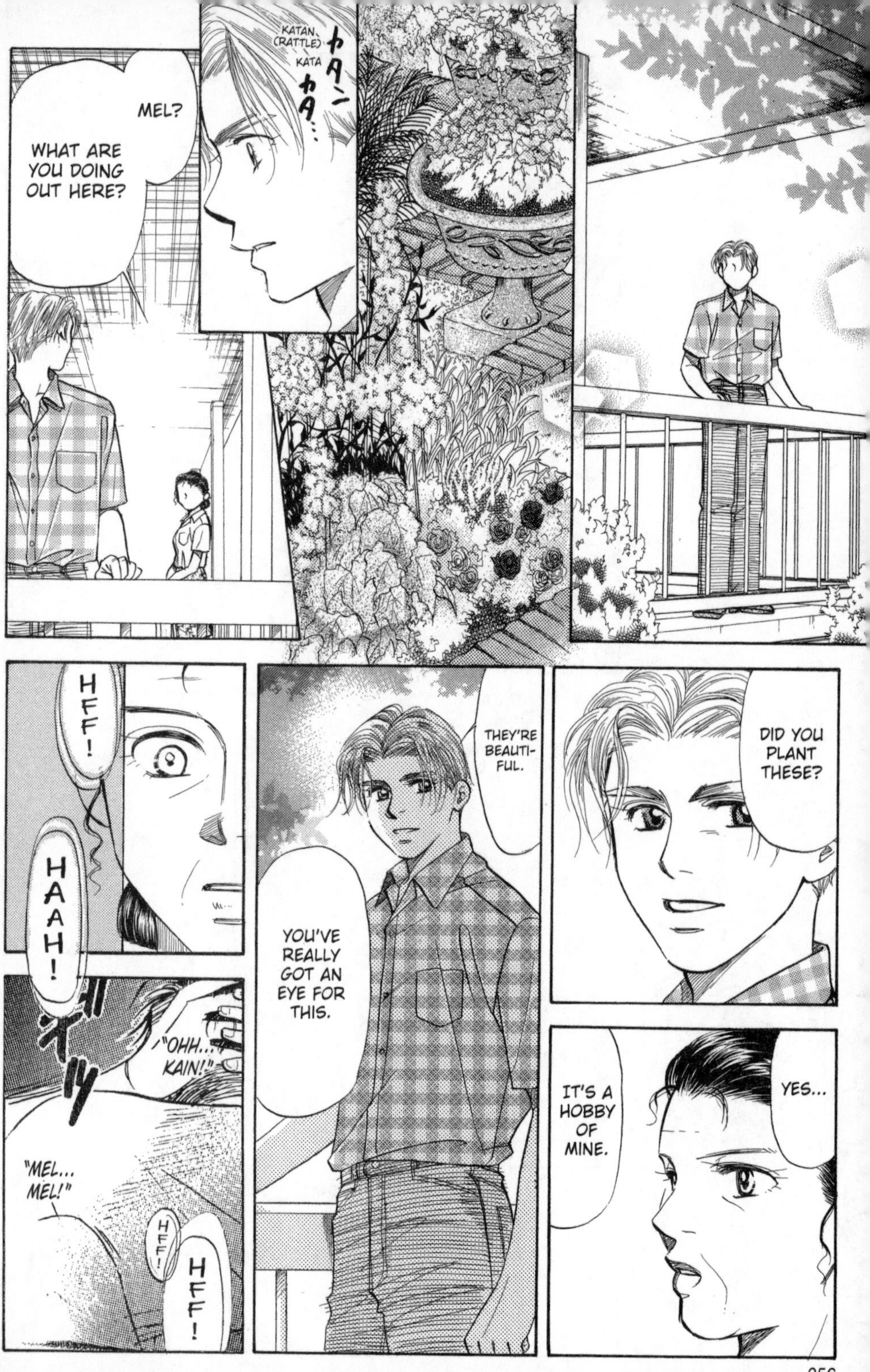
KATAN (RATTLE)
KATA
MEL?
WHAT ARE YOU DOING OUT HERE?
DID YOU PLANT THESE?
YES...
IT'S A HOBBY OF MINE.
THEY'RE BEAUTIFUL.
YOU'VE REALLY GOT AN EYE FOR THIS.
HFF!
HAAAH!
"OHH... KAIN!"
"MEL... MEL!"
HFF!
HFF!

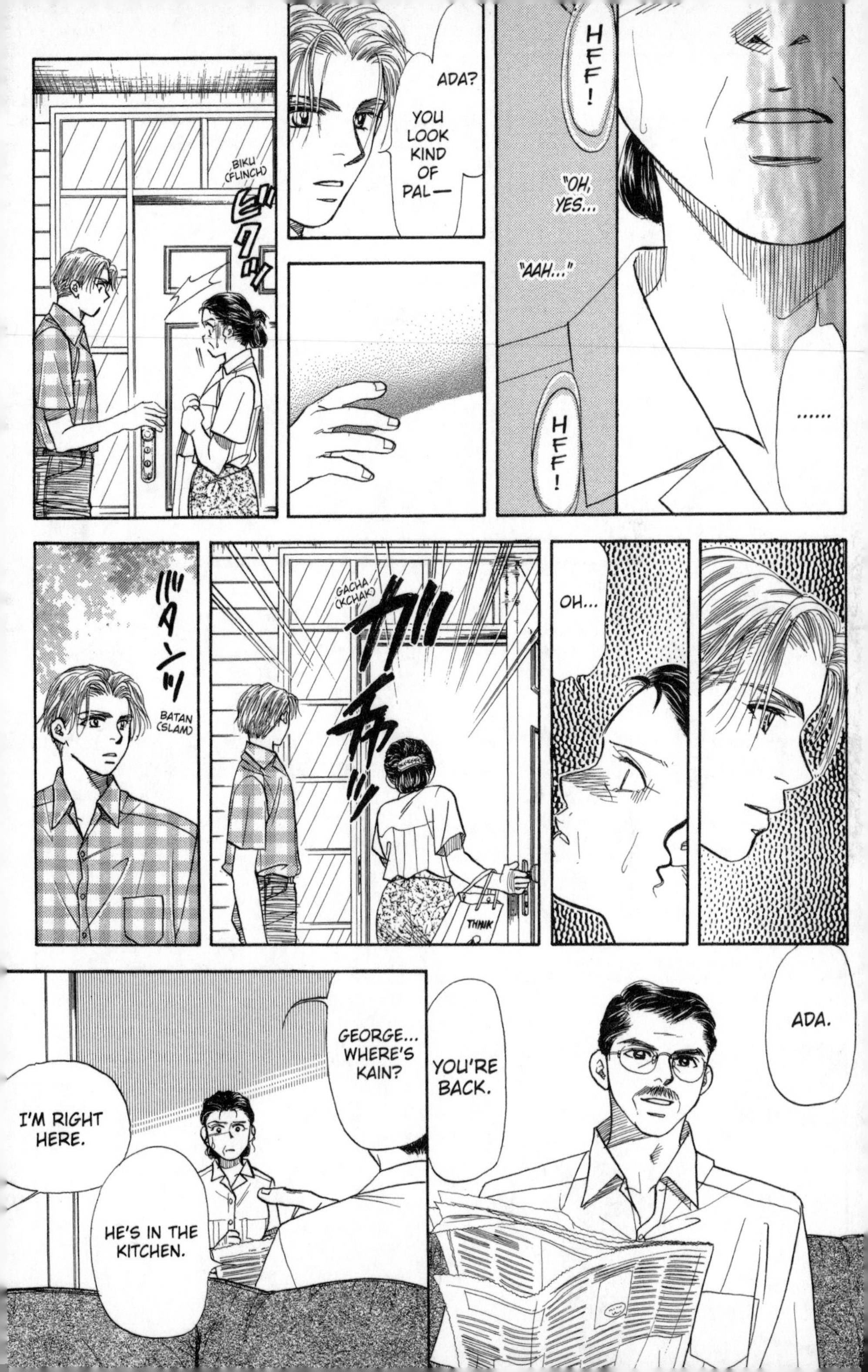
......
HFF!
"OH, YES...
"AAH..."
HFF!
ADA?
YOU LOOK KIND OF PAL—
BIKU (FLINCH)
OH...
GACHA (KCHAK)
THNK
BATAN (SLAM)
ADA.
YOU'RE BACK.
GEORGE... WHERE'S KAIN?
I'M RIGHT HERE.
HE'S IN THE KITCHEN.

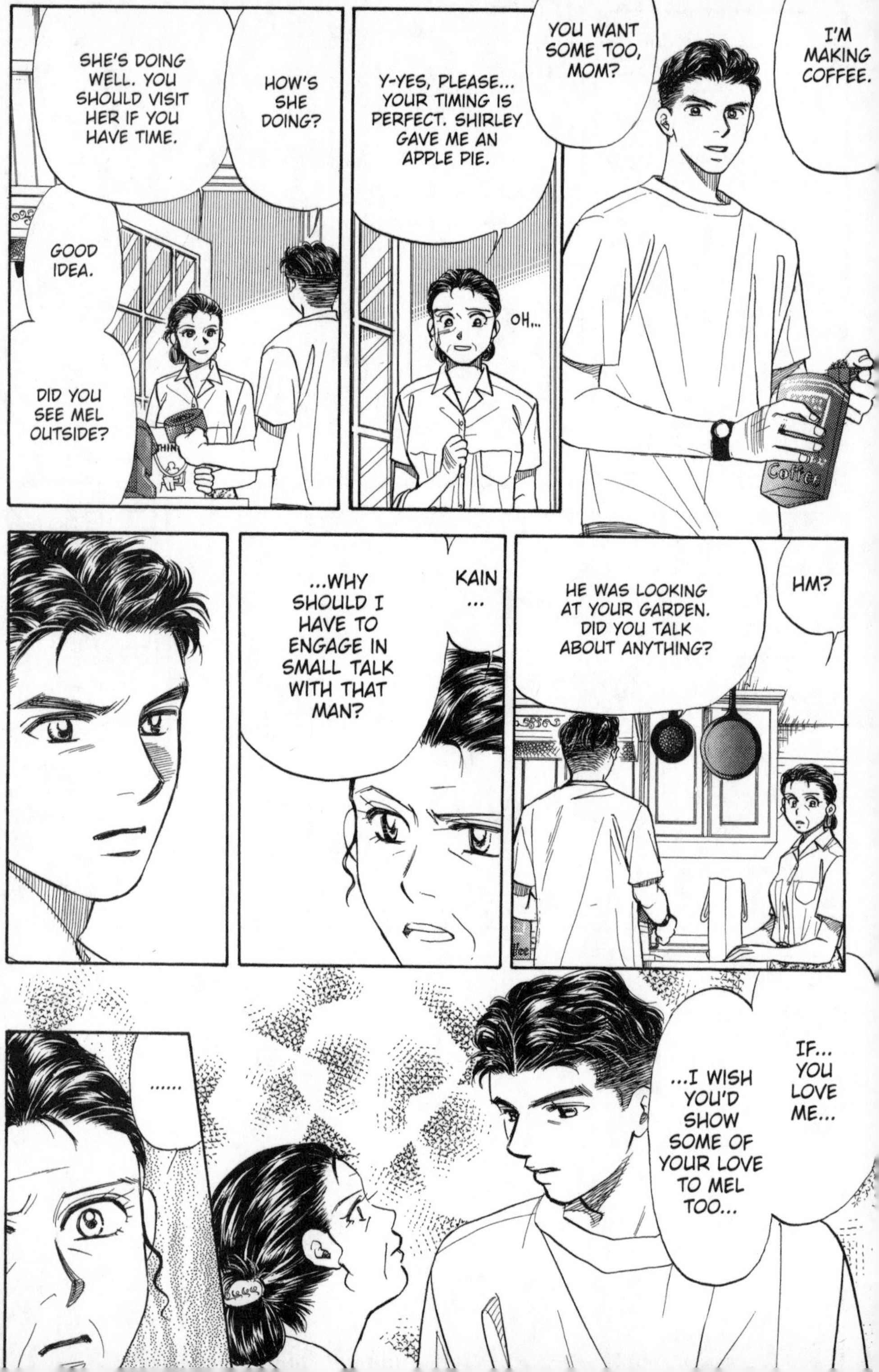
I'M MAKING COFFEE.
YOU WANT SOME TOO, MOM?
Coffee
Y-YES, PLEASE... YOUR TIMING IS PERFECT. SHIRLEY GAVE ME AN APPLE PIE.
OH...
HOW'S SHE DOING?
SHE'S DOING WELL. YOU SHOULD VISIT HER IF YOU HAVE TIME.
GOOD IDEA.
DID YOU SEE MEL OUTSIDE?
HM?
HE WAS LOOKING AT YOUR GARDEN. DID YOU TALK ABOUT ANYTHING?
KAIN ...
...WHY SHOULD I HAVE TO ENGAGE IN SMALL TALK WITH THAT MAN?
IF... YOU LOVE ME...
...I WISH YOU'D SHOW SOME OF YOUR LOVE TO MEL TOO...
......

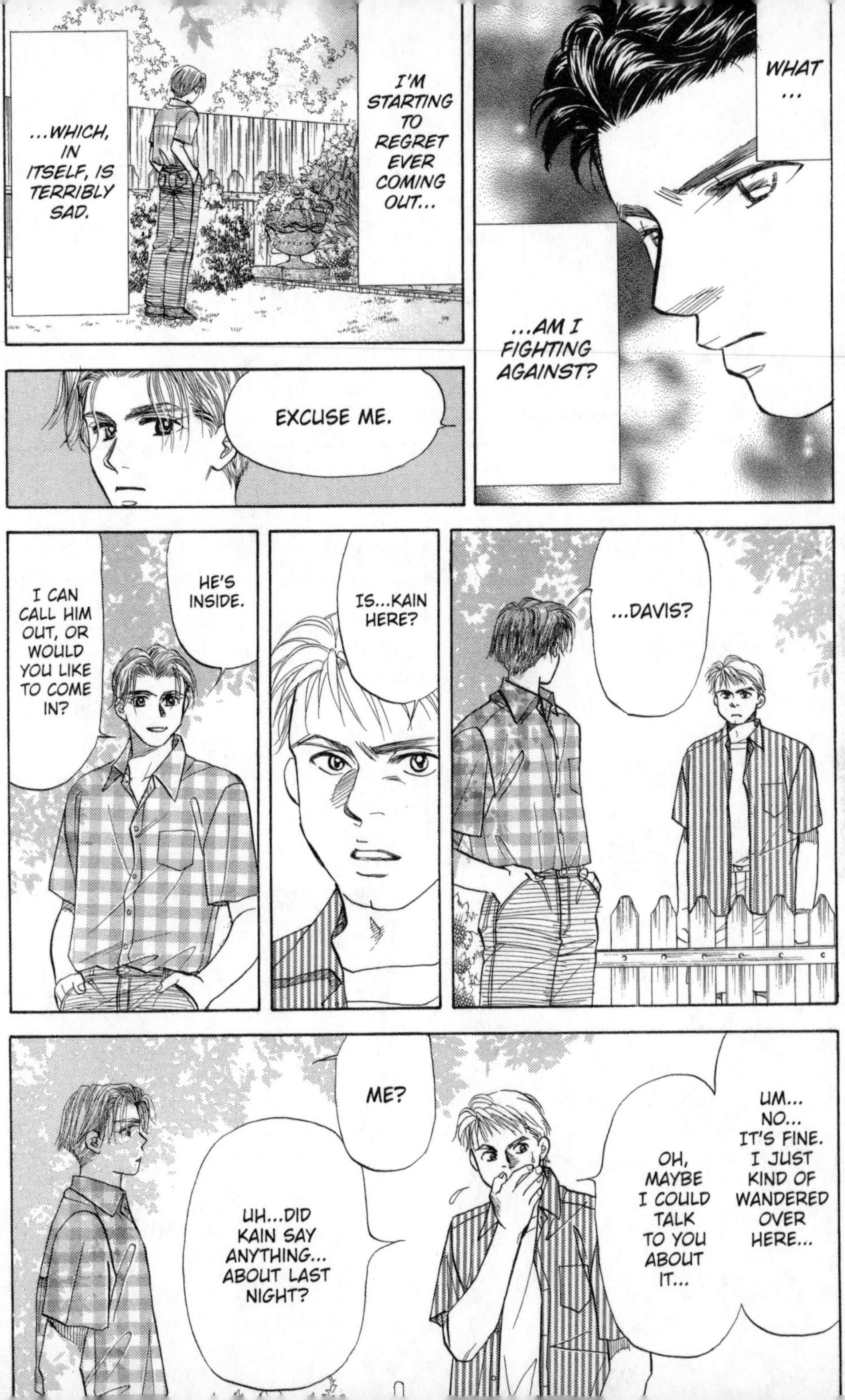

WHAT...
...AM I FIGHTING AGAINST?
I'M STARTING TO REGRET EVER COMING OUT...
...WHICH, IN ITSELF, IS TERRIBLY SAD.
EXCUSE ME.
...DAVIS?
IS...KAIN HERE?
HE'S INSIDE.
I CAN CALL HIM OUT, OR WOULD YOU LIKE TO COME IN?
UM... NO... IT'S FINE. I JUST KIND OF WANDERED OVER HERE...
OH, MAYBE I COULD TALK TO YOU ABOUT IT...
ME?
UH...DID KAIN SAY ANYTHING... ABOUT LAST NIGHT?

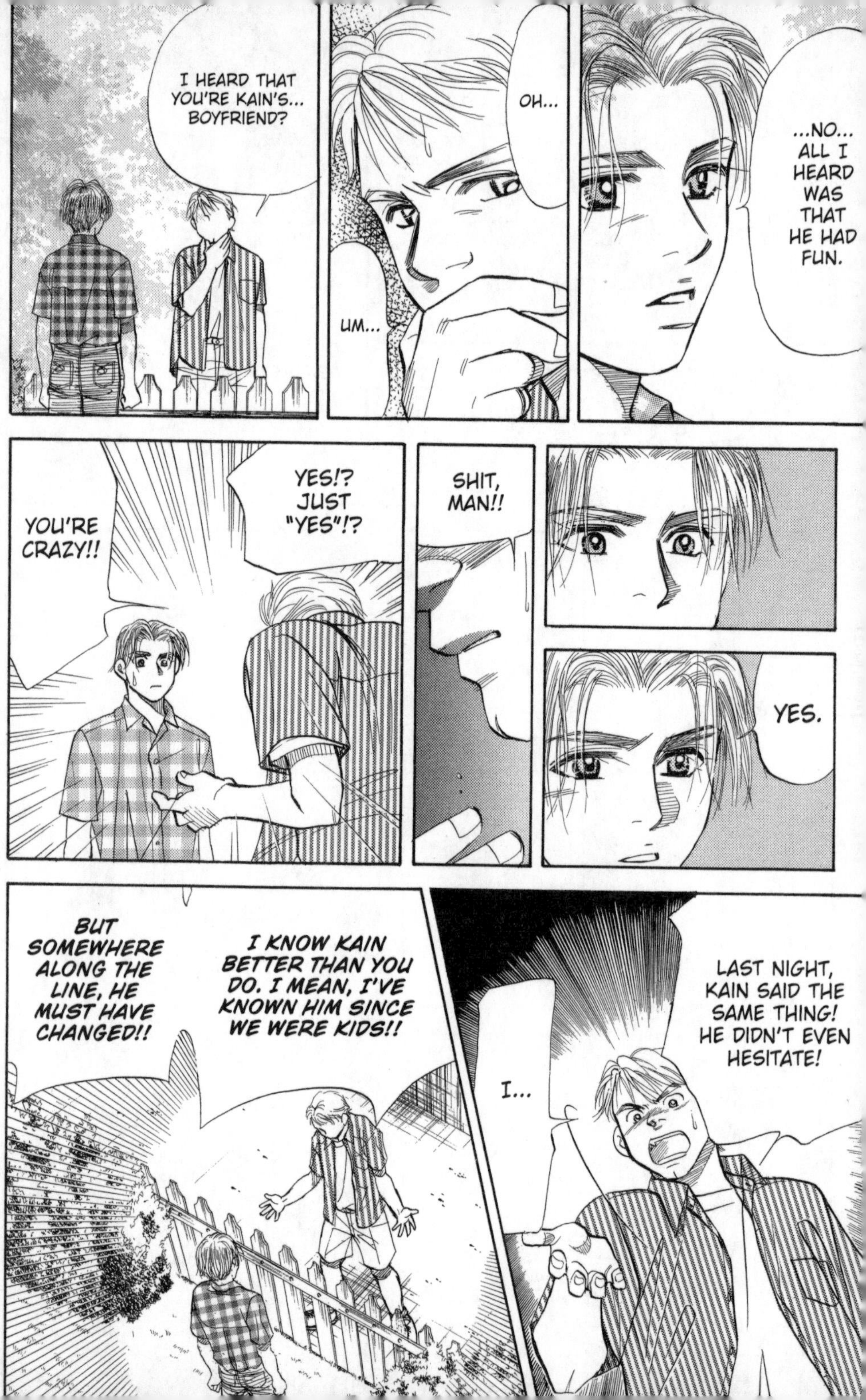
...NO... ALL I HEARD WAS THAT HE HAD FUN.
OH...
UM...
I HEARD THAT YOU'RE KAIN'S... BOYFRIEND?
YES.
SHIT, MAN!!
YES!? JUST "YES"!?
YOU'RE CRAZY!!
LAST NIGHT, KAIN SAID THE SAME THING! HE DIDN'T EVEN HESITATE!
I...
I KNOW KAIN BETTER THAN YOU DO. I MEAN, I'VE KNOWN HIM SINCE WE WERE KIDS!!
BUT SOMEWHERE ALONG THE LINE, HE MUST HAVE CHANGED!!

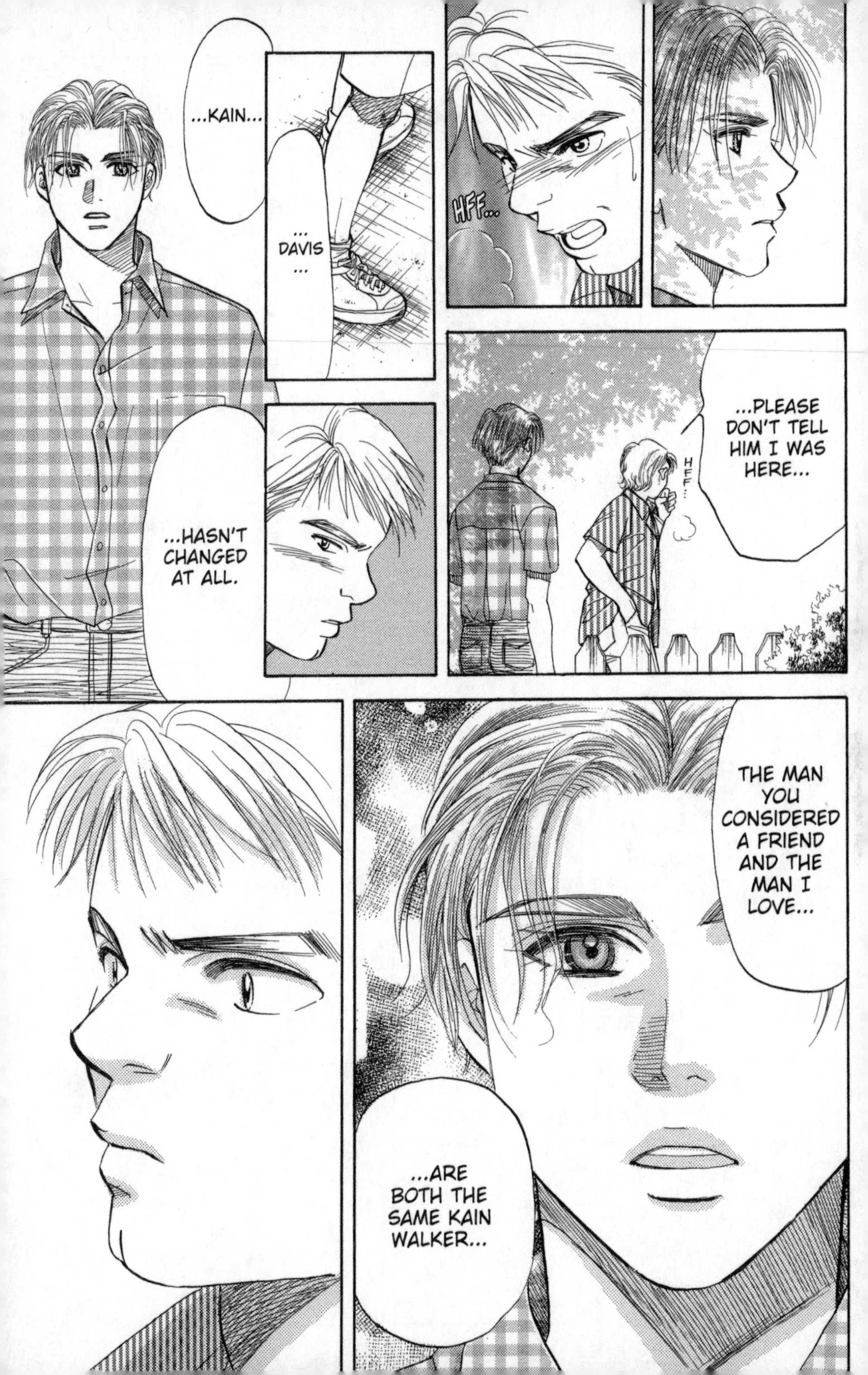
HFF...
...
DAVIS
...
...PLEASE DON'T TELL HIM I WAS HERE...
HFF...
...KAIN...
...HASN'T CHANGED AT ALL.
THE MAN YOU CONSIDERED A FRIEND AND THE MAN I LOVE...
...ARE BOTH THE SAME KAIN WALKER...

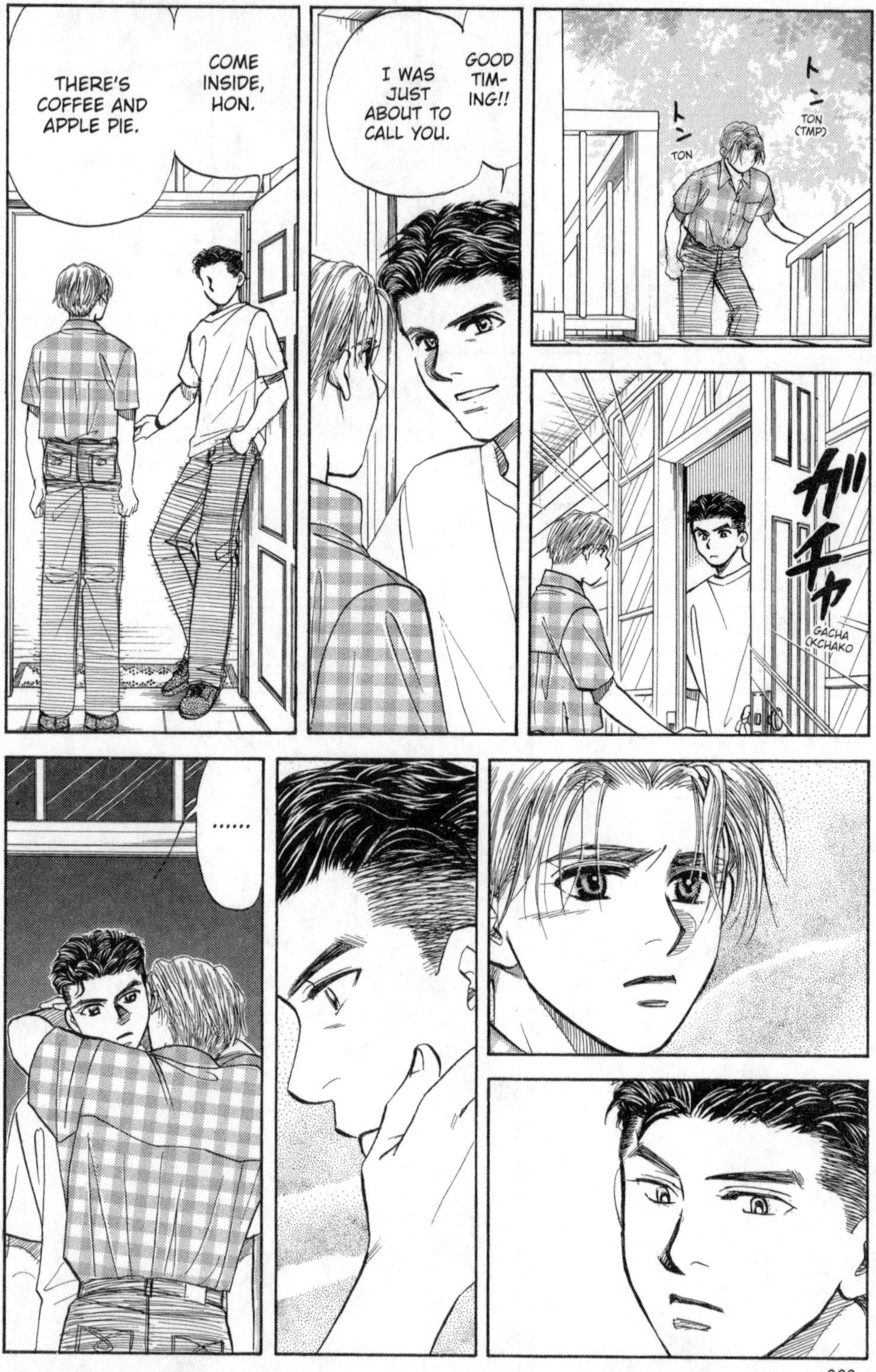
トン
TON (TMP)
トン
TON
ガチャ
GACHA CKCHAKO
GOOD TIM-ING!!
I WAS JUST ABOUT TO CALL YOU.
COME INSIDE, HON.
THERE'S COFFEE AND APPLE PIE.
......

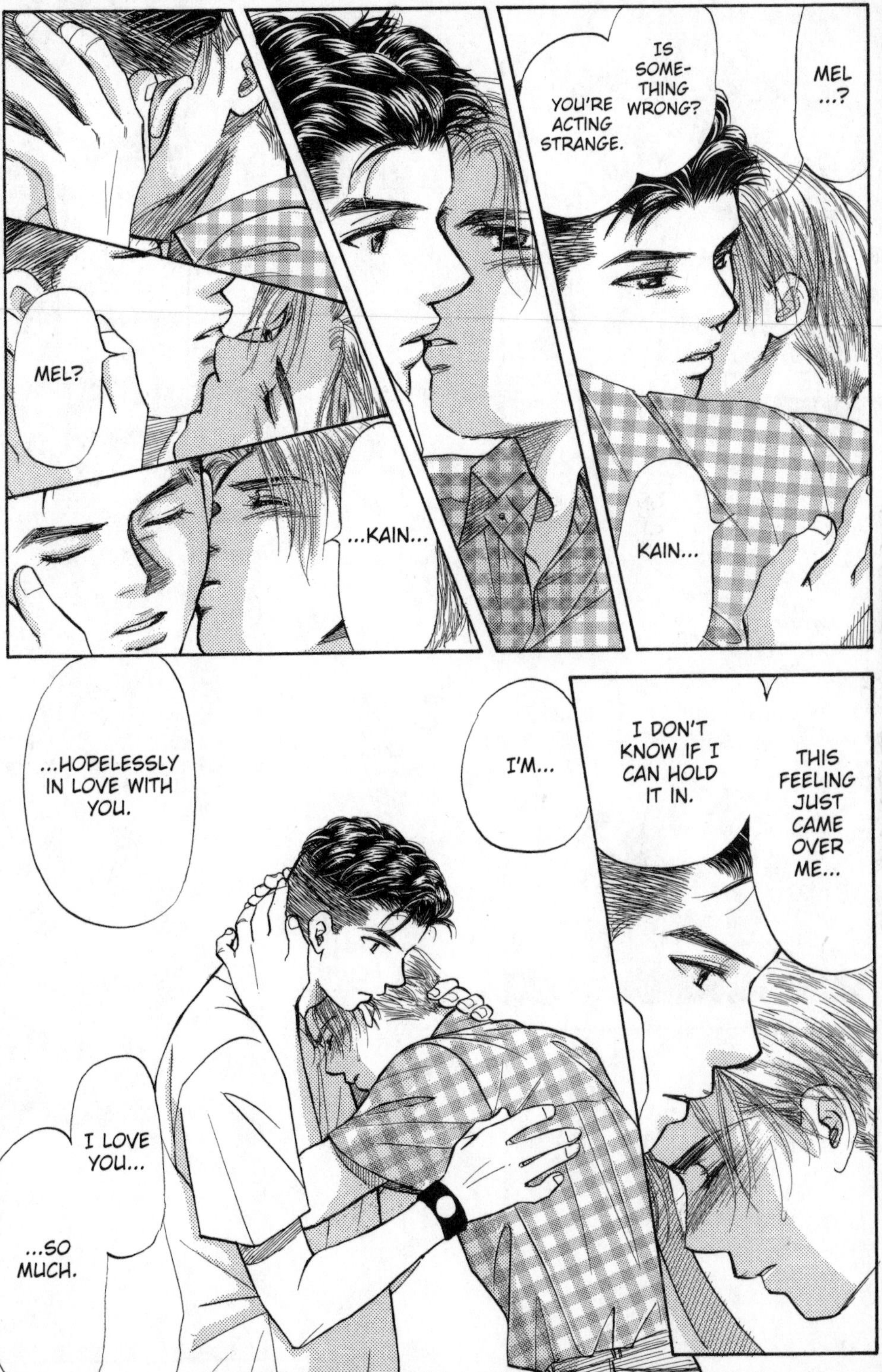
MEL ...?
IS SOME-THING WRONG?
YOU'RE ACTING STRANGE.
KAIN...
...KAIN...
MEL?
THIS FEELING JUST CAME OVER ME...
I DON'T KNOW IF I CAN HOLD IT IN.
I'M...
...HOPELESSLY IN LOVE WITH YOU.
I LOVE YOU...
...SO MUCH.

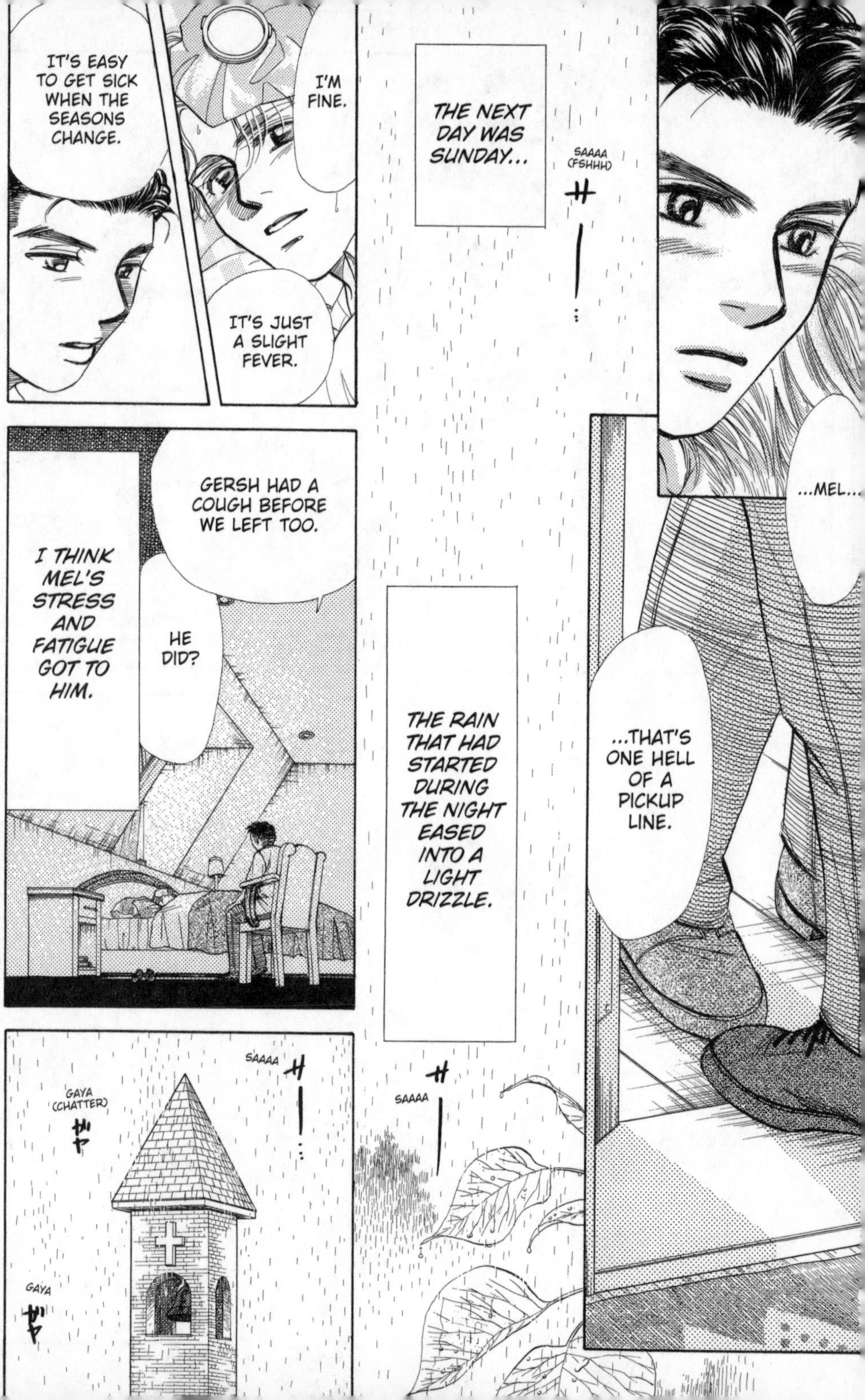
...MEL...
...THAT'S ONE HELL OF A PICKUP LINE.
THE NEXT DAY WAS SUNDAY...
SAAAA (FSHHH)
THE RAIN THAT HAD STARTED DURING THE NIGHT EASED INTO A LIGHT DRIZZLE.
SAAAA
I'M FINE.
IT'S EASY TO GET SICK WHEN THE SEASONS CHANGE.
IT'S JUST A SLIGHT FEVER.
GERSH HAD A COUGH BEFORE WE LEFT TOO.
HE DID?
I THINK MEL'S STRESS AND FATIGUE GOT TO HIM.
SAAAA
GAYA (CHATTER)
GAYA

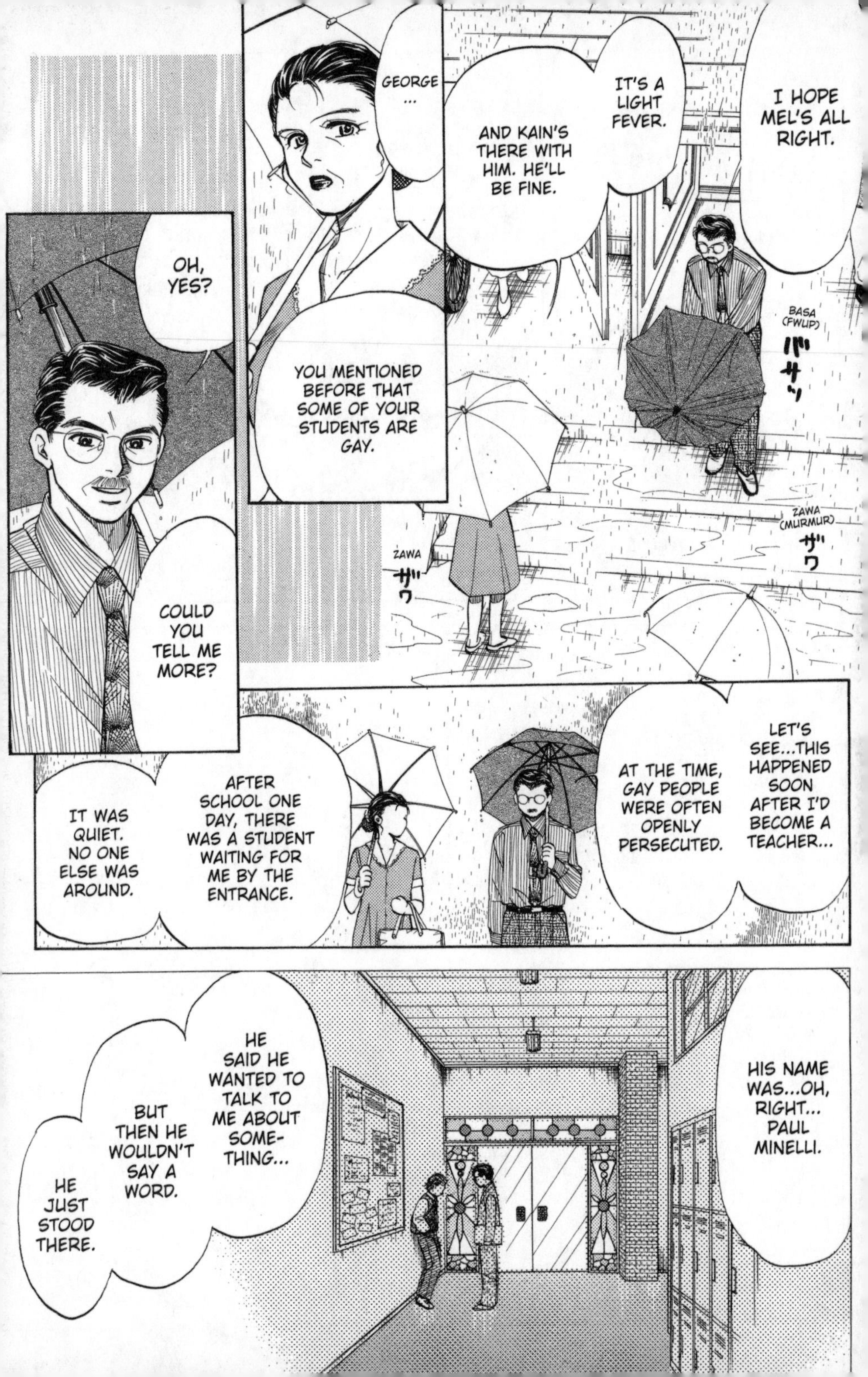
I HOPE MEL'S ALL RIGHT.
IT'S A LIGHT FEVER.
AND KAIN'S THERE WITH HIM. HE'LL BE FINE.
BASA (FWUP)
バサッ
ZAWA (MURMUR)
ザワ
ZAWA
ザワ
GEORGE...
YOU MENTIONED BEFORE THAT SOME OF YOUR STUDENTS ARE GAY.
OH, YES?
COULD YOU TELL ME MORE?
LET'S SEE...THIS HAPPENED SOON AFTER I'D BECOME A TEACHER...
AT THE TIME, GAY PEOPLE WERE OFTEN OPENLY PERSECUTED.
AFTER SCHOOL ONE DAY, THERE WAS A STUDENT WAITING FOR ME BY THE ENTRANCE.
IT WAS QUIET. NO ONE ELSE WAS AROUND.
HIS NAME WAS...OH, RIGHT... PAUL MINELLI.
HE SAID HE WANTED TO TALK TO ME ABOUT SOME-THING...
BUT THEN HE WOULDN'T SAY A WORD.
HE JUST STOOD THERE.

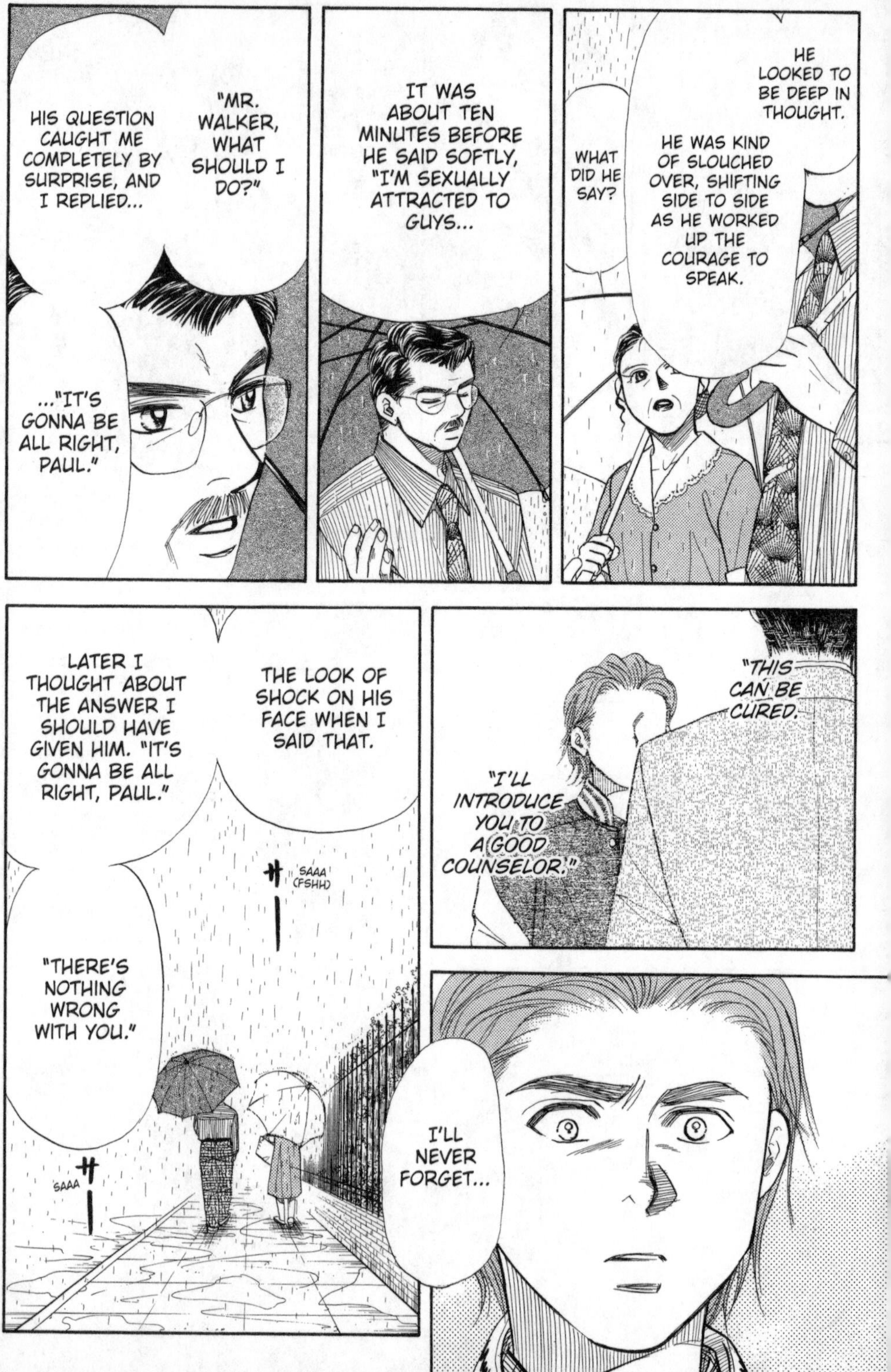
HE LOOKED TO BE DEEP IN THOUGHT.
HE WAS KIND OF SLOUCHED OVER, SHIFTING SIDE TO SIDE AS HE WORKED UP THE COURAGE TO SPEAK.
WHAT DID HE SAY?
IT WAS ABOUT TEN MINUTES BEFORE HE SAID SOFTLY, "I'M SEXUALLY ATTRACTED TO GUYS...
"MR. WALKER, WHAT SHOULD I DO?"
HIS QUESTION CAUGHT ME COMPLETELY BY SURPRISE, AND I REPLIED...
..."IT'S GONNA BE ALL RIGHT, PAUL."
"THIS CAN BE CURED.
"I'LL INTRODUCE YOU TO A GOOD COUNSELOR."
I'LL NEVER FORGET...
THE LOOK OF SHOCK ON HIS FACE WHEN I SAID THAT.
LATER I THOUGHT ABOUT THE ANSWER I SHOULD HAVE GIVEN HIM. "IT'S GONNA BE ALL RIGHT, PAUL."
SAAA (FSHH)
"THERE'S NOTHING WRONG WITH YOU."
SAAA

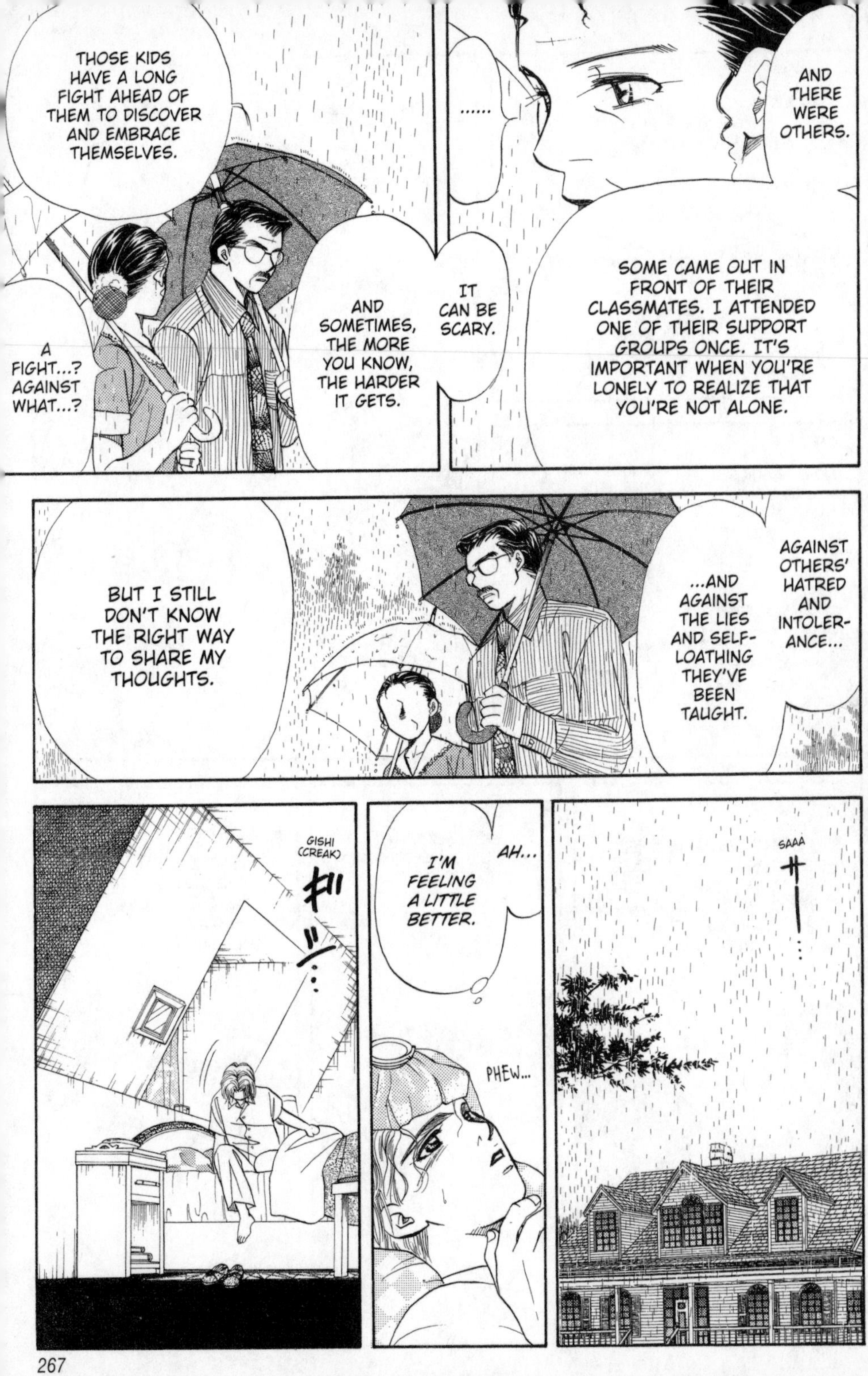
AND THERE WERE OTHERS.
......
SOME CAME OUT IN FRONT OF THEIR CLASSMATES. I ATTENDED ONE OF THEIR SUPPORT GROUPS ONCE. IT'S IMPORTANT WHEN YOU'RE LONELY TO REALIZE THAT YOU'RE NOT ALONE.
IT CAN BE SCARY.
AND SOMETIMES, THE MORE YOU KNOW, THE HARDER IT GETS.
THOSE KIDS HAVE A LONG FIGHT AHEAD OF THEM TO DISCOVER AND EMBRACE THEMSELVES.
A FIGHT...? AGAINST WHAT...?
AGAINST OTHERS' HATRED AND INTOLER-ANCE...
...AND AGAINST THE LIES AND SELF-LOATHING THEY'VE BEEN TAUGHT.
BUT I STILL DON'T KNOW THE RIGHT WAY TO SHARE MY THOUGHTS.
SAAA
AH...
I'M FEELING A LITTLE BETTER.
PHEW...
GISHI (CREAK)

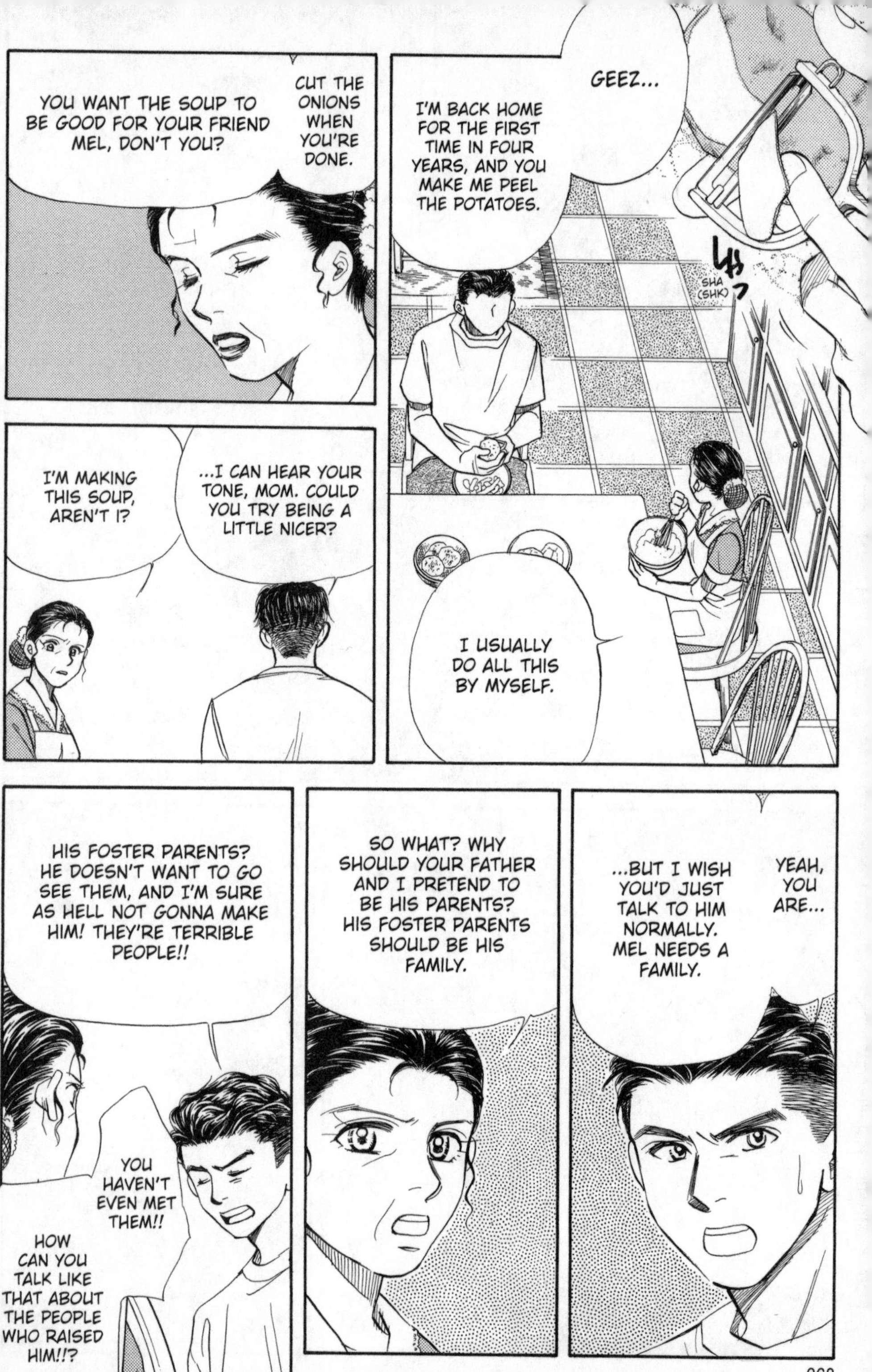
GEEZ...
I'M BACK HOME FOR THE FIRST TIME IN FOUR YEARS, AND YOU MAKE ME PEEL THE POTATOES.
SHA (SHK)
I USUALLY DO ALL THIS BY MYSELF.
CUT THE ONIONS WHEN YOU'RE DONE.
YOU WANT THE SOUP TO BE GOOD FOR YOUR FRIEND MEL, DON'T YOU?
...I CAN HEAR YOUR TONE, MOM. COULD YOU TRY BEING A LITTLE NICER?
I'M MAKING THIS SOUP, AREN'T I?
YEAH, YOU ARE...
...BUT I WISH YOU'D JUST TALK TO HIM NORMALLY. MEL NEEDS A FAMILY.
SO WHAT? WHY SHOULD YOUR FATHER AND I PRETEND TO BE HIS PARENTS? HIS FOSTER PARENTS SHOULD BE HIS FAMILY.
HIS FOSTER PARENTS? HE DOESN'T WANT TO GO SEE THEM, AND I'M SURE AS HELL NOT GONNA MAKE HIM! THEY'RE TERRIBLE PEOPLE!!
YOU HAVEN'T EVEN MET THEM!!
HOW CAN YOU TALK LIKE THAT ABOUT THE PEOPLE WHO RAISED HIM!!?

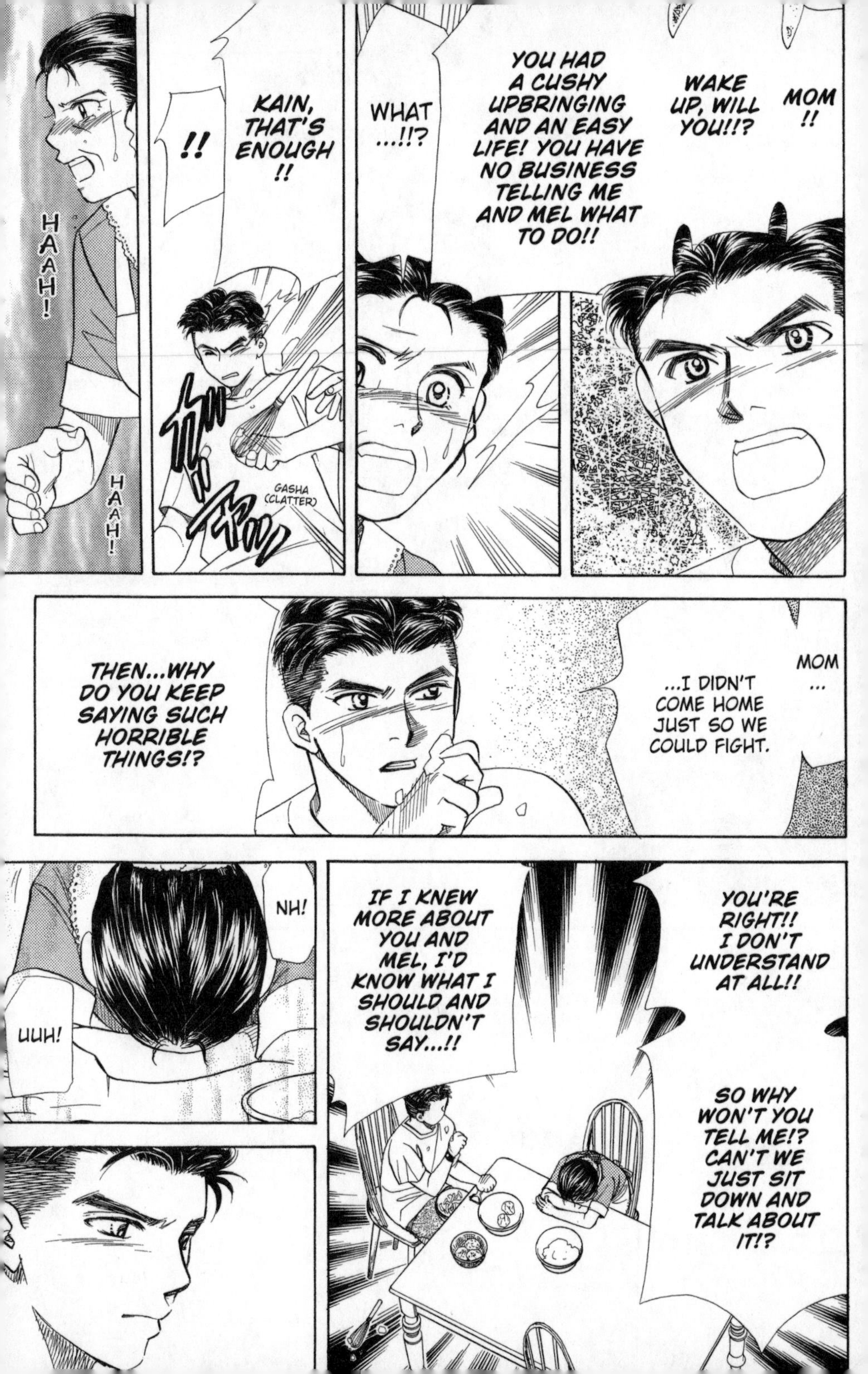
MOM !!
WAKE UP, WILL YOU!!?
YOU HAD A CUSHY UPBRINGING AND AN EASY LIFE! YOU HAVE NO BUSINESS TELLING ME AND MEL WHAT TO DO!!
WHAT ...!!?
KAIN, THAT'S ENOUGH !!
!!
GASHA (CLATTER)
HAAAH!
HAAAH!
MOM ...
...I DIDN'T COME HOME JUST SO WE COULD FIGHT.
THEN...WHY DO YOU KEEP SAYING SUCH HORRIBLE THINGS!?
YOU'RE RIGHT!! I DON'T UNDERSTAND AT ALL!!
IF I KNEW MORE ABOUT YOU AND MEL, I'D KNOW WHAT I SHOULD AND SHOULDN'T SAY...!!
SO WHY WON'T YOU TELL ME!? CAN'T WE JUST SIT DOWN AND TALK ABOUT IT!?
NH!
UUH!

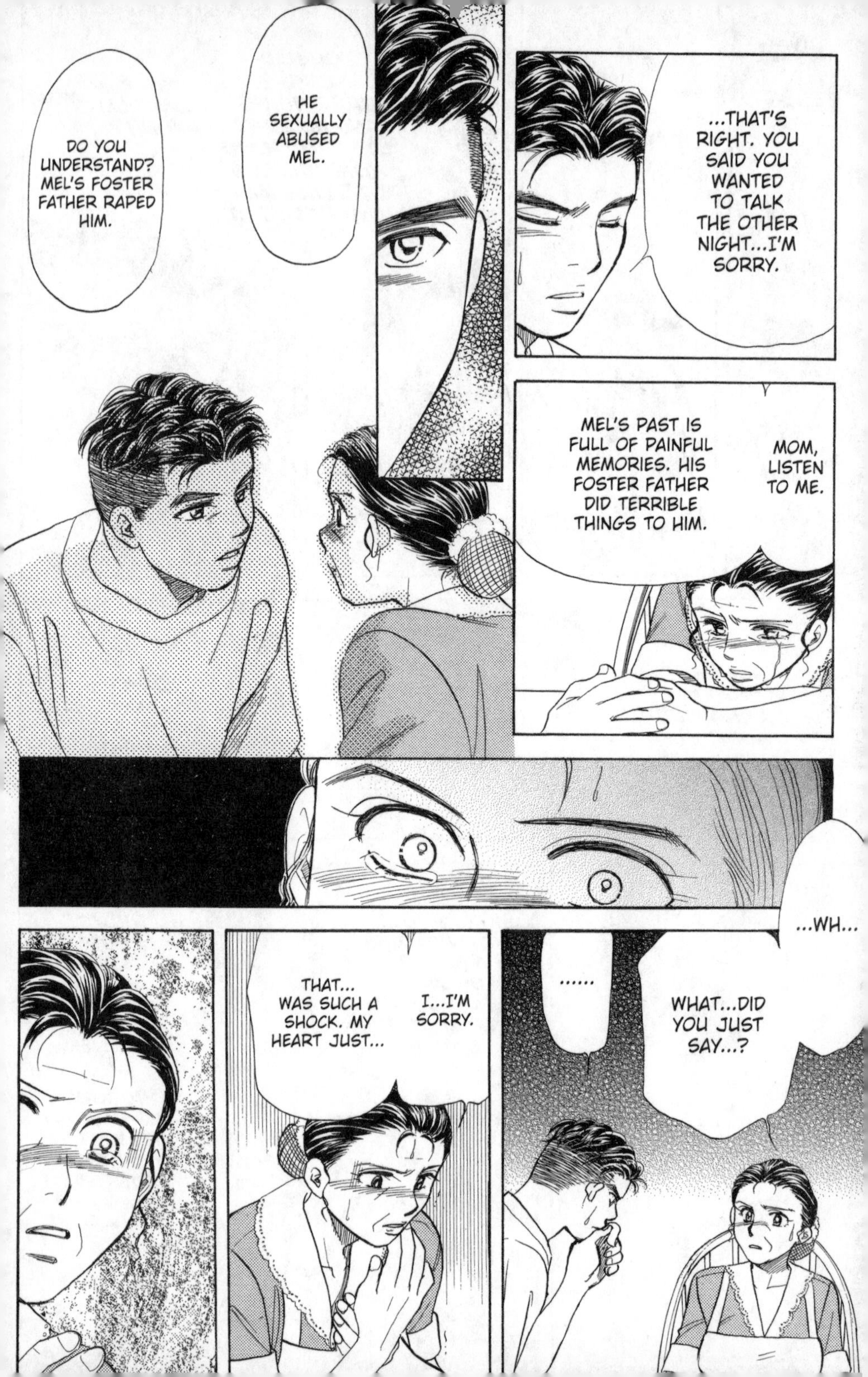
...THAT'S RIGHT. YOU SAID YOU WANTED TO TALK THE OTHER NIGHT...I'M SORRY.
MOM, LISTEN TO ME.
MEL'S PAST IS FULL OF PAINFUL MEMORIES. HIS FOSTER FATHER DID TERRIBLE THINGS TO HIM.
HE SEXUALLY ABUSED MEL.
DO YOU UNDERSTAND? MEL'S FOSTER FATHER RAPED HIM.
...WH...
WHAT...DID YOU JUST SAY...?
......
I...I'M SORRY.
THAT... WAS SUCH A SHOCK. MY HEART JUST...

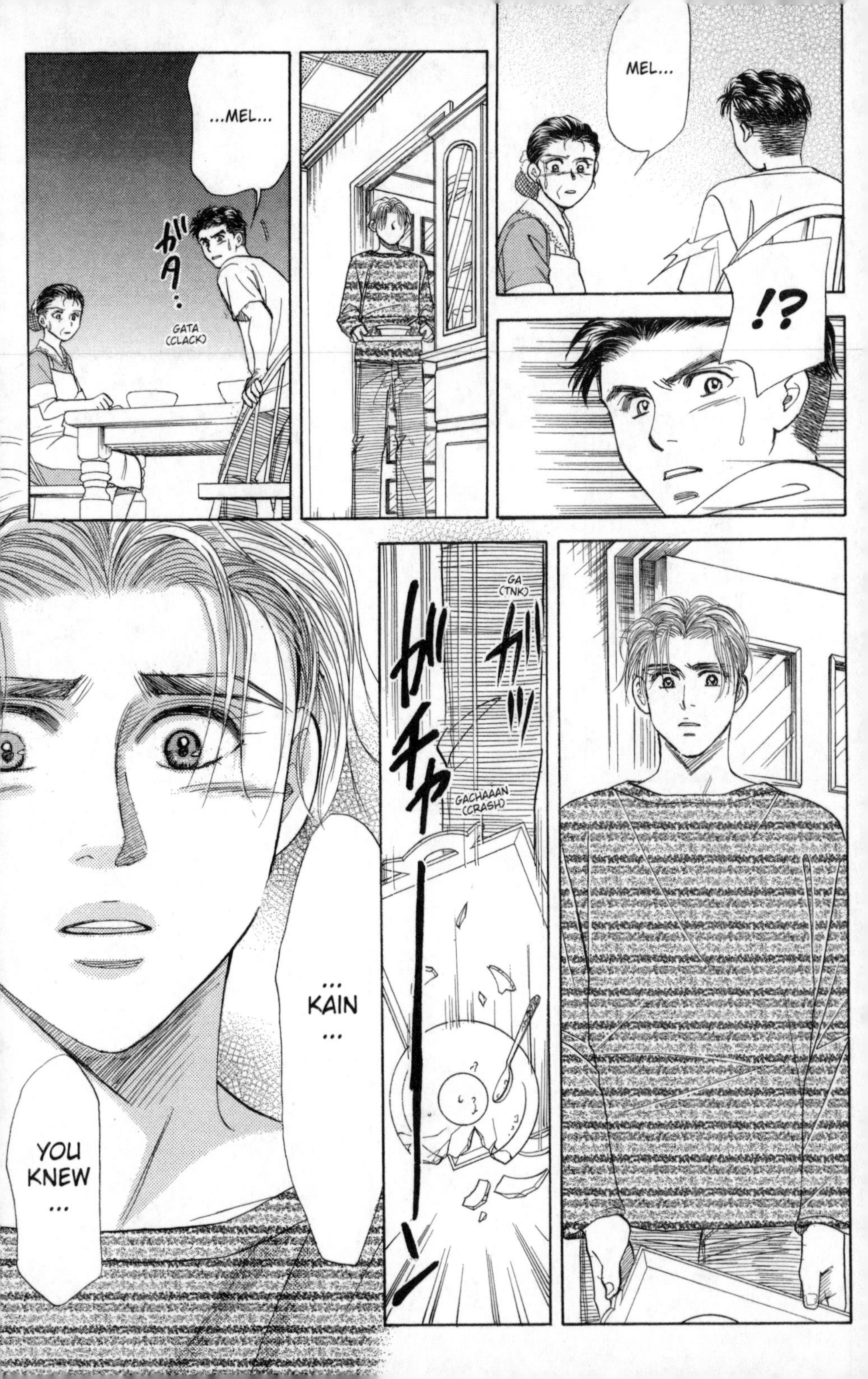
MEL...
!?
...MEL...
GATA (CLACK)
GA (TNK)
GACHAAN (CRASH)
... KAIN ...
YOU KNEW ...

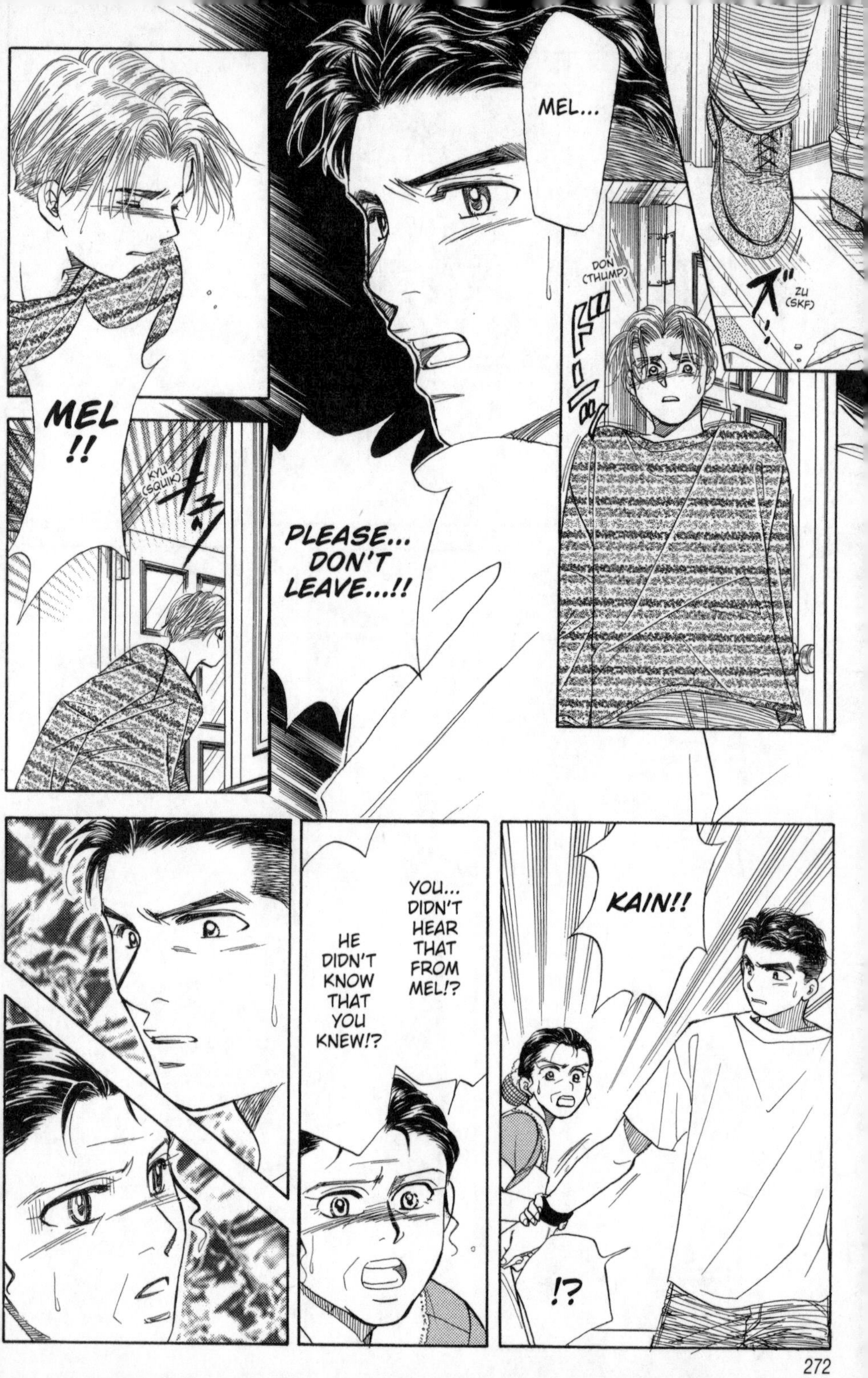
ZU (SKF)
DON (THUMP)
MEL...
PLEASE... DON'T LEAVE...!!
MEL !!
KYU (SQUIK)
KAIN!!
!?
YOU... DIDN'T HEAR THAT FROM MEL!?
HE DIDN'T KNOW THAT YOU KNEW!?

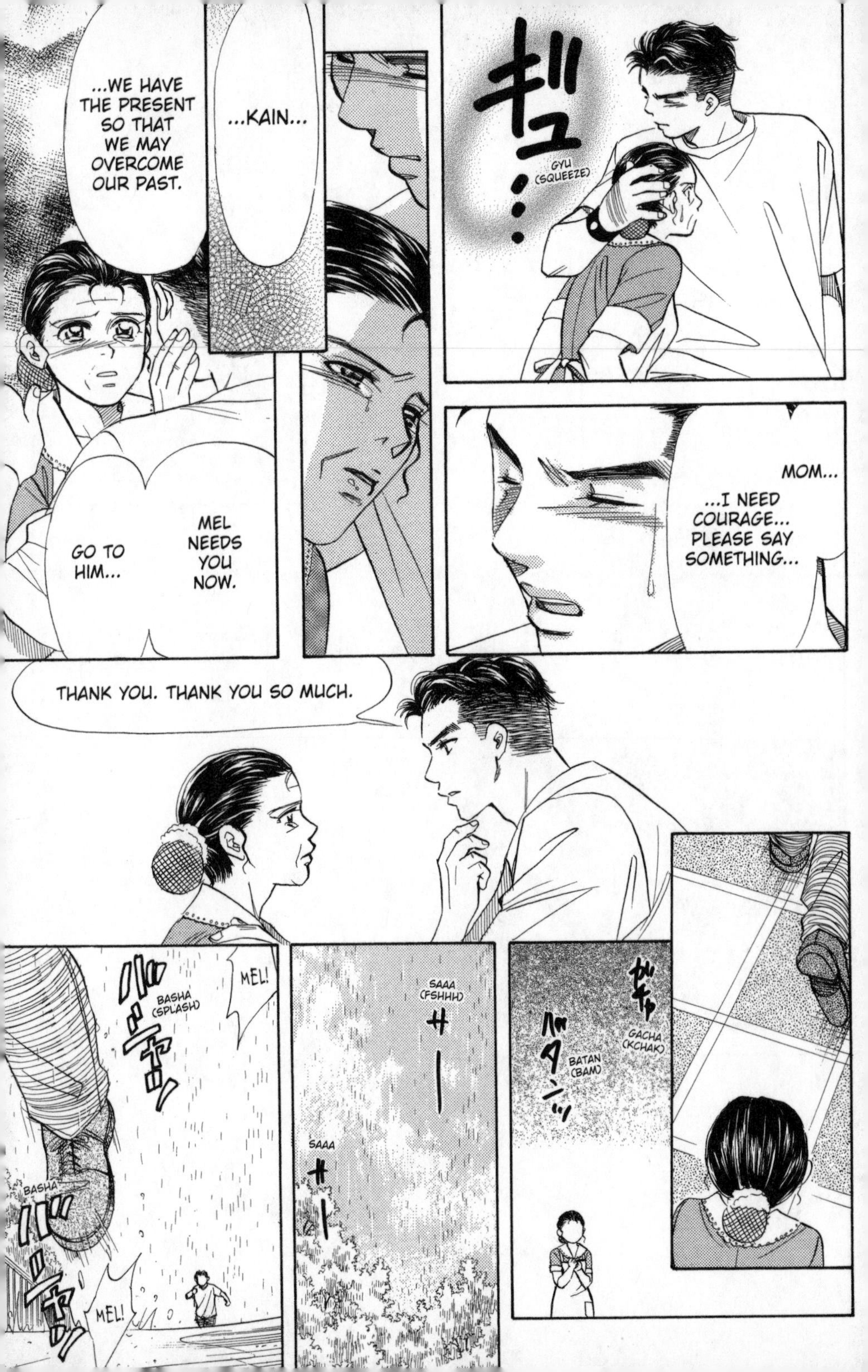
GYU (SQUEEZE)
MOM...
...I NEED COURAGE... PLEASE SAY SOMETHING...
...KAIN...
...WE HAVE THE PRESENT SO THAT WE MAY OVERCOME OUR PAST.
MEL NEEDS YOU NOW.
GO TO HIM...
THANK YOU. THANK YOU SO MUCH.
GACHA (KCHAK)
BATAN (BAM)
SAAA (FSHHH)
SAAA
MEL!
BASHA (SPLASH)
BASHA
MEL!

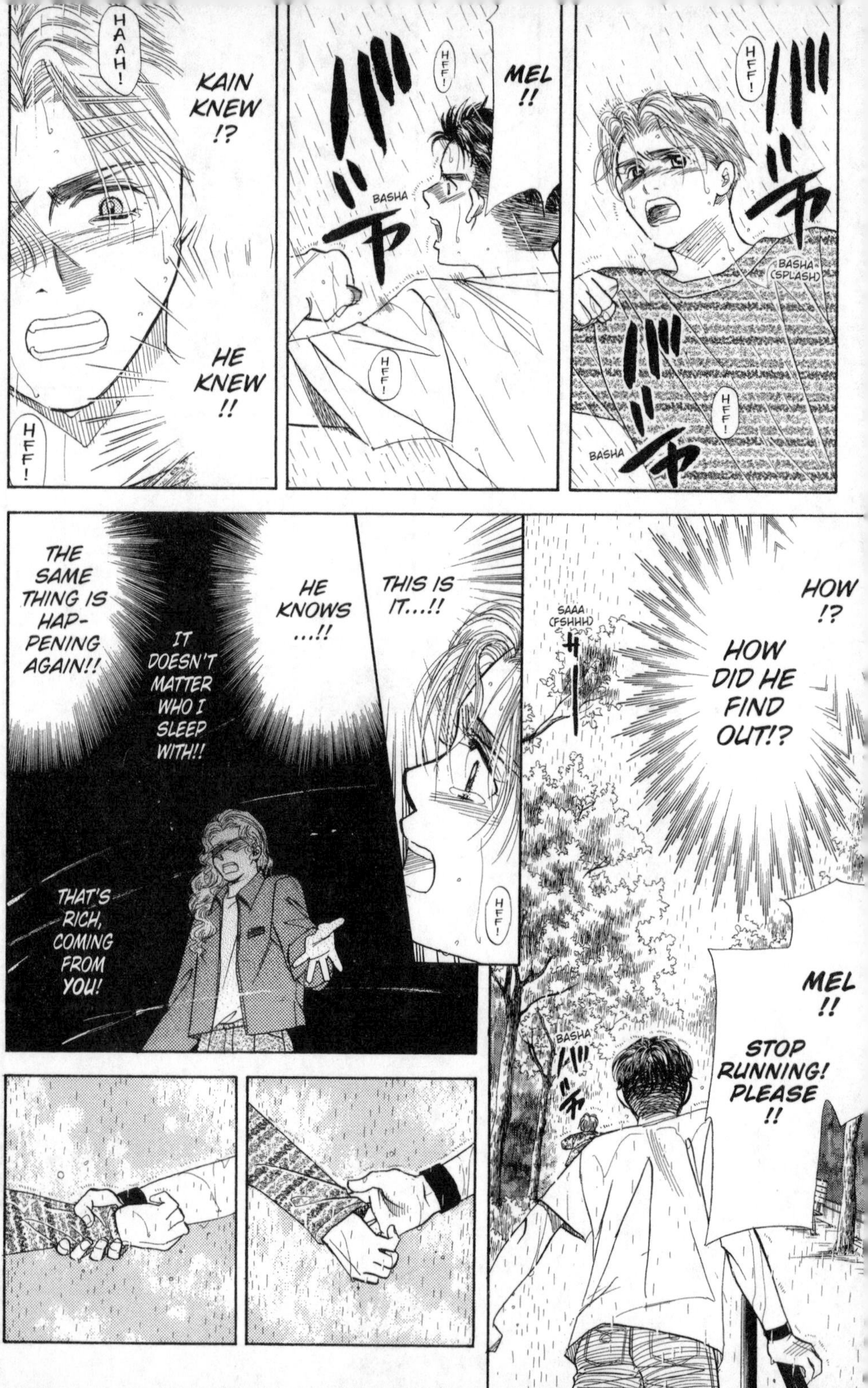
HFF!
BASHA (SPLASH)
HFF!
BASHA
MEL !!
HFF!
BASHA
HFF!
HAAAH!
KAIN KNEW !?
HE KNEW !!
HFF!
SAAA (FSHHH)
HOW !?
HOW DID HE FIND OUT!?
BASHA
MEL !!
STOP RUNNING! PLEASE !!
THIS IS IT...!!
HE KNOWS ...!!
HFF!
THE SAME THING IS HAP-PENING AGAIN!!
IT DOESN'T MATTER WHO I SLEEP WITH!!
THAT'S RICH, COMING FROM YOU!

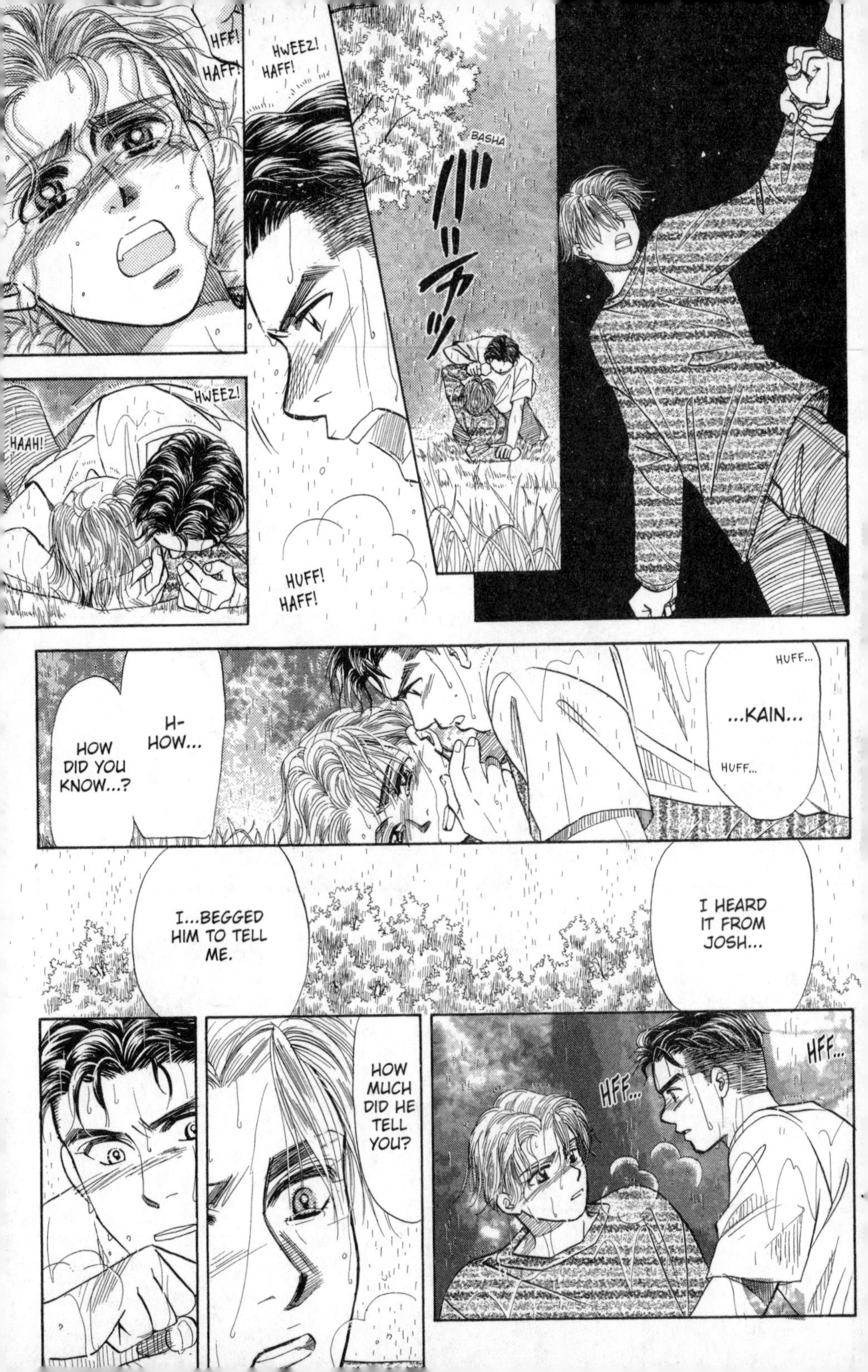
BASHA
HWEEZ! HAFF!
HUFF! HAFF!
HFF! HAFF!
HWEEZ!
HAAH!
HUFF...
...KAIN...
HUFF...
H- HOW...
HOW DID YOU KNOW...?
I HEARD IT FROM JOSH...
I...BEGGED HIM TO TELL ME.
HFF...
HFF...
HOW MUCH DID HE TELL YOU?

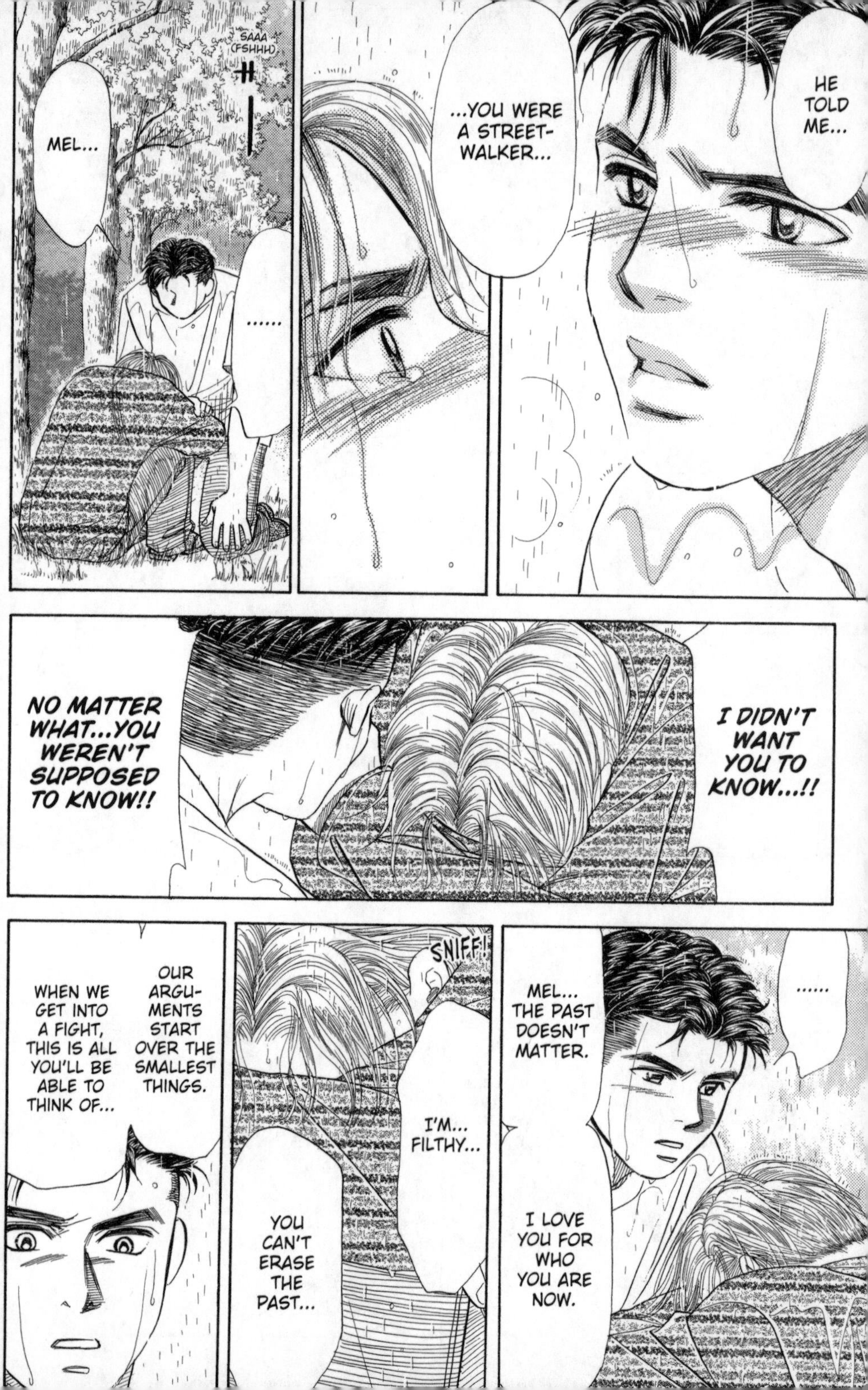
HE TOLD ME...
...YOU WERE A STREET-WALKER...
SAAA (FSHHH)
......
MEL...
I DIDN'T WANT YOU TO KNOW...!!
NO MATTER WHAT...YOU WEREN'T SUPPOSED TO KNOW!!
......
MEL... THE PAST DOESN'T MATTER.
I LOVE YOU FOR WHO YOU ARE NOW.
SNIFF!
I'M... FILTHY...
YOU CAN'T ERASE THE PAST...
OUR ARGU-MENTS START OVER THE SMALLEST THINGS.
WHEN WE GET INTO A FIGHT, THIS IS ALL YOU'LL BE ABLE TO THINK OF...

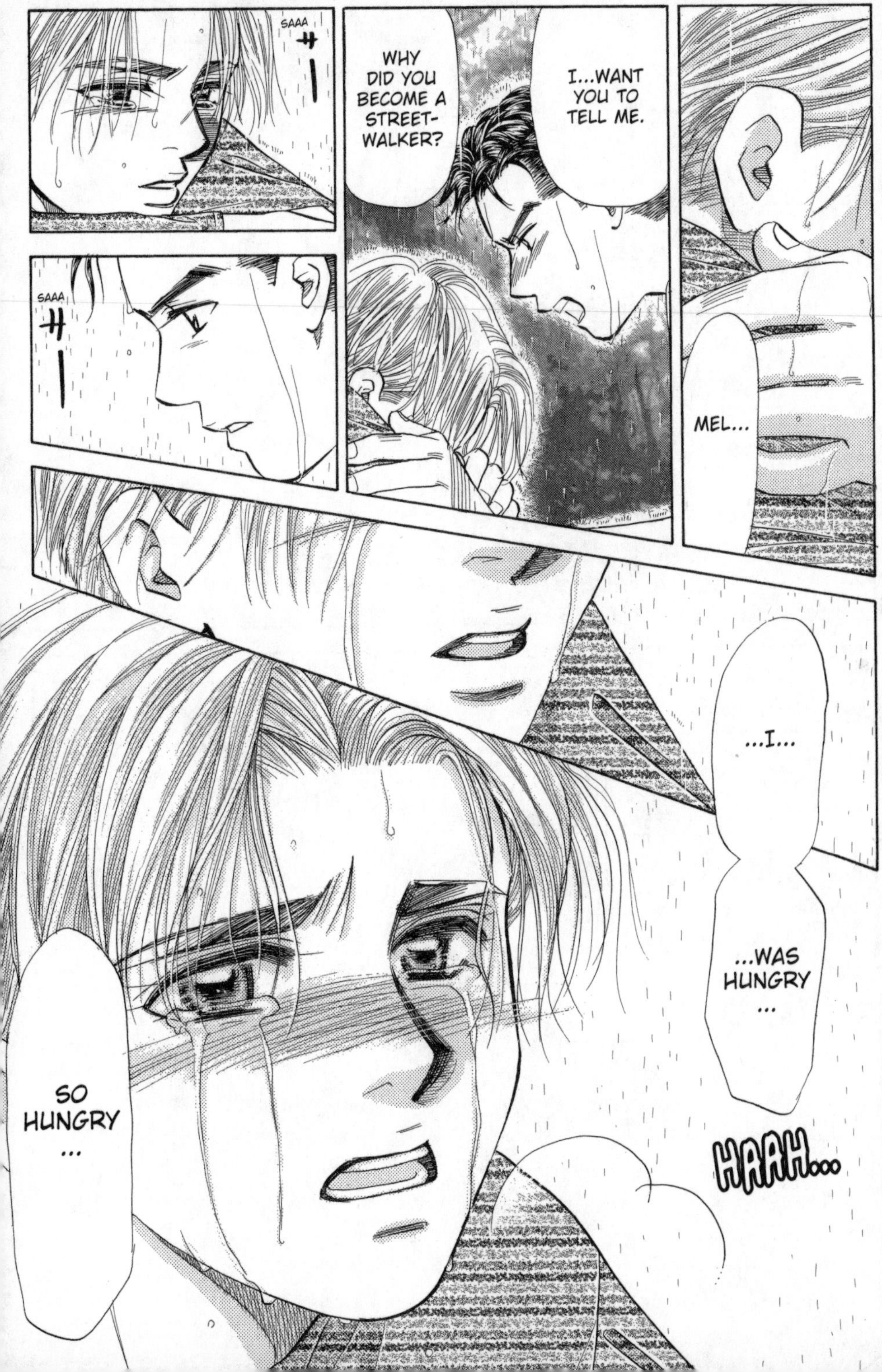
MEL...
I...WANT YOU TO TELL ME.
WHY DID YOU BECOME A STREET-WALKER?
SAAA
SAAA
...I...
...WAS HUNGRY...
HAAH...
SO HUNGRY...

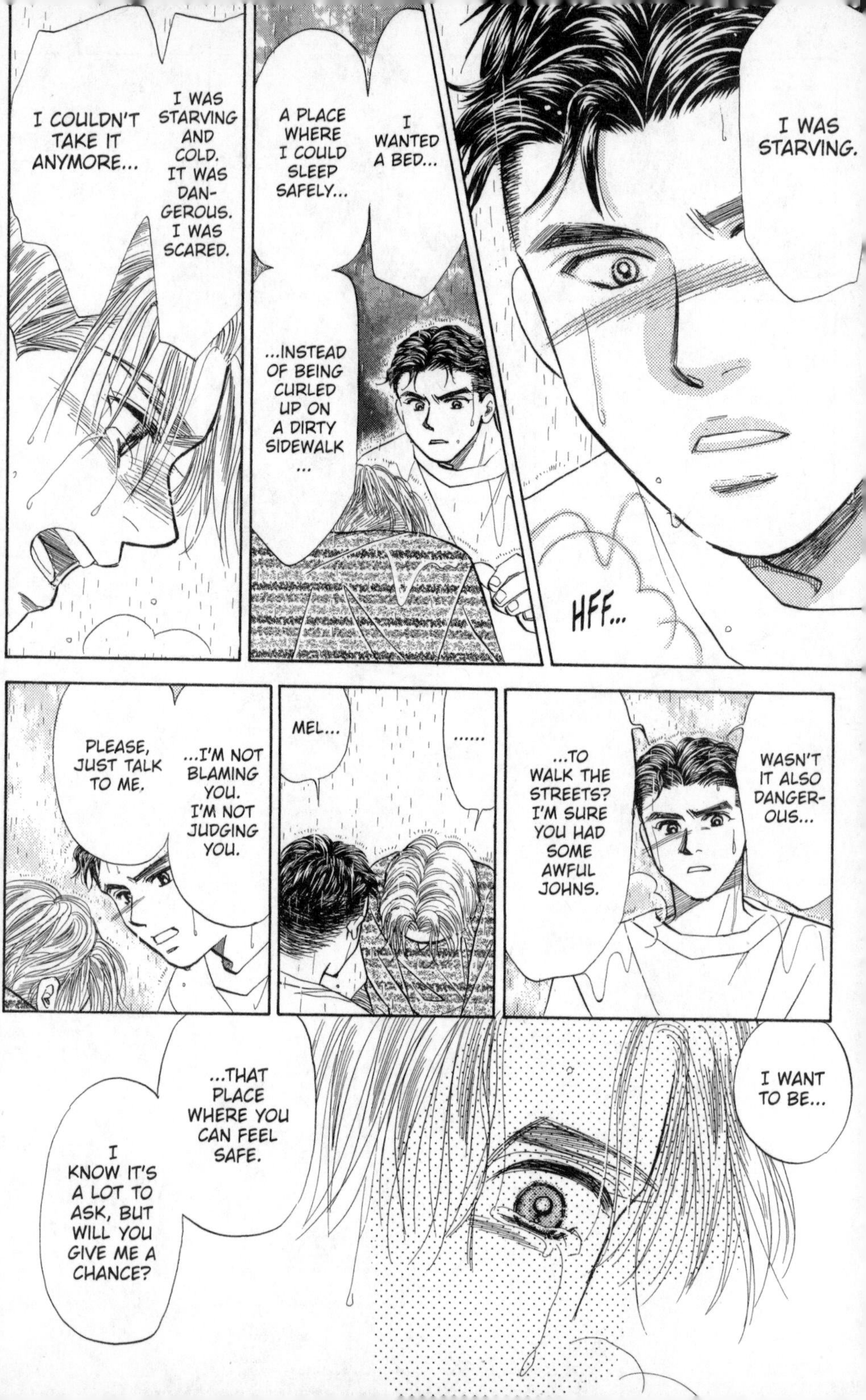
I WAS STARVING.
HFF...
I WANTED A BED...
A PLACE WHERE I COULD SLEEP SAFELY...
...INSTEAD OF BEING CURLED UP ON A DIRTY SIDEWALK ...
I WAS STARVING AND COLD. IT WAS DAN-GEROUS. I WAS SCARED.
I COULDN'T TAKE IT ANYMORE...
WASN'T IT ALSO DANGER-OUS...
...TO WALK THE STREETS? I'M SURE YOU HAD SOME AWFUL JOHNS.
......
MEL...
...I'M NOT BLAMING YOU. I'M NOT JUDGING YOU.
PLEASE, JUST TALK TO ME.
I WANT TO BE...
...THAT PLACE WHERE YOU CAN FEEL SAFE.
I KNOW IT'S A LOT TO ASK, BUT WILL YOU GIVE ME A CHANCE?

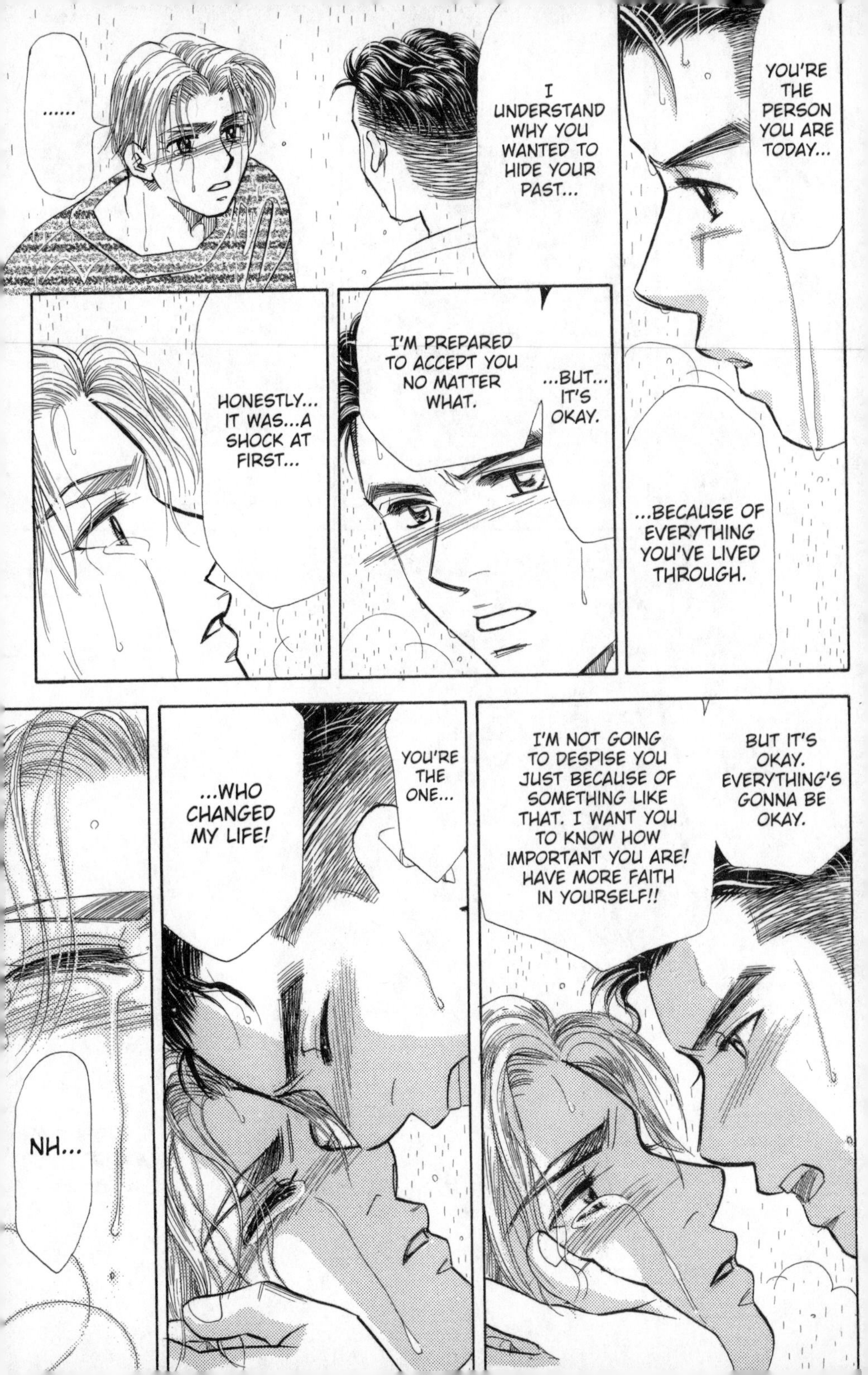
YOU'RE THE PERSON YOU ARE TODAY...
...BECAUSE OF EVERYTHING YOU'VE LIVED THROUGH.
I UNDERSTAND WHY YOU WANTED TO HIDE YOUR PAST...
......
...BUT... IT'S OKAY.
I'M PREPARED TO ACCEPT YOU NO MATTER WHAT.
HONESTLY... IT WAS...A SHOCK AT FIRST...
BUT IT'S OKAY. EVERYTHING'S GONNA BE OKAY.
I'M NOT GOING TO DESPISE YOU JUST BECAUSE OF SOMETHING LIKE THAT. I WANT YOU TO KNOW HOW IMPORTANT YOU ARE! HAVE MORE FAITH IN YOURSELF!!
YOU'RE THE ONE...
...WHO CHANGED MY LIFE!
NH...

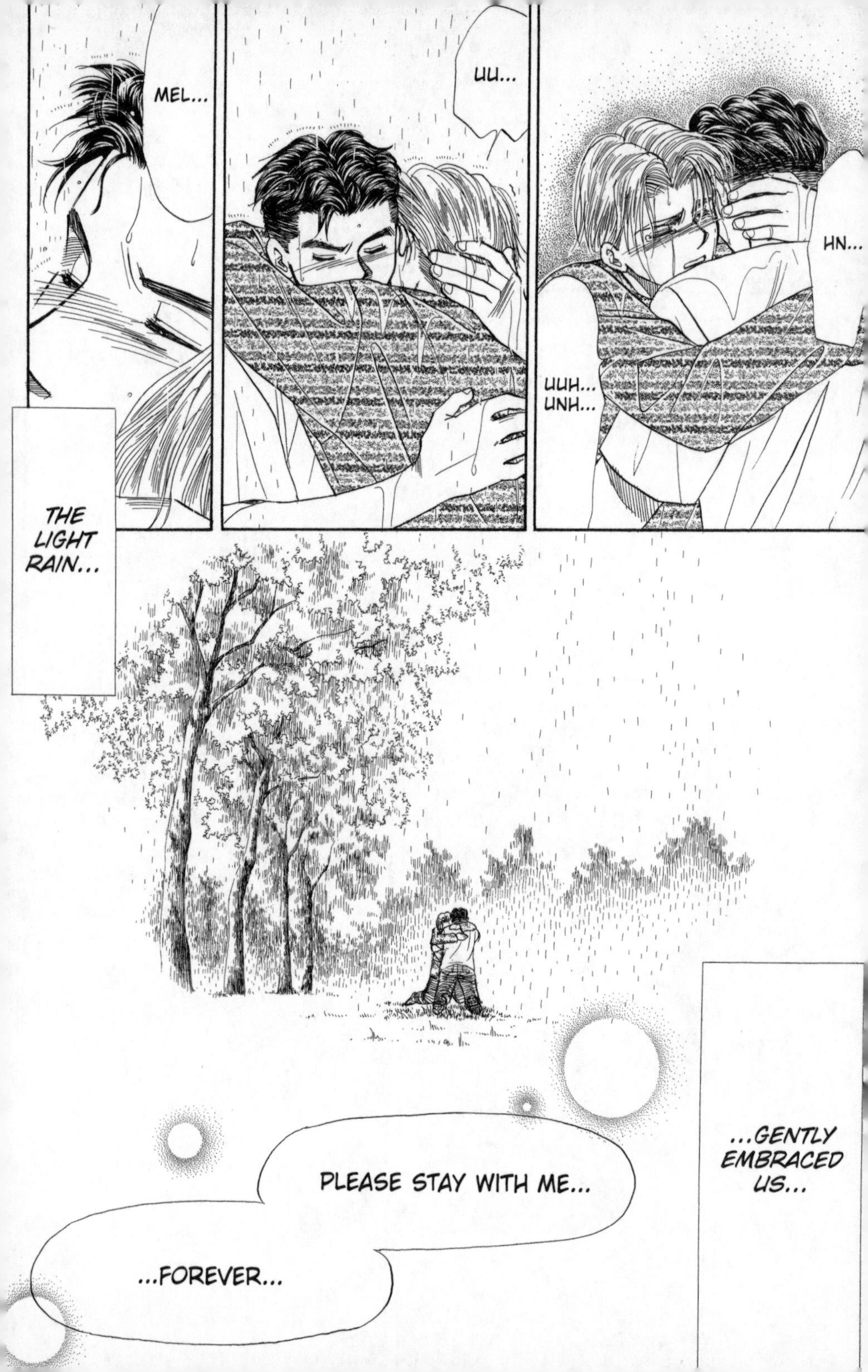
HN...
UUH... UNH...
UU...
MEL...
THE LIGHT RAIN...
...GENTLY EMBRACED US...
PLEASE STAY WITH ME...
...FOREVER...

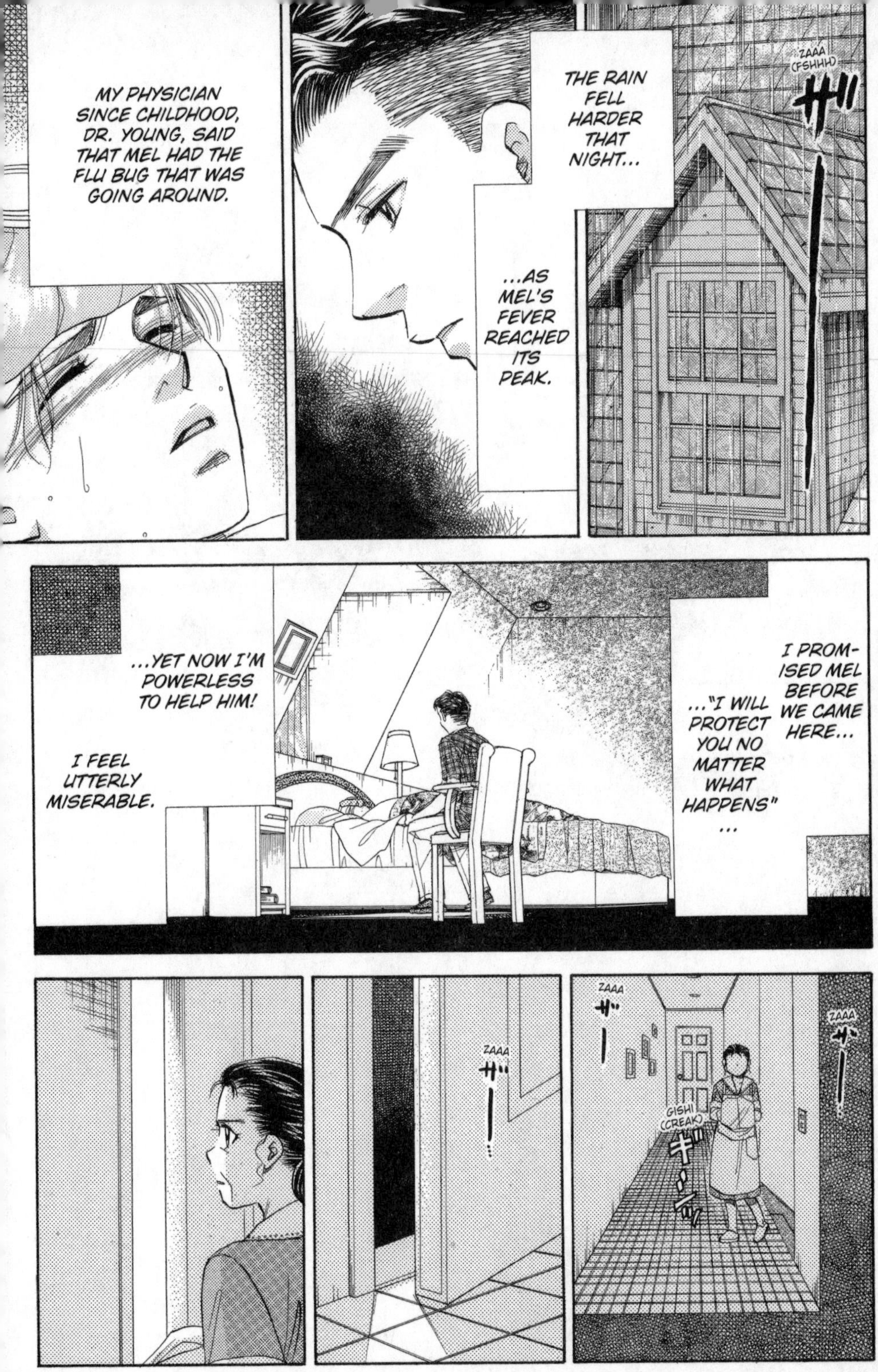
ZAAA (FSHHH)
THE RAIN FELL HARDER THAT NIGHT...
...AS MEL'S FEVER REACHED ITS PEAK.
MY PHYSICIAN SINCE CHILDHOOD, DR. YOUNG, SAID THAT MEL HAD THE FLU BUG THAT WAS GOING AROUND.
I PROMISED MEL BEFORE WE CAME HERE...
..."I WILL PROTECT YOU NO MATTER WHAT HAPPENS"...
...YET NOW I'M POWERLESS TO HELP HIM!
I FEEL UTTERLY MISERABLE.
ZAAA
ZAAA
GISHI (CREAK)
ZAAA

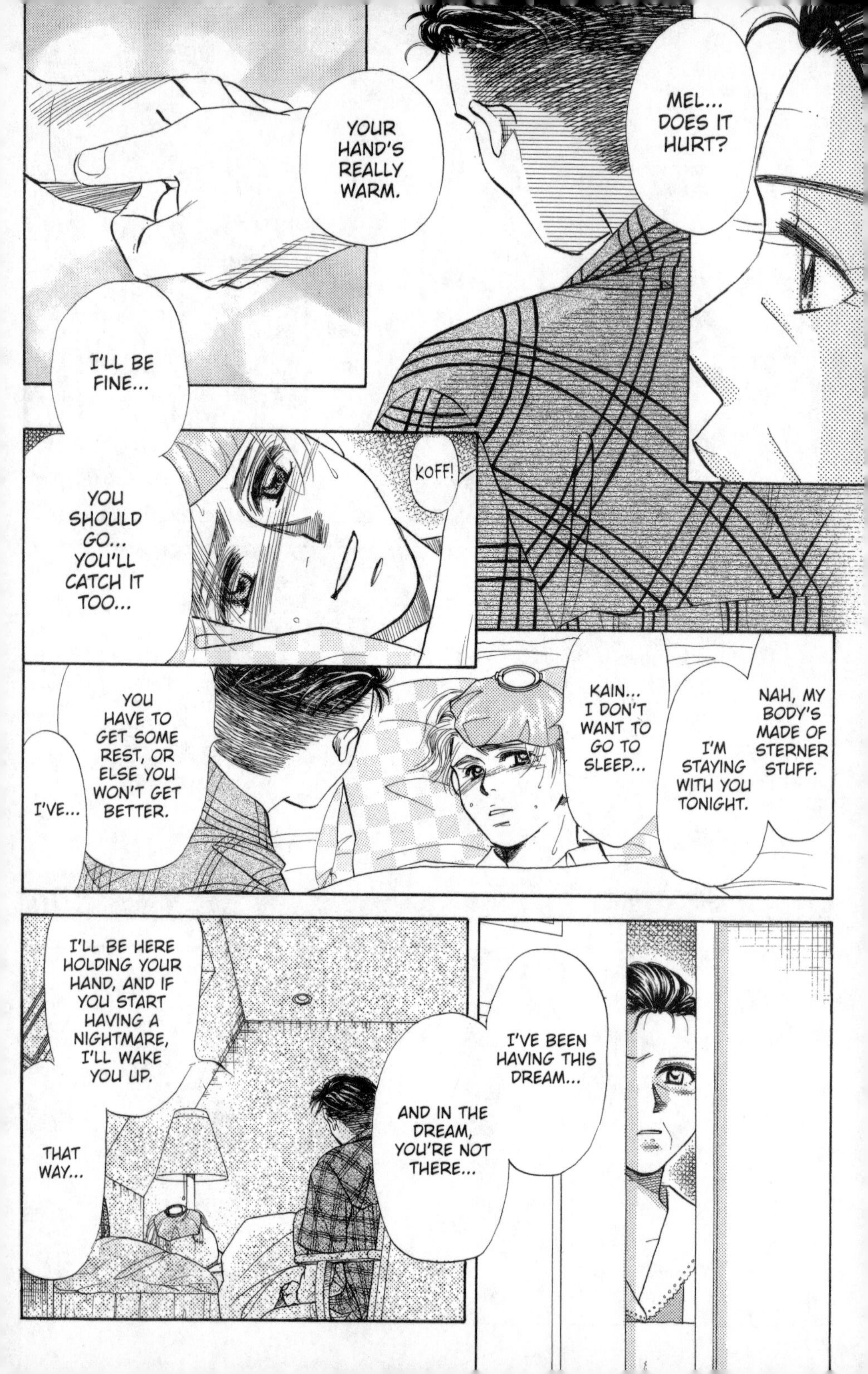
MEL... DOES IT HURT?
YOUR HAND'S REALLY WARM.
KOFF!
I'LL BE FINE...
YOU SHOULD GO... YOU'LL CATCH IT TOO...
NAH, MY BODY'S MADE OF STERNER STUFF.
I'M STAYING WITH YOU TONIGHT.
KAIN... I DON'T WANT TO GO TO SLEEP...
YOU HAVE TO GET SOME REST, OR ELSE YOU WON'T GET BETTER.
I'VE...
I'VE BEEN HAVING THIS DREAM...
AND IN THE DREAM, YOU'RE NOT THERE...
I'LL BE HERE HOLDING YOUR HAND, AND IF YOU START HAVING A NIGHTMARE, I'LL WAKE YOU UP.
THAT WAY...

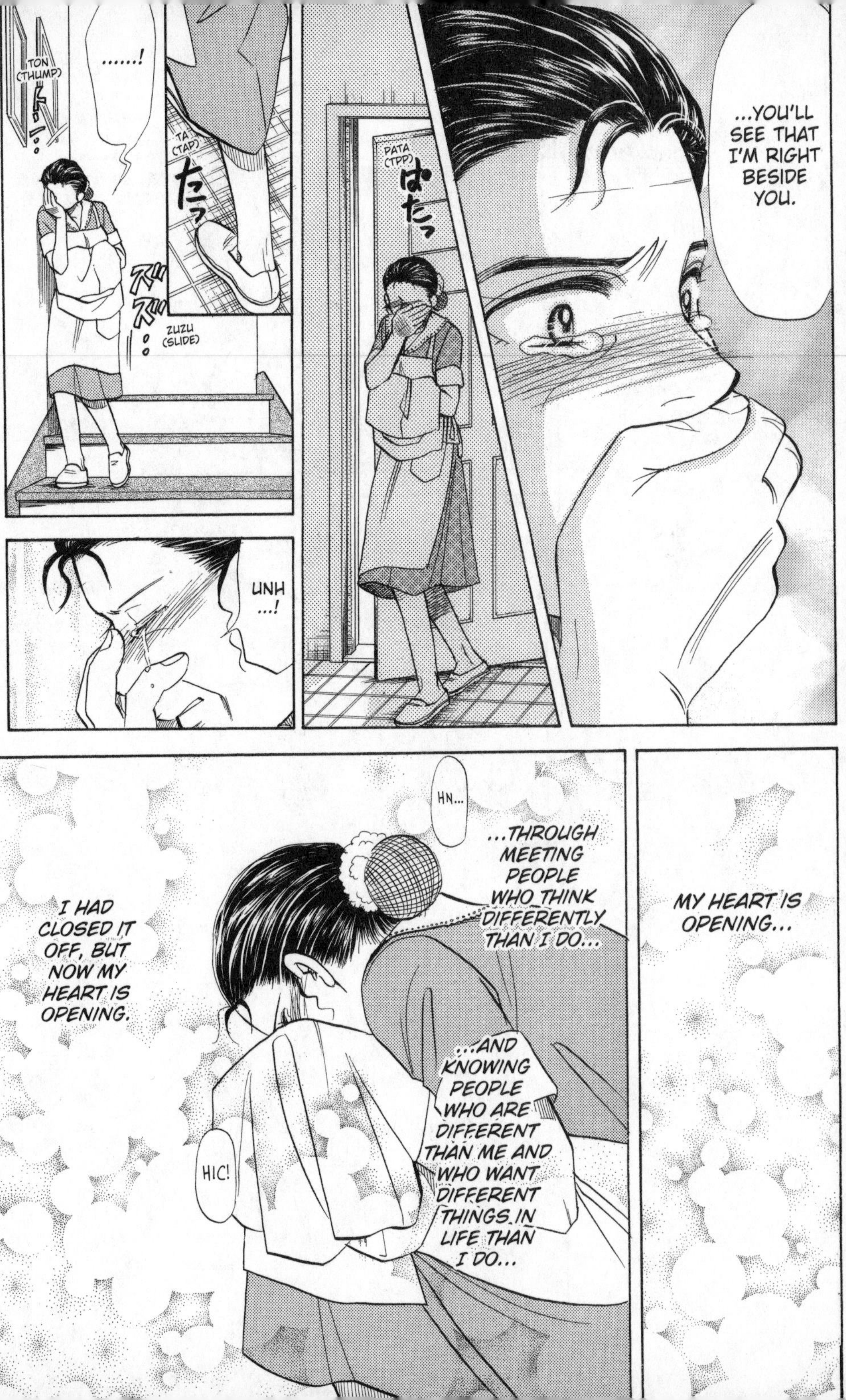
...YOU'LL SEE THAT I'M RIGHT BESIDE YOU.
PATA (TPP)
ぱたっ
......!
TA (TAP)
たっ
TON (THUMP)
ZUZU (SLIDE)
ズズ‥
UNH ...!
MY HEART IS OPENING...
HN...
...THROUGH MEETING PEOPLE WHO THINK DIFFERENTLY THAN I DO...
I HAD CLOSED IT OFF, BUT NOW MY HEART IS OPENING.
...AND KNOWING PEOPLE WHO ARE DIFFERENT THAN ME AND WHO WANT DIFFERENT THINGS IN LIFE THAN I DO...
HIC!

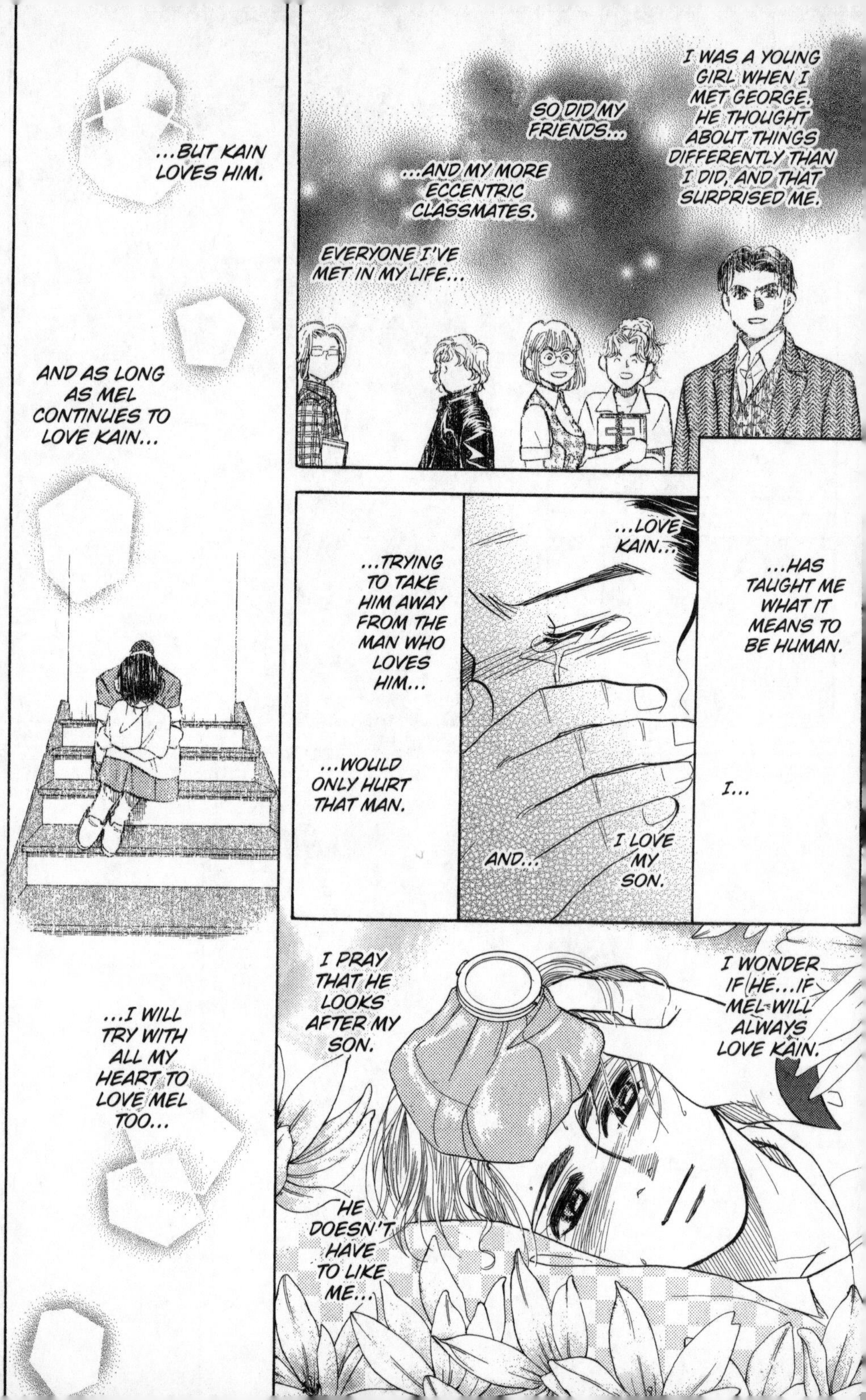
I WAS A YOUNG GIRL WHEN I MET GEORGE. HE THOUGHT ABOUT THINGS DIFFERENTLY THAN I DID, AND THAT SURPRISED ME.
SO DID MY FRIENDS...
...AND MY MORE ECCENTRIC CLASSMATES.
EVERYONE I'VE MET IN MY LIFE...
...HAS TAUGHT ME WHAT IT MEANS TO BE HUMAN.
I...
...LOVE KAIN...
I LOVE MY SON.
AND...
...TRYING TO TAKE HIM AWAY FROM THE MAN WHO LOVES HIM...
...WOULD ONLY HURT THAT MAN.
I WONDER IF HE...IF MEL WILL ALWAYS LOVE KAIN.
I PRAY THAT HE LOOKS AFTER MY SON.
HE DOESN'T HAVE TO LIKE ME...
...BUT KAIN LOVES HIM.
AND AS LONG AS MEL CONTINUES TO LOVE KAIN...
...I WILL TRY WITH ALL MY HEART TO LOVE MEL TOO...

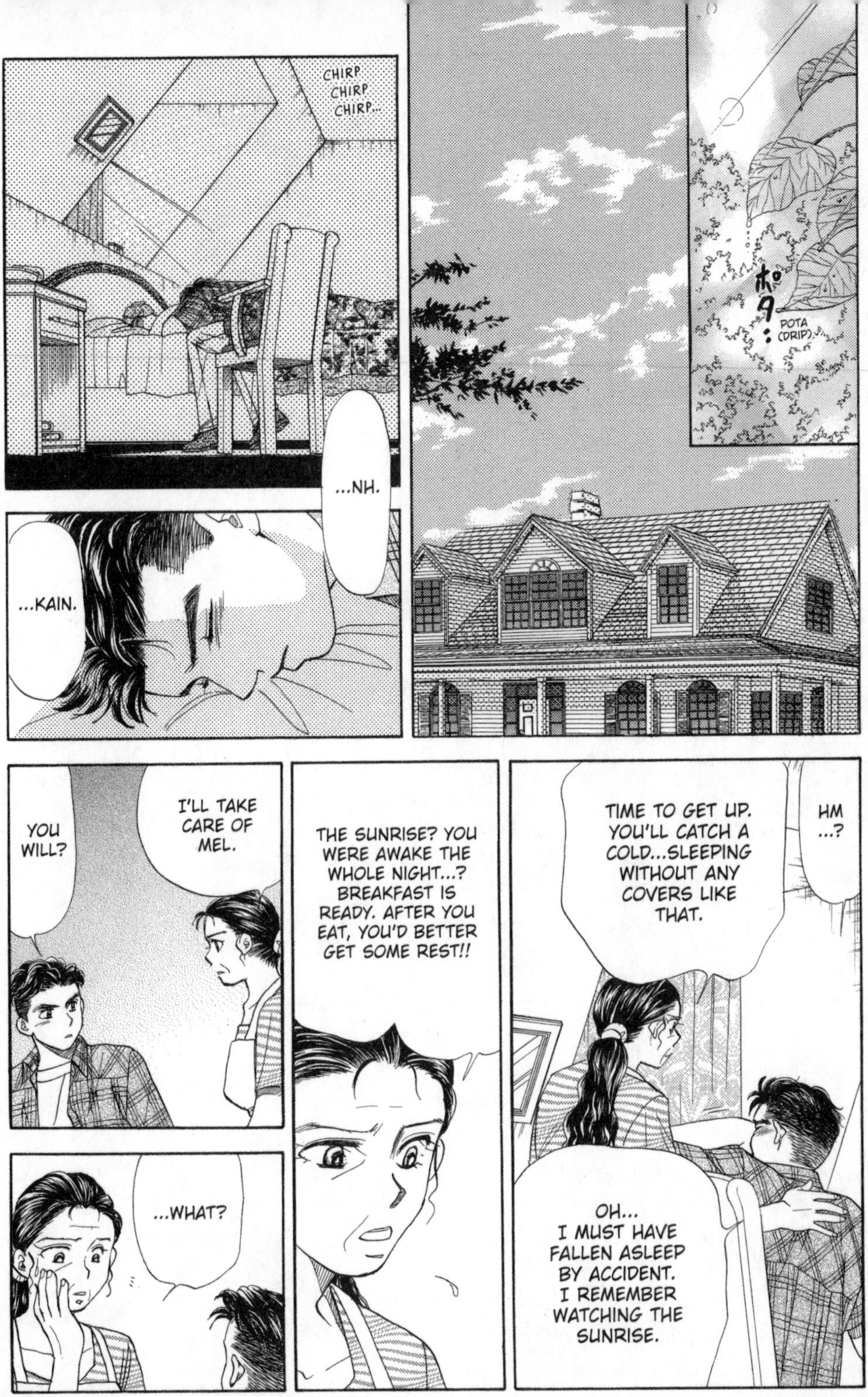
ポタ
POTA (DRIP)
CHIRP CHIRP CHIRP...
...NH.
...KAIN.
HM ...?
TIME TO GET UP. YOU'LL CATCH A COLD...SLEEPING WITHOUT ANY COVERS LIKE THAT.
OH... I MUST HAVE FALLEN ASLEEP BY ACCIDENT. I REMEMBER WATCHING THE SUNRISE.
THE SUNRISE? YOU WERE AWAKE THE WHOLE NIGHT...? BREAKFAST IS READY. AFTER YOU EAT, YOU'D BETTER GET SOME REST!!
I'LL TAKE CARE OF MEL.
YOU WILL?
...WHAT?

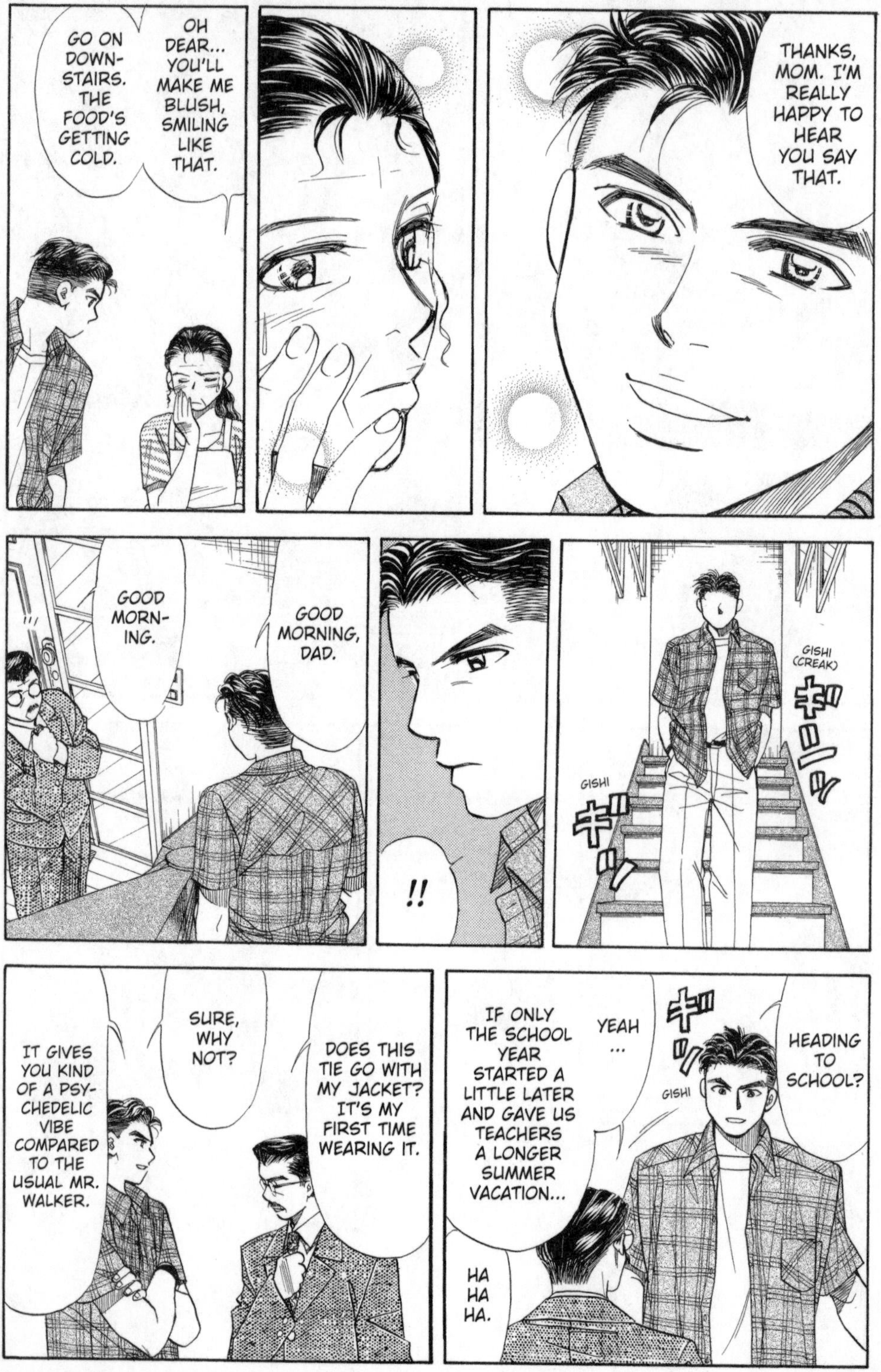
THANKS, MOM. I'M REALLY HAPPY TO HEAR YOU SAY THAT.
OH DEAR... YOU'LL MAKE ME BLUSH, SMILING LIKE THAT.
GO ON DOWN-STAIRS. THE FOOD'S GETTING COLD.
GISHI (CREAK)
GISHI
!!
GOOD MORNING, DAD.
GOOD MORN-ING.
HEADING TO SCHOOL?
GISHI
YEAH ...
IF ONLY THE SCHOOL YEAR STARTED A LITTLE LATER AND GAVE US TEACHERS A LONGER SUMMER VACATION...
HA HA HA.
DOES THIS TIE GO WITH MY JACKET? IT'S MY FIRST TIME WEARING IT.
SURE, WHY NOT?
IT GIVES YOU KIND OF A PSY-CHEDELIC VIBE COMPARED TO THE USUAL MR. WALKER.

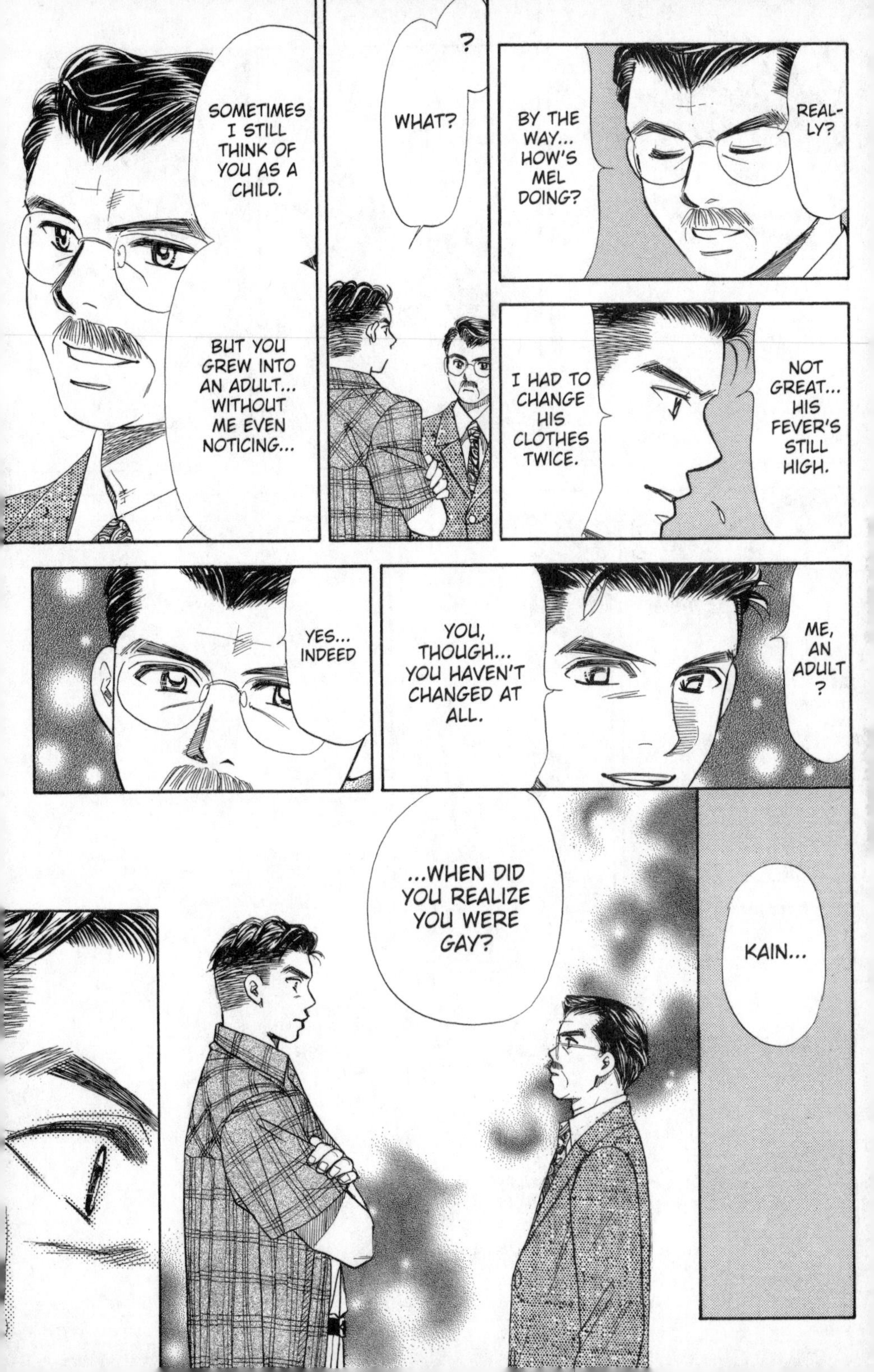
REAL-LY?
BY THE WAY... HOW'S MEL DOING?
NOT GREAT... HIS FEVER'S STILL HIGH.
I HAD TO CHANGE HIS CLOTHES TWICE.
?
WHAT?
SOMETIMES I STILL THINK OF YOU AS A CHILD.
BUT YOU GREW INTO AN ADULT... WITHOUT ME EVEN NOTICING...
ME, AN ADULT?
YOU, THOUGH... YOU HAVEN'T CHANGED AT ALL.
YES... INDEED
KAIN...
...WHEN DID YOU REALIZE YOU WERE GAY?

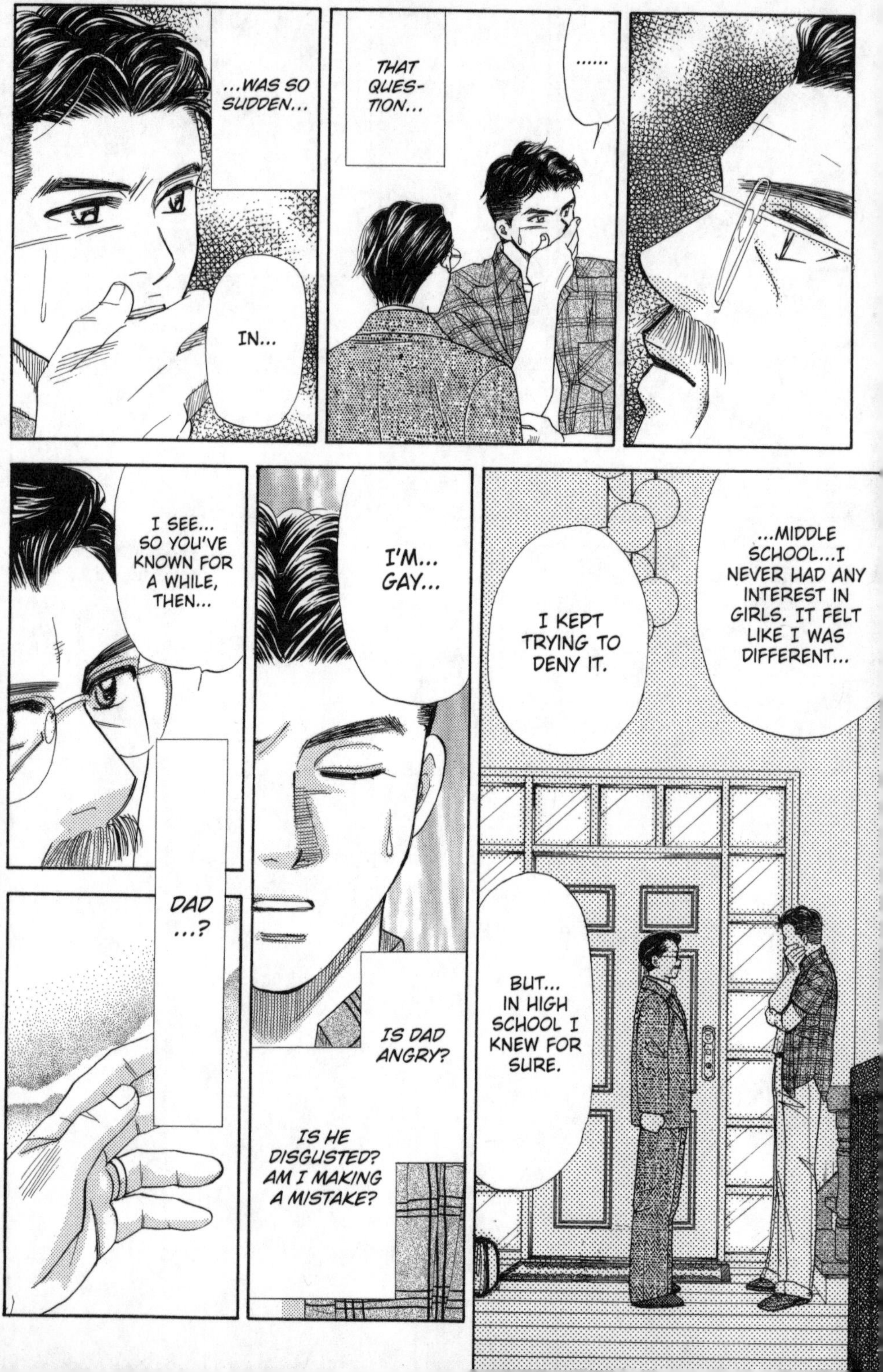
......
THAT QUES-TION...
...WAS SO SUDDEN...
IN...
...MIDDLE SCHOOL...I NEVER HAD ANY INTEREST IN GIRLS. IT FELT LIKE I WAS DIFFERENT...
I KEPT TRYING TO DENY IT.
BUT... IN HIGH SCHOOL I KNEW FOR SURE.
I'M... GAY...
IS DAD ANGRY?
IS HE DISGUSTED? AM I MAKING A MISTAKE?
I SEE... SO YOU'VE KNOWN FOR A WHILE, THEN...
DAD ...?

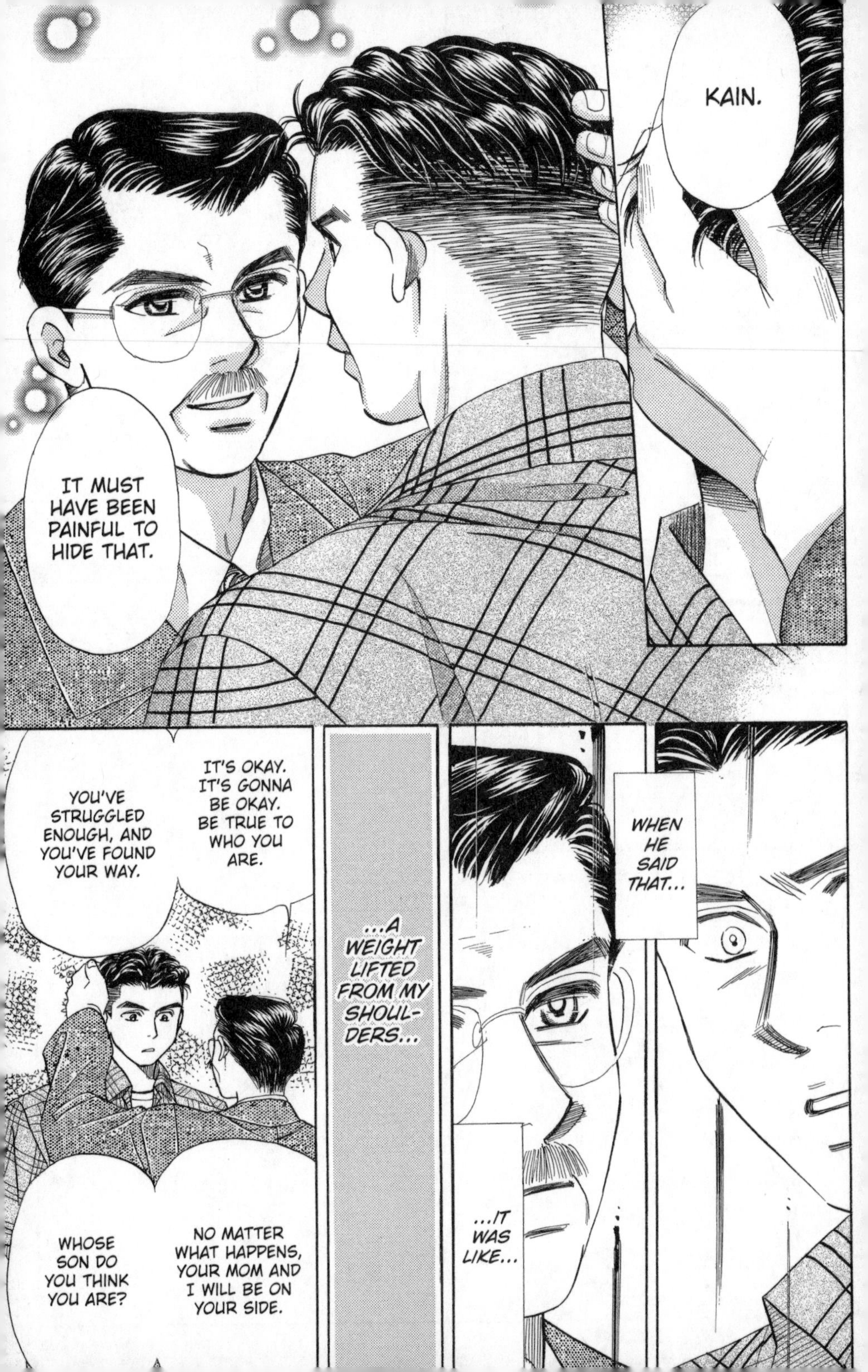
KAIN.
IT MUST HAVE BEEN PAINFUL TO HIDE THAT.
WHEN HE SAID THAT...
...IT WAS LIKE...
...A WEIGHT LIFTED FROM MY SHOUL-DERS...
IT'S OKAY. IT'S GONNA BE OKAY. BE TRUE TO WHO YOU ARE.
YOU'VE STRUGGLED ENOUGH, AND YOU'VE FOUND YOUR WAY.
NO MATTER WHAT HAPPENS, YOUR MOM AND I WILL BE ON YOUR SIDE.
WHOSE SON DO YOU THINK YOU ARE?

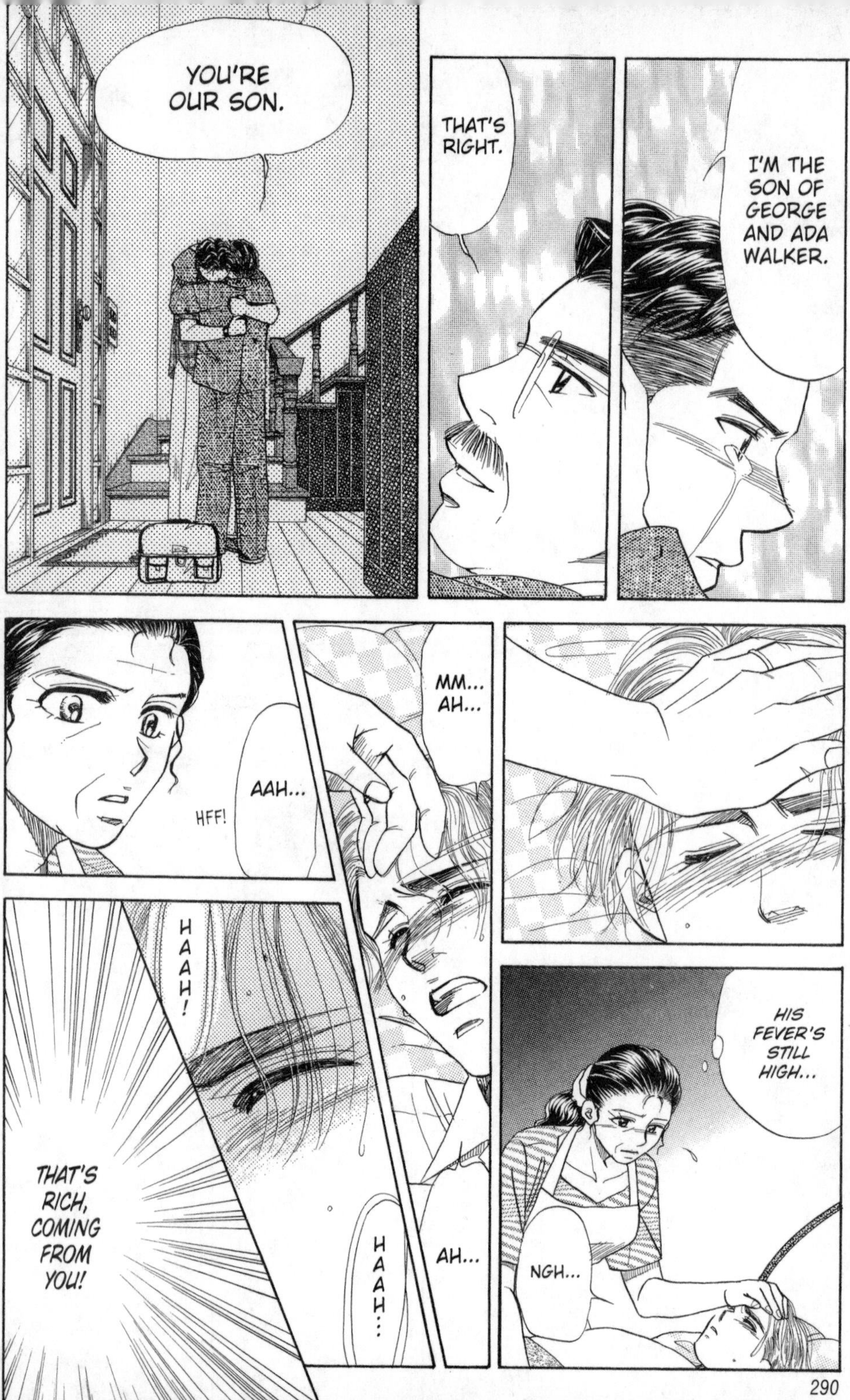
I'M THE SON OF GEORGE AND ADA WALKER.
THAT'S RIGHT.
YOU'RE OUR SON.
MM... AH...
AAH...
HFF!
HIS FEVER'S STILL HIGH...
NGH...
AH...
HAAAH...
HAAAH!
THAT'S RICH, COMING FROM YOU!

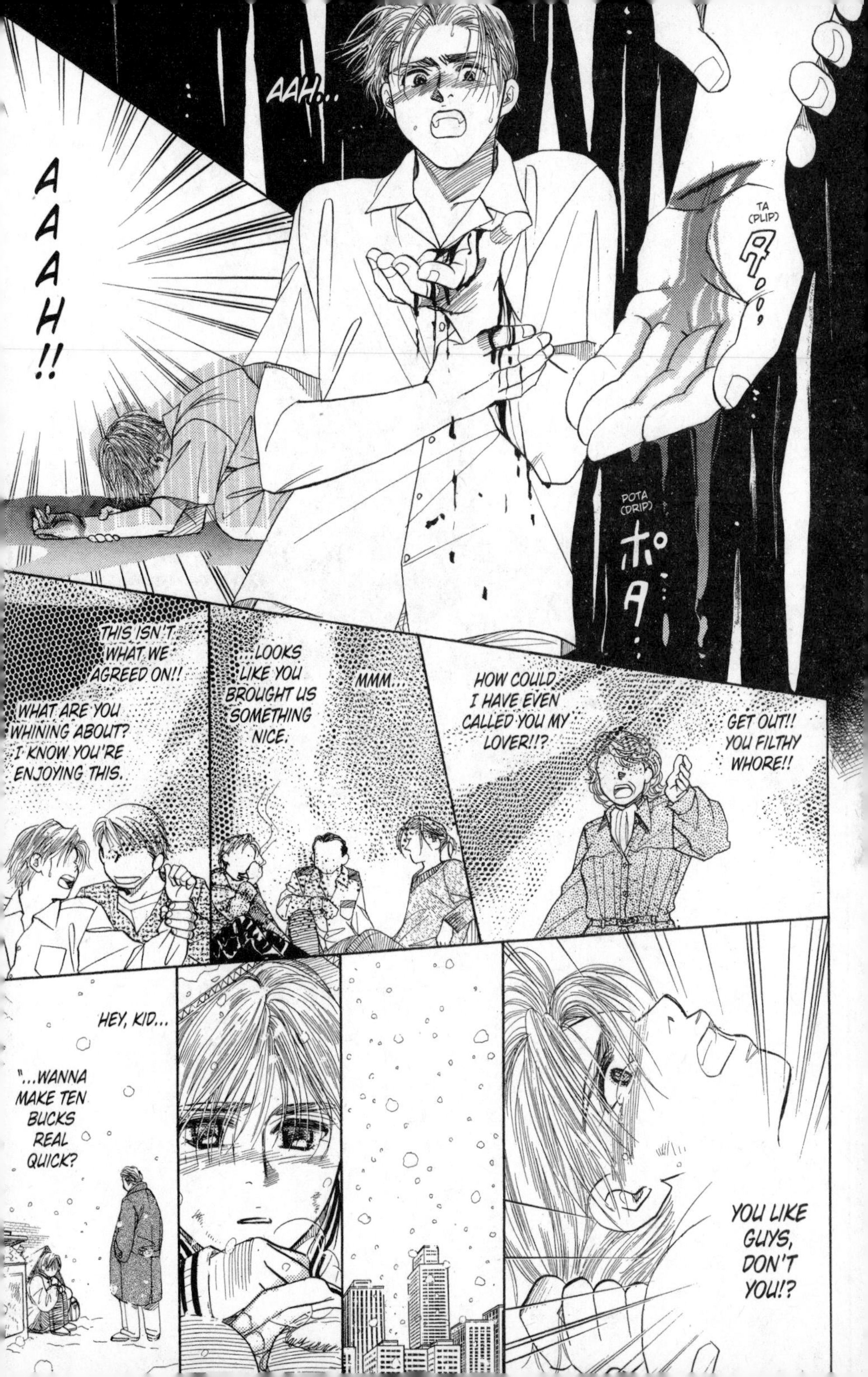
TA (PLIP)
タ
AAH...
AAAAH!!
POTA (DRIP)
ポタ
HOW COULD I HAVE EVEN CALLED YOU MY LOVER!!?
GET OUT!! YOU FILTHY WHORE!!
MMM...
...LOOKS LIKE YOU BROUGHT US SOMETHING NICE.
THIS ISN'T WHAT WE AGREED ON!!
WHAT ARE YOU WHINING ABOUT? I KNOW YOU'RE ENJOYING THIS.
YOU LIKE GUYS, DON'T YOU!?
HEY, KID...
"...WANNA MAKE TEN BUCKS REAL QUICK?

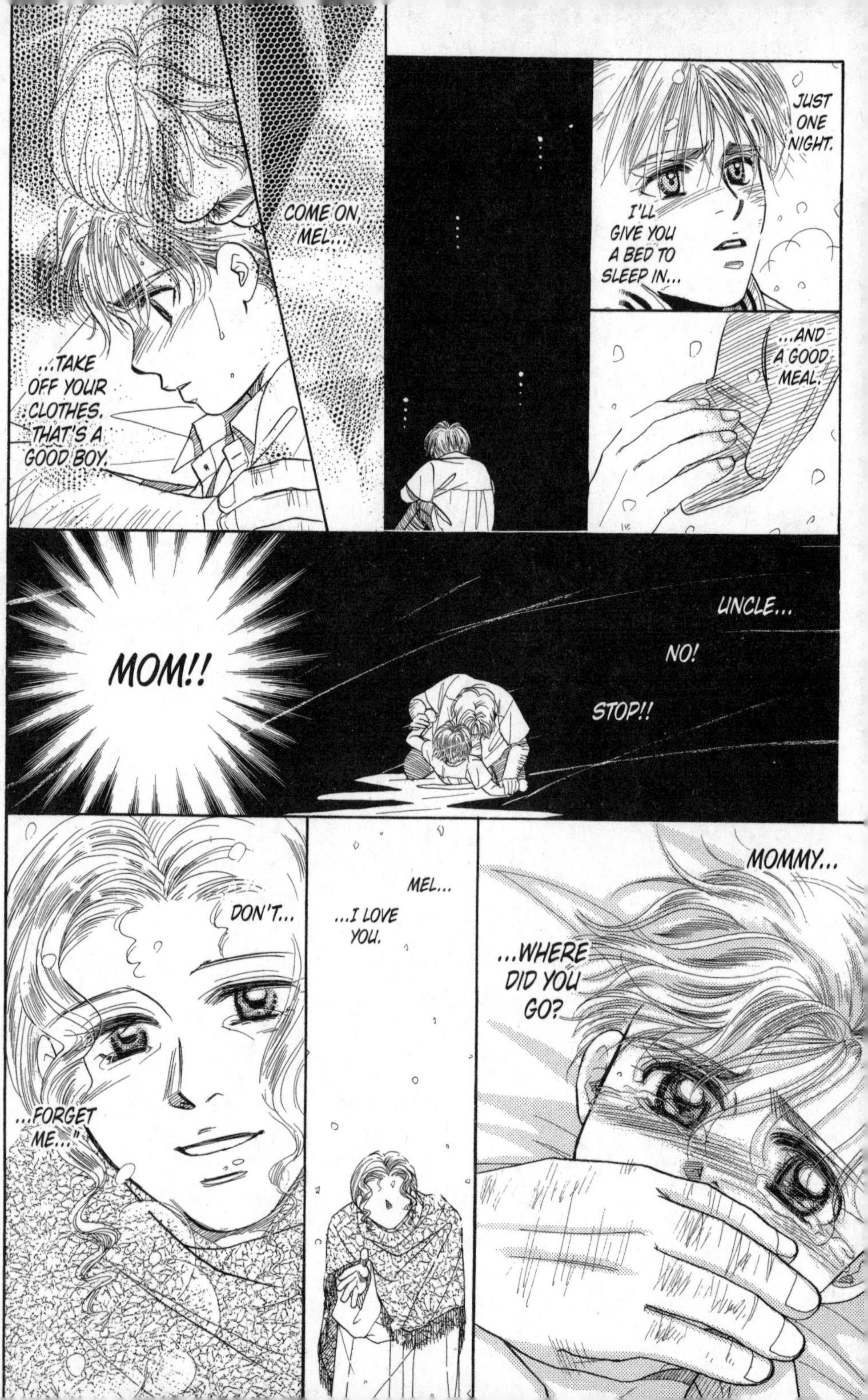
JUST ONE NIGHT.
I'LL GIVE YOU A BED TO SLEEP IN...
...AND A GOOD MEAL.
COME ON, MEL...
...TAKE OFF YOUR CLOTHES. THAT'S A GOOD BOY.
UNCLE...
NO!
STOP!!
MOM!!
MOMMY...
...WHERE DID YOU GO?
MEL...
...I LOVE YOU.
DON'T...
...FORGET ME..."

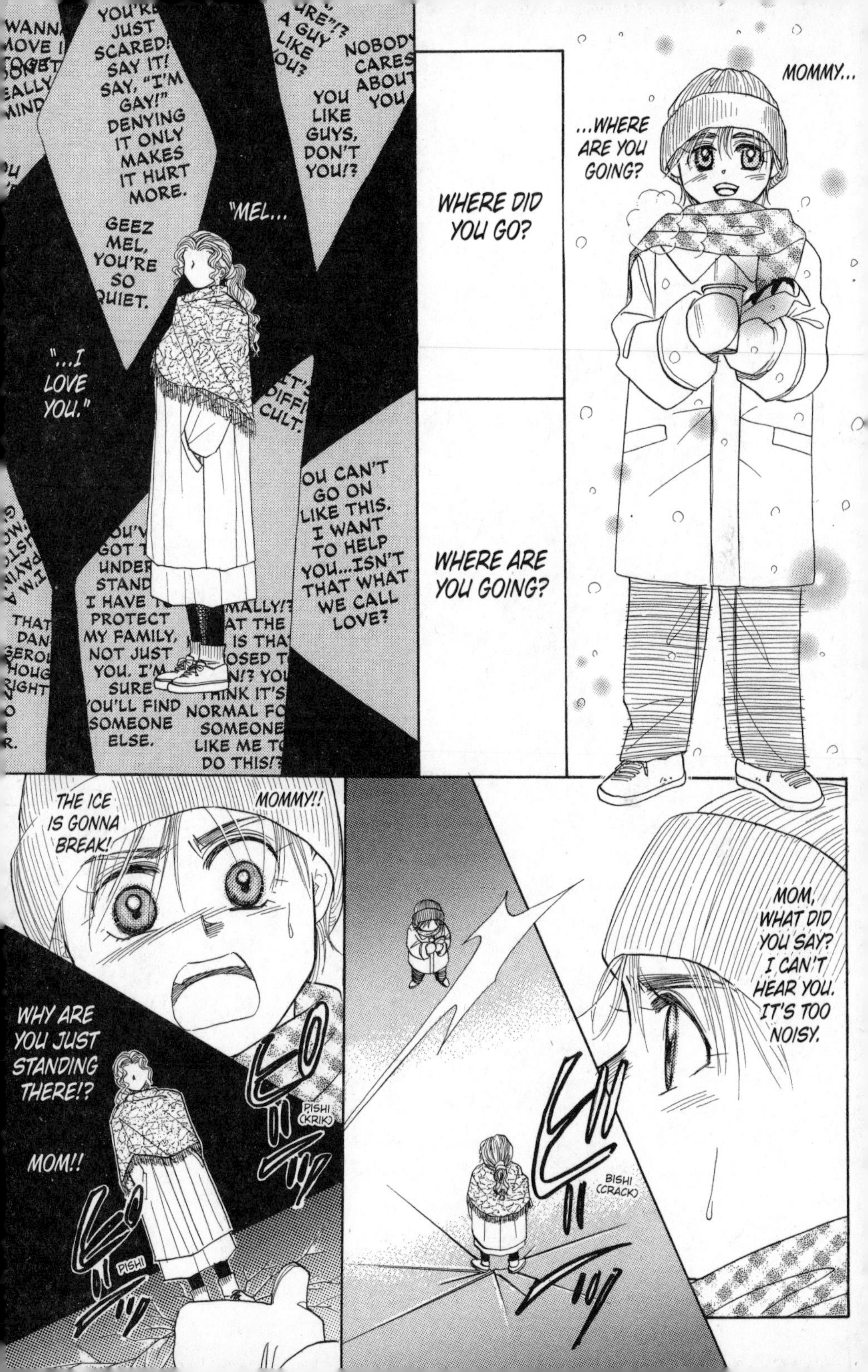
MOMMY...
...WHERE ARE YOU GOING?
WHERE DID YOU GO?
WHERE ARE YOU GOING?
NOBODY CARES ABOUT YOU
YOU LIKE GUYS, DON'T YOU!?
A GUY LIKE
JUST SCARED! SAY IT! SAY, "I'M GAY!" DENYING IT ONLY MAKES IT HURT MORE.
"MEL...
GEEZ MEL, YOU'RE SO QUIET.
"...I LOVE YOU."
CULT.
OU CAN'T GO ON LIKE THIS. I WANT TO HELP YOU...ISN'T THAT WHAT WE CALL LOVE?
NORMAL FO SOMEONE LIKE ME T DO THIS!?
PROTECT MY FAMILY, NOT JUST YOU. I'M SURE OU'LL FIND SOMEONE ELSE.
MOM, WHAT DID YOU SAY? I CAN'T HEAR YOU. IT'S TOO NOISY.
BISHI (CRACK)
MOMMY!!
THE ICE IS GONNA BREAK!
WHY ARE YOU JUST STANDING THERE!?
MOM!!
PISHI (KRIK)
PISHI

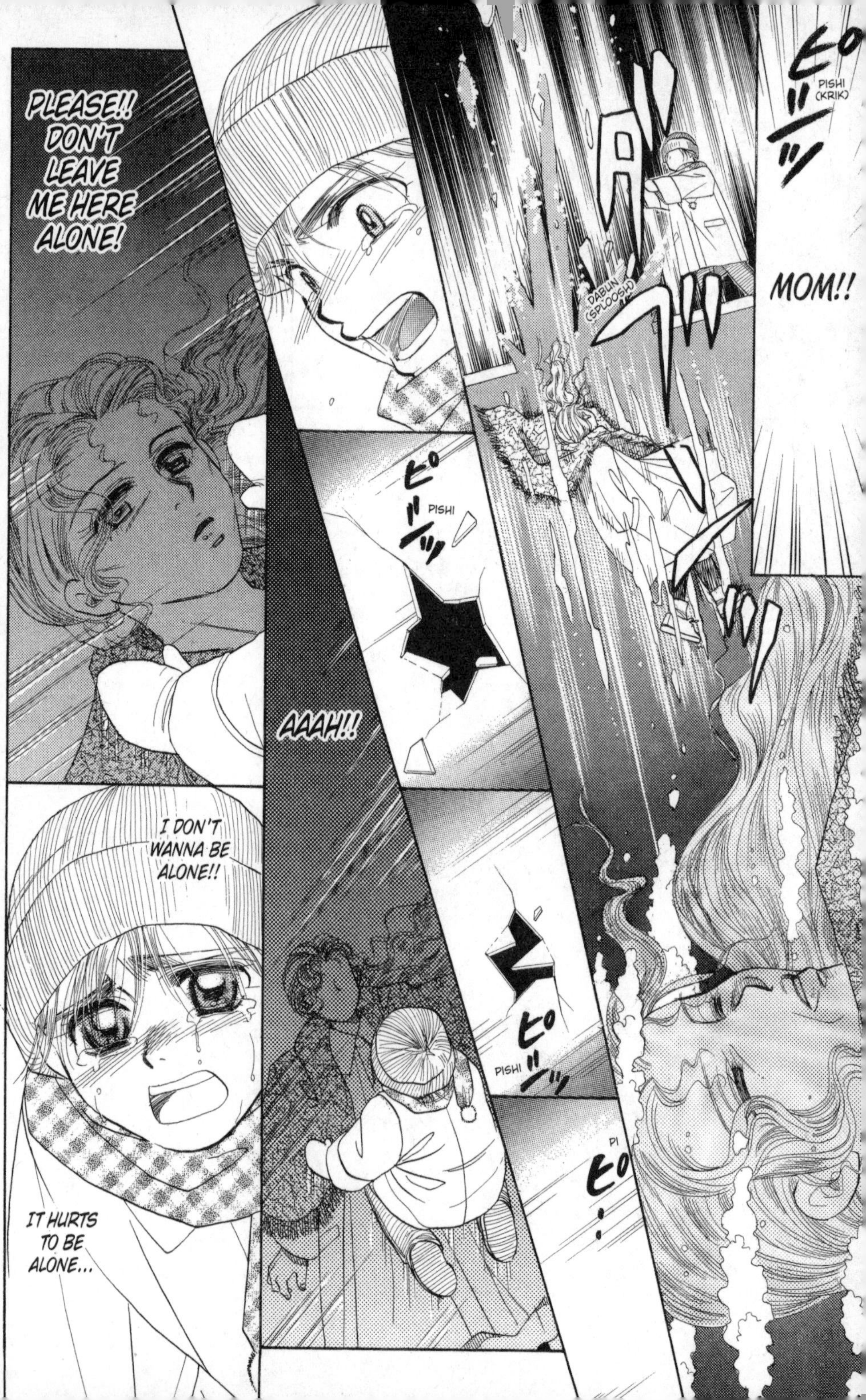
PISHI (KRIK)
MOM!!
DABUN (SPLOOSH)
PISHI
AAAH!!
PLEASE!! DON'T LEAVE ME HERE ALONE!
PISHI
PI
I DON'T WANNA BE ALONE!!
IT HURTS TO BE ALONE...

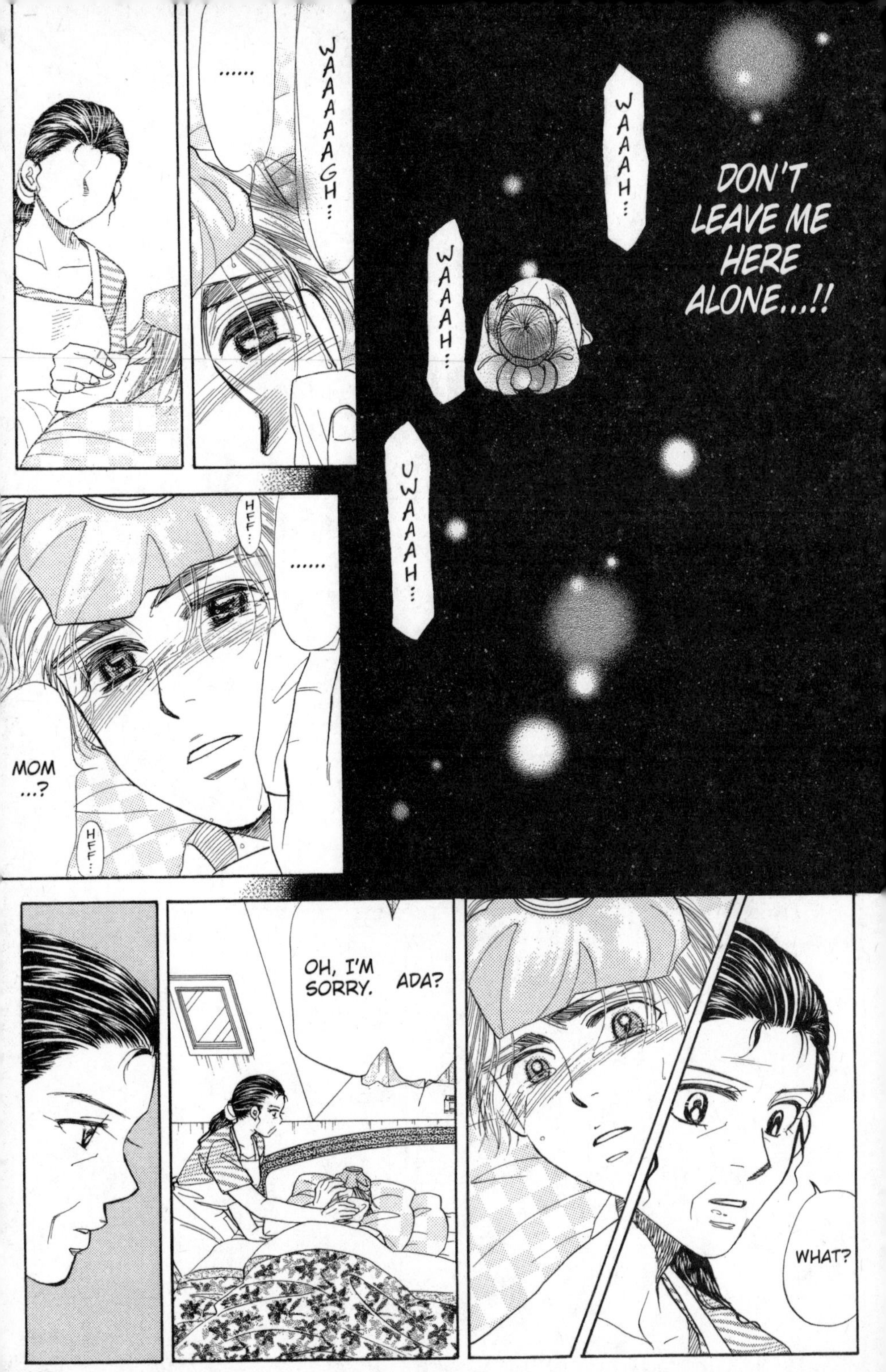
DON'T LEAVE ME HERE ALONE...!!
WAAAAH...
WAAAAH...
UWAAAAH...
WAAAAAAGH...
......
HFF...
......
MOM ...?
HFF...
WHAT?
ADA?
OH, I'M SORRY.

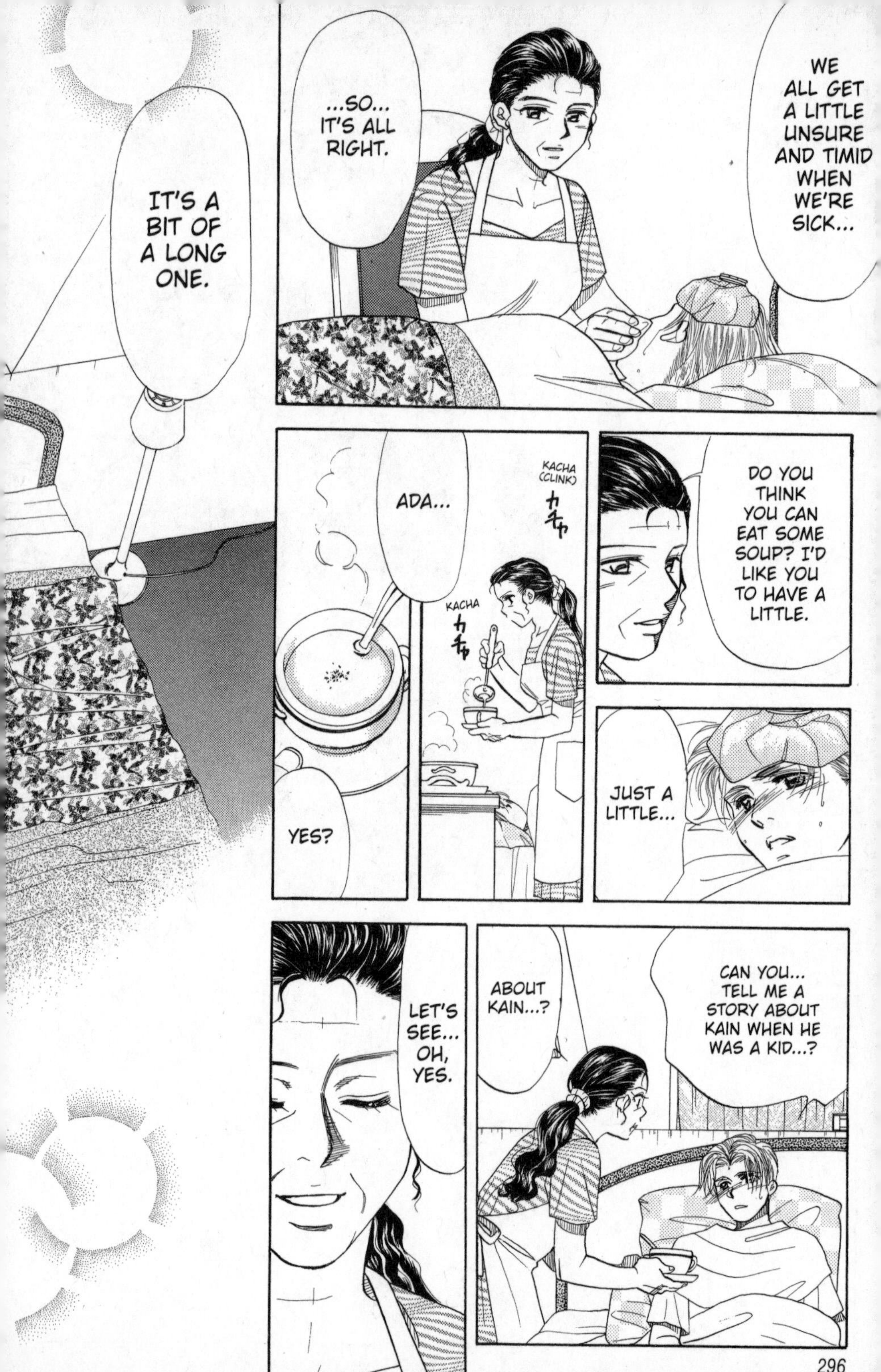
WE ALL GET A LITTLE UNSURE AND TIMID WHEN WE'RE SICK...
...SO... IT'S ALL RIGHT.
DO YOU THINK YOU CAN EAT SOME SOUP? I'D LIKE YOU TO HAVE A LITTLE.
JUST A LITTLE...
KACHA (CLINK)
カチャ
KACHA
カチャ
ADA...
YES?
CAN YOU... TELL ME A STORY ABOUT KAIN WHEN HE WAS A KID...?
ABOUT KAIN...?
LET'S SEE... OH, YES.
IT'S A BIT OF A LONG ONE.

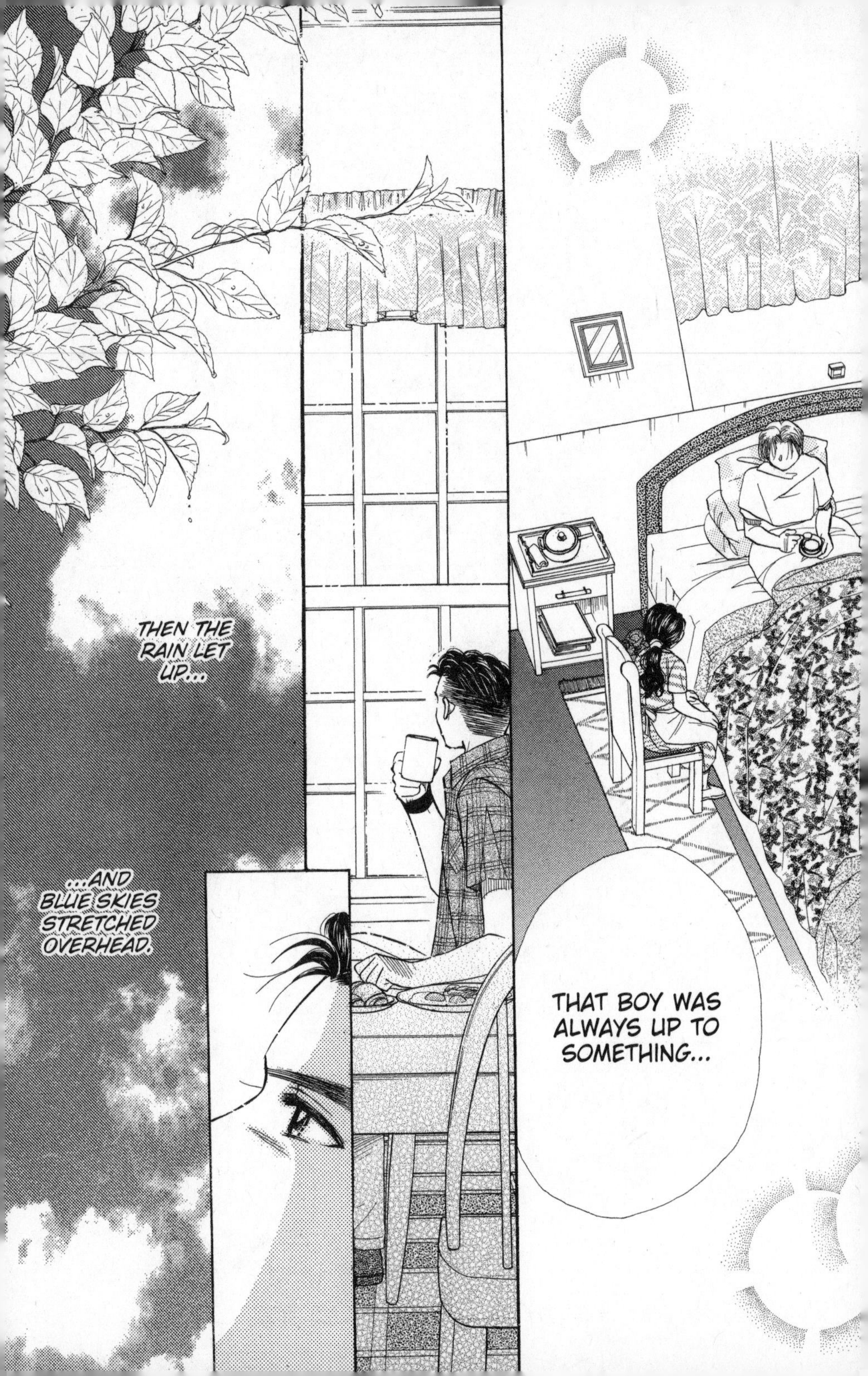
THAT BOY WAS ALWAYS UP TO SOMETHING...
THEN THE RAIN LET UP...
...AND BLUE SKIES STRETCHED OVERHEAD.

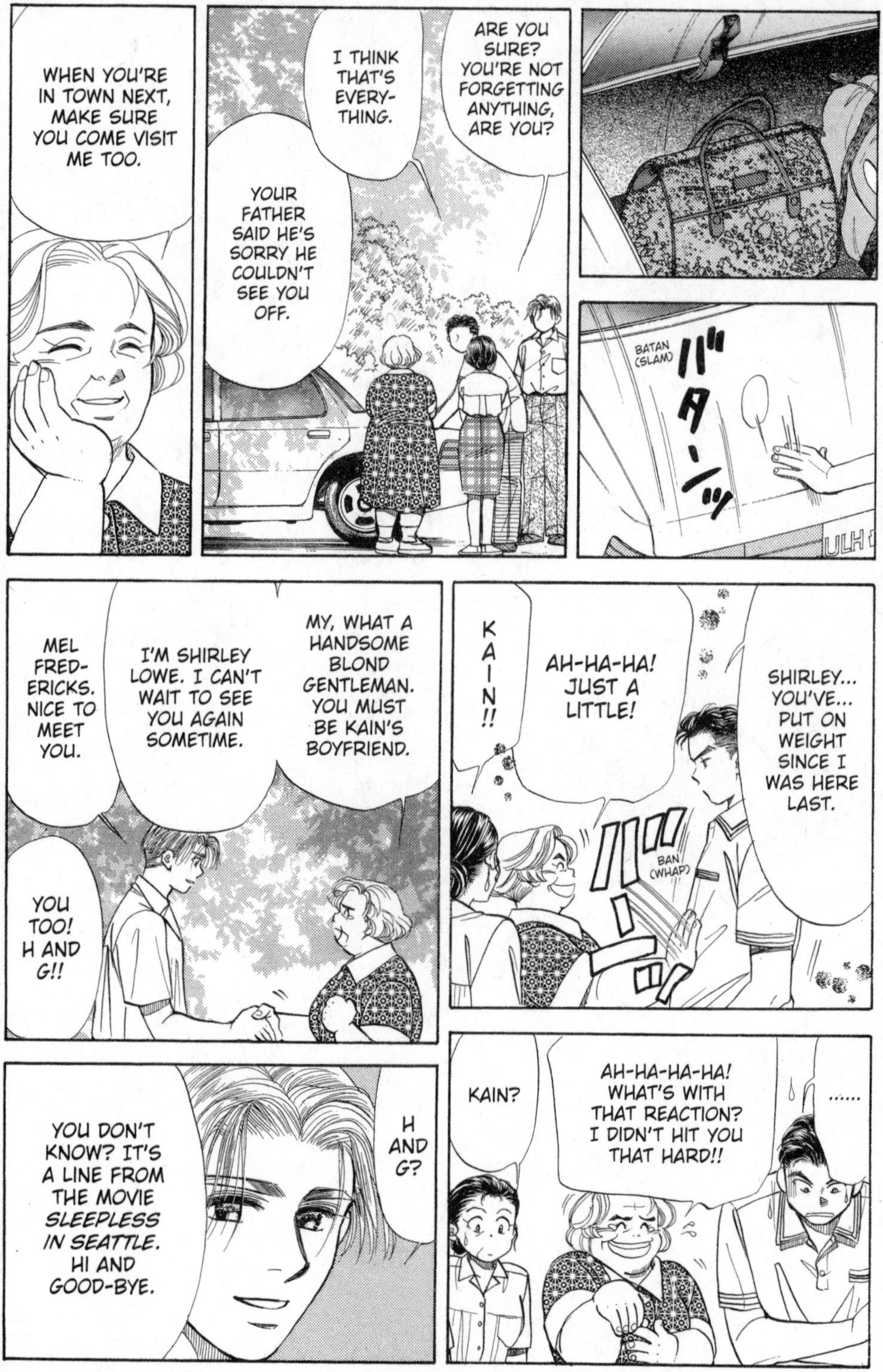
BATAN (SLAM)
バタンッ
ARE YOU SURE? YOU'RE NOT FORGETTING ANYTHING, ARE YOU?
I THINK THAT'S EVERY-THING.
YOUR FATHER SAID HE'S SORRY HE COULDN'T SEE YOU OFF.
WHEN YOU'RE IN TOWN NEXT, MAKE SURE YOU COME VISIT ME TOO.
SHIRLEY... YOU'VE... PUT ON WEIGHT SINCE I WAS HERE LAST.
AH-HA-HA! JUST A LITTLE!
KAIN!!
BAN (WHAP)
MY, WHAT A HANDSOME BLOND GENTLEMAN. YOU MUST BE KAIN'S BOYFRIEND.
I'M SHIRLEY LOWE. I CAN'T WAIT TO SEE YOU AGAIN SOMETIME.
MEL FRED-ERICKS. NICE TO MEET YOU.
YOU TOO! H AND G!!
......
AH-HA-HA-HA! WHAT'S WITH THAT REACTION? I DIDN'T HIT YOU THAT HARD!!
KAIN?
H AND G?
YOU DON'T KNOW? IT'S A LINE FROM THE MOVIE *SLEEPLESS IN SEATTLE.* HI AND GOOD-BYE.

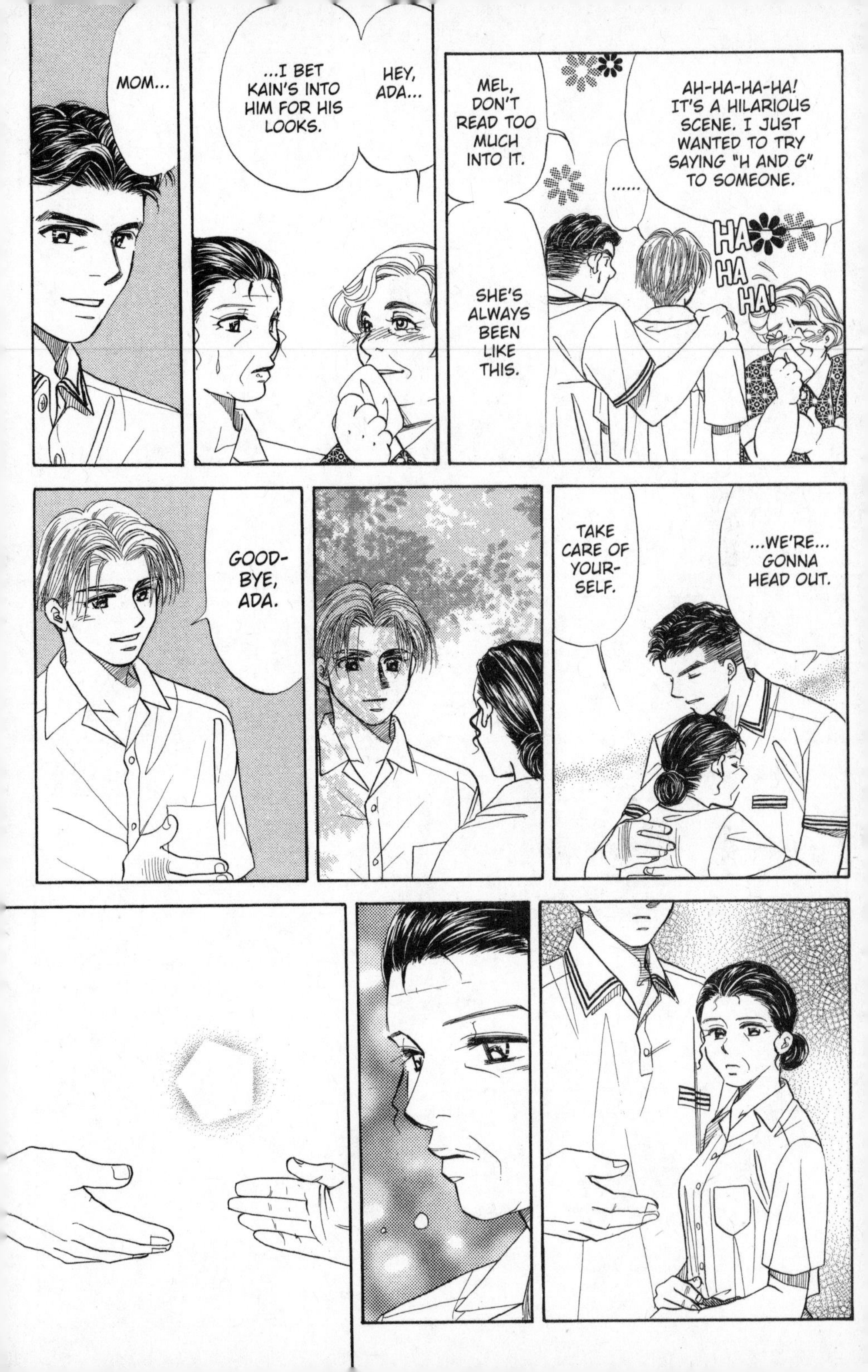
AH-HA-HA-HA! IT'S A HILARIOUS SCENE. I JUST WANTED TO TRY SAYING "H AND G" TO SOMEONE.
MEL, DON'T READ TOO MUCH INTO IT.
......
HA HA HA!
SHE'S ALWAYS BEEN LIKE THIS.
HEY, ADA...
...I BET KAIN'S INTO HIM FOR HIS LOOKS.
MOM...
...WE'RE... GONNA HEAD OUT.
TAKE CARE OF YOUR-SELF.
GOOD-BYE, ADA.

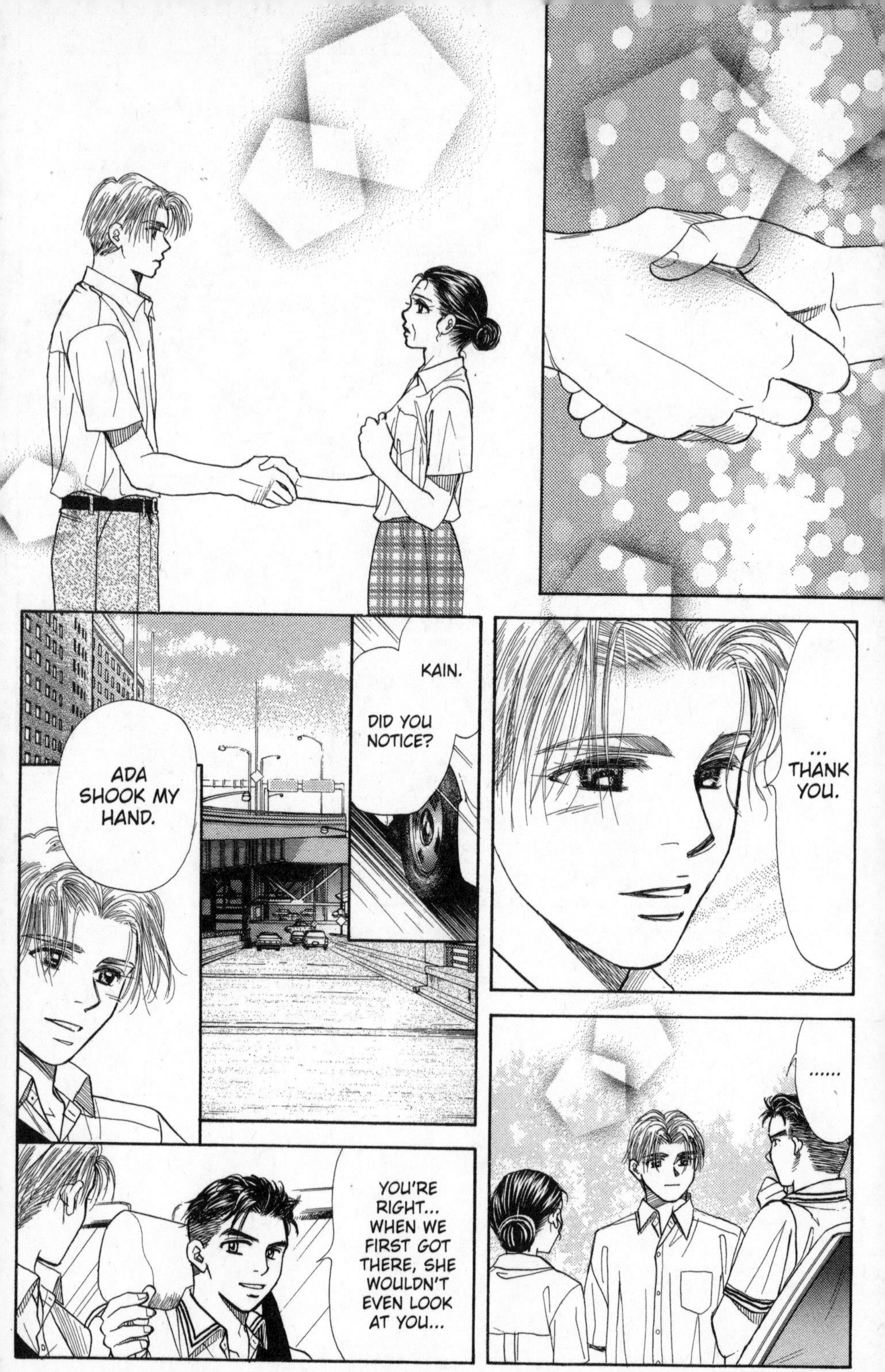
... THANK YOU.
KAIN.
DID YOU NOTICE?
ADA SHOOK MY HAND.
......
YOU'RE RIGHT... WHEN WE FIRST GOT THERE, SHE WOULDN'T EVEN LOOK AT YOU...

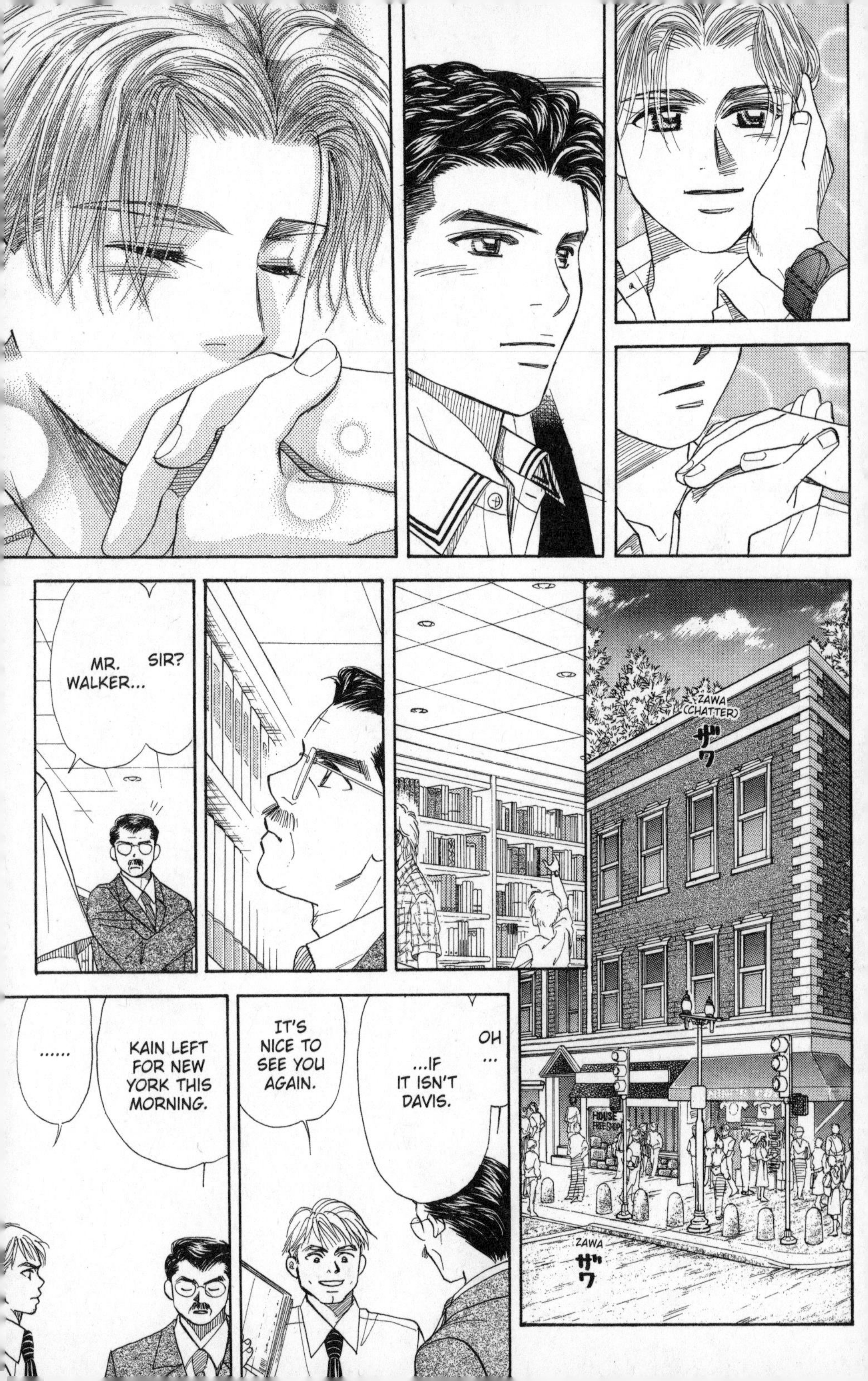
ZAWA (CHATTER)
ザワ
ZAWA
ザワ
MR. WALKER... SIR?
OH ...
...IF IT ISN'T DAVIS.
IT'S NICE TO SEE YOU AGAIN.
KAIN LEFT FOR NEW YORK THIS MORNING.
......

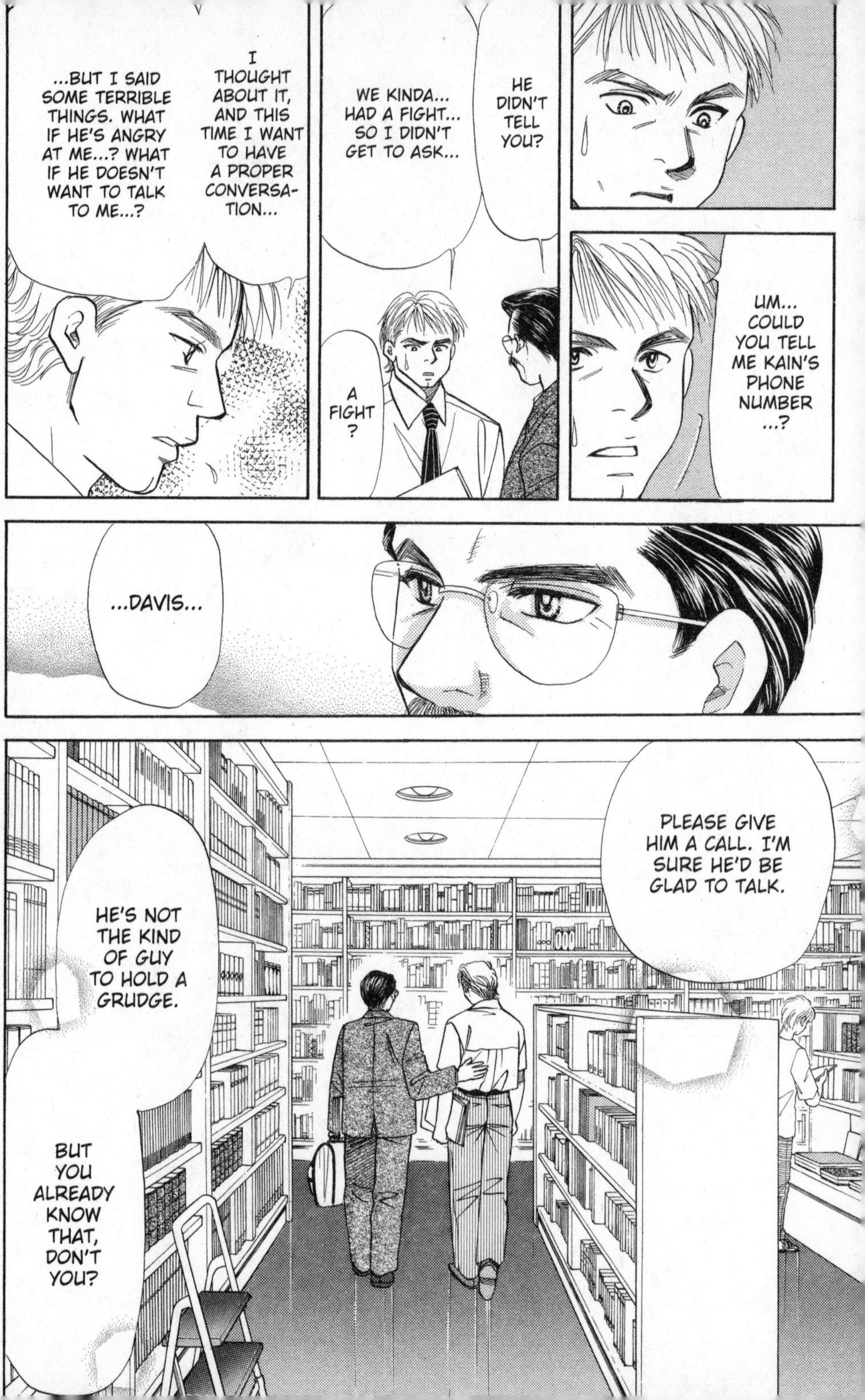
UM... COULD YOU TELL ME KAIN'S PHONE NUMBER ...?
HE DIDN'T TELL YOU?
WE KINDA... HAD A FIGHT... SO I DIDN'T GET TO ASK...
A FIGHT ?
I THOUGHT ABOUT IT, AND THIS TIME I WANT TO HAVE A PROPER CONVERSATION...
...BUT I SAID SOME TERRIBLE THINGS. WHAT IF HE'S ANGRY AT ME...? WHAT IF HE DOESN'T WANT TO TALK TO ME...?
...DAVIS...
PLEASE GIVE HIM A CALL. I'M SURE HE'D BE GLAD TO TALK.
HE'S NOT THE KIND OF GUY TO HOLD A GRUDGE.
BUT YOU ALREADY KNOW THAT, DON'T YOU?

EPISODE III

SCENE 1

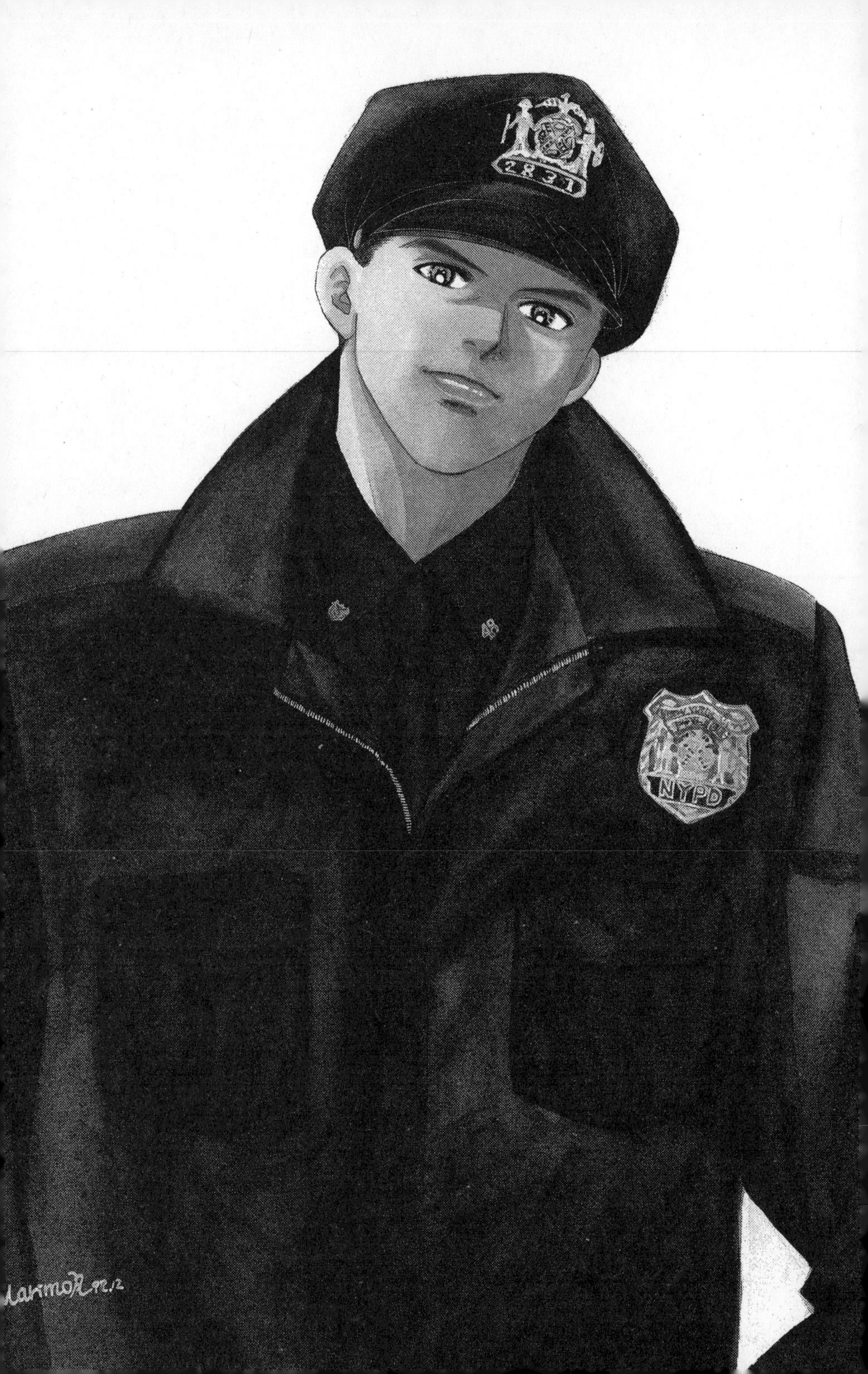
NYPD

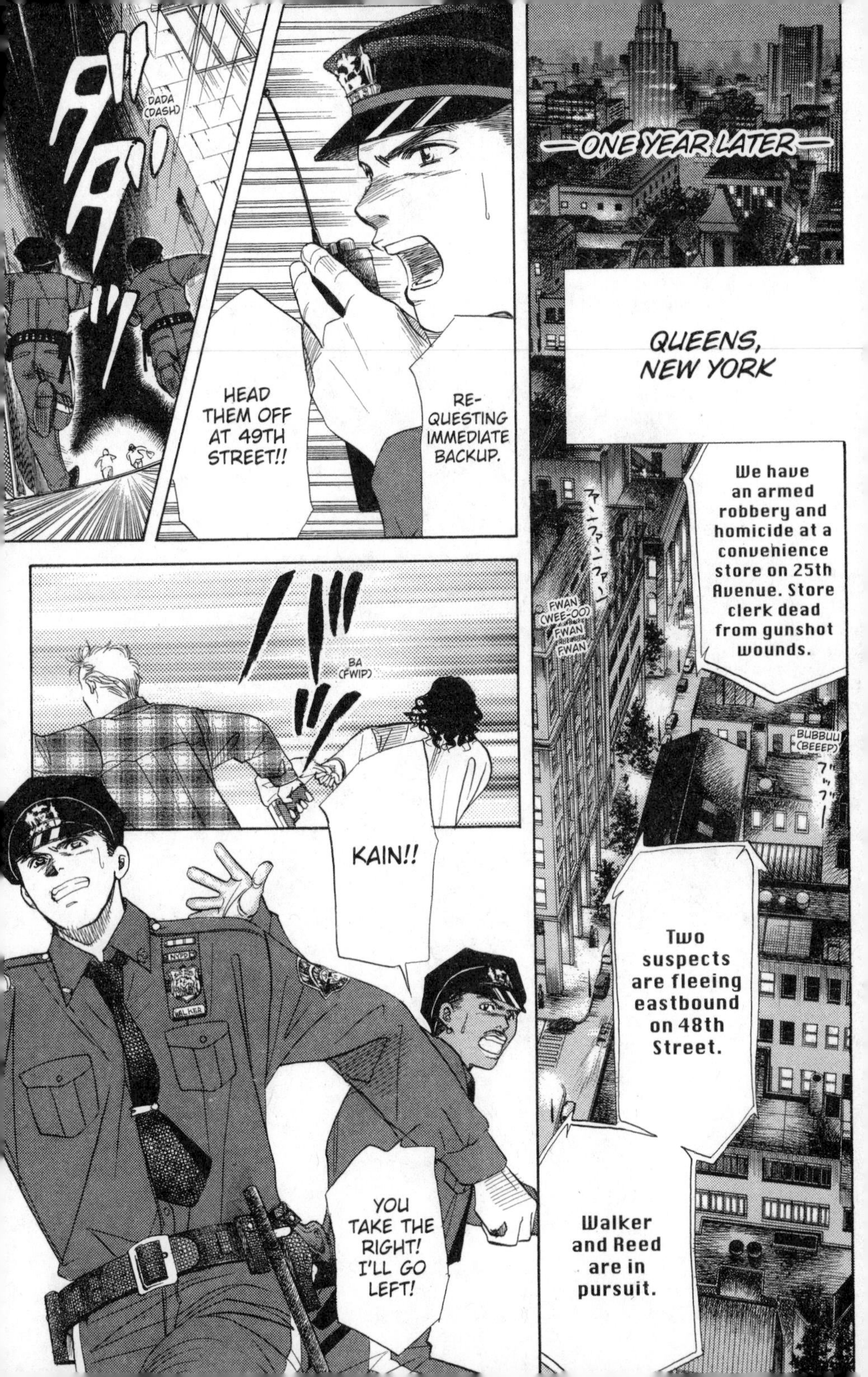
—ONE YEAR LATER—
QUEENS, NEW YORK
We have an armed robbery and homicide at a convenience store on 25th Avenue. Store clerk dead from gunshot wounds.
FWAN (WEE-OO) FWAN FWAN
BUBBUU (BEEEP)
Two suspects are fleeing eastbound on 48th Street.
Walker and Reed are in pursuit.
RE-QUESTING IMMEDIATE BACKUP.
HEAD THEM OFF AT 49TH STREET!!
DADA (DASH)
BA (FWIP)
KAIN!!
YOU TAKE THE RIGHT! I'LL GO LEFT!

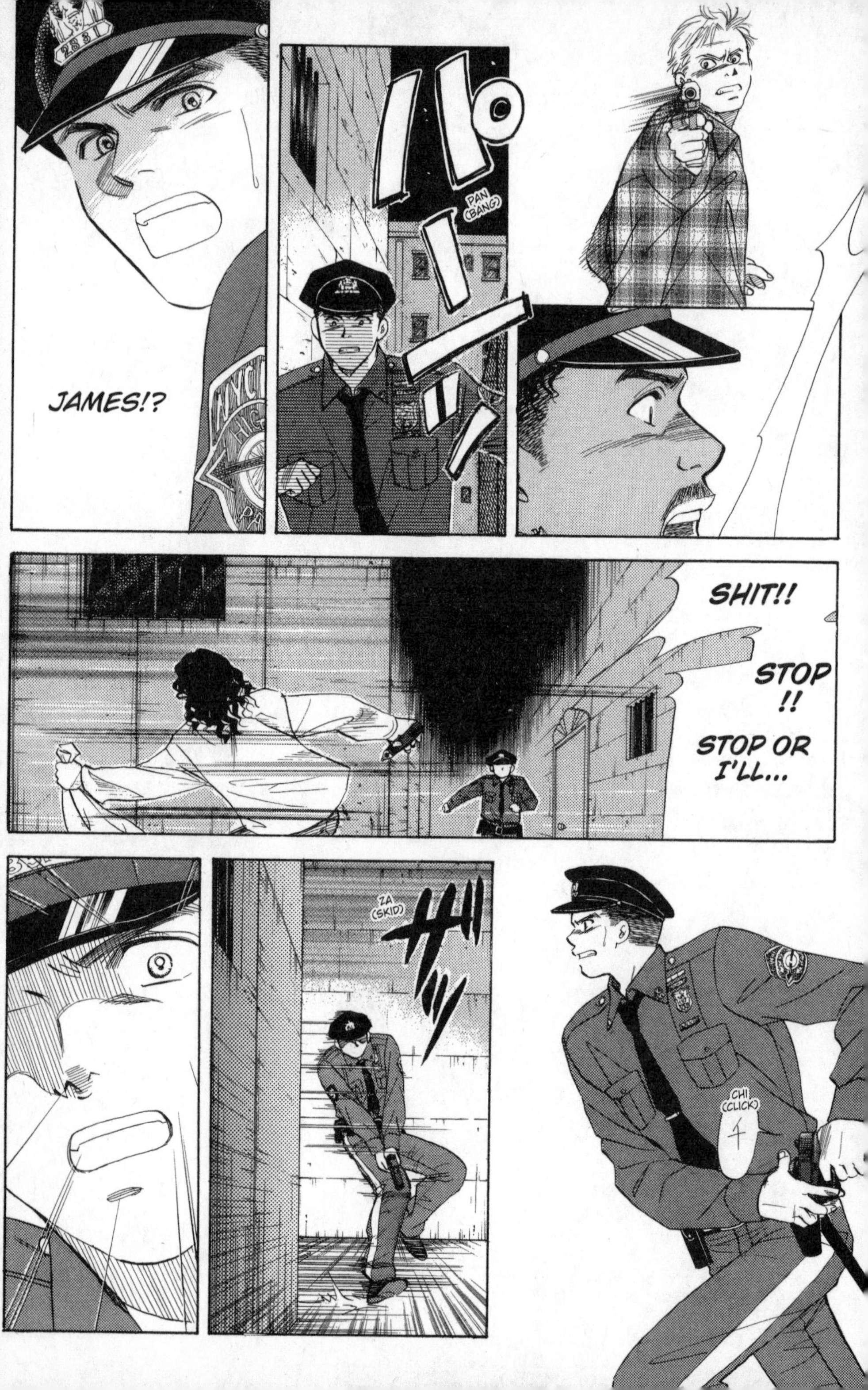
PAN (BANG)
JAMES!?
SHIT!!
STOP !!
STOP OR I'LL...
CHI (CLICK)
ZA (SKID)

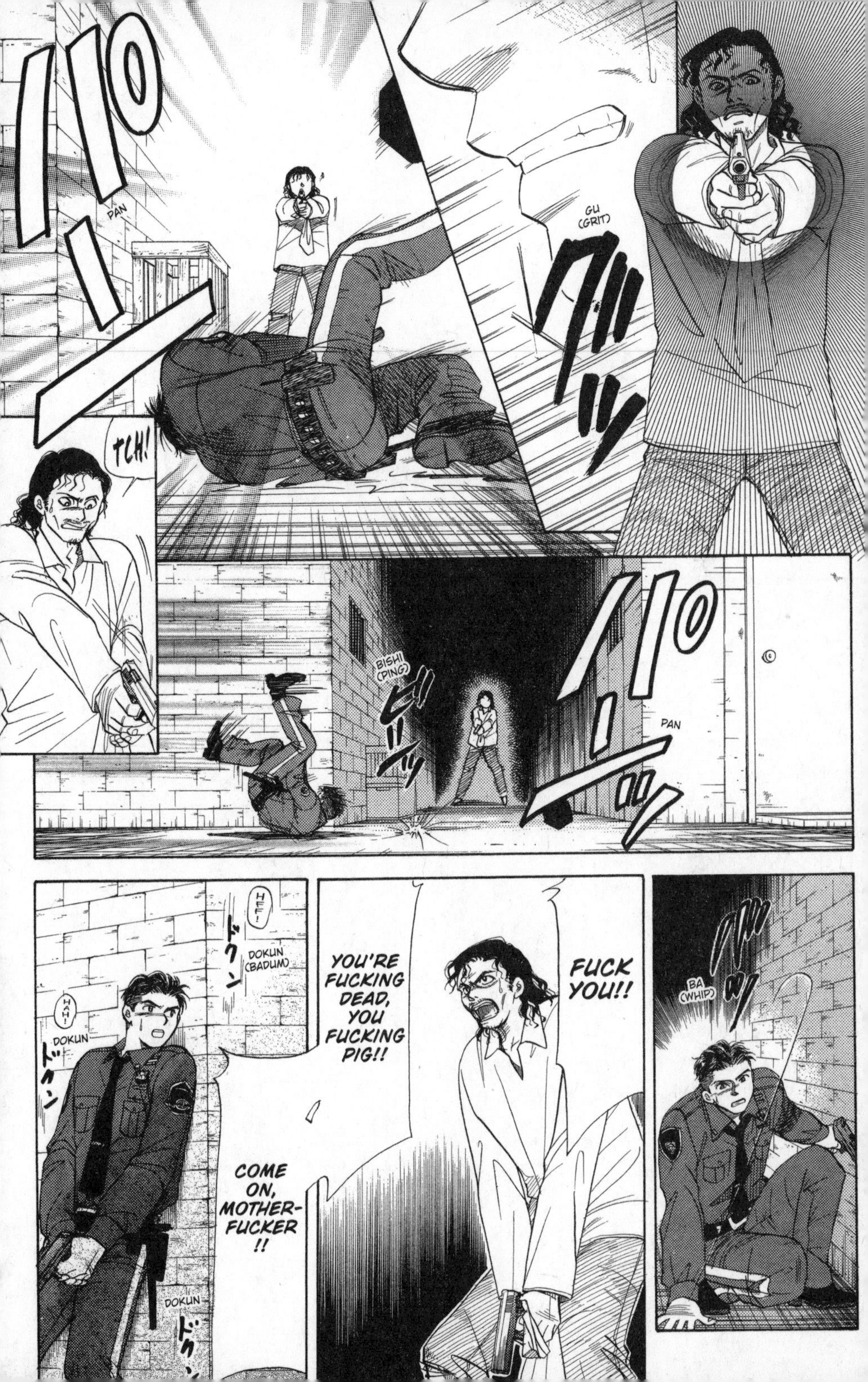
GU
(GRIT)
PAN
TCH!
PAN
BISHI
(PING)
BA
(WHIP)
FUCK
YOU!!
YOU'RE
FUCKING
DEAD,
YOU
FUCKING
PIG!!
COME
ON,
MOTHER-
FUCKER
!!
HEF!
DOKUN
(BADUM)
HAH!
DOKUN
DOKUN

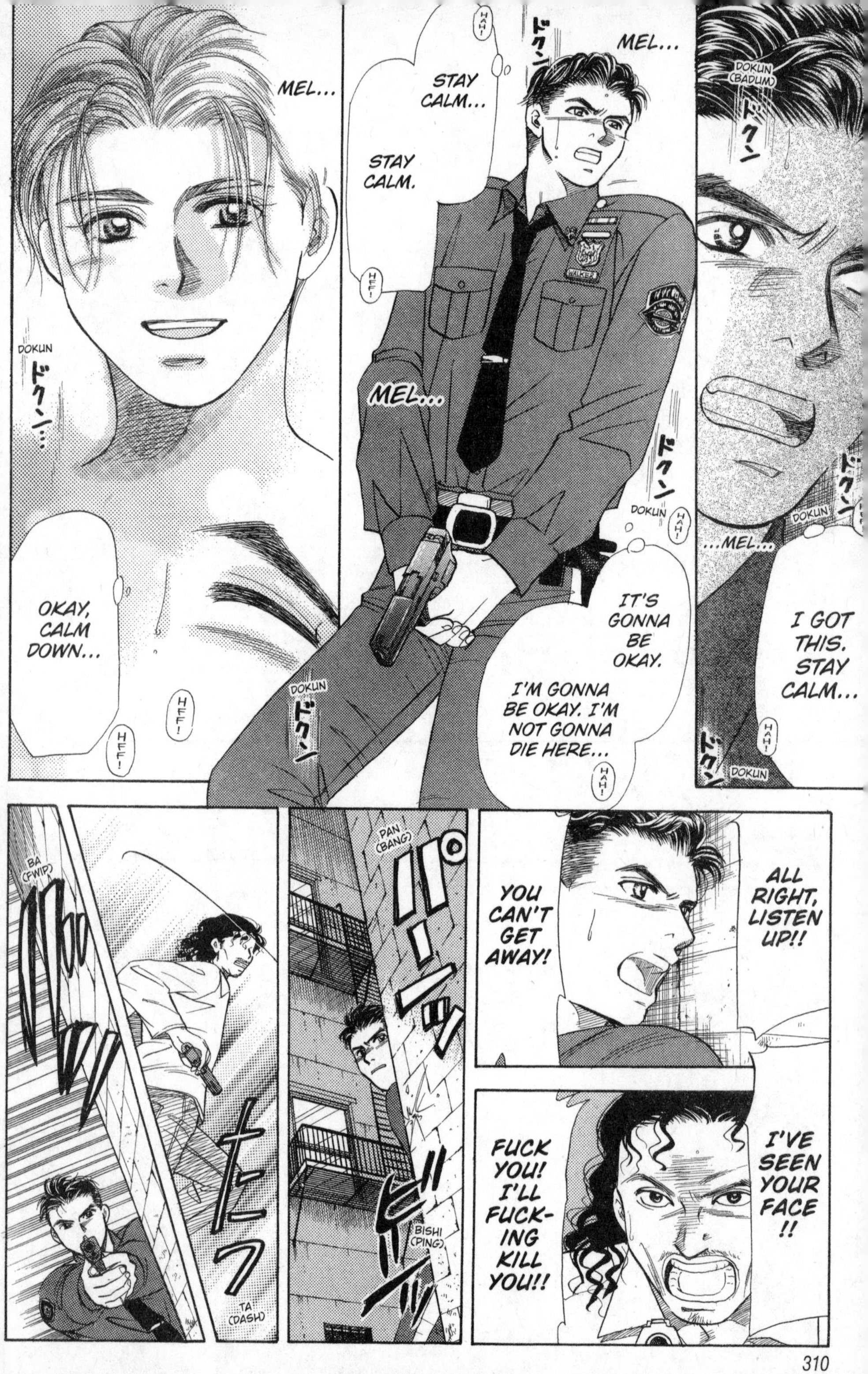
DOKUN (BADUM)
...MEL...
DOKUN
I GOT THIS. STAY CALM...
HAH!
DOKUN
MEL...
HAH!
STAY CALM...
STAY CALM.
HFF!
MEL...
DOKUN
HAH!
IT'S GONNA BE OKAY.
I'M GONNA BE OKAY. I'M NOT GONNA DIE HERE...
HAH!
DOKUN
MEL...
DOKUN
OKAY, CALM DOWN...
HFF!
HFF!
ALL RIGHT, LISTEN UP!!
YOU CAN'T GET AWAY!
I'VE SEEN YOUR FACE!!
FUCK YOU! I'LL FUCK-ING KILL YOU!!
PAN (BANG)
BISHI (PING)
BA (FWIP)
TA (DASH)

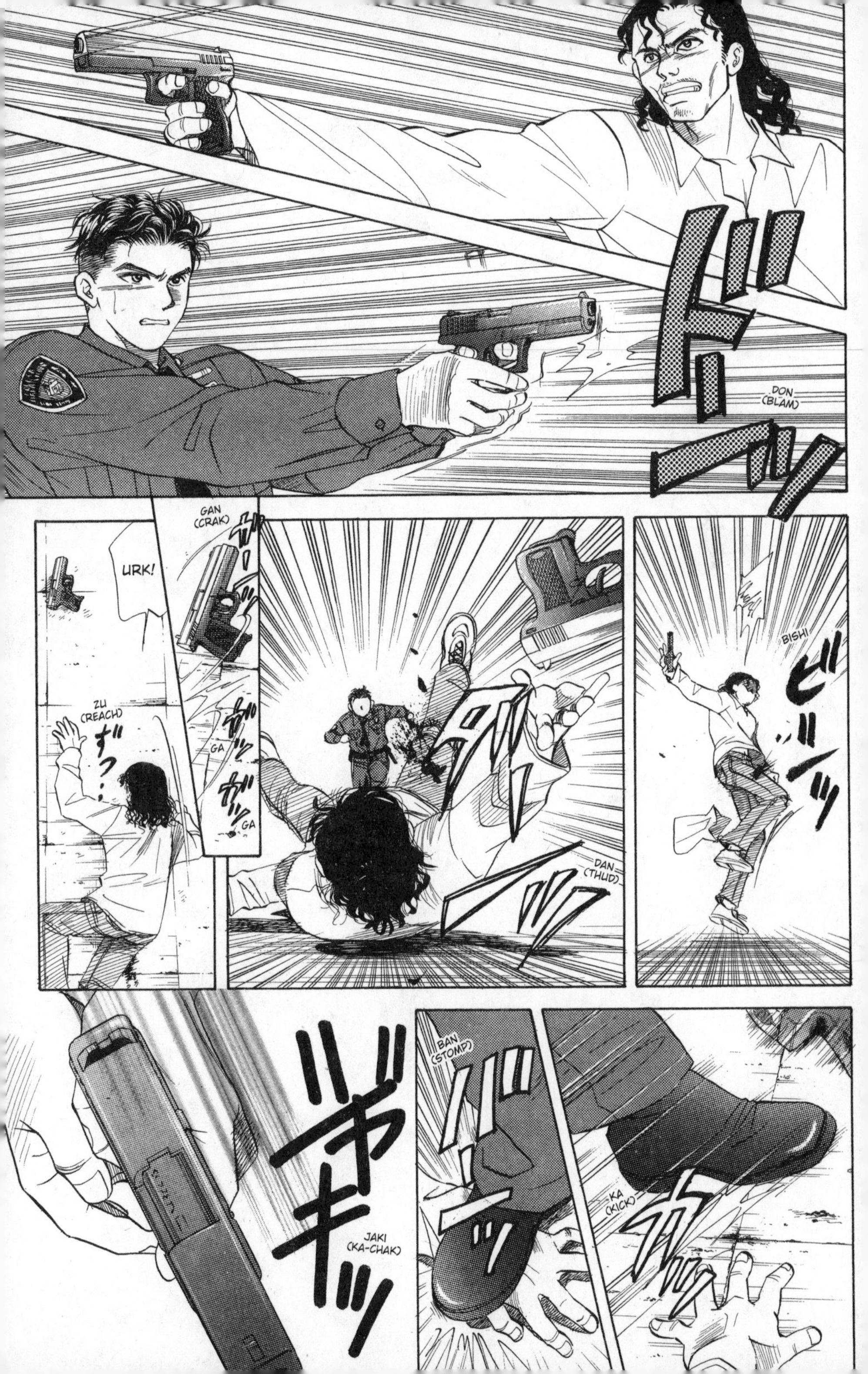
DON (BLAM)
BISHI
DAN (THUD)
GAN (CRAK)
URK!
GA
GA
ZU (REACH)
KA (KICK)
BAN (STOMP)
JAKI (KA-CHAK)

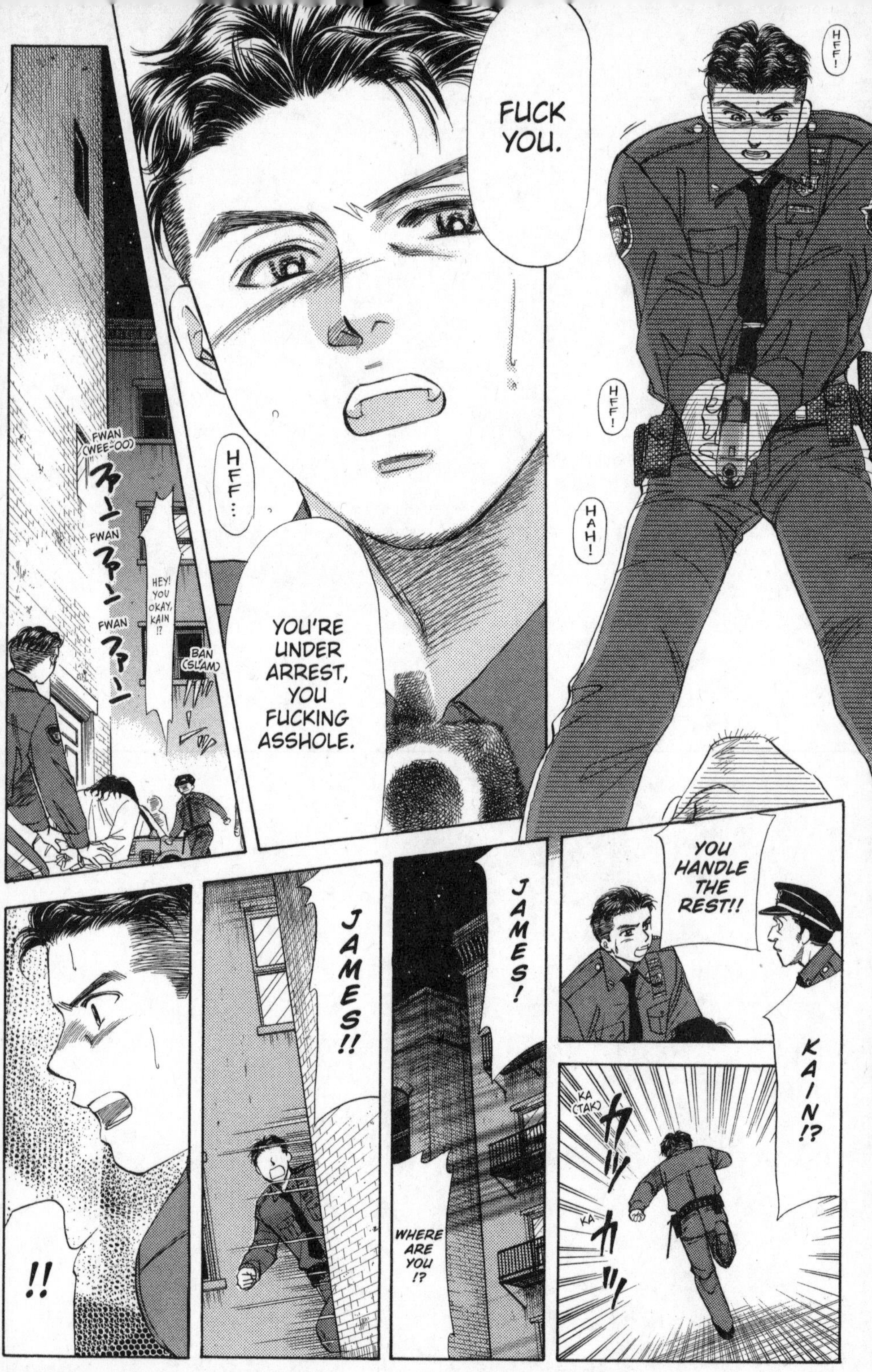
HFF!
HFF!
HAH!
FUCK YOU.
HFF...
YOU'RE UNDER ARREST, YOU FUCKING ASSHOLE.
FWAN (WEE-OO)
FWAN
FWAN
HEY! YOU OKAY, KAIN!?
BAN (SLAM)
YOU HANDLE THE REST!!
KAIN!?
KA (TAK)
KA
JAMES!
WHERE ARE YOU!?
JAMES!!
!!

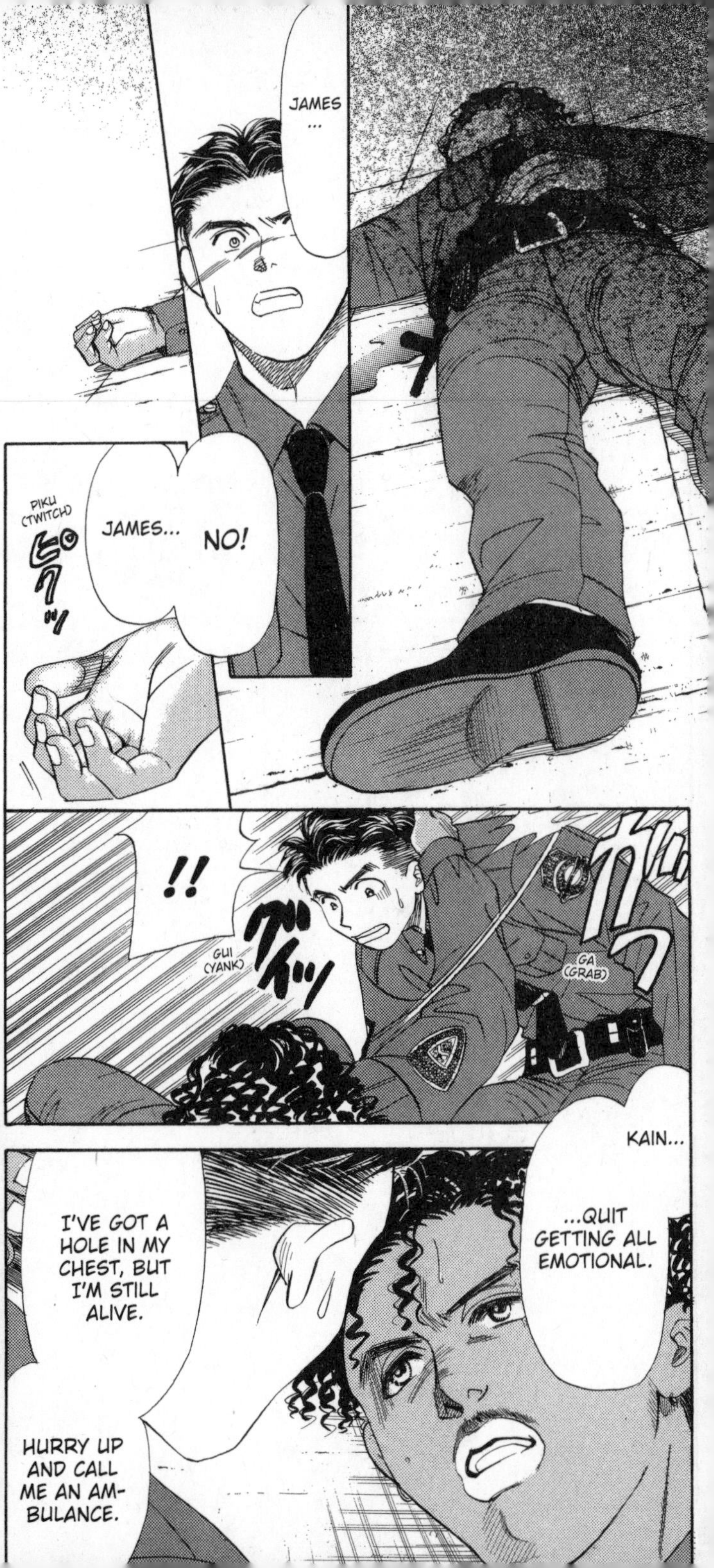
JAMES ...
NO!
JAMES...
PIKU (TWITCH)
GA (GRAB)
!!
GUI (YANK)
KAIN...
...QUIT GETTING ALL EMOTIONAL.
I'VE GOT A HOLE IN MY CHEST, BUT I'M STILL ALIVE.
HURRY UP AND CALL ME AN AM-BULANCE.
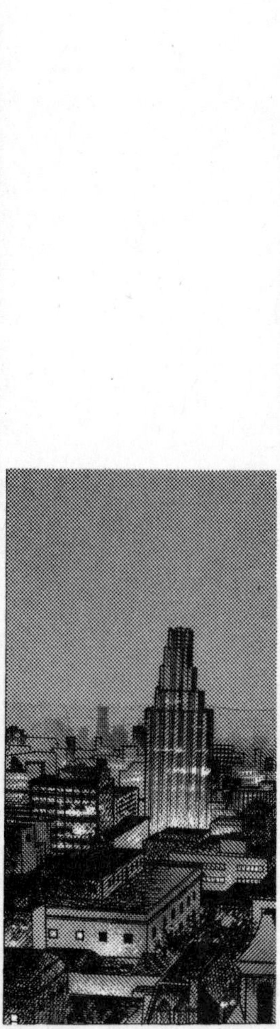

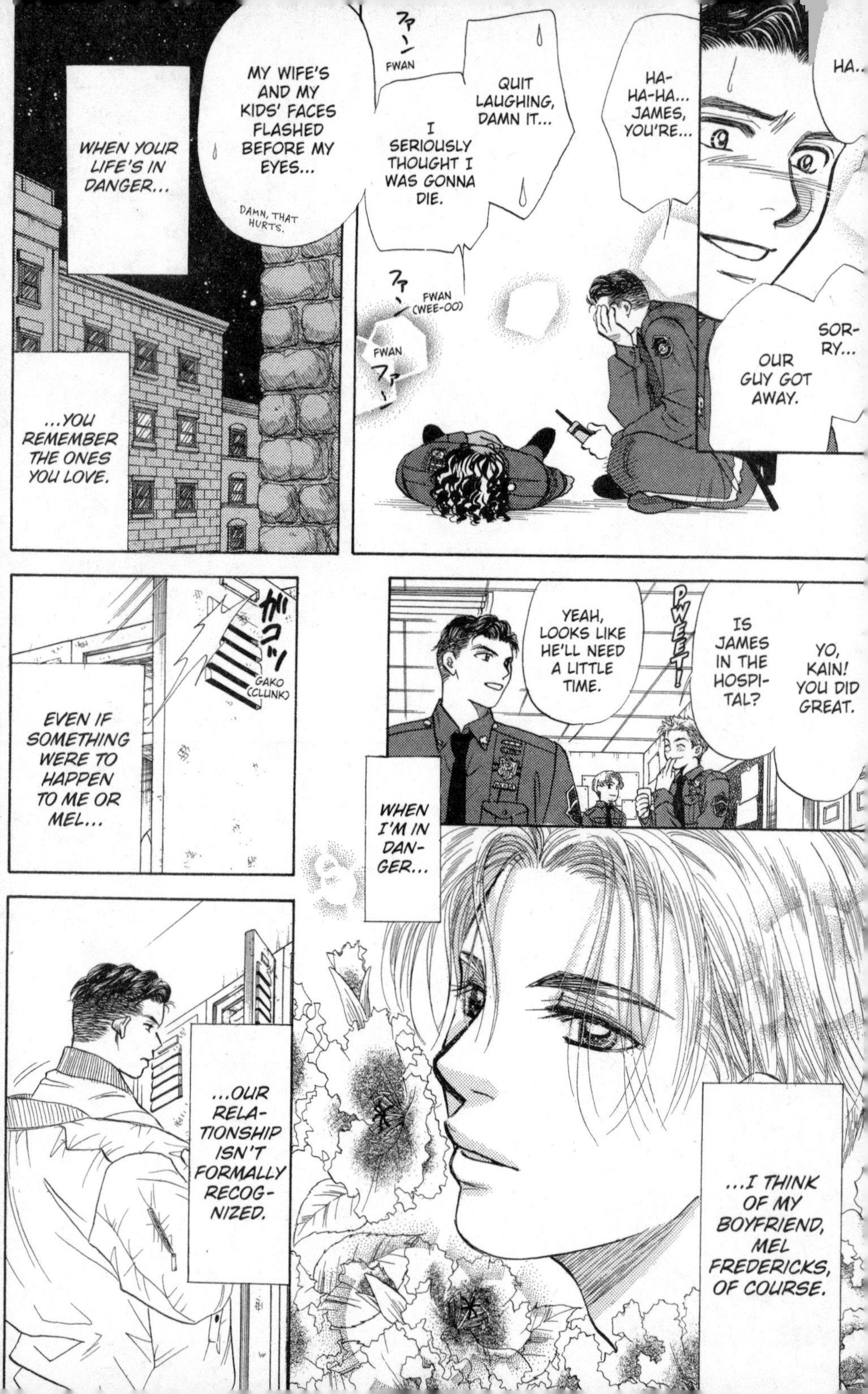
HA..
SORRY...
OUR GUY GOT AWAY.
ファン
FWAN
HA-HA-HA... JAMES, YOU'RE...
QUIT LAUGHING, DAMN IT...
I SERIOUSLY THOUGHT I WAS GONNA DIE.
ファン
FWAN (WEE-OO)
FWAN
ファン
MY WIFE'S AND MY KIDS' FACES FLASHED BEFORE MY EYES...
DAMN, THAT HURTS.
WHEN YOUR LIFE'S IN DANGER...
...YOU REMEMBER THE ONES YOU LOVE.
YO, KAIN! YOU DID GREAT.
IS JAMES IN THE HOSPITAL?
PWEET!
YEAH, LOOKS LIKE HE'LL NEED A LITTLE TIME.
WHEN I'M IN DANGER...
...I THINK OF MY BOYFRIEND, MEL FREDERICKS, OF COURSE.
ガコッ
GAKO (CLUNK)
EVEN IF SOMETHING WERE TO HAPPEN TO ME OR MEL...
...OUR RELATIONSHIP ISN'T FORMALLY RECOGNIZED.

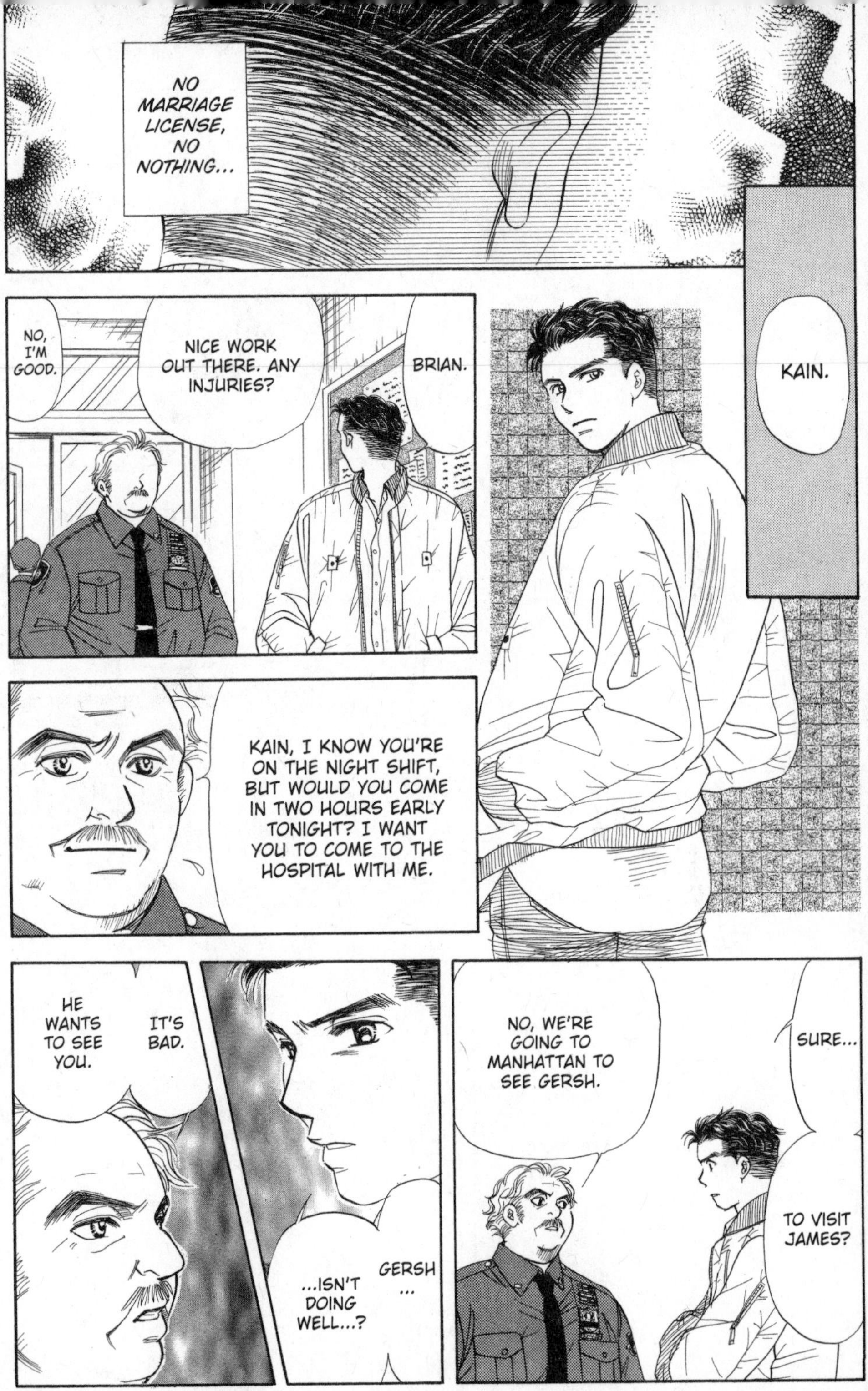
NO MARRIAGE LICENSE, NO NOTHING...
KAIN.
BRIAN.
NICE WORK OUT THERE. ANY INJURIES?
NO, I'M GOOD.
KAIN, I KNOW YOU'RE ON THE NIGHT SHIFT, BUT WOULD YOU COME IN TWO HOURS EARLY TONIGHT? I WANT YOU TO COME TO THE HOSPITAL WITH ME.
SURE...
TO VISIT JAMES?
NO, WE'RE GOING TO MANHATTAN TO SEE GERSH.
GERSH...
...ISN'T DOING WELL...?
IT'S BAD.
HE WANTS TO SEE YOU.

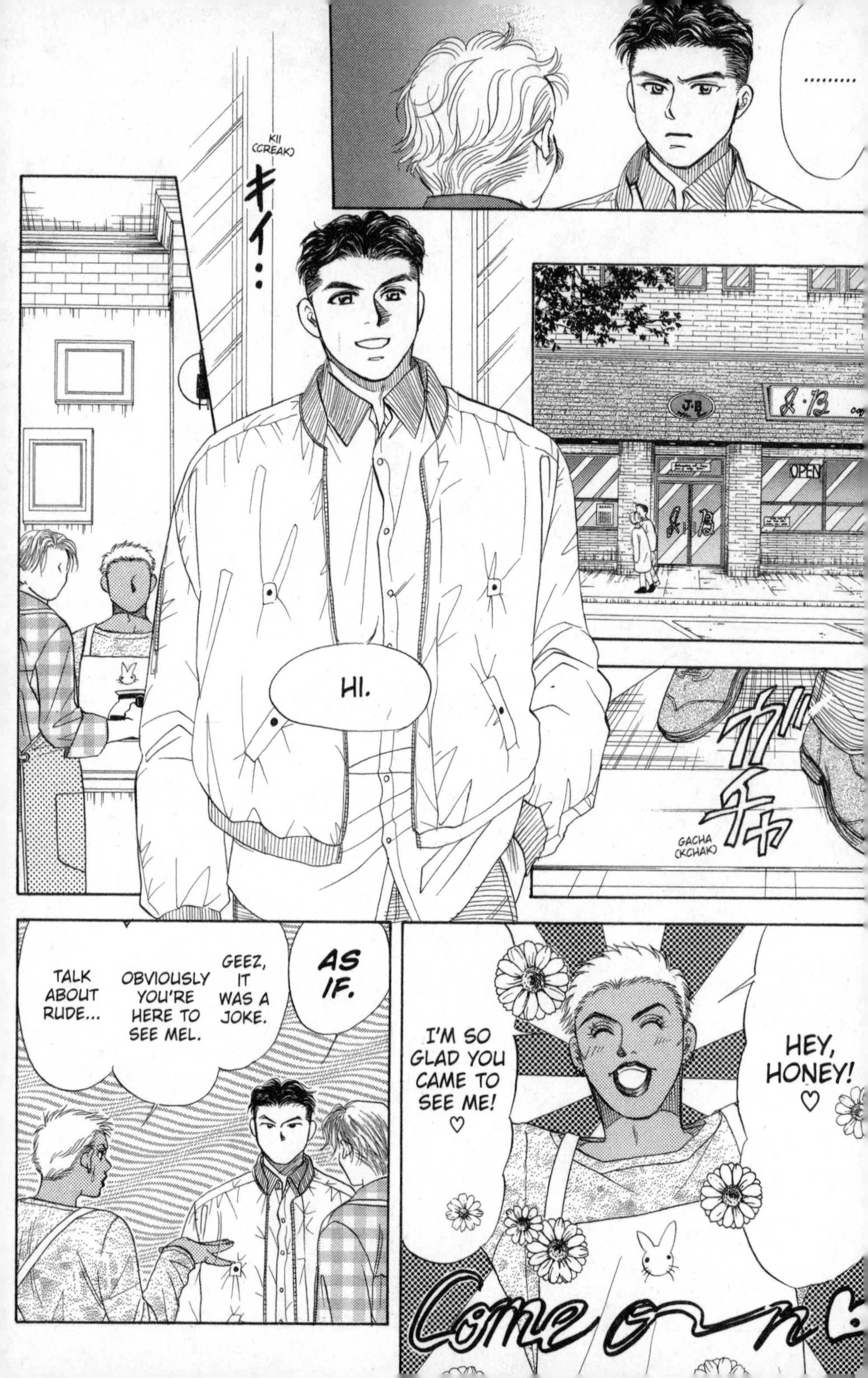

....
ガチャ
GACHA (KCHAK)
KII (CREAK)
キイ・・
HI.
HEY, HONEY! ♡
I'M SO GLAD YOU CAME TO SEE ME! ♡
Come on
AS IF.
GEEZ, IT WAS A JOKE.
OBVIOUSLY YOU'RE HERE TO SEE MEL.
TALK ABOUT RUDE...

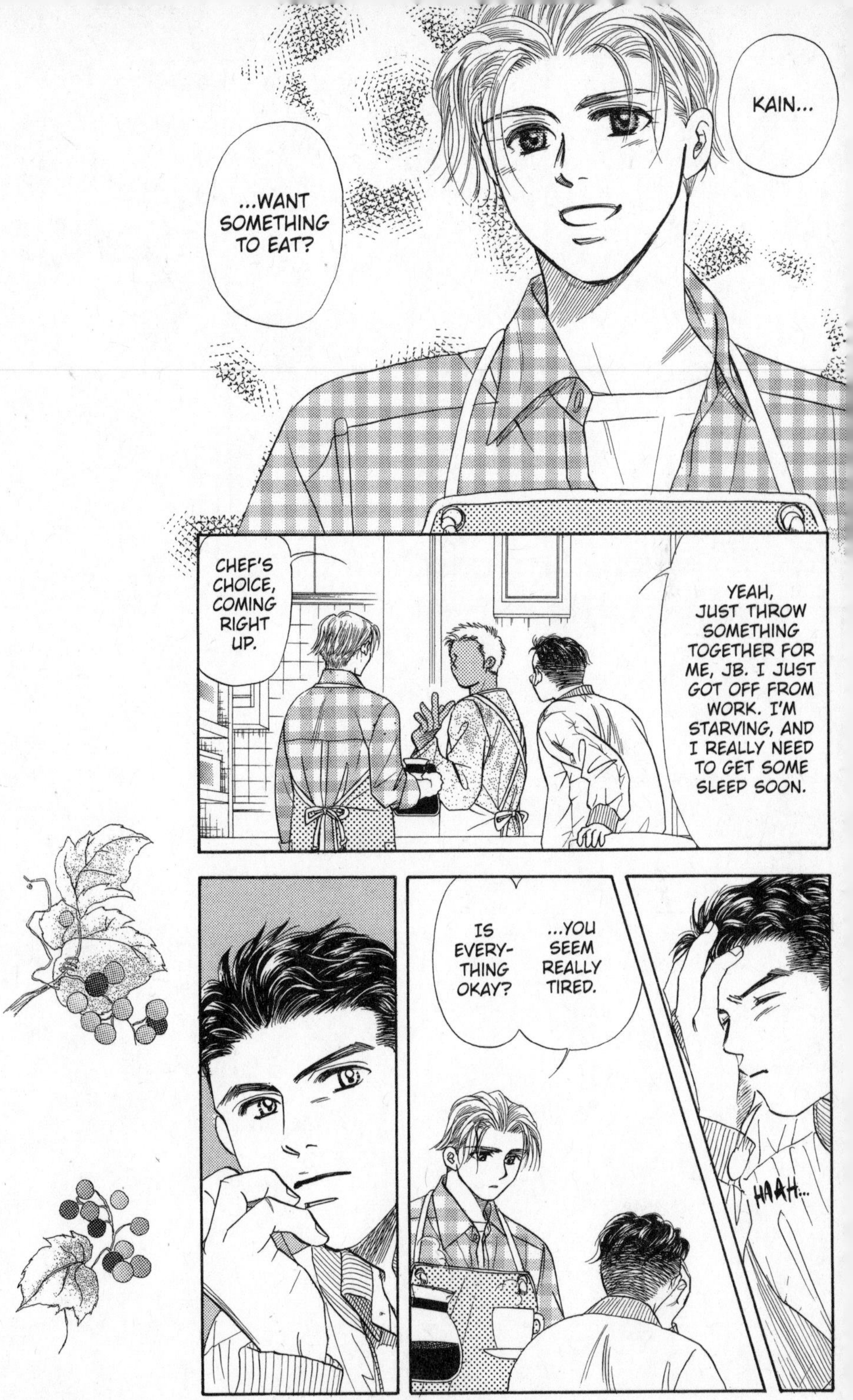
KAIN...
...WANT SOMETHING TO EAT?
YEAH, JUST THROW SOMETHING TOGETHER FOR ME, JB. I JUST GOT OFF FROM WORK. I'M STARVING, AND I REALLY NEED TO GET SOME SLEEP SOON.
CHEF'S CHOICE, COMING RIGHT UP.
HAAH...
...YOU SEEM REALLY TIRED.
IS EVERY-THING OKAY?

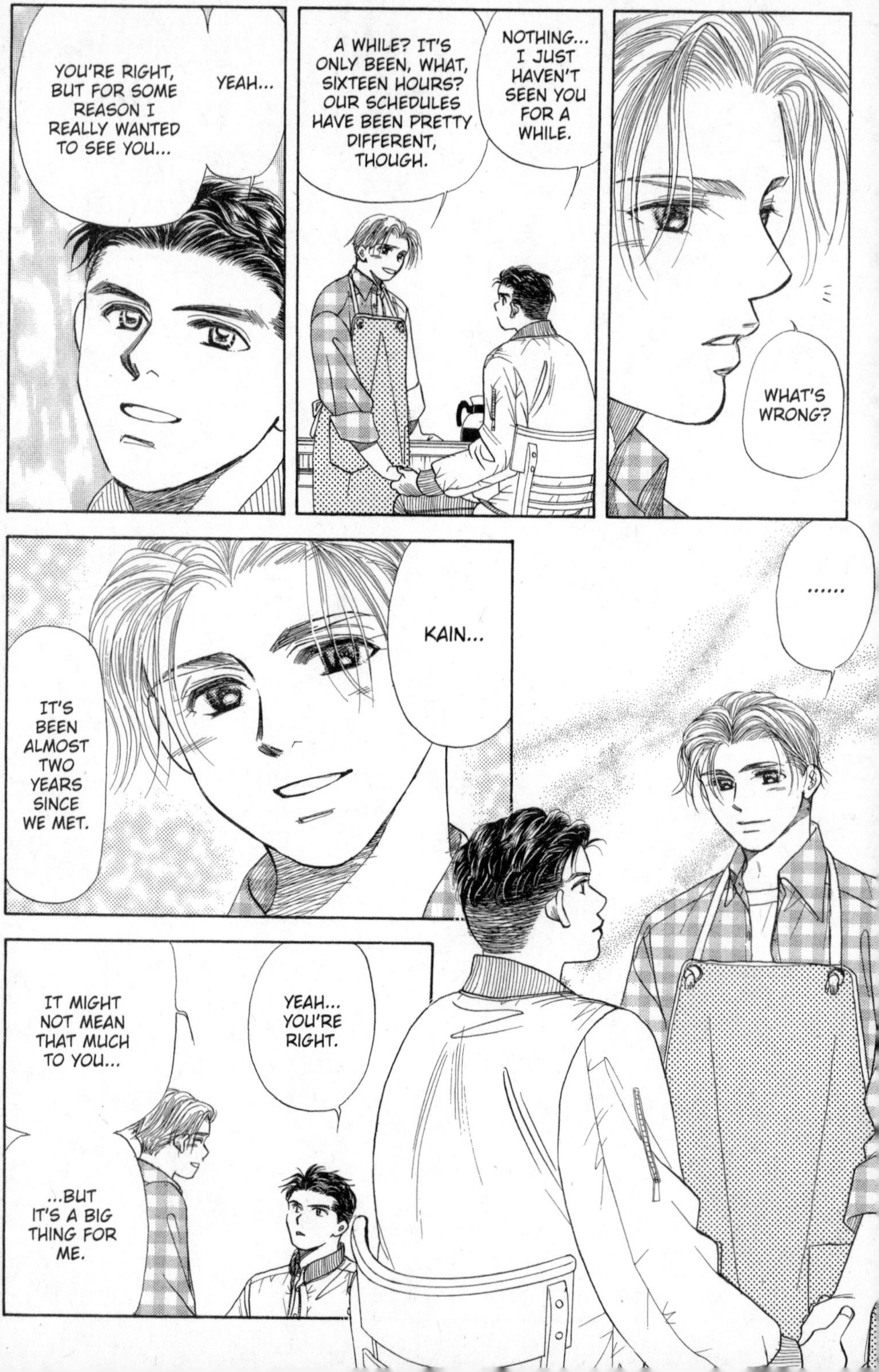
WHAT'S WRONG?
NOTHING... I JUST HAVEN'T SEEN YOU FOR A WHILE.
A WHILE? IT'S ONLY BEEN, WHAT, SIXTEEN HOURS? OUR SCHEDULES HAVE BEEN PRETTY DIFFERENT, THOUGH.
YEAH...
YOU'RE RIGHT, BUT FOR SOME REASON I REALLY WANTED TO SEE YOU...
......
KAIN...
IT'S BEEN ALMOST TWO YEARS SINCE WE MET.
YEAH... YOU'RE RIGHT.
IT MIGHT NOT MEAN THAT MUCH TO YOU...
...BUT IT'S A BIG THING FOR ME.

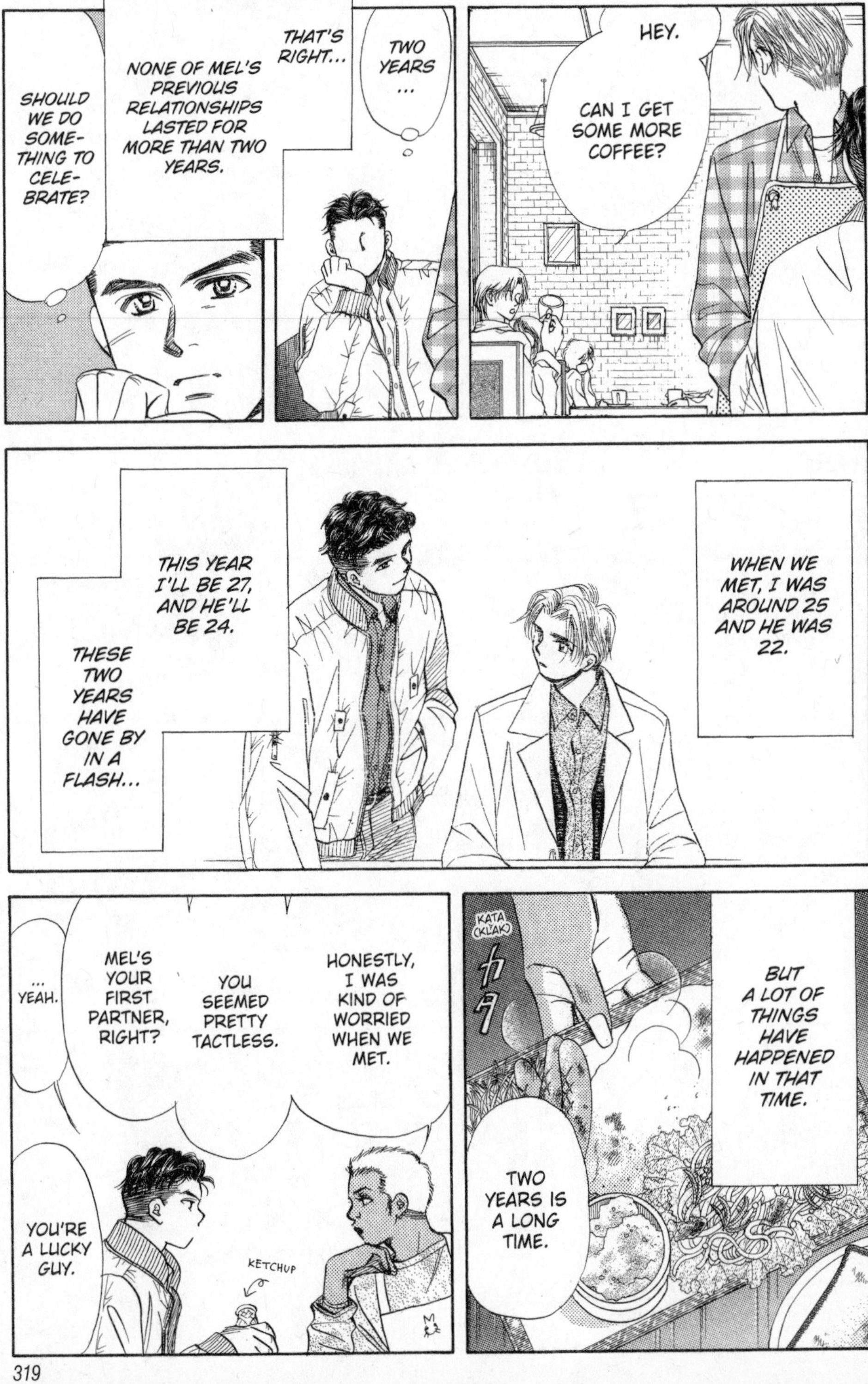
HEY.
CAN I GET SOME MORE COFFEE?
TWO YEARS ...
THAT'S RIGHT...
NONE OF MEL'S PREVIOUS RELATIONSHIPS LASTED FOR MORE THAN TWO YEARS.
SHOULD WE DO SOME-THING TO CELE-BRATE?
WHEN WE MET, I WAS AROUND 25 AND HE WAS 22.
THIS YEAR I'LL BE 27, AND HE'LL BE 24.
THESE TWO YEARS HAVE GONE BY IN A FLASH...
KATA (KLAK)
カタ
BUT A LOT OF THINGS HAVE HAPPENED IN THAT TIME.
TWO YEARS IS A LONG TIME.
HONESTLY, I WAS KIND OF WORRIED WHEN WE MET.
YOU SEEMED PRETTY TACTLESS.
MEL'S YOUR FIRST PARTNER, RIGHT?
... YEAH.
YOU'RE A LUCKY GUY.
KETCHUP

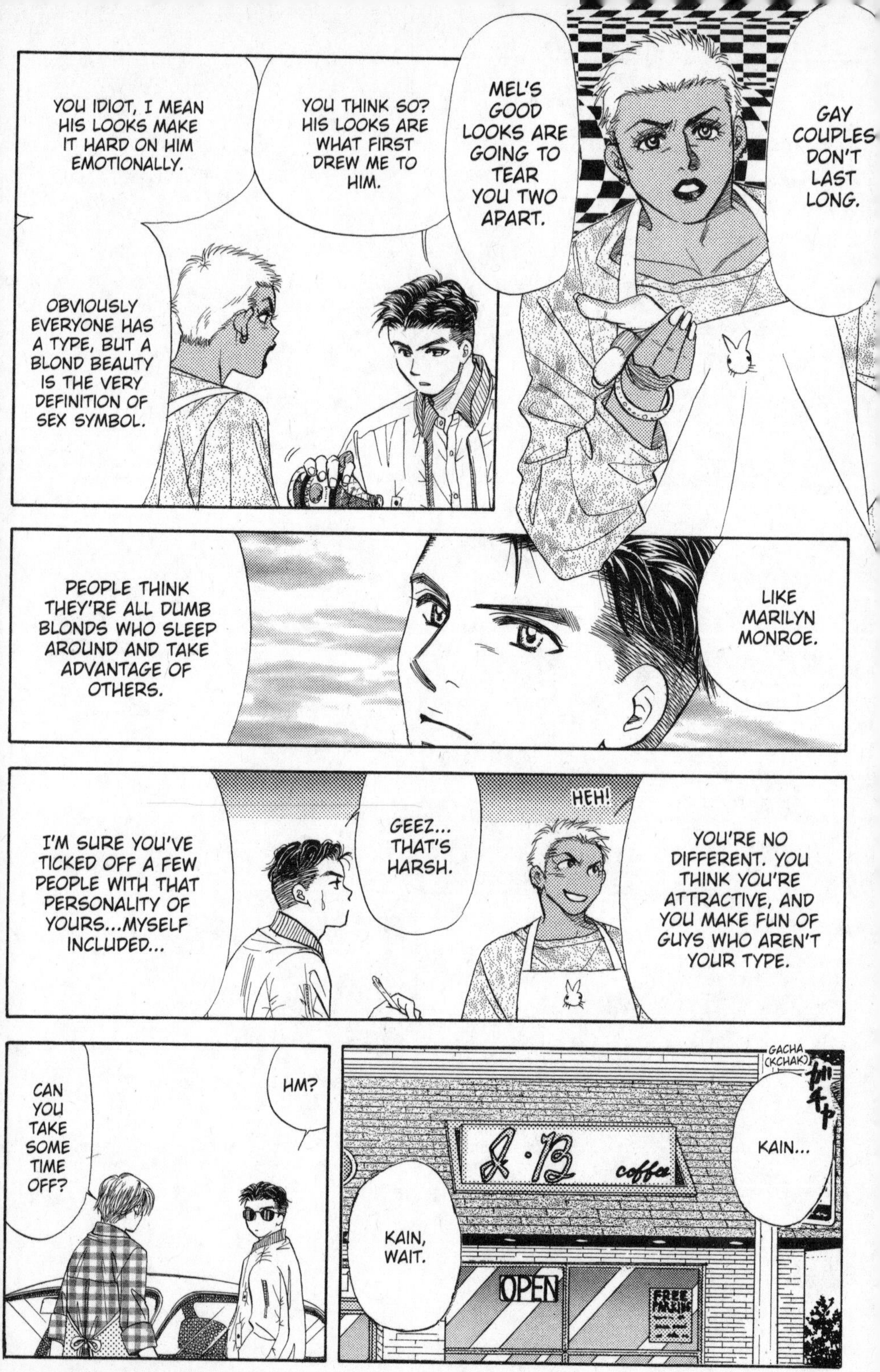
GAY COUPLES DON'T LAST LONG.
MEL'S GOOD LOOKS ARE GOING TO TEAR YOU TWO APART.
YOU THINK SO? HIS LOOKS ARE WHAT FIRST DREW ME TO HIM.
YOU IDIOT, I MEAN HIS LOOKS MAKE IT HARD ON HIM EMOTIONALLY.
OBVIOUSLY EVERYONE HAS A TYPE, BUT A BLOND BEAUTY IS THE VERY DEFINITION OF SEX SYMBOL.
LIKE MARILYN MONROE.
PEOPLE THINK THEY'RE ALL DUMB BLONDS WHO SLEEP AROUND AND TAKE ADVANTAGE OF OTHERS.
HEH!
YOU'RE NO DIFFERENT. YOU THINK YOU'RE ATTRACTIVE, AND YOU MAKE FUN OF GUYS WHO AREN'T YOUR TYPE.
GEEZ... THAT'S HARSH.
I'M SURE YOU'VE TICKED OFF A FEW PEOPLE WITH THAT PERSONALITY OF YOURS...MYSELF INCLUDED...
GACHA (KCHAK)
ガチャ
KAIN...
coffee
OPEN
FREE PARKING
KAIN, WAIT.
HM?
CAN YOU TAKE SOME TIME OFF?

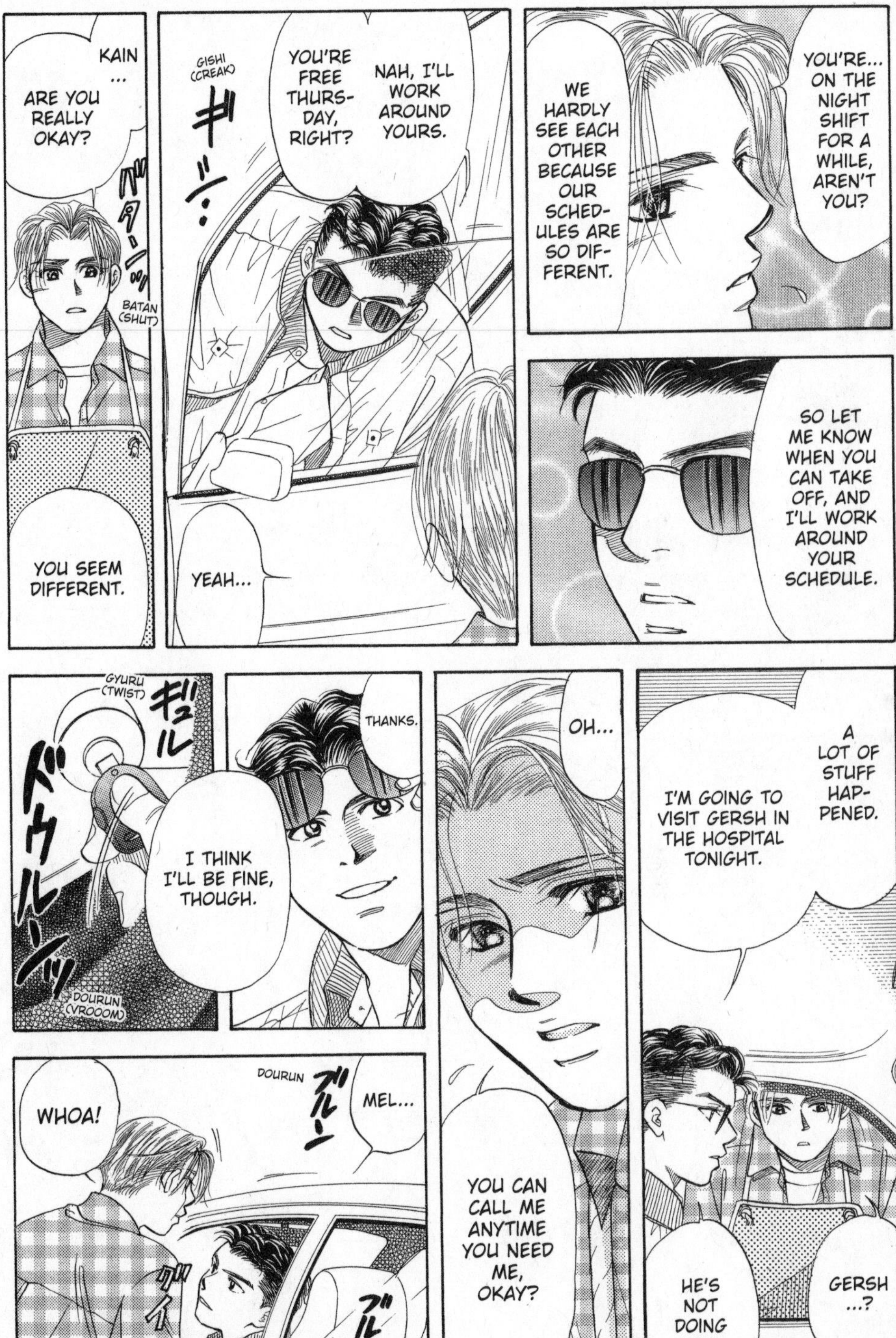
YOU'RE... ON THE NIGHT SHIFT FOR A WHILE, AREN'T YOU?
WE HARDLY SEE EACH OTHER BECAUSE OUR SCHED-ULES ARE SO DIF-FERENT.
SO LET ME KNOW WHEN YOU CAN TAKE OFF, AND I'LL WORK AROUND YOUR SCHEDULE.
NAH, I'LL WORK AROUND YOURS.
YOU'RE FREE THURS-DAY, RIGHT?
GISHI (CREAK)
YEAH...
KAIN ...
ARE YOU REALLY OKAY?
BATAN (SHUT)
YOU SEEM DIFFERENT.
A LOT OF STUFF HAP-PENED.
I'M GOING TO VISIT GERSH IN THE HOSPITAL TONIGHT.
GERSH ...?
HE'S NOT DOING WELL.
OH...
YOU CAN CALL ME ANYTIME YOU NEED ME, OKAY?
THANKS.
I THINK I'LL BE FINE, THOUGH.
GYURU (TWIST)
DOURUN (VROOOM)
DOURUN
MEL...
WHOA!
GUI (TUG)
DOURUN

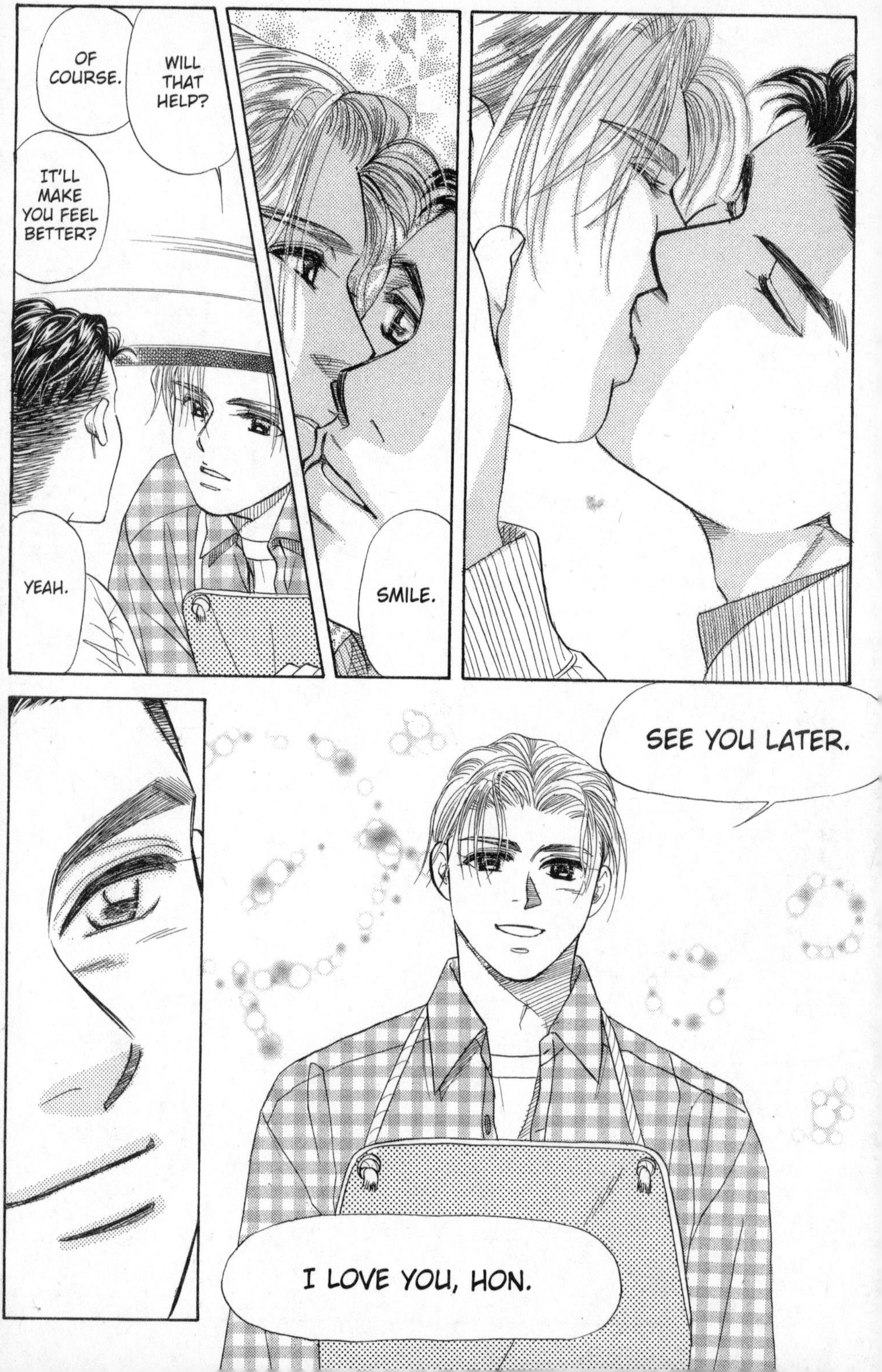
SMILE.
WILL THAT HELP?
OF COURSE.
IT'LL MAKE YOU FEEL BETTER?
YEAH.
SEE YOU LATER.
I LOVE YOU, HON.

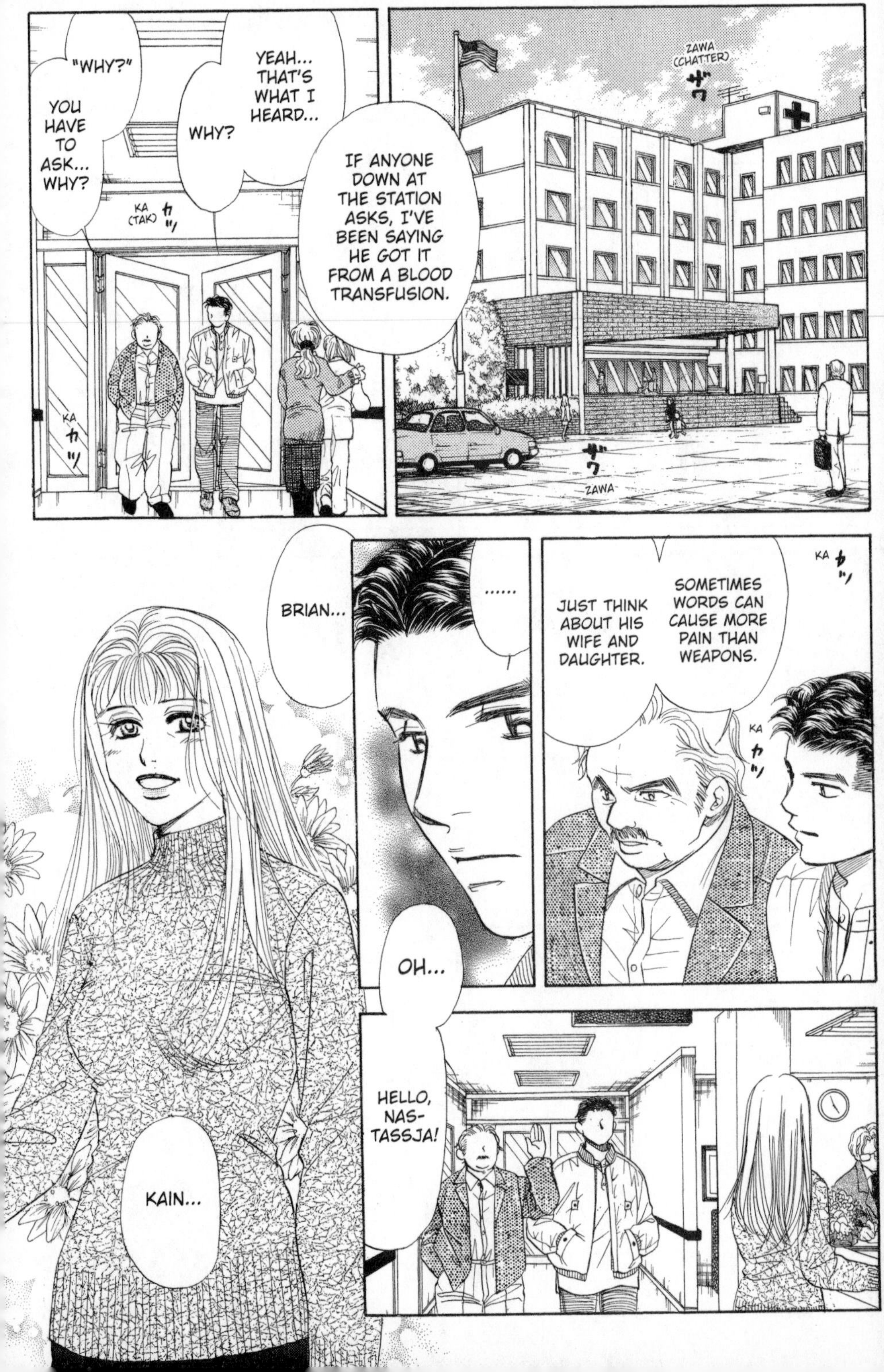
ZAWA (CHATTER)
ザワ
ザワ
ZAWA
IF ANYONE DOWN AT THE STATION ASKS, I'VE BEEN SAYING HE GOT IT FROM A BLOOD TRANSFUSION.
YEAH... THAT'S WHAT I HEARD...
WHY?
"WHY?"
YOU HAVE TO ASK... WHY?
KA (TAK) カツ
KA カツ
KA カツ
SOMETIMES WORDS CAN CAUSE MORE PAIN THAN WEAPONS.
JUST THINK ABOUT HIS WIFE AND DAUGHTER.
KA カツ
......
OH...
HELLO, NAS-TASSJA!
BRIAN...
KAIN...

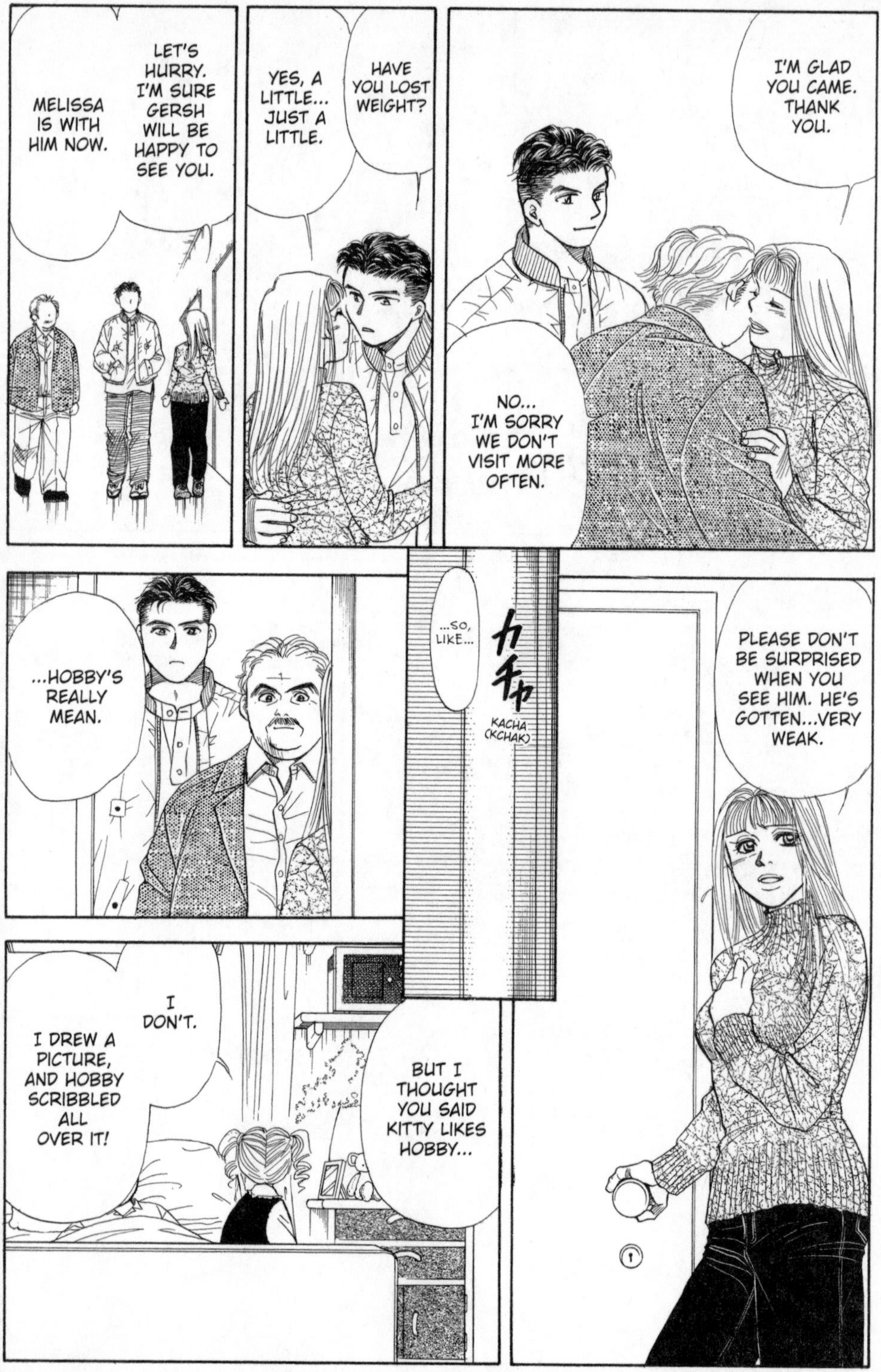
I'M GLAD YOU CAME. THANK YOU.
NO... I'M SORRY WE DON'T VISIT MORE OFTEN.
HAVE YOU LOST WEIGHT?
YES, A LITTLE... JUST A LITTLE.
LET'S HURRY. I'M SURE GERSH WILL BE HAPPY TO SEE YOU.
MELISSA IS WITH HIM NOW.
PLEASE DON'T BE SURPRISED WHEN YOU SEE HIM. HE'S GOTTEN...VERY WEAK.
カチャ
KACHA (KCHAK)
...SO, LIKE...
...HOBBY'S REALLY MEAN.
BUT I THOUGHT YOU SAID KITTY LIKES HOBBY...
I DON'T.
I DREW A PICTURE, AND HOBBY SCRIBBLED ALL OVER IT!

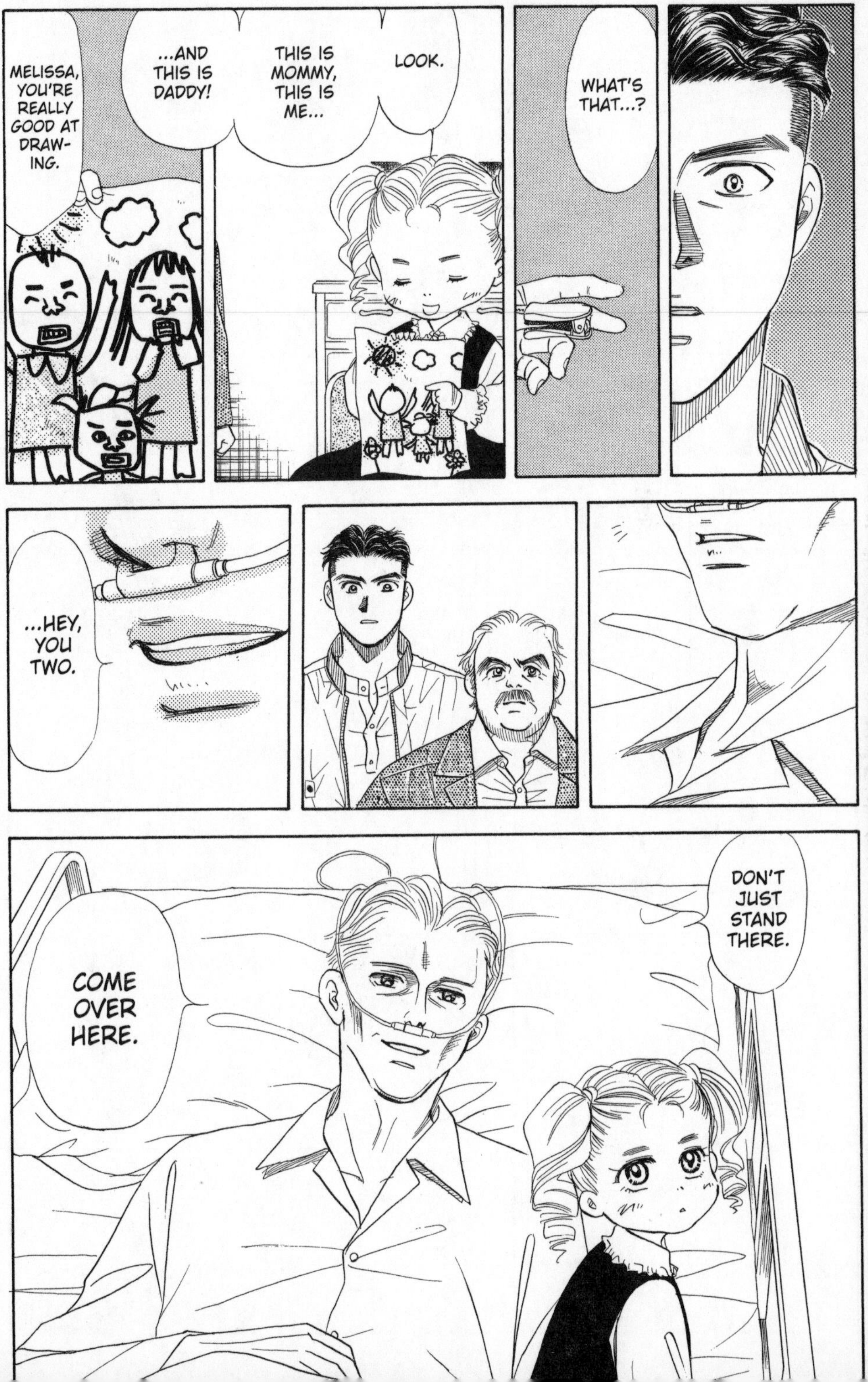
WHAT'S THAT...?
LOOK.
THIS IS MOMMY, THIS IS ME...
...AND THIS IS DADDY!
MELISSA, YOU'RE REALLY GOOD AT DRAW-ING.
...HEY, YOU TWO.
DON'T JUST STAND THERE.
COME OVER HERE.

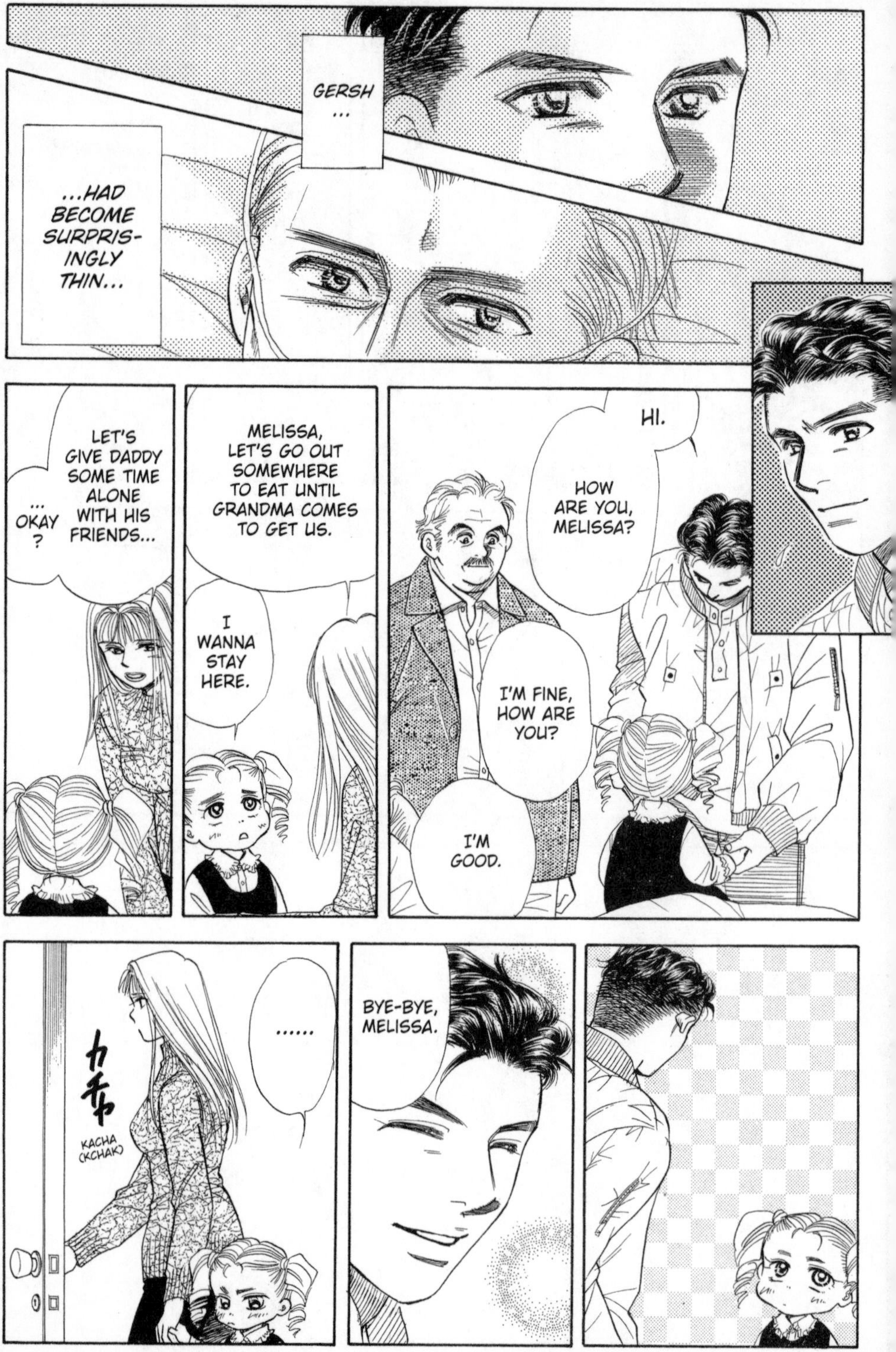
GERSH ...
...HAD BECOME SURPRISINGLY THIN...
HI.
HOW ARE YOU, MELISSA?
I'M FINE, HOW ARE YOU?
I'M GOOD.
MELISSA, LET'S GO OUT SOMEWHERE TO EAT UNTIL GRANDMA COMES TO GET US.
I WANNA STAY HERE.
LET'S GIVE DADDY SOME TIME ALONE WITH HIS FRIENDS...
... OKAY?
BYE-BYE, MELISSA.
......
カチャ
KACHA (KCHAK)

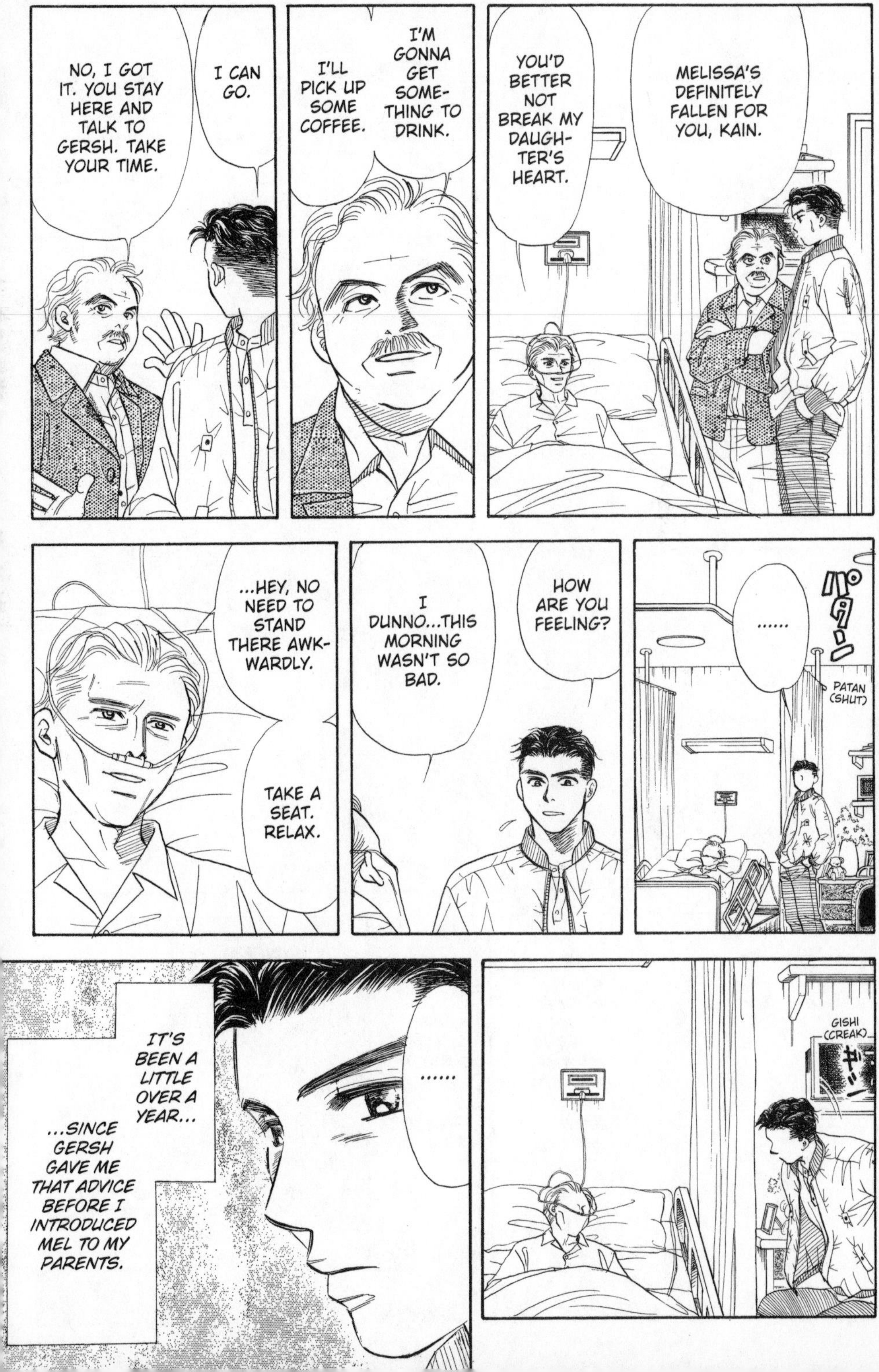
MELISSA'S DEFINITELY FALLEN FOR YOU, KAIN.
YOU'D BETTER NOT BREAK MY DAUGHTER'S HEART.
I'M GONNA GET SOMETHING TO DRINK.
I'LL PICK UP SOME COFFEE.
I CAN GO.
NO, I GOT IT. YOU STAY HERE AND TALK TO GERSH. TAKE YOUR TIME.
......
PATAN (SHUT)
HOW ARE YOU FEELING?
I DUNNO...THIS MORNING WASN'T SO BAD.
...HEY, NO NEED TO STAND THERE AWKWARDLY.
TAKE A SEAT. RELAX.
GISHI (CREAK)
......
IT'S BEEN A LITTLE OVER A YEAR...
...SINCE GERSH GAVE ME THAT ADVICE BEFORE I INTRODUCED MEL TO MY PARENTS.

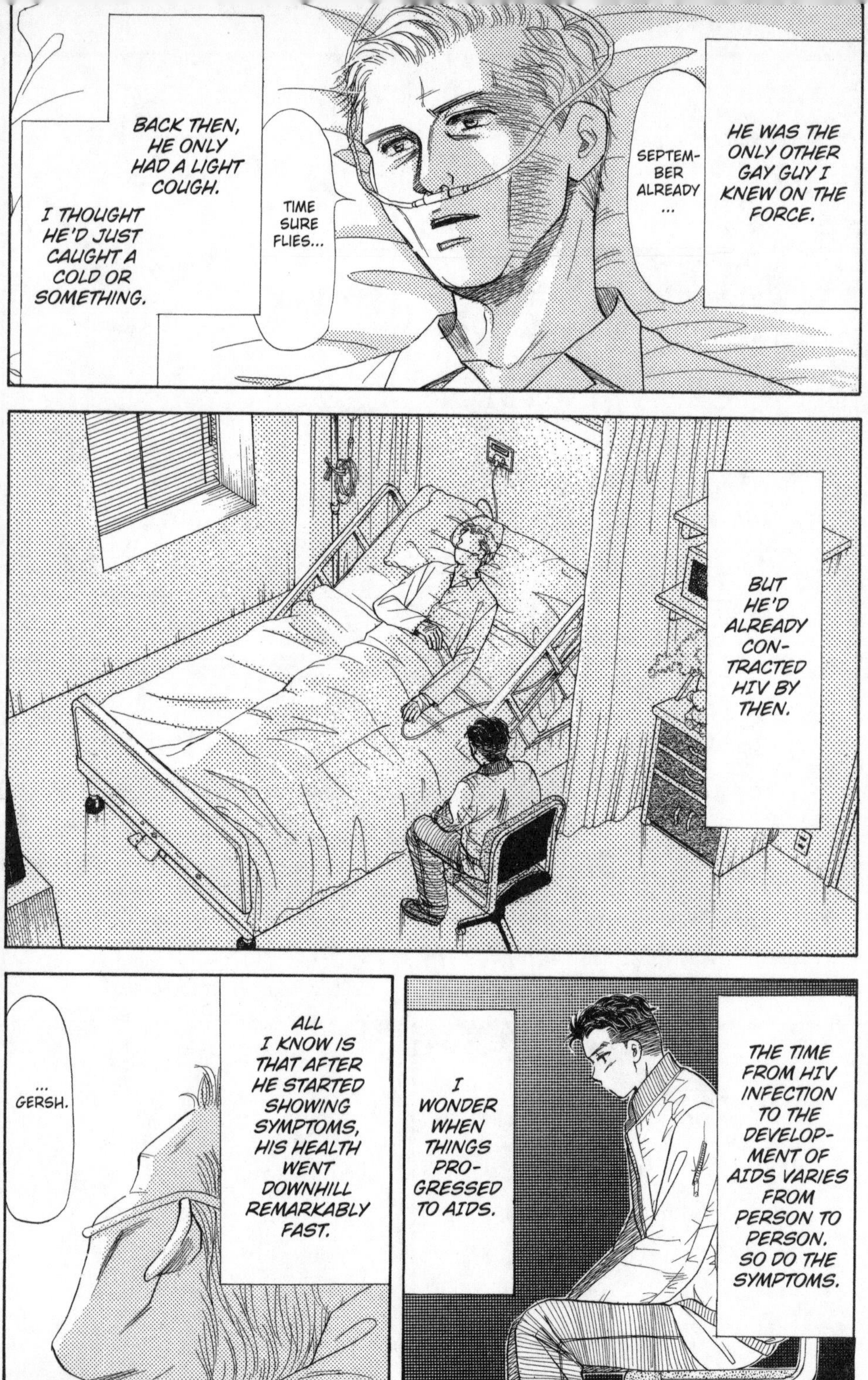
HE WAS THE ONLY OTHER GAY GUY I KNEW ON THE FORCE.
SEPTEMBER ALREADY...
TIME SURE FLIES...
BACK THEN, HE ONLY HAD A LIGHT COUGH.
I THOUGHT HE'D JUST CAUGHT A COLD OR SOMETHING.
BUT HE'D ALREADY CONTRACTED HIV BY THEN.
THE TIME FROM HIV INFECTION TO THE DEVELOPMENT OF AIDS VARIES FROM PERSON TO PERSON. SO DO THE SYMPTOMS.
I WONDER WHEN THINGS PROGRESSED TO AIDS.
ALL I KNOW IS THAT AFTER HE STARTED SHOWING SYMPTOMS, HIS HEALTH WENT DOWNHILL REMARKABLY FAST.
...GERSH.

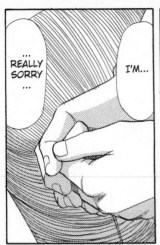

I'M SORRY...
I DON'T KNOW WHAT TO SAY...
I'M...
...REALLY SORRY...
KAIN... THAT'S NOT LIKE YOU.
WHAT HAPPENED TO THE RUDE GUY WITH THE BAD JOKES?
IT'S NICE TO SEE...
...YOUR CYNICAL SARCASM HASN'T CHANGED.
GERSH...
...REMEMBER THAT TIME WHEN I ASKED YOU IF I'D EVER DONE OR SAID SOMETHING HURTFUL TO YOU?
YEAH... I REMEMBER.
YOU DIDN'T GIVE ME AN ANSWER THEN...
...BUT...CAN YOU GIVE ME AN ANSWER NOW...?
GEEZ... KAIN...
...YOU HAVEN'T DONE ANYTHING TO HURT ME.

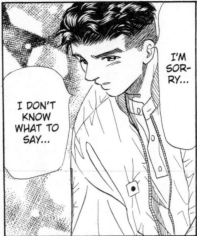

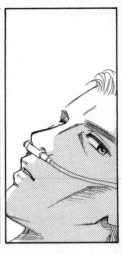

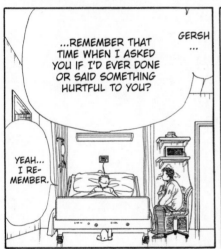

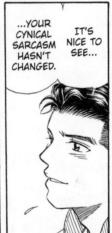

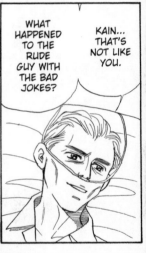

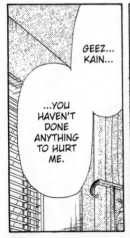

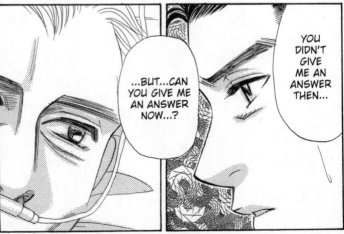

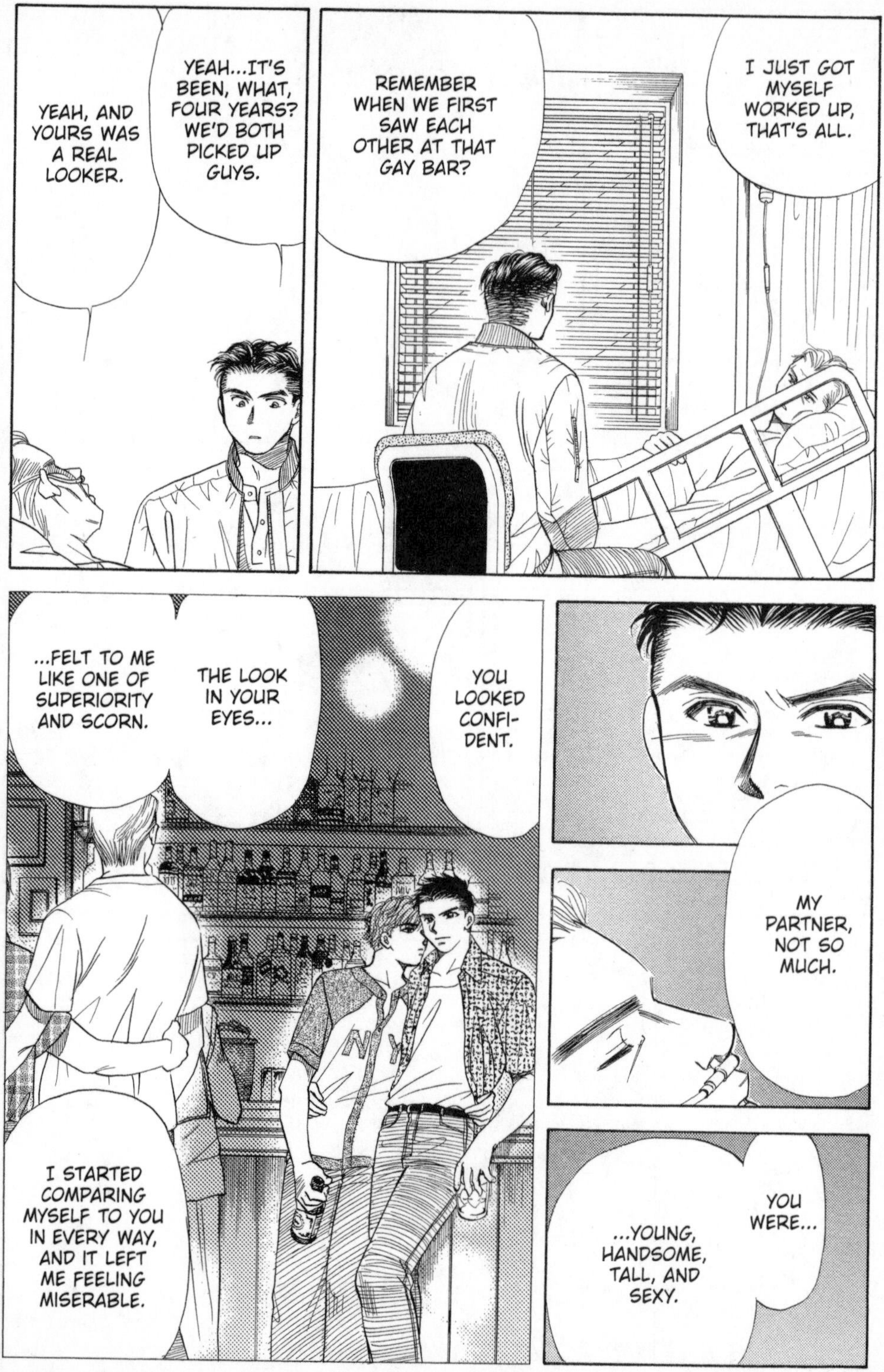
I JUST GOT MYSELF WORKED UP, THAT'S ALL.
REMEMBER WHEN WE FIRST SAW EACH OTHER AT THAT GAY BAR?
YEAH...IT'S BEEN, WHAT, FOUR YEARS? WE'D BOTH PICKED UP GUYS.
YEAH, AND YOURS WAS A REAL LOOKER.
MY PARTNER, NOT SO MUCH.
YOU WERE...
...YOUNG, HANDSOME, TALL, AND SEXY.
YOU LOOKED CONFIDENT.
THE LOOK IN YOUR EYES...
...FELT TO ME LIKE ONE OF SUPERIORITY AND SCORN.
I STARTED COMPARING MYSELF TO YOU IN EVERY WAY, AND IT LEFT ME FEELING MISERABLE.

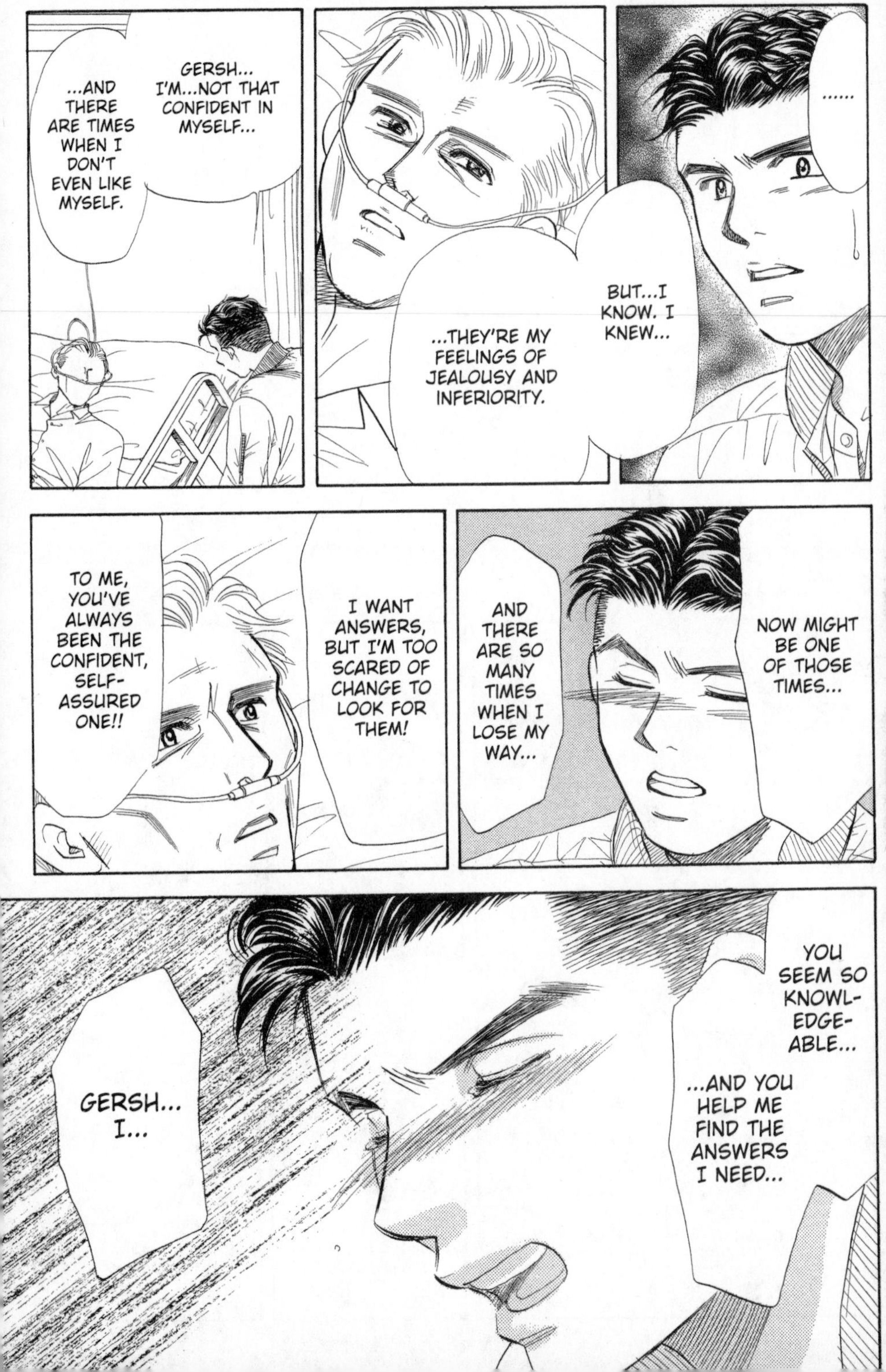
......
BUT...I KNOW. I KNEW...
...THEY'RE MY FEELINGS OF JEALOUSY AND INFERIORITY.
GERSH... I'M...NOT THAT CONFIDENT IN MYSELF...
...AND THERE ARE TIMES WHEN I DON'T EVEN LIKE MYSELF.
NOW MIGHT BE ONE OF THOSE TIMES...
AND THERE ARE SO MANY TIMES WHEN I LOSE MY WAY...
I WANT ANSWERS, BUT I'M TOO SCARED OF CHANGE TO LOOK FOR THEM!
TO ME, YOU'VE ALWAYS BEEN THE CONFIDENT, SELF-ASSURED ONE!!
YOU SEEM SO KNOWL-EDGE-ABLE...
...AND YOU HELP ME FIND THE ANSWERS I NEED...
GERSH... I...

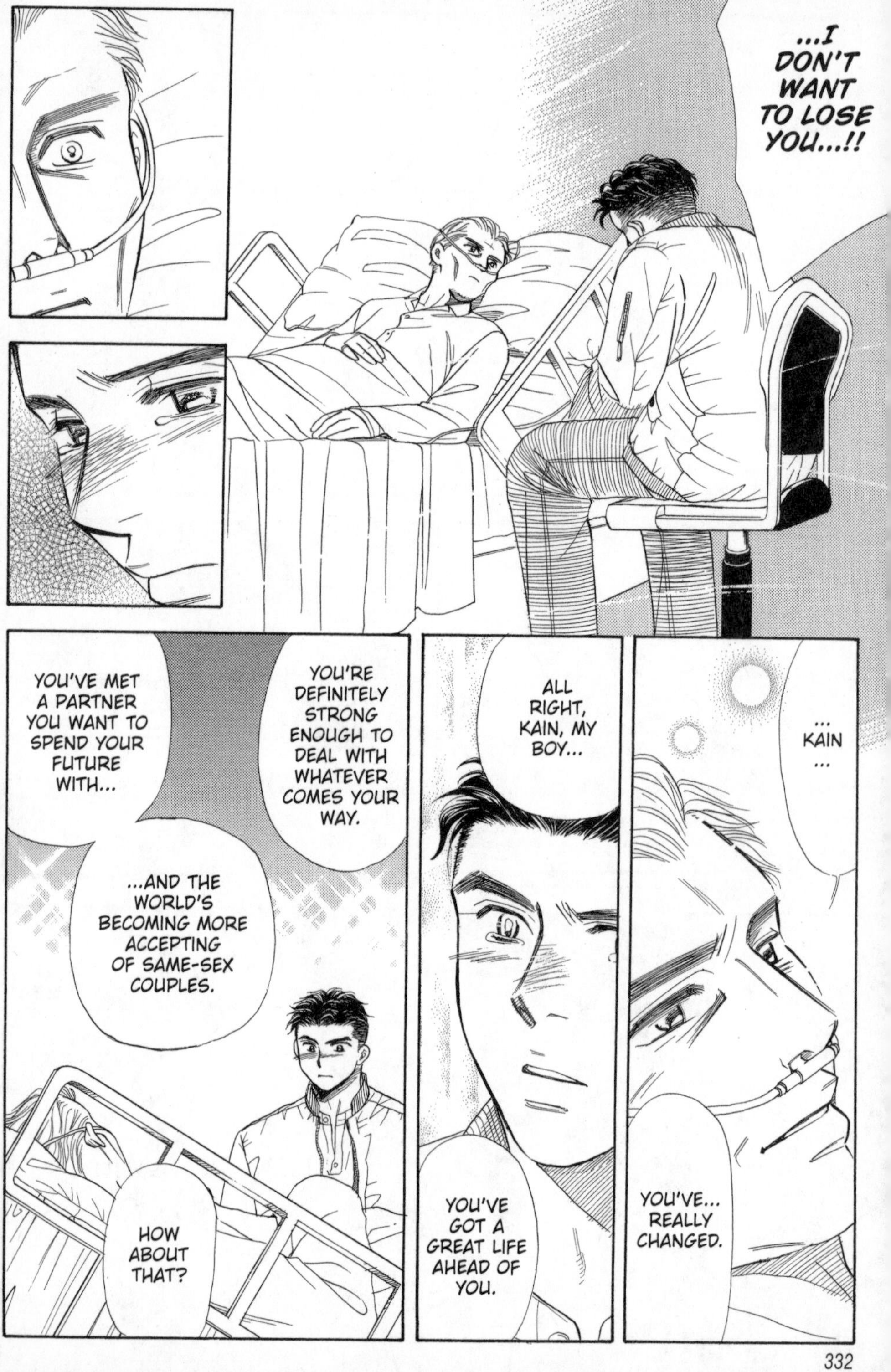
...I DON'T WANT TO LOSE YOU...!!
... KAIN ...
YOU'VE... REALLY CHANGED.
ALL RIGHT, KAIN, MY BOY...
YOU'VE GOT A GREAT LIFE AHEAD OF YOU.
YOU'RE DEFINITELY STRONG ENOUGH TO DEAL WITH WHATEVER COMES YOUR WAY.
YOU'VE MET A PARTNER YOU WANT TO SPEND YOUR FUTURE WITH...
...AND THE WORLD'S BECOMING MORE ACCEPTING OF SAME-SEX COUPLES.
HOW ABOUT THAT?

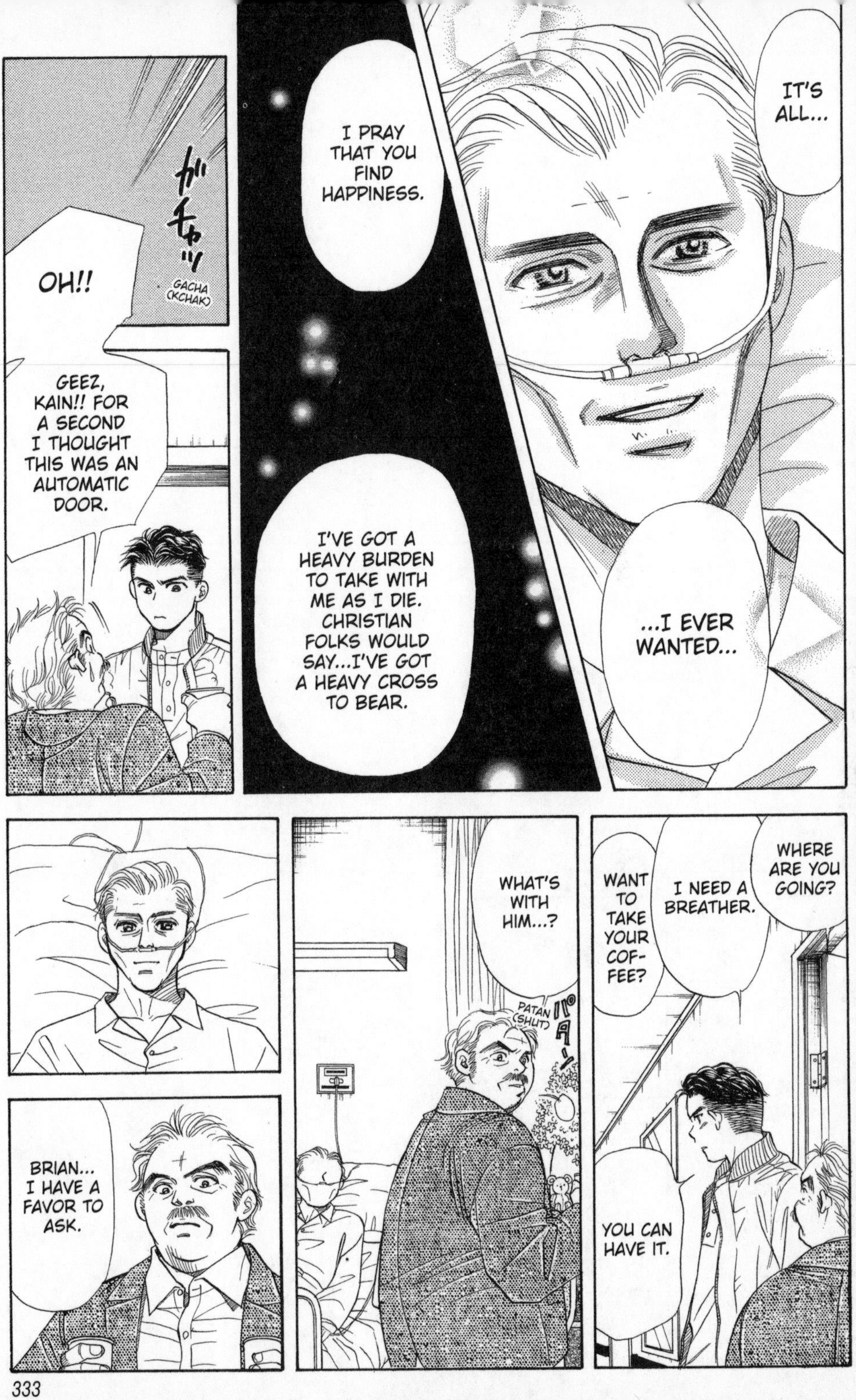
IT'S ALL...
...I EVER WANTED...
I PRAY THAT YOU FIND HAPPINESS.
I'VE GOT A HEAVY BURDEN TO TAKE WITH ME AS I DIE. CHRISTIAN FOLKS WOULD SAY...I'VE GOT A HEAVY CROSS TO BEAR.
ガチャッ
GACHA (KCHAK)
OH!!
GEEZ, KAIN!! FOR A SECOND I THOUGHT THIS WAS AN AUTOMATIC DOOR.
WHERE ARE YOU GOING?
I NEED A BREATHER.
WANT TO TAKE YOUR COF-FEE?
YOU CAN HAVE IT.
WHAT'S WITH HIM...?
パタン
PATAN (SHUT)
BRIAN... I HAVE A FAVOR TO ASK.

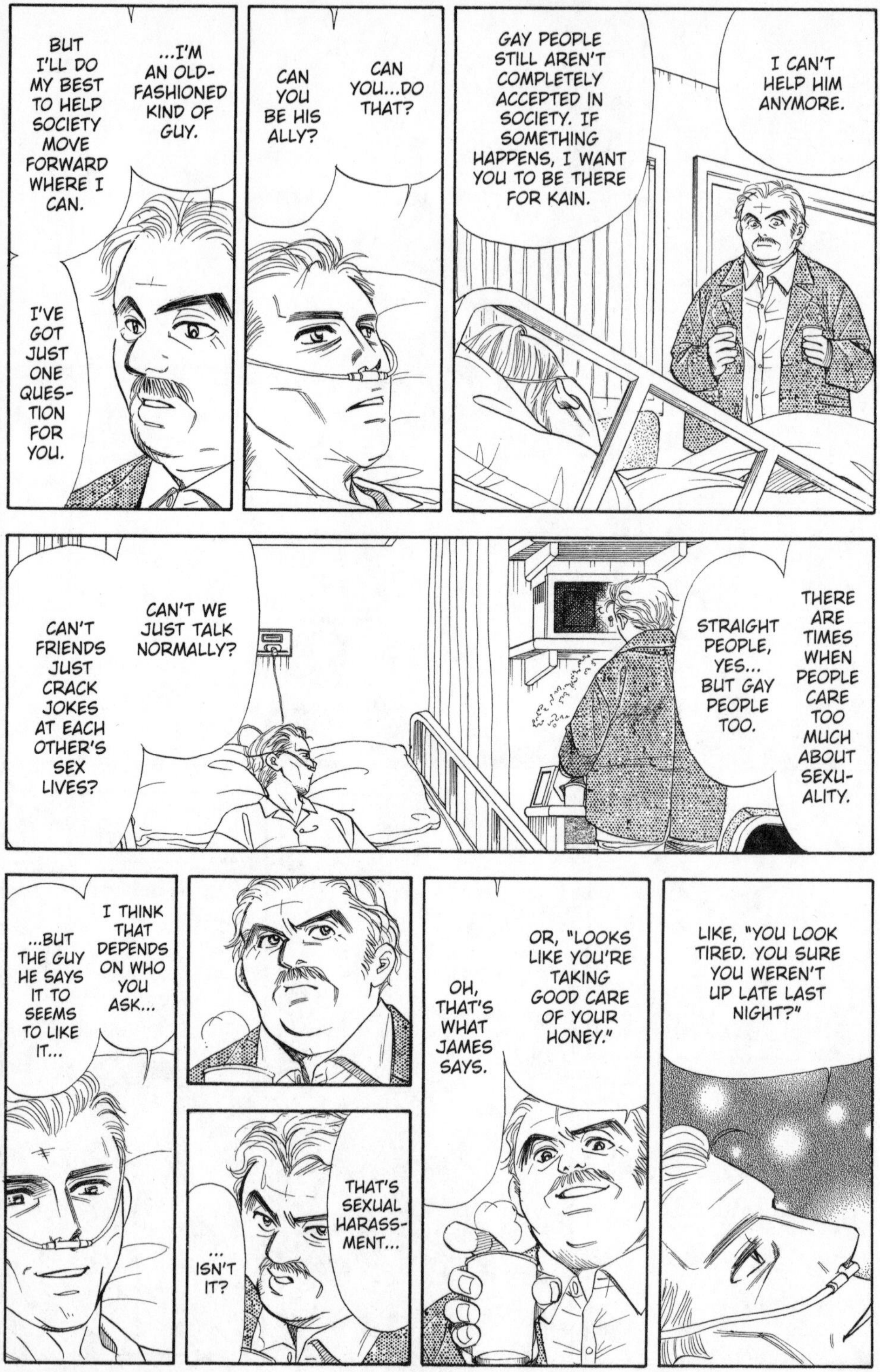
I CAN'T HELP HIM ANYMORE.
GAY PEOPLE STILL AREN'T COMPLETELY ACCEPTED IN SOCIETY. IF SOMETHING HAPPENS, I WANT YOU TO BE THERE FOR KAIN.
CAN YOU...DO THAT?
CAN YOU BE HIS ALLY?
...I'M AN OLD-FASHIONED KIND OF GUY.
BUT I'LL DO MY BEST TO HELP SOCIETY MOVE FORWARD WHERE I CAN.
I'VE GOT JUST ONE QUES-TION FOR YOU.
THERE ARE TIMES WHEN PEOPLE CARE TOO MUCH ABOUT SEXU-ALITY.
STRAIGHT PEOPLE, YES... BUT GAY PEOPLE TOO.
CAN'T WE JUST TALK NORMALLY?
CAN'T FRIENDS JUST CRACK JOKES AT EACH OTHER'S SEX LIVES?
LIKE, "YOU LOOK TIRED. YOU SURE YOU WEREN'T UP LATE LAST NIGHT?"
OR, "LOOKS LIKE YOU'RE TAKING GOOD CARE OF YOUR HONEY."
OH, THAT'S WHAT JAMES SAYS.
THAT'S SEXUAL HARASS-MENT...
...ISN'T IT?
I THINK THAT DEPENDS ON WHO YOU ASK...
...BUT THE GUY HE SAYS IT TO SEEMS TO LIKE IT...

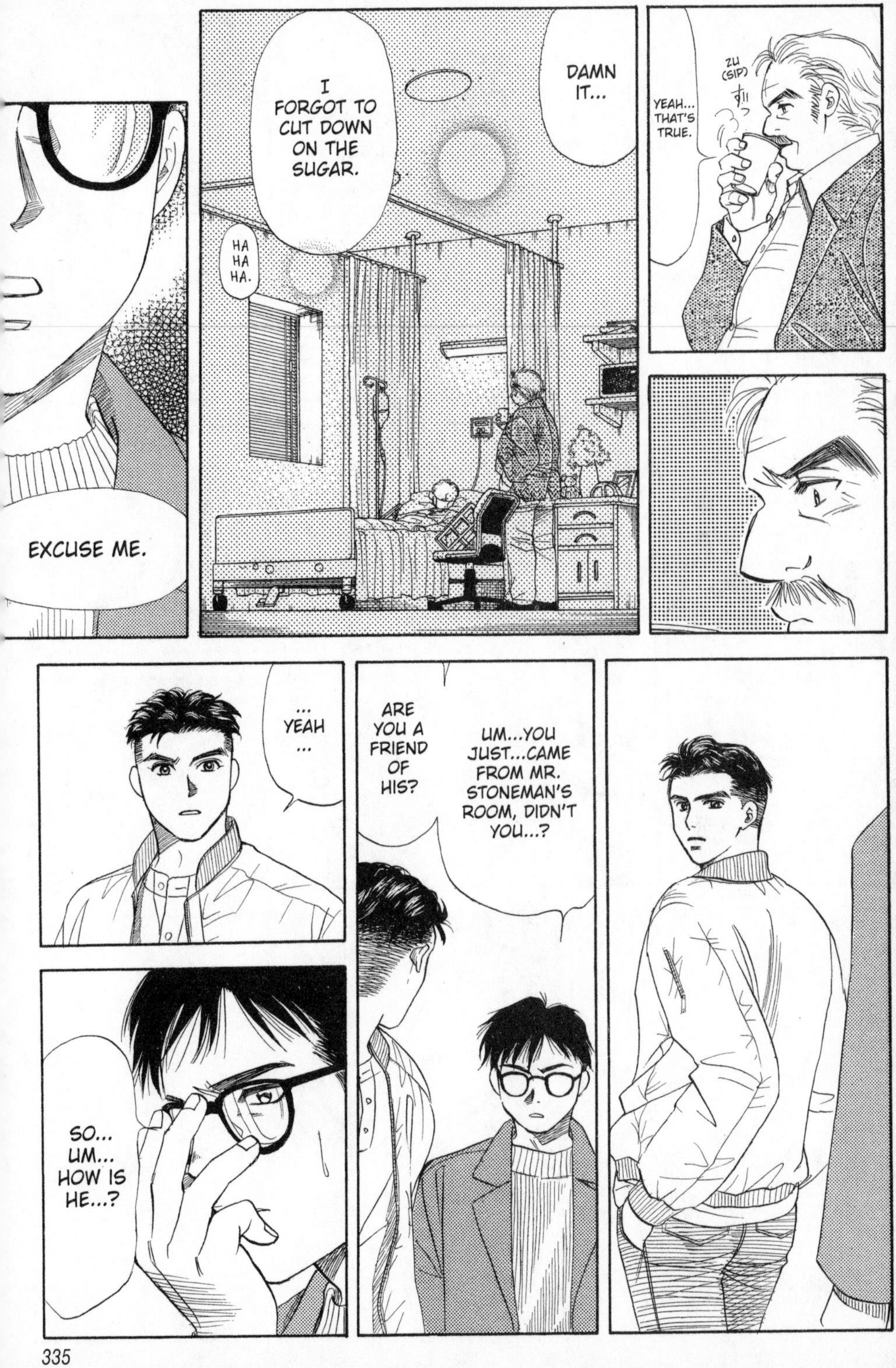
ZU (SIP)
YEAH... THAT'S TRUE.
DAMN IT...
I FORGOT TO CUT DOWN ON THE SUGAR.
HA HA HA.
EXCUSE ME.
UM...YOU JUST...CAME FROM MR. STONEMAN'S ROOM, DIDN'T YOU...?
ARE YOU A FRIEND OF HIS?
...YEAH...
SO... UM... HOW IS HE...?

AH... NO...I...

...I DON'T THINK I SHOULD...

WHAT'S UP WITH YOU? IF YOU'RE ONE OF GERSH'S FRIENDS, YOU SHOULD GO PAY HIM A VISIT.

...DOESN'T SEEM TO BE DOING SO HOT.

GERSH...

SORRY. UM... UH...

GOSO (RUSTLE)

SNRK!

THANK YOU.

ALL RIGHT...

......

I DON'T KNOW THE DETAILS.

HOW LONG DOES HE HAVE?

......

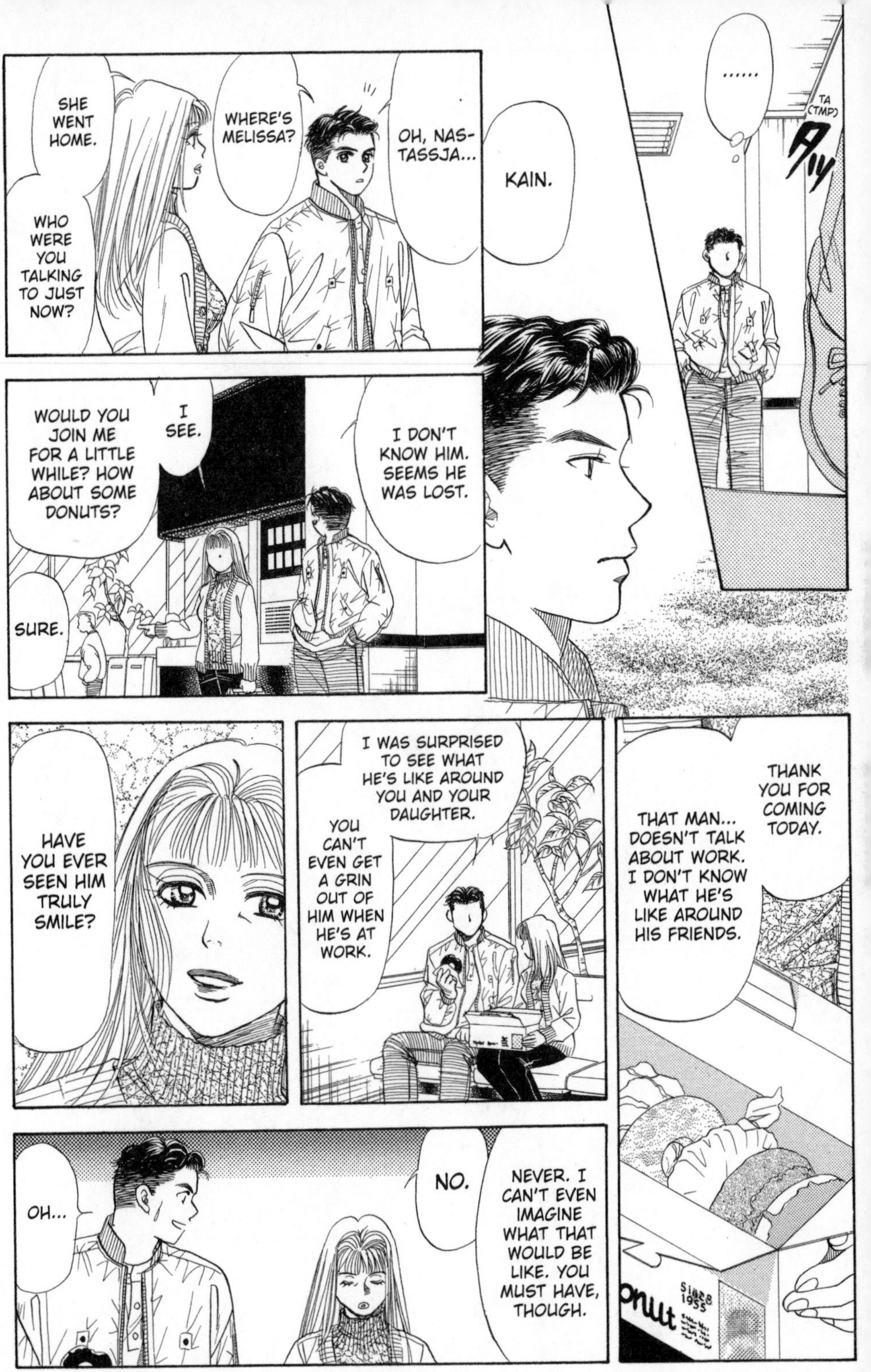
......
TA (TMP)
KAIN.
OH, NASTASSJA...
WHERE'S MELISSA?
SHE WENT HOME.
WHO WERE YOU TALKING TO JUST NOW?
I DON'T KNOW HIM. SEEMS HE WAS LOST.
I SEE.
WOULD YOU JOIN ME FOR A LITTLE WHILE? HOW ABOUT SOME DONUTS?
SURE.
THANK YOU FOR COMING TODAY.
THAT MAN... DOESN'T TALK ABOUT WORK. I DON'T KNOW WHAT HE'S LIKE AROUND HIS FRIENDS.
I WAS SURPRISED TO SEE WHAT HE'S LIKE AROUND YOU AND YOUR DAUGHTER.
YOU CAN'T EVEN GET A GRIN OUT OF HIM WHEN HE'S AT WORK.
HAVE YOU EVER SEEN HIM TRULY SMILE?
Since 1955
NO.
NEVER. I CAN'T EVEN IMAGINE WHAT THAT WOULD BE LIKE. YOU MUST HAVE, THOUGH.
OH...

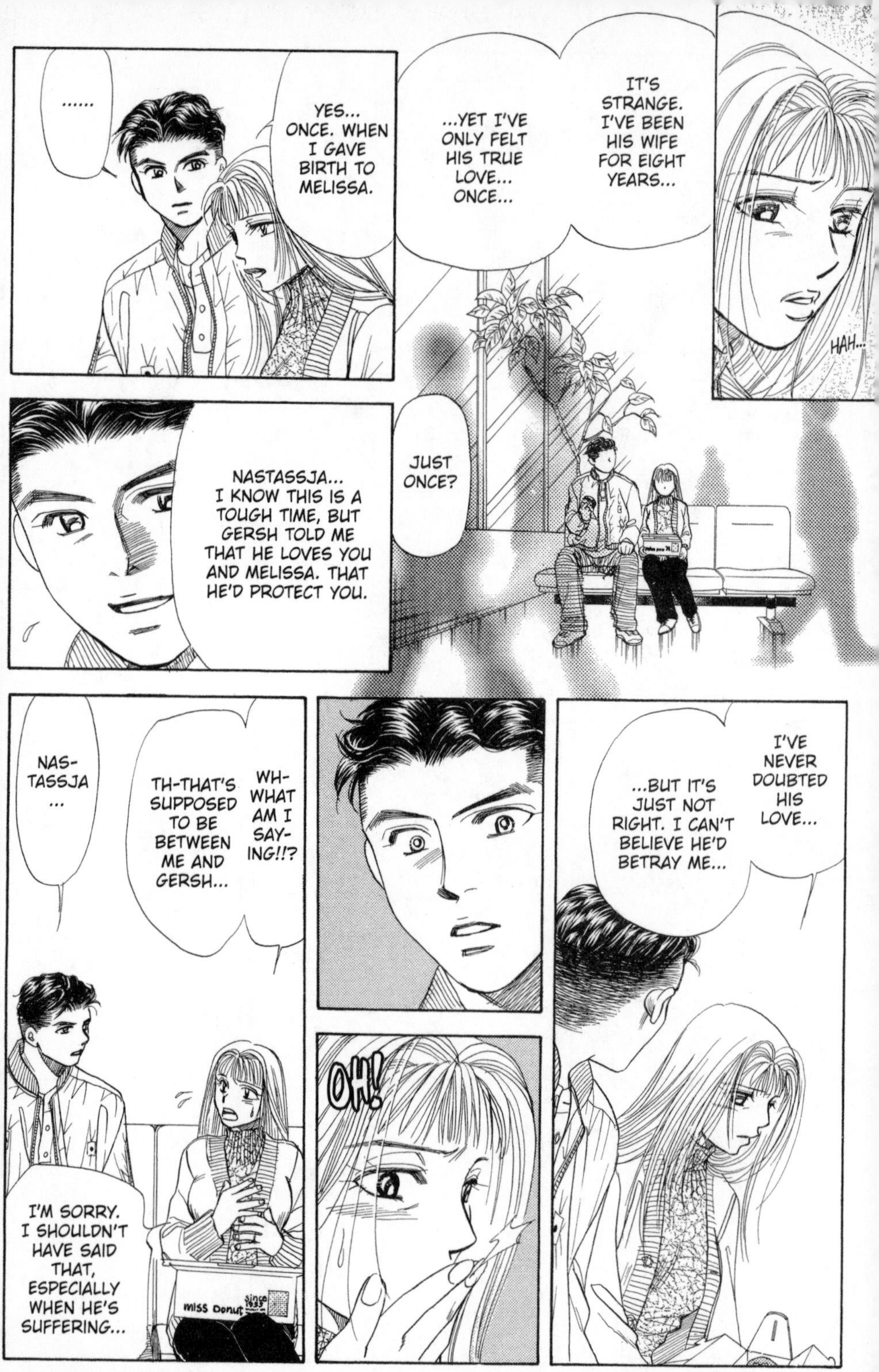
HAH...
IT'S STRANGE. I'VE BEEN HIS WIFE FOR EIGHT YEARS...
...YET I'VE ONLY FELT HIS TRUE LOVE... ONCE...
JUST ONCE?
YES... ONCE. WHEN I GAVE BIRTH TO MELISSA.
......
NASTASSJA... I KNOW THIS IS A TOUGH TIME, BUT GERSH TOLD ME THAT HE LOVES YOU AND MELISSA. THAT HE'D PROTECT YOU.
I'VE NEVER DOUBTED HIS LOVE...
...BUT IT'S JUST NOT RIGHT. I CAN'T BELIEVE HE'D BETRAY ME...
OH!
WH-WHAT AM I SAY-ING!!?
TH-THAT'S SUPPOSED TO BE BETWEEN ME AND GERSH...
NAS-TASSJA ...
I'M SORRY. I SHOULDN'T HAVE SAID THAT, ESPECIALLY WHEN HE'S SUFFERING...

THIS MUST BE HARD ON YOU TOO.

HE CAME OUT TO YOU, DIDN'T HE?

IT'S OKAY. I THINK I KNOW THE GIST OF IT ANYWAY.

NAS-TASSJA...

TO THINK... HE GOT HIV FROM SLEEPING WITH A MAN...

I'M SORRY... I HAVEN'T HAD ANYONE TO TALK TO ABOUT THIS...

NAS-TASSJA... UM...DO YOU HAVE IT TOO?

HNH...

...WE HAVEN'T HAD SEX EVEN ONCE SINCE MELISSA WAS BORN.

AND...

NO...MY TEST CAME BACK NEGATIVE.

MISS Donut

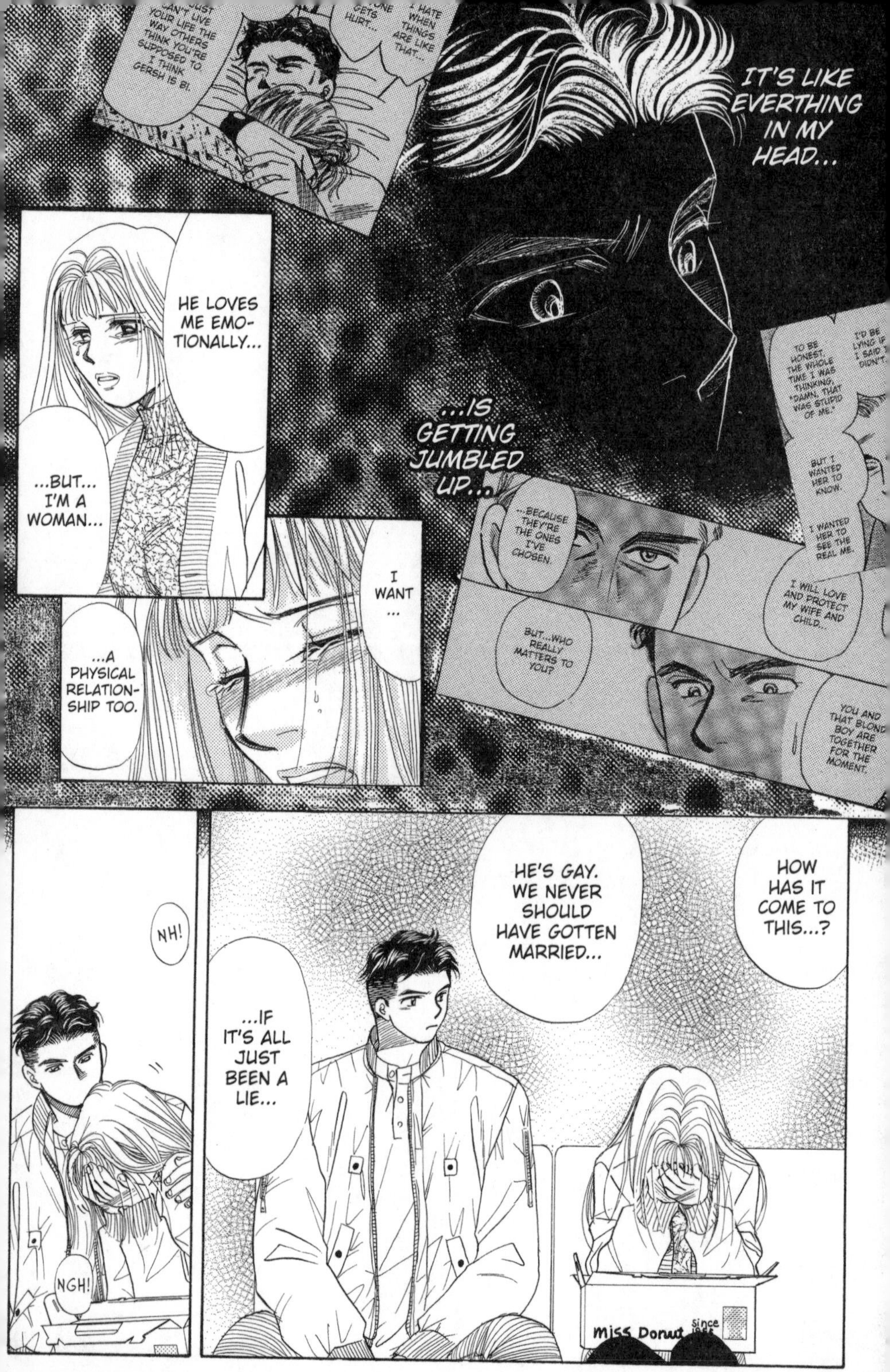
IT'S LIKE EVERTHING IN MY HEAD...
I HATE WHEN THINGS ARE LIKE THAT...
GETS HURT...
CAN'T JUST LIVE YOUR LIFE THE WAY OTHERS THINK YOU'RE SUPPOSED TO. I THINK GERSH IS BI.
I'D BE LYING IF I SAID I DIDN'T.
TO BE HONEST, THE WHOLE TIME I WAS THINKING, "DAMN, THAT WAS STUPID OF ME."
BUT I WANTED HER TO KNOW.
I WANTED HER TO SEE THE REAL ME.
...IS GETTING JUMBLED UP...
I WILL LOVE AND PROTECT MY WIFE AND CHILD...
...BECAUSE THEY'RE THE ONES I'VE CHOSEN.
YOU AND THAT BLOND BOY ARE TOGETHER FOR THE MOMENT.
BUT...WHO REALLY MATTERS TO YOU?
HE LOVES ME EMO-TIONALLY...
...BUT... I'M A WOMAN...
I WANT ...
...A PHYSICAL RELATION-SHIP TOO.
HOW HAS IT COME TO THIS...?
HE'S GAY. WE NEVER SHOULD HAVE GOTTEN MARRIED...
...IF IT'S ALL JUST BEEN A LIE...
Miss Donut
NH!
NGH!

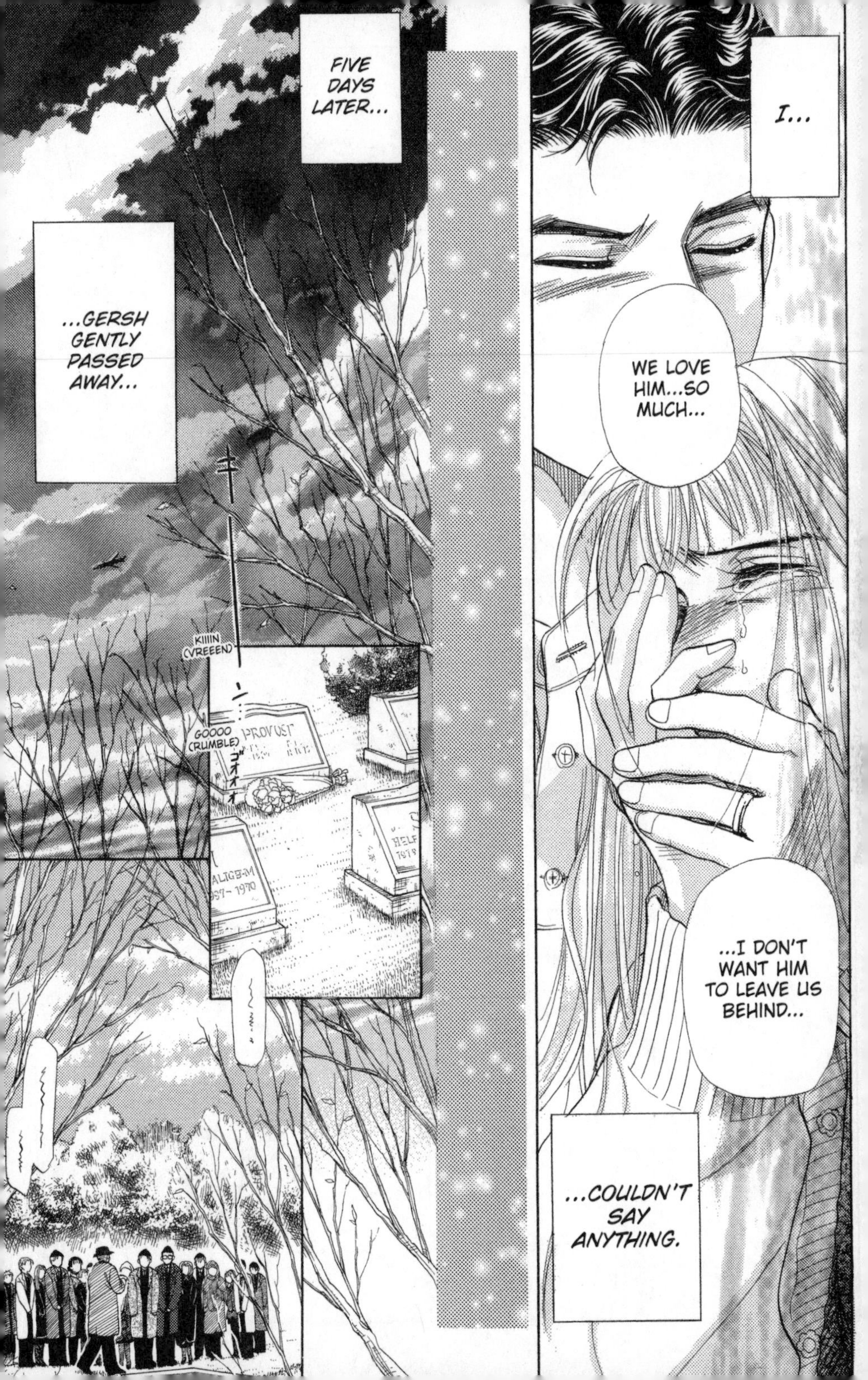
I...
WE LOVE HIM...SO MUCH...
...I DON'T WANT HIM TO LEAVE US BEHIND...
...COULDN'T SAY ANYTHING.
FIVE DAYS LATER...
...GERSH GENTLY PASSED AWAY...
KIIIN (VREEEN)
GOOOO (RUMBLE)
ゴオオオ

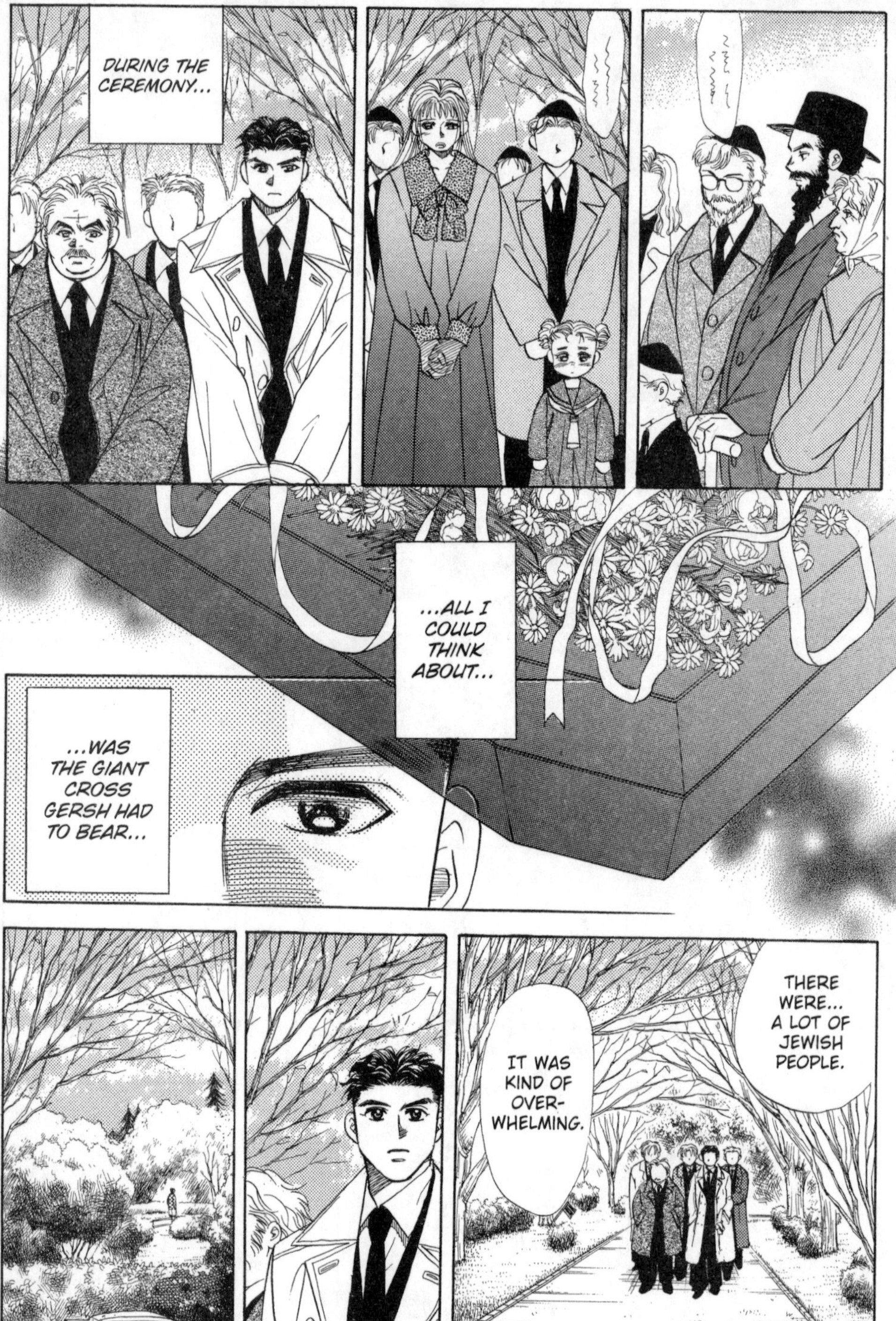
DURING THE CEREMONY...
...ALL I COULD THINK ABOUT...
...WAS THE GIANT CROSS GERSH HAD TO BEAR...
THERE WERE... A LOT OF JEWISH PEOPLE.
IT WAS KIND OF OVER-WHELMING.

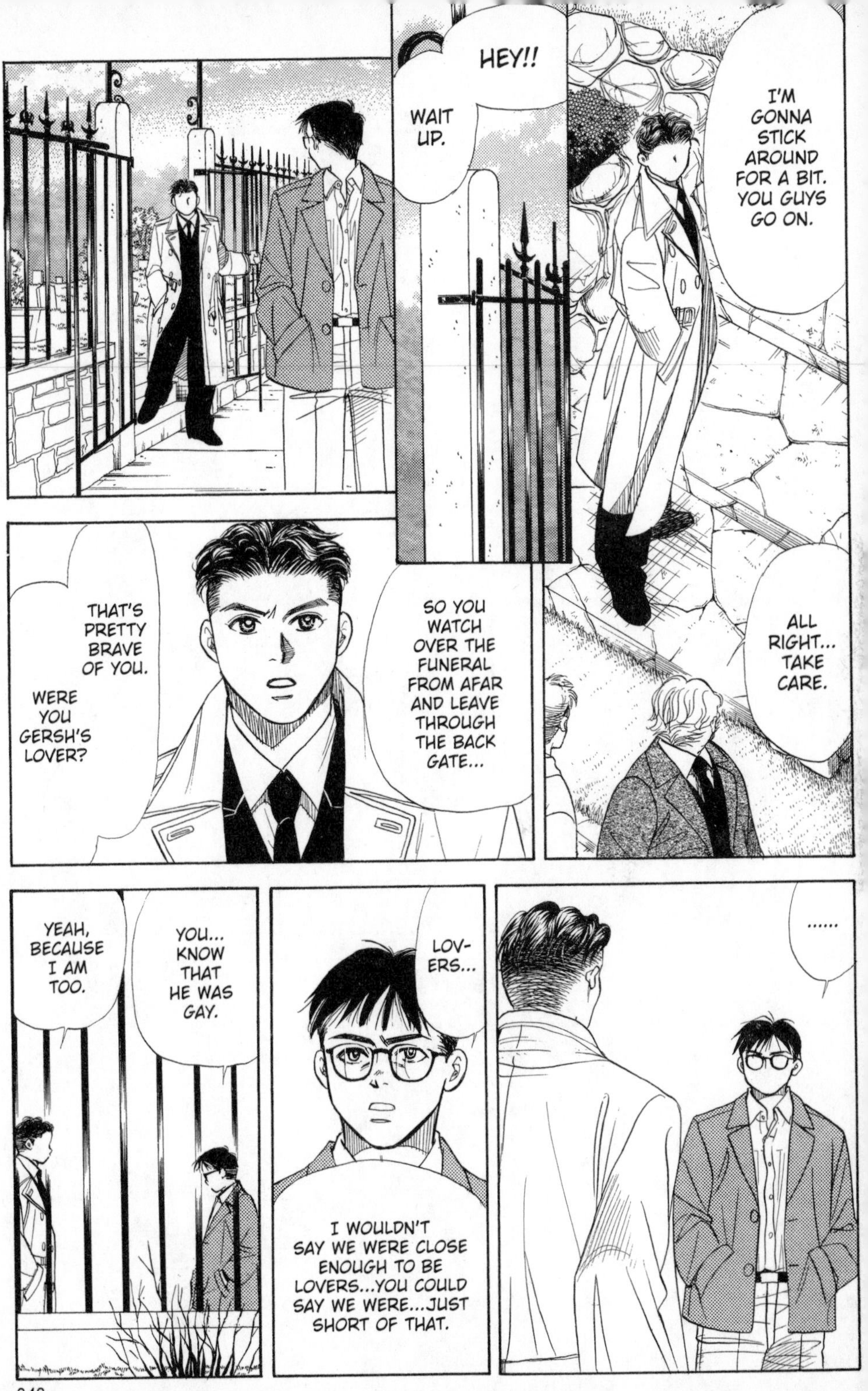
I'M GONNA STICK AROUND FOR A BIT. YOU GUYS GO ON.
ALL RIGHT... TAKE CARE.
HEY!!
WAIT UP.
SO YOU WATCH OVER THE FUNERAL FROM AFAR AND LEAVE THROUGH THE BACK GATE...
THAT'S PRETTY BRAVE OF YOU.
WERE YOU GERSH'S LOVER?
......
LOVERS...
I WOULDN'T SAY WE WERE CLOSE ENOUGH TO BE LOVERS...YOU COULD SAY WE WERE...JUST SHORT OF THAT.
YOU... KNOW THAT HE WAS GAY.
YEAH, BECAUSE I AM TOO.

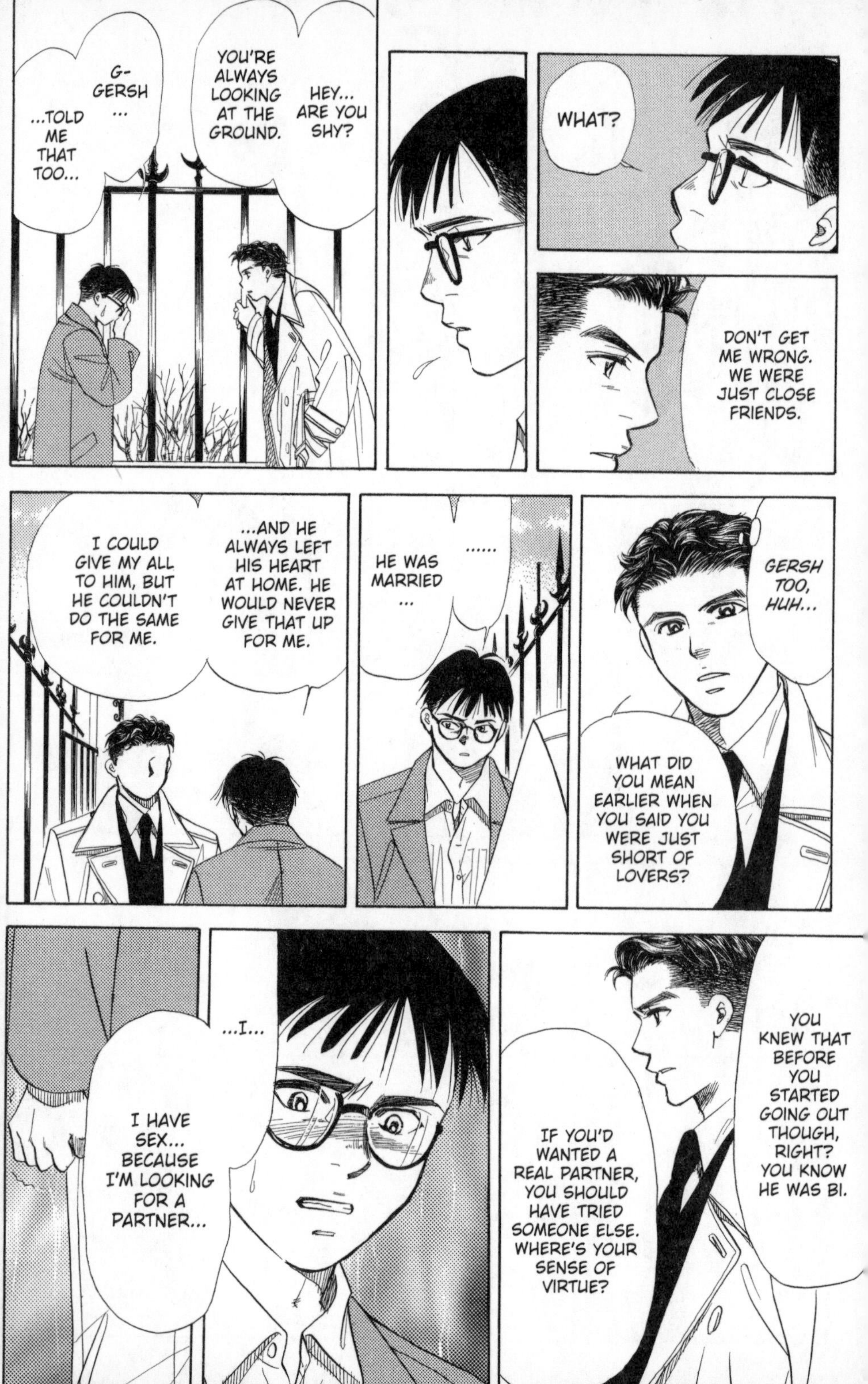
WHAT?
DON'T GET ME WRONG. WE WERE JUST CLOSE FRIENDS.
HEY... ARE YOU SHY?
YOU'RE ALWAYS LOOKING AT THE GROUND.
G-GERSH...
...TOLD ME THAT TOO...
GERSH TOO, HUH...
WHAT DID YOU MEAN EARLIER WHEN YOU SAID YOU WERE JUST SHORT OF LOVERS?
......
HE WAS MARRIED...
...AND HE ALWAYS LEFT HIS HEART AT HOME. HE WOULD NEVER GIVE THAT UP FOR ME.
I COULD GIVE MY ALL TO HIM, BUT HE COULDN'T DO THE SAME FOR ME.
YOU KNEW THAT BEFORE YOU STARTED GOING OUT THOUGH, RIGHT? YOU KNOW HE WAS BI.
IF YOU'D WANTED A REAL PARTNER, YOU SHOULD HAVE TRIED SOMEONE ELSE. WHERE'S YOUR SENSE OF VIRTUE?
...I...
I HAVE SEX... BECAUSE I'M LOOKING FOR A PARTNER...

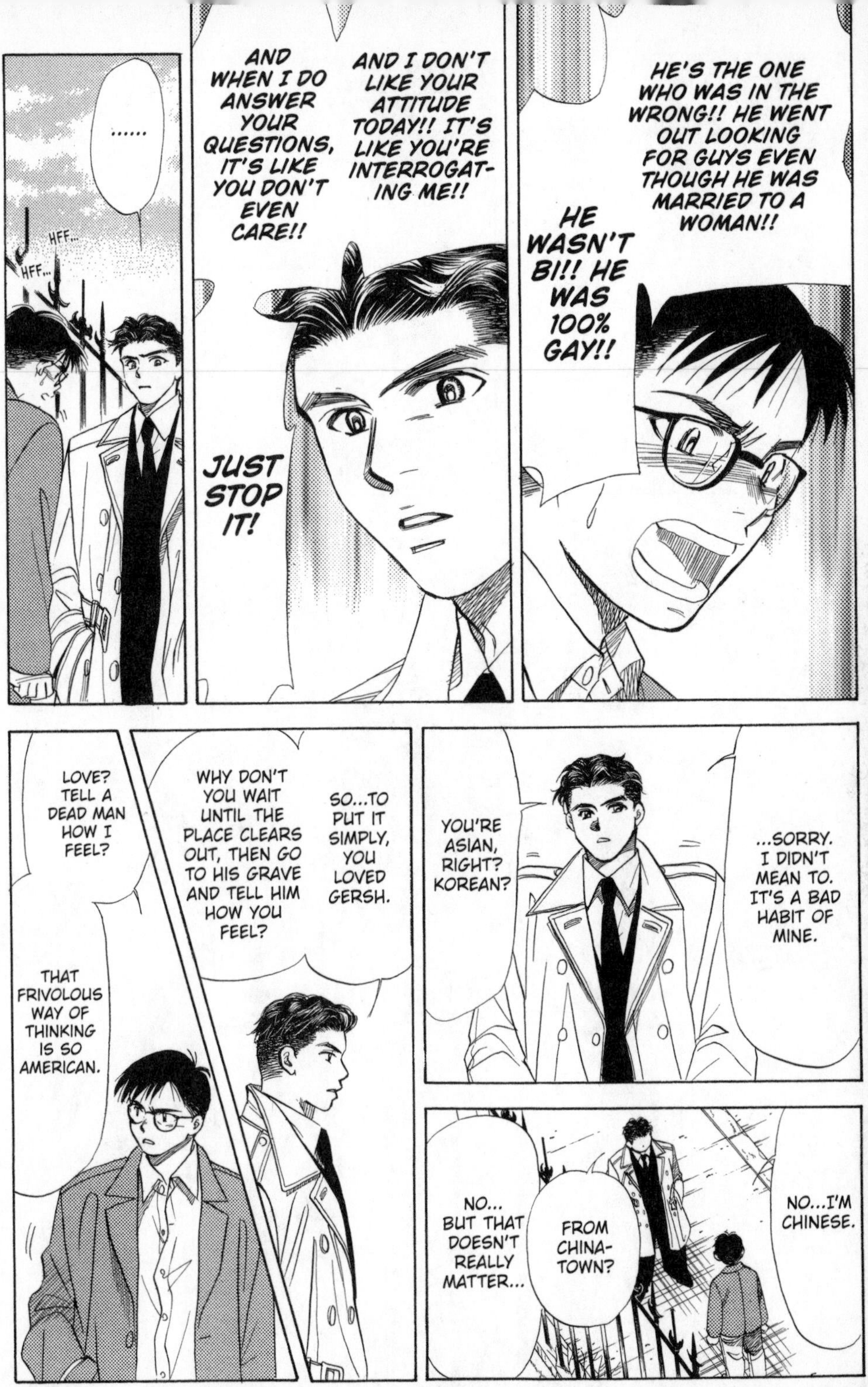
HE'S THE ONE WHO WAS IN THE WRONG!! HE WENT OUT LOOKING FOR GUYS EVEN THOUGH HE WAS MARRIED TO A WOMAN!!
HE WASN'T BI!! HE WAS 100% GAY!!
AND I DON'T LIKE YOUR ATTITUDE TODAY!! IT'S LIKE YOU'RE INTERROGATING ME!!
AND WHEN I DO ANSWER YOUR QUESTIONS, IT'S LIKE YOU DON'T EVEN CARE!!
JUST STOP IT!
......
HFF...
HFF...
...SORRY. I DIDN'T MEAN TO. IT'S A BAD HABIT OF MINE.
YOU'RE ASIAN, RIGHT? KOREAN?
NO...I'M CHINESE.
FROM CHINA-TOWN?
NO... BUT THAT DOESN'T REALLY MATTER...
SO...TO PUT IT SIMPLY, YOU LOVED GERSH.
WHY DON'T YOU WAIT UNTIL THE PLACE CLEARS OUT, THEN GO TO HIS GRAVE AND TELL HIM HOW YOU FEEL?
LOVE? TELL A DEAD MAN HOW I FEEL?
THAT FRIVOLOUS WAY OF THINKING IS SO AMERICAN.

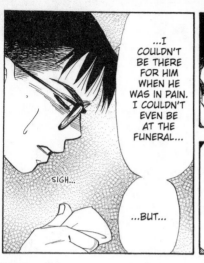

...I COULDN'T BE THERE FOR HIM WHEN HE WAS IN PAIN. I COULDN'T EVEN BE AT THE FUNERAL...

SIGH...

...BUT...

SNRK!

...I...

SNIFF!

SNIFF! I'M SORRY.

......

GOSO (RSTL)

EVERYONE AT THE FUNERAL GAVE HER THEIR SYMPATHIES AND COMFORT.

...HIS WIFE COULD BE THERE.

I GOT HIV FROM GERSH.

IT'S LIKE I DON'T EVEN EXIST. WHERE DO I FIT IN THE PICTURE?

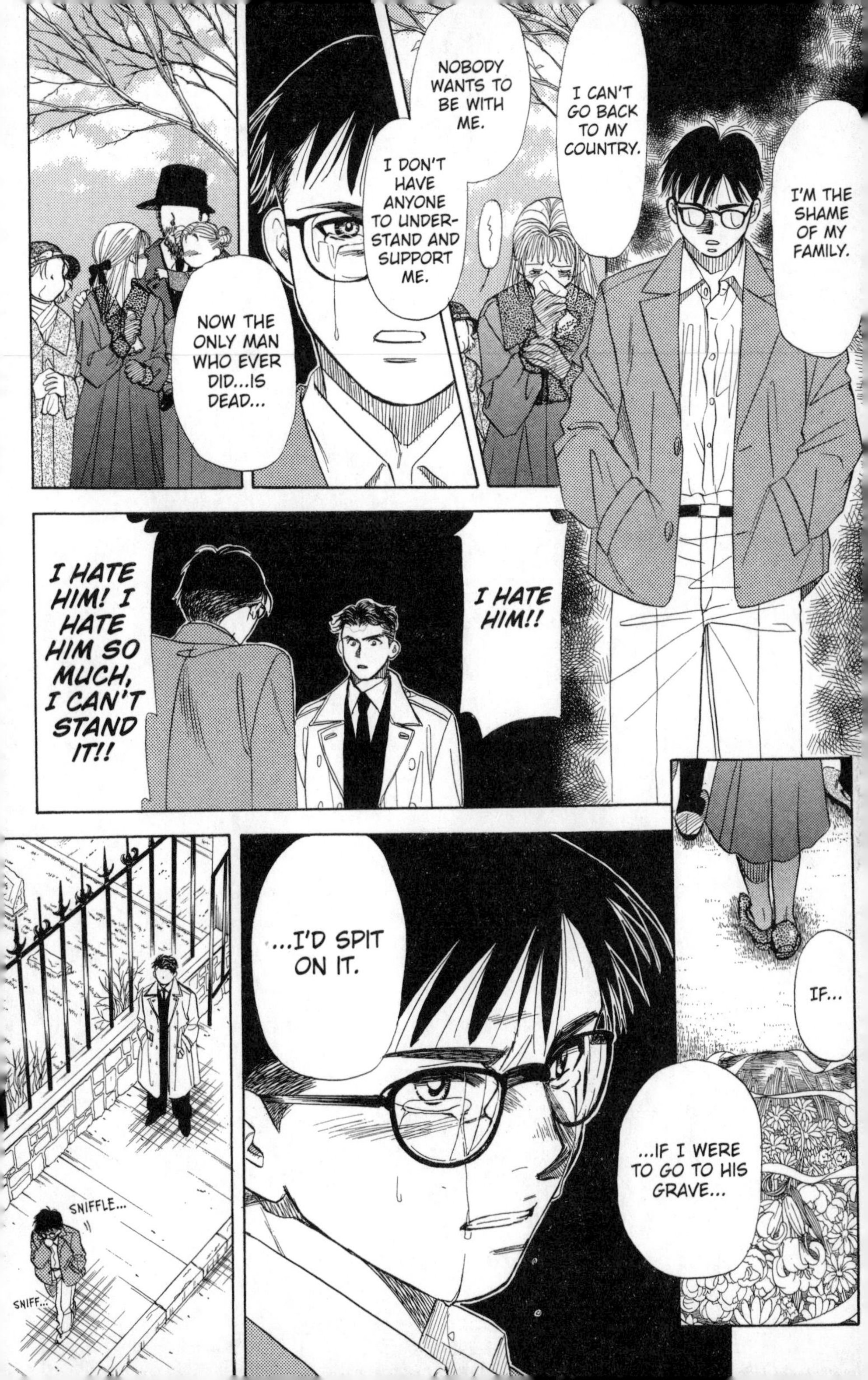
I'M THE SHAME OF MY FAMILY.
I CAN'T GO BACK TO MY COUNTRY.
NOBODY WANTS TO BE WITH ME.
I DON'T HAVE ANYONE TO UNDER-STAND AND SUPPORT ME.
NOW THE ONLY MAN WHO EVER DID...IS DEAD...
I HATE HIM!!
I HATE HIM! I HATE HIM SO MUCH, I CAN'T STAND IT!!
IF...
...IF I WERE TO GO TO HIS GRAVE...
...I'D SPIT ON IT.
SNIFFLE...
SNIFF...

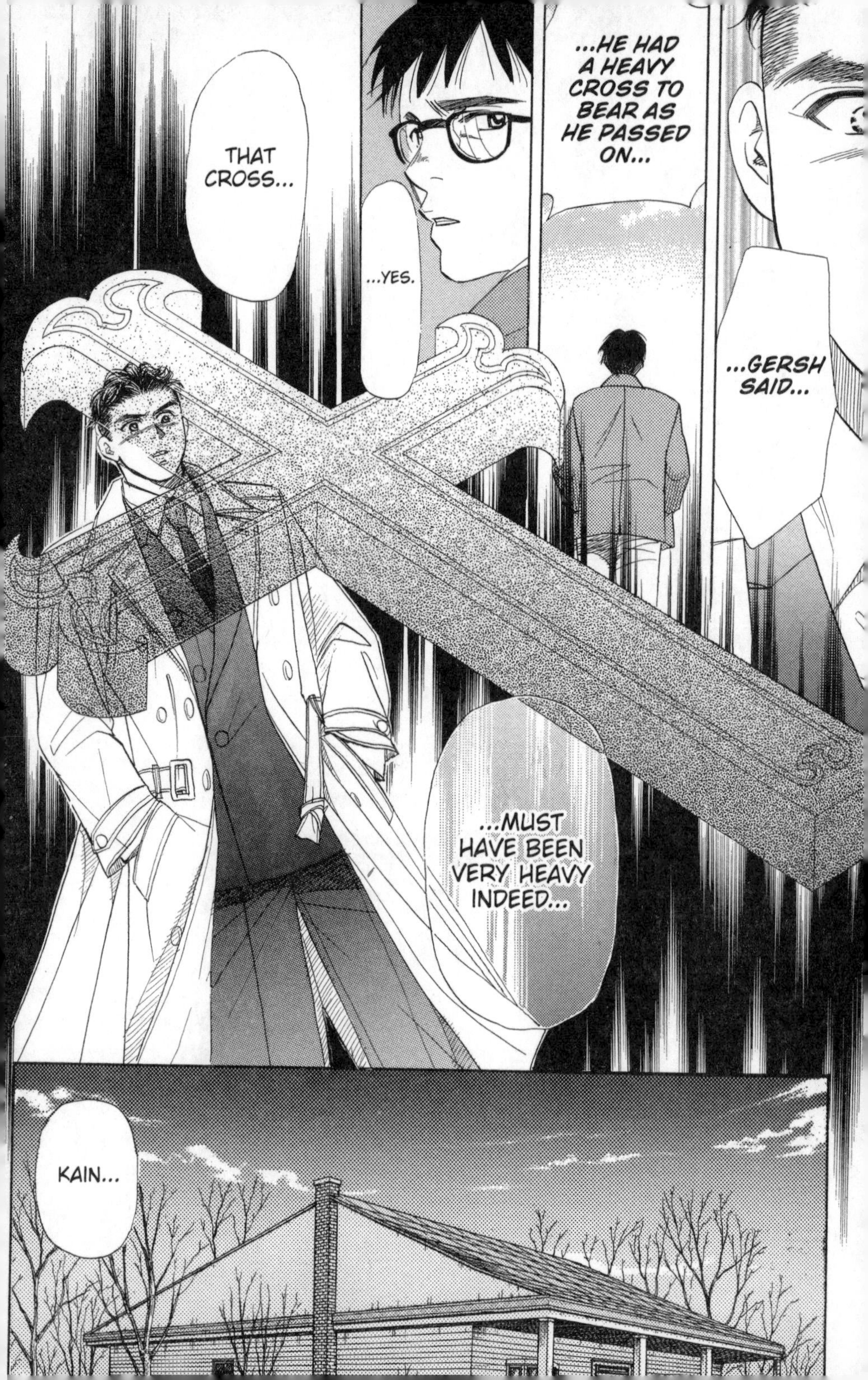
...GERSH SAID...
...HE HAD A HEAVY CROSS TO BEAR AS HE PASSED ON...
...YES.
THAT CROSS...
...MUST HAVE BEEN VERY HEAVY INDEED...
KAIN...

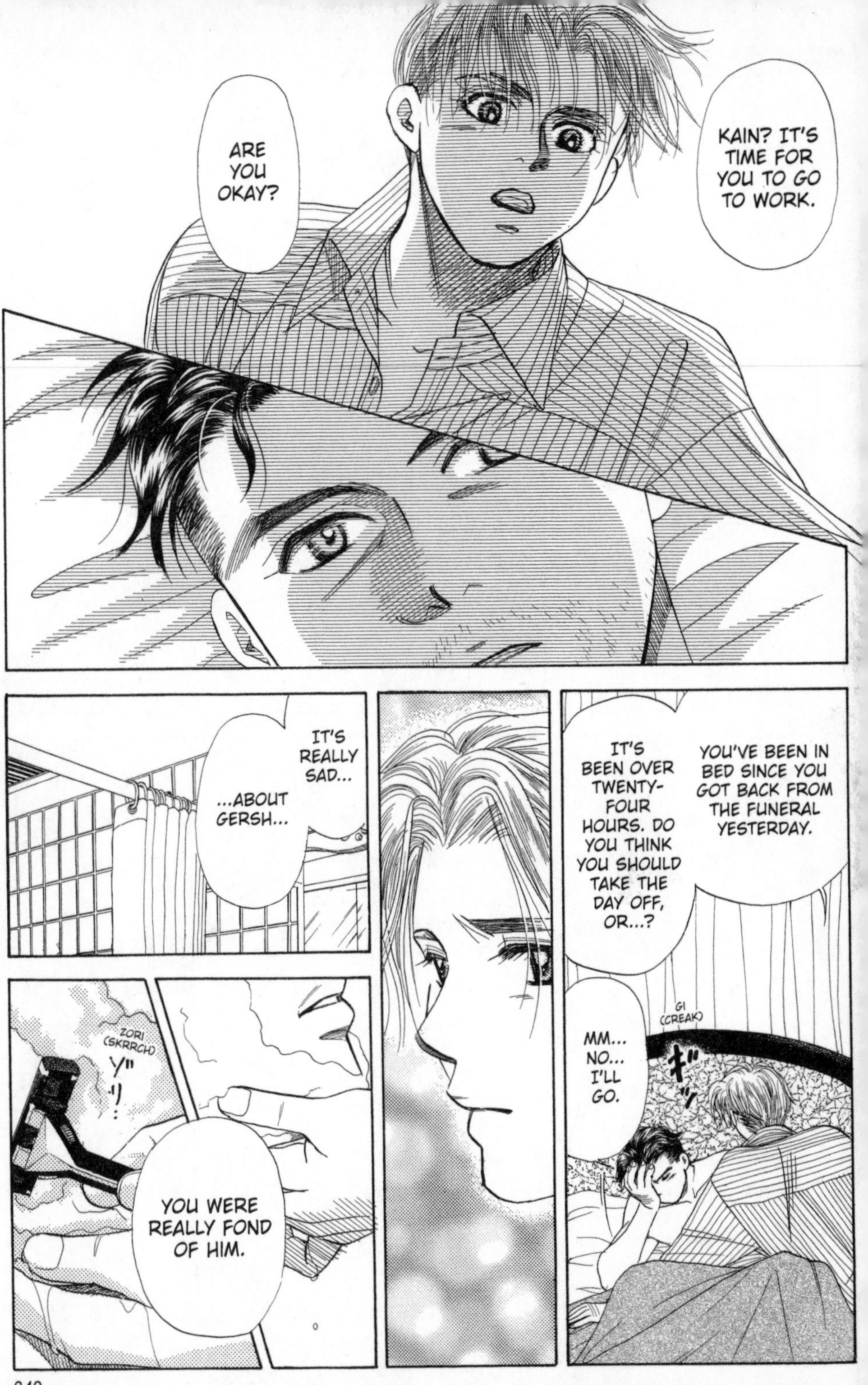
KAIN? IT'S TIME FOR YOU TO GO TO WORK.
ARE YOU OKAY?
YOU'VE BEEN IN BED SINCE YOU GOT BACK FROM THE FUNERAL YESTERDAY.
IT'S BEEN OVER TWENTY-FOUR HOURS. DO YOU THINK YOU SHOULD TAKE THE DAY OFF, OR...?
GI (CREAK)
ギッ
MM... NO... I'LL GO.
IT'S REALLY SAD...
...ABOUT GERSH...
ZORI (SKRRCH)
ゾリ…
YOU WERE REALLY FOND OF HIM.

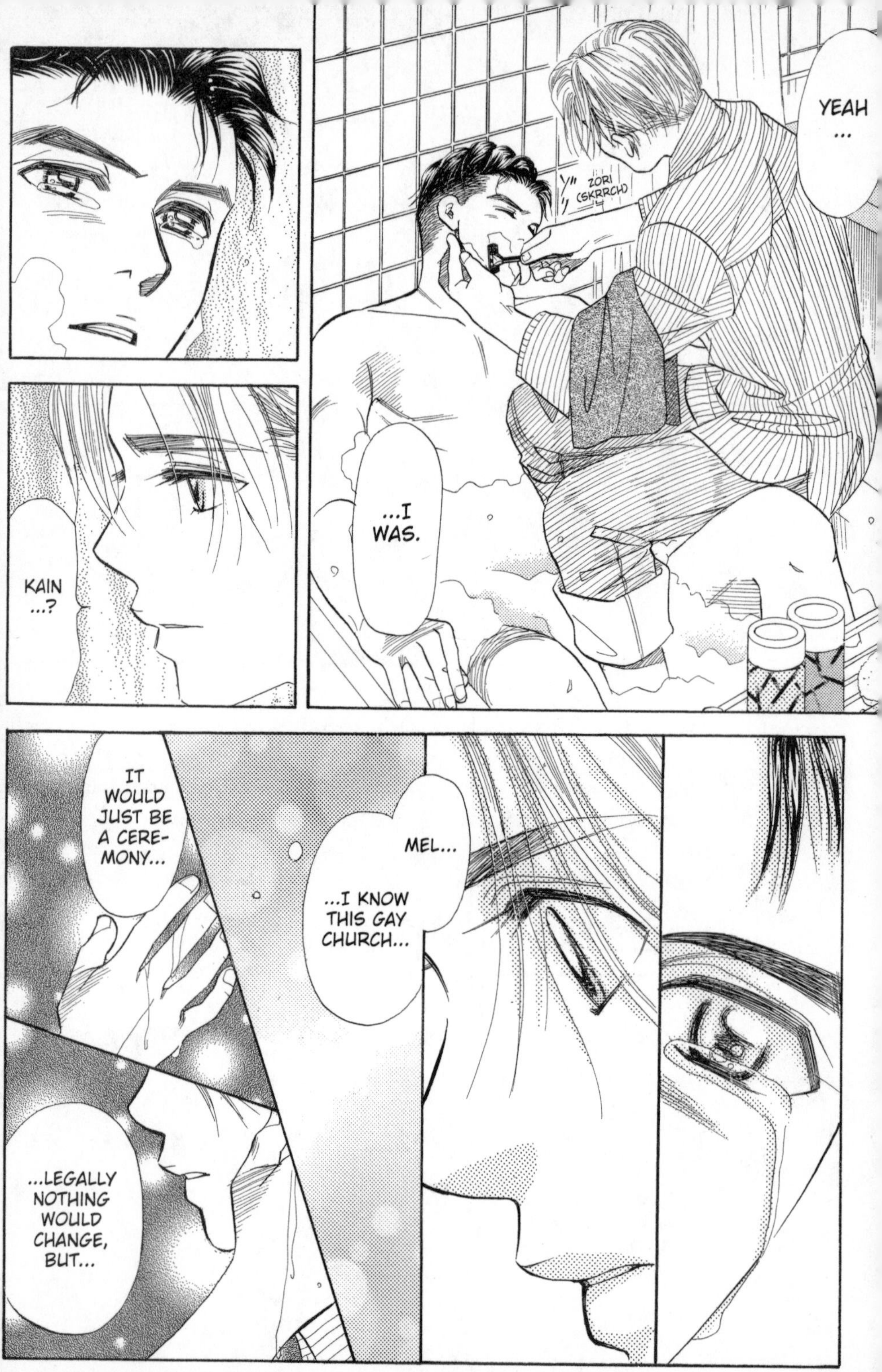
YEAH ...
ZORI (SKRRCH)
...I WAS.
KAIN ...?
MEL...
...I KNOW THIS GAY CHURCH...
IT WOULD JUST BE A CERE-MONY...
...LEGALLY NOTHING WOULD CHANGE, BUT...

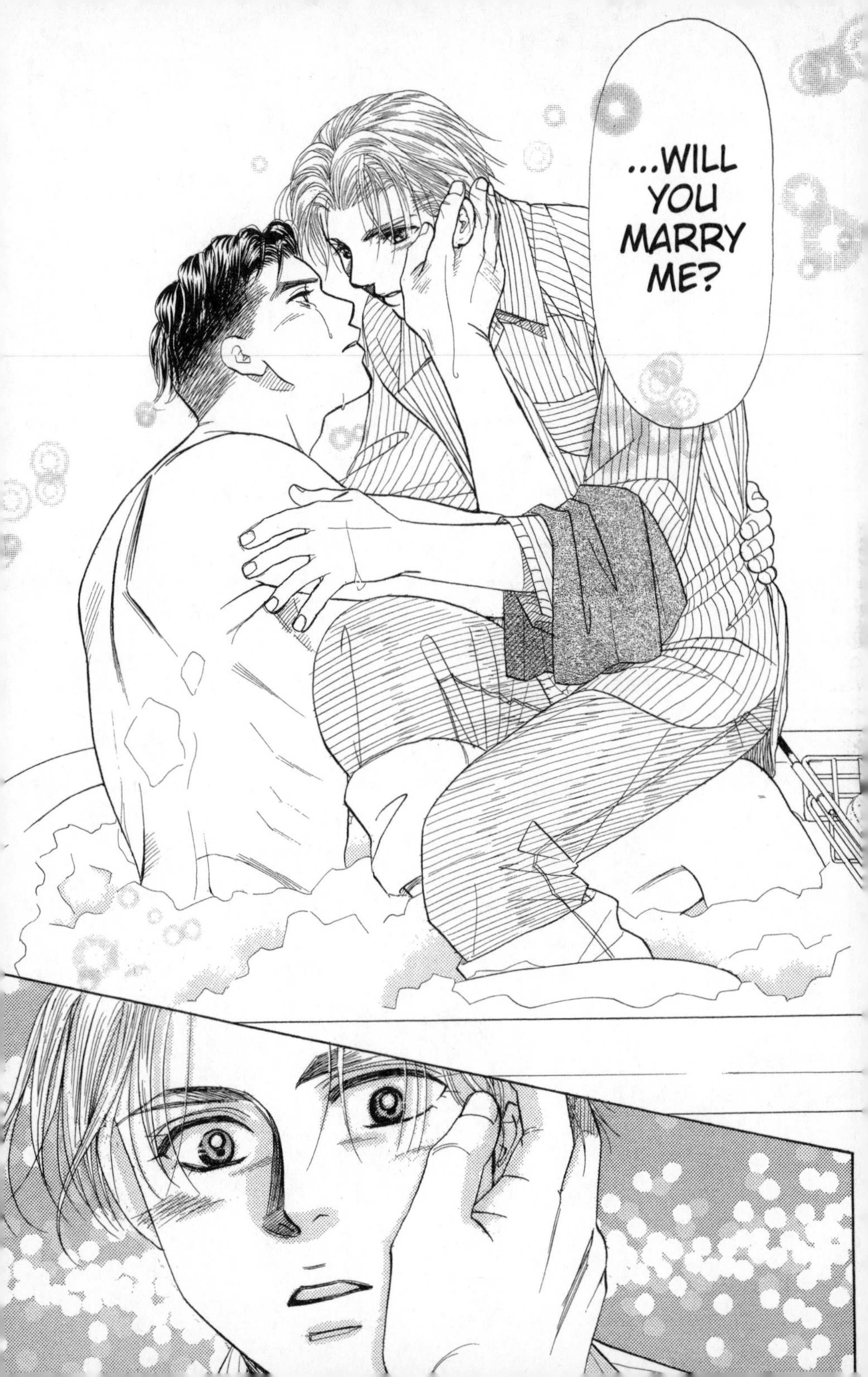
...WILL YOU MARRY ME?

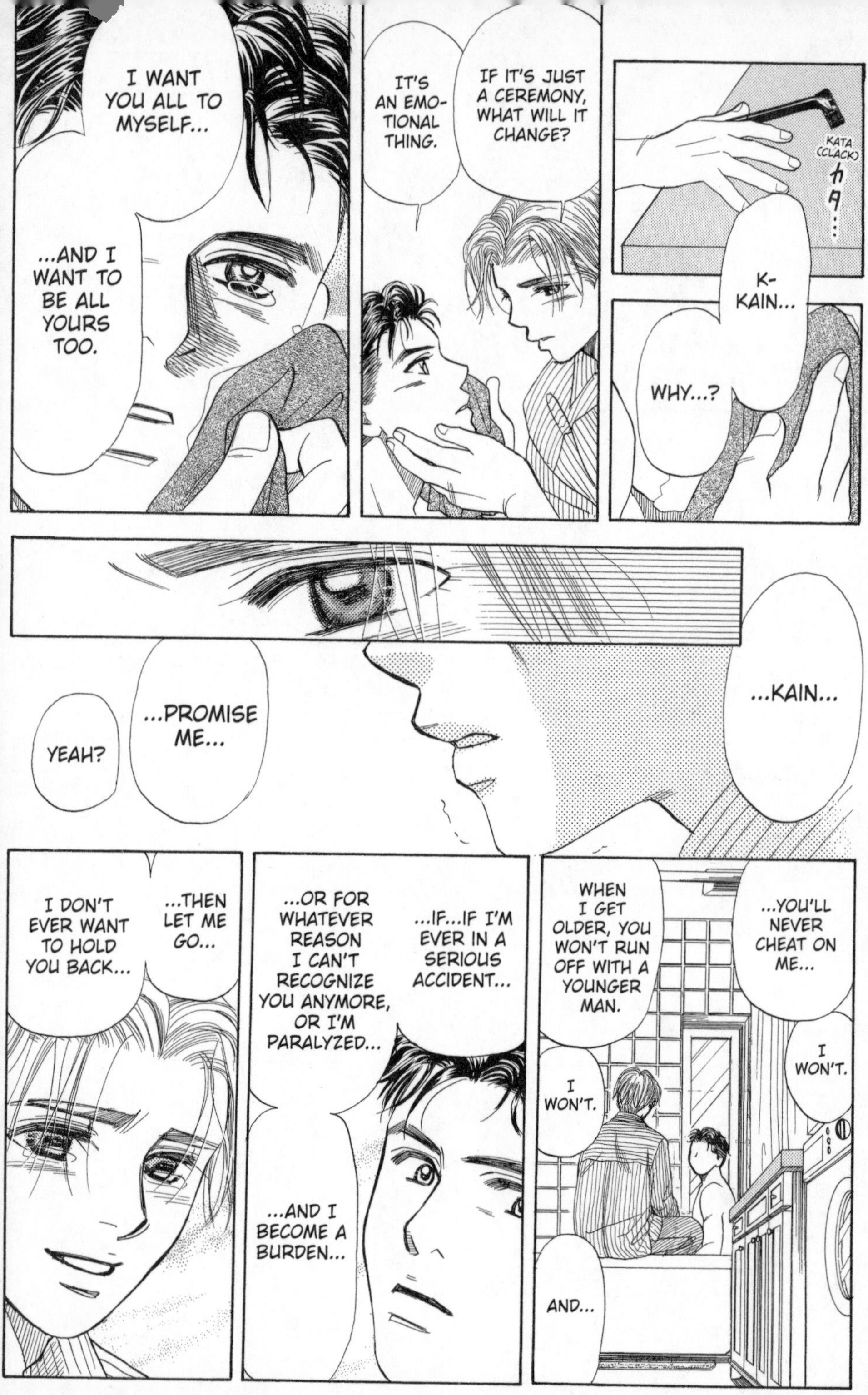
KATA (CLACK)
カタ…
K-KAIN…
WHY…?
IF IT'S JUST A CEREMONY, WHAT WILL IT CHANGE?
IT'S AN EMOTIONAL THING.
I WANT YOU ALL TO MYSELF…
…AND I WANT TO BE ALL YOURS TOO.
…KAIN…
…PROMISE ME…
YEAH?
…YOU'LL NEVER CHEAT ON ME…
I WON'T.
WHEN I GET OLDER, YOU WON'T RUN OFF WITH A YOUNGER MAN.
I WON'T.
AND…
…IF…IF I'M EVER IN A SERIOUS ACCIDENT…
…OR FOR WHATEVER REASON I CAN'T RECOGNIZE YOU ANYMORE, OR I'M PARALYZED…
…AND I BECOME A BURDEN…
…THEN LET ME GO…
I DON'T EVER WANT TO HOLD YOU BACK…

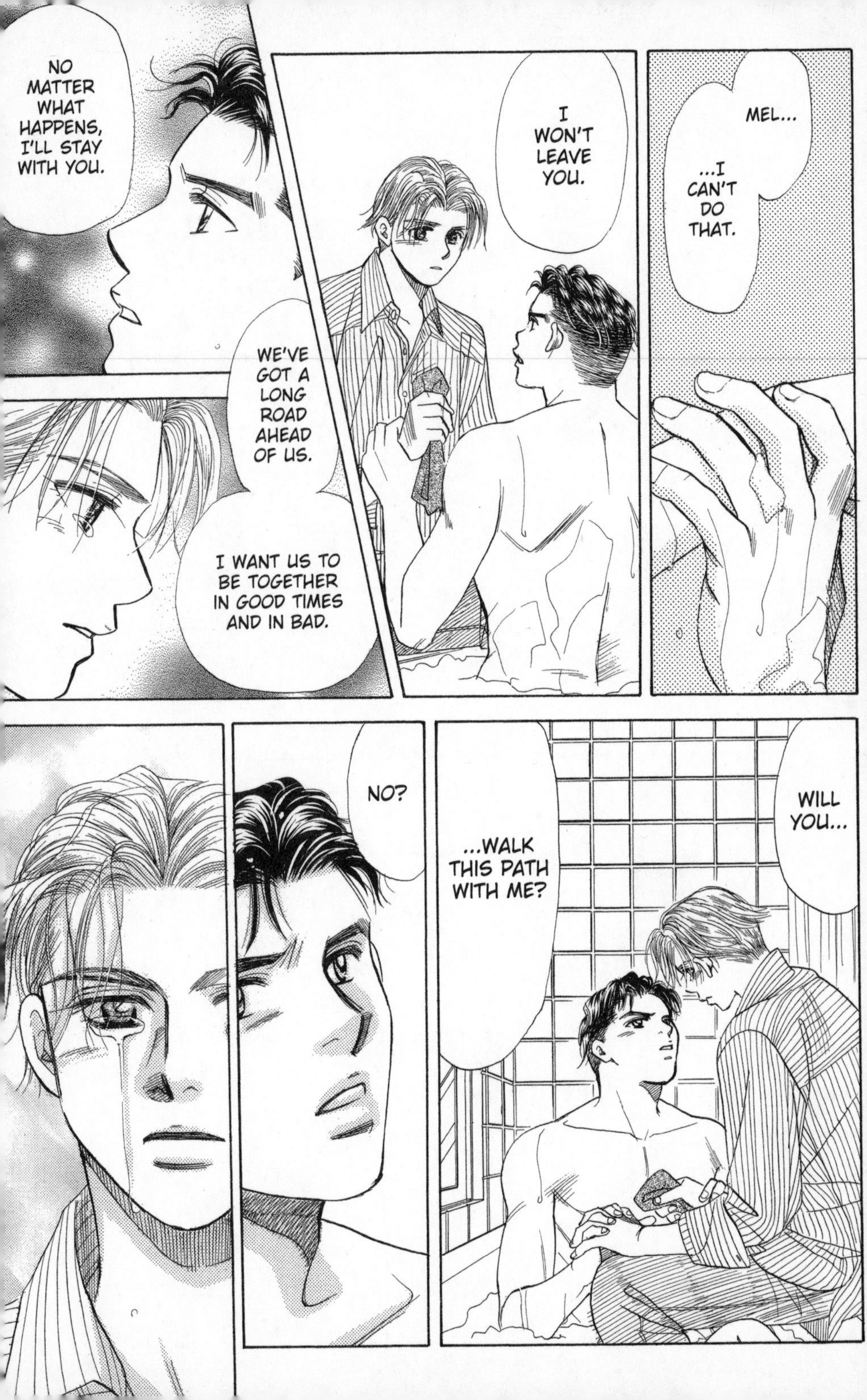
MEL...
...I CAN'T DO THAT.
I WON'T LEAVE YOU.
NO MATTER WHAT HAPPENS, I'LL STAY WITH YOU.
WE'VE GOT A LONG ROAD AHEAD OF US.
I WANT US TO BE TOGETHER IN GOOD TIMES AND IN BAD.
WILL YOU...
...WALK THIS PATH WITH ME?
NO?

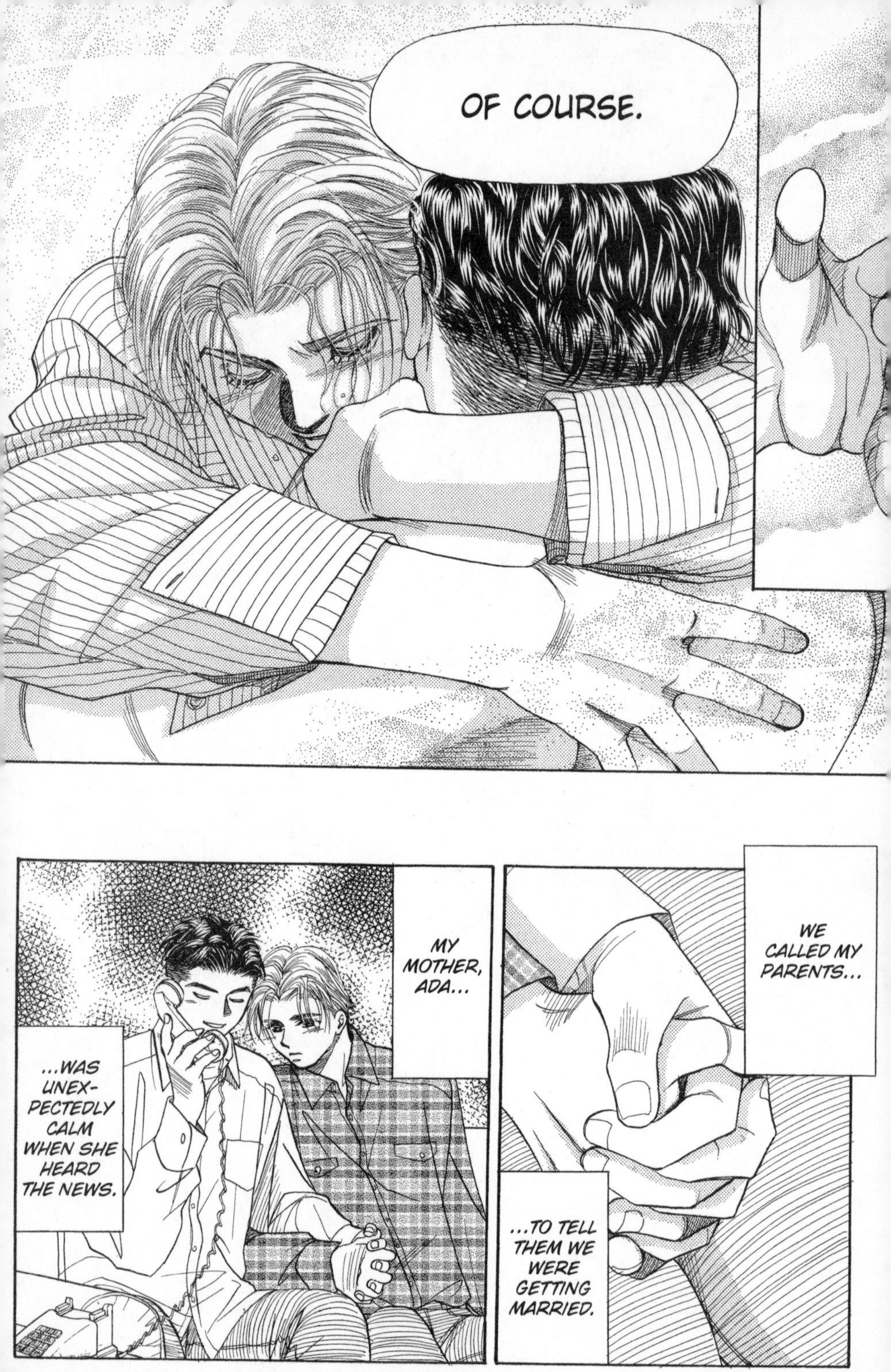
OF COURSE.
WE CALLED MY PARENTS...
...TO TELL THEM WE WERE GETTING MARRIED.
MY MOTHER, ADA...
...WAS UNEX-PECTEDLY CALM WHEN SHE HEARD THE NEWS.

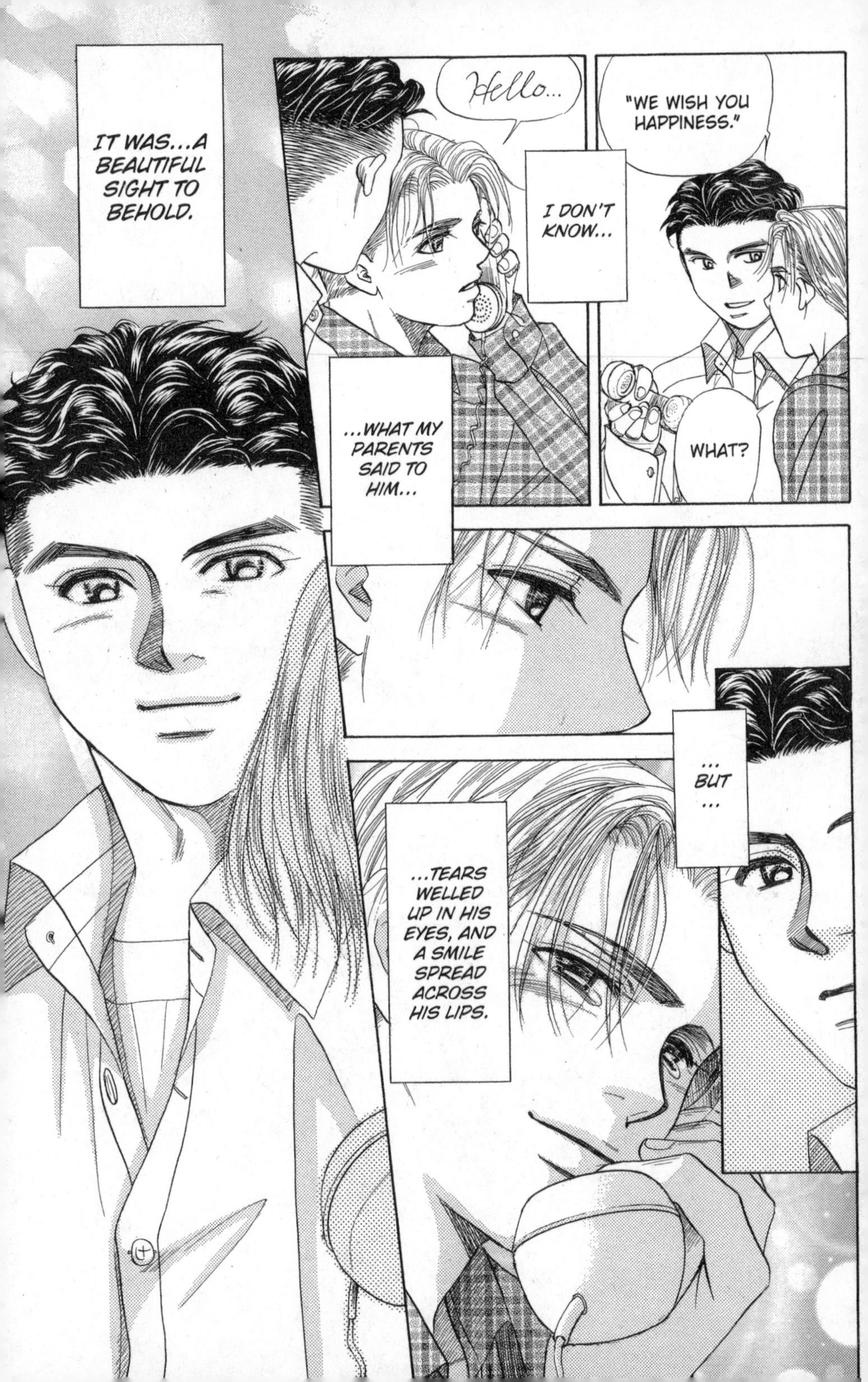
"WE WISH YOU HAPPINESS."
WHAT?
Hello...
I DON'T KNOW...
...WHAT MY PARENTS SAID TO HIM...
...BUT...
...TEARS WELLED UP IN HIS EYES, AND A SMILE SPREAD ACROSS HIS LIPS.
IT WAS...A BEAUTIFUL SIGHT TO BEHOLD.

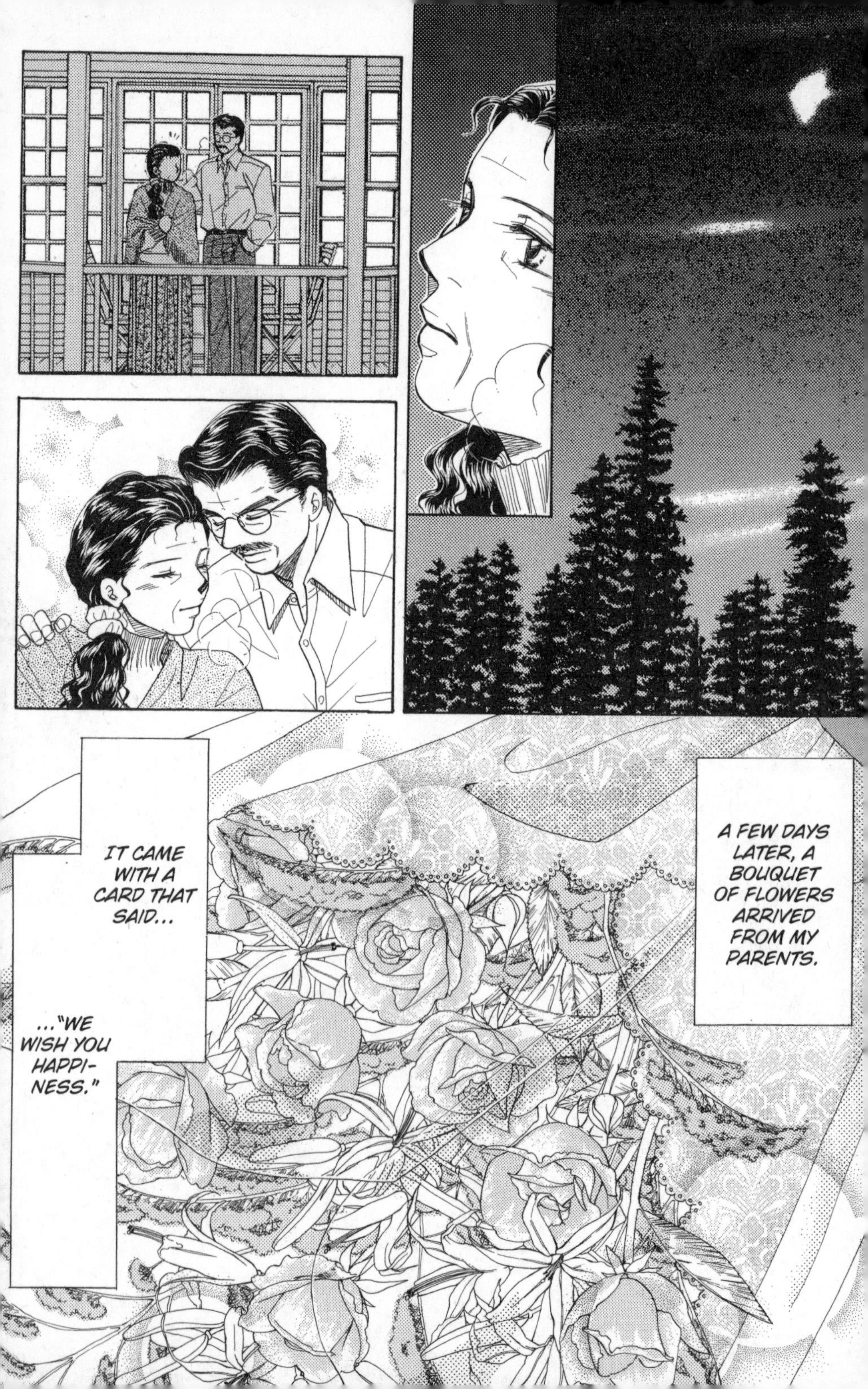
A FEW DAYS LATER, A BOUQUET OF FLOWERS ARRIVED FROM MY PARENTS.
IT CAME WITH A CARD THAT SAID...
..."WE WISH YOU HAPPI-NESS."

SHY GUY
Words & Music by Diana King, Andy Marvel, Kingsley Gardner, Hamish Stuart, Steve Ferrone, Alan Gorrie, Roger Ball, Malcolm Duncan and Owen Mcintyre
© DEKOPA MUSIC LTD. and KINGSLEY GARDNER MUSIC

NEW YORK, NEW YORK 1 · END

NEW YORK, New York, 1

Marimo Ragawa

Translation:
Preston Johnson-Chonkar

Retouch: Lys Blakeslee

Lettering: Abigail Blackman

Library of Congress Control
Number: 2021943180

ISBNs: 978-1-9753-2535-0
       (paperback)
       978-1-9753-2536-7
       (ebook)

10 9 8 7 6 5 4 3 2 1

WOR

Printed in the United States
of America

NEW YORK, NEW YORK by Marimo Ragawa
©Marimo Ragawa 2003
All rights reserved.
First published in Japan in 2003 by HAKUSENSHA,
INC., Tokyo.
English translation rights in U.S.A., Canada and U.K.
arranged with HAKUSENSHA, INC., Tokyo
through TUTTLE-MORI AGENCY, INC., Tokyo.

English translation © 2022
by Yen Press, LLC

Yen Press
150 West 30th Street, 19th Floor
New York, NY 10001

Visit us at yenpress.com
facebook.com/yenpress
twitter.com/yenpress
yenpress.tumblr.com
instagram.com/yenpress

First Yen Press Edition: February 2022

Yen Press is an imprint of Yen Press, LLC.
The Yen Press name and logo are trademarks of
Yen Press, LLC.